The **Rough**

Los Angeles

written and researched by

JD Dickey

NEW YORK • LONDON • DELHI

www.roughguides.com

Contents

3

◀ Desert Garden, Getty Center

Introduction to

Los Angeles

Los Angeles is California's biggest, most stimulating city – though an unconventional one by any standard. Indeed, its multiple personalities and lack of any unifying design make it seem, at first, a daunting place: a maddening collection of freeways and beaches, fast-food joints and theme parks, seedy suburbs and high-gloss neighborhoods. Once the free-spirited chaos of the place takes hold, though, you'll be hard-pressed to resist.

Made up of scores of distinct municipalities, LA is a model for modern city development, having traded urban centralization for suburban sprawl and high-rise corporate towers for strip malls. Although the city had a significant Spanish and Mexican presence through the mid-nineteenth century, it was only after it became part of the booming state of California that LA began to grow into a metropolis, marketing itself as a sunny arcadia full of orange groves and open space. When the film and aerospace industries were added to the mix in the early twentieth century, the place truly boomed, eventually displacing Chicago as America's second-largest city. Nowadays, LA's explosive population growth continues to add to its vibrant, unique character: a giant funfair filled with eye-popping billboards, painted murals of publicity-hungry starlets, all-night delis with their own weird cabarets, and a tumult of peoples and languages from nearly every corner of the earth – and the entire scene playing out in a freeway-covered landscape of glaring neon signs and towering palm trees.

Despite this uniqueness, LA has much in common with other major US cities. With the largest port in the country (and biggest in the world outside of China), LA is a center for transpacific trade and a dominant financial hub in its own right. Meanwhile, LA's social gaps are quite broad, and there appears to be no end in sight for the nasty racial divisions broadcast to the world during the 1992 riots. Still, the metropolis has slowly accommodated its multicultural character and even widened the spectrum – newcomers from Armenia to Zimbabwe can all be found here in pockets large and small. Mexican-Americans in particular, whether newly arrived or ancient in lineage, are doing much to remind this city of the Hispanic cast and culture that it's always had.

Unlike more conventional cities, LA does not reward an attraction-oriented itinerary, going from one museum or official exhibit to the next. While there are world-class institutions here – the Getty Center foremost among them – the sights that are most worth seeing tend to be separated by vast distances, and you'll doubtless spend most of your time on the freeway

Suggested itineraries

LA can be experienced in an endless number of ways, depending on what you're most interested in seeing – theme parks, Hollywood studios, art museums, and so on. The following are suggested **itineraries** for trips up to a week – while giving you an idea of what's possible to see in one day. They're mainly designed around the key sights and include suggestions for where and when to have lunch. Of course if any of the days seem too sight-oriented for you, don't be afraid to skip the museums and just wander – or drive – around.

Two days
• Disney Hall; Griffith Park; Hollywood Boulevard/Sunset Strip (lunch); Melrose Avenue; Rodeo Drive.
• Getty Center; Third Street Promenade (lunch); Santa Monica Pier; Venice Boardwalk.

Four days
• Disney Hall; Museum of Contemporary Art; Little Tokyo (lunch); Exposition Park.
• Griffith Park; Hollywood Boulevard/Sunset Strip (lunch); Miracle Mile; Los Angeles County Museum of Art.
• Melrose Avenue; Rodeo Drive (lunch); Greystone Mansion; Westwood; Getty Center.
• Venice Boardwalk; Santa Monica Pier; Third Street Promenade (lunch); Malibu; Santa Monica Mountains.

One week
As above plus . . .
• Old Pasadena (lunch); Norton Simon Museum and Gamble House, or Universal Studios.
• Palos Verdes Peninsula; Wayfarer's Chapel; Downtown Long Beach (lunch); *Queen Mary*; Aquarium of the Pacific.
• Disneyland or Magic Mountain.

▼ Beachside on Santa Monica Bay

if you try to see them all. Rather, the best approach to LA is to experience those activities that really make the city a great place to spend a week – the free-spirited bars, upscale restaurants, dynamic clubs, and quirky shopping strips and boardwalks that most define Southern California.

Surprisingly for such a sprawling metropolis, many of these activities are located in fairly compact neighborhoods, from Venice to Old Pasadena, so you can leave your car in a parking lot or just use public transit to get there. In fact, it's possible to have a memorable time in LA simply by taking in the bars of Hollywood, the clubs of West Hollywood, and the restaurants of West LA and Santa Monica. To really get into the urban spirit, make sure to try a bit of spontaneous wandering around the city's less glitzy zones, stumbling upon that perfect Indian diner or funky shoe store, discovering the hidden charms of the city away from the theme parks and klieg lights.

What to see

Most of the city of Los Angeles lies in a flat basin, contained within and around the Santa Monica, San Gabriel, Santa Ana, and Verdugo mountains, and hemmed in by the Pacific Ocean to the west – a geography best appreciated from the crest of the Hollywood Hills, where on any given night you're likely to see the city lights spread out before you in a seemingly endless illuminated grid. Though hosting a vast network of freeways, the landscape also features undulating hills, coastal bluffs, mountain ranges, and rocky canyons – all places that are variously home to movie stars, shopping malls and theme parks, not to mention impressive museums, rugged parks, and expansive gardens.

Starting in the center of the region, at the junction of the Hollywood, Santa Monica, Harbor, and Santa Ana freeways, **Downtown** has always been the hub of LA's political and financial life, a district that has long tried to match the cultural cachet of the Westside and Hollywood – to no avail. Still, there's nowhere else in the city with as much variation of class, culture, and design, all within a fairly compact, centralized area. Just west, the loosely defined district of **Mid-Wilshire**, built around part of the commercial strip of Wilshire Boulevard, is home to some of LA's best Art Deco architecture and finest residential designs, and is also a good place to take in some culture along "Museum Row," which overlaps the old Miracle Mile commercial zone, and further north, the chic grunginess of Melrose Avenue.

Due north is LA's most famous zone, **Hollywood**. Despite its longstanding patina of grime, the birthplace of the American movie business is still an essential stop, the site of grand old cinema palaces like the Chinese Theatre and the ever-popular "Walk of Fame." Hollywood, Sunset, and Santa Monica boulevards are the district's main drags, all of which lead into the chic boutiques and trendy clubs of **West Hollywood**, a center for gays, seniors, and Russian immigrants. In the hills above Hollywood, you can pick out your favorite cliff-hanging mansion or take a break in **Griffith Park**, location of LA's famed observatory.

Stargazing in LA

If you really want to catch a glimpse of the glitterati in LA, you can do much better than riding around on a tour bus staring at the locked iron gates of the homes of the rich and famous – and paying plenty for the privilege. In fact, with just a little preparation, you can quickly find yourself within sight of your favorite movie hero, TV star, or
pseudo-celebrity. To catch the stars while they're playing instead of working, the city's latest trendy bars and clubs are the places to visit (you can find such haunts in the *LA Times'* weekly Calendar Live entertainment section), as are the celebrity-oriented restaurants listed in the box on p.287. For a more intimate encounter, you can sometimes get movie stars to **sign autographs** if you avoid acting like the typical tourist. To wit: it's best to approach the rich and/or famous when they're "performing" for the public – attending a movie premiere, showing off their new duds at a flashy club, or doing anything in the company of a publicist or reporter. They're much less likely to blow you off in full public view than they are if you have the temerity to invade their privacy in a secluded beach cabana, back-corner dining booth, or on the Stairmaster at an upscale gym.

Traffic and smog

Whatever you may have heard about the unpleasant side of Los Angeles, it's more likely you'll only face the typical pitfalls of traffic and smog. The latter, while still virulent, has slowly improved in recent decades. Smog reports, broken down by geographic area, are published daily in the *LA Times*. As for traffic hassles, gridlock can sometimes be avoided if you stick to one place, as many neighborhoods are surprisingly compact and can be seen on foot. Still, you'll likely need a car to jump around from place to place, or to see any semblance of the city sprawl. Driving on LA's myriad freeways can be a challenge, but as long as you don't try to emulate some of the crazier local motorists, you should have few problems. Whatever your transportation plan, make sure to budget plenty of time for your travels. While you can theoretically go from Santa Monica to Downtown LA in twenty minutes by freeway, most likely it will take twice that amount of time, or more than seventy-five minutes on side streets.

▲ The Fox Westwood Village theater

West of here, in the heart of the city's Westside, **Beverly Hills** and **West LA** are where visitors often base themselves, keeping close to the all-out glitz of Rodeo Drive or Westwood's movie theaters and affordable shops. In the latter district, there's also the picturesque UCLA campus, and further west, in the Sepulveda corridor, sits LA's showpiece, the colossal Getty Center.

Santa Monica and **Venice** lie at the ocean's edge, sixteen miles from Downtown. These towns give LA its popular beach image (though the waters are somewhat cleaner further north), and are highlighted by such favorite attractions as the relaxed Santa Monica Pier, the shopping strip of the Third Street Promenade, and the freewheeling Venice Boardwalk and adjacent body shrine of Muscle Beach.

Well off the path of most tourists and dogged by crime, **South Central** holds a few scattered but notable sights like the fine array of historic architecture along West Adams and several good cultural institutions in Exposition Park. East of Downtown, **East LA** is the heart of the city's Mexican-American community, with a fairly vibrant street life. To the south, the largely residential and industrial **South Bay** and **LA Harbor** feature some compelling oceanside scenery and charming architecture, plus a few unpretentious beachfront towns, including the port cities of San Pedro and Long Beach – best known for holding the *Queen Mary* ocean liner. Back up the coast, Manhattan Beach and Hermosa Beach are small, middle-class beachfront towns, while at the southwestern edge of LA, the Palos Verdes Peninsula is home to some of the city's most dramatic ocean vistas.

The sprawling suburbs of the **San Gabriel** and **San Fernando valleys**, east and north of the Hollywood Hills, have become increasingly popular for dining, shopping, and a range of culture activities, from Burbank's working movie studios and Glendale's famed Forest Lawn cemetery to the historic town of Pasadena. The best natural turf in LA, however, is around **Malibu** and **the Santa Monica Mountains**, where the many state and regional parks are ideal for exploring on foot, or by car along the scenic Mulholland Highway. Nearby, the exclusive enclave of Pacific Palisades is home to a handful of architectural highlights, while the city of Malibu to the north is a surfside celebrity enclave whose beaches are famously difficult, though not impossible, to access.

More beach options abound in the increasingly populous communities of **Orange County**, though the area is better known for sights like Knott's Berry Farm and Disneyland, along with the Richard Nixon Library. The

▲ Santa Monica Pier and Pacific Park

most distant attractions will take you almost halfway to San Diego, where you can chase the swallows of Mission San Juan Capistrano or visit Nixon's old haunt of San Clemente.

▸ Freeway interchange, South LA

When to go

Los Angles holds several types of warm **climate zones**, including desert, semi-arid, and Mediterranean areas, and differences between constituent cities' temperatures can be great: for example, Pasadena is ten to fifteen degrees hotter on average than Santa Monica, which can resemble a maritime climate at times. Due to the enclosed geographic design of the LA basin, high levels of smog are possible, worst during the summer months in the eastern parts of the region; torrential rainstorms occur during the winter months; and disastrous fires and mudslides affect hillside neighborhoods across the city with uneasy frequency. That said, monthly city temperatures range less than twenty degrees throughout the year. In general, toasty air and sunny skies reign: summer and fall months are fairly warm and dry; winter and spring periods are cooler and wetter, but still quite warm. More than most cities, then, the right time to travel to Los Angeles is more dependent on cultural events – parades, festivals, movie previews, surfing tournaments – than it is on the weather alone.

Average daytime temperatures in LA

	Jan	Feb	Mar	Apr	May	Jun	Jul	Aug	Sep	Oct	Nov	Dec
Max °F	65	66	68	71	73	77	83	82	81	77	73	68
Min °F	47	48	49	53	55	60	63	63	60	57	53	49
Max °C	18	19	20	22	23	25	28	28	27	25	23	20
Min °C	8	9	9	12	13	16	17	17	16	14	12	9

21

things not to miss

It goes without saying that whether you're staying for a weekend or a month, it's impossible to take in all of the attractions and activities of Los Angeles. What follows is a selective and subjective taste of the city's highlights, which includes everything from major museums to verdant mountain parks, arranged in five color-coded categories. All highlights have page references to take you further into the Guide, where you can get a more detailed description of each attraction.

01 **Disney Hall** Page **65** • Although Frank Gehry's architectural marvel was designed in 1987, it took sixteen years for it to finally get built; it now serves as the home of the LA Philharmonic.

02 **Pacific Coast Highway** Page **217** and Page **237**• A favorite setting for biker flicks and road movies, the sinewy stretch of asphalt winds around coastal cliffs and legendary beaches from Malibu to Orange County.

03 **Disneyland** Page **230** • Much more than a theme park, the "Magic Kingdom" is a carefully planned resort where you can eat, sleep, and take a spin on the family-oriented rides without ever leaving its gates.

04 **Neon cruises** Page **76** • Sponsored by the Museum of Neon Art, these evening tours are the best way to catch a look at LA's remaining heritage of splashy mid-century neon signs.

06 **Venice Boardwalk**
152 • Mix with itinerant artis
rollerbladers, street preachers, T-sl
trinket vendors, and hordes of tour
this free-spirited beachside strip.

05 **Queen Mary** Page **187** • Docked in Long Beach, a striking Art Deco–styled ocean liner that's open for tours, on which you can also step inside a Russian sub moored nearby.

07 **Sunset Strip** Page **121** • The essential axis of the California music scene, jammed with groovy bars and clubs as well as swanky hotels, oddball boutiques, and towering billboards advertising fashion, liquor, and starlets.

08 Canter's Deli Page 268

One of LA's better delis and an inspired 24hr spectacle, with brassy waitresses, an eclectic clientele, and an adjoining cabaret.

09 Bradbury Building Page 71

Seen in movies from *Citizen Kane* to *Blade Runner*, this office building features a beautiful 1893 lobby boasting some of the best-preserved Victorian decor around.

10 Watts Towers Page 171

These spiny towers built from cast-off glass and pottery are a welcome sight in South Central LA, where their graceful silhouettes lend an otherworldly touch.

11 Golden Triangle/ Rodeo Drive Page 124

A compact section of downtown Beverly Hills featuring countless jewelry, fashion, and beauty merchants, catering both to elite buyers and window-shopping tourists.

12 **Egyptian Theatre** Page **108** • The stylishly preserved zenith of movie palaces in the 1920s, with ancient-looking columns, scarabs, and friezes, and solid diet of art-house and independent fare.

13 **Warner Bros Studio Tour** Page **210** • The best of the movie-studio tours in LA offers a chance to wander around real sets and soundstages and perhaps even sneak a peek of the stars at work.

14 **Getty Center** Page **135** • This colossal, modernist arts center, looming above West LA and stuffed with the treasures of the Old World, has done much to help Los Angeles shake off its reputation as a culture-free zone.

15 **Mulholland Drive** Page **118** • The winding concourse that climbs through the Hollywood Hills, offering stunning views of the metropolis, especially at night when the city's boulevards spread out in a glowing, multicolor grid.

16 **Whisky-a-Go-Go** Page **312** • Perhaps the most famous rock club on the West Coast, a proving ground for punk and metal groups and a classic venue that's hosted the likes of Buffalo Springfield, Janis Joplin, and the Doors.

17 Museum of Jurassic Technology
Page **142** • One of the city's best-kept secrets is home to fascinating exhibits of cultural oddities, including the likes of this micro-sculpture of hand-painted birds perched on an actual human hair.

18 Third Street Promenade
Page **149** • Santa Monica's pedestrianized shopping strip hosts a mix of upscale retailers, fronted by a vivid array of street characters, from impromptu jazz bands to hollering preachers.

19 Griffith Park
Page **102** • A verdant swath of urban greenery on the hills overlooking the city, containing several museums, bucolic glades, a bird sanctuary and zoo, and the signature Observatory.

20 Gamble House
Page **201** • This 1908 Craftsman style treasure is one of Pasadena's gems, blending elements of rustic native design with touches of Swiss-chalet and Japanese decoration.

21 Malibu Creek State Park
Page **226** • Expansive park in the Santa Monica Mountains offering terrific camping and hiking, as well as striking natural vistas memorable from many movies and TV shows, including *M*A*S*H*.

Basics

Basics

Getting there

Unless you are within a half-day's drive of Southern California, the quickest way to get to Los Angeles is by flying into Los Angeles International Airport (LAX) or Orange County's John Wayne International. Amtrak trains provide an alternate approach to LA within the US and Canada, though this is typically a rather leisurely and expensive choice, while Greyhound buses are a cheaper, if much less enjoyable, option. If you're driving to LA, as many do, it pays to familiarize yourself with the freeway layout beforehand.

Airfares always depend on the season, with the highest prices charged during summer and around Christmas; you'll get the best prices during the low season, mid-January to the end of February, and October to the end of November; shoulder seasons cover the rest of the year. You might make major **savings** by shifting your departure date by a week – or even a day. Note also that flying on weekends ordinarily adds around $30–50 to the round-trip fare; price ranges quoted in the text assume midweek travel.

While it's worth checking with the airlines directly to inquire about fares, you'll often cut costs by going through a **specialist flight agent** – either a **consolidator**, who buys up blocks of tickets from the airlines and sells them at a discount, or a **discount agent** who, in addition to dealing with discounted flights, may also offer special student and youth fares and a range of other travel-related services such as rail passes, car rental, tours, and the like. Bear in mind, though, that changing your plans can be costly.

Some agents specialize in **charter flights**, often cheaper than anything available on a scheduled flight, but again departure dates are fixed and withdrawal penalties are high: be sure to check the refund policy. If you travel a lot, **discount travel clubs** are another option – the annual membership fee may be worth it for benefits such as cut-price air tickets and car rental. Considering the popularity of Los Angeles, you might even find it cheaper to pick up a bargain **package deal** from a tour operator and then find your own accommodation when you get there.

Overseas visitors can buy air, train, and bus **passes** for discounted travel throughout the United States, though these usually have to be purchased in advance of your trip. All prices in this section are given in US dollars, unless otherwise stated.

Online booking agents and general travel sites

Many airlines and discount travel websites offer you the opportunity to book your tickets **online**, cutting out the costs of agents and middlemen. Good deals can often be found through discount or auction sites, as well as through the airlines' own websites.

ⓦ **www.cheapflights.com**, ⓦ **www.cheaptickets.co.uk**, ⓦ **www.cheaptickets.ca**, ⓦ **www.cheaptickets.com.au** Flight deals and packages (listed by country of access), and good links to relevant destination sites.

ⓦ **www.ebookers.com** Low fares on an extensive selection of flights.

ⓦ **www.etn.nl/discount** A hub of consolidator and discount agent links, maintained by the nonprofit European Travel Network.

ⓦ **www.expedia.com**, ⓦ **www.expedia.co.uk** Discount airfares, all-airline search engine and daily deals.

ⓦ **www.flyaow.com** "Airlines of the Web" – online air travel info and reservations.

ⓦ **www.hotwire.com** Bookings from the US only. Last-minute savings of up to forty percent on regular published fares. Travelers must be at least 18 and there are no refunds, transfers, or changes allowed.

ⓦ **www.lastminute.com** UK site offering good last-minute holiday package and flight-only deals.

ⓦ **www.opodo.co.uk** Popular and reliable source of low UK airfares. Owned by, and run in conjunction with, nine major European airlines.

ⓦ **www.orbitz.com** Comprehensive Web travel source, with the usual flight, car hire, and hotel deals but also great follow-up customer service.

Ⓦ**www.priceline.com,** Ⓦ**www.priceline.co.uk**
Name-your-own-price websites with deals around
forty percent off standard fares.

Ⓦ**www.seatguru.com** Highly useful site with
numerous diagrams showing aircraft amenities and
location of the best and worst seats, broken down by
air carrier and airplane model. Particularly valuable
when planning a long flight.

Ⓦ**www.skyauction.com** Bookings from the
US only. Auctions tickets and travel packages to
destinations worldwide.

Ⓦ**travel.yahoo.com** Incorporates Rough Guide
material in its coverage of destination countries, with
information about places to eat and sleep, etc.

Ⓦ**www.travelocity.com,** Ⓦ**www.travelocity
.co.uk** Destination guides with deals for car rental,
lodging, and air fares.

Ⓦ**www.travelzoo.com** Great resource for news
on the latest airline sales, cruise discounts, and hotel
deals. Links bring you directly to the carrier's site.

Traveling from the US and Canada

As the major hub for domestic and international travel on the West Coast, LA is
well served by air, rail, and road networks.
The best means of getting to LA from most
places in North America is to fly, as many
airlines offer daily service to LA from across
the US and Canada. Rail travel is a distant
second, while the cheapest way is to go by
bus, but it's also the least comfortable and
the most time-consuming. And of course,
you could follow the lead of millions of tourists and simply drive to LA.

By plane

The most convenient airport for domestic
arrivals into LA is **Los Angeles International Airport,** known as "LAX," and
located just south of the major beach
cities of Santa Monica and Venice. Most
flights into LA use LAX, but if you're arriving
from elsewhere in the US or Mexico, you
can land at one of the **smaller airports**
in the LA area – at John Wayne Airport in
Orange County, Long Beach, Burbank, Van
Nuys, or Ontario (thirty miles east of Downtown LA).

With many air carriers experiencing
economic troubles in recent years, week-
to-week **prices** can vary dramatically,
with some financially strapped airlines

reducing their flight schedules and range
of bargains, and tacking on fees for meal
service and nonstop routes. The cheapest
round-trip prices from New York generally start at around $200, or $170 from
Chicago, $300 from Miami, and $400 from
Toronto or Montréal. Flights from major US
air hubs, such as Denver and Atlanta, will
often cost you less than shorter trips from
smaller airports closer to LA, unless you're
flying on a **regional carrier,** in which case
you can expect to pay much less – in some
cases less than $100 round-trip from west-
ern US cities.

Travelers **from Canada** may find that, with
less competition on direct routes, fares are
somewhat higher – typically US$100–150
– than flights originating in the US. You may
often find that it's worth getting to a US city
first and flying on to LA from there.

Airlines

Air Canada ℡1-888/247-2262, Ⓦwww
.aircanada.ca
Alaska ℡1-800/252-7522, Ⓦwww.alaska-air
.com
America West ℡1-800/235-9292, Ⓦwww
.americawest.com
American ℡1-800/433-7300, Ⓦwww.aa.com
American Trans Air ℡1-800/225-2995, Ⓦwww
.ata.com
Continental domestic ℡1-800/523-3273,
international ℡1-800/231-0856, Ⓦwww
.continental.com
Delta domestic ℡1-800/221-1212, international
℡1-800/241-4141, Ⓦwww.delta.com
Frontier ℡1-888/241-7821, Ⓦwww
.frontierairlines.com
Hawaiian ℡1-800/367-5320, Ⓦwww
.hawaiianair.com
Horizon ℡1-800/547-9308, Ⓦwww.horizonair
.com
JetBlue ℡1-800/538-2583, Ⓦwww.jetblue.com
Midwest ℡1-800/452-2022, Ⓦwww
.midwestairlines.com
Northwest/KLM domestic ℡1-800/225-5252,
international ℡1-800/447-4747, Ⓦwww.nwa.com
or Ⓦwww.klm.com
Southwest ℡1-800/435-9792, Ⓦwww
.southwest.com
United domestic ℡1-800/241-6522, international
℡1-800/538-2929, Ⓦwww.ual.com
US Airways domestic ℡1-800/428-4322,
international ℡1-800/622-1015, Ⓦwww.usair
.com

Discount travel agents

Airtech ☎212/219-7000, ⊛www.airtech.com. Standby seat broker; also deals in consolidator fares.
Educational Travel Center ☎1-800/747-5551, ⊛www.edtrav.com. Low-cost fares worldwide, student/youth discount offers, car rental, and tours.
Flightcentre US ☎1-866/WORLD-51, ⊛www.flightcentre.com; Canada ☎1-888/WORLD-55, ⊛www.flightcentre.ca. Rock-bottom fares worldwide.
STA Travel US ☎1-800/329-9537, Canada ☎1-888/427-5639, ⊛www.statravel.com. Worldwide specialists in independent travel; also student IDs, travel insurance, car rental, rail passes, and more.
Student Flights ☎1-800/255-8000, ⊛www.isecard.com/studentflights. Student/youth fares, plus student IDs and bus passes.
Travel Avenue ☎1-800/333-3335, ⊛www.travelavenue.com. Full-service travel agent that offers discounts in the form of rebates.
Travel Cuts US ☎1-800/592-CUTS, Canada ☎1-888/246-9762, ⊛www.travelcuts.com. Popular, long-established student-travel organization, with worldwide offers.
Travelers Advantage ☎1-877/259-2691, ⊛www.travelersadvantage.com. Discount travel club, with cash-back deals and discounted car rental. Membership required ($1 for 3 months' trial).
Worldtek Travel ☎1-800/243-1723, ⊛www.worldtek.com. Discount travel agency for worldwide travel.

Package tours

Booked **in the US**, a typical three-night jaunt to Los Angeles – including round-trip flight plus three-star room-only accommodation – starts at about $450 per person from the West Coast or about $600 from the East Coast. Add an additional $150–200 or so to upgrade to a four-star hotel.
American Express Vacations ☎1-800/346-3607, ⊛www.americanexpress.com/travel. Flights, hotels, last-minute specials, city-break packages, and myriad specialty tours involving LA.
Amtrak Vacations ☎1-800/YES-RAIL, ⊛www.amtrak.com/services/vacations/html. Train or Amtrak Air Rail trips on the West Coast, along with hotel reservations, car rental, and sightseeing tours to LA.
Collette Vacations ☎1-800/340-5158, ⊛www.collettevacations.com. Packages range from five-night LA visits ($1400) to thirteen-day trips up and down the West Coast ($2200).
Contiki Holidays ☎1-888/CONTIKI, ⊛www.contiki.com. Youth-oriented sightseeing and national-park trips, with one- to two-week treks including LA for $600 to $1600.
Globus Journeys ☎1-866/755-8581, ⊛www.globusandcosmos.com. Options include five-day LA visits for the Rose Parade ($1100) to eight-day treks between California cities ($1600).
Insight Vacations ☎1-800/582-8380, ⊛www.insightvacations.com. Ten- to fourteen-day trips ($1600–2200) incorporate LA as part of Southwest trips through the rest of California, as well as Arizona and Nevada.
Suntrek ☎1-800/SUNTREK, ⊛www.suntrek.com. Two-week trips including San Francisco and other California cities (from $900) to month-long journeys from New York across the US (from $1880).
Trek America US and Canada ☎1-800/221-0596, ⊛www.trekamerica.com. One-week trips in Southern California (from $650) up to three-week treks around the Southwestern US ($1500). Aimed mainly at 18–38-year-old travelers.
United Vacations ☎1-888/854-3899, ⊛www.unitedvacations.com. Chain and boutique hotel accommodation, car rental, and other options for LA visits, plus various Disneyland packages.

By train

If you don't want to fly, **Amtrak** (☎1-800/USA-RAIL, ⊛www.amtrak.com) is a leisurely but expensive option. Although financially precarious for years, the company has managed to keep running – though rarely ever on time. Expect delays when traveling by rail, and the trains themselves vary in style, amenities, and speed, so it can be worth checking ahead on the type of train that services your route.

To arrive by way of the Midwest and Southwest, ride on the **Southwest Chief**, which begins in Chicago and travels through Kansas City, Albuquerque, and Flagstaff before reaching LA (Las Vegas is connected by bus line to this route through Needles, California). The **Sunset Limited** covers more of the South and the Southwest, taking you from Orlando through New Orleans, Houston, and Tucson, and arriving in LA via Palm Springs and Pomona. Another memorable route is the **Coast Starlight**, which runs between Seattle and San Diego and passes some of the most appealing scenery anywhere, from coastal whale-watching between San Luis Obispo and Santa Barbara, to an evening

Amtrak rail passes

General types of **Amtrak rail passes** are listed below, and include travel in different areas beyond LA, from just the western US, to the entire country, to a North American version that includes the US and Canada – the latter known as "**Explore North America**" and including Canadian routes on VIA Rail (☏1-888/842-7245, ⊛www.viarail.ca). A **California rail pass** ($159, all year) is also available for seven days of travel over a three-week period.

The above passes are available to all. Otherwise, 45-day "**Explore America**" fares are aimed at domestic travelers, while shorter-term **USA Rail passes** are aimed at foreign visitors only; both cover the entire country or sections such as the West. Finally, all passes must be purchased before your trip at travel agents, or at Amtrak stations in the US, on production of a passport issued outside the US or Canada.

	15-day (June–Aug)	15-day (Sept–May)	30-day (June–Aug)	30-day (Sept–May)	45-day (June–Aug)	45-day (Sept–May)
West (Explore America)	-	-	-	-	$309	$288
National (Explore America)	-	-	-	-	$515	$443
West (USA Rail)	$325	$210	$405	$270	-	-
National (USA Rail)	$440	$295	$550	$385	-	-
North America	-	-	$729	$516	-	-

Outside the US, Amtrak rail passes are available through the following companies:

Australia Asia Pacific Travel Marketing, St David's Hall, 17 Arthur St, Surry Hills, Sydney ☏612/9319 6624, ⊛www.aptms.com.au

Ireland USIT, 19/21 Aston Quay, O'Connell Bridge, Dublin ☏01/602 1600, ⊛www.usitworld.ie

New Zealand Walshes World, Ding Wall Building, 87 Queen St, Auckland ☏09/379 3708, or from almost any travel agent

UK lastminute.com, 4 Buckingham Gate, London SW1E 6JP ☏0871/222 5969, ⊛www.lastminute.com

trip around Mount Shasta and a journey through the wooded terrain of the Pacific Northwest. The shortest route of all, the **Pacific Surfliner**, connects San Diego to San Luis Obispo, with LA roughly on the mid-point of the journey.

One-way cross-country fares can be as low as $175 during the offseason, or as high as twice that much during peak periods; always check for **online discounts** of up to 70 percent first, though such fares are offered irregularly. While Amtrak's basic fares are good value, the cost rises quickly if you want to travel more comfortably. **Sleeping compartments**, which include small toilets and showers, start at around $100 for one or two people, but can climb as high as $400, depending on the class of compartment, number of nights, season, and so on, but all include three meals per day.

Amtrak also offers package deals combining hotels, rental cars, and other services for American travelers, as well as rail passes; see the box above.

By bus

Bus travel is a slow, often agonizing way to get to LA, and in the end you won't really save that much money. **Greyhound** (☏1-800/231-2222, ⊛www.greyhound.com) is the sole long-distance operator servicing LA, and charges around $200 round-trip, paid at least seven days in advance, from major cities like New York, Chicago, and Miami. The main reason to take Greyhound is if you're planning to visit other places en route; the company's domestic **Discovery Pass** (⊛www.discoverypass.com) is good for unlimited travel within a set time: 7 days of travel costs $219; 15 days, $319; 30 days, $419; and 60 days, $589; passes for overseas travelers run about five percent less. Other variants cover Canada and the US, for 15 ($399) to 60 days ($639) of travel, or the West Coast of both countries, for 10 ($279) and 21 days ($359). Domestic passes are valid from the date of purchase, so it's a bad idea to buy them in advance; overseas visitors, however, can buy passes before leaving home, and they will be validated at the start of the trip.

An alternative to Greyhound is the colorful **Green Tortoise** line, whose buses come complete with bunks, foam cushions, coolers and sound systems, and who offer a handful of routes to get you to Southern California. The company's "Hostel Hopper" links LA with San Francisco, Las Vegas, and/or selected national parks on one- or two-day adventure trips ($129–349), with express routes available if you just want to go to the cities on overnight quick trips ($39–59). Additionally, the five-day "Western Trail" outing ($334) orients you with the California coastline, the Sierra Nevada mountains, Yosemite National Park, and San Francisco. From April to September, on two routes, they also cross the country between New York and San Francisco; there's also a Greyhound connection for LA travelers at Bakersfield in California. These trips amount to mini-tours of the country, taking twelve to fourteen days (for $700–820), and allowing plenty of stops for hiking, river rafting, and hot springs. For details, call ☎1-800/TORTOISE or visit ⓦwww.greentortoise.com.

By car

Obviously, for a city built on concrete and asphalt, LA is the perfect place to reach by **car**, and although there are numerous freeways within the region to hasten your trip

Discovery Pass outlets outside the US

Australia STA Travel, 855 George St, Sydney 2007 ☎1300/733 035, ⓦstatravel.com.au

Ireland DUST, Students Union House 6, Trinity College, Dublin ☎01/677 5076

New Zealand Discovery Holidays, 1 Montrose Terrace, Suite 5A, Mairangi Bay, Auckland ☎09/479 6555, ⓦwww.discoveryholidays.com

UK STA Travel, 85 Shaftesbury Ave, Soho, London ☎020/7432 7474, ⓦwww.sta-travel.co.uk

(see "City transportation," p.35), there are three main routes outside Southern California leading to the metropolis: **Interstate 5**, the north–south corridor that connects LA to Mexico and Canada along the West Coast; **I-10**, a transcontinental east–west route that begins in Jacksonville, Florida, and ends in Santa Monica; and **I-15**, running along a mostly deserted stretch of desert before it reaches Las Vegas and drops down into LA's eastern San Gabriel Valley. Another option is **US Highway 101**, the famed coastal route that takes you along cliffs overhanging the Pacific Ocean and terminates in Downtown LA, after traveling through the San Fernando Valley and Hollywood, where it is known as the "Hollywood Freeway." If traveling on Hwy-101 beyond LA to the north, you can expect almost double the travel time as on Interstate 5, which goes in the same general direction.

Flights from the UK and Ireland

There are daily **nonstop flights** to LA **from London Heathrow** with Air New Zealand, American Airlines, British Airways, Continental, United, and Virgin Atlantic. Although you can fly to the US from any of the regional airports, the only nonstop flights from the UK to Los Angeles are from London (around 11 hours). Tailwinds ensure that return flights are always an hour or two shorter than outward journeys. Because of the time difference between Britain and the West Coast (eight or nine hours, depending on Daylight Savings Time), flights usually leave Britain mid-morning, while flights back from the US tend to arrive in Britain early in the morning. Most other airlines serving LA, including Delta and KLM/Northwest, fly **from London Gatwick** via their respective American or European hubs. These flights take an extra two to five hours each way, depending on how long you have to wait for the connection. Additionally, Air Canada, Air France, and Lufthansa connect Heathrow with LAX via Toronto, Paris, and Frankfurt, respectively. Whether direct or one-stop, return **fares** to Los Angeles from London and Manchester typically cost around £480 between July and August and at Christmas, falling to £270 in winter.

There are no nonstop flights from **Ireland** to LA, though most carriers connecting the

UK with the US offer service from Dublin (14–17hr), usually with a stopover in Atlanta, New York, or London, regardless of ticket price. The cheapest flights – if you're under 26 or a student – are available from USIT. Student-only round-trip fares range from €470 to €700. Ordinary Apex fares are only marginally higher.

If you've got some time, or want to see more of the US, it's possible to **stop over** in another city – eg, New York – and fly on from there for little more than the cost of a direct flight to LA. If the US is only one stop on a longer journey, you might also want to consider buying a **Round-the-World** (RTW) ticket. Some travel agents can sell you an "off-the-shelf" RTW ticket that will have you touching down in about half a dozen cities (Los Angeles is on many itineraries); others will have to assemble one for you, which can be tailored to your needs but is apt to be more expensive.

Packages

Packages – fly-drive, flight/accommodation deals and guided tours (or a combination of all three) – can work out cheaper than arranging the same trip yourself, especially for a short stay. The obvious drawbacks are the loss of flexibility and the fact that most operators use hotels in the mid-range bracket, but there is a wide variety of options to choose from. High-street travel agents have plenty of brochures and information detailing the various combinations.

Fly-drive deals, which give cut-rate (sometimes free) car rental when buying a transatlantic ticket, always work out cheaper than renting on the spot and give especially great value if you intend to do a lot of driving. On the other hand, you'll probably have to pay more for the flight than if you booked it through a discount agent. Competition between airlines and tour operators means that it's well worth calling to check on special promotions. Watch out for hidden extras, such as local taxes and **"drop-off"** charges, which can be as much as a week's rental, and Collision Damage Waiver insurance. Remember, too, that while you can drive in the States with a British license, there can be problems renting vehicles if you're under 25.

For more car-rental and driveaway details, see p.35.

There are plenty of specialist **touring and adventure packages** that include transportation, accommodation, food, and a guide. These work best if you're planning on seeing more of California than just Los Angeles, though many companies offer specific city-breaks as well. Some of the more adventurous carry small groups around on minibuses and use a combination of budget hotels and campgrounds (equipment, except a sleeping bag, is provided).

There's no end of combined **flight and accommodation deals** to Los Angeles, and although you can often do things cheaper independently, you won't be able to do the *same* things cheaper – in fact, the equivalent room booked separately will normally be a lot more expensive. Discount agents can set up basic packages for just around £500 each. A handful of tour operators offer more deluxe packages: a week in LA plus a round-trip ticket should run you anywhere from £750–1000.

Airlines

Aer Lingus ☎01/886 8844, ⊛www.aerlingus.ie
Air Canada ☎0871/220 1111, ⊛www.aircanada.com
Air France ☎0845/0845 111, ⊛www.airfrance.com/uk
Air New Zealand ☎020/8741 2299, ⊛www.airnz.co.uk
American ☎0845/7789 789 or 020/8572 5555, ⊛www.aa.com
British Airways ☎0845/773 3377, ⊛www.ba.com
Continental ☎0800/776 464, ⊛www.flycontinental.com
Delta ☎01/676 8080 or 1-800/768 080, ⊛www.delta.com
KLM/Northwest ☎0870/507 4074, ⊛www.klmuk.com
United ☎0845/844 4777, ⊛www.unitedairlines.co.uk
Virgin Atlantic ☎01293/747 747, ⊛www.virgin-atlantic.com

Tour operators

American Holidays Belfast ☎028/9023 8762, Dublin ☎01/673 3840, ⊛www.american-holidays.com. Full range of package deals from Ireland to all parts of the US and Canada. LA options are focused more on theme parks, but include a half-dozen hotel deals in Hollywood and Beverly Hills.

Bales Worldwide UK ☎0870/241 3208, ⓦwww .balesworldwide.com. Family-owned company offering quality escorted tours. Uses LA as an initial base for exploring California state and national parks.

British Airways Holidays ☎0870/240 0747, ⓦwww.baholidays.co.uk. Exhaustive range of package and tailor-made holidays around the world, using British Airways and other international airlines.

Contiki Tours UK ☎020/8290 6777, ⓦwww .contiki.co.uk. Trips for the 18–38-year-old crowd; one- to two-week treks including LA for $600 to $1600.

Kuoni Travel UK ☎01306/747 002, ⓦwww.kuoni .co.uk. Runs flexible package holidays to long-haul destinations worldwide. Build your own holiday package, selecting hotels (three- to five-star), flights, car rental, and other services.

Thomas Cook Holidays ☎0870/0100 437, ⓦwww.thomascook.co.uk. City breaks in either three- or four-star accommodation.

TravelScene ☎0870/777 4445, ⓦwww .travelscene.co.uk. Good-value city breaks, with a choice of four hotels (two-star to four-star) in top locations.

TrekAmerica ☎01295/256 777, ⓦwww .trekamerica.co.uk. Youth-oriented (18–38-year-olds) camping tours including LA as part of larger tours of the region.

United Vacations UK ☎0870/606 2222, ⓦwww .unitedvacations.co.uk. One-stop agent for tailor-made holidays, city breaks, fly-drive deals, pre-booked sightseeing tours, etc.

Virgin Holidays UK ☎0870/220 2788, ⓦwww .virginholidays.co.uk. Packages to a wide range of California destinations.

Flight and travel agents

Apex Travel Ireland ☎01/241 8000, ⓦwww .apextravel.ie. Specialists in flights to Australia, East Asia & USA. Consolidators for BA, American and SAS Scandinavian.

Bridge the World UK ☎0870/444 7474, ⓦwww .bridgetheworld.com. Specializing in round-the-world tickets, with good deals aimed at backpackers.

Destination Group UK ☎020/7400 7045, ⓦwww.destination-group.com. Good discount airfares, as well as Far East and US packages.

ebookers UK ☎0870/010 7000, ⓦwww .ebookers.com. Low fares on an extensive selection of scheduled flights.

Flight Centre UK ☎0870/890 8099, ⓦwww .flightcentre.co.uk. Rock-bottom fares worldwide.

Flights4Less UK ☎0871/222 3423, ⓦwww .flights4less.co.uk. Good discount airfares. Part of Lastminute.com.

Flynow UK ☎0870/444 0045, ⓦwww.flynow.com. Large range of discounted tickets.

McCarthy's Travel Ireland ☎021/427 0127, ⓦwww.mccarthystravel.ie. Established Irish travel agent now part of the Worldchoice chain of travel shops. Featuring flights, short breaks, and group holidays.

North South Travel UK ☎01245/608 291, ⓦwww.northsouthtravel.co.uk. Discounted fares worldwide – profits are used to support projects in the developing world, especially the promotion of sustainable tourism.

Premier Travel Northern Ireland ☎028/7126 3333, ⓦwww.premiertravel.uk.com. Discount flight specialists.

STA Travel UK ☎0870/1600 599, ⓦwww .statravel.co.uk. Worldwide specialists in low-cost flights and tours for students and those under 26, though other customers welcome.

Trailfinders UK ☎020/7938 3939, ⓦwww .trailfinders.com, Ireland ☎01/677 7888, ⓦwww .trailfinders.ie. One of the best-informed and most efficient agents for independent travelers.

Travel Bag UK ☎0870/890 1456, ⓦwww .travelbag.co.uk. Discount flights to Australia, New Zealand, the US, and the Far East.

Usit NOW Republic of Ireland ☎0818/200 020, Northern Ireland ☎028/9032 7111, ⓦwww .usitnow.ie. Specialists in student, youth, and independent travel – flights, trains, study tours, visas, and more.

World Travel Centre Ireland ☎01/416 7007, ⓦwww.worldtravel.ie. Excellent fares worldwide.

Flying from Australia and New Zealand

Los Angeles is the main American entry point for flights from Australia or New Zealand, so there are plenty of **direct flights** from those countries – though very little price difference between airlines. Air passes and round-the-world tickets can be good value if you're planning on covering more ground than just Los Angeles. The travel time between Auckland or Sydney and LA is 12–14 hours on a nonstop flight – though some flights do allow for stopovers in Honolulu and a number of the South Pacific islands.

From **Australia**, fares to Los Angeles from eastern capitals cost much the same; from Perth they're about A$380–450 more. There are **daily nonstop** flights from Sydney to LA on American, United, Air New Zealand, and Qantas for around A$1650 in low season, or $300–400 more in high season. Similar rates apply for stopping over in New Zealand via Auckland, or in Honolulu, Fiji, Tonga, or Papeete, generally starting at A$1600. The best deal for flying via Asia is on JAL during low season (A$1850), which includes a night's stopover accommodation in Tokyo; fares on Korean Air, via Seoul, start at around A$1900.

From **New Zealand**, you can go nonstop from Auckland to LAX (about 12 hr, or 90min less than from Sydney) for around NZ$1800 in low season, $2500 in high; Air New Zealand, American, Qantas, and United all offer direct flights. JAL offers the best fares via Asia, starting at NZ$1800/2150 for low and high seasons, with a transfer or stop–over in Tokyo, while Korean Air via Seoul costs from NZ$2000.

If you plan to visit LA as part of a world trip, a **round-the-world** (RTW) ticket offers the best value for the money. The most US-oriented are the fifteen airlines (among them Air New Zealand, Lufthansa, and United) making up the "Star Alliance" network (Ⓦwww.star-alliance.com), which offers a minimum of three and up to fifteen stopovers worldwide, with a total trip length from ten days to a year, up to 39,000 miles in total. An alternative option includes the eight carriers of the "One World Alliance" (such as Qantas, Cathay Pacific, American, and British Airways; Ⓦwww.oneworldalliance.com), which bases its rates on travel to and within the six major continents, allowing two to six possible stopovers per each continent. Costs for both plans can be as low as A$150/NZ$160 per segment, with the total cost for low-season fares around A$2400/NZ$2750 and high-season rates at A$3500/NZ$3800.

Packages

A variety of **package holidays** to Los Angeles are available to travelers from Australia and New Zealand, but few include international flights. Occasionally Qantas or Air New Zealand, in conjunction with wholesalers, offers flight-accommodation packages to LA, but most are for land travel only. These can be booked through most travel agents;

before you book, ask about any special conditions or hidden costs that may apply, as full refunds on package holidays are uncommon.

In addition, a number of operators specialize in overland **adventure trips and sightseeing tours** from LA, including Trek America (Ⓦwww.trekamerica.com), which offers a three-week "Western Sun" tour with stops in San Francisco, San Diego, and Las Vegas, plus eye-opening visits to the Grand Canyon, Yosemite, and Death Valley; prices start from A$2000/NZ$2150, with a similar mix of accommodation.

Airlines

Air New Zealand Australia ☎13 24 76, New Zealand ☎800/737 000, Ⓦwww.airnz.co.nz
America West Australia ☎02/9267 2138 or 1300/364 757, New Zealand ☎0800/866 000, Ⓦwww.americawest.com
American Australia ☎1300/130 757, New Zealand ☎0800/887 997, Ⓦwww.aa.com
British Airways Australia ☎1300/767 177, New Zealand ☎0800/274 847 or 09/356 8690, Ⓦwww.britishairways.com
Cathay Pacific Australia ☎13 17 47 or 1300/653 077, New Zealand ☎09/379 0861 or 0508/800 454, Ⓦwww.cathaypacific.com
Continental Australia ☎1300/361 400, New Zealand ☎09/308 3350, Ⓦwww.continental.com
Delta Australia ☎02/9251 3211 or 1800/500 992, New Zealand ☎09/379 3370, Ⓦwww.delta-airlines.com
Japan Airlines Australia ☎02/9272 1111, New Zealand ☎09/379 9906, Ⓦwww.jal.com
KLM/Northwest Australia ☎1300/303 747, New Zealand ☎09/309 1782, Ⓦwww.klm.com
Korean Air Australia ☎02/9262 6000, New Zealand ☎09/914 2000, Ⓦwww.koreanair.com.au
Lufthansa Australia ☎1300/655 727, New Zealand ☎0800/945 220, Ⓦwww.lufthansa.com
Malaysia Australia ☎13 26 27, New Zealand ☎0800/777 747, Ⓦwww.malaysia-airlines.com
Qantas Australia ☎13 13 13, New Zealand ☎09/357 8900, Ⓦwww.qantas.com
Singapore Australia ☎13 10 11, New Zealand ☎09/303 2129, Ⓦwww.singaporeair.com
United Australia ☎13 17 77, New Zealand ☎09/379 3800 or 0800/508 648, Ⓦwww.unitedairlines.com
Virgin Atlantic Australia ☎02/9244 2747, New Zealand ☎09/308 3377, Ⓦwww.virgin-atlantic.com

Travel agents

Flight Centre Australia ☎13 31 33, ⓦwww
.flightcentre.com.au, New Zealand ☎0800 243
544, ⓦwww.flightcentre.co.nz. Rock-bottom fares
worldwide.
Holiday Shoppe New Zealand ☎0800/808 480,
ⓦwww.holidayshoppe.co.nz. Great deals on flights,
hotels, and holidays.
OTC Australia ☎1300/855 118, ⓦwww.otctravel
.com.au. Deals on flights, hotels, and holidays.
STA Travel Australia ☎1300/733 035, New Zealand
☎0508/782 872, ⓦwww.statravel.com. Worldwide
specialists in low-cost flights, overlands, and holiday
deals. Good discounts for students and under-26s.
Student Uni Travel Australia ☎02/9232 8444,
ⓦwww.sut.com.au, New Zealand ☎09/379 4224,
ⓦwww.sut.co.nz. Great deals for students.
Trailfinders Australia ☎02/9247 7666, ⓦwww
.trailfinders.com.au. One of the best-informed and
most efficient agents for independent travelers.
travel.com Australia ☎1300/130 482 or 02/9249
5444, ⓦwww.travel.com.au, New Zealand
☎0800/468 332, ⓦwww.travel
.co.nz. Comprehensive online travel company, with
discounted fares.

Specialist agents and operators

Adventure World Australia ☎02/8913 0755,
ⓦwww.adventureworld.com.au, New Zealand
☎09/524 5118, ⓦwww.adventureworld.co.nz.
Agents for a vast array of international adventure-
travel companies that operate trips to every

continent. The two-day "Pacific Coast Explorer"
tour encompasses LA to San Francisco along the
shoreline, while the five-day "Golden West" links LA to
Phoenix and the desert Southwest.
Canada and America Travel Specialists
Australia ☎02/9922 4600, ⓦwww.canada
-americatravel.com.au. North American specialists
– accommodation, train travel, adventure sports, car
and RV rentals, Greyhound and other long-distance
bus passes, cruises, escorted tours, independent
travel, and more. LA trips include four-day jaunts
around Hollywood, Beverly Hills, and Disneyland.
Contiki Holidays Australia ☎02/9511 2200,
New Zealand ☎09/309 8824, ⓦwww.contiki
.com. Frenetic tours for 18–38-year-old party
animals. "Wild Western" tour is a major, thirteen-day
trek through California, down to Tijuana, and including
Las Vegas and Phoenix as well – the whole thing
begins and ends in LA.
Sydney Travel ☎02/9250 9320, ⓦwww
.sydneytravel.com.au. US flights, accommodation,
city stays, and car rental. Twelve-day "Western
Bonanza" trip across the Southwest includes two days
in Beverly Hills and Hollywood, plus the Getty Center.
United Vacations ☎1300/887 870, ⓦwww
.unitedvacations.com.au. Tailor-made city stays or
wider American holidays, with departures available
from several Australian airports; specials on airfare and
accommodation to LA and other US cities available.
Viator ⓦwww.viator.com. Bookings for local tours and
sightseeing trips in destinations around the world. Many
different LA trips, with a good number focusing on the
beaches, theme parks, and Hollywood attractions.

Red tape and visas

Keeping up with the constant changes to US entry requirements since 9/11 can
sometimes feel like a hopeless task. Seemingly every few months, the American
government announces new restrictions on foreign entry into the country, adding
considerably to the red tape involved in visiting it. Nonetheless, there are several
basic rules that apply to these requirements, which are detailed (and should be
frequently checked for updates) on the US State Department website ⓦtravel
.state.gov.

As of 2005, under the **Visa Waiver Program**,
if you're a citizen of the UK, Ireland, Australia,
New Zealand, most Western European

states, or other selected countries like
Singapore, Japan, and Brunei (27 in all), and
visiting the United States for less than ninety

days, you need an onward or return ticket, a Machine Readable Passport (MRP), and a visa waiver form. The MRP requirement is a recent manifestation of America's security clampdown, and requires certain high-tech protections built into the passport against fraud, counterfeiting, and so on. It is up to the various countries covered by the Visa Waiver Program to provide such passports to its citizens; for more information, inquire at American embassies or consulates. The **Visa Waiver Form** (an I-94W) will be provided by the airline, and must be presented to Immigration on arrival. The same form covers entry across the US borders with Canada and Mexico. If you're in the Visa Waiver Program and intend to work, study, or stay in the country for more than ninety days, you must apply for a regular visa through your local US embassy or consulate. UK citizens must apply in person at the US Embassy in London, under rules adopted in 2003, and have "British Citizen" stated on their passports.

Canadian citizens, who have not always needed a **passport** to get into the US, should have their passports on them when entering the country. If you're planning to stay for more than ninety days, you'll need a visa, which can be applied for by mail through the US embassy or nearest US consulate. If crossing the US border by car, be prepared for US Customs officials to search your vehicle. Remember, too, that without the proper paperwork, Canadians are barred from working in the US.

Citizens of all other countries should contact their local US embassy or consulate for details of current entry requirements, as they are often required to have both a valid passport and a **non-immigrant visitor's visa**. To obtain such a visa, complete the application form available through your local American embassy or consulate, and send it with the appropriate fee, two photographs, and a passport – valid for at least six months from the end of your planned stay. Beyond this, you can expect additional hassles to get a visa, including one or more in-depth interviews, supplemental applications for

students and "high-risk" travelers, and long delays in processing time. Visas are not issued to convicted criminals or those with ties to radical political groups; complications also arise if you are HIV positive or have TB, hepatitis, or other major communicable diseases. Furthermore, the US government now fingerprints all visitors to the US from countries not covered by the Visa Waiver Program, and applies spot background checks looking for evidence of past criminal or terrorist connections.

For further information or to get a visa extension before your time is up, contact the nearest **US Citizenship and Immigration Service office**, whose address will be at the front of the phone book, under the Federal Government Offices listings, or call ☎1-800/877-3676. You can also contact the National Customer Service Center at ☎1-800/375-5283. Immigration officials will assume that you're working in the US illegally, and it's up to you to prove otherwise. If you can, bring along an upstanding American citizen to vouch for you, and be prepared for potentially hostile questioning. Under no circumstances are visitors who have been admitted under the Visa Waiver Program allowed to extend their stays beyond ninety days.

US embassies abroad

For a more complete list around the world, check ⓦusembassy.state.gov. Details of foreign consulates in LA are given in "Directory," p.372.

Australia Moonbah Place, Yarralumla, Canberra, ACT ☎02/6214 5600, ⓦusembassy-australia .state.gov/embassy
Canada 490 Sussex Drive, Ottawa, ON K1P 5T1 ☎613/238-5335, ⓦwww.usembassycanada.gov
Ireland 42 Elgin Rd, Ballsbridge, Dublin 4 ☎01/668-7122, ⓦwww.usembassy.ie
New Zealand 29 Fitzherbert Terrace, Thorndon, Wellington ☎04/462 6000, ⓦwww.usembassy .org.nz
UK 24 Grosvenor Square, London W1A 1AE ☎020/7499 9000, visa hotline ☎09068/200 290, ⓦwww.usembassy.org.uk

Insurance

Although not compulsory, international travelers should have some form of travel insurance. The US has no national healthcare system, and it can cost an arm and a leg (so to speak) having even minor medical treatment. Many insurance policies are adaptable to reflect the coverage you want – for example, sickness and accident benefits can often be excluded or included at will. If you do take medical coverage, verify if benefits will be paid during treatment or only after your return home, and whether there is a 24-hour medical emergency phone number. If you need to make a claim, keep receipts for medicines and medical treatment. Also, if you have anything stolen from you, you must obtain an official statement from the police.

A typical **travel insurance** policy also provides coverage for the loss of baggage, tickets, and a certain amount of cash or travelers checks, as well as the cancellation or curtailment of your trip. Most policies exclude so-called dangerous sports unless an extra premium is paid; in the US, this can apply to rock climbing, white-water rafting, and windsurfing. Therefore, if you're visiting LA as part of a wider trip and planning to do water sports or similar activities, you'll most likely have to pay extra.

Before buying travel insurance, check that you're not already covered. Credit-card companies, home insurance policies, and private medical plans sometimes cover you and your belongings when you're abroad. Most travel agents, tour operators, banks, and insurance brokers will be able to help you, or you could consider the travel insurance offered by Rough Guides. Remember that when securing baggage insurance, make sure that

the per-article limit – typically under $800/£500 – will cover your most valuable possession.

Health matters

For **emergencies** or ambulances, dial ℡911. If you have medical or dental problems that don't require an ambulance, most hospitals will have a walk-in emergency room; for the nearest hospital, check with your hotel or dial ℡411. Should you need to see a **doctor**, lists can be found in the *Yellow Pages* under "Clinics" or "Physicians and Surgeons." A basic consultation fee is around $60–130, and medications aren't cheap either – keep all your receipts for later insurance claims. Many minor ailments can be remedied by items available in **drugstores**. Foreign visitors should bear in mind that some pills available over-the-counter at home need a prescription in the US, and local brand names can be confusing; ask for advice at any drugstore's pharmacy.

Rough Guides travel insurance

Rough Guides has teamed up with Columbus Direct to offer **travel insurance** that can be tailored to suit the needs of individual travelers. Readers can choose from many different travel-insurance products, including a low-cost backpacker option for long stays; a short break option for city getaways; a typical holiday package option; and many others. There are also annual multi-trip policies for those who travel regularly, with variable levels of cover available. Different sports and activities (trekking, skiing, etc) can be covered if required on most policies.

Rough Guides travel insurance is available to the residents of 36 different countries with different language options to choose from via our website – ⊛www.roughguides insurance.com – where you can also purchase the insurance. Alternatively, US citizens should call ℡1 800/749/4922; UK residents should call ℡0800/083 9507; Australians should call ℡1300/669 999. All other nationalities should call ℡+44 870/890 2843.

Information, websites, and maps

The best way to get free information and maps about LA is to write or call any of its constituent cities' visitors bureaus, from LA itself to Beverly Hills and Santa Monica down to Orange County. These promotional offices will send you copious material on their respective areas, including glossy promos advertising the swanky hotels and restaurants, plugs for the top sights, and, occasionally, a simple map or two. However, in a region like LA, there are numerous ways to get lost, so you're better off investing a few extra dollars in a detailed map book, just so you stay on the right boulevards and freeways.

Information

The **Los Angeles Convention and Visitors Bureau** (LACVB) is the main source of **information** about the city, with offices Downtown and in Hollywood. Independent offices in smaller LA cities also offer valuable material, which relate more to their own specific attractions. For information on Southern California, as well as the entire state, call or write to California Tourism, PO Box 1499, Sacramento, CA 95812-1499 (☎916/444-4429 or 1-800/862-2543, 🖰www.visitcalifornia.com), or visit the office's welcome centers at 8500 Beverly Blvd, Suite 150, Los Angeles, 90048 (☎310/854-7616, 🖰visitcwc.com), and in an Orange County mall at 800 N Main St, Suite 112, Santa Ana, 92705 (☎714/667-0400). British travelers can contact the Office of Tourism's representative, McCluskey and Associates, 50 Sullivan Rd, London SW6 3DX (☎020/7371 8900).

You can also pick up free promotional material such as maps, hotel and restaurant pamphlets, and magazine-sized city guides at small kiosks across the city, or at stands in most hotels.

Visitors bureaus

Beverly Hills 239 S Beverly Drive (Mon–Fri 8.30am–5pm) ☎310/248-1000, 🖰www.beverlyhillscvb.com
Downtown LA 685 S Figueroa St (Mon–Fri 9am–5pm) ☎213/689-8822, 🖰www.lacvb.com
Hollywood Hollywood & Highland mall, 6801 Hollywood Blvd (Mon–Sat 10am–10pm, Sun 10am–7pm) ☎323/467-6412

Long Beach 1 World Trade Center, Suite 300 (Mon–Fri 9am–5pm) ☎562/436-3645, 🖰www.visitlongbeach.com
Orange County near Disneyland, 640 W Katella Ave (daily 8am–8pm) ☎714/239-1340, 🖰www.anaheim411.com, 🖰www.anaheimoc.org
Pasadena 171 S Los Robles Ave (Mon–Fri 8am–5pm, Sat 10am–4pm) ☎626/795-9311, 🖰www.pasadenacal.com
Santa Monica 1400 Ocean Ave (daily 10am–4pm) ☎310/393-7593, 🖰www.santamonica.com. Also at Santa Monica Place mall, Colorado Blvd at Third St (daily 10am–6pm) ☎1-800-544-5319
West Hollywood Pacific Design Center, 8687 Melrose Ave #M38 (Mon–Fri 9am–5pm) ☎310/289-2525, 🖰www.visitwesthollywood.com

Websites

Whether you're planning your trip or checking to see what's on in the clubs, LA's role as a center for commercial entertainment makes it the subject of some interesting and offbeat **websites** devoted to the local color and culture. Selected sites are listed below.

Art and architecture

ArtScene 🖰artscenecal.com/index.html. Copious, regularly updated listing of galleries and museums in Southern California, broken down by geography.
Los Angeles Conservancy 🖰www.laconservancy.org. A great place to begin exploring the wealth of classic architecture in Downtown and other parts of the city (the Conservancy itself offers periodic tours as well – see p.40). An excellent related site, 🖰www.modcom.org, covers more Pop-oriented architecture from the mid-twentieth century.
Los Angeles County Museum of Art 🖰www.lacma.org. Besides offering an online tour of the

museum's exhibitions and permanent collection, this site gives a rundown on movie programs at the Bing Theater ($3 matinees of Hollywood classics) and music concerts in the museum's forecourt.

Mural Conservancy of LA Ⓦ www.lamurals.org. Excellent listing by neighborhood of the many murals across the city – from resplendent Madonnas in East LA to Botticelli's Venus in Venice – accompanied by photos and maps.

Roadside Peek Ⓦ www.roadsidepeek.com. Easily the best and most entertaining site about Southern California's Pop architecture (as well as select parts of the US), focusing on such subjects as "googie" diners, retro-bowling alleys, neon signs, Route 66 motels, and buildings shaped like donuts and dinosaurs.

Disneyland

Intercot West: Disneyland Inside and Out Ⓦ www.intercotwest.com. A first-rate source of news, information, and advice about the Mouse House in Anaheim, from getting good rates on tickets to avoiding the worst lines at the best rides.

Yesterland Ⓦ www.yesterland.com. A guide to long-lost Disneyland attractions, including such favorites as the Main Street Electrical Parade, the PeopleMover, and the legendary House of the Future, which once boasted that "the floors on which you are walking, the gently sloping walls around you, and even the ceilings are made of plastics."

Entertainment and general listings

@LA Ⓦ www.at-la.com. Extensive but straightforward listing of sights, products, and services in the LA region, from laundromats to theme parks to windsurfing.

Calendar Live Ⓦ www.calendarlive.com. The most comprehensive daily listing of all the city's entertainment options, updated regularly by the *LA Times*. Subscriber content can be accessed for free for two weeks with site registration.

Citysearch LA Ⓦ losangeles.citysearch.com. The LA site of a nationwide listings guide for major US cities, somewhat useful for navigating the metropolis, though not as frequently updated as other listings websites.

Club LA Ⓦ www.clubLA.com. Searchable lists and reviews of trendy bars, dance clubs, and comedy spots, plus fashion advice and gossip tidbits.

Downtown LA Visitors Guide Ⓦ www .downtownnews.com/dtvg/index1.html. Easy-to-use website featuring the high points of Downtown's sights, restaurants, and clubs, with good accounts of historical background and cultural lore.

Hollywood history and celebrity culture

LA Grim Society Ⓦ www.grimsociety.com. Surprisingly cheerful look at the books, movies, and events relating to death in LA, past and present, with the expected focus on celebrity deaths and murder sites. Infrequently updated, though.

Rock and Roll Road Map Ⓦ www .rockandrollroadmap.com. Visit the sites that made local, and national, music history in the LA area.

Seeing Stars Ⓦ www.seeing-stars.com. Comprehensive guide to tracking down celebrities wherever they hide out, from hotels and restaurants to churches, beaches, and beauty parlors. Also offers a good assortment of pages detailing movie palaces, film memorabilia, and almost anything connected with Hollywood – including a schedule for the latest Walk of Fame inductions.

Virtual Hollywood Walking Tour Ⓦ www .historicla.com/hollywood/index.html. Wander through movie history online by way of Hollywood Boulevard and learn about the famous sights and surroundings of this faded, but still colorful, stretch.

Miscellaneous

California Surf Report Ⓦ www.surfrider.org /surfreport. The latest surfing news and weather for the Southern California counties of Los Angeles and Ventura, plus related stories and photos.

LA Nocturne Ⓦ www.nocturne.com. Reviews of pool halls, diners, and clubs, plus books and movies that explore the dark side of LA, as well as the metropolis after dark.

LA Observed Ⓦ www.laobserved.com. The best web log about LA, covering a wide spectrum of city affairs, from overlooked news stories to media reviews to assorted quirks of the urban experience. A good tool to get a deeper sense of the city beyond the familiar stereotypes and PR campaigns.

Southern California Earthquake Map Ⓦ www .crustal.ucsb.edu/scec/webquakes. Disturbing (but interesting) "up-to-the-minute" map showing the regional sites of the last 500 or so quakes picked up by local seismographs, plus informative earthquake links.

Union Station: Los Angeles Rail Transit Ⓦ www.westworld.com/~elson/larail. Fares, schedules, system maps, and other practical information about the subways, trains, and light-rail options available in LA, along with history and trivia about the Angel's Flight funicular railway.

Maps

The **maps** in this book should be sufficient in helping you find your way around the main parts of town and their key attractions, with the exception of the Hollywood Hills, whose serpentine passages and switchbacks require highly detailed maps to navigate (and even then, with difficulty). For a folding map, try Gousha Publications' *Los Angeles City Map* ($3.95), available from vending machines in visitor centers and some hotel lobbies, Rand McNally's excellent Los Angeles/Hollywood map ($4.95) focusing on central LA, or our own rip-proof *Los Angeles Rough Guide Map* ($8.95).

For a more detailed view of the city, Thomas Brothers Publishing has the hefty, spiral-bound *LA County Thomas Guide* ($19.95), and *Thomas Guide to Los Angeles and Orange Counties* ($34.95), sold at most bookstores. Published yearly for counties across Southern California, the Thomas guides are the best maps available for regional travel, especially for venturing beyond the easily accessed parts of the city into more unfamiliar territory – like the northern deserts, eastern suburbs, or Hollywood Hills. If you're staying for several weeks, consider purchasing one if you're traveling anywhere outside central LA. If you're interested in highly detailed views of rural terrain, as well as the urban layout, consider DeLorme's large-format *Atlas and Gazetteer of Southern and Central California* ($19.95, last updated in 2000), which best shows national forests, parkland, hiking trails, and minor dirt and gravel roads. The colorful *Benchmark California Road and Recreation Atlas* ($24.95, published 2002) is also excellent for showing the same features; though it's now out of print, used copies are cheap and available.

If you happen to be a member, the Automobile Club of Southern California, 2601 S Figueroa St, south of Downtown (Mon–Fri 9am–5pm; ☎213/741-3686, ⓦwww.aaa-calif.com), hands out free maps, guides, and other information to member motorists and even bicyclists; while the national office of the AAA also provides maps and assistance to its members, as well as to British members of the AA and RAC, and Canadian members of the CAA (☎1-800/222-4357, ⓦwww.aaa.com).

LA-area travel bookshops can be found under "Shopping," p.367.

Map and travel-book outlets

In the US and Canada

110 North Latitude US ☎336/369-4171, ⓦwww.110nlatitude.com
Book Passage 51 Tamal Vista Blvd, Corte Madera, CA 94925, and in the historic San Francisco Ferry Building ☎1-800/999-7909, ⓦwww.bookpassage.com
Elliot Bay Book Company 101 S Main St, Seattle, WA 98104 ☎1-800/962-5311, ⓦwww.elliotbaybook.com
Globe Corner Bookstore 28 Church St, Cambridge, MA 02138 ☎1-800/358-6013, ⓦwww.globecorner.com
Longitude Books 115 W 30th St #1206, New York, NY 10001 ☎1-800/342-2164, ⓦwww.longitudebooks.com
Map Town 400 5 Ave SW #100, Calgary, AB T2P 0L6 ☎403/266-2241, ⓦwww.maptown.com
Powells Travel Books 701 SW Sixth Ave, Portland, OR 97204 ☎503/228-1108, ⓦwww.powells.com
Rand McNally US ☎1-800/333-0136, ⓦwww.randmcnally.com. Dial ext 2111 or check the website for the nearest location.
Travel Bug Bookstore 3065 W Broadway, Vancouver, BC, V6K 2G9 ☎604/737-1122, ⓦwww.travelbugbooks.ca
World of Maps 1235 Wellington St, Ottawa, ON, K1Y 3A3 ☎613/724-6776, ⓦwww.worldofmaps.com

In the UK and Ireland

Blackwell's Map Centre 50 Broad St, Oxford OX1 3BQ ☎01865/793 550, ⓦmaps.blackwell.co.uk. Branches in Bristol, Cambridge, Cardiff, Leeds, Liverpool, Newcastle, Reading, and Sheffield.
The Map Shop 30a Belvoir St, Leicester LE1 6QH ☎0116/247 1400, ⓦwww.mapshopleicester.co.uk
National Map Centre 22–24 Caxton St, London SW1H 0QU ☎020/7222 2466, ⓦwww.mapsnmc.co.uk
National Map Centre Ireland 34 Aungier St, Dublin ☎01/476 0471, ⓦwww.mapcentre.ie
Stanfords 12–14 Long Acre, London WC2E 9LP ☎020/7836 1321, ⓦwww.stanfords.co.uk. Also at 39 Spring Gardens, Manchester ☎0161/831 0250, and 29 Corn St, Bristol ☎0117/929 9966.
The Travel Bookshop 13–15 Blenheim Crescent, London W11 2EE ☎020/7229 5260, ⓦwww.thetravelbookshop.co.uk
Traveller 55 Grey St, Newcastle-upon-Tyne NE1 6EF ☎0191/261 5622, ⓦwww.newtraveller.com

In Australia and New Zealand

Map Centre ⓦ www.mapcentre.co.nz
Mapland Australia 372 Little Bourke St, Melbourne ☏ 03/9670 4383, ⓦ www.mapland .com.au
Map Shop Australia 6–10 Peel St, Adelaide ☏ 08/8231 2033, ⓦ www.mapshop.net.au

Map World Australia 371 Pitt St, Sydney ☏ 02/9261 3601, ⓦ www.mapworld.net.au. Also at 900 Hay St, Perth ☏ 08/9322 5733, Jolimont Centre, Canberra ☏ 02/6230 4097, and 1981 Logan Road, Brisbane ☏ 07/3349 6633.
Map World New Zealand 173 Gloucester St, Christchurch ☏ 0800/627 967, ⓦ www.mapworld .co.nz.

Arrival

Depending on how you travel, arriving in LA can place you at any number of locations scattered across the city – from the train and bus stations Downtown to the main air terminal by the ocean to the freeways coming in from all directions. However you arrive, you're faced with an unending sprawl that can be a source of bewilderment even for those who've lived in it for years. Provided you don't panic, however, this ungainly beast of a city can be managed and even easily navigated, if not necessarily tamed.

By air

Most people arrive in Los Angeles **by air**. Many domestic flights and also Asian and European flights touch down at Los Angeles International Airport (☏ 310/646-5252, ⓦ www.los-angeles-lax.com), known as LAX, sixteen miles southwest of Downtown along the ocean. **Shuttle buses** "B" and "C" serve their respective parking lots round the clock (disabled travelers should call ☏ 310/646 8021 for special lifts). If you're not planning to rent a car (in which case see "Driving," p.35), local **buses** (the citywide MTA and individual lines to Santa Monica, Culver City, and Torrance) pick up by parking lot "C" – see "City transportation" on p.35 for more details.

The most convenient way into town is to ride a minibus such as **LAX Chequer Shuttle** (☏ 1-800/545-7745, ⓦ www.laxchequer .com) or **Super Shuttle** (☏ 310/782-6600 or 1-800/258-3826, ⓦ www.supershuttle.com), which run to Downtown, Hollywood, West LA, and Santa Monica (the SuperShuttle also goes to Long Beach and Disneyland) and have signs on their windshields advertising their general destination. Fares vary depending on your destination, but are generally around $25–30, plus tip. The shuttles run around the clock from outside the baggage reclaim areas, and you should never have to wait more than twenty minutes; pay the fare when you board.

Taxis charge at least $35 to West LA or Hollywood, $90 to Disneyland, and a flat $38 to Downtown, and a $2.50 surcharge applies for all trips starting from LAX; for more information check out ⓦ www.taxicabsla.org. Unlicensed taxi operators may approach you and offer flat fares to your destination; such offers are best avoided.

Using the **Metro** system to get to your destination from LAX is difficult. The nearest light-rail train, the **Green Line**, stops miles from the airport, and the overall journey involves three time-consuming transfers before you even arrive Downtown. If you'd like to try anyway, shuttle service leaves from the lower level of the terminal to access the Metro stop at Aviation Station.

Most flights into LA use LAX, but if you're arriving from elsewhere in the US or Mexico, you can land at one of the **smaller airports** in the LA area – at Burbank, Long Beach, Ontario, or Orange County's John Wayne

Airport in Costa Mesa (see "Directory" for more information; p.372). These are similarly well served by car rental firms; if you want to use public transportation, phone the MTA Regional Information Network for specific details upon arrival (Mon–Fri 6am–7pm, Sat 8am–6pm; ☎213/626-4455, 1-800/COMMUTE or outside LA 1-800/2LA-RIDE, ⓦwww.mta.net).

By train

Arriving in LA by **train**, you'll disembark at Union Station (☎213/624-0171), on the north side of Downtown at 800 N Alameda St. (You can also connect to regional bus lines next door at the Gateway Transit Center.) Union Station is the hub for three main rail lines: **Metrorail**, the subway and light-rail system (see p.36), **Metrolink**, a commuter rail line servicing distant suburbs (see p.37), and Amtrak (☎1-800/USA-RAIL, ⓦwww.amtrak.com), whose long-distance trains also stop at outlying stations in the LA area.

Amtrak: departures for Downtown		
Anaheim	10 daily	40min
Fullerton (for Disneyland)	10 daily	35min
Las Vegas	1 daily	10hr, with bus connection
Oxnard	6 daily	1hr 35min
Palm Springs	2 daily	2hr 35min
Sacramento	1 daily	14hr
San Bernardino	1 daily	2hr
San Diego	10 daily	2hr 50min
San Francisco	3 daily	9–12hr, with bus connection
San Juan Capistrano	10 daily	1hr 15min
Santa Barbara	5 daily	2hr 35min
Tucson	2 daily	9hr 30min
Ventura	4 daily	1hr 50min

By bus

The main **Greyhound** bus terminal, at 1716 E Seventh St (☎213/629-8401, ⓦwww.greyhound.com), is in a seedy section of Downtown – though access is restricted to ticket holders and it's safe enough inside. There are other Greyhound terminals elsewhere in LA handling fewer services: in Hollywood at 1715 N Cahuenga Blvd

(☎323/466-6381); Pasadena at 645 E Walnut St (☎626/792-5116); North Hollywood at 11239 Magnolia Blvd (☎818/761-5119); Long Beach at 1498 Long Beach Blvd (☎562/218-3011); and Anaheim at 101 W Winston Rd (☎714/999-1256). Only the Downtown terminal is open around the clock.

Greyhound: departures for Downtown		
Las Vegas	18 daily	5–8hr
Palm Springs	7 daily	3hr 30min
Phoenix	10 daily	7–9hr
Portland	5 daily	20–23hr
Reno	9 daily	12–15hr
Sacramento	12 daily	7–10hr
Salt Lake City	4 daily	16hr
San Diego	24 daily	3hr
San Francisco	17 daily	8–12hr
Seattle	5 daily	25–28hr
Tijuana, Mexico	10 daily	3hr 30min
Tucson	9 daily	10–12hr

By car

The **main routes** by car into LA are the interstate highways, all of which pass through or by Downtown. From the east, I-10, the **San Bernardino Freeway**, runs south of Downtown then heads to the Westside and the coast, where it's called the **Santa Monica Freeway**. US-60, the **Pomona Freeway**, parallels the faster I-10 through the eastern suburbs, providing a less hair-raising interchange than I-10 when it reaches Downtown. The **Foothill Freeway**, I-210 (formerly Route 66), mainly serves the San Gabriel Valley; while the **Golden State Freeway**, or I-5, is the chief north–south access corridor, with the **San Diego Freeway**, I-405, used commonly as a Westside alternative.

Alternative routes into the city include US-101, the scenic route from San Francisco known as the **Ventura F reeway**, which cuts across the San Fernando Valley and Hollywood into Downtown. Hwy-1 follows the entire coast of California and links up with US-101 in Ventura County, but once in LA it's known as **Pacific Coast Highway** (PCH), and uses surface streets through Santa Monica, the South Bay, and Orange County.

City transportation

The only certainty when it comes to getting around LA is that wherever and however you're going, you should allow plenty of time to get there. This is partly due to the sheer size of the city, but the tangle of freeways and the gridlock common throughout the day can make car trips lengthy undertakings – and with most local buses stopping on every corner, bus travel is hardly a speedy alternative. The Metrorail subway and light-rail system are increasingly attractive options, though at present they serve too few parts of the city to be your only transit option.

Driving and car rental

The best way to get around LA is to **drive**. All the major car rental firms have branches throughout the city, and most have their main office close to LAX, linked to each terminal by a free shuttle bus. A number of smaller rental companies specialize in everything from Gremlins to Bentleys; the best known, and one of the cheapest, is Rent-a-Wreck.

Parking is a particular problem Downtown, along Melrose Avenue's trendy Westside shopping streets, and in Beverly Hills and Westwood – the latter with one of the nation's most aggressive meter-enforcement policies. Also watch out for **restrictions** – some lampposts boast as many as four placards listing dos and don'ts; it's better to shell out $5 for valet parking than get stuck with a $35 ticket for parking in a residential zone. If you're staying at a major chain hotel in a high-ticket area (especially Downtown and Beverly Hills), be prepared to plunk down an average of $20–30 per day for hotel parking; otherwise, at cheap motels and hotels in lower-rent areas, it'll cost you nothing to keep your vehicle overnight.

Car rental companies

Ace ℡ 1-800/831-5556, Ⓦ www.acerentacar.com
Advantage ℡ 1-800/777-5500, Ⓦ www.arac.com
Alamo ℡ 1-800/462-5266, Ⓦ www.alamo.com
Avis ℡ 1-800/230-4898, Ⓦ www.avis.com
Budget ℡ 1-800/527-0700, - Ⓦ www
.budgetrentacar.com
Dollar ℡ 1-800/800-3665, Ⓦ www.dollar.com
Enterprise ℡ 1-800/325-8007, Ⓦ www
.enterprise.com
Fox Rent-a-Car ℡ 1-800/225-4369,
Ⓦ foxrentacar.com
Hertz ℡ 1-800/654-3131, in Canada
℡ 1-800/263-0600, Ⓦ www.hertz.com
National ℡ 1-800/962-7070, Ⓦ www.nationalcar
.com
Payless ℡ 1-800/729-5377, Ⓦ www
.paylesscarrental.com
Rent-a-Wreck ℡ 310/826-7555 or 1-800/995-
0994, Ⓦ www.rentawreck.com
Thrifty ℡ 1-800/847-4389, Ⓦ www.thrifty.com

LA's freeways

Despite traffic being bumper-to-bumper much of the time, the **freeways** are the only way to cover long distances quickly; with more than 250 miles of asphalt and twenty major routes, the LA freeway system is the largest in the world, carrying up to six million cars a day.

The system, however, can be confusing, especially since each stretch might have two or three names (often derived from its eventual destination, however far away) as well as a number. Out of an eye-popping, four-level interchange known as "**The Stack**," four major freeways fan out from Downtown: the Hollywood Freeway (a section of US-101) heads northwest through Hollywood into the San Fernando Valley; the Santa Monica Freeway (I-10) runs south of Mid-Wilshire and West LA to Santa Monica; the Harbor Freeway (I-110) goes south to San Pedro – heading northeast it's called the Pasadena Freeway; and the Santa Ana Freeway (I-5) passes Disneyland and continues south through Orange County – north of Downtown it's called the Golden State Freeway. **Other freeways** include the San Diego Freeway (I-405), which roughly follows the coast through West LA and the South Bay; the Ventura Freeway (Hwy-134), which links Burbank, Glendale, and Pasadena to US-101 in the San Fernando Valley; the Long Beach Freeway (I-710), a truck-heavy route connecting East LA and Long Beach; and short routes like Hwy-2, which serves the San Gabriel Valley, and Hwy-90, which runs through Marina del Rey. For **shorter journeys**, especially between Hollywood and West LA, the wide avenues and boulevards are a better option (sometimes the only one), not least because you get to see more of the city.

Freeway driving strategies

Visitors exploring most places between Hollywood and the coast can side-step LA's **freeways** by traveling on surface streets. However, those headed to more far-flung parts of LA will find them unavoidable. Although LA freeway travel presents its own unique challenges, keeping a few things in mind will go some way toward reducing the time spent in gridlock. For one, alternate route planning is critical, especially when traveling to Orange County, because **gridlock** can occur at any time of the day. To assist your planning, AM news radio stations (see p.48) provide frequent **traffic updates** identifying where the nasty tie-ups are.

The **busiest roads** are Highway 101 and the 405 freeway, with particularly hellish confluences at the Downtown "Stack" and the section of the 405 at the 10 freeway, one of the busiest junctions in LA. Individual roads present their own difficulties, including the 101 south through Universal City, where you only have a few yards to accelerate from a dead stop to 55mph, or the antiquated 110 freeway in Highland Park, where exit-ramp speeds suddenly drop to 5mph. At the LA River, transferring from the south 5 to the south 110 is a hair-raising merge around the base of a cliff, while following the 10 freeway through East LA plunges you briefly, and chaotically, into the confusion of Interstate 5. Finally, tractor-trailer trucks are almost ubiquitous on the Terminal Island Expressway, a short road near the harbor, and on the Long Beach Freeway, or 710, which offers the added pitfalls of narrow lanes and uneven, rutted asphalt.

Public transportation

The bulk of LA's **public transportation** is run by the LA County Metropolitan Transit Authority (MTA or "Metro"), whose massive **Gateway Transit Center**, Downtown to the east of Union Station on Vignes Street, serves commuters traveling by Metrorail, light rail, commuter rail, Amtrak, and regional buses. The Center comprises **Patsaouras Transit Plaza**, from where buses depart, the glass-domed **East Portal**, which leads to train connections, and the 26-story Gateway Tower, which has an MTA **customer service office** on the ground floor (Mon–Fri 6am–6.30pm; ❾www.mta.net).

Metrorail

LA's **Metrorail** subway and light-rail system has tried for fifteen years to expand and access areas of the city that its critics claimed it would never reach. The system has generally been successful in reaching its geographic goals, and more commuters are riding it each year. For tourists, much depends on location – if you're staying in Hollywood, Pasadena, or Long Beach and want to go Downtown without a car (or vice versa), it's pretty useful. Otherwise, the city's other popular areas – notably the Westside – are well out of its reach.

At present, the system encompasses four major lines, though extensions are planned in coming years, along with the August 2005 completion of a new **Orange Line** crossing the San Fernando Valley and linking Canoga Park with North Hollywood. The latter area already provides the northern terminus for the underground **Red Line**, which heads south under the Hollywood Hills to connect Central Hollywood and Downtown (stopping at the Gateway Transit Center, as with all Downtown routes). Of more use to residents than tourists, the **Green Line** runs between industrial El Segundo (from where you can pick up an LAX shuttle at Aviation Station; see p.33) and colorless Norwalk, along the middle of the Century Freeway. The **Blue Line** leaves Downtown and heads overland through South Central to Long Beach, while the more appealing **Gold Line** is also a light-rail route, connecting Downtown with northeast LA, Highland Park, and Old Pasadena,

MTA offices and information

For **MTA route and transfer information**, phone ☎213/626-4455 or 1-80〔
COMMUTE (Mon–Fri 7.30am–3.30pm); be prepared to wait, and be ready t〔
precise details of where you are and where you want to go. Otherwise, you
check out the MTA website (☜www.mta.net) or go in person to Downtown's
Transit Center, Chavez Avenue at Vignes Street (Mon–Fri 6am–6.30pm), or to three
other centrally located offices: in Downtown at 515 S Flower St, on level C of Arco
Plaza (Mon–Fri 7.30am–3.30pm); Mid-Wilshire at 5301 Wilshire Blvd (Mon–Fri 9am–
5pm); and 14435 Sherman Way, in the San Fernando Valley (Mon–Fri 10am–6pm).

before ending at drab Sierra Madre. **Fares** are $1.25 one way, with one-hour-long transfers available for 25¢ and day passes available for $3. Trains run daily 5am– 12.30am, with peak-hour routes at five- to six-minute intervals, and at other times every ten to fifteen minutes. No smoking, eating, or drinking is allowed while on board.

Other forms of rail transit mainly serve more distant parts of the city. Amtrak, for example, connects to points in Ventura, Riverside, and Orange counties and beyond (see p.34).

Metrolink

As one rail alternative, **Metrolink** commuter trains operate primarily inter-suburban to Downtown routes on weekdays, though can be useful if you find yourself in any such far-flung districts, among them places in Orange, Ventura, Riverside, and San Bernardino counties. Although casual visitors may find the service useful mainly for reaching the more outlying corners of the San Fernando Valley, the system does reach as far as Oceanside in San Diego County, from which you can connect to that region's Coaster commuter rail and avoid the freeways altogether. One-way fares range from $3.50–11.25, depending on when you're traveling (most routes run during daily business hours, often to LA in the morning and back to the suburbs in the evening) and how far you're going. For information on specific routes and schedules, call ☎1-800/371-LINK or visit ☜www.metrolinktrains.com.

Buses

Car-less Angelenos not lucky enough to live near a train route have to settle for **buses**.

Although initially bewildering, the MTA network is really quite simple: the main routes run east–west (eg, between Downtown and the coast) and north–south (eg, between Downtown and the South Bay). Establishing the best transfer point if you need to change buses can be difficult, but with a bit of planning you should have few problems – though always allow plenty of time.

Free brochures are available from MTA offices, as are diagrams and timetables for individual bus routes, as well as regional bus maps showing larger sections of the metropolis. Buses on the major arteries between Downtown and the coast run roughly every fifteen minutes between 5am and 2am; other routes, and the **all-night services** along the major thoroughfares, are less frequent, usually every thirty minutes or hourly. At night be careful not to get stranded Downtown waiting for connecting buses.

The standard **one-way fare** is $1.25, except for night routes (9pm–5am), when the cost is only 75¢; **transfers**, which can be used in one direction within the time marked on the ticket (usually three hours), cost 25¢ more; and **express buses** (a limited commuter service), and any others using a freeway, are usually $1.75–2.25, but can be as much as $4 depending on length of trip and the number of zones you pass through, as shown on station maps. Put the correct money (coins or notes) into the slot when getting on. If you're staying a while, save some money with a **weekly**, semi-monthly, or monthly pass, which cost $14, $27, and $52, respectively (with monthly student passes for $27), and also give reductions at selected shops and travel agents. Finally, "**EZ Transit**" passes give you the option of traveling on MTA and DASH buses, as well etrorail trains, for a flat $58 per month.

In the coming years, the MTA is planning to continue rolling out more of the new **Metro Rapid** routes throughout the region, offering modified bus service (along special #700 lines) with special red-colored identification, waiting kiosks with enhanced displays, and technology to reduce waiting times at green lights. There is no extra charge for these nine routes, and in Central LA they currently serve Wilshire, Ventura, and La Cienega boulevards, Vermont Avenue, Broadway, and the 405 freeway – though LAX is not yet connected. There are also the mini **DASH** buses, which operate through the LA Department of Transportation, or LADOT (☎808-2273 for area codes 213, 310, 323, and 818, ⓦwww.ladottransit .com), with a flat fare of 25¢. Six routes run through Downtown every five to ten minutes between 6.30am and 6pm on weekdays, and every fifteen to twenty minutes between 10am and 5pm on Saturdays and Sundays. Other DASH routes travel widely throughout the metropolis, including the Mid-Wilshire area, Pacific Palisades, Venice, and South Central LA, usually every fifteen to thirty minutes on weekdays, less often on Saturdays, and not at all on Sundays. The LADOT also operates quick, limited-stop routes called **commuter express**, though these cost a bit more (90¢–$3.10) depending on how far you're traveling.

Other **local bus services** include those for Orange County (OCTD; ☎714/636-7433, ⓦwww.octa.net), Long Beach (LBTD; ☎562/591-2301, ⓦwww.lbtransit .org), Culver City (☎310/253-6500, ⓦwww .culvercity.org/depts_bus.html), and Santa Monica (☎310/451-5444, ⓦwww.bigblue-bus.com) – the latter two systems provide the best options for reaching the Getty Center.

Bus routes

MTA's bus routes fall into six categories, as outlined below. Whatever bus you're on, if traveling alone, especially at night, it's best to sit up front near the driver.

#1–99 Local routes to and from Downtown
#100–299 Local routes to other areas
#300–399 Limited-stop routes (usually rush hour only)

#400–499 Express routes to and from Downtown
#500–599 Express routes for other areas
#600–699 Special service routes (for sports events and the like)
#700–799 Metro Rapid Service

Major LA bus lines

From LAX bus center to:
Beverly Hills #220
Downtown #42, #439
Long Beach #232
San Pedro #225
Watts Towers #117
West Hollywood #220 (for Hollywood change to #4 along Santa Monica Boulevard)

To and from Downtown along:
Broadway (through Downtown) #45, #46
Hollywood Blvd #2, #4, #10, #20, #21 (connect at **La Brea Ave** to #212 or #312 northbound)
Melrose Ave #10, #11
Olympic Blvd #28
Santa Monica Blvd #4, #304
Sunset Blvd #2, #302
Venice Blvd #33
Wilshire Blvd #20, #21, #320

From Downtown to:
Beverly Hills #20, #21, #320
Burbank Studios #96
Exposition Park #38, #81
Forest Lawn Cemetery, Glendale #90, #91
Getty Center #2, #302 (transfer at UCLA to #761)
Hollywood #2, #302
Huntington Library #78, #79
Long Beach #60, #360
Manhattan Beach/Hermosa Beach/ Redondo Beach #439
Orange County, Knott's Berry Farm, Disneyland #460
Palos Verdes #444
San Pedro #445, #446, #447, transfer to DASH #142 for Catalina
Santa Monica #4, #20, #434
Venice #33, #333

Taxis

You can find **taxis** at most terminals and major hotels. Otherwise you'll need to call for a pick-up; among the more reliable companies are Independent Cab Co (☎1-800/521-8294), Checker Cab (☎1-800/200-1085), and United Independent Taxi (☎1-800/411-0303). Fares are set by the city at $2, plus $1.60 for each mile (or 40¢ per minute of waiting time), with a $2.50 surcharge if you're picked up at LAX: the driver won't know every street in LA but will know the major ones; ask for the nearest junction and give directions from there. If you encounter problems, call ☎1-800/501-0999, or visit ⓦwww.taxicabsla.org.

Bikes

Cycling in LA may sound perverse, but in some areas, notably away from the freeways, it can be one of the better ways of getting around. There is an excellent **beach bike-path** between Santa Monica and Redondo Beach, and from Long Beach to Newport Beach, and many equally enjoyable inland routes, notably around Griffith Park and the grand mansions of Pasadena (the LA River route, however, is justifiably notorious, loaded with broken glass and bands of budding criminals). Contact the AAA, 2601 S Figueroa St (Mon–Fri 9am–5pm; ☎213/741-3686, ⓦwww.aaa-calif.com), or the LA office of the state Department of Transportation, known as CalTrans, 120 S Spring St (Mon–Fri 8am–5pm; ☎213/897-3656, ⓦwww.dot.ca.gov), for maps and information. The best place to **rent a bike** for the beaches is on Washington Street around Venice Pier, where numerous outlets include Spokes 'n' Stuff, 4175 Admiralty Way (☎310/306-3332) and 1700 Ocean Ave (☎310/395-4748); in summer, bike rental stands line the beach. Prices range from $8–10 a day for a clunker to $15–20 a day or more for a mountain bike. Many beachside stores also rent **roller skates** and **rollerblades**.

City tours

One quick and easy way to see something of LA is from the window of a tour bus. Guided tours vary greatly in cost and quality, with the mainstream operators taking busloads of tourists around the major sights and only worth considering if you're pushed for time – none covers anything that you couldn't see for yourself for less money. Specialist tours, tailored to suit particular interests, usually take smaller groups and are often a better value, while studio tours of film and TV production areas are covered on day-trips by most of the mainstream operators, though again you'll save money by showing up independently.

Mainstream tours

By far the most popular of the mainstream tours Is the half-day "**stars' homes**" – usually including the Farmers Market, Sunset Strip, Rodeo Drive, the Hollywood Bowl, and Chinese Theatre, but the "stars' homes" themselves are often no more than the gates of B-list or long-forgotten celebrities. These tours are typically the most visible to newcomers, and the area around the Chinese Theatre is usually thick with tourists queuing for their tickets. Other programs include detours around the Westside at night, to the beach areas, the *Queen Mary*, day-long excursions to Disneyland, and shopping trips into Mexico and Tijuana. Most of these can be taken at a reduced cost by staying at one of the major hostels (see "Accommodation," p.260), which offer special package trips that are often more affordable, and fun, than the usual variety.

Costs are $30–95 minimum per person, with some simple hour-long trips around Hollywood for around $15; assorted leaflets are strewn over hotel lobbies and visitor centers. You can make reservations at (and be picked up from) most hotels; otherwise contact one of the following booking offices, all of them located in Hollywood proper:

Hollywood Fantasy Tours 6671 Hollywood Blvd ☏323/469-8184, ⍟www.hollywoodfantasytours .com

LA Tours 1617 Gower St ☏323/460-6490, ⍟www.latours.net

Red Line Tours 6773 Hollywood Blvd ☏323/402-1072, ⍟www.redlinetours.com

Starline Tours 6925 Hollywood Blvd ☏323/463-3333, ⍟www.starlinetours.com

VIP Tours 9830 Bellanca Ave ☏310/641-8114, ⍟www.viptoursandcharters.com

Specialist tours

The specialist tours listed below generally cost $30 or more per person. For more suggestions, pick up the free *LA Visitors Guide* from hotels and visitor centers.

Architecture Tours LA ☏323/464-7868, ⍟www .architecturetoursla.com. Driving tours of the major buildings of the LA region, with packages focusing on Hollywood, West LA, Pasadena, and Downtown.

Architours ☏323/294-5821 or 1-866/227-2448, ⍟www.architours.com. Walking, driving, and custom tours of the art and architecture highlights of certain parts of the city. Multi-day trips also available.

Black LA Tours ☏323/750-9267, ⍟www .soulofamerica.com/tours/tour_la.html. Black historical and entertainment tours of once-renowned Central Avenue and important sites for African-American society and culture.

Googie Tours ☏323/666-9623. Pilgrimages to Southern California's remaining space-age glass and formica diners, quirky cocktail lounges, classic fast-food joints, and other gems of pop architecture.

Heli USA 16303 Waterman Drive, Van Nuys ☏818/994-1445 or 1-877/TO-FLY-LA, ⍟www .toflyla.com. Tours by helicopter of some of the more prominent visual sights in the region, such as movie studios, skyscrapers, and the Hollywood sign, for $150–270, with dinner packages available.

Hiking tours Sierra Club (☏323/387-4287, ⍟www.sierraclub.org); State Parks Department (☏818/880-0350, ⍟www.parks.ca.gov); Santa Monica Mountains National Recreation Area (☏818/597-1036, ☏www.nps.gov/samo). Free weekend guided hikes are available through these organizations, traversing the wilds of the Santa Monica Mountains and Hollywood Hills.

LA Conservancy Tours ☏213/623-CITY, ⍟laconservancy.org. Excellent walking treks of Downtown, rich with Art Deco movie palaces, once-opulent financial monuments, and architectural gems like the Bradbury Building. Every Saturday, Downtown tours leave the *Biltmore Hotel* at 10am (reservations required; $10); alternately, you can tour Angelino Heights, Highland Park, and San Pedro for the same fee.

Neon Cruises 501 W Olympic Blvd, Downtown ☏213/489-9918, ⍟www.neonmona.org/cruise .html. Three-hour-long, eye-popping evening tours of LA's best neon art, led once a month on Saturdays by the Museum of Neon Art. These very popular tours often book up months in advance.

Off 'n' Running Tours 1129 Cardiff Ave, West LA ☏310/246-1418, ⍟www.offnrunningtours.com. Offbeat four-to-six-mile jogging tours of the stars' homes, plus sprightly jaunts around Beverly Hills and West LA.

SPARC tours: the Murals of LA 685 Venice Blvd, Venice ☏310/822-9560, ⍟www.sparcmurals.org. Public art is alive and well in LA, and these thoroughly enlightening tours of the "mural capital of the world" are worth a look. Pricey two-hour mural tours ($400) are personalized to your interests and may include discussions with the artists.

Studio tours

For some small insight into how a film or TV show is made, or just to admire the special effects, there are **guided studio tours** at NBC ($7; ☏818/840-3537), Paramount ($35; ☏323/956-1777, ⍟www.paramount .com/studio), Sony ($20; ☏323/520-TOUR), Universal ($50; ⍟www.universalstudioshollywood.com), and Warner Bros. Studios ($35; ☏818/972-8687); all are near Burbank except for Sony, which is in Culver City, and Paramount, in Hollywood. If you want to be part of the **audience** in a TV show, Hollywood Boulevard, just outside the Chinese Theatre, is the spot to be: TV company reps regularly appear handing out free tickets, and they'll bus you to the studio and back. All you have to do once there is be willing to laugh and clap on cue. For more information on seeing your favorite shows in person, contact Audiences Unlimited (see box, p.115).

Phones, mail, and email

Like most major US cities, LA has an excellent communications infrastructure, with countless high-tech links to the rest of the country and the world. Although some areas are better hooked up than others – the Westside, for example – most communication services are more than adequate throughout the region, especially telephone service and email; the US mail is comparatively slow, if usually quite reliable.

Telephones

If you're making a **telephone** call, Los Angeles has about half a dozen area codes (listed below) that, with the rise of ten-digit dialing, you may need to use even if calling from within the same area code. A local call on a public phone usually costs 50¢. Outside the immediate calling zone, you'll have to dial a 1, plus the area code, then the telephone number. Unless you're using a cell phone (and not paying a roaming fee), you'll be charged quite a bit more for out-of-area-code calls than for calls within them. For detailed information about calls, area codes, and rates in the LA area, consult the front *White Pages* of the telephone directory.

Calling from your **hotel room** will cost considerably more than if you use a public phone. Fancy hotels often charge a connection fee of at least $1 for most calls (waived if they're toll-free), and international calls will cost a small fortune. While an increasing number of public phones accept credit cards, these can incur astronomical charges for long-distance service, including a high "connection fee" that can bump charges up to as much as $7 a minute.

Long-distance and international calls dialed direct are most expensive during daylight hours (7am–6pm), with evening charges slightly reduced (6–11pm) and early morning hours cheapest of all (11pm–7am). Detailed rates are listed at the front of the local *White Pages*.

Any number with ☎800, ☎866, ☎877, or ☎888 in place of the area code is **toll-free**. Most major hotels, government agencies, and car rental firms have toll-free numbers, though some can be used only within the state of California – dialing is the only way to find out. Numbers with a ☎1-900 prefix are toll calls, typically sports information lines, psychic hotlines, and phone-sex centers, and will cost you a variable, though consistently high, fee for just a few minutes of use.

Telephone charge cards

Most long-distance companies enable customers to make **calling-card** calls billed to their home number. Call your company's customer-service line to find out if it provides this service, and if so, what the toll-free access code is.

An alternative to telephone charge cards is cheap, **pre-paid phone cards** allowing calls to virtually anywhere in the world. Most convenience stores sell them; look for signs posted in shop windows advertising rates, which can vary dramatically, and check the fine print to make sure you're getting a good deal. Some cards allow you to add time to them as their minutes elapse through the use of a unique PIN number, while others only have a set number of minutes available. Finally, pre-paid calling-card companies may change their rates, policies, or deals on a month-to-month basis, or go out of business altogether, so if you're buying a card, make sure to use it within a reasonable amount of time, lest you end up with a worthless piece of plastic.

Useful telephone numbers

Emergencies ☏911 for fire, police, or ambulance
Police ☏213/625-3311
Sheriff ☏213/526-5541
Operator ☏0
Local directory information ☏411
Long-distance directory information
☏1 +area code/555-1212

International calls to Los Angeles:
Dial your country's international access code + 1 for the US + LA area code + phone number
International calls from Los Angeles:
Dial ☏011 + country code + phone number
Country codes: Australia ☏61, Ireland ☏353, New Zealand ☏64, United Kingdom ☏44. For all other codes, dial ☏0 for the operator or check the front of the local White Pages.

LA area codes

213	Downtown
310	West Hollywood, Beverly Hills, West LA, Westwood, Santa Monica, Venice, Malibu, South Bay, San Pedro
323	Mid-Wilshire, Hollywood, South Central LA, East LA
562	Long Beach, Whittier, Southeast LA
626	Pasadena, Arcadia, San Gabriel Valley
714	Northern Orange County – Anaheim, Garden Grove, Huntington Beach
805	Santa Clarita, Lancaster, northern deserts
818	Burbank, Glendale, San Fernando Valley
909	Pomona, Inland Empire
949	Southern Orange County – Costa Mesa, Newport and Laguna beaches

Cell phones

If visiting from overseas and you still want to use your **cell phone**, check with your phone provider if it will work abroad, and what the call charges are. Unless you have a tri-band phone, it is unlikely that a mobile bought for use outside the US will work inside the States and vice versa, with many only working within the region designated by the area code in the phone number – ☏213, ☏310, etc. If you have a phone that works Stateside, inform your phone provider before going abroad to get international access switched on. You may get charged extra for this and you're also likely to be charged extra for incoming calls when abroad, as the people calling you will be paying the usual rate. If you want to **retrieve messages** while you're away, you'll have to ask your provider for a new access code, as your home one is unlikely to work abroad. **Tri-band phones** will automatically switch to the US frequency, but these can be pricey, so you may want to rent a phone if you're traveling to the US. For further information on this subject, check out ⊕www.telecomsadvice.org.uk/features/using_your_mobile_abroad.

Mail

Post offices are usually open Monday through Friday, from 9am to 5pm, although some are open on Saturday from 9am to noon or 1pm.

Ordinary **mail** sent within the US costs 37¢ (at press time) for letters weighing up to an ounce, while standard postcards cost 23¢. For anywhere outside the US, airmail letters weighing up to an ounce cost 80¢; postcards and aerogrammes 70¢. Airmail between the US and Europe, for instance, may take a week, and 12–14 days to Australia and New Zealand. Drop mail off at any post office or in the blue mailboxes found on street corners throughout LA. Domestic letters that don't carry a **zip code** are liable to get lost or at least seriously delayed; phone books list zip codes for their service area, and post offices – even abroad – should have zip-code directories for major US cities.

You can have mail sent to you c/o General Delivery (known elsewhere as poste restante), at the main post office in Downtown LA, next to Union Station, at 760 N Main St, Los Angeles, CA 90012 (☏213/617-4405 or 1-800/275-8777), which will hold mail for thirty days before returning it to the sender – so make sure the envelope has a return address. You can pick up general delivery mail from the main post office Monday to Friday, 8am to 3pm (otherwise, regular hours are Mon–Fri 8am–7pm, Sat 8am–4pm). Alternatively, any decent hotel will hold mail for you, even in advance of your arrival.

If you want to send packages overseas from LA, check the front of telephone directories for packaging requirements. Bear in mind that you'll need to fill in a green customs declaration form, which is available from post offices. International parcel rates for items weighing less than a pound run from $5 to $17, depending on the package's size and destination, and how quickly you want it to arrive.

Email

Email is often the cheapest and most convenient way to keep in touch. **Cyber-cafés** are found throughout LA, including *CyberJava*, 7080 Hollywood Blvd, Hollywood (☎323/466-5600, ⊛www.cyberjava.com), and the *Newsroom Café*, 120 N Robertson Blvd, West LA (☎310/652-4444), with the

going rate at least 10 cents per minute. Additionally, many public **libraries** have computers that provide free Internet access (notably the Central Library in Downtown LA, see p.75, and the Beverly Hills public library, see p.126) – though there may be a waiting list at peak hours.

If neither of these options fit the bill, or if you just need a fast machine to visit the Net, then find a commercial **photocopying** and printing shop such as FedEx Kinko's (look under "Copying" in the *Yellow Pages*). They'll charge around 25¢ a minute for use of their computers, but you're guaranteed fast access; the same goes for Internet stations available in the terminals at LAX. Most upscale hotels also offer email and Internet access – though often at a steep price.

Opening hours, public holidays, and festivals

The opening hours of specific attractions – including museums, theme parks, public offices, and homes open for tours – are given throughout the Guide, with phone numbers for those sights that are open irregularly, closed until further notice, or require a reservation to visit. It's always worth checking ahead, especially if you're planning to visit attractions far from central LA.

Opening hours

As a general rule, most **museums** are **open** Tuesday through Saturday, from 10am until 5 or 6pm, though a select few stay open until 7 or 8pm. Those that don't tend to stay open late one evening a week – usually Thursday, when ticket prices are sometimes reduced. **Government offices**, including post offices, are open during regular business hours, typically 8 or 9am until 5pm, Monday through Friday (with the odd post office also open for a few hours on Saturday, often 9am–2pm). Most **stores** are open daily from 10am and close at 5 or 6pm, while specialty stores can be more erratic, usually opening and closing later in the day (from noon to 2pm until 8–10pm)

and remaining shuttered for two days of the week. **Malls** tend to be open from 10am until 7 or 8pm daily, though individual stores may close before the mall does.

While many diners stay open around the clock, the more typical **restaurants** open daily around 11am or noon for lunch and close between 9.30 and 11pm. Places that serve breakfast, however, open early between 6 to 8am and serve lunch later, closing in the early or mid-afternoon. Dance and live-music **clubs** often won't open until 9 or 10pm (or even later, in some cases), and many will serve liquor until 2am and then either close for the night or stay open until dawn without serving booze. **Bars** that close at 2am – when they're legally obligated to quit serving booze – may reopen as early as 6am to grab bleary-eyed customers in need of a liquid breakfast.

Finally, the big-name **theme parks** are open throughout the year, usually daily during summer, from 9 or 10am until 10 or 11pm, and with reduced hours during the offseason (ie Mon–Fri 10am–6pm, Sat & Sun 9am–9pm). The two exceptions are Disneyland, which generally has longer hours throughout the year, and water parks, which are often accessible during the summer only.

Public holidays and festivals

On the national **public holidays** listed below, banks, government offices, and many museums are liable to be closed all day. Small stores, as well as some restaurants and clubs, are usually closed as well, but shopping malls, supermarkets, and department and chain stores increasingly remain open. Most parks, beaches, and cemeteries stay open during holidays, as do theme parks, which draw some of their biggest crowds during such times. The **summer tourism season**, when many attractions have extended hours, runs from Memorial Day to Labor Day.

The LA region hosts a wide variety of **festivals** during the year; the highlights are described in "Festivals and events," p.341. Most of LA may hold parades, set off fireworks and indulge in general merriment for New Year's Day, the Fourth of July, Halloween, and the assorted Christmas light shows. Except for Pasadena's signature Rose Parade, LA has no equivalent to New York's holiday parades, and is rather subdued except for the chaotic spectacle at the local shopping malls, marking the beginning of the Christmas buying season – a four-week shopping orgy that is perhaps LA's biggest festival of all.

Official national holidays

January
New Year's Day
3rd Monday: Dr Martin Luther King Jr's birthday
February
3rd Monday: Presidents' Day
May
Last Monday: Memorial Day
July
4: Independence Day
September
1st Monday: Labor Day
October
2nd Monday: Columbus Day
November
11: Veterans Day
4th Thursday: Thanksgiving
December
25: Christmas

Costs, money, and banks

Given the historically low value of the American dollar, there's rarely been a better time for foreign travelers to visit LA. The city is less expensive than San Francisco or New York, and with a minimum of effort you can find plenty of bargains and reasonably priced goods and services, though of course you won't lack for choice should you want to splurge at one of the city's swankier restaurants or trendy bars.

Average costs

Accommodation is likely to be your biggest single **expense** in LA: adequate lodging is rarely available for less than $50 per night, although hostels will of course be cheaper (usually $15–22 per night in a dorm bed). Any reasonable hotel room will run from $75–100, with fancier hotels costing much more – upwards of $400 in some cases.

Camping in LA is an alternative, but only if you're staying in more isolated areas like San Clemente, where you can get into a campground for around $16–21 per night (see "Accommodation," p.261).

Unlike accommodation, prices for good **food** range widely, as do the types of places that serve it, from hot-dog stands to chic restaurants. You could get by on as little as $15 a day, but realistically you should aim for around $50 – and remember, too, that LA has plenty of great spots for a splurge. Beyond restaurants, the city has many bars, clubs, and live-music venues to suit all tastes and wallets.

In terms of **transportation**, your best bet is probably to rent a car from any of the rental outlets around the airport, especially if you're traveling with a group. Regional distances are huge, and if you're headed anywhere beyond central LA, or more specifically beyond the Westside, you'll undoubtedly find public transit to be a time-consuming hassle. US gas prices, moreover, are still relatively cheap compared to those in the rest of the world and especially Europe.

Added to the cost of most items you purchase is an 8.25 percent sales **tax**. Additionally, many municipalities tack on a hotel tax of around 14–15 percent, which can drive up accommodation costs dramatically.

Finally, expect to **tip about 15 percent** to waiters in restaurants (unless the service is truly wretched), and 20 percent in upscale establishments or for excellent service. About the same amount should be added to taxi fares – and round them up to the nearest 50¢ or dollar. A hotel porter should get $1 per bag; chambermaids $1–2 a day; and valet attendants $1.

For attractions in the main part of the Guide, **prices** are quoted for adults, with children's rates listed only if they are more than a few dollars less; at some spots, kids get in for half price, or for free if they're under 8. Seniors may sometimes get a break, too, usually running a few dollars less than the standard adult rate. The city also has a few **free** attractions for everyone, but these are mostly historical and cultural monuments like adobes and old railroad stations – with the major exception of the Getty Center (though parking is $7).

Banks and ATMs

With an **ATM card**, you'll be able to withdraw cash just about anywhere in LA, though you'll be charged $2–4 for using a different bank's network. Foreign cash-dispensing cards linked to international networks, such as Plus or Cirrus, are also widely accepted – ask your home bank or credit company which branches you can use. To find the location of the nearest ATM in LA, call: American Express ☎1-800/CASH-NOW; Cirrus ☎1-800/4-CIRRUS; The Exchange ☎1-800/237-ATMS; or Plus ☎1-800/843-7587. Make sure you have a **personal identification number** (PIN) that's designed to work overseas.

Bank hours are generally from 9am to 4pm or 5pm Monday to Thursday, and from 10am to 6pm on Friday; the big local names are Wells Fargo and Bank of America. For banking services – especially currency exchange – outside normal business hours and on weekends, try major hotels or Travelex outlets.

Travelers' checks

US **travelers' checks** are the safest way for overseas visitors to carry money, and the better-known travelers' checks, such as those issued by American Express and Visa, are treated as cash in most shops. The usual fee for travelers' check sales is one or two percent, though this fee may be waived if you buy the checks through your home bank. It pays to get a selection of denominations, but particularly tens and twenties. Keep the purchase agreement and a record of **check serial numbers** safe and separate from the checks themselves. In the event that checks are lost or stolen, the issuing company will expect you to report the loss immediately (see p.51 for emergency numbers). Most companies claim to replace lost or stolen checks within 24 hours.

Credit and debit cards

Credit cards are the most widely accepted form of payment for major hotels, restaurants, and retailers, even though a few smaller merchants still do not accept them. You'll be asked to show a credit card when renting a car, bike, windsurfer, or other such item, or to

Money: a note for foreign travelers

Given the recent decline in value of the **US dollar**, at the time of writing one pound sterling will buy $1.70–1.90, a euro $1.15–1.35, a Canadian dollar 70–85¢, an Australian dollar 65–80¢, and a New Zealand dollar 50–70¢ – all of which makes visiting LA an attractive budget vacation.

US currency comes in bills of $1, $5, $10, $20, $50, and $100 **denominations**. All are the same size, though denominations of $10 and higher have in the last few years been changing shades from their familiar drab green. These days such bills offer more colorful pastels of faint red, yellow, and blue, and other embedded inks and watermarks – all to deter would-be counterfeiters. The dollar comprises one hundred cents, made up of combinations of one-cent pennies, five-cent nickels, ten-cent dimes, and 25-cent quarters. Quarters bearing individual state names and related historical designs are being rolled out one month at a time until 2008 (including California's own design – an easy-to-find souvenir). Quarters are most useful for buses, vending machines, parking meters, and telephones, so always carry plenty.

start a "tab" at hotels for incidental charges; in any case, you can always pay the bill in cash when you return the item or check out of your room. Most major credit cards issued by foreign banks are honored in the US. Visa, MasterCard, American Express, and Diners Club are the most widely used.

Credit cards can also come in handy as a backup source of funds, and they can save on exchange-rate commissions. Make sure you have a personal identification number, or PIN, that's designed to work overseas. Remember that all cash advances are treated as loans, with **interest** accruing daily from the date of withdrawal (there may be a transaction fee on top of this).

If your credit cards are **stolen**, you'll need to provide information on where and when you made your last transactions, and the specific numbers of the (emergency numbers are given on p.51).

Wiring money

Wiring money from home using one of the companies listed below is never convenient or cheap, and should be considered a last resort. It's also possible to have money wired directly from a bank in your home country to a bank in the US, even though this is somewhat less reliable as it involves two separate institutions. If you choose this option, the person making the transfer will include the address of the branch bank where you want to pick up the money, and the address and

telex number of the bank to which the funds are being sent. Money wired this way will take two working days to arrive.

The quickest way to have money wired to you is to have someone take the cash to the nearest American Express Moneygram office (☏1-800/543-4080; also available at participating Travelex branches) and have it instantaneously wired to you, minus a ten-percent commission that varies according to the amount sent – the entire process should take no longer than ten minutes. For similar, if slightly pricier, services, Western Union has offices throughout LA (information at ☏1-800/325-6000 in the US; ☏0800/833 833 in the UK; and ☏1-800/649 565 in Australia; ⊛www.westernunion.com), with credit card payments subject to an additional $10 fee.

International Money Transfers can be made from any bank in Australia and New Zealand to a nominated bank abroad; fees run around A$25/NZ$30, but be warned – the whole process can take anywhere from a couple of days to several months. If you desperately need money, wire services are faster, but about twice as expensive.

If you have a few days' leeway, sending a postal **money order**, exchangeable at any post office through the mail, is a cheaper option. The equivalent for foreign travelers is the international money order, for which you need to allow up to seven days in international air mail before arrival.

The media

BASICS | The media

Although LA's local press has a deserved reputation for sensationalism, known for its helicopter pursuits of police chases and constant celebrity gossip, you can still find good regional and national media outlets, typically of the print variety. With the growth of cable TV, there are more television viewing choices than ever, though since most channels are owned by the same handful of multinational corporations, the quality has not improved one bit. The same is true for area radio stations; hunt down LA's public-radio affiliates for relief from the inane talk-show chatter and rigid pop-music playlists.

Newspapers and magazines

For such a large city, LA supports surprisingly few daily **newspapers**. At the top of the list is the *Los Angeles Times* (35¢; www.latimes.com), the most widely read newspaper in Southern California, available at news boxes and dealers throughout town. Friday's "Calendar" section is an essential source for entertainment and cultural listings (with much of the information also available online for a fee at www.calendarlive.com). Upscale hotels often distribute the newspaper to your door for free, sometimes along with a copy of the *New York Times* or *Wall Street Journal*. However, most other major newspapers, whether domestic or foreign, tend to be found mainly at city and university libraries, and a few large magazine stands.

As far as **other dailies** go, the *Los Angeles Daily News* (www.dailynews.com) is more conservative than the *LA Times*, with a near-militant San Fernando Valley slant; while *La Opinion* (www.laopinion.com) is one of the country's major Spanish-language newspapers, and has a large readership in LA. The *Orange County Register* (www.ocregister .com), a right-of-center paper, is mainly found in its namesake macro-suburb and offers little for LA readers. Smaller weekly papers include such names as the *Watts Times*, *Downtown News,* and *Los Angeles Independent*, each focusing on more local concerns within a particular district or community.

There are a few good **alternative weeklies**, most notably the free *LA Weekly* (www.laweekly.com), found at libraries and retailers everywhere, providing engaging investigative journalism and copious entertainment listings. The *OC Weekly* (www .ocweekly.com), the liberal Orange County counterpart of the *LA Weekly*, is a fine alternative source.

Every community of any size has at least a few free newspapers that cater to the local scene. Like the *LA Weekly*, many of these are also good sources for listings for bars, restaurants, and nightlife within their areas. Both the USC and UCLA campuses have libraries carrying recent overseas newspapers, while day-old **foreign papers** are on sale in Hollywood at Universal News Agency, 1645 N Las Palmas Ave (daily 7am–midnight), and the 24-hour World Book and News, 1652 N Cahuenga Blvd.

LA has a few style-conscious **magazines**, foremost among them the monthly *Los Angeles* magazine ($3.95; lamag.com), packed with gossipy news and profiles of local movers and shakers, as well as reviews of the city's trendiest restaurants and clubs. There are also dozens of less glossy, more erratically published **zines** focusing on LA's diverse gay and lesbian culture and nightclubs. As for **free** magazines, the touristy *Where LA* (www.wherela.com) is a monthly public-relations magazine found in many hotel rooms, and has both glossy reviews and more straightforward listings.

Television

LA **network television** generally offers a steady diet of talk shows, sitcoms, soap operas, and the ubiquitous "reality shows," with some Spanish-language and Asian stations on the UHF portion of the dial. An ad-free alternative to the standard fare is KCET, on UHF channel 28 (🌐www.kcet .org), LA's public television station and one of the nation's top producers of educational programs.

Most motel and hotel rooms are hooked up to some form of **cable TV**, though the number of channels available to guests depends on where you stay. (See the daily papers for channels, schedules, and times.) Most cable stations are actually no better than the big broadcast networks, though some of the specialized channels are occasionally interesting. Cable News Network (CNN) and Headline News both have round-the-clock news, with Fox News providing a right-wing slant on the day's events. ESPN is your best bet for all kinds of sports, MTV for youth-oriented music videos and programming, and VH-1 for Baby Boomer shows. Home Box Office (HBO) and Showtime present big-budget Hollywood flicks and excellent TV shows such as *The Sopranos*, while Turner Classic Movies takes its programming from the Golden Age of Hollywood cinema (1930s to 1950s).

Many major **sporting events** are transmitted on a pay-per-view basis, and watching an event like a heavyweight boxing match will set you back at least $50, billed directly to your motel room. Most hotels and motels also offer a choice of **recent movies** that have just finished their theatrical runs, at around $10 per film.

Broadcast television stations

KCBS CBS channel 2
KNBC NBC channel 4
KTLA WB channel 5
KABC ABC channel 7
KCAL unaffiliated channel 9
KTTV Fox channel 11
KCOP UPN channel 13
KCET PBS channel 28 UHF
KMEX Spanish-language Univision channel 34 UHF

Radio

Radio stations are even more abundant than broadcast TV stations, and the majority stick to mainstream commercial formats. **AM stations** are best for news, traffic reports, and talk radio, while **FM stations**, particularly

the federally and subscriber-funded **public** and **college stations** found between 88 and 92 FM, broadcast diverse programming, from bizarre underground rock to obscure local theater (for some of the more interesting stations we've included websites for program details). Of these stations, KCRW (89.9) has some of the most diverse programming in LA, from public affairs to dance music, which at night can be anything from trance, dub, and trip-hop to ambient. LA also has a range of decent **specialist music** stations – classical, jazz, and so on – as well as a sizable number of Spanish-language stations. Finally, check out LA Radiowatch (🌐www .radiowatch.com) for information on up-and-coming **Internet** stations playing tunes over the Web – often more unusual and daring than their broadcasted counterparts (we've listed a few below as a sample).

LA radio stations

AM

KFI 640 right-wing talk radio
KFWB 980 news, traffic, talk, and Dodger baseball
KNX 1070 traffic, news, and sports reports
KXTA 1150 sports and talk

FM

KKJZ 88.1 blues and jazz; 🌐www.kkjz.org
KUCR 88.3 eclectic and alternative
KXLU 88.9 alternative, progressive, and eclectic 🌐www.kxlu.com
KPCC 89.3 news, talk, arts, and NPR 🌐www .scpr.org
KCRW 89.9 one of the country's best NPR affiliates, with new music, transatlantic imports, and world news 🌐www.kcrw.com
KPFK 90.7 leftist opinions, news, and music, Pacifica affiliate; 🌐www.kpfk.org
KUSC 91.5 classical and opera 🌐www.kusc.org
KCBS 93.1 classic rock
KZLA 93.9 country
KLOS 95.5 album rock
KLSX 97.1 talk
KSSE 97.5 Latin pop and salsa
KKBT 100.3 soul, R&B, and rap
KRTH 101.1 golden oldies
KIIS 102.7 Top 40 pop
KBIG 104.3 pop and dance
KMZT 105.1 classical
KPWR 106 rap and R&B
KROQ 106.7 indie and grunge rock

Internet

Groove Radio classic electronica, with famous and underground cuts ⓦ www.grooveradio.com

KNAC heavy metal favorites, plus contemporary grunge and headbanging ⓦ www.knac.com
UCLA Radio pure college playlists, featuring eclectic music and talk programming ⓦ www.uclaradio.com

B

BASICS | Crime and personal safety

Crime and personal safety

Hollywood revels in its stereotypes of LA as a lawless land of rampant muggings and drive-by shootings. In reality, members of the notorious LA street gangs – who figure in most of the news headlines for acts of random violence – target each other rather than tourists, and many violent crimes can be avoided by steering clear of rough or dicey neighborhoods.

Most places in LA, from Downtown to the coast, are fairly nonthreatening during the daytime, especially in the major tourist zones, while the number of safe spots diminishes at night. Much of **Downtown**, west of Skid Row at least, is walkable during the morning and afternoon hours, while at night you should stay in your hotel room if you're staying anywhere away from the Downtown core of Bunker Hill – the area closes up after dark anyway. **Mid-Wilshire** should be treated like Downtown, with special care given to the dicey Temple-Beaudry, Pico-Union, and Westlake neighborhoods, and the area both south of Wilshire and east of La Brea Avenue. **Hollywood** is best explored on foot, and is, while dodgy in some places, a prime spot for after-hours dancing and drinking, if you don't mind a few prostitutes in your midst. **West Hollywood** is busy and safe throughout the day and night, especially along the Sunset Strip, as are most **West LA** areas from Beverly Hills to Santa Monica – with the notable exception of Venice's small but dicey ghetto between Electric Avenue and Lincoln Boulevard. Most of **South Central LA** should only be visited during the day, with some areas like Compton off-limits at all times to unaccustomed visitors.

Further out, you should have few problems in the major tourist areas – Burbank, Pasadena, coastal Long Beach, Malibu, coastal Orange County. There are some scattered places where the street gangs are particularly visible – large sections of Southeast and East LA, North Long Beach, Pacoima in the San Fernando Valley, and Orange County towns like Santa Ana – and the attractions therein should be approached with caution.

Following the terrorist attacks of September 11, 2001, and the US invasion of Iraq in March 2003, there have been major **security clampdowns** at governmental buildings and institutions in LA, as with the rest of the country. If you visit an airport, local city hall, or a federal building, you can expect to get scanned or patted down, but most museums and other public entities haven't yet reached this level of official paranoia. Still, always have your ID ready just in case.

Mugging and theft

Because LA attracts so many tourists, it certainly has its share of **petty crime**, with pickpocketing and the odd mugging accounting for most of the problems. As a general rule, try to keep your wits about you in crowds, make sure your wallet or purse is secured, and, of course, avoid parks, parking lots, and dark streets in dicey areas at night.

Always be careful when using **ATMs**, especially in nontourist areas. Try to use machines near major hotels, shops, or offices, and during the daytime. If the worst

49

does happen, it's advisable to hand over your money and afterwards find a phone and dial ☎911, or go to the nearest police station. Here, report the theft and get a reference number on the report so you can claim insurance and/or travelers' check refunds.

To avoid being the victim of **hotel room theft**, lock your valuables in the room safe when you leave, and always keep doors locked when you're in the room. Don't open the door to anyone you don't know or aren't expecting, and if a questionable visitor claims to be a hotel representative, phone the front desk to verify their identity.

Having bags that contain travel documents stolen can be a big headache, so make photocopies of everything important before you travel and keep them separate from the originals. **If your passport is stolen** (or if you lose it), call your country's consulate (see list on p.372), and pick up an application form, or have one sent to you. Complete the application and submit it with a notarized photocopy of your ID and a reissuing fee, often around $30. The process of issuing a new passport can take up to six weeks, so plan accordingly.

Keep a record of the numbers of your **travelers' checks** separate from the actual checks; if you lose them, call the issuing company on the toll-free number below. They'll ask you for the check numbers, the place you bought them, when and how you lost them, and whether or not you contacted the police. The missing checks should be reissued within a couple of days, and you can request an emergency advance to tide you over in the meantime.

Finally, remember that you should never flash money around, leave your wallet open or count money in public, and look panicked, even if you are. Also, it goes without saying that you should never hitchhike anywhere in LA.

Women's safety

A **woman traveling** alone is not as conspicuous a target in LA as she might be in other American metropolises, but common sense still applies. If you can, try not to travel at night by public transportation, especially in the city's dodgier parts – South Central, Boyle Heights, the barrios east of Downtown LA, and so on. If this is your only means of transit, sit as close to the bus driver as possible. Also on the danger list is walking through desolate, unlit streets at night; you're better off taking cabs to your destination, if even for just a few blocks. If you don't appear confused, scared, or drunk, and project a serious or wary countenance instead, your chances of attack may be lessened.

If you listen to the advice of locals, and stick to safer parts of town, going into **bars and clubs** should pose no problems, as women's privacy is often respected, especially in dance and rock clubs. However, sexual harassment is more common for single women in country-and-western clubs, and the bars of East LA are very male-oriented and should be strictly avoided, as should those in Southeast and South Central LA. If in doubt, Westside bars

Breaking the law

Whether intentionally or not, foreign visitors may find themselves **breaking US laws** on occasion. Aside from **speeding** or **parking violations**, one of the most common ways visitors bring trouble on themselves is through **jaywalking**, or crossing the road against red lights or away from intersections. Fines can be stiff, and the police will most assuredly not take sympathy on you if you mumble that you "didn't think it was illegal."

Drinking laws provide another source of irritation to visitors, particularly as the law prohibits drinking liquor, wine, or beer in most public spaces like parks and beaches, and liquor is officially off-limits to anyone under 21. And although possessing small amounts of **marijuana** is a misdemeanor in California, it may get you thrown out of the country if you're a foreigner – or into jail for larger amounts. Other infringements include insulting a police officer (ie, arguing with one), and riding a bicycle at night without proper lights and reflectors.

Emergency numbers for lost cards and checks

American Express cards
☎1-800/528-4800, ⓦwww
.americanexpress.com
American Express checks
☎1-800/221-7282
Citicorp checks ☎1-800/645-6556,
ⓦwww.citicorp.com
Diners Club ☎1-800/234-6377,
ⓦwww.dinersclub.com

Discover ☎1-800/DISCOVER,
ⓦwww.discovercard.com
MasterCard ☎1-800/826-2181,
ⓦwww.mastercard.com
Thomas Cook/MasterCard checks
☎1-800/223-9920, ⓦwww.travelex
.com or ⓦwww.thomascook.co.uk
Visa cards ☎1-800/847-2911,
ⓦwww.visa.com
Visa checks ☎1-800/227-6811

and clubs are usually safe choices, and gay and lesbian bars are generally trouble-free alternatives.

If disaster strikes, rape **counseling services** are available throughout the city (check the *Yellow Pages* under "Rape services" or "Crisis intervention"), and can also be accessed through the sheriff's office, which can make arrangements for personal help and counseling.

Car crime and safety

Crimes committed against tourists driving **rental cars** made headlines in the 1990s, but there are certain precautions you can take to keep yourself safe. In major urban areas like LA, any car you rent should have nothing on it – such as a special license plate – to distinguish it as a rental car. When driving, under no circumstances should you stop in unlit or deserted urban areas, and especially not if someone is waving at you and claiming there's something wrong with your vehicle. Similarly, if you are "accidentally" rammed by the driver behind you, do not stop immediately but instead drive on to the nearest well-lit and busy spot and phone the police at ☎911. Keep doors locked and hide valuables out of sight, either in the trunk or the glove compartment – any valuables

you don't need for your journey should be left in your hotel safe.

Should a relatively uncommon "**carjacking**" occur, in which you're asked to hand over your car at gunpoint, flee the vehicle as quickly as possible and get away from the scene, then call the police. There is absolutely no reason why you should die for the sake of an automobile – even in LA.

If your car **breaks down** at night while on a boulevard or major street, activate the emergency flashers to signal a police officer for assistance, or, if possible during the day, find the nearest phone book and call for a tow truck. Should you be forced to stop your car on a freeway, pull over to the right shoulder of the highway – never the left, as countless motorists have been killed by oncoming traffic – and activate your flashers. Wait for assistance either in your vehicle while strapped in by a seat belt or on a safe embankment nearby. If necessary, you can use one of the "**call boxes**" found every half-mile or so along freeways in LA. No matter the situation, never do "on the spot" repair work to your vehicle beside an LA highway; numerous would-be mechanics have been killed in recent years while adjusting engines, fixing headlights, and changing flat tires.

Travelers with disabilities

Travelers with mobility challenges or physical disabilities will find LA, along with the US in general, more amenable to their needs than many places in the world. Because of the passage of the 1990 Americans with Disabilities Act, or ADA, all public buildings must be wheelchair-accessible and have suitable toilets (though the US Supreme Court has limited the reach of the ADA in recent years to exclude certain work-related disorders and personal injuries). Accordingly, the city has sloped curbs at most street corners, subways have elevator access, and city buses have lifts, along with space and handgrips for wheelchair users. Most hotels and restaurants, especially those built within the last decade, also have adequate accommodations for wheelchairs. Even movie theaters – that last hold-out for equal access – have been forced by courts in recent years to allow people in wheelchairs to have a reasonable, unimpeded view of the screen.

Transportation

Airlines in the US must by law accommodate those with disabilities, some of them even allowing attendants of those with serious conditions to accompany them for a reduced fare. Similarly, almost every **Amtrak** train includes one or more cars with accommodation for disabled passengers, along with wheelchair assistance at train platforms, adapted on-board seating, free travel for guide dogs, and fifteen percent discounts on fares, with 24 hours' advance notice. Passengers with hearing impairment can get information by calling ☏1-800/523-6590 or checking out ⊛www.amtrak.com.

However, traveling by **Greyhound** and Amtrak Thruway service is often problematic. Buses are not equipped with platforms for wheelchairs, though intercity carriers are required by law to provide assistance with boarding, and disabled passengers may be able to get priority seating. Those unable to travel alone, and in possession of a doctor's certificate, may receive two-for-one fares to bring a companion along. Call Greyhound's ADA customer assistance line for more information (☏1-800/752-4841, ⊛www .greyhound.com).

Along with wheelchair lifts, area **Metro** buses provide reduced fares to physically challenged passengers (monthly passes for $12), and visual aids to help with signaling buses; get more information by calling ☏213-626-4455, or TDD/TTY ☏1-800/252-9040, or visiting ⊛www.mta.net. Also, fixed-route "paratransit" services offer door-to-door service for those who cannot access regular mass transit; call ☏1-800/827-0829 for information.

The city's major **car rental** firms provide vehicles with hand controls for drivers with leg or spinal disabilities. The American Automobile Association, locally at 2601 S Figueroa St (Mon–Fri 9am–5pm; ☏213/741-3686, ⊛www.aaa-calif.com), produces the *Handicapped Driver's Mobility Guide*, and parking regulations for disabled motorists are uniform: licenses for the disabled must carry a three-inch-square international access symbol, and placards bearing this symbol must be hung from the car's rear-view mirror (blue colors signify permanent disability, while red signifies a temporary condition of up to six months). Additionally, self-service gas stations are required to provide full service to disabled motorists at self-service prices.

Disabled access

The LA County Commission on Disabilities, 500 W Temple St, Los Angeles, CA 90012 (☏213/974-1053 or TDD ☏213/974-1707), is the best source of material on the range of **services** available in the city; other disabled information in the county is provided through the general county access line at ☏1-800/339-6993.

The major hotel and motel chains are the best bet for accessible accommodation. At the higher end of the scale, *Embassy Suites* (voice ☎1-800/362-2779, TDD ☎1-800/458-4708, ⊛www.embassysuites.com) has been working to comply with new standards of access that meet or, in some cases, exceed ADA requirements, involving building new facilities, retrofitting older hotels, and providing special training to all employees. To a somewhat lesser degree, the same is true of *Hyatt Hotels* (voice ☎1-800/233-1234, TDD ☎1-800/228-9548, ☎www.hyatt.com) and the other big hoteliers in town.

Citizens or permanent residents of the US who have been "medically determined to be blind or permanently disabled" can obtain the **Golden Access Passport** (⊛www.nps .gov/fees_passes.htm), a free lifetime pass to federally operated parks, monuments, historic sites, and recreation areas that charge admission fees. The pass must be picked up in person, from the sites described, and it also provides a 50 percent discount on fees charged at facilities for camping, boat launching, and parking. The **Golden Bear Pass**, also free to the disabled, offers similar benefits for California state-run parks, beaches, and historic sites that charge admission fees (⊛www.parks.ca.gov for details).

Information and contacts

Major US **organizations** for the disabled include the Society for the Advancement of Travelers with Handicaps (SATH) and Mobility International. *Easy Access to National Parks*, by Wendy Roth and Michael Tompane, explores every national park from the points of view of people with disabilities, senior citizens, and families with children, and *Disabled Outdoors* is a quarterly magazine focusing on facilities for travelers with disabilities who wish to get into the countryside.

United States

Access-Able PO Box 1796, Wheat Ridge, CO 80034 ☎303/232-2979, ⊛www.access-able.com. Information service and network that assists travelers with disabilities by putting them in contact with other people with similar conditions.
California Office of Tourism 801 K St, Suite 1600, Sacramento, CA 95814-3520 ☎1-800/GO-CALIF or

916/322-2881, ⊛www.visitcalifornia.com. Publishes a free, 200-page *Travel Planning Guide* that lists disabled facilities for state accommodations and attractions.
Directions Unlimited 720 N Bedford Rd, Bedford Hills, NY 10507 ☎1-800/533-5343 or 914/241-1700. Tour operator with customized tours for people with disabilities.
Easy Access Travel 5386 Arlington Ave, Riverside, CA 92504 ☎1-800/920-8989, ⊛www .easyaccesstravel.com. Travel consulting services with comprehensive tour packages.
Mobility International USA PO Box 10767, Eugene, OR 97440 ☎541/343-1284, ⊛www .miusa.org. Answers travel questions and operates an exchange program for the disabled. Annual membership ($35) includes quarterly newsletter.
Society for the Advancement of Travelers with Handicaps (SATH) 347 Fifth Ave, #610, New York, NY 10016 ☎212/447-7284, ⊛www.sath .org. Nonprofit organization comprising travel agents, tour operators, hotels, and airlines, and travelers with disabilities.
Twin Peaks Press Box 129, Vancouver, WA 98666-0129 ☎360/694-2462, ⊛home.pacifier .com/~twinpeak. Publishes the *Directory of Travel Agencies for the Disabled*, listing more than 370 agencies worldwide, as well as *Travel for the Disabled*.
Wheels Up! ☎1-888/38-WHEELS, ⊛www .wheelsup.com. Online service that provides discounted air fares, tour and cruise prices for disabled travelers, and publishes a free monthly newsletter.

Canada

Canadian National Institute for the Blind (CNIB) ☎604/431-2121, ⊛www.cnib.ca. Assistance and information for the visually impaired.
Canadian Paraplegic Association offices in every province. Main office at Suite 230, 1101 Prince of Wales Drive, Ottawa, ON K2C 3W7 ☎613/723-1033 or ☎1-800/720-4933, ⊛www.canparaplegic.org. Lots of information on travelling in specific provinces, and most of its regional offices produce a free guide on the most easily accessed sites.
Western Institute for the Deaf and Hard of Hearing 2125 W 7th Ave, Vancouver V6K 1X9 ☎604/736-7391 (voice) or 604/736-2527 (TDD), ⊛www.widhh.ca. Travel advice for the hearing-impaired.

UK and Ireland

Access Travel 6, The Hillock, Astley, Lancashire M29 7GW ☎01942/888 844, ☎01942/891 811, ⊛www.access-travel.co.uk. Helps travelers secure wheelchair-accessible accommodations, adapted vehicles, nursing services, and more.

Holiday Care 7th floor Sunley House, 4 Bedford Park, Croydon, Surrey CRO 2AP ☎0845/124 9971, ☎0845/124 9972, Minicom ☎0845/124 9976, ⊛www.holidaycare.org.uk. Offers free lists of accessible accommodation in the US and other destinations. Information on financial help for holidays available.

Irish Wheelchair Association Blackheath Drive, Clontarf, Dublin 3 ☎01/818 6400, ⊛www.iwa.ie. Useful information provided about traveling abroad with a wheelchair.

Mencap Holiday Services Optium House, Clippers Quay, Salford Quays, Manchester M52 2XP ☎0161/888 1200, ⊛www.mencap.org.uk. Provides information on holiday travel for the disabled, including an annual guide.

Royal Association for Disability and Rehabilitation (RADAR) 12 City Forum, 250 City Rd, London EC1V 8AF ☎020/7250 3222, Minicom ☎020/7250 4119, ⊛www.radar.org.uk.

General information and advice on holidays and travel.

Tripscope The Vassall Centre, Gill Avenue, Bristol BS16 2QQ ☎08457/585 641, ⊛www.tripscope .org.uk. Registered charity providing a national telephone information service offering free advice on UK and international transport for those with mobility problems.

Australia and New Zealand

ACROD Australian Council for Rehabilitation of the Disabled PO Box 60, Curtin, ACT 2605 ☎02/6282 4333, ⊛www.acrod.org.au. Provides lists of travel agencies and tour operators.

Barrier-Free Travel 36 Wheatley St, North Bellingen, NSW 2454 ☎02/6655 1733. Disabled travel-access information, for a fee.

Disabled Persons Assembly Level 4, Wellington Trade Centre, 173–175 Victoria St, Wellington ☎04/801 9100, ⊛www.dpa.org.nz. Resource center with lists of travel agencies and tour operators.

The City

The City

Downtown LA

One of the most enduring stereotypes about Los Angeles is that it has never had any kind of urban center, and is merely an endless series of flat, disconnected suburbs. While modern LA does indeed have an aspect of such sprawl, historically **DOWNTOWN LA** was the social and cultural hub of the region, where the masses worked, dined, shopped, and came to be entertained. Since the advent of the automobile, however, Angelenos have been moving away from their ostensible city center, paving over orange groves and beanfields in their continuous march outward. Today, with its serviceable array of skyscrapers, Downtown is mainly a hub for commercial activity: most of the middle and working classes have long since escaped, or been forced out when their homes were destroyed by dubious urban-renewal schemes.

Still, for all its failings, boosters keep trying to make Downtown into an actual attraction for visitors – if not exactly the center of LA social activity, at least one of its many nodes. In this they have succeeded, as Downtown has re-emerged as an enjoyable place to visit during the day (though this corporate-dominated zone still shuts down at night), with a smattering of refurbished adobes and grand old movie palaces, some modern museums and a few interesting pieces of architecture – along with some of the city's best hotels and restaurants.

It's only fairly recently that Downtown has become vertical at all, easily spotted by car at a distance. Until 1960, **City Hall** was, at 28 stories, the town's tallest structure, but from the 1960s to the end of the 1980s, LA saw a building boom spurred on largely by Canadian and Japanese venture capital, which replaced the creaky Victorians atop Bunker Hill with glass curtain-walls and Brutalist concrete monsters. The boom faded during LA's near-depression during the early 1990s, but in the last decade, the area has made a slow recovery. To many, the monumental construction of Disney Hall is the singular symbol of Downtown's long-awaited rebirth, while less high-minded souls point to the sports complex of the Staples Center as providing the real lifeblood of the area.

Although the gleaming modernity of Bunker Hill is immediately tempting, a trip Downtown is best experienced beginning at **the Plaza**, the original nineteenth-century town site and now the remodeled focus of a spruced-up zone known as "**El Pueblo de Los Angeles**," which also holds the historic, if over-commercialized, **Olvera Street**. To the south, LA's **Civic Center** is a shamefully bland seat of local government, enlivened only by the classic form of City Hall and a scant few other structures.

Further south stand the antique facades along **Spring Street** and **Broadway**. Since their heyday in the 1920s as the respective financial and cultural axes of the city, the two streets have changed considerably. Broadway is still a thriving commercial area, but now has a Hispanic flavor, with T-shirt stands

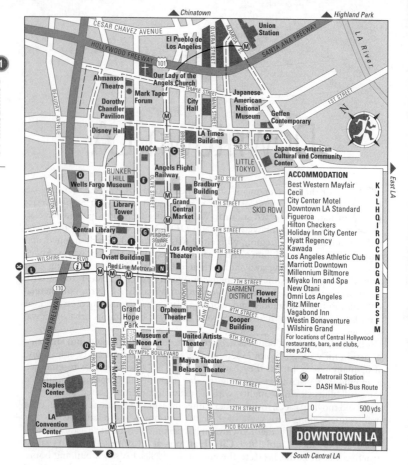

▲ Chinatown   ▲ Highland Park

CESAR CHAVEZ AVENUE

HOLLYWOOD FREEWAY

El Pueblo de Los Angeles

Union Station

SANTA ANA FREEWAY

LA River

101

Ahmanson Theatre

Our Lady of the Angels Church

TEMPLE STREET

Mark Taper Forum

Dorothy Chandler Pavilion

City Hall

Japanese-American National Museum

Geffen Contemporary

Disney Hall

LA Times Building

MOCA

BUNKER HILL

Angels Flight Railway

LITTLE TOKYO

Japanese-American Cultural and Community Center

Wells Fargo Museum

Bradbury Building

3RD STREET

SKID ROW

Library Tower

Grand Central Market

4TH STREET

Central Library

5TH STREET

PERSHING SQUARE

Oviatt Building

Los Angeles Theater

6TH STREET

Red Line Metrorail

WILSHIRE BLVD

7TH STREET

GARMENT DISTRICT

Flower Market

Grand Hope Park

Orpheum Theater

8TH STREET

Cooper Building

Museum of Neon Art

United Artists Theater

9TH STREET

OLYMPIC BOULEVARD

Mayan Theater

Belasco Theater

11TH STREET

Staples Center

12TH STREET

LA Convention Center

PICO BOULEVARD

▼ South Central LA

ACCOMMODATION

Best Western Mayfair	K
Cecil	J
City Center Motel	L
Downtown LA Standard	H
Figueroa	Q
Hilton Checkers	I
Holiday Inn City Center	R
Hyatt Regency	O
Kawada	C
Los Angeles Athletic Club	N
Marriott Downtown	D
Millennium Biltmore	G
Miyako Inn and Spa	A
New Otani	B
Omni Los Angeles	E
Ritz Milner	P
Vagabond Inn	S
Westin Bonaventure	F
Wilshire Grand	M

For locations of Central Hollywood restaurants, bars, and clubs, see p.274.

Ⓜ Metrorail Station
--- DASH Mini-Bus Route

0   500 yds

DOWNTOWN LA

and fast-food vendors lining its corridor, and many of its once-grand movie palaces now host fiery evangelist churches, hectic swap meets, or the occasional Hollywood action flick. Spring Street, on the other hand, became largely deserted through the 1980s and 90s, but since then some of its grand Neoclassical buildings have been renovated into artist's lofts and a few smart shops and restaurants.

Replacing Spring Street as LA's financial axis, **Bunker Hill** has, despite its colossal cache of new development, rather limited charms – mainly museums and modernist architecture. North and east of Downtown, **Chinatown** and **Little Tokyo** are interesting for their predictable wealth of ethnic restaurants, though neither is a vital cultural center – the city's Asian immigrants tend to migrate toward livelier and more authentic places like Monterey Park and Alhambra. Central American newcomers, by contrast, often end up in **Westlake**, west of Downtown, comprising the bulk of the population in the busy, and sometimes dangerous, **MacArthur Park** and **Echo Park** areas. To the northeast of Downtown, the **Southwest Museum**, **Lummis House**, and **Heritage**

Square offer more sedate trips through local culture and history, with a smattering of worthwhile artist's studios and galleries open to the public.

Finally, sealing off Downtown from the spiderweb of freeways to the east, the **LA River** is a bleak concrete channel designed for flood control and, not surprisingly, the forbidding setting for assorted TV shows and Hollywood action flicks.

Downtown can easily be seen in a day, and if your feet get tired you can hop aboard the **DASH buses** that run every five to ten minutes on six loops to major tourist destinations (look for the silver-signed bus stops). The area is also the hub of the MTA networks and easily accessible by public transportation, based around the colossus of Union Station. **Parking** in lots is expensive on weekdays ($7–10 per hour), but on weekends is more affordable (a flat $5–8 for up to eight hours); street parking is a good alternative, except on Bunker Hill, where the meters cost at least $2 per hour.

Some history

For more than two hundred years, the center of Downtown LA has been slowly shifting. **Spanish colonizers** constructed the first town site, the Plaza, in 1781, but the tract was soon destroyed by fire and rebuilt further southeast in 1818, at the present site of El Pueblo de Los Angeles. Encompassing the historic Pico House and Plaza Church, the district was the focus of commercial activity during the Mexican years of rule and the early American period, though even then other parts of the LA basin were developing as alternative areas for housing and commerce.

By the end of the nineteenth century, Downtown's **commercial hub** had relocated to Broadway, thick with department stores and vaudeville theaters, while Spring Street had become the financial center. The Plaza was left to decay until the 1920s, when renovation projects slowly brought the area back, this time as a tourist center. Meanwhile, Broadway and Spring were, along with City Hall (completed in 1928), the most visible emblems of LA as an emerging American **metropolis** – by then numbering over a million people in its city limits and over two million in the surrounding LA County – sending San Francisco into permanent eclipse as the largest and most powerful California city.

Although the Civic Center is still LA's seat of government, its financial and cultural counterparts have since relocated to the south. Cold War–era urban renewal projects shoved the city center six blocks to the west and doomed the great boulevards in the process. Bunker Hill replaced Spring Street in the 1960s as Downtown's financial nucleus, thanks to a drastic facelift engineered by LA's fumbling **Community Redevelopment Agency (CRA)**. While Spring Street's financial center re-emerged on the western side of Downtown, nothing so far has re-created Broadway's buzzing entertainment zone. The Museum of Contemporary Art, plunked down at the top of the hill in the 1980s, was one attempt to draw back the crowds, as was the placement of nearby cultural facilities such as the Mark Taper Forum, Dorothy Chandler Pavilion, and Ahmanson Theater – all of which failed in resurrecting the social vitality that once existed along Broadway. It took a handful of huge new showpieces, most prominently Disney Hall, Our Lady of the Angels Catholic Church, and the Staples Center, to begin drawing the city's attention back from the Westside, with the hopes of civic boosters and investment gurus riding on the public's appreciation for eye-catching architecture and sports enthusiasm – so far, a successful gamble.

The Plaza and around

Because so much of LA's architectural heritage has been destroyed, it is surprising that **the Plaza** still exists. From the early 1920s on, city planners wanted to demolish it to make way for a larger, even more imposing Civic Center. Luckily, the area was saved by its 1953 designation as **El Pueblo de Los Angeles State Historic Park**, 845 N Alameda St (daily 9am–5pm; free; ☏213/628-2381, ⓦwww.ci.la.ca.us/ELP). Comprising thirty buildings, a third of them open to the public, the park is an essential stop on any history trek through LA. In the immediate vicinity of the Plaza, **Union Station** and the adjacent **Gateway Transit Center** make up a sizable hub for train and bus activity throughout the region, while just north sits the latest version of LA's rather uninspiring **Chinatown**.

Olvera Street

Within El Pueblo de Los Angeles Historic Park, the former urban center of LA – the square known as **the Plaza** – was in 1870 reconstructed into the circular design located just off North Los Angeles Street. However, the true focus of the early settlement was the **zanja madre**, or "mother ditch," which ran from the then-wild Los Angeles River through what is now **Olvera Street**. The canal was used for domestic and agricultural purposes as early as 1781; in the 1870s, pioneering hydrologist **William Mulholland** had an early job "ditch-digging" on the watercourse, moving up to all-powerful water superintendent in eight short years. Then, just as now, *agua* was serious business, and it's no accident that a key route like Olvera Street follows the path of an antique irrigation ditch.

Open to pedestrian traffic only (daily 10am–7pm; free; ⓦwww.olvera-street .com), Olvera Street has been closed since 1930 to automobiles; you can trace the original path of the *zanja madre* by a series of marked bricks throughout. The street is at its best when taken over for numerous **festivals** throughout the year, like the Day of the Dead on November 2, and regularly features strolling mariachi bands, Aztec and Mexican-themed processions, and various dancers and artisans.

The street's re-emergence was the work of one **Christine Sterling**, who, with help from the city government, tore down the slum she found here in 1926 and created much of what remains today. For the next twenty years, she organized fiestas and worked to popularize the city's Mexican heritage while living in the early nineteenth-century **Avila Adobe** at 10 Olvera St – touted as the oldest structure in Los Angeles, from 1847, though almost entirely rebuilt out of reinforced concrete following the 1971 Sylmar earthquake. Inside the house are two **museums** (both daily 9am–3pm; free): one featuring an idealized view of pueblo-era domestic life and of Ms. Sterling herself; the other, across the landscaped courtyard, telling the sanitized "History of the Water in Los Angeles" – ie, how local authorities connived to steal a water supply from upstate farmers (for the real story, see box on p.208, or watch the fairly accurate Hollywood version in *Chinatown*).

Across the street, the **Sepulveda House**, 125 Paseo de la Plaza (Mon–Sat 10am–3pm; free; ☏213/628-1274), is a quaint 1887 Eastlake Victorian and the park's **visitor center**, with rooms highlighting different eras in Hispanic cultural history and an informative free film (Mon–Sat 11am & 2pm) on the history of LA. Free **guided walking-tours** (on the hour Wed–Sat 10am–noon) leave from the information booth at 130 Paseo de la Plaza, where self-guided tour brochures are also available.

South and West of Olvera Street

Just west of the Plaza, the Catholic Plaza Church, or **La Placita**, 535 N Main St (daily 8am–8pm; ☎213/629-3101, ⊛www.laplacita.org), is a small adobe structure with a gabled roof that has long been a sanctuary for Central American refugees. From 1861 to 1923 the building was remodeled or reconstructed four times, but it still evokes a sense of the local heritage. If you'd like to take part in one of the church **masses** (occasionally with mariachi bands), they occur three or four times daily (Mon–Fri 6.30am, 8am, noon & 5.30pm, Sat 7.30am, 12.30pm & 5.30pm), with twelve Eucharist services on Sunday. To the south, the red-brick **Old Plaza Firehouse** (Tues–Sun 10am–3pm; free) was only operational for thirteen years, beginning in 1884, subsequently becoming a saloon, lodging house, and pool hall before reaching museum status in 1960. If you like old firefighting equipment, this is the place for you.

Two adjacent structures remain closed to the public: the handsome Mission-style **Pico House** was once the home of the last Mexican governor of California, Pio Pico, while LA's most luxurious hotel when it opened in 1870, the **Merced Theater**, was also the city's first indoor theater. The **Old Masonic Hall** next door (Tues–Fri 10am–3pm; free) was the first of its kind in the city when built in 1858 and still holds the occasional Freemason meeting, as well as a cache of artifacts including swords, compasses, and jewels. Close by, LA's original Chinese settlement was centered on the **Garnier Building**, an 1850 brick-and-stone structure that reopened in 2003 as the **Chinese American Museum**, 425 N Los Angeles St (Tues–Sun 10am–3pm; $3; ⊛www.camla.org). Inside, local Chinese history, society, and culture is detailed, with items from the nineteenth and twentieth centuries including revealing letters, photos, and documents, as well as a smattering of contemporary art and the re-creation of a Chinese herb shop c.1900.

Lastly, three blocks west, at the junction of Sunset Boulevard and Hill Street, the **Fort Moore Pioneer Memorial** is a series of bas reliefs depicting early LA political and social figures who provided "for its citizens water and power for life and energy." This inscription is written on the interior wall of what has been described as "the most spectacular man-made waterfall in the United States": an 80-foot-wide, 50-foot-high wall of water serving as a colossal monument to the city's aqueous needs. Not surprisingly, it was shut off a quarter-century ago.

Union Station and around

The Mission-style **Union Station**, across from the Plaza at 800 N Alameda St, is an impressive, if underused, architectural landmark that was an early site of LA's Chinatown, though the local Chinese community was forcibly evicted when the station was constructed in the 1930s. Despite rail travel's precipitous decline in the US, the terminus remains one of the city's best-preserved monuments to the golden age of railways, replete with grand arches, a high clock tower, Spanish-tiled roof, and Art Deco motifs such as geometric designs and Streamline Moderne lettering. And while it's no longer the heart of the region's transit system, the station continues to serve as the confluence for Amtrak, Metrolink, and Metroline commuter trains, as well as the occasional shooting location for all kinds of Hollywood movies – most memorably in *Blade Runner*, as the gloomy, atmospheric police station where Harrison Ford's Deckard is given his mission to kill off four alien "replicants."

Less interesting is **Gateway Transit Center**, connected to Union Station by tunnel below the train tracks and comprising three distinct parts: the

26-story **Gateway Tower**, with a customer service center on its ground floor; **Patsaouras Transit Plaza**, the bus mall itself, decorated with insipid public art and worth avoiding at night; and, under a glass ceiling, the **East Portal**, a light and airy space marred by an Orwellian-looking mural supposedly celebrating LA's ethnic diversity. There's nothing much to see beyond here, just the largest municipal **jail** in the US – where actors like Robert Downey Jr have cooled their heels – and the similarly imposing **Metropolitan Detention Center**, with its razor-wire-style decor, providing the memorable cover of Mike Davis's modern history of LA, *City of Quartz*.

Chinatown

If you visit LA's **CHINATOWN** expecting to see a bustling affair, you will be sadly disappointed. Located between North Broadway and North Hill streets, the enclave is rather small and hemmed in by wide boulevards, a maze of ersatz-Chinese architecture, and narrow pedestrian alleys with inauthentic names like Bamboo Lane. The area was established in 1938 along North Broadway and North Spring Street following its residents' abrupt transplant from the current site of Union Station. Unless it's Chinese New Year, when there's a parade of dragons and firework celebrations, there's little point in turning up here except to eat in one of the good, affordable restaurants. Apart from this, official Chinese culture consists of a handful of small shopping malls, where you can pick up an assortment of lanterns, teapots, and jade jewelry – more aimed at tourists than residents. For a truer sense of contemporary Chinese culture, visit **Alhambra** and **Monterey Park**, both lively ethnic suburbs located several miles east of Downtown.

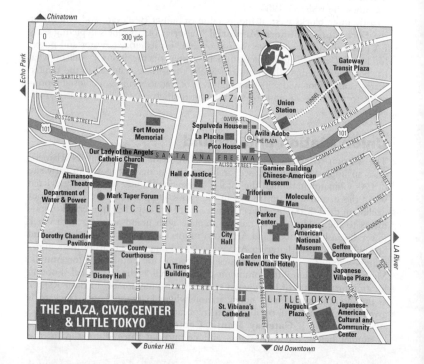

THE PLAZA, CIVIC CENTER & LITTLE TOKYO

Civic Center

Marked by City Hall's great white pillar, the **Civic Center** is the seat of government for the city and county of LA, with various state and federal entities also occupying space in the district. Bounded on the east and west by San Pedro and Figueroa streets and on the north and south by the Hollywood Freeway and First Street, this unexciting hive of bureaucracy offers only a few interesting cultural and architectural sights. Even in the face of this, LA's political bigwigs have spent significant time and money vainly trying to pump some life into the area, resulting in the strange scene of desperate homeless people wandering in an often-deserted landscape of spartan modern architecture and ugly public artworks.

City Hall and around

City Hall, 200 N Spring St, is still visible in TV reruns as *Dragnet*'s imposing symbol of civic virtue and as the Daily Planet office in the original *Superman*

△ City Hall

show. Once LA's tallest structure, its silhouette is now dwarfed by the office blocks of Bunker Hill. The building's crown is as close as most visitors will ever get to seeing the Mausoleum at Halicarnassus, one of the seven ancient wonders of the world, which provided a curious, only-in-LA architectural inspiration. You can still get a good look at the inside of the building on free **tours**, which include its 28th-story 360-degree observation deck (daily 10am–1pm; reserve on ☎213/485-4423, ⊛www.lacityhall.org); for a more in-depth, 1hr 45min view of the building and its architecture, the LA Conservancy offers monthly tours (first Sat of month 11am; $5; ⊛laconservancy.org) as well.

Less inspiringly, there's plenty of bad, unavoidable public art hereabouts, especially at the corner of Main and Temple, where the monstrous **Triforium**, from 1975, is decorated with shafts of colored glass and long-silent loudspeakers strategically placed between its massive concrete legs. More compelling is **Molecule Man**, 255 E Temple St, in which sculptor Jonathan Borofsky's perforated figures supposedly illustrate the watery composition of the human body, even as some see them as

The LA Times family dynasty

The *Los Angeles Times* began life in 1881 as the mouthpiece for **Harrison Gray Otis**, the arch-conservative publisher whose virulently anti-labor opinions and actions led union chiefs to call him the most "unfair enemy of trades unionism on the North American continent." Tensions he fostered with unions and leftists turned violent in 1910, when the original Times building was bombed. After the explosion, Otis not only rebuilt the structure, but he emerged even stronger and more powerful than ever, when partial blame was assigned to his political nemesis **Job Harriman** (for defending the accused, but later convicted, bombers in court and in public), who otherwise would have become the city's first and only Socialist mayor. Having already kept the Southern Pacific Railroad from monopolizing development of the LA Harbor, Otis also engineered public support for the giant construction projects that stole water from Northern California's Owens Valley and carried it to LA, or more precisely, to the San Fernando Valley, where he and other investors made a fortune in shady real-estate dealings.

The *LA Times* directly reflected Otis's sharp opinions and, when he died in 1917, his legacy was passed to his son-in-law, **Harry Chandler**, who maintained the paper's fight against unions and political reform until his death in 1941. With a personal fortune worth up to a billion dollars, he made much of it in San Fernando Valley real estate, thanks in large part to the newfound water source irrigating freshly built suburbs. Chandler was a plutocrat and mayoral kingmaker who usually got his way with city politicians, controlling them much like his father-in-law had. His one great defeat was the 1937 election of reformist mayor Fletcher Bowron, who replaced the scandal-tainted figure of Frank Shaw.

In 1960, the paper changed course dramatically with the ascension of Harry's son **Otis** to the publishing throne. Through his progressive efforts, the *LA Times* finally rejected its provincial conservatism and became nationally recognized for its journalistic quality. In later decades, with the demise of rivals like William Randolph Hearst's once-powerful *Los Angeles Herald-Tribune*, the *Times* would nearly monopolize local journalism and emerge as an international news organization, with bureaus around the world. More recently, however, the paper was gobbled up in a media mega-merger by the *Chicago Tribune*, and some fear that under the influence of its new overseer, it's now reverting to its conservative, hidebound former ways.

bullet-riddled bodies – a jab at the adjacent **Parker Center**, headquarters of the LAPD.

Just to the south, near Spring and First streets, the concrete and glass **Times-Mirror Complex** houses the production facilities for the *Los Angeles Times*, the West Coast's biggest newspaper. Built in the colossal PWA Moderne style in the mid-1930s, and given a drab expansion in 1973, the building supplanted an earlier version, closer to Broadway, that was bombed, rebuilt, then torn down. Take one of its free **public tours** (by reservation only at ☏213/237-5757, ◉www.latimes.com) if you're interested in seeing how the paper operates.

Civic Center West

The municipal buildings in the **Civic Center West** are largely functional, though not entirely without interest. The **Department of Water and Power Building**, at the corner of Hope and First streets, is a pleasing modern pile that casts an appealing glow at night with its narrow horizontal bands of light – though its array of once-gleaming fountains have been turned off to save water. Nearby is the 1925 **Hall of Justice**, Broadway and Temple streets, famous for the turbulent trial of the Manson Family and a compelling counterpart to City Hall, with high granite columns typifying the late Beaux Arts style of the time. It's now closed, but re-development plans are always in the works.

Further west, LA has lumped together three leading music and theater venues – the Dorothy Chandler Pavilion, Ahmanson Theatre, and Mark Taper Forum – as the bland **Music Center**, north of First Street at 135 Grand Ave (see "Performing arts and film," p.315). However, **Disney Hall**, on the border of Bunker Hill at First Street at Grand Avenue, is a true jewel of modern architecture, a headline-grabbing spectacle based on a 1987 design by architect Frank Gehry and similar to his later-designed but already-built Guggenheim Museum in Bilbao, Spain. Finally finished in 2003, the Hall is a 2300-seat acoustic showpiece whose stainless-steel exterior resembles something akin to colossal broken eggshells – and so shiny that in 2005 the county ordered the metallic facade be sanded down to reduce glare. The interior is just as impressive, with rich, warm acoustics and a mammoth, intricate pipe organ; indeed, it's already considered one of the best places to hear music in the country, which you can do courtesy of the LA Philharmonic (◉laphil.org; see p.316). Unfortunately, the self-guided **audio tours** (9am–10.30am, or 3pm if no matinees; $10; reserve at ☏323/850-2000) only shunt you around the garden and anterooms of the building, not into the stunning auditorium itself; for that, you'll have to attend a concert.

A long block north is LA's other modern colossus, **Our Lady of the Angels** Catholic church, 555 W Temple St (Mon–Fri 6.30am–7pm, Sat 9am–7pm, Sun 7am–7pm; tours Mon–Fri 1pm; free; ◉www.olacathedral.org). The $200-million centerpiece of the local archdiocese, this is a truly massive structure in its own right – eleven stories tall and capable of holding three thousand people – and solidly built of concrete. Dressed in an unattractive shade of ochre, the church's fortress-like exterior suggests a parking garage or prison. Still, the interior is the undeniable highlight, with its grand marble altar and giant bronze doors, tapestries of saints and ultra-thin alabaster screens for diffusing light, plus $30 million worth of art and furnishings laid out in a space longer than a football field.

△ Interior of Our Lady of the Angels

Little Tokyo and around

Southeast of the Civic Center, **LITTLE TOKYO** is a more vital ethnic core than Chinatown – if not quite a flourishing residential neighborhood – full of smart shops and restaurants, well-heeled visitors, and a handful of business and cultural institutions. Originally named in 1908, the area, bound by First and Third streets north and south, and Central Avenue and San Pedro Street east and west, was home to 30,000 Japanese immigrants before they were forced into internment camps in 1942. While the district has returned to prominence, most Japanese-Americans now live well outside the area.

Little Tokyo

Little Tokyo is best explored on foot, starting at the **Japanese American Cultural and Community Center**, 244 S San Pedro St (ⓦwww.jaccc.org), reached via the gentle contours and heavy basalt rocks of **Noguchi Plaza**, designed by modern sculptor Isamu Noguchi, who grew up in nearby Boyle Heights. Inside the center, the **Doizaki Gallery** (Tues–Fri noon–5pm, Sat & Sun 11am–4pm; free) shows traditional and contemporary Japanese drawing and calligraphy, along with costumes, sculptures, and other media. Also on site is the **Japan America Theater**, which hosts cultural events such as kabuki theater, as well as more contemporary plays. Shoehorned between the two and easy to miss, the stunning **James Irvine Garden** (daily 9am–5pm; free), with a 170-foot stream running along its sloping hillside, is a cultural treasure. Although named after its biggest donor, it really owes its existence to the efforts of two hundred volunteers who gave up their Sundays to carve the space out of a flat lot, turning it into the "garden of the clear stream" and making the area seem a world away from LA's expanse of asphalt and concrete. Nearby, the more authentically Japanese **Garden in the Sky**, 120 S Los Angeles St, located on the *New Otani Hotel*'s third-floor terrace, uses local materials native to Japan. This half-acre strolling garden, or *shuyu*, works the skyline into the setting – a technique known as "borrowed scenery" – allowing you to contemplate the grandeur of City Hall during your walk around the premises.

The most active part of Little Tokyo is **Japanese Village Plaza** (daily 11am–pm), an outdoor mall near First Street and Central Avenue lined with sushi bars, upscale retailers, and Zen rock gardens. Adjacent to the plaza is the area's signature icon: the **Fire Tower**, a small canopy sitting atop slender wooden beams. Across First Street, the **Japanese American National Museum** (Tues–Sun 10am–5pm, Thurs closes at 8pm; $8; ☎213/625-0414, ⓦwww.janm .org), housed in a former Buddhist temple constructed in 1925, has exhibits on everything from origami to traditional furniture and folk craftwork to the internment of Japanese-Americans during World War II.

Across from the museum is the **Geffen Contemporary**, Central Avenue at First Street (same hours and website as MOCA, to which a ticket entitles same-day admission). Occupying an old city warehouse and police garage, the Frank Gehry–designed museum was initially opened in 1983 as overflow space for the main facility on Bunker Hill, but its success has been such that it was kept on as an alternative exhibition space to its more mainstream sibling. Here you're likely to find anything from exhibits on the latest LA architecture to small abstract paintings lining the walls to huge installations occupying similarly huge galleries.

West of Little Tokyo, **St Vibiana's Cathedral**, 114 E Second St, is a modest replica of Barcelona's church of San Miguel del Mar, with a simple white Italianate design. For years the regional seat of the Catholic Church, as well as a sanctuary for recently arrived Latin American immigrants, the 1871 cathedral fell on tough times after it was damaged in the 1994 Northridge earthquake and the archdiocese abandoned it to build Our Lady of the Angels further west. Saved from demolition, the cathedral is being redeveloped as a performing-arts complex (with an adjacent public library), the centerpiece of the ongoing re-emergence of this formerly down-at-heel area.

East of Little Tokyo

East of Little Tokyo, not far from the LA River, intriguing art is on display in the **Freight Depot** of the Southern California Institute of Architecture, 960 E Third St (daily 10am–6pm; free; ⓦwww.sciarc.edu), housed in a renovated train depot from 1907. Devoting its flowing horizontal spaces to architectural instruction, "Sci-Arc" was founded by current Pritzer Prize (architecture's highest honor) winner Thom Mayne in 1972, and now has as its director the great modernist maverick Eric Owen Moss, whose own work in Culver City alone merits a visit to that town (see p.141). Not surprisingly, the depot's public gallery hosts all manner of quirky and avant-garde exhibits by its students and faculty, from high-tech computer models to complex installations that riddle the gallery with Escher-like stairways, catwalks, pipes, and ladders. In the neighborhood just west of the Depot, an independent art scene is developing around classic old industrial buildings that have been renovated into lofts and eateries. There are no official sights here yet, but some visitors drop in for the handful of funky bars or cafés; if arriving by night, take a cab, as the area's a bit too close to Skid Row for comfort.

Old Downtown

Spring Street and Broadway form the axes of **Old Downtown**, a once thriving district that has in recent years tried to recapture its old spark with new investment. To the east, the **Garment District** and **Flower Market** are hives of mercantile energy, representing an urban vitality that the antique banking corridor of Spring Street can only hope to achieve with a smattering of new condos and cafés. Paralleling Spring to the west, Broadway buzzes with colorful street life, though its character has changed, too: whereas movie palaces and fine restaurants once drew white middle-class crowds, its current swap meets and bargain discounters now draw working-class Hispanics.

Spring Street

As the one-time "Wall Street of the West," the imperious banking and commercial buildings of **Spring Street** no longer serve their original functions, almost all of them victims of Downtown's financial relocation to Bunker Hill. Still, for those with an interest in LA history, or with a nose for sniffing out the area's emerging arts scene, Spring Street may offer a few worthwhile attractions (many of which are viewable on LA Conservancy tours of the old strip; see p.40). South from the Civic Center, begin your wanderings at peaceful **Biddy Mason Park**, 333 S Spring St (daily 8am–8pm, weekends open 9am; free), which commemorates a former midwife and slave who won her freedom in an 1855 legal challenge. The small memorial provides a timeline of her life, from when she was purchased for $250 (on the property that is now the park), to when she became one of the founders of the local First African Methodist Episcopal Church.

Less than a block away begins the strip that redevelopers have christened as the "**Old Bank District**," a collection of stately Beaux Arts buildings from one hundred years ago that are now, in various stages, being converted into yuppie housing, upmarket shops, chic eateries, and the like. At 408 Spring St, the 1904 Braly Block is home to the **Continental Building**, which was LA's first "skyscraper," though it only boasts twelve stories. Now transformed into artists' lofts and condos, the imposing structure serves the same function as the nearby **Farmers and Merchants Bank**, at no. 401, an eye-catching Neoclassical pile from 1908. Also close, at no. 433, the striking **Title Insurance and Trust Company** houses municipal agencies as well as the LA Design Center, an uneven collection of art dealers and jewelry merchants (open to the public), featuring an appealing Art Deco design in the Zigzag style of the late 1920s. Also remodeled, the **Security Trust and Savings Bank**, no. 514, is home to four small theaters presenting intermittent productions and special events. Further south, the one-time **Pacific Coast Stock Exchange**, no. 618, bears an inscription stating that it was "created for the economic welfare of the community, state and nation." Ironically, the Moderne structure was completed in 1930 – the first full year of the Great Depression. These days, the *Stock Exchange* is a weekend disco for Bunker Hill yuppies (see "Bars and clubs," p.306). Nearby, at Spring Street's intersection with Seventh Street, the 1910 **I.N. Van Nuys Building** celebrates one of the city's early titans, a San Fernando Valley land baron and wheat farmer, in grand Beaux Arts style, with ornamental Ionic columns and white terracotta walls adorning the old office space.

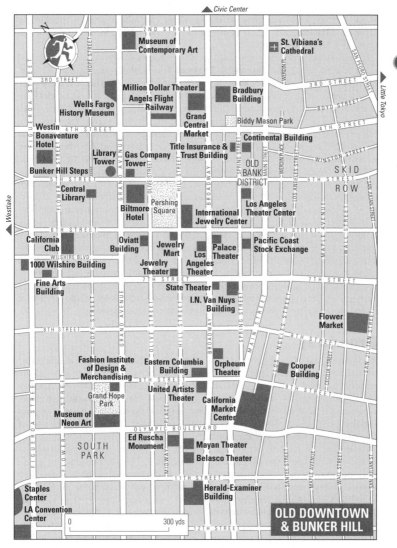

Little Tokyo ▶

◀ Westlake

OLD DOWNTOWN & BUNKER HILL

0 — 300 yds

Skid Row and the Garment District

East of Spring Street, a good portion of LA's homeless population, estimated at anywhere between 60,000 and 200,000, can be found on **Skid Row**, which begins just south of Little Tokyo and continues down past Seventh Street, at its seediest along Fifth Street between San Pedro and Los Angeles streets – a stretch known as "the Nickel." Unless you're looking for exceptionally gritty inspiration – as did the Doors (who posed in these parts for the cover of their *Morrison Hotel* album) and Charles Bukowski – you're best off skipping Skid

Row entirely. However, those daring enough can take a tour of the **Union Rescue Mission**, 545 S San Pedro St (☎213/347-6300), for a grim, up-close view of LA's dispossessed.

If Skid Row is precisely the kind of place visitors to Downtown LA would most like to avoid, the **Garment District** (or, euphemistically, the "Fashion District"; ☎213/488-1153, ⊛www.fashiondistrict.org), further south, is one of the area's most appealing attractions, with twenty square blocks of clothing manufacturers and discounters selling everything from fabric for as little as $2 per yard, to cut-rate designer suits and exquisite silk and velvet draperies. The biggest retailer here, the **California Market Center**, at Ninth and Los Angeles streets (☎213/630-3600, ⊛www.californiamarketcenter.com), fills three million square feet and seemingly has just as many visitors, especially during the hectic autumn "Fashion Week" (⊛www.fashionweekla.com), while just across Los Angeles Street at Santee, the **Cooper Building** (☎213/627-3754, ⊛www .cooperdesignspace.com) offers designer merchandise at bargain prices; indeed, most shrewd Angelenos avoid the high-priced Westside boutiques and head to this district to do their clothes buying. To plunge into the shopping experience at its most colorful and chaotic, head for the area along Maple Avenue between Sixth and Ninth streets, where businesses (often run by first-generation immigrant families) sell bolts of serviceable fabrics for ultra-cheap prices. Keep in mind, however, that street parking is meager and traffic maddening. Nearby, at the atmospheric early-morning **Flower Market**, 766 Wall St (Mon, Wed & Fri 8am–noon, Tues, Thurs & Sat 6am–noon; entry $2, Sat $1; ⊛www.laflowerdistrict .com), you can buy flowers for a fraction of the prices elsewhere.

Broadway

Broadway was once the axis of LA's most fashionable shopping and entertainment district, brimming with movie palaces and department stores. Beyond the handful of jewelers who've stuck around since the old days, today Broadway is largely taken over by the clothing and knickknack stores of a bustling Hispanic community, which operate out of the ground floors of otherwise empty hundred-year-old buildings, the salsa music and street scene making for one of the city's most electric environments.

An instructive place to begin exploring the strip's former color is at its southern end, with the **Herald-Examiner Building**, 1111 S Broadway, a grand Mission-style edifice occupying a city block and featuring blue-and-yellow domes and ground-level arcades. The building was first home to William Randolph Hearst's *Los Angeles Examiner*, the progressive counterpart of the *Los Angeles Times*, which grew to have the widest afternoon circulation of any daily in the country. After it merged with Hearst's *Herald-Express*, though, trouble soon began, and the paper went out of business in 1989. Although the building is currently closed to the public, redevelopment plans are slowly taking shape and it frequently hosts movie crews because of its opulent setting – fitting, considering that Orson Welles had the news magnate and the building in mind when he directed his thinly veiled critique of Hearst, *Citizen Kane*.

One block to the west, the Theater District begins at 1040 S Hill St, where the wild **Mayan Theater** is a stunning remnant of the pre-Columbian revival, its ornamental design, including sculpted reliefs of Aztec gods and bright paintings of dragons and birds, every bit as outlandish as its Chinese Theatre counterpart in Hollywood. The building is still in use as the *Mayan* dance club (see p.305). The neighboring **Belasco Theater**, 1050 S Hill St, has similar brash appeal, with a Spanish Baroque design and a bright green color, though its partially restored interior is only open to film crews as a shooting location – which is true of a number of the shuttered theaters on this stretch, if they haven't been renovated and "improved" beyond repair.

Nearby, the **United Artists Theater**, 929 S Broadway, is a 1927 Spanish Gothic movie palace with a lobby designed after a cathedral nave – appropriate, since the theater is now the site of a church. A block away, stuck amidst the theaters, is the Art Deco **Eastern Columbia Building**, 849 S Broadway, with terracotta walls of gold and aquamarine, a giant clock face, and sleek dark piers on its roof, all essential viewing for anyone remotely interested in 1920s architecture. Further along, at no. 744, the **Globe Theater** is a Beaux Arts design that has been clumsily converted into a flea market.

The street continues with a rash of old moviehouses, notably the **Los Angeles**, 615 S Broadway, built in ninety days for the world premiere of Charlie Chaplin's *City Lights* in 1931, crowning what had become the largest concentration of film theaters in the world. Considered by some to be the best movie palace in the city, the theater's plush lobby behind the triumphal arch facade is lined by marble columns supporting an intricate mosaic ceiling, while the 1800-seat auditorium is enveloped by trompe l'oeil murals and lighting effects. Although it's no longer open to the public for regular screenings, a June program called *Last Remaining Seats* draws huge crowds to this and the nearby **Orpheum Theatre**, 842 S Broadway – a still-open monumental French Renaissance palace of grand staircases and chandeliers – to watch revivals of classic Hollywood films. If you're in town at the time, don't miss it (tickets $20 per film, often with live entertainment; call ☎213/623-CITY for details). Near the Los Angeles theater, the monumental Renaissance Revival charm of the **State Theatre**, 630 S Broadway, is also on display during occasional film screenings and public events; check entertainment listings for details.

A few blocks north, the **Million Dollar Theater**, no. 307, has appeared in numerous Hollywood movies and is renowned for its whimsical terracotta facade, mixing buffalo heads with bald eagles. The former moviehouse was built in 1906 by theatres magnate Sid Grauman, who went on to build the Egyptian and Chinese theaters in Hollywood. It's now closed to the public, and its projector has been removed; still, there's always talk of refurbishing it someday. Across the street, the 1893 **Bradbury Building**, no. 304 (Mon–Sat 9am–5pm; free), has perhaps the finest atrium of any structure in the city, each level of its glazed-brick court adorned in wrought-iron railings and open-cage elevators, all atmospherically lit by a skylight. The lobby, which is as far as the public can go, should be recognizable to most from films such as *Citizen Kane* and *Blade Runner*, and LA Conservancy tours often begin here. As you exit on Third Street, the colorful **Grand Central Market**, between Third and Fourth (daily 9am–6pm; ⊛www.grandcentralsquare.com), provides a good taste of modern Broadway – everything from apples and oranges to pickled pig's feet and sheep's brains.

Pershing Square and around

The city's oldest park, the uninspiring but unavoidable **Pershing Square**, acts as a buffer between Bunker Hill and Old Downtown. Constructed in 1866 and known variously as Public Square, City Park, La Plaza Abaja, and St Vincent's Park, it was renamed for the last time in 1918, in honor of World War I general **John Pershing**. By the 1960s, the place had deteriorated considerably, and decades of efforts to revitalize the park have resulted only in a bright purple campanile towering over charmless concrete benches and a lack of grass and other plants.

The buildings around the square hold more visual appeal, including the **Biltmore Hotel**, on the west side of the park, its three brick towers rising from a Renaissance Revival arcade along Olive Street. Inside, the grand old lobby has an intricately painted Spanish-beamed ceiling, plus all manner of Baroque flourishes and an elegant bar, exquisite ballrooms, and a dark, luminous pool facility. If you don't mind paying a top-dollar rate, the hotel's accommodation is also outstanding (see p.247). To the east, the **International Jewelry Center**, 550 S Hill St, holds more than six hundred jewelers and dealers in precious stones and metals. If this doesn't satisfy your passion for pricey shopping, try the other **Jewelry Mart**, 607 S Hill St, a green Art Deco gem, or the **Jewelry Theater**, 411 W Seventh St, which occupies the former Pantages Theater, maintaining its grand Hollywood look with its own wraparound marquee.

At 617 S Olive St, the Art Deco **Oviatt Building** is another sumptuous survivor that recalls the vibrant nature of Old Downtown in vivid color. The ground floor once housed LA's most elegant haberdashery, catering to dapper types such as Clark Gable and John Barrymore, but has since been converted into the *Cicada* restaurant (see p.275). The building's elevators, which open onto the street-level exterior lobby, feature hand-carved oak paneling designed and fashioned by elegant Parisian craftsman René Lalique. Equally striking is the intricate 1928 design of the building's exterior, especially its grand sign and clock high above.

Bunker Hill

Developed as a middle-class neighborhood in the 1870s, **Bunker Hill** was an upscale district for just a few decades; by the 1940s it was little more than a collection of fleabag dives and crumbling Victorian mansions, providing the seedy *film noir* backdrop for detective films such as the apocalyptic 1955 Mike Hammer movie *Kiss Me Deadly*. With its middle class having long since moved to the suburbs, in the 1960s the whole thing was plowed under, and Bunker Hill became the nucleus for Downtown's massive redevelopment as a high-rise corporate enclave, a hive of activity from nine-to-five, and deserted after hours. These days, the power brokers are trying to alter the character of the district they made, but establishing a bona fide street life may still be more dream than reality.

The best way to approach Bunker Hill's **Financial District** used to be the **Angels Flight Railway**, a short section of track that leads up from the corner of Hill and Fourth streets to the top of Bunker Hill. The funicular was a throwback to the long-departed Victorian era, but the inclined train cars were removed in 1969 during the urban-renewal period, later to be restored and repainted orange and black in 1996. The railway was again closed in 2001 after the death of a passenger in an accident, but it's slated to begin operation once more by 2006. As an alternative, an **escalator** at the corner of Olive and Fourth streets will give you the same views of the city for free.

The Museum of Contemporary Art

The largest and most ambitious development in Bunker Hill is the **California Plaza** on Grand Avenue, a billion-dollar complex of offices and luxury

Breaching the fortress of Bunker Hill

One of the first things newcomers to Downtown LA realize is how truly unpleasant it is to walk around **Bunker Hill**, filled with freeway access ramps, giant boulevards without sidewalks, walled-off corporate landscapes, and even signs prohibiting pedestrians. **Mike Davis**, LA's pre-eminent chronicler of official wickedness, posited after the 1992 riots that politicians, architects, and businessmen had conspired to keep the masses away from Bunker Hill by constructing it as a veritable **fortress**, with automatically controlled security doors and private guards as the modern equivalent of moats and mercenaries. And that it worked perfectly according to plan when the riots came, with the crowds focusing their rage elsewhere, far away from the banking towers and elite institutions at the top of the hallowed hill.

The reality may be less conspiratorial, but is almost as disturbing. Like most of LA's city planners throughout the twentieth century, the forces behind Bunker Hill probably never even considered creating a pedestrian-friendly space Downtown and simply followed the logic of much late-modern design: bigger is better, impersonal is ideal, and cars are always king – a formula that, unfortunately, still persists in much of LA's municipal planning.

Still, there are a few **remedies** for dealing with Bunker Hill's layout if you're on foot. The first is to explore the area from the north or south – via Flower and Hope streets and Grand Avenue. Because of poor planning and a greater incline, the east and west sides of the hill are its most "fortified" and difficult to navigate. But if you are coming from the east, the Angels Flight Railway (when running) or a nearby escalator at Fourth and Olive streets are among the few good choices. If coming from the west, try Fifth Street, as the east–west streets to the north are among the most inaccessible to pedestrians. Motorists should also realize that while Bunker Hill was made expressly for their driving pleasure, it was not made for convenient, or cheap, parking. Find a lot below the hill and hike up the incline from there, or be prepared to cough up $2 in quarters per hour for street parking. Finally, resist the temptation to walk under the hill by way of the Third Street Tunnel; despite its gleaming appearance in films like *Blade Runner*, it remains quite deadly to careless pedestrians.

condos centering on the **Museum of Contemporary Art** (MOCA; Mon & Fri 11am–5pm, Thurs 11am–8pm, Sat & Sun 11am–6pm; $8, students $5, free Thurs; ☎213/621-2766, ⊛www.moca.org), the leading institution for contemporary art in Southern California, representing an excellent selection of post–World War II American art in all its manifestations, from Abstract Expressionist to Minimalist to postmodern. Built in 1986 and designed by showman architect **Arata Isozaki** as a "small village in the valley of the skyscrapers," it justifies a look for the building alone, its playful red pyramids a welcome splash of color among the corporate piles.

Of particular note are the weekly "**Immersion**" events (Thurs 5–8pm; free) that bring forth artists and lecturers to discuss their ideas, musicians to set the tone, and happy-hour cocktails to make it all go down more easily. To head straight for the art, go past the barrel-vaulted entrance pavilion on Grand Avenue, which opens out to an outdoor sculpture plaza, and follow the stairs down from the upper plaza to the smaller courtyard, between the café and the main entrance to the galleries.

Much of the gallery is used for temporary exhibitions – where you're apt to see anything from Donald Judd's prefabricated metal boxes to Ed Kienholz's perverse assemblage art. The bulk of the **permanent collection** draws heavily from the Abstract Expressionist period, including pieces by Franz Kline and

△ A Nancy Rubins Sculpture at MOCA

Mark Rothko, an important Jackson Pollock work – his imposing, hypnotic *Number Three* – plus ten of Sam Francis's vivid splashes of color. You'll also find plenty of Pop Art, in Claes Oldenburg's papier-mâché representations of hamburgers and gaudy fast-foods, Andy Warhol's print-ad black telephone, and Robert Rauschenberg's *Coca-Cola Plan*, a battered old cabinet containing three soda bottles and angelic wings tacked onto the sides. Jasper Johns' well-known *Map* is also here, a blotchy diagram of the US states. Don't be surprised to find a few Minimalist creations, either, with drawings and photos of the massive earthworks of Robert Smithson as a definite point of interest.

Many newer art-world stars are represented as well – including Alexis Smith's quirky collages, Charles Ray's Amazon-sized mannequins, and Martin Puryear's anthropomorphic wooden sculptures – and the museum is also strong on **photography**, exhibiting the work of Diane Arbus, Larry Clark, and Robert Frank. Also not to be missed is the impressive selection of **Southern California artists**, which range from Lari Pittman's spooky, sexualized silhouettes to Robert Williams' feverishly violent and satiric comic-book-styled paintings.

The theater on the lower floor of MOCA hosts some bizarre multimedia shows and performances, as well as more straightforward lectures and seminars (☎213/621-2766 for details). The best time to visit MOCA is during an **evening concert** in summer, when entry is free, and jazz and classical music is played outdoors under the red pyramids. At other times, a ticket to MOCA also entitles you to same-day entrance to the Geffen Contemporary, the museum's renovated-warehouse exhibition space on the east side of Downtown, and to the branch at the Pacific Design Center out in West Hollywood.

The Financial District

South of MOCA is the bulk of office towers that make Downtown visible from a distance, though from this close-up vantage, their mostly bland architecture and blocky forms are not particularly inspiring. Known as the **Financial District**, this zone replaced the antique buildings of Spring Street and the Old Bank District thanks to hamfisted 1960s urban renewal. A good place to start exploring is the **Wells Fargo History Museum**, just down the street from MOCA at 333 S Grand Ave (Mon–Fri 9am–5pm; free; ⊛www.wellsfargohistory.com). Located at the base of the Wells Fargo Center, the museum displays photographs, a two-pound chunk of gold, a re-created assay office from the nineteenth century, and a simulated stagecoach journey from St Louis to San Francisco.

A block away, the shining glass tubes of the **Westin Bonaventure Hotel**, 404 S Figueroa St (see p.248), have become one of LA's most unusual landmarks since the late 1970s. The only LA building by architect John Portman, the structure doubles as a shopping mall and office complex, and is built with a flurry of ramps, concrete columns, and catwalks in a soaring atrium that is one of the city's most eye-popping interiors. Step inside for a ride in the glass elevators that climb up the outside walls of the building (famously showcased in Clint Eastwood's *In the Line of Fire*), giving views over much of Downtown and beyond. From the hotel's rotating skyline bar, *Top of Five* (see p.299), you'll get a bird's-eye view of Bunker Hill's skyline, including the **Gas Company Tower**, 555 W Fifth St, a stunning modern high-rise whose crown symbolizes a blue natural-gas flame on its side, and the **1000 Wilshire Building**, one of Downtown's few postmodern creations, with ridiculously oversized windows, sitting right off the 110 freeway.

The biggest of the skyscrapers, though, is the cylindrical **Library Tower**, at Grand Avenue and Fifth Street, designed by I.M. Pei's firm and, at 73 stories, the tallest building west of Chicago. Now owned by U.S. Bank, the tower is mostly off-limits to the public, though occasionally open to tours run through operators such as Red Line Tours (see p.40). In exchange for planning permission and air rights, the developers of the tower agreed to pay some fifty million dollars toward the restoration of the neighboring **Richard J. Riordan Central Library**, 630 W Fifth St (Mon–Fri 10am–8pm, Sat 10am–6pm, Sun 1–5pm; ☎213/228-7000, ⊛www.lapl.org/central), named for LA's billionaire mayor of the 1990s. The concrete walls and piers of the lower floors form a pedestal for the squat central tower, which is topped by a brilliantly colored pyramid roof. The library, built in 1926, was the last work of architect Bertram Goodhue, and its striking, angular lines set the tone for many LA buildings, most obviously City Hall. Across Fifth Street, Lawrence Halprin's huge **Bunker Hill Steps**, supposedly modeled after the Spanish Steps in Rome, curve up Bunker Hill between a series of terraces with uneventful outdoor cafés, and ultimately end at the **Source Figure**, one of sculptor Robert Graham's small, creepy nudes, at the top.

On the downslope, a reminder of old LA sits at Sixth and Flower streets. **The California Club**, an exclusive men's social club, was a favorite spot for the **Committee of 25**, an informal group of conservative politicians and bigwigs who secretly decided important issues behind the club's (still) closed doors. Just over a block away, the more welcoming **Fine Arts Building**, 811 W Seventh St (Mon–Fri 7am–9.30pm, Sat & Sun 8am–6pm), is notable for its grand entry arch featuring gargoyles and griffins, and an eye-catching lobby where you'll find medieval-flavored carvings and art exhibits under gloomy lighting.

Finally, the peripheral attractions in the area include two of artist Kent Twitchell's massive murals. The first, **Harbor Freeway Overture**, decorates the side of a parking lot and is visible from the northbound 110 freeway at Seventh Street. In it, members of the LA Chamber Orchestra stare relentlessly out at the traffic, with the mural sponsor, and CEO of Mitsubishi, hiding somewhere among the musicians. Several blocks to the southeast, at 1031 S Hill St, Twitchell's **Ed Ruscha Monument** was the piece that first brought the muralist to fame, showing the quintessential California artist Ruscha looming high above a parking lot, with the blank expression and rigid pose of Frankenstein's monster.

icinity of the Ruscha mural, the mostly colorless blocks south of Hill have been named "**South Park**" by developers apparently _____ irony or access to cable TV. Serene **Grand Hope Park**, a grassy public space between Grand Avenue and Hope Street, just south of Ninth Street, was designed by Lawrence Halprin, and features a red-and-yellow clock tower, wooden canopies, and concave fountains with gilt mosaics. Less impressive are the lines of doggerel on the canopies, such as "Dawn is a tale of intrigue carved in citrus and jasmine." The park is popular with visitors to the neighboring **Museum of Neon Art**, 501 W Olympic Blvd (Wed–Sat 11am–5pm, Sun noon–5pm; $5; ☎213/489-9918, ⊛www.neonmona.org), recognizable by the adulterated visage of Mona Lisa smiling through blue-and-yellow neon squiggles. The museum's small exhibition space showcases contemporary neon designs and a range of strange kinetic art, plus some great old neon theater signs – notably the sweeping, streamlined lettering of the Melrose Theater – and runs monthly bus tours of LA's best neon sights (see p.40). Across the park, the **Fashion Institute of Design and Merchandising**, 919 S Grand Ave (10am–4pm Mon–Sat; free; ☎213/624-1200, ⊛www.fashionmuseum.org), trains would-be couturiers and costume designers, throwing the odd fashion exhibition, with items drawn from its collection of ten thousand pieces of costume and apparel. While the French gowns, Russian jewels, and quirky shoes sometimes on display are appealing, the highlight is the annual "**Art of Motion Picture Costume Design**" show that runs from February to April – roughly Oscar time – displaying colorful outfits from the golden age of cinema to the present, from Liz Taylor's Cleopatra garb to Austin Powers' retro-60s outfits.

Finally, three blocks to the southwest, the LA **Convention Center** and the **Staples Center**, 865 S Figueroa St (☎213/624-3100, ⊛www.staplescenter.com), are sleek modern structures that have led the way for the redevelopment of the area, but otherwise offer little of interest beyond conventions and Lakers games.

Around Downtown

Just west of the Harbor Freeway, the **Temple-Beaudry** and **Pico-Union** barrios are home to thousands of newly arrived immigrants from Central America, areas more depressed in many ways than the noted ghettos of South Central LA – so avoid getting lost on one of the side streets. Also potential trouble, **MacArthur Park** and the **Westlake** neighborhood along Wilshire Boulevard, despite the appeal of their faded Victorian architecture, should only be viewed by car – petty theft and drug dealing are rampant. (The one essential reason to come here is the renowned *Langer's Deli*, p.267, which luckily offers curbside pick-up.) North of Westlake, **Echo Park** has a pleasantly faded charm, and, like **Angelino Heights** to its east, is safer and quite picturesque. Further east is car-friendly **Elysian Park**, a green space that surrounds **Dodger Stadium**. Finally, **Highland Park**, northeast of Downtown, has some decent museums, none very far from the stark concrete channel of the **LA River**.

Westlake and MacArthur Park

Westlake is the tumultuous center for countless newcomers to the city, thronged with Panamanians, Hondurans, Salvadorans, and other recent arrivals waiting for American citizenship or trying to avoid deportation by much-despised immigration agents. The activity centers on the intersection of **Wilshire and Alvarado**, where street vendors hawk their wares in front of busy swap meets, overlooked by the classy sign for the departed **Westlake Theater**, 638 Alvarado St, now overlooking a grubby flea market. A few Angelenos drop by the area for cheap and tasty Mexican food; tourists are advised to be wary.

Across Alvarado, **MacArthur Park** was developed in the 1890s when its surrounding area was a prime LA suburb; these days it's busy with drug dealing and gang activity. Although the Red Line subway passes under the park, you're best off traveling during the day and not venturing up to the surface. To the south, **Bonnie Brae Street** and **Alvarado Terrace** still have a number of quaint Victorian houses, such as the striking mix of Queen Anne and French chateau styles at 1036 S Bonnie Brae St. The one functional museum of note in the area, and a respite of relative safety, is the **Grier–Musser Museum**, 403 S Bonnie Brae St (Wed–Sat noon–4pm; $6; ☎213/413-1814, ◉home.comcast.net/~gmuseum), offering a glimpse of the luxurious furnishings and stylish architecture of the nineteenth century, when this now-decrepit neighborhood was a pleasant middle-class suburb, and the local Victorian homes boasted copious Gothic turrets, gingerbread detail, and Italianate windows.

Echo Park and Angelino Heights

About a mile north of Westlake along Glendale Boulevard, **Echo Park**, a tranquil arrangement of lotuses and palm trees set around an idyllic lake, was the setting for several scenes in Roman Polanski's film *Chinatown*. In one memorable sequence, detective Jake Gittes follows the town water-boss to a clandestine meeting, spying on him in a rowboat – the kind which you can still rent (along with paddleboats; typically $10 per hour) from vendors along Echo Park Avenue, running along the eastern edge of the lake. In the large, white **Angelus Temple** on the northern side of the lake, the evangelist **Aimee Semple McPherson** used to preach to some five thousand people, with thousands more listening in on the radio. The first in a long line of media evangelists, "Sister Aimee" was tainted by a later romantic scandal and died in 1944, but the building is still used for services by her Four Square Gospel ministry, which dunks converts in its huge water tank during mass baptisms.

Just east of Echo Park on a hill overlooking the city, **Angelino Heights** was LA's first suburb, laid out in the flush of a property boom at the end of the 1880s and connected by streetcar to Downtown. Although the boom soon went bust, the elaborate houses that were built here, especially along **Carroll Avenue**, have survived and been restored as reminders of the optimism and energy of the city's early years. There's a dozen or so in all, and most repay a look for their catalog of late-Victorian details – wraparound verandas, turrets, and pediments, set oddly against the Downtown skyline and occasionally used in ads for paint, among other things. One, with a weird pyramid roof, was even used as the set for the haunted house in Michael Jackson's *Thriller* video. The best of the lot is the **Sessions House**, no. 1330, a Queen Anne masterpiece with Moorish detail, decorative glass, and a circular "moon window." The neighborhood has been decreed a "Historic Preservation Overlay Zone" – about as close as LA gets to an official designation of preservation – and on the first Saturday of the month, you can take a two-and-a-half-hour tour of the neighborhood through the LA Conservancy (Sat 10am; $10; reserve at ☏213/623-CITY, ⊛www.laconservancy .org), and visit the interiors of two of these classic homes as well.

Elysian Park

Two miles north of the Civic Center, quiet **Elysian Park** was laid out in 1886 and has been shrinking ever since. The LA Police Academy first commandeered a chunk of the park for its training facility; later, the Pasadena Freeway sliced off another section. Finally, after city bureaucrats booted a good number of poor tenants from the land (who lived a rural lifestyle, vividly documented in the book *Chavez Ravine 1949*; see p.405), **Dodger Stadium** was constructed in the early 1960s to host the transplanted Brooklyn baseball team, and the park became a fraction of its former self. However, even crisscrossed by winding roads, it's still worth a look, especially for its awe-inspiring views of the metropolis – when the smog doesn't intercede. **Angels Point**, on the upper western rim of the park, is your best vantage point, marked by an abstract sculpture with a palm tree growing out of its center.

Highland Park

Beside the freeway, a mile from Elysian Park, Highland Park is one of several neighborhoods north of Downtown that has established a surprising beachhead for the arts in a once-depressed part of the city (see box opposite). It was the very first district annexed to LA, in 1895, and has recently become linked up with the Gold Line Metrorail. It's also home to the **Southwest Museum** (Tues–Sun 10am–5pm; $7.50; ☏323/221-2164, ⊛www.southwestmuseum.org), the oldest museum in LA, dating from 1907. Its name is a bit deceptive: there are in fact displays of Native American artifacts from all over North America, from pre-Columbian pottery and coastal Chumash rock art to a full-sized Cheyenne tepee. Its traveling exhibitions, educational programs, and theatrical events have made it an international center for indigenous American cultures, and its Braun Research Library has a superlative collection of recordings and photographs of Native Americans from the Bering Strait to Mexico. On the way out, there's a small gift shop where you can sift through Navajo rugs, kachina dolls, and turquoise jewelry, plus an extensive selection of books and specialist publications. Nearby, the museum administers **Casa de Adobe**, 4603 N Figueroa St, a 1917 re-creation of a Mexican hacienda with a small museum inside detailing LA history into the nineteenth century. However, the Casa is only open for special events (call ☏213/221-2163 for more information). Note that the Southwest Museum and Griffith Park's Museum of the American West offer a joint ticket to both museums for $12 – though you'll probably need a car to get to both easily.

Just down the road, at 200 E Ave 43, the **Lummis House** (Fri–Sun 1–4pm; free; ☏323/222-0546, ⊛www.socalhistory.org) is the well-preserved home of Charles F. Lummis, the city librarian who helped develop the Southwest Museum and was at the heart of LA's nineteenth-century boom. An early champion of civil rights for Native Americans, and one who worked to save and preserve many of the missions, Lummis built his home as a cultural center of turn-of-the-century Los Angeles, where the literati of the day would meet to discuss poetry and the art and architecture of the Southwest. He built the house in an ad hoc mixture of Mission and Medieval styles, naming it "El Alisal" after the many large sycamore trees that shade the gardens, and constructing the

Art in post-industrial LA

Although spots like West Hollywood, Venice, and Santa Monica grab most of the attention for attracting artists, in recent years the leading edge of LA's underground art movement has been located much further east, in the neighborhoods of **northeast Los Angeles**, which have increasingly drawn some of the city's most interesting and enterprising painters, sculptors, and architects. Setting up homes in the contiguous districts of **Highland Park**, **Eagle Rock**, **Mount Washington**, and **Lincoln Heights**, these artists have done much to revitalize a previously dilapidated, industrial dead-zone of LA. While there is no one center where artists reside or work, there are a few highlights that are definitely worth a look.

A good place to start is **The Brewery**, north of Downtown at 676 S Ave 21 (information at ☎323/222-0222, ⊛www.oversight.com), a renovated 1920s complex of twenty buildings that's gone from brewing suds to exhibiting designers and architects, with some three hundred artists occupying space in a variety of galleries and art annexes that are open to the public. Most prominent in the complex is Michael Rotundi's striking **Carlson-Reges Residence**, a converted electrical utility building, noteworthy for its jagged architecture and post-industrial decor. (It's not open to the public, but is viewable from outside.) Other worthwhile sites include the **Judson Gallery for Contemporary and Traditional Art**, in Highland Park at 200 S Ave 66 (Mon–Fri 10am–3pm; free; ☎323/255-0131, ⊛www.judsonstudios.com), which displays contemporary stained glass along with periodic exhibitions in a variety of media, and **Gallery Figueroa**, also in Highland Park at 6122 N Figueroa St (Fri–Sun noon–5pm; free; ☎323/258-5939, ⊛www.galleryfigueroa.com), where the wide-ranging shows include everything from photography and etchings to murals.

To learn more about northeast LA's art scene, check out the websites of the community-oriented **Northeast LA Network** (⊛www.nelanet.org) and the more comprehensive **Arroyo Arts Collective** (☎323/850-8566, ⊛www.ArroyoArtsCollective.org), which also organizes an annual November **Discovery Tour** ($10 in advance, $15 on the day), a self-guided tour of around eighty of the best and quirkiest of the area's galleries and private studios.

thick walls out of rounded granite boulders taken from the nearby riverbed, and the beams over the living room of old telephone poles. The solid wooden front doors are similarly built to last, reinforced with iron and weighing tons, while the plaster-and-tile interior features rustic, hand-cut timber ceilings and home-made furniture. It's all a fitting reflection of its rugged owner, one of the few individuals to reach LA by walking – from Cincinnati.

Across the Pasadena Freeway, **Heritage Square**, 3800 Homer St (grounds Fri 10.30am–3.30pm, Sat & Sun noon–3pm, tours on the hour Sat & Sun noon–3pm; $6; ⊛www.heritagesquare.org), is an outdoor museum – critics call it an architectural "petting zoo" – featuring a jumble of Victorian structures collected from different places in the city, most transported from Bunker Hill. The strip uncomfortably sites a railway station next to an octagonal house next to a Methodist church, and although the buildings are interesting enough, the adjacent freeway makes this a less than ideal spot to imagine a Victorian world of buggies and gingerbread.

The LA River

"A beautiful, limpid little stream with willows on its banks" is how water czar William Mulholland once described the **LA River**, the long gutter that serves as Downtown's eastern border. While the river may have often been tranquil, it was also quite volatile, periodically flooding neighboring communities until, in 1938, a typically drastic solution was imposed: its muddy bottom was transformed into cement and its earthy contours into a hard, flat basin. The river mutated into a flood channel, which it remains, snaking through the city for 58 miles. Although some of the northern sections of the river (mainly through the San Fernando Valley) have been re-seeded with foliage, efforts to return the Downtown stretch to its natural state have met with predictable bureaucratic resistance. Still, the fight continues, with groups like **Friends of the LA River** (☎1-800/LA-RIVER, ⊛www.folar.org) arguing for the restoration of the watercourse's old natural contours, and hosting curious monthly "**river walks**" (April–Nov: third Sun of month 3.30pm; $5) exploring the high- and lowlights of different sections of its length. To learn more about the character of the waterway and the potential for resurrecting its much-abused ecosystem, you can stop by the idyllic **Los Angeles River Center and Gardens**, 570 W Ave 26 (Mon–Fri 9am–5pm; free; ☎323/221-8900), for its informative "living river" exhibit. The center itself, set amid copious greenery and fountains, is home to various environmental and preservation groups, as well as a **bike-staging area** that has a repair station, restroom, and basic facilities for cyclists making the rugged trek along the various trails that link this terrain with the more verdant expanses of Pasadena's Arroyo Seco (see p.201).

Throughout Downtown you're not allowed to poke around the river, but you can get a vivid taste of its history and visual character by visiting ⊛www .deliriousla.net/lariver. You can also get a good Downtown view by driving across several eastside bridges, designed in various revival styles – from Gothic to Baroque – or by renting movies. The empty riverbed has been used in numerous films, notably *Grease*, in which the channel hosts a wild drag race, and the *Terminator* series, in which cyborgs run amok in its bleak setting.

Mid-Wilshire and the Miracle Mile

The ethnically diverse territory of **MID-WILSHIRE** takes in the general area around **Wilshire Boulevard** between Downtown and Beverly Hills, running parallel to Hollywood to the north. Beyond motoring down the prime traffic corridor of Wilshire itself, many visitors overlook the area, despite its being one of LA's best bets for revisiting the architecture of the early twentieth century, having escaped much of the redevelopment that has drastically transformed the more famous parts of town. Because Wilshire was the principal route of LA's first major suburban expansion in the 1920s, when the middle class began migrating west along the expanding strip – you can literally take a chronological tour of LA history simply by driving west from Downtown along it, from the Art Deco piles of its eastern end, to the auto-centric precinct of the mid-century Miracle Mile, to today's upscale shops and office blocks of the Westside.

The Wilshire corridor groups together communities of middle-income Asians, old-money whites, working-class African-Americans, and diverse groups of Hispanics within a few miles of each other. Although the area is perhaps most well-known to outsiders for being a target of the 1992 riots, **Koreatown** has since then experienced renewed growth with a slew of modernist office towers and three-story malls. To the west, just north of Wilshire Boulevard, many of the old Anglo-Saxon estates in places like **Hancock Park** visually recall their 1920s heyday, and are now populated by a mix of Asians, Jews, and African-Americans.

Further along Wilshire, the **Miracle Mile** is a classic shopping strip that boasts enough remaining Art Deco architecture to make a visit worthwhile, while the area's western side has been reincarnated as **Museum Row**, a collection of institutions celebrating everything from tar-soaked fossils to automobile culture, but especially noted for the presence of the huge **LA County Museum of Art** – one of the city's essential stops. **Fairfax Avenue**, west of Museum Row, takes you through the human hive of the **Farmers Market** to the heart of the city's Jewish population. Further west, the **Third Street** shopping district, along with **La Brea Avenue** to the east, is where the hip and trendy buy the latest designer clothes, eat in the smartest cafés, and hobnob with other would-be bohemians. These same activities occur more conspicuously on the celebrated **Melrose Avenue**, bordering the southern edge of Hollywood, though its lower-end junk stores and quirky boutiques are sadly being edged out in favor of blander designer shops. Fittingly perhaps, the west side of Mid-Wilshire is marked by an imposing symbol of mass consumerism, the concrete monstrosity of the **Beverly Center** mall.

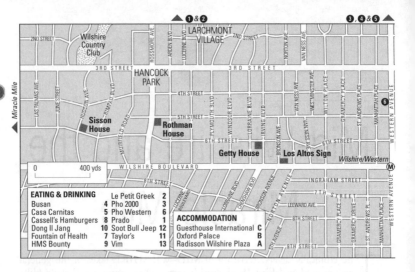

EATING & DRINKING

Busan	4	Le Petit Greek	2
Casa Carnitas	5	Pho 2000	3
Cassell's Hamburgers	8	Pho Western	6
Dong Il Jang	10	Prado	1
Fountain of Health	7	Soot Bull Jeep	12
HMS Bounty	9	Taylor's	11
		Vim	13

ACCOMMODATION

Guesthouse International	C
Oxford Palace	B
Radisson Wilshire Plaza	A

Wilshire Boulevard

Named for oil magnate and socialist H. Gaylord Wilshire, a unique individual even for LA, **Wilshire Boulevard** runs from Downtown to Beverly Hills and Santa Monica, but is at its most historic from Vermont to Fairfax avenues. This

Henry Gaylord Wilshire

Aline Barnsdall, the 1920s heiress who commissioned Frank Lloyd Wright to build her Hollyhock House in Hollywood (see p.101), was not the only socialist who became rich thanks to overflowing oil profits. Decades before, **Henry Gaylord Wilshire** gained his notoriety from the petroleum industry (also making a fortune selling an electrical device that claimed to restore gray hair to its original color), and like Barnsdall was a scion of a family dynasty, as well as an entrepreneur. By the time he was 30, in the 1880s, he had already come to California and founded the Orange County town of Fullerton. Shortly thereafter, he became heavily involved in progressive causes and took up the **Socialist** banner in two unsuccessful runs for Congress, losing both in New York and California. These defeats did not deter his frenetic activity, however, and before long he was in London hanging out with members of the **Fabian Society**, as well as a then-unknown George Bernard Shaw. The turn of the century found him back in LA, this time buying up chunks of land from Pasadena to Santa Monica, including some of the Westlake neighborhood a few miles west of Downtown, site of now-decrepit MacArthur Park.

Although Wilshire is often credited with creating his eponymous boulevard, the strip had actually been a wagon trail well before the Spanish had begun to settle in the area and had by Wilshire's time become known as the **"Old Road,"** though it was actually little more than an uneven dirt path. The oil baron soon developed the street and the property around it, eventually helping the boulevard to connect Downtown with the ocean and creating one of the city's biggest thoroughfares in the process. Wilshire, though, had worse luck than the street he named. After another failed congressional attempt, he lost much of his money in foolhardy investments, managing to drop a cool $3 million. Still, he survived long enough to see his beloved route become one of the city's most important boulevards, a role that it holds to this day.

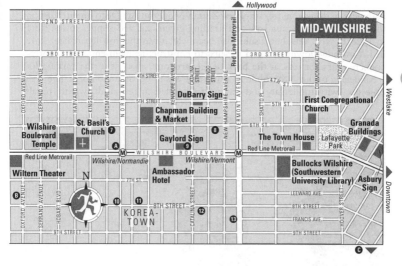

MID-WILSHIRE

Westlake

2ND STREET
3RD STREET
4TH STREET
DuBarry Sign
Chapman Building
& Market
5TH STREET
St. Basil's
Church ❼
Wilshire
Boulevard
Temple
Gaylord Sign ❾
3RD STREET
First Congregational
Church
Granada
Buildings
The Town House   Lafayette
                  Park
Red Line Metrorail

Red Line Metrorail   Wilshire/Normandie   Wilshire/Vermont
Wiltern Theater   N   Ambassador
                        Hotel
                                          Bullocks Wilshire
                                          (Southwestern
                                          University Library) Asbury
                                          LEEWARD AVE.   Sign
KOREA-
TOWN

Downtown

MID-WILSHIRE AND THE MIRACLE MILE | East of Vermont Avenue

stretch of road was for many decades LA's prime shopping strip, until the same
middle class that supported this "**linear city**" in the 1920s and 1930s disappeared for good in the 1970s and 1980s. After a couple of lean decades, many
of the once-vacant buildings have begun to re-emerge as the homes of cheap
ethnic diners, offices for entertainment companies, and various independent
businesses. While many of the Art Deco facades need renovation, they continue
to serve as beacons of a faded era, when Zigzag and Streamline Moderne
architecture were the rage, and designers built apartment blocks to resemble
Egyptian temples and French castles.

East of Vermont Avenue

The section of Mid-Wilshire closest to grim MacArthur Park and Westlake
is predictably dicey, but around **Lafayette Park**, between Wilshire and Sixth
Avenue, are a few excellent examples of these early styles. The Romanesque
Revival **Park Plaza Hotel**, 607 S Park View St, was once the celebrity-
frequented Elks Lodge, built in 1925 and adorned by intricately crafted
sculptures of stern angels on the facade, with an exquisite marble lobby
regularly used in film shoots; and the **First Congregational Church**, 540 S
Commonwealth Ave, is a 1930 English Gothic–styled cathedral known for its
huge and glorious set of pipe organs (free recitals Thurs 12.10pm) and, appropriately, the annual Bach Festival (information at ☎213/385-1345, ⌨www
.fccla.org). The best example of the period-revival styles may be the historic
Granada Buildings, 672 S Lafayette Park Place, a shopping and residential
complex posing as a charming Spanish Colonial village. It was here that the
great Hollywood photographer George Hurrell shot many of the greats of
the golden age, including Greta Garbo, and where today (at Starlight Studios)
you can watch many of the better films of the era in special weekly screenings
(Sat 7.30pm; screenings free, pre-show lecture $10; ☎213/383-2448, ⌨www
.thestarlightstudio.com).

Overall, though, the best and most famous icon in the neighborhood is the
former **Bullocks Wilshire** department store, 3050 Wilshire Blvd, the most

complete and unaltered example of Zigzag Moderne Art Deco architecture in the city, with a terracotta base and dazzling green oxidized-copper tower. Built in 1928, in what was then a suburban beanfield, it was the first department store in LA outside Downtown, and the first to construct its main entrance, a porte-cochère entry for cars, at the back of the structure adjacent to the parking lot – pandering to the automobile in a way that was to become the norm. The era's obsession with modernity and transport extended to the inside, where murals

△ The Bullocks Wilshire building

and mosaics featured planes and ocean liners abuzz with activity. Badly vandalized during the 1992 riots, the store subsequently closed, but the building has since reopened as the law library of adjacent **Southwestern University**, which in October 2004 completed a monumental, $29million restoration to bring the old beauty back to its original glamour. To see the high style of this building up close, you'll have to reserve space for one of the school's periodic "Tea and Tour" events (information at ☎213/738-8240, ⓦwww.swlaw.edu/bullockswilshire), though more regular monthly tours are planned for the future.

West of Vermont Avenue

In a far different condition than the former Bullocks Wilshire is the **Ambassador Hotel**, just west of Vermont Avenue at 3400 Wilshire Blvd, a sprawling Mediterranean Revival complex that can be viewed only behind chain-link fencing – and whose fate is still up in the air, under constant threat of demolition for the last fifteen years. Across the street from the hotel, another of LA's icons has been bizarrely re-sited. The **Brown Derby** restaurant, once the city's prime example of programmatic architecture (or buildings shaped like objects – in this case, a hat), has now been relocated to the roof of a minimall, where a coat of orange paint and a stripped brim have made it all but unrecognizable.

The fate of the Ambassador Hotel

From the early 1920s to the late 1940s, the **Ambassador Hotel** was one of the essential centers of LA's social, political, and entertainment worlds. Occupying a sizable tract of land in what where then the automobile-suburbs of the city, the hotel, when built in 1921, stood out prominently in the landscape of low-slung development and a few remaining agricultural tracts. But LA developed quickly, and the complex soon became the winter home of transient Hollywood celebrities, and its **Cocoanut Grove** club was a favorite nightspot, attracting singers and musicians like Bing Crosby and Duke Ellington on stage (its glossy character was recently re-created in Martin Scorsese's *The Aviator*). The large ballroom also hosted some of the early Academy Award ceremonies, and appeared in the first two versions of *A Star is Born*. Politically, too, it hosted events with significant consequences: **Richard Nixon** wrote his immortal "Checkers" speech here in 1952, and on June 5, 1968, **Bobby Kennedy** was fatally shot in the hotel kitchen as he tried to avoid the press after winning the California presidential primary.

Despite its considerable history and impressive architecture, though, the building's future has been in doubt since the hotel **closed** some fifteen years ago – a victim of LA's relentless expansion westward and of the neighborhood's fading glamour and lack of capital investment. At first, Donald Trump battled the **LA Unified School District** to win control of the site, and the latter won the legal fight many years after, only to dither over the hotel's fate for some time, and then in late 2004 to announce that most of the complex would be unceremoniously **destroyed** and replaced with a high school. However, the LA Conservancy, in a coalition of historians, architects, and celebrities, has since filed a lawsuit to stop this planned demolition, and the entire matter is now under review by the courts – which may mean years more of delay before the *Ambassador's* fate is decided. For more on this seemingly endless saga, visit ⓦwww.laconservancy.org. To get a view of the massive hotel, you can peer through the fence on Wilshire or be on a Hollywood film crew – as with other abandoned buildings, this one is a favorite shooting location for filmmakers desiring an opulent real-world setting without interference by movie-mad gawkers.

A few blocks west, the strikingly modern **St Basil's Roman Catholic Church**, 3611 Wilshire Blvd, was once the seat of the Church in Los Angeles (now Downtown at Our Lady of the Angels; see p.65), and is still LA's foremost example of contemporary ecclesiastical architecture, dating from 1969, with twelve looming concrete columns interspersed with colored-glass sculptures, resplendent teak altars and pews, and a ceiling decorated with over two thousand twisted aluminum tubes. For a particularly vivid experience, come during one of the church's periodic **choral concerts** (for information, check listings or call ☎213/381-6191). Built forty years earlier and somewhat more traditional, the lustrous mosaics, marble, and gold of the Byzantine **Wilshire Boulevard Temple**, nearby at no. 3633, are appropriately stunning. At the corner of Wilshire and Western Avenue, you can find one of LA's great Art Deco monuments: the **Wiltern Theater**, a former movie palace featuring a bluish Zigzag Moderne facade and narrow windows that make the building seem larger than it actually is. Not to be missed is the theater's dazzling interior, notable for its opulent sunburst motifs and grand Art Deco columns and friezes. Known as the Warner Bros Western Theater upon its completion in 1930, the building was nearly demolished in the 1980s until conservationists stepped in; it has since been converted into a concert hall (see p.311), and you'll need a ticket for a look inside.

Decades ago, countless **neon signs** used to illuminate the bustling blocks of the Wilshire corridor, some of which still survive. City redevelopment money has helped to relight a few, though the repair list is quite long and most landlords cannot afford the upkeep and electric cost that the signs require. Because there's no guarantee that these signs will be lit when you arrive, neon lovers may want to hedge their bets by viewing them in the daylight. Notable signs include the elegant **Gaylord**, 3355 Wilshire Blvd, the stylishly Art Deco **Asbury**, 2505 W Sixth St, the faux-French of the **Du Barry**, 500 S Catalina Ave, and the gentle cursive of the **Los Altos Hotel**, 4121 Wilshire Blvd. The Museum of Neon Art in Downtown LA offers monthly tours of these, and many other historic signs in the region (see p.40).

Koreatown

To get a good look at LA's cultural diversity, head south to Olympic Boulevard, between Vermont and Western avenues, to find the center of **KOREATOWN**, the largest concentration of Koreans outside Korea (more than 100,000 people) and five times bigger than touristy Chinatown and Little Tokyo combined. Unlike the latter two, Koreatown is an active residential and commercial district, noticeably lacking the low-rise buildings and mom-and-pop stores that fit the stereotype of ethnic enclaves elsewhere: the district is loaded with glossy modern buildings and huge, multistory minimalls that contain several of the city's better restaurants, especially for Korean barbecue (see p.278). Except for dining, though, you'll probably not linger as there aren't enough key sites to make a lengthy trip here worthwhile. A good place to start any visit, however, is the **Korean Cultural Center**, further west at 5505 Wilshire Blvd (Mon–Fri 9am–5pm; free; ☎323/936-7141, ⊛www .kccla.org). Along with a museum displaying photographs, antiques, and craftwork from Korea and local immigrants, the center features an art gallery with rotating exhibits of fine art, folk work and applied crafts, and puts on periodic theatrical and performing arts productions.

Hancock Park and around

Further west, Wilshire passes through the sloping, tree-lined neighborhood of **Hancock Park**, named after yet another oil magnate, G. Allan Hancock, who developed this expansive parcel of real estate in the 1920s as an elite suburb. The area has managed to retain its charm thanks to its well-preserved Historic Revival architecture, especially the restored 1920 **Getty House**, 605 S Irving at Sixth Street, the mayor's official residence and something of an architectural oddity, its green-and-cream Tudor design bucking the stereotype of the sprawling mayoral mansion. The house is open periodically for free tours (check ⊛www.gettyhouse .org for details), but can be readily appreciated from the street. As for the suggestive name, J. Paul Getty himself didn't reside here – his oil company owned it, along with the surrounding blocks, before donating it to the city in 1975.

There are plenty of other lovely houses, mock-Tudor and otherwise, in the neighborhood, though none, unfortunately, are open to the public. Still, you can check out some grand exteriors, such as Paul R. Williams' magnificent **Rothman House**, 541 Rossmore Ave, a half-timbered Tudor jewel, and further west, a bizarre example of Medieval Norman, the **Sisson House**, Hudson Avenue at Sixth Street, featuring a gloomy facade and three-story tower.

Bordering Hancock Park to the west and Wilshire Boulevard to the north, the Mid-Wilshire blocks of **La Brea Avenue** have emerged as one of the city's trendier shopping districts, with weekend visitors coming to sample the edgy galleries, hip boutiques and restaurants, and antique furniture dealers. As a more relaxed, though similarly well-heeled, alternative, **Larchmont Village** also has its share of high-end shops and restaurants, located just around Larchmont and Beverly boulevards, on the northern edge of Hancock Park.

The Miracle Mile

Like so many of LA's iconic districts, the **Miracle Mile**, along Wilshire Boulevard between La Brea and Fairfax avenues, was created by a property developer, in this case A.W. Ross, who realized the growing importance of the city's auto culture and quickly began developing this stretch of road in 1921. Though it never became LA's version of Fifth Avenue as Ross thought it would be, the Miracle Mile was quite a successful enterprise in its time, luring big-name department stores like Coulter's, Desmond's, Orbach's, and May Company to the then fringes of the city. Inevitably, the westward suburban shift that helped create the Miracle Mile also doomed it, and by the 1970s the area had fallen into decline, its vivid Art Deco designs left to fade and crumble after its department stores had moved away. In recent years, however, the strip has experienced a minor commercial upturn, with the arrival of celebrity-owned nightclubs, stylish galleries, ethnic diners, and offices for movie producers and agents. If you're really interested in taking in all the history and architecture, the Los Angeles Art Deco Society will happily assist you, offering two-hour **walking tours** of the strip on the third Saturday of every other month beginning at 10am ($10; reserve at ☎310/659-3326, ⊛www.adsla.org).

The route begins in earnest with the **Security Pacific Bank Building**, just east of La Brea Avenue at 5209 Wilshire Blvd, which gives you a small hint of what LA's greatest Art Deco structure, the **Richfield Building** Downtown, must have looked like before it was summarily destroyed in 1968. Both the original, and the current black-and-gold version, were designed by the firm of Morgan, Walls and Clements, perhaps LA's greatest purveyor of Art Deco and Historic Revival styles (see box, below). Just past this is the **Wilson Building**, 5217 Wilshire Blvd, a grand Zigzag tower known for the colossal neon ad on its roof, and the former **Dark Room**, no. 5370, a Streamline Moderne retail shop with a facade shaped like a huge camera, now transformed into a restaurant. Another Art Deco classic is the former home of **Desmond's Department Store**, no. 5514, with its bold Moderne tower and wraparound corners, which has been partially restored. The most vibrant classic Deco building may be the **El Rey Theater**, no. 5519, a thriving concert venue (see p.311) with its sleek king's head and flashy neon marquee, unmistakable amid the modern concrete boxes. Just to the north, a series of **period-revival apartment blocks**, between Burnside and La Brea avenues around Sixth Street, manages to impress with wild 1920s and 1930s styling, everything from French chateaux to Hansel-and-Gretel cottages to pop-Baroque confections, many of them preserved with their original designs.

LA's greatest unknown architects

Frank Lloyd Wright's forays into pre-Columbian styles in 1920s Los Angeles are well known, as are Rudolf Schindler's and Richard Neutra's early modernist efforts. However, the firm of **Morgan, Walls and Clements** had equal, if not greater, success in the age of Art Deco, even though its name is now largely forgotten.

The most conspicuous works of Octavius Morgan, J.A. Walls and Stiles O. Clements were the beloved **Art Deco movie palaces** that have survived the years and re-emerged as shrines to the golden age of Hollywood. The old Warner Bros Western Theater, now called the **Wiltern** and transformed into a performing-arts complex, was a triumph of the Zigzag Moderne style saved from the wrecking ball by community activism in the 1980s. Other of the firm's theaters, such as the **El Capitan**, have survived through massive renovation, or by being converted into nightclubs, as in the pre-Columbian fantasy of the **Mayan Theater**. Moviehouses aside, the firm's best work included a variety of commercial buildings throughout Mid-Wilshire and Hollywood in a range of styles, from the Spanish churrigueresque of the former **Hollywood Chamber of Commerce**, on Sunset Boulevard at Hudson Avenue, to the monumental Assyrian design of the Samson Tyre and Rubber Company, now **The Citadel** shopping complex – an ersatz temple stranded alongside a busy freeway.

Besides being skilled in period-revival architecture, Morgan, Walls and Clements also produced superb early Beaux Arts designs, as in Downtown's **I.N. Van Nuys Building**, and the Streamline Moderne, shown best in the radiant pylon of the **KFL Building**, 133 N Vermont Ave, and the sleek and towering **Owl Drug Company**, 6380 Hollywood Blvd (now a florist). Perhaps their most impressive remaining structure is the Spanish Colonial **Chapman Building and Market**, at Sixth Street and Alexandria Avenue, a fanciful creation occupying a full city block and hiding an interior courtyard with assorted clubs and restaurants.

Although many of the firm's extant structures are closed to the public, their Andalusian-styled **Adamson House** in Malibu, Pacific Coast Highway at Serra Road (p.223), is not, offering the best chance to see what made their romantic escapist designs of the period so appealing to the architecture world.

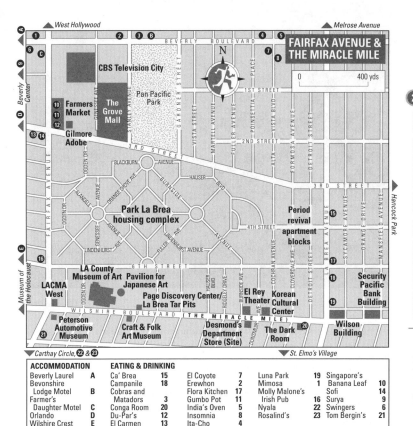

West Hollywood   *Melrose Avenue*

FAIRFAX AVENUE & THE MIRACLE MILE

CBS Television City

Pan Pacific Park

N

0   400 yds

10 Farmers Market   The Grove Mall

11

12

13 **14** Gilmore Adobe

BLACKBURN AVENUE

HAUSER BLVD

Park La Brea housing complex

Period revival apartment blocks **15**

16

17

LA County Museum of Art   Pavilion for Japanese Art

LACMA West

Page Discovery Center/ La Brea Tar Pits

El Rey Theater   Korean Cultural Center

18 Security Pacific Bank Building

19

WILSHIRE BOULEVARD (THE MIRACLE MILE)

Peterson Automotive Museum **21**   Craft & Folk Art Museum   Desmond's Department Store (Site)   The Dark Room **20**   Wilson Building

Carthay Circle, **22** *&* **23**   *St. Elmo's Village*

Beverly Center

Museum of the Holocaust

Hancock Park

ACCOMMODATION		EATING & DRINKING							
Beverly Laurel	A	Ca' Brea	15	El Coyote	7	Luna Park	19	Singapore's	
Bevonshire		Campanile	18	Erewhon	2	Mimosa	1	Banana Leaf	10
Lodge Motel	B	Cobras and		Flora Kitchen	17	Molly Malone's		Sofi	14
Farmer's		Matadors	3	Gumbo Pot	11	Irish Pub	16	Surya	9
Daughter Motel	C	Conga Room	20	India's Oven	5	Nyala	22	Swingers	6
Orlando	D	Du-Par's	12	Insomnia	8	Rosalind's	23	Tom Bergin's	21
Wilshire Crest	E	El Carmen	13	Ita-Cho	4				

Museum Row

As you continue west, the Art Deco monuments of the Miracle Mile give way to the cultural behemoths of **Museum Row**. The museums begin at **La Brea Tar Pits**, Wilshire at Curson Avenue, where a large pool of smelly tar (*la brea* in Spanish) surrounds full-sized models of mastodons struggling to free themselves from the grimy muck, a re-creation of prehistoric times when such creatures tried to drink from the thin layer of water covering the tar in the pits, only to become entrapped. Millions of bones belonging to the animals (and one set of human bones) have been found here and reconstructed in the adjacent **George C. Page Discovery Center**, 5801 Wilshire Blvd (daily 9.30am–5pm, Sat & Sun opens 10am; $7, students $4.50; ⊛www.tarpits.org), a Westside branch of the Natural History Museum in Exposition Park. Besides watching research-ers clean and categorize the bones of recent finds behind glass, you can also examine the mounted remains of many early or extinct creatures, including bison, saber-toothed tigers, and giant ground sloths, their skeletons stained brown from the goo. More recently, oil drillers pumped the liquid black gold from the ground and created an industry as endemic to Southern California as

△ La Brea Tar Pits

the movie business. In fact, it was a petroleum geologist, **William Orcutt**, who found the modern world's first saber-toothed tiger skull here in 1916, and an oil magnate, G. Allan Hancock, who in the same year donated this property to the county (not far from his later Hancock Park development). Outside, tar still seeps through the grass, but most of it oozes behind chain-link fences.

Across the street, the **Craft and Folk Art Museum**, 5814 Wilshire Blvd (Wed–Sun 11am–5pm; $3.50; ⊛www.cafam.org), has a small selection of handmade objects – rugs, pottery, clothing, and the like. The fairly limited gallery space also hosts rotating exhibitions, among them pottery bowls and vases designed by Picasso, international carnival costumes, and local examples of "low-rider" bicycles. Further west, at the intersection of Fairfax Avenue, the **Petersen Automotive Museum**, 6060 Wilshire Blvd (Tues–Sun 10am–6pm; $10, parking $6; ☎323/930-2277, ⊛www.petersen.org), is spread over three floors, showcasing cars of all makes and models, from the splashiest muscle cars to "million-dollar" vehicles like the 1919 Bentley and 1961 Ferrari. On the ground floor, an asphalt path leads you on a winding trek through the city's vehicular past, heading past dioramas of LA car worship past and present – from the reconstruction of a Streamline Moderne gas station to a mock-1950s car-hop diner to a 1960s hot-rod body shop in a suburban garage. The museum's most memorable image may be its re-creation of the *Dog Café*, a departed LA landmark of roadside pop architecture shaped like a giant bulldog smoking a pipe.

The Los Angeles County Museum of Art

On the west side of the La Brea Tar Pits, the **LA County Museum of Art**, or **LACMA**, 5905 Wilshire Blvd (Mon, Tues & Thurs noon–8pm, Fri noon–9pm, Sat & Sun 11am–8pm; $9, students $5; ⊛www.lacma.org), comprises an ugly cluster of oversized beige-and-green blocks, which were plopped down along the Miracle Mile in 1965 and have been mostly scorned ever since. Because of this disregard, the museum plans to undergo a massive **rebuilding** project, which originated in 2001 from an architectural contest won by Rem Koolhaas, whose radical redesign would have torn down most of the eyesores and replaced them with a three-level structure under a translucent roof. Stodgy LA voters, however, chose not to fund this project, and so the reconstruction was turned over to Renzo Piano and will be partially funded by private donations. Piano's version of the new LACMA, unfortunately, involves keeping many of the giant blocks and tying them loosely together under a rather vaguely designed scheme – making it highly unlikely that the complex will ever come close to rivaling the Getty Center or Disney Hall for aesthetic appeal.

Unless you come during a period of reconstruction (the schedule is still up in the air), make sure to check out as much of LACMA's wide-ranging stock of art as you can, some of which is among the best in the world. And if you arrive on a Tuesday before 1pm, check out the schedule of classic Warner Bros films playing in the **Leo S. Bing Theater**, where you can see anything from a film *noir* to a screwball comedy for only $2 (regular evening ticket prices are $9).

LACMA is enormous, and there's no way you could see it all at once: you're best off either focusing on the contemporary art and traveling exhibitions in the **Anderson Building** or diving into the fine selection of world art in the **Ahmanson Building**. Either way, get a **map** of the complex from the information desk in the central courtyard.

The Ahmanson Building

Upon entering the **Ahmanson Building** on the first floor, you'll encounter the museum's surprisingly spotty collection of **American art**; although the collection is rotated, highlights may include the work of John Singleton Copley (the regal *Portrait of a Lady*) and Winslow Homer (the dusty realism of the *Cotton Pickers*). Better is the impressive assortment of American and Western **furniture**, including bureaus from the Federal period, rough-hewn Craftsman designs, and machine-molded 1950s modern seats. Also on the first floor, across the atrium, is a selection of Central and South American art, the highlight of which is the **Fearing Collection**, consisting of funeral masks and sculpted guardian figures from the early civilizations of pre-Columbian Mexico.

Below the first floor, on a small lower level, is the museum's growing collection of **Chinese and Korean art**, of primary interest for its ancient lacquerware trays, hanging scrolls, bronze drinking vessels, glazed stone bowls, and jade figurines all covering nearly seven thousand years of East Asian history. Outside, in the museum forecourt, the **B. Gerald Cantor Sculpture Garden** is mostly noteworthy for its cast of characters from Rodin's *Gates of Hell*, as well as his towering *Balzac*, along with a few other of the great French sculptor's works.

The central attractions of the second floor are undoubtedly the **European art rooms**, which begin with a good overview of Greek and Roman art and continue into the medieval era with religious sculptures, notably a series of stone carvings of the Passion cycle and various shards of ecclesiastical architecture such as Romanesque capitals, Gothic reliefs, and so on. The Renaissance and Mannerist eras are represented by compelling works such as Veronese's *Two Allegories of Navigation*, great Mannerist figures filling the frame from an imposing low angle; El Greco's *The Apostle Saint Andrew*, an uncommonly reserved portrait; and Titian's *Portrait of Giacomo Dolfin*, a carefully tinted study by the great Venetian colorist. Northern European painters are well represented by Hans Holbein's small, resplendent *Portrait of a Young Woman with White Coif*, a number of Frans Hals' pictures of cheerful burghers, and Rembrandt's probing *Portrait of Marten Looten*.

The people vs Ed Kienholz

Twenty years before Robert Mapplethorpe and Andres Serrano stirred up controversy in the art world of the 1980s, **Ed Kienholz** was making waves with his *Back Seat Dodge '38*, a broken-down old Dodge with faded blue paint and dim headlights sitting on an artificial grass mat surrounded by empty beer bottles. An open door reveals two wire-mesh bodies, their grubby clothes ripped and torn, intertwined in an act of sexual frenzy and looking thoroughly decomposed. Ominous, crackly music adds to the sordid effect. Now recognized as a triumph of early social-protest art, Kienholz's piece was called many other things upon its debut in the mid-1960s – indecent, morally depraved, pornographic.

LA County Supervisor **Kenneth Hahn** was one of the loudest voices to vilify both Kienholz and the museum for exhibiting the work, calling for the museum to be shut down unless it was removed. The battle that ensued was resolved with an appropriately ridiculous solution: the piece would be left in the gallery, but its car door would have to be closed most of the time, and opened only infrequently by a museum guard stationed nearby. Both Kienholz and Hahn moved on from the fight relatively unscathed: Hahn became a local legend for securing support for rapid transit, building Martin Luther King Jr General Hospital, creating the freeway emergency "call box" system, and funding sports complexes (he had earlier successfully lured the Dodgers away from Brooklyn); Kienholz went on to establish an international reputation for daring assemblage art, becoming especially influential in Europe, though largely unheralded in his native country.

Appropriately, Kienholz carried his fixation with cars to the grave. When he was buried in 1994, in a strangely modern version of an Egyptian funeral rite, his wife drove him and his possessions down into the grave, burying him along with his favorite car – a Packard.

In adjacent galleries are Georges de la Tour's *Magdalen with Smoking Flame*, a Caravaggio-influenced chiaroscuro work of a girl ruminating by candlelight while holding an ominous skull; Jean-Jacques Feuchère's wickedly grotesque bronze sculpture, *Satan*; and an excellent cache of Rodin's smaller works. Elsewhere are some lesser works by Degas, Gauguin, Renoir, and the like, as well as the dramatic prints and drawings of the **Robert Gore Rifkind Center for German Expressionist Studies**, which includes a library of magazines and tracts from Weimar Germany. Rounding out the second floor are a few rooms containing ancient **Egyptian and Persian** sculptures and icons, including bronze figures and stone reliefs of Egyptian deities dating back to 3000 BC.

The third floor is most interesting for its **South and Southeast Asian and Islamic art**, notably the selection of richly detailed sculptures of Buddha in copper and polychromed wood, watercolor images of Tibetan monks inlaid with gold, and a pantheon of Hindu gods carved in stone, copper, and marble. The adjacent **costume and textile gallery** presents a wide assortment of fabrics and clothing from many different eras and cultures – including ancient Persian rugs, embroidered Jacobean gauntlets made of gold and silk, kimonos from feudal Japan, and nineteenth-century New England quilts – but really draws the crowds with occasional shows on **Hollywood costume design**, featuring elegant gowns and outlandish headpieces from the likes of studio legends Edith Head and Adrian.

The Anderson Building

Contemporary art is showcased in the ugly **Anderson Building**, a giant concrete cube that abuts Wilshire Boulevard with a huge, sheer wall, and the adjoining **modern sculpture garden**, a largely ignored selection of uninspired works around a stagnant pond. Rotating exhibitions are presented on the ground floor, while on the second and third floors, American and international **modernist art** is the focus (though this collection, too, rotates on occasion); among the more prominent pieces of twentieth-century art are works by Picasso and Magritte, and abstract expressionists like Mark Rothko and Franz Kline. Less celebrated, but just as appealing, is Mariko Mori's hypnotic video presentation *Miko No Inori*, in which the platinum-blonde artist stares at the viewer with ice-blue eyes, manipulating a glowing orb to a hushed and haunting soundtrack; Bill Viola's *Slowly Turning Narrative*, a huge, rotating projection screen displaying discordant images; and Ed Kienholz's *Back Seat Dodge '38*, looking just as perverse as it did in the 1960s when it caused political outrage (see box, opposite). On a similar note, Michael McMillen's multimedia assemblage *Central Meridian* is a creepy walk-in garage, decorated with occult symbols and other mysterious ornaments, that showcases an old beater propped up on blocks and eerily lit by red neon under its chassis.

The Pavilion for Japanese Art
On the north side of LACMA, adjacent to the tar pits, is the **Pavilion for Japanese Art**, easily the most effective building in the museum complex with its striking design, and the only one that will be completely spared when the LACMA remodeling job begins. This traditional–modern hybrid was designed by maverick architect Bruce Goff, and modeled after traditional *shoji* screens to filter varying levels and qualities of light through to the interior. Rivaling the holdings of the late Emperor Hirohito as the most extensive in the world, the pavilion's collection includes delicately painted screens and scrolls, while elegant ceramics and lacquerware are arranged beside a gradually sloping ramp that starts at the entrance and meanders down through the building, until it reaches a small, ground-floor waterfall that trickles pleasantly in the near-silence of the gallery.

LACMA West
LACMA continues on to the western end of Museum Row (and the Miracle Mile), inside the former May Company department store at Fairfax Avenue. Built in 1934 as a great westward leap over other local retail stores, the building – whose eye-catching facade brings to mind an oversized perfume bottle – is home to **LACMA West**, an exhibition annex to the larger museum down the road (daily noon–5pm, Sat & Sun opens 11am, closed Wed; $9, also good for LACMA admission). When this annex isn't showing big-ticket blockbusters, it presents a good selection of experimental work, historic and contemporary pieces by Native American artists, and children's art in a special gallery – with pieces made to be jumped on, played with, and laughed at.

Around Museum Row

Just **west of Museum Row** beyond Fairfax is the harrowing **Museum of the Holocaust**, 6435 Wilshire Blvd #303 (Mon–Thurs 10am–4pm, Fri 10am–2pm; free; ⊛www.lamuseumoftheholocaust.org), which recounts the history of anti-Semitism and serves as a memorial to those who died in the Holocaust, as well as an affecting presentation of survivors' thoughts and memories; look for the intricate model of the Sobibor death camp, created by one of its survivors. Different sections of the museum reflect on Nazi atrocities, and illustrate the various means of resistance – violent or non-violent – employed by victims, and offer the overall timeline by which German hatred of Jewish people and culture led to the Nuremberg laws, Kristallnacht, and eventually the "Final Solution" of state mass murder. All manner of vividly evocative and disturbing photos, film, artifacts, and icons make this trip through the blackest page of modern European history a grim, but essential, stop.

On a very different note, a few blocks **south of Wilshire**, around San Vicente Boulevard, the period-revival architecture of **Carthay Circle**, a 1920s property development, is one of LA's best spots to see classic Spanish Colonial homes. A few more blocks to the south, **South Carthay** preserves plenty of 1920s and 1930s Historic Revival styles, and also has the added benefit of being one of the region's few protected architectural areas (and toured periodically by the LA Conservancy; see p.40). On the western edge of the neighborhood, the attractive **Center for Motion Picture Study**, 333 S La Cienega Blvd (Mon, Tues, Thurs & Fri 10am–6pm; ⊛www.oscars.org/mhl), houses the esteemed **Margaret Herrick Library**, whose voluminous and non-circulating collection includes books on actors, filmmaking, and festivals, as well as screenplays, film production photographs, and etchings. Formerly the home of the Beverly Hills Water Department, it was given a 1988 renovation by the Academy of Motion Picture Arts and Sciences, though its original spirit was kept intact – a municipal shrine to water, designed to look like a Spanish Mission church.

A mile from Wilshire down La Brea Avenue, **St Elmo's Village**, 4836 St Elmo Drive (☎323/931-3409, ⊛www.stelmovillage.org), is a community arts project now 35 years old, worth a look for its colorful murals and sculptures, with many of the local artists present for Sunday-afternoon presentations. It's now also the site of the **Festival of the Art of Survival**, an annual celebration of folk and popular art and music held each Memorial Day, and August jazz and October poetry events.

Fairfax Avenue and around

Just beyond Museum Row, **Fairfax Avenue**, between Santa Monica and Wilshire boulevards, was long the backbone of the city's Jewish culture, full of temples, yeshivas, kosher butcher-shops, and delicatessens. The ethnic presence is still around, even as encroaching development from all sides threatens to turn the area into another homogenized LA retail zone.

At Fairfax's junction with Third Street are the ramshackle buildings and white-clapboard tower of the **Farmers Market** (Mon–Fri 9am–9pm, Sat 9am–8pm, Sun 10am–7pm; free; ⊛www.farmersmarketla.com), created in the 1930s in an act of civic boosterism to highlight the region's agrarian heritage, much of which was being paved over to make way for new suburbs. Inside the market is a bustling warren of food stalls and produce stands, popular with locals and out-of-towners to the point where it now sees 40,000 visitors daily. This growth has helped fund a monstrous mall next door: **The Grove**, a three-level, $100million complex that has taken over much of the market's parking lot. Also on the Farmers Market property is the 1852 **Gilmore Adobe**, named for the company that financed the Grove's creation and has also helped renovate some of the classic structures of Downtown's Old Bank District. As one of the oldest dwellings in LA, the adobe was once surrounded by a dairy farm, but has since been converted into private corporate offices.

Just north, **CBS Television City** is a thoroughly contemporary, sprawling black cube – and something of an architectural eyesore – but also a worthwhile destination if you're in town to sit in an audience for a sitcom, game show, or the network's *Late Late Show* (call ☎323/852-2624 for more information); note, however, that many sitcoms – including those on other networks such as Fox – are taped in the San Fernando Valley at CBS Studio Center (🖰www.cbssc .com; to attend a taping, call Audiences Unlimited at ☎818/753-3470). To the east up on Third Street, pleasant **Pan Pacific Park** once featured the wondrous Pan Pacific Auditorium, a masterpiece of late Art Deco architecture and filming location for the Olivia Newton John kitsch classic *Xanadu*. Although the structure burned down in a 1989 fire, a hint of its breezy architectural style is still visible in the lettering and curving pylon of an adjacent sports facility. Also at the site is a moving **Holocaust Memorial**, featuring six black-granite columns (each representing a million Jews killed by the Nazis) inscribed with the events of that dark period from 1933 to 1945.

West of the Farmers Market, the **Third Street** shopping district, running from La Jolla Avenue to La Cienega Boulevard, is another of LA's trendy retail zones, though with a bit less flash than most. Although there are numerous good antique stores, restaurants, and coffee shops, most visitors are actually drawn by the huge shopping mall nearby – the imposing **Beverly Center**, Third Street at La Cienega Boulevard, a hideous brown-plaster fortress that serves as the hub of weekend activity for LA teenagers.

Melrose Avenue

The unofficial border between Mid-Wilshire and Hollywood, **Melrose Avenue** is, outside of Rodeo Drive, LA's most famous shopping strip. Running south of Hollywood starting at Hoover Street in Silver Lake, Melrose becomes liveliest between La Brea and Fairfax avenues, where it shifts from being a grimy traffic corridor to a busy shopping zone with a wide range of retailers and chains. In its heyday, Melrose was an eccentric world of its own, but since the 1990s a crush of designer boutiques, salons, and restaurants has been gaining ground at

The rise and fall of bohemian Melrose

Synonymous to many with Los Angeles itself – splashy, anarchic, vulgar – **Melrose Avenue** came to national prominence in the 1980s by featuring stores with edgy veneers and irreverent attitudes, with the garish duds at Retail Slut being only one of many such examples (see "Shopping," p.358). And although the exteriors of the 1990s soap opera *Melrose Place* were shot at an actual apartment complex in the area – further east in Los Feliz (see p.100) – that program's blow-dried beautiful people were a world away from the black-clad Gen-Xers and grungy hipsters of the real Melrose. More than anything else, though, what really defined the Melrose experience in its heyday was its widely eclectic selection of shops – junk emporia, perverse novelty stores, tarot-card readers, fetish lingerie dealers, etc – and colorful, eye-popping decór, making a stroll along the strip a truly odd experience. Unfortunately, in the last decade, many of the shops that once defined the avenue have been edged out by steep rents and forced to move to newer digs in zones like Silver Lake, Venice, and Downtown's northeastern fringe. Predictably enough, they've been replaced by the types of chain-clothing dealers, pricey boutiques, pretentious salons, and other overpriced merchants you can find practically everywhere on the Westside.

the expense of the older, quirkier tenants, diluting the strip's funky allure. As for **parking**, you won't find it easily on the avenue itself, but free spots exist on the side streets a block or two north and south of Melrose – as always, though, check the signs for parking restrictions.

The west end of Melrose is rather dull and mainstream, and beyond Fairfax Avenue the street turns self-consciously chic and pricey until it reaches West Hollywood, where its color and vitality dissolve into an uninspiring stretch of elite boutiques, and most of the window-shoppers also vanish.

Hollywood and West Hollywood

Ever since movies and their stars became international symbols of the good life, **HOLLYWOOD** has epitomized the American dream of glamour, money, and overnight success, acting as a magnet to both tourists and hopefuls drawn by the prospect of riches and glory. Even if their real chances of success were infinitesimal, enough people were taken in by the dream to make Hollywood what it is today – a charged combination of optimism and despair. Nathanael West memorably captured its dark side in his 1938 novel *The Day of the Locust*, Raymond Chandler made a career out of telling bleak stories of its violence and corruption, and James Ellroy has mined its depravity in lurid detail. Nonetheless, this dark side has only served to enhance Hollywood's romantic appeal.

The far eastern boundary of Hollywood begins just beyond Echo Park at **Silver Lake**, initial home of the movie studios and now a center for Latin American immigrants and a well-established gay community. To the north, **Los Feliz** was home in the 1920s to many of the residences of Hollywood bigwigs, and nowadays is a charming mixed-income community with a few examples of notable architecture on its northern slope. Further north lies **Griffith Park**, the site of LA's famed **observatory**, among other less well-known institutions, and offering some excellent recreational opportunities.

The district's main drag, **Hollywood Boulevard**, is still essential viewing – the basis for much LA myth and lore, epitomized by the ever-popular **Walk of Fame**. This strip and its southern neighbor, **Sunset Boulevard**, were the central axes of the golden age of Hollywood, from the 1920s through the early 1950s; even now the stars live above it in exclusive homes in the **Hollywood Hills**, perched on snaking driveways behind locked gates – the most tangible reminders of the wealth generated in the city. In recent decades, though, the economic core of the area has migrated west and now resides in **WEST HOLLYWOOD**, actually a separate city, attracting a diverse mix of gays and lesbians, pensioners, bohemians, and a fast-growing community of Russian immigrants. Youthful poseurs and music lovers congregate on the legendary **Sunset Strip**, a traffic corridor loaded with nightclubs, bars, and huge billboards.

Some history

Although you'd never believe it these days, Hollywood started life as a **temperance colony**, created to be a sober, God-fearing alternative to raunchy

Downtown LA, eight miles away by rough country road. Purchased and named by a pair of devout Methodists in 1887, the district remained autonomous until 1911, when residents were forced, in return for a regular water supply, to be annexed as an LA suburb. The film industry, meanwhile, gathering momentum on the East Coast, needed a place with guaranteed sunshine, cheap labor, low taxes, diverse scenery, and most importantly, enough distance to dodge Thomas Edison's patent trust, which tried to restrict filmmaking nationwide. Southern California was the perfect spot.

A few offices affiliated to Eastern film companies started appearing Downtown in 1906 and the first true studios opened in nearby Silver Lake, but independent hopefuls soon discovered the cheaper rents in Hollywood (for the full story, see "The Rise of Hollywood," p.389). Of considerable influence was **Thomas Ince**, a producer who set up shop here and established a production studio that would become a template for later filmmaking companies. While Hollywood soon vaulted to domestic economic success, its international rise was only assured after the first world war; the World War II crippled Europe's vibrant film industry, ensuring American pop-culture hegemony until the 1950s. At this time, government antitrust actions, television, and revitalized European competition damaged the US movie industry, and by the 1960s large-scale financial flight further weakened LA's film business.

In recent decades, even the industrial companies involved in motion pictures – support facilities for editing, lighting, and props – have been underbid by outside competitors based in North Carolina, Toronto, and Vancouver, and shooting locations have migrated to those areas – along with more far-flung spots such as Eastern Europe – mainly because of lower taxes and cheaper labor. While offices for big-name producers, directors, actors, and agents are still based in LA, all of the major studios, except for **Paramount**, have long since moved from Hollywood to digs in Burbank, Culver City, and elsewhere.

Although the district has been hobbled by the departure of the studios, tourism has helped to make up some of the economic loss, and city redevelopment schemes are always in the works – including the massive **Hollywood and Highland mall**, site of the Academy Awards. While Hollywood may never be totally sanitized, most of its denizens – rock musicians, struggling writers, club-hoppers, and petty criminals – prefer it to stay that way.

Silver Lake and Los Feliz

As the original home of the region's film studios, **Silver Lake** and **Los Feliz** are fitting places to begin any in-depth tour of Hollywood. Unfortunately, Silver Lake's movieland heritage survives in only a few dusty pockets, and it's more noteworthy now for its striking views of the city and fine modern architecture. Los Feliz has preserved slightly more of its history and maintains a number of landmark buildings, thanks to the financial wherewithal of its richer residents, and remains a pleasantly low-key area with less of the pretension found in the Hollywood Hills.

Silver Lake

As a body of water, **SILVER LAKE** is not a pretty sight – little more than a utilitarian reservoir, built in 1907, just before the area around it briefly became

LA's movie capital. The neighborhood that bears the same name, however, features a number of fine homes and sweeping views of the LA basin. Divided into the wealthier sections in the hills and the poorer, mainly Hispanic parts near Sunset Boulevard, Silver Lake also has sizable white and Latino gay populations, and the combination gives the place a real vitality, especially evident in the area's varied bars and clubs, where you're apt to come across anything from old-fashioned cocktail lounges to free-wheeling drag shows. The intersection of **Sunset and Silver Lake boulevards** is the funky heart of the neighborhood, crowded with grubby-chic dance clubs, dingy bars, art studios, offbeat shops, and cheap restaurants. The best time to come is during the **Sunset Junction Street Fair** in August (see p.344), a bohemian carnival known for its loud music, ethnic food, and vintage-clothing stalls, which draws everyone from aging hippies with their families to pierced and tattooed youth looking for a little raucous amusement.

Above Sunset, Silver Lake's hills rise around the reservoir, and from the aptly-named **Apex Street** to the east, wealthy residents are afforded great views of the city, which you can get too, if you don't mind driving up the precipitously steep incline to reach the top. The hills to the west are peppered with prime examples of modernist homes by the likes of Gregory Ain, Richard Neutra, R.M. Schindler, and Harwell Harris. Two bravura examples of mid-twentieth-century design are Schindler's cliff-hugging masterpiece of projecting roofs and glass corners, the **Van Patten House**, 2320 Moreno Drive, and John Lautner's **Silvertop House**, 2138 Micheltorena St (best viewed from 2100 Redcliff Drive), with its cantilevered roofs and balconies, wraparound glass windows, and sweeping concrete curves.

The east side of Silver Lake is an area once known as **Edendale**. Although most of the district's movie history has been paved over or altered beyond recognition (such as an early Walt Disney studio at 2719 Hyperion Ave, now a grocery store), an indication of its fleeting glory is at 1712 Glendale Blvd, currently a storage facility but once the place where movie pioneer Mack Sennett's **Keystone Film Company** employed such legends as Fatty Arbuckle, Charlie Chaplin, Gloria Swanson, and the Keystone Kops, using much of the surrounding terrain for shooting locations. If you're a devotee of Laurel and Hardy, wander south to one such location on Vendome Street where, near no. 930, a **long stairway** saw the duo trying to move a grand piano up its incline, in the 1932 film *The Music Box*.

Los Feliz

Named after nineteenth-century soldier and landowner José Feliz, **LOS FELIZ** is a mixed-class neighborhood with large numbers of Hispanic and gay residents, though it used to hold the glittering mansions of movie stars and studio bosses, a legacy that has left it with no small amount of eye-opening architecture. Just northwest of Silver Lake and occupying a prime perch below Griffith Park, the district numbered among its 1920s denizens Cecil B. DeMille, W.C. Fields, and Walt Disney. The legendary animator had his first "studio" here, at 4649 Kingswell Ave, which was actually little more than rental space in a realty office, where the bathroom had to double as a darkroom (Disney's first true studio complex was at 2719 Hyperion Ave, now a parking lot). Other early movie companies in the area include **KCET Studios**, 4401 Sunset Blvd, constructed in 1912 and Hollywood's oldest film studio in continuous use, and the old **Vitagraph Studios**, 4151 Prospect Ave, since reincarnated as **ABC Television Center**, which mainly uses the facility for taping soap operas

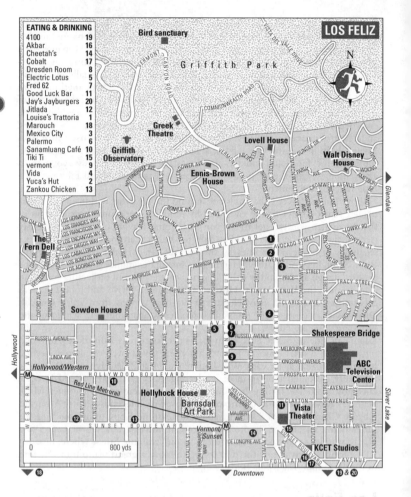

EATING & DRINKING
4100	19
Akbar	16
Cheetah's	14
Cobalt	17
Dresden Room	8
Electric Lotus	5
Fred 62	7
Good Luck Bar	11
Jay's Jayburgers	20
Jitlada	12
Louise's Trattoria	1
Marouch	18
Mexico City	3
Palermo	6
Sanamluang Café	10
Tiki Ti	15
vermont	9
Vida	4
Yuca's Hut	2
Zankou Chicken	13

like *General Hospital* (call ☎310/557-7777 for free tickets). Melodrama and mystery junkies may also want to pass by **4616 Greenwood Place**, the apartment complex that was used as the exterior of TV's *Melrose Place*, and where Raymond Chandler lived in the 1930s.

More atmospheric is the **Vista Theater**, at the convergence of Sunset and Hollywood boulevards, a lovely, quasi-Egyptian moviehouse. Across the street is the vacant site where **D.W. Griffith** constructed his Babylonian set for the 1916 film **Intolerance**, which cost $2 million and employed fifteen thousand extras. The movie was a parable about social bigotry and a response to critics of his earlier hit, *The Birth of a Nation*, which glorified the Ku Klux Klan; however, audiences were largely intolerant of *Intolerance*, and as a reminder of the movie's failure, the colossal film set (featuring elephant statues, hanging gardens, and massive pillars) sat for three years, becoming a perverse sort of tourist attraction as it became more decrepit. You won't see anything like it at the intersection today, but as an odd epilogue, a stripped-down "re-creation" of the gargantuan film set is now the centerpiece of the giant Hollywood and Highland mall in Central Hollywood (see p.109), and of a Disneyland fake studio lot (see p.233).

Just after the original movie set's destruction, Frank Lloyd Wright began constructing his first LA house up the road, on a picturesque hillside overlooking the city. The 1921 **Hollyhock House**, close to the junction of Vermont Avenue at 4800 Hollywood Blvd (Wed–Sun 1hr tours every hour 12.30–3.30pm, Wed–Fri by reservation only at ☎323/644-6269, ⊛www.hollyhockhouse .net; donation), was largely supervised by Wright's student, **Rudolf Schindler**. Covered with Mayan motifs and stylized, geometric renderings of the hollyhock flower, the house is an intriguingly obsessive dwelling, whose original furniture (now replaced by detailed reconstructions) continued the conceptual flow. The bizarre building was obviously too much for its oil-heiress owner, Aline Barnsdall, who lived here only for a short time before donating both the house and the surrounding land to the city authorities, now the **Barnsdall Art Park** (Wed–Sun noon–5pm; free). Renovated in the last five years and featuring a number of art galleries, the complex makes for a pleasant stop while waiting for the Hollyhock tour to begin.

Further into the residential heart of Los Feliz are a number of notable sights, including the **Shakespeare Bridge** on Franklin Avenue near St George Street, a 1925 charmer with turrets, which leads toward the **Walt Disney House**, 4053 Woking Way, an oversized cartoon cottage perched on a high slope. Further into the hills, Richard Neutra's **Lovell House**, 4616 Dundee Drive, is a stack of blindingly white concrete slabs balanced on delicate stilts that looks quite contemporary for a 1929 building. One of LA's landmarks of early modernism, the so-called "Health House" was used to striking effect in the film *L.A. Confidential*, as the home of a wily pornographer. More garish is the **Sowden House**, 5121 Franklin Ave, a pink box with concrete jaws designed by Frank Lloyd Wright's son Lloyd; though not open for tours, you can get a pretty good look at this curiosity from the street.

Much higher on the slopes above Los Feliz, the **Ennis-Brown House**, 2655 Glendower Ave, is the elder Wright's own design, a fascinating experiment built

△ Hollyhock House

ndreds of bulky concrete blocks to look like a monumental Mayan ___ one of four similar Wright oddities in LA. The house's imposing, ___bian appearance has added atmosphere to over thirty TV shows ___vies, from Vincent Price's *The House on Haunted Hill* to David Lynch's *Twin Peaks*. Unfortunately, due to an ongoing renovation, the house has been closed for extended periods; check the latest status at ☎323/660-0607, ⓦwww .ennisbrownhouse.org.

Griffith Park

Griffith Park (daily 6am–10pm, mountain roads close at dusk; ⓦwww.cityofla .org/RAP/grifmet/gp), north of Los Feliz, is the nation's largest municipal park, a sprawling combination of gentle greenery and rugged mountain slopes acquired by mining millionaire **Griffith J. Griffith** in 1884. Almost immediately, Griffith wanted to be rid of it, but could find no buyers and, in 1896, deeded the space to the city for public recreation. With its picture-postcard vistas and striking silhouette, it has since become a standard field trip for grade-school kids and a requisite stop for anyone taking a trip through Hollywood. Above the

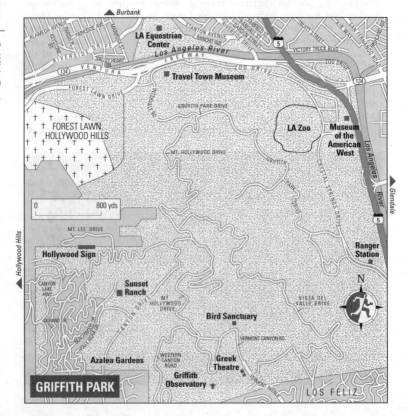

Park activities

The steeper parts of Griffith Park, which blend into the foothills of the Santa Monica Mountains, offers a variety of **hiking trails**. You can get maps from the ranger station, at 4400 Crystal Springs Rd (daily during daylight hours; ☎323/662-6573) – also the starting point for guided hikes and atmospheric evening hikes, held whenever there's a full moon. The rangers also have maps for drivers that detail the best vantage points for views over the whole of Los Angeles, including the highest place in the park – the summit of Mount Hollywood. If you'd rather go horseback riding, the **Sunset Ranch**, 3400 N Beachwood Drive, provides 90min horse rides through the area for $50 (first-come first-served, Fri 4.30pm; ☎323/469-5450, ⊛www.sunsetranchhollywood.com), and the **LA Equestrian Center**, just across the LA River at 480 Riverside Drive, offers horse rentals for $20 per hour or evening rides for $40 (☎818/840-8401, ⊛www.la-equestriancenter.com). Lastly, **bicycles** can also be rented throughout the year from Spokes 'n Stuff, behind the ranger station (weekends during daylight hours; $6–10 per hour; ☎323/662-6573), and at a facility around the Travel Town Museum (see overleaf).

landscaped flat sections, where the crowds gather to picnic, play sports, or visit the fixed attractions, the hillsides are rough and wild, marked only by foot and bridle paths, leading into appealingly unspoiled terrain that gives great views over the LA basin and out towards the ocean.

In its five square miles, the park contains 53 miles of **trails** and many opportunities for exploring its natural beauty. Near the entrance to the park off of Los Feliz Boulevard, Fern Dell Drive leads into the **Fern Dell**, a bucolic glade of ferns that acts as a border between the park to the east and an exclusive neighborhood to the west. Along Canyon Drive to the northwest, a hiking trail leads past a rock quarry to the lush **azalea gardens**, tucked away in a little-traveled section of the park. If you'd rather just view the park's animals, there's a **bird sanctuary** on Vermont Canyon Road (daily 10am–5pm; free), set within a modest wooded canyon, though as the birds aren't in captivity you might not see them. Across the road is the **Greek Theatre** (☎323/665-1927, ⊛www.greektheatrela.com), an open-air amphitheater that seats nearly five thousand beneath its quasi-Greek columns – though if you're not coming for a show (mostly summertime rock, jazz, and country concerts), you'll see just the bland exterior.

Elsewhere in the park, caged animals are plentiful in the **LA Zoo**, 5333 Zoo Drive (daily 10am–5pm, summer closes 6pm; $10, kids $5; ⊛www.lazoo.org), one of the biggest zoos in the country and home to more than 1600 creatures, divided by continent, with pens representing various parts of the world. Despite the zoological inventory, it's crammed and uninspired, especially compared to its San Diego counterpart, two hours south. The park also has a **recreation center**, Los Feliz Boulevard at Riverside Drive, offering a swimming pool and various indoor and outdoor sports; an old-fashioned **carousel** with sprightly horses first carved in 1926 (Sat & Sun 11am–5pm, daily in summer); and a **ranger station** that has information and maps on hiking paths (see box, above). In the summer the park hosts periodic, free classical-music **concerts** (information at ⊛www.symphonyintheglen.org).

The Griffith Observatory

The **Griffith Observatory**, at 2800 East Observatory Rd, is unquestionably one of LA's monuments, a domed Art Deco shrine to science, and a favorite shooting location for Hollywood filmmakers, but it got off to a less than auspicious start. Just after the turn of the twentieth century, Griffith J. Griffith offered $700,000 to the city to build the observatory and theater on the parkland he had previously donated. The city declined, principally because "the Colonel" had just been released from California's San Quentin Prison for trying to murder his wife – a 1903 incident in which Griffith, drunk and convinced that his wife was plotting a papal conspiracy, shot Mary Griffith through the eye. Although convicted of attempted murder, Griffith only spent a year in prison, and it wasn't until 1919, after his death, that LA finally took his money and later built the observatory and theater.

The observatory, finished in 1935, is perhaps most familiar from its use as a backdrop in *Rebel Without a Cause* and numerous sci-fi flicks, ranging from *The Amazing Colossal Man* to *The Terminator*. Though one of the city's most enjoyable spots, it is nonetheless closed for renovation until May 2006, including its Hall of Science, planetarium, laserium, and massive telescope. Until then, more modest exhibits are on view at a **satellite facility** in the northeast section of the park, at 4800 Western Heritage Way (Tues–Fri 1–10pm, Sat & Sun 10am–10pm; free; information at ☎323/664-1191, ⊛www .griffithobs.org).

Northern Griffith Park

The **northern end** of the park, over the hills in the San Fernando Valley, is best reached directly by car from the Golden State Freeway (I-5), although you can take the park roads (or explore the labyrinth of hiking trails) that climb the park's hilly core, past some of its wildlife lurking in the brush. The most worthwhile museum in these parts is undoubtedly the **Museum of the American West**, near the junction of the Ventura and Golden State freeways at 4700 Western Heritage Way (Tues–Sun 10am–5pm, Thurs closes 8pm; $7.50, students $5, combo ticket with Southwest Museum for $12; ⊛www .museumoftheamericanwest.org). The museum was founded by **Gene Autry**, the "singing cowboy" who cut over six hundred discs from 1929 and was the star of Hollywood Westerns during the 1930s and 1940s as well as his own TV show in the 1950s. Autry fans hoping for a shrine to the man who penned the immortal *That Silver-Haired Daddy of Mine* are in for a surprise, however: the **collection** – from buckskin jackets and branding irons to Frederic Remington sculptures of turn-of-the-century Western life and the truth about the shoot-out at the OK Corral – is a serious and thoughtful examination of Western history and legends. The comprehensive collection of artifacts is organized into engaging sections on native peoples, European exploration, nineteenth-century pioneers, the Wild West, Asian immigrants, and, of course, Hollywood's versions of all of the above. Catholic missionaries, gunslinging criminals, tribal medicine men, Romantic painters, and Tinseltown directors are but a few of the colorful figures the museum honors, and sometimes criticizes.

Less intriguing is the nostalgic **Travel Town Museum**, 5200 Zoo Drive (Mon–Fri 10am–4pm, Sat & Sun 10am–5pm; free; ⊛traveltown.org), touted as a transportation museum but more a dumping ground for old trains and fire trucks. Bounding Griffith Park's northwest rim, **Forest Lawn Hollywood Hills**, 6300 Forest Lawn Drive (daily 8am–5pm; ⊛www.forestlawn.com), is a cemetery of the stars that, while not quite as awe-inspiringly vulgar as its Glendale counterpart (see p.209), is no less pretentious, with showy gravestones and fancy memorials to such luminaries as Buster Keaton, Stan Laurel, Marvin Gaye, and Charles Laughton, as well as the likes of Andy Gibb, Liberace, and Jack Webb.

Hollywood Boulevard

From the 101 freeway to the edge of West Hollywood, the central section of Hollywood is appropriately based around **Hollywood Boulevard**, containing the densest concentration of faded glamour and film mythology in the world, with a pervasive sense of nostalgia that makes the area deeply appealing in a way no measure of commercialism can diminish. The decline that blighted the area from the early 1960s is slowly receding in the face of prolonged efforts by local authorities – including repaving Hollywood Boulevard with a special glass-laden tarmac that sparkles in the streetlights and inviting all manner of new malls to take root here. Nevertheless the place still gets hairy after dark away from the main tourist zones, when the effects of homelessness, drug addiction, and prostitution are more evident, and petty thieves go hunting for the odd purse or wallet. The contrasting qualities of faded glamour, modern hype, and deep-set seediness also make Hollywood one of LA's best spots for funky bar-hopping and nightclubbing, with a range of cheap, affordable options.

Once you cross the freeway and reach Gower Street, you enter the most celebrated stretch of the boulevard, which drops off in interest beyond La Brea Avenue. An unofficial dividing line between the east and west sides of this historic district is **Highland Avenue**.

East of Highland Avenue

Perhaps the most famous intersection in Los Angeles, the junction of **Hollywood and Vine** still tingles the spines of dedicated Hollywoodphiles. During the early years of film, the rumor spread that any budding star had only to parade around this junction to be "spotted" by big-name film directors, who nursed coffees behind the windows of neighboring restaurants, as the major studios were in those days all concentrated nearby. In typical Hollywood style,

---

Sidewalk stargazing

As practically any visitor to Hollywood knows, the **Walk of Fame** is a series of metallic stars inlaid into the sidewalk throughout the district, honoring various actual, quasi- and pseudo-celebrities of the past and present, from big-name actors to obscure radio commentators to people only famous for being famous. The laying of the stars began in 1960, instigated by the local **Chamber of Commerce**, which thought that by enshrining the big names in radio, television, movies, music, and theater, it could somehow restore the boulevard's past glamour and boost tourism. However, for every Laurence Olivier or Dustin Hoffman, plenty of dubious choices are also made; the Rolling Stones, for example, took decades to gain a star, long after they were past their prime, while such questionable picks as TV's *Rugrats* cartoon characters are enshrined frequently. Selected stars have to part with several thousand dollars for the privilege of being included: among them Marlon Brando (1717 Vine St), Marlene Dietrich (6400 Hollywood Blvd), Michael Jackson (6927 Hollywood Blvd), Elvis Presley (6777 Hollywood Blvd), and Ronald Reagan (6374 Hollywood Blvd). (For the full rundown, visit ⓦ www.hollywoodchamber.net.) Almost every month there's a ceremony for some new luminary or curiosity to be "inducted" into the street; check the local newspapers for upcoming ceremonies. Strangely enough, the one major figure to actually die on the Walk of Fame was TV actor William Frawley – better known as Fred Mertz on *I Love Lucy* – who had a heart attack a short distance from his own star at 6322 Hollywood Blvd.

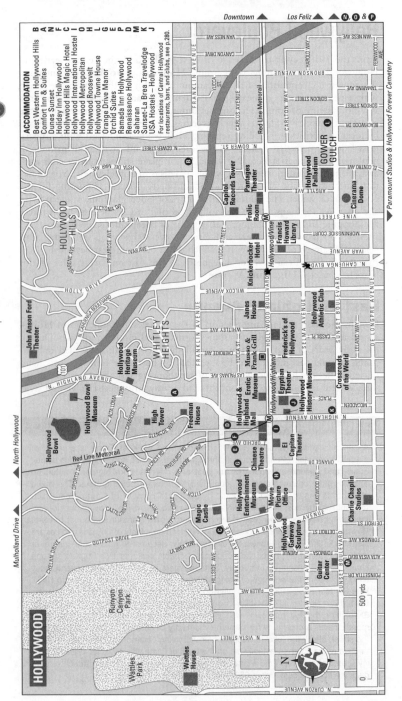

HOLLYWOOD

ACCOMMODATION

Best Western Hollywood Hills	B
Comfort Inn & Suites	A
Dunes Sunset	N
Holiday Inn Hollywood	F
Hollywood Hills Magic Hotel	C
Hollywood International Hostel	I
Hollywood Metropolitan	O
Hollywood Roosevelt	H
Hollywood Towne House	L
Orange Drive Manor	G
Orchid Suites	E
Ramada Inn Hollywood	P
Renaissance Hollywood	D
Saharan	M
Sunset-La Brea Travelodge	K
USA Hostels – Hollywood	J

For locations of Central Hollywood restaurants, bars, and clubs, see p.280.

Downtown ▲   Los Feliz ▲   ▲ N, O & P

▶ Paramount Studios & Hollywood Forever Cemetery

◀ Mulholland Drive   ◀ North Hollywood

0   500 yds

N

the whole tale was blown wildly out of proportion, and while many real stars like Tom Mix and Rudolph Valentino did pass by, it was only briefly on their way to and from work. The most notable thing marking the legend today is located underground, where the **Red Line** subway stops on its way from Downtown up to North Hollywood in the San Fernando Valley. This subterranean station is decorated with film reels and familiar cinematic imagery – one of the few artistically interesting stops in LA's mass transit network. For a look at this and other subway-art highlights, the MTA transit system sponsors free two-hour tours of the most noteworthy and eye-catching installations (information at ☎213/922-2738 or ⊛www.mta.net/metroart).

Nowadays, few aspiring stars loiter at Hollywood and Vine, but many visitors do come to trace the **Walk of Fame**, which officially begins here (see box, p.105), and just north of Hollywood and Vine is a small cache of historic pop-culture buildings. The most familiar, the **Capitol Records Tower**, 1750 Vine St, resembles a stack of 45rpm records and continues to serve as the music company's headquarters. Nearby, at 6233 Hollywood Blvd, the 1929 **Pantages Theater** has a bland facade but one of the city's greatest interiors, a melange of Baroque styling and ornate Art Deco friezes that mainly sees touring stage productions these days, but also served as the glossy site of the Academy Awards throughout the 1950s. Next door, the **Frolic Room** is an old-time watering hole (see p.300) that has appeared in countless movies, notable for its dynamic neon sign and interior mural of the stars drawn by the cartoonist Al Hirschfeld.

Around the corner, a bit of literary history can be found at 1817 Ivar Ave, the site of the fleabag rooming house where author and screenwriter **Nathanael West** lived during the 1930s after coming west in an unsuccessful attempt to revive his flagging finances. (The author vividly described Ivar Avenue as "Lysol Alley.") Gazing over the street's assortment of extras, hustlers, and make-believe cowboys, he penned the classic satirical portrait of Hollywood, *The Day of the Locust*, whose apocalyptic finale was inspired by West's witnessing of the Hollywood Hills wildfires in the summer of 1935 (and which, oddly enough, includes a character named Homer Simpson). Across the street, the former **Knickerbocker Hotel**, 1714 Ivar Ave, now a retirement center, was the spot where, in the 1950s, the likes of Elvis Presley and Jerry Lee Lewis stayed, and where the widow of legendary magician Harry Houdini conducted a rooftop seance in an attempt to help her late spouse make the greatest escape of all.

Further south on Ivar, between Sunset and Hollywood boulevards, the popular **Hollywood Farmers Market** (Sun 8am–1pm; ⊛www.farmernet.com) has been doling out agrarian goodies for more than a decade, its hundred vendors selling their wares to locals and tourists alike; while at 1623 Ivar Ave, the **Francis Howard Library** – named after the socialite wife of movie pioneer Sam Goldwyn – is a branch of LA's library system designed by Frank Gehry, and one of the master's less inspired works: fortress architecture with blank walls, a faceless facade, and maximum security above all. More inviting is the **Janes House**, back up on 6541 Hollywood Blvd, a 1903 Queen Anne dwelling that is now the last remaining residential site on central Hollywood Boulevard, though it's surrounded by a bland retail complex; the structure and its surroundings were renovated in 2004 to make way for splashy eateries and shops. A block west, you can find the well-worn dining booths of the **Musso and Frank Grill**, no. 6667, a 1919 restaurant that has been a fixture since the days of silent cinema. Here, writers, actors, and studio bosses would meet (and still do, occasionally) to slap backs, cut deals, and drink potent lunches. It's no accident that this was the place where, in Tim Burton's *Ed Wood*, the title character goes to drown his sorrows, only to encounter a loaded Orson Welles doing the same thing.

Across the street, at no. 6608, is the garish purple-and-pink **Frederick's of Hollywood**, a local landmark that sells racy lingerie and offers visitors a glimpse of famous undergarments from the 1940s to the present in its **lingerie museum** (Mon–Fri 10am–9pm, Sat 10am–6pm, Sun noon–6pm; free), where the center-piece of the collection is the **Celebrity Lingerie Hall of Fame**, showcasing underclothing donated by a host of famous wearers: Zsa Zsa Gabor's girdle, Cyd Charisse's leotard, Ava Gardner's skirt, and Madonna's bustier, among many others. If you're sufficiently fired up by all of the displays, wander another block down to the recently opened **Erotic Museum**, 6741 Hollywood Blvd (Sun–Thurs noon–9pm, Fri & Sat noon–midnight; $13; ⊛www.theeroticmuseum .com), Hollywood's latest stab at contextualizing (and profiting from) the sleaze that's available for free on the streets outside. The museum is something of an intellectual attempt to probe the mysteries of libido, covering such high-minded topics as sex and technology, biology, art, and so forth.

Egyptian Theatre

Across from the Erotic Museum, the **Egyptian Theatre**, 6708 Hollywood Blvd, is a unique, essential Hollywood icon: the very first Hollywood premiere (*Robin Hood*, an epic swashbuckler starring Douglas Fairbanks Sr), took place here in 1922. Financed by impresario Sid Grauman, in its heyday the Egyptian was a glorious fantasy, modestly seeking to re-create the Temple of Thebes, with usherettes dressed as Cleopatra. This great, restored building is managed by the American Cinematheque film foundation, and now plays an assort-ment of Hollywood classics, avant-garde flicks, and foreign films to small but appreciative crowds. Tourists, however, are encouraged to check out a short documentary, presented hourly, chronicling the rise of Hollywood as Ameri-ca's movie capital (Sat & Sun 2pm & 3.30pm; $7; ⊛egyptiantheatre.com). Alternatively, you can get the grand tour of the theater itself in hour-long visits to sights like the backstage dressing rooms and projection booth, usually presented twice monthly (10.30am only; $9; call for details at ☏323/461-2020 ext 115). Much less appealing, the eastern corners of the Hollywood and Highland intersection feature a handful of dreary tourist traps – wax museum, oddities gallery, world-record exhibit – that are worthwhile only if you're very easily amused.

The Hollywood Heritage and Hollywood History museums

A five-minute walk north of the Hollywood and Highland intersection, the **Hollywood Heritage Museum**, 2100 N Highland Ave (Sat & Sun 11am–4pm; $3; ☏323/874-4005, ⊛www.hollywoodheritage.org), occupies a historic horse barn that originally stood at the corner of Selma and Vine streets. In 1913, Cecil B. DeMille, Jesse Lasky, and Sam Goldfish (later Goldwyn) rented one half of the structure while the barn's owner continued to stable horses in the other. From this base, the three collaborated to make *The Squaw Man*, Hollywood's first true feature film, whose success propelled them to move their operation – including the barn itself – to the current Paramount lot at Marathon Street and Van Ness Avenue. The barn was eventually brought to its present location as a monument to Hollywood history.

Just south of the Hollywood and Highland crossing, the **Hollywood History Museum**, 1660 Highland Blvd (Thurs–Sun 10am–5pm; $15; ⊛thehollywoodmuseum.com), exhibits on its four levels the fashion, sets, make-up, and special-effects taken from a broad swath of movie history, with particular focus on the clothing, art design, models, special effects and props from the latest Hollywood spectaculars. However, even though located in America's film capital, the museum pales in comparison to the much more comprehensive and informative Museum of Television and Radio in Beverly Hills.

West of Highland Avenue

Looming on the west side of its eponymous intersection, the **Hollywood and Highland** complex (@www.hollywoodandhighland.com) must rank as one of LA's most frustrating attractions. After nearly a billion dollars of public and private investment, the commitment of a major hotel, boutiques, and restaurants, and the relocation of the Oscars to the specially designed **Kodak Theater** on site, this towering beacon of commerce – which was supposed to revitalize Hollywood and give the district a cultural renaissance – is no better than your average suburban shopping mall. Its chosen, and perhaps unintentionally ironic, theme is the Babylonian set from the 1916 D.W. Griffith film *Intolerance*, from which the mall borrows heavily in its super-sized columns, elephant statues, and colossal archway. Unrivaled in film history for almost fifty years, the movie was Hollywood's first real financial disaster.

One site that the mall has nearly swallowed up is the **Chinese Theatre**, 6925 Hollywood Blvd, now enveloped by a curving stucco wall and expanded into a multiplex (beyond the three theaters predating the mall). As for what remains of the building, it's an odd version of a classical Chinese temple, replete with dubious Chinese motifs and upturned dragontail flanks, and the lobby's Art Deco splendor and the grand chinoiserie of the auditorium make for interesting viewing. Afterward, on the street outside the theater, you can hop aboard a tour bus for a look at the "homes of the stars," along with hundreds of other sightseers (see "City tours," p.40).

Similarly, the **El Capitan Theater**, no. 6834, is a colorful 1926 movie palace, with Baroque and Moorish details and a wild South Seas–themed interior of sculpted angels and garlands, plus grotesque sculptures of strange faces and creatures. Twice restored in recent years, the theater also has one of LA's great marquees, a multicolored profusion of flashing bulbs and neon tubes. The Disney-owned theater, which mostly shows cartoons and comedies, is worth the price of a ticket to glimpse the eye-popping old Hollywood architecture

Hollywood impressions at the Chinese Theatre

Opened in 1927 as a lavish setting for premieres of swanky new productions, the **Chinese Theatre** was for many decades *the* spot for movie first nights, and the public crowded behind the rope barriers in the thousands to watch the movie aristocrats arriving for the screenings – a familiar scene memorably satirized in the classic musical *Singin' in the Rain*. The main draw has always been the array of cement **handprints** and **footprints** embedded in the theater's forecourt. The idea came about when actress Norma Talmadge "accidentally" stepped in wet cement (some say it was a deliberate publicity stunt) while visiting the construction site with owner **Sid Grauman**, a local P.T. Barnum of movie exhibitors who, with the Egyptian Theatre down the block and other such properties, established a reputation for creating movie palaces with gloriously vulgar designs based on exotic themes. The first formally to leave their marks were Mary Pickford and Douglas Fairbanks Sr, who ceremoniously dipped their hands when arriving for the opening of *King of Kings*, and the practice continues today. It's certainly fun to work out the actual dimensions of your favorite film stars, and to discover if your hands are smaller than Julie Andrews' or your feet are bigger than Rock Hudson's (or both).

△ Chinese Theatre

(you can also drop in for the frat-house jokes of ABC's *Jimmy Kimmel Live* talk show; reserve a spot at ☎866/546-6984).

A few doors down, at no. 7000, the **Hollywood Roosevelt** was movieland's first luxury hotel (see p.249). Opened in the same year as the Chinese Theatre, it fast became the meeting place of top actors and screenwriters, its *Cinegrill* restaurant feeding and watering the likes of W.C. Fields and F. Scott Fitzgerald. In 1929 the first Oscars were presented here, too. Look inside for a view of the fountains and elegantly weighty wrought-iron chandeliers of its marble-floored lobby, and for the pictorial **History of Hollywood** on the second floor. The place is thick with legend: on the staircase from the lobby to the mezzanine, Bill "Bojangles" Robinson taught Shirley Temple to dance; and the ghost of Montgomery Clift (who stayed here while filming *From Here to Eternity*) reputedly haunts the place.

Across the street, the **Hollywood Entertainment Museum**, 7021 Hollywood Blvd (summer daily 10am–6pm; winter Thurs–Sun 11am–6pm; $10; ☎323/465-7900, ⑩www.hollywoodmuseum.com), occupies a lower level of the crudely "futuristic" Hollywood Museum Center. While highlighted by the full set of the show *Cheers* and the bridge of the Enterprise from *Star Trek*, along with rotating exhibitions of antiques and curios from Hollywood history, the museum is a rather amateurish collection of odds and ends from old TV programs and movies, largely presented without context or any apparent purpose.

If you still can't get enough of all the filmland spectacle on display, you can also drop by a local **film office**, the Entertainment Industry Development Corporation, 7083 Hollywood Blvd, 5th Floor (Mon–Fri 9am–5.30pm; ☎323/957-1000, ⑩www.eidc.com), which provides public information on the day's shoots for films, TV shows, commercials, and so on – pointing out what locations are publicly accessible and what kinds of access visitors are allowed.

The Hollywood Gateway and around

Hollywood Boulevard's historic stretch largely ends where it hits La Brea Avenue, on the corner of which stands Karl West's **Hollywood Gateway**. This iconic 1993 sculpture features a towering pylon and metallic Art Deco–styled roof supported by caryatids of movie goddesses Dorothy Dandridge, Dolores del Rio, Anna May Wong, and Mae West – supposedly an homage to diversity in Tinseltown history, though the reality is more complex. The first three actresses had to struggle mightily against the stereotypes of their eras, and even West herself was the target of small-minded censors with no patience for her "lascivious" antics. One long block north, at 7001 Franklin Ave, the **Magic Castle** is a spooky Victorian mansion and private club that puts on magic shows and other spectacles; the only nonmembers allowed a look inside are guests at the adjacent *Hollywood Hills Magic Hotel* (see p.249).

For a respite from the Hollywood scene, the **Wattles House and Park**, further west at 1824 N Curson Ave (tours by appointment only; ☎323/874-4005, ⑩www.hollywoodheritage.org), is a relaxing spot at the edge of the Hollywood Hills. This 1907 estate contains an expansive park with picturesque grounds, several gardens with Japanese, Italian, and native-plant themes, and a palm court. The park is usually accessible if you call ahead; the house is more difficult to visit, though no less interesting, with its Mission Revival design, impressive arcade, and Craftsman detail.

Sunset and Santa Monica boulevards

Although Hollywood Boulevard is the undisputed hub of Tinseltown legend, the area around **Sunset and Santa Monica boulevards** was the actual focus of the early film industry. In the 1910s and 20s, these streets hosted five of the seven major film studios, but a decade later, four had left for more spacious lots in cities like Burbank, which offered huge parcels of land to these studios, with lower taxes than LA. Ultimately, only **Paramount** stayed in its Hollywood location.

Today, both these streets are less touristy than Hollywood Boulevard, and their attractions are more modest and intermittent. Most of the interesting spots are grouped in pockets and should be explored by car, not on foot, as both strips can get dicey at night – drugs and prostitution being the major industries these days.

③ **Sunset Boulevard**

Famous as the title of the classic 1950 movie that featured Gloria Swanson as an aging, predatory silent-film star, **Sunset Boulevard** runs through Hollywood into West Hollywood, where it becomes the colorful Sunset Strip. Apart from **RKO Studios** to the south (which went under in 1955) and then-tiny **Universal** (which left in 1915), three filmmaking giants left sizable holes in the landscape when they departed more than six decades ago. **Warner Bros** (1918–29), **Columbia** (1920–1934), and **William Fox Studios** (1924–35) were located within twelve blocks of each other, but all their studio buildings have been changed or destroyed – the former Warner facility, 5858 Sunset Blvd, is now a TV station. Other, smaller, studios also occupied space along Sunset, and many actors would frequently try to get the attention of movie producers or casting directors by loitering around the corner of Sunset and Gower Street, the so-called **Gower Gulch**. Here, film extras in need of a few days' work would make appearances in the hope of being hired for the latest B-grade Western, as extras or emergency stuntmen. The gulch's air of desperation earned it the moniker "**Poverty Row**," which also collectively described the town's smaller studios, such as nearby Columbia, which Harry Cohn founded (along with Universal), before it grew to become one of the majors – after it left the area.

Adjacent to the old Warner Bros studios, the **Hollywood Palladium**, 6215 Sunset Blvd, was best known for hosting the big names in swing, jazz, and big-band music, notably Glenn Miller and Lawrence Welk, who played here for a solid fifteen years, and the place still puts on concerts today, though of the rock, punk, and rap variety (see p.311). Down a few blocks, at no. 6360, the white concrete **Cinerama Dome** is an unmistakable sight, its hemispheric auditorium now part of a larger retail complex of theaters, shops, and eateries; the AFI organization also has regular screenings of Hollywood classics and art films here ($11; tickets at ☎323/464-4226, ⊛www.afi.com). The dome was originally built to screen the three-projector films sweeping Hollywood at the end of the 1950s, but the movie fad faded even before the theater was completed; however, you can still see blockbusters in the dome on its large, curved screen. Nearby, the delectable Spanish Revival building at no. 6525, was, from the 1920s until the 1950s, known as the **Hollywood Athletic Club**. Another of Hollywood's legendary watering holes, the likes of Charlie Chaplin, Clark Gable, and Tarzan himself (Johnny Weismuller) lounged beside its Olympic-sized pool, while Johns Barrymore and Wayne held olympic drinking parties in the apartment levels above, with the Duke himself prone to chucking billiard balls at passing cars below. After standing empty for 25 years, the building reopened in the 1990s as a pool hall and restaurant, only to close again and remain shuttered, though it still hosts special parties and events; check ⊛www .hollywoodathleticclub.com to see if any are open to the public.

Continuing west, the business complex at **Crossroads of the World**, 6672 Sunset Blvd, was, when finished in 1936, one of LA's major tourist attractions: its very first mall. The central plaza supposedly resembles a ship, surrounded by shops designed with Tudor, French, Italian, and Spanish motifs – the idea being that the shops are the ports into which the shopper would sail. Time has been kind to this place, and it has a definite, if muted, charm as the headquarters of the iconoclastic publisher Taschen (whose appealing Beverly Hills bookstore is also worth a visit; see p.367).

Further along, **Charlie Chaplin Studios**, just south of Sunset at 1416 N La Brea Ave, was a 1918 creation, built a year before the Little Tramp teamed with other celebrities to create the United Artists studio. Now owned by a different (independent) studio, the complex is not open to the public but does exhibit a bit of whimsical, Tudor-flavored architecture from the street. A few blocks to the west, the **Guitar Center**, 7425 Sunset Blvd, a musical-instrument store, features handprints of your favorite guitar gods – Eddie Van Halen, Slash, and so on. You might even see some of these virtuosos – with their axes in tow – at the so-called **"Rock 'n' Roll" Denny's**, 7373 Sunset Blvd, which has long been a hangout for musicians who've just performed on the Sunset Strip the night before.

Santa Monica Boulevard

For a street with such a familiar name, **Santa Monica Boulevard** has few noteworthy attractions, at least in Hollywood proper. Often plied by prostitutes and drug dealers, the boulevard is home to a mix of Russian immigrants, pensioners, and working-class gays. For excitement, you're better off heading further west into West Hollywood, where the street becomes a bit more lively – and safer. Still, despite its seediness, this stretch does have the distinction of bordering Hollywood's last remaining studio and most famous graveyard.

Hollywood Forever cemetery

Not surprisingly for a town obsessed with marketing and PR, even the cemeteries in LA – and not just the actors – are renamed to draw the crowds. Thus the former Hollywood Memorial Park is now **Hollywood Forever**, 6000 Santa Monica Blvd (daily dawn–dusk; free; ⓦwww.hollywoodforever.com), though at least the graves have been kept in the same places. Close to the junction of Santa Monica and Gower and overlooked by the famous water tower of neighboring Paramount Studios, the cemetery displays myriad resting places of dead celebrities, most notably in its southeastern corner, a cathedral mausoleum that includes, at no. 1205, the resting place of **Rudolph Valentino**. In 1926, 10,000 people packed the cemetery when the celebrated screen lover died aged just 31, and to this day on each anniversary of his passing (August 23), at least one **"Lady in Black"** will likely be found mourning – a tradition that started as a publicity stunt in 1931 and has continued ever since. While here, spare a thought for the more contemporary screen star, Peter Finch, who died in 1977 before being awarded a Best Actor Oscar for his role in the film *Network* ("I'm as mad as hell, and I'm not going to take it any more!"). His crypt is opposite Valentino's and tourists often lean their butts against it while photographing the marker for the "White Sheik."

Fittingly, outside the mausoleum, the most pompous grave belongs to **Douglas Fairbanks Sr**, who, with his wife Mary Pickford (herself buried at Forest Lawn Glendale), did much to introduce social snobbery to Hollywood. Even in death Fairbanks keeps a snooty distance from the pack, his ostentatious memorial (complete with sculptured pond), only reachable by a shrubbery-lined path from the mausoleum. If you revel in Tinseltown's postmortem pretensions, there are countless self-important obelisks and grandiose grave-markers throughout the park. More visually appealing, on the south side of Fairbanks' memorial lake, stands the appropriately black bust of **Johnny Ramone**, erected in 2004 following his death, and showing the seminal punk pioneer rocking out with dark, mop-top intensity. Further west, one of the cemetery's more animated arrivals was **Mel Blanc**, "the man of a thousand voices" – among them Bugs Bunny, Porky Pig, Tweety Pie, and Sylvester – whose epitaph simply reads "That's All, Folks."

Despite its morbid glamour, the cemetery also has a contemporary function. As you'll see around the Blanc memorial, there are many tightly packed rows of glossy black headstones with Orthodox crosses and Cyrillic lettering. These mark the resting places of **Russian and Armenian immigrants**, who increasingly populate the graveyard just as their living counterparts populate Central and West Hollywood.

△ Johnny Ramone's grave At Hollywood Forever cemetery

Paramount Studios and around

South of here, at 5555 Melrose Ave (but not anywhere near the celebrated stretch of Melrose, for which see p.95), are the grand gates of **Paramount Studios** (2hr tour Mon–Fri 10am & 2pm; $35; by reservation at ☎323/956-1777, ⓦwww.paramount.com/studio), though the original entrance – which Gloria Swanson rode through in *Sunset Boulevard* – is now inaccessible. The tour isn't quite up to the standard of Universal's theme-park madness or Warner Bros' close-up visit, but if you want to poke around soundstages and a mildly interesting backlot (and have plenty of cash to spare), it may be worth it. However, fans of drawling TV shrink Dr. Phil don't need to shell out to watch their hero in action: the lot is readily open to those who've reserved space in the audience for his and other, less familiar, programs (call the studio for details).

There are only two other interesting sights along this stretch of Santa Monica Boulevard, the first of which is the **Formosa Café**, no. 7156, where celebrities from Humphrey Bogart to Marilyn Monroe came to drown their sorrows. It's still open, and its colorful ambience, though faded, makes it an excellent spot to savour authentic Hollywood spirits. Nearby, at 1041 Formosa Ave, is the independent production facility now known as **The Lot**, which used to be owned by Warner Bros, and before that housed **United Artists Studios** (starting in 1928), the production company of Charlie Chaplin (his second), Douglas Fairbanks Sr, Mary Pickford, and D.W. Griffith, until 1975. With their studio as the symbol of the **star system** in the silent era, these four artists controlled their careers through the company, at least for a while, and helped craft the Hollywood marketing machine that sold movies by celebrity appeal, a system that endures to this day, for better or worse. If you want to venture inside the historic confines, you'll have to reserve space in the audience for whatever TV show might be taping there at the time you arrive; for information, call Audiences Unlimited (see box, below).

The Hollywood Hills

Once the exclusive domain of Hollywood's glitterati, and still a lofty location for the city's up-and-comers, the **HOLLYWOOD HILLS** are perhaps the best-known urban mountains in the US, synonymous with the legendary LA image of celebrities sipping champagne high above the urban sprawl. Roughly paralleling Hollywood itself, and forming the eastern end of the Santa Monica Mountains chain, these canyons and slopes offer truly striking

---

Laughing on cue

For many visitors, there's no greater highlight of a trip to LA than sitting in a **studio audience** and chuckling or applauding on cue to the would-be laughs generated by a TV sitcom. While not for everyone, such visits are required viewing for any proper television fanatic or old-movie buff – many production facilities are based in movie studios like Disney and Fox that would otherwise be off-limits to interlopers. Unless stated otherwise in the text, the main agency that handles the business of drumming up eager crowds for (live) laugh tracks is Audiences Unlimited. To be a member of an audience and experience the up-close taping of shows from *According to Jim* to *Will & Grace*, call ☎818/753-3470 or visit ⓦwww.tvtickets.com.

views of the basin at night, when LA spreads out like a huge illuminated grid in all directions, seemingly without end. Beyond the stunning views, most of the appealing sights in this area are located just north of Hollywood Boulevard, on narrow, snaking roads that are easy to get lost on. If you want to do serious exploring in these hills, bring a detailed map, such as a *Thomas Guide*, or prepare to be befuddled.

The eastern Hollywood Hills

On the eastern side of the area, Beachwood Drive heads into the hills north of Franklin Avenue and was the axis of the **Hollywoodland** residential development, a 1920s product of *Los Angeles Times* news baron **Harry Chandler**, who found ample time for real-estate speculation when he wasn't strong-arming city politicians. The pretentious **stone gates** of the development sit at Beachwood's intersection with Westshire and Belden drives; the chief reason most people come to the area is for the view of the **Hollywood sign** at the top of Mount Lee above (see box, below). Unfortunately, there's no public road to the sign (Beachwood comes nearest, but ends at a closed gate) and you'll incur minor cuts and bruises while scrambling to get anywhere near. In any case, infrared cameras and radar-activated zoom lenses have been installed to catch trespassers, and innocent tourists who can't resist a close look are liable for a steep fine. For a much simpler look, check out ⓦ www.hollywoodsign.org, where the letters are visible day or night, along with a virtual-reality tour of it.

If you've seen the disaster epic *Earthquake*, you may remember **Lake Hollywood**'s dam bursting and flooding the LA basin; however, this man-made body of water is anything but apocalyptic – just a pleasant, rustic refuge in the heart of the city. The clear, calm waters, actually a reservoir intended for drought relief, are surrounded by clumps of pines in which squirrels, lizards, and a few scurrying skunks and coyotes easily outnumber humans. You can't get too near the water, as metal fences protect it from the general public, but the footpaths that encircle it make for a relaxed stroll, especially for a glimpse of the stone **bear heads** that decorate the reservoir's curving front wall.

Tales of the Hollywood sign

The **Hollywood sign** began life in 1923 as a billboard for the Hollywoodland development and originally contained its full name; however, in 1949 when a storm knocked down the "H" and damaged the rest of the sign, the "land" part was removed and the rest became the familiar icon of the district. Unfortunately, the current incarnation has literally lost its radiance: it once featured four thousand light bulbs that beamed the district's name as far away as LA Harbor, but a lack of maintenance and frequent theft put an end to that practice.

The public's easy access to the sign is as distant a memory as the bright lights, for it has gained a reputation as a suicide spot, ever since would-be movie star Peg Entwistle terminated her career and life here in 1932, aged 24. It was no mean feat: from the end of Beachwood Drive she picked a path slowly upward through the thick brush and climbed the fifty-foot-high "H," eventually leaping from it to her death. However, stories that this act led a line of failed starlets to make their final exit from Tinseltown's best-known marker are untrue – though many troubled souls may have nearly died of exhaustion while trying to get to it. Less fatal mischief has been practiced by students of nearby Cal Tech, who on one occasion took to renaming the sign for their school, and by other, less accomplished, vandals.

You can only reach the lake by car. Although opening and closing times vary widely throughout the year, the **lake access road** is generally open from 7am until noon and 2pm until 7pm on weekdays, and 7am till 7.30pm on weekends: to get to it, go north on Cahuenga Boulevard past Franklin Avenue, turn right onto Dix Street and left to Holly Drive and climb up to Deep Dell Place; from there it's a sharp left on Weidlake Drive. Follow the winding little street to the main gate.

Whitley Heights

West across Cahuenga Boulevard, pristine **Whitley Heights** is a small pocket of Spanish Colonial architecture, worth a look for its well-maintained houses and great city views. The district, accessible from Milner Road off Highland Avenue, was laid out in 1918 by business tycoon **Hobart J. Whitley**, an Owens Valley water conspirator who engineered the sale of San Fernando Valley real estate (under his aptly named corporation, "Suburban Homes"). He was also known as the "Father of Hollywood," as his Whitley Heights soon became a movie-star subdivision for such silent-screen greats as Marie Dressler, Gloria Swanson, Rudolph Valentino, and the first "Ben Hur," Francis X. Bushman. The area is fairly well protected from unrestrained development, though its residents are not particularly friendly toward outside publicity. Thus, you won't find any free tourist brochures available, but will still be able to enjoy a revealing look at an elegant, ungated "Old Hollywood" neighborhood – a far cry from modern celebrity enclaves like the well-guarded Malibu Colony.

The Hollywood Bowl and around

Near the Hollywood Freeway at 2301 N Highland Ave, the **HOLLYWOOD BOWL** is an open-air auditorium that opened in 1921 and has since gained more fame than it probably deserves. The Beatles played here in the mid-1960s, but the Bowl's principal function is as the occasional summer home of the Los Angeles Philharmonic, which gives evening summer concerts (July–Sept; information at ☎323/850-2000, ⊛www.hollywoodbowl.org), along with the pops-oriented Hollywood Bowl Orchestra. As you might imagine, many of the latter events feature spirited crowd-pleasers like *Victory at Sea* and the *1812 Overture*, as well as selections of smooth jazz, film music, and other inoffensive fare. Although not always a choice spot for lovers of fine music, the venue can still be fun, with ticket prices starting at $1 (and up to $100 and beyond). If you're really broke, come to the Bowl during summer mornings (Tues, Thurs & Fri 9am–noon) and listen to rehearsals for free.

More about the Bowl's history can be gleaned from the video inside the **Hollywood Bowl Museum** (July to mid-Sept Tues–Sat 10am–8pm, Sun 4–7.30pm; mid-Sept to June Tues–Sat 10am–4.30pm; free; ☎323/850-2000) near the entrance. With a collection of musical instruments from around the world, the museum also features recordings of notable symphonic moments in the Bowl's history and architectural drawings by Lloyd Wright, Frank's son (more famous for his Wayfarer's Chapel), who contributed a design for one of the Bowl's many shells. The fifth and newest of these shells dates from 2004.

One of the elder Wright's memorable 1920s residences, the **Freeman House**, is just south of the Bowl at 1962 Glencoe Way (information at ☎323/851-0671): a squat, Mayan-modern hybrid made of concrete "knit-blocks," which doesn't actually seem like much from the outside, but inside you'll get an outstanding panoramic view of Hollywood, and a close-up look at Wright's geometric decorations and motifs. The house has been closed for long periods of time for repair from earthquake damage and acid rain decay, and is only open intermittently. Another early1920s design, the **High Tower**, is notable for a different reason. Inaccessible to the public, though viewable at the end of High Tower Drive, the Italian-styled campanile is the literary home of Raymond Chandler's Philip Marlowe – and Elliott Gould, playing Marlowe, lived in a dumpy apartment at the tower's apex in Robert Altman's 1973 film *The Long Goodbye* (see review, p.398).

The western Hollywood Hills

When he was directing *Chinatown*, Roman Polanski spent many hours in Jack Nicholson's house on **Mulholland Drive**, and later remarked of LA, "[t]here's no more beautiful city in the world ... provided it's seen at night and from a distance." With its striking panorama after dark of the illuminated city-grid, stretching nearly to the horizon, Mulholland easily justifies the director's wry comment – and makes the **western Hollywood Hills** a good place to get a glimpse of the LA good life.

From its starting point near the 101 freeway to its terminus at LA County's beachside boundary, the road travels 21 miles through winding mountain passes and steep canyons, and offers a stunning overview of the region's size and character. The stretch between the 101 and 405 freeways is the best, especially at night, when alternating views of brightly lit LA and the San Fernando Valley, to the north, keep drivers dangerously distracted. Although parking is forbidden at night, daytime views are best experienced at a **roadside park**, at 7320 Mulholland Drive just west of Hillside Drive. Here, telescopes allow you to peek at Hollywood, Downtown, and the many palatial homes.

Further west lies the northern edge of **Runyon Canyon Park** (🔞www .runyon-canyon.com), which actually improves on the views from Mulholland's crest. Park your car in the dirt near its chained gate and wander inside to a rocky outcrop that overlooks the city. Below, a path winds down to closer views of Hollywood until it eventually reaches the base of the hills themselves. If you have the stamina, take the long hike back up the hill to Mulholland, and keep a look out for B-list celebrities walking their dogs or burning off a few pounds for their next roles; otherwise, leave the park at Fuller Street (the only southern exit) and call a cab to take you back up to the top. From here, follow Mulholland west past the Woodrow Wilson Drive entrance to the elite subdivision of **Mount Olympus**, a residential exercise in 1950s vulgarity that is to Neoclassical architecture what a toga party is to ancient drama, with faux palazzos, pseudo-Roman statuary, goofy marble urns, and snarling stone lions added pell-mell to charmless stucco boxes. Much more appealing is the **Chemosphere**, 776 Torreyson Drive, architect John Lautner's giant UFO-like house, balanced on a huge space-age pedestal and overlooking the San Fernando Valley to the north. Today it's home to Benedikt Taschen, publisher of art and architecture books that celebrate quirky structures just like this one.

Other architectural treats can be found with sufficient effort as well, notably the stunning **Case Study House #21**, 9038 Wonderland Park Ave, Pierre Koenig's hillside glass-and-steel box, part of the influential Case Study Program (see box, opposite). Unfortunately, most of the area's other houses are hidden away, and there's no real way to explore in depth without your own car, a copy of the latest *Thomas Guide* map and, if possible, a detailed guide to LA architecture. If you're more interested in peeking at the homes of the stars, check out one of the many tours designed expressly for celebrity gazing (see "Mainstream tours," p.40), or look up a master list on the Internet (🔞www.seeing-stars.com is a good place to start). Notable movie-star houses include Rudolph Valentino's

The Case Study Program

Of all the popular architectural images to appear in the decades after World War II, perhaps none has been as recognizable or influential as the one of two women reclining in their evening gowns inside a glass-enclosed home overlooking the illuminated grid of Los Angeles. The photograph was of Case Study House #22, at 1635 Woods Drive in the Hollywood Hills, one of the 36 **Case Study Houses** planned in the LA area in the two decades after the war.

Created by the editor of the influential *Arts and Architecture* magazine, **John Entenza**, the Case Study Program was designed to show how industrial materials like glass and steel could be used for elegant, affordably modern homes, using "open-floor" plans to eliminate dining rooms and unnecessary walls – all revolutionary concepts at the time. Surprisingly, for a program that showcased what were then rather avant-garde structures, it was quite popular locally; selected homes were displayed for the public, and nearly 400,000 visitors took a walk through the first six of these open houses. Especially influential in design circles, the low-cost houses used construction materials that were often donated for free by various building-supply companies, with a free plug in the magazine as an incentive. However, despite its popularity and influence, the program never really came close to its goal of converting the broader American public to the modern mindset, though it did create some pretty impressive works (check out Elizabeth A.T. Smith's *Blueprints for Modern Living* for more details; see "Books," p.407).

With designs chosen by Entenza and his staff at the magazine, the houses were numbered in the order they were planned, irrespective of when, or if, they were ever built (23 eventually were, all but two in LA). The eighth house in the series was its first masterpiece, Charles and Ray Eames' colorful 1949 steel-and-glass complex of 1949, the **Eames House and Studio**, a modular construction on the bluffs of Pacific Palisades. Eventually, many of the biggest names in LA architecture – Richard Neutra, Raphael Soriano, Gregory Ain, among 27 others – took a stab at the program, with Craig Ellwood's #16 house, 1811 Bel Air Rd – a rigid exercise in steel, glass, and stone – and Neutra's wood-and-brick **Bailey House**, near the Eames House at 219 Chautauqua Blvd, among the finest examples. Unfortunately, for a program that was designed to have a great public impact, almost all these houses are now closed to the public, so a drive-by look will have to suffice if you're interested in seeing them. The only exception is the prominent Eames House, which offers lectures, seminars, and tours of the grounds by appointment.

extravagant **Falcon Lair** (1436 Bella Drive), Errol Flynn's **Mulholland House** (7740 Mulholland Drive), and the former home of actress Sharon Tate – and studio of Trent Reznor of Nine Inch Nails – at **10066 Cielo Drive**, where some of the Manson killings took place.

Mulholland Drive continues past a series of enjoyable parks, including **Fryman Canyon Overlook**, a good place for a hike in the Santa Monica Mountains, and **Coldwater Canyon Park**.

West Hollywood

Between Hollywood proper and Beverly Hills, **WEST HOLLYWOOD** was for many years the vice capital of LA, with prostitution, gambling, and drugs all occupying prominent places on the debauched **Sunset Strip**, where a whole criminal subculture flourished in the absence of effective law-enforcement and with the tacit approval of lethargic locals. The area was incorporated in 1984, a move meant partly to clean up the place and partly to represent the interests of gays, seniors, and renters. West Hollywood has since gone on to become one of the most dynamic parts of the region, especially notable for its freewheeling bars and clubs. However, this success has not entirely eliminated strife, and the new waves of Russian and Armenian immigrants making their homes near Santa Monica Boulevard have made for an uneasy mix with the city's long-standing residents. Not surprisingly, West Hollywood is in many ways more akin to Hollywood, in its progressive character and attitudes, than it is to the prosaic wealth of Beverly Hills.

Except for the Sunset Strip – the well-known asphalt artery that features LA's best nightlife and billboards – West Hollywood's principal attractions lie west of **La Cienega Boulevard** around the colossal **Pacific Design Center**. The area to the east generally blends with the less inviting parts of lower Hollywood and has little appeal beyond a few clubs and restaurants.

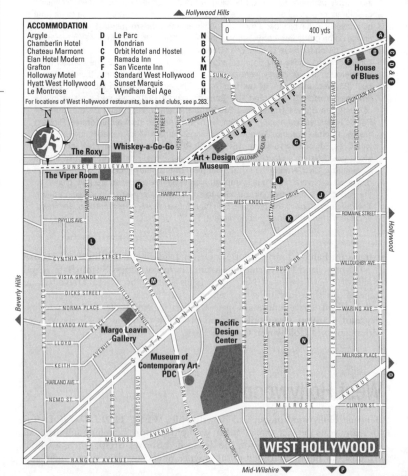

▲ Hollywood Hills

ACCOMMODATION

Argyle	D	Le Parc	N
Chamberlin Hotel	I	Mondrian	B
Chateau Marmont	C	Orbit Hotel and Hostel	O
Elan Hotel Modern	P	Ramada Inn	K
Grafton	F	San Vicente Inn	M
Holloway Motel	J	Standard West Hollywood	E
Hyatt West Hollywood	A	Sunset Marquis	G
Le Montrose	L	Wyndham Bel Age	H

For locations of West Hollywood restaurants, bars and clubs, see p.283.

0   400 yds

House of Blues

The Roxy   Whiskey-a-Go-Go

Art + Design Museum

The Viper Room

Margo Leavin Gallery

Pacific Design Center

Museum of Contemporary Art-PDC

Beverly Hills ◄

Hollywood ►

Mid-Wilshire ▼   ▼

WEST HOLLYWOOD

The Sunset Strip

Sunset Boulevard from Crescent Heights Boulevard to Doheny Drive, long known as the **Sunset Strip**, is a roughly two-mile-long assortment of chic restaurants, plush hotels, and swinging nightclubs. These establishments first appeared during the 1920s, along what was then a dirt road serving as the main route between the Hollywood movie studios and the early Westside "homes of the stars." F. Scott Fitzgerald and friends spent many leisurely afternoons over drinks here, around the swimming pool of the long-demolished *Garden of Allah* hotel, and the nearby *Ciro's* nightclub was *the* place to be seen in the 1940s, surviving today as the *Comedy Store* (see p.321). With the demise of the studio system, the Strip declined, only reviving in the 1960s when a happening scene developed around the landmark *Whisky-a-Go-Go* club, which featured seminal rock bands such as Love, the Doors, and Buffalo Springfield. Since the incorporation of West Hollywood, the striptease clubs and head shops have been phased out and this fashionable area now rivals Beverly Hills for movie-industry executives per square foot.

Some tourists come to the Strip just to see the enormous **billboards**, which take advantage of a very permissive, longstanding municipal policy that allows all kinds of gargantuan signs to pop up along the road. The ruddy-faced Marlboro Man is now gone, but there are many more along the Strip to attract your eye: fantastic commercial murals animated with bright colors, movie ads with stars' names in massive letters, and self-promotions for mysterious actresses – note the amply bosomed "Angelyne" looming in Day-Glo splendor.

The Strip starts in earnest at the huge Norman castle of the **Chateau Marmont Hotel**, towering over the east end of Sunset Strip at no. 8221. Built in 1927 as luxury apartments, this stodgy block of concrete has long been a Hollywood favorite for its elegant private suites and bungalows (see p.250). Howard Hughes used to rent the entire penthouse so he could keep an eye on the bathing beauties around the pool below, and the hotel made headlines in 1982 when comedian John Belushi died of a heroin overdose in the hotel bungalow that he used as his LA home. Across the street, the **House of Blues**, no. 8430, is a corrugated tin shack, with an imported dirt floor from the Deep South, that is one of the area's chief tourist attractions (and the flagship branch of an international chain), although it pales in comparison with the more authentic scene found around the **Whisky-a-Go-Go**, no. 8901, and the **Roxy**, no. 9009, both famed for their 1960s pedigree. Other spots, like the **Viper Room**, no. 8852, and the **Sunset Hyatt**, no. 8401, have their own notorious histories – Johnny Depp's trendy lair for rockers is where River Phoenix overdosed, and the upscale hotel (known then as the "Riot House") was the staging ground for the antics of The Who and Led Zeppelin, who took to racing motorcycles down its hallways and engaging in carnal acts with a fish (cited as the "Sleaziest Moment in Rock History," according to *Spin* magazine).

On a higher-minded note, for a dose of chic WeHo art check out the **Art + Design Museum**, in a business complex at 8650 Sunset Blvd (Mon–Sat 10am–6pm, Sun noon–6pm; free; ⊛www.aplusd.org), which puts on rotating exhibits of the latest trends in art, photography, and architecture, with most of the famous international names represented.

La Cienega Boulevard

La Cienega Boulevard divides Hollywood roughly down the middle, separating the funky seediness to the east and the snooty affluence to the west. The street holds a mixture of excellent hotels, clubs, and restaurants, along with Cesar Pelli's **Pacific Design Center**, 8687 Melrose Ave, a hulking complex known as the "Blue Whale," loaded with interior-design boutiques and furniture dealers. Completely out of scale to the low-scaled neighborhood around it, the entire Center is open to the public for viewing, but purchasing anything inside requires the assistance of a professional designer. Still, you're likely to be satisfied just snooping around, not so much in the octagonal **Center Green** – also called the "Green Apple," and largely vacant – but in **Center Blue**, a massive barn with a mix of showrooms and boutiques. The center also features a Westside branch of the **Museum of Contemporary Art** (Tues–Fri 11am–5pm, Thurs closes 8pm, Sat & Sun 11am–6pm; free), focusing on architecture and industrial and graphic design with a sleek, modern bent, and often participating in multi-site exhibitions with the two Downtown branches.

Other architectural novelties exist on the surrounding streets, including the **Margo Leavin Gallery**, 817 N Hilldale Ave, notable for its striking facade: a giant Claes Oldenburg–designed knife cutting through the stucco. If you really have a taste for bizarre architecture, there's even more to be found on the streets around the area, which are home to any number of fancy designers, art galleries, and trendy boutiques.

Schindler House

Back east of La Cienega Boulevard, the **Schindler House**, 835 N Kings Rd (Wed–Sun 11am–6pm, tours on the hour Sat & Sun 11.30am–2.30pm, and by appointment; $6), was for years the blueprint of California modernist architecture, with sliding canvas panels designed to be removed in summer, exposed roof rafters, and open-plan rooms facing onto outdoor terraces. Coming from his native Austria via Frank Lloyd Wright's studio to work on the Hollyhock House (see p.101), R.M. Schindler was so pleased with the California climate that he built this house without any bedrooms, romantically planning to sleep outdoors year-round in covered sleeping baskets on the roof. However, like other newcomers unfamiliar with the region's erratic climate, he misjudged the weather and soon moved inside. Now functioning as the **MAK Center for Art and Architecture**, the house plays host to a range of avant-garde music, art, film, and design exhibitions, from the work of famous modernists like John Cage and Eric Owen Moss to lesser known photographers, artists, and architects (program information at ☎323/651-1510, ⦿www.makcenter.com).

Beverly Hills and West LA

Although Downtown and Hollywood are richer in historic and cultural attractions, **Beverly Hills** and **West LA** are where most tourists spend their time. Along with neighboring West Hollywood, they boast the best hotels and restaurants, and relentlessly market themselves as the height of fashion – with an ersatz European flair. Of course, with its diverse architecture and plentiful gardens, there's more to Beverly Hills than just the elite boutiques of **Rodeo Drive**, but for most visitors, the focus lies within the three sides of the shopping zone known as the **Golden Triangle**. Above Beverly Hills, the canyon roads lead into the well-guarded enclaves of rich celebrities, while to the west, the bleak modern towers of **Century City** rise in the distance, with the district's main attraction being its large, eponymous mall.

As with the similar term "Westside," West LA has an amorphous definition, anything from the vaguely defined area between Beverly Hills and Santa Monica to everything west of Hollywood. Whatever the case, it's crossed by the 405 freeway and extends from the mountain foothills to the I-10 freeway. One of West LA's main districts, **Westwood**, is a sunless corridor of towering office blocks along Wilshire Boulevard, but closer to **UCLA** Westwood becomes pedestrian-friendly in the so-called "Village," and the university itself is full of resplendent buildings and gardens. To the west, along the **Sepulveda Pass**, the residents hiding in the wooded wealth of **Bel Air** and **Brentwood** are less than welcoming, but the hilltop **Getty Center** is a travertine icon of monumental proportions that's one of LA's crown jewels of art and architecture. West LA's southern neighbor, **Culver City**, is far less conspicuous than other areas, even though it contains several historic movie studios and a trove of eye-catching, experimental buildings.

Beverly Hills

The world over, **BEVERLY HILLS** is synonymous with images of suntanned Mercedes-drivers, fur-clad poodle-walkers, and outrageously priced designer clothes, illustrating how successful this city has been in marketing itself to the rest of the world. Inevitably, this self-promotion doesn't quite match reality,

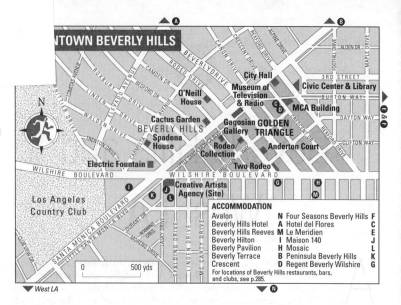

but if you've come here to fawn over celebrities and press your nose against the display windows, you won't leave disappointed. Beverly Hills' sparkling image is also kept up in part by a formidable local police force – with more cops per capita than any other city in the world – that keeps the streets free of panhandlers. The glossy heart of Beverly Hills is **Rodeo Drive**, which slices through downtown with much pomp and circumstance. More picturesque sights are tucked away in the slopes and canyons north of here, but even there you'll find gated-off mansions to match the area's super-exclusive stores.

Wilshire Boulevard

From the east, a trip into Beverly Hills begins in grand style on **Wilshire Boulevard**, where you encounter the **Academy of Motion Picture Arts and Sciences (AMPAS)**, 8949 Wilshire Blvd, the headquarters of the organization that puts on the Oscars each year (see box, opposite). The association also offers occasional public screenings in its excellent theater, along with regular exhibits in its **galleries** showcasing items from classic and contemporary American films, from scripts and storyboards to still photographs and animation cels (Tues–Fri 10am–5pm, Sat & Sun noon–6pm; free; ☎310/247-3000, ⦿www .oscars.org/foundation). This stretch of Wilshire features other classic venues for movies, including the Zigzag Moderne **Wilshire Theater**, no. 8440 (☎323/468-1770), built in 1930, and nowadays a home to traveling stage productions; the exuberant neon of the **Fine Arts Theater**, no. 8556 (☎310/652-1330), a theatrical stage built in 1936, and now a well-restored, Art Deco–flavored spot to catch a film; and the once–grand, now subdivided, **Music Hall Theater**, no. 9036 (☎310/274-6869).

The Golden Triangle

Downtown Beverly Hills, successfully labeled the **Golden Triangle** by the city's PR department, is a ritzy wedge between Rexford Drive and Wilshire and Santa Monica boulevards, dotted with some of LA's top retailers, hotels, and eateries. Street parking is tough to come by in the area, though there are a few scattered public lots, two of them just off Beverly Drive, north of Brighton Way and Dayton Way, respectively.

Rodeo Drive

Most people's chief reason for visiting Beverly Hills is, of course, **Rodeo Drive**, which cuts right through a three-block area boasting the most exclusive names in international fashion. Some of the bigger names include Barney's, 9570 Wilshire Blvd; Chanel, 400 N Rodeo Drive; Giorgio Armani, 436 N Rodeo Drive; Gucci, 347 N Rodeo Drive; and Neiman-Marcus, 9700 Wilshire Blvd, which sells everything from $5 Swiss truffles to his'n'hers leopard skins. As yet,

The Academy and the Oscar

The **Academy of Motion Picture Arts and Sciences** was formed in 1927 by titans of the film industry such as Louis B. Mayer, Cecil B. DeMille, Mary Pickford, and Douglas Fairbanks. Officially created to advance the cause of filmmaking, it was actually intended to combat trade-union expansion in Hollywood, which it tried to do, unsuccessfully, for ten years. After that, the Academy concentrated instead on standardizing the **technical specifications** of movie-making – including everything from screenwriting to sound and lighting. To expand its membership and appeal, the Academy began to include notable artists and craftworkers from most segments of the business and to promote its award show as an event of national significance – if not quite an arts festival on the level of Cannes or Venice, at least an opportunity for starlets to parade past the footlights in the latest haute couture.

This show was, of course, the **Academy Awards**, which began two years after the organization's creation and was designed to give the industry's stamp of approval to its own film product. Called the **Oscar**, an award with many dubious explanations for its name – everything from its being a forgotten acronym to the name of Academy librarian Margaret Herrick's uncle – the Academy's official blessing was a much sought-after honor even in its early years. From their infancy, however, the Oscars have generally recognized the best work produced by the **studio system**, not necessarily the best films overall, so as not to bite the hand that feeds it. This is why landmark works such as *Citizen Kane*, *Vertigo*, and *Taxi Driver* have typically been ignored and event films like *The Greatest Show on Earth*, *Cavalcade*, and *Out of Africa* have grabbed the accolades. Even in recent years, despite the renowned strength of independent studios (though most are subsidiaries of the majors), the top awards have gone to old-fashioned tub-thumpers and tearjerkers like *Gladiator*, *Million Dollar Baby*, and *A Beautiful Mind*, leaving the lower-budgeted films to clean up in "minor" categories like screenwriting and cinematography.

The awards are not above the occasional debacle, though. The appearance of a **streaker** during the 1974 show is the most notorious example, and actors Marlon Brando and George C. Scott publicly refused their awards in the early 1970s, with Scott describing the awards as a "meat parade." More recently, the awards ceremony has moved to a seemingly permanent home at the **Kodak Theater**, inside the colossal Hollywood and Highland mall. Ironically, at a time when movie grosses seem to be breaking box-office records with each passing year, the **TV ratings** of the awards show have nose-dived, and efforts to hasten the interminable ceremony have had little success. You're still apt to see award-winning actors blurting out cringe-inducing hosannas (Sally Field's "You really, really like me!") or, more frequently, reading laundry-list thank-yous to all the people in town who *really* matter: executive producers, agents, managers, publicists, ad infinitum.

none of the stores charges for admission, though some do require an invitation. (For details on each store, see "Shopping," p.352.) Adjacent to Rodeo Drive and Wilshire Boulevard, **Two Rodeo** is the area's mock-European tourist corridor, where a cobblestoned street leads visitors into a curving shopping alley designed to resemble an old-world footpath, or at least a Disney version of one. True to its LA identity, the Continental fantasy is built on top of a parking garage.

Just to the north of these snooty shops is Frank Lloyd Wright's decidedly unstodgy **Anderton Court**, now called "Tallarico," at 328 N Rodeo Drive, which resembles a boxy, miniature version of the Guggenheim museum crowned by a jagged horn, and is home to a few cramped retailers who must contend with Wright's awkward experiment in space and light. For a complete overview of the shopping zone, including Rodeo Drive and beyond, take a trip on the **Beverly Hills Trolley** (July & Aug Tues–Sat noon–5pm; May & June & Sept–Nov Sat noon–4pm; $5), which offers tourists a 40-minute glimpse of the town's highlights, departing hourly from the corner of Rodeo and Dayton Way; also worthwhile is the special Art & Architecture trolley tour (May–Dec Sat 11am; $5; information at ☎310/285-2438), a 50-minute trip through the city's aesthetic high points.

The Museum of Television and Radio and around

A few more interesting sights lie in and around Rodeo's elite commercial zone, most prominently the **Museum of Television and Radio**, 465 N Beverly Drive (Wed–Sun noon–5pm; $10, students $5; ☎310/786-1000, ⊛www.mtr .org), featuring a collection of more than 75,000 TV and radio programs, sometimes put together in informative exhibits, on such subjects as political image-making, famous advertising characters, and the best of radio and TV sitcoms, dramas, and thrillers. The museum, LA's only real attempt at providing a media museum of scholarly value, has a well-designed theater for public screenings of old and recent shows, including programs celebrating the golden age of 1950s TV and examining the role of the electronic media in reporting, and creating, the news. The building itself is immaculate white geometry from the leading practitioner of this style, Richard Meier – more famous for his Getty Center – whose other noteworthy Beverly Hills work is his spartan, garage-like **Gagosian Gallery**, just two blocks west at 456 N Camden Drive (Tues–Sat 10am–5.30pm; free; ⊛www.gagosian.com), featuring modern painting, photography, and sculpture by the likes of Cindy Sherman, Eric Fischl, David Salle, and Chris Burden.

A few blocks away at 360 Crescent Drive is the former **MCA Building**, architect Paul R. Williams' Georgian-style mansion with a central Florentine fountain and surrounding gardens – one of the few buildings in Beverly Hills with an eighteenth-century flair, despite being constructed in 1940. Appropriately for LA, all this glory is in the service of a Hollywood talent agency. Another architectural triumph is the adjacent **Beverly Hills City Hall**, a 1932 concoction of Spanish Revival and Art Deco architecture that resembles a squat version of LA's City Hall, except for the ornate dome dripping with Baroque details and vivid colors. Within the complex, the new **Beverly Hills Municipal Art Gallery**, 450 N Crescent Drive (Mon–Fri 10am–4pm; free; ☎310/285-1045), regularly offers programs of some interest, focusing on arts and crafts, furniture, antiques, and photography. On Rexford Drive, the **Civic Center and Library** complex is built in Charles Moore's postmodern design with Art Deco elements, though remains much less appealing than City Hall.

Outside the triangle

Just west of the triangle is the **Electric Fountain**, created in 1930 by the Beverly Hills Women's Club, through the efforts of comedian Harold Lloyd's mother. Depicting the history of the West on a circular frieze running along its base, the fountain spews water from the hands of a nameless Native American sitting atop its central column, deep in a rain prayer. Across from here, at the intersection of Wilshire and Santa Monica boulevards, sits the headquarters of **Creative Artists Agency**, where powerbrokers, led by Mike Ovitz, made their company into one of the most feared institutions in town in the 1980s and early 90s. With its white-marble curtain wall and curved glass, the I.M. Pei design befits the former attitude of the company, but agents don't reign quite as supreme these days, and CAA is selling the behemoth and moving to Century City.

Meanwhile, along Santa Monica Boulevard, the entire north side of the road in Beverly Hills is lined with a continuous strip of green known as **Beverly Gardens**. The most appealing stretch, between Camden and Bedford drives, is home to one of the largest municipal collections of cacti in the world, and a tranquil setting despite the abundance of prickly plants, littered here and there with a few middling sculptures.

Further north is the residential side of Beverly Hills, with its winding, palm-lined streets and Mercedes-filled driveways. Although a number of lesser-known stars live on these streets, the real interest is the fanciful architecture. Without a doubt the most peculiar item is the **Spadena House**, Carmelita Drive at Walden Avenue, whose sagging roof, gnarled windows, and pointed wooden fence have earned it the nickname the "Witch's House." Built as the headquarters for a Culver City movie company in the 1920s, the house was later moved here. Another outlandish design, the **O'Neill House**, 507 N Rodeo Drive, looks like a melting birthday cake, with its undulating lines and lopsided, vaguely Art Nouveau shape.

The increasingly curvaceous roads head into the hills and become more upmarket, converging on the pink-plaster **Beverly Hills Hotel**, on Sunset and Rodeo (see p.251), constructed in 1912 to attract wealthy settlers to what was then a town of just five hundred people. Much has changed in the intervening years, and the hotel's Mission style has been updated by a slew of renovations, though the core design of the building and its attendant gardens remain intact. Will Rogers, W.C. Fields, and John Barrymore were but a few of the celebrities known to frequent the bar here, and the hotel's social cachet still makes its *Polo Lounge* a prime spot for movie execs to power-lunch.

The northern hills and canyons

Above the *Beverly Hills Hotel*, in the northern hills and canyons, a number of well-concealed gardens and parks offer a respite from the shopping frenzy below. One such place, the wooded **Virginia Robinson Gardens**, 1008 Elden Way (tours Tues–Thurs 10am & 1pm, Fri 10am; $10, students $5; by appointment only at ☎310/276-5367), spreads across six acres of flora, with more than a thousand varieties, including some impressive Australian King Palm trees. The heiress to the Robinson's department-store chain bequeathed the land and the attached Mediterranean-style estate (not open to the public) to LA County. To the east, the grounds of the biggest house in Beverly Hills, **Greystone Mansion**, 905 Loma Vista Drive, are now maintained as a public **park** by the city (daily 10am–5pm; free), which uses it to disguise a massive underground reservoir. The fifty-thousand-square-foot manor was once the property of oil

The Beverly Hills oil baron

The 1920s were a busy time for millionaire oil magnate **Edward L. Doheny**. Not only did the former mining prospector build the mansion of his dreams, **Greystone**, at the end of the Beverly Hills street that would one day bear his name, but he was also granted the title of Knight of the Equestrian Order of the Holy Sepulchre in the Roman Catholic Church. Unfortunately, he was also involved in one of the biggest political scandals in US history.

Some three decades before, in 1892, Doheny and partner Charles Canfield struck **black gold** in the Temple-Beaudry district west of Downtown – a spot that quickly became the city's most lucrative terrain and which is now, ironically, one of its most desperate slums. But around 1909, petro-dollars made Doheny wealthy beyond all imagining, and he put some of his fortune into his elegant mansion in the Exposition Park district (which is still a marvel; see p.168) and invested even more into new wells throughout the city.

By 1921, the one-time miner was a formidable force in both the local and national economy, and he probably didn't need to offer a bribe to the newly installed Interior Secretary, **Albert Fall**, one of President Warren Harding's many corrupt minions, in exchange for preferential drilling leases in the Elk Hills region of Southern California. But he did just that, putting $100,000 in the secretary's wallet. Three years later, after Harding's untimely death, a national scandal was unearthed in Wyoming, where another bribery deal – this one engineered by oil titan Harry Sinclair – had been made over the lucrative **Teapot Dome** lease. Soon enough, the corrupt bargain for the Elk Hills property was uncovered, and Doheny was prosecuted. Over the next six years until 1930, the government tried to put him in prison, but two trials only resulted in acquittals on technicalities. Although the legal result was favorable for Doheny – though not for Fall, who served time – the damage was significant, and the scandal forever blackened his reputation. In a tragic coda to the story, Doheny's son, whom he had originally used to deliver Fall's bribe, died in a mysterious shooting in 1929.

titan Edward Doheny, who was not only a huge figure in LA history, but also a major player in the Teapot Dome scandal of the 1920s (see box, above). The house itself is rarely open to the public, except for periodic **Music at the Mansion** classical-music concerts (☎310/550-4796). At other times, you can admire the mansion's limestone facade and intricately designed chimneys, then stroll through the sixteen-acre park, with its koi-filled ponds and expansive views of the LA sprawl.

Two miles northwest, **Franklin Canyon**, an isolated niche of the Santa Monica Mountains National Recreation Area, features two idyllic reservoirs and a ranch, and it routinely sees picnickers, joggers, and even wedding parties. Although reaching the area may require a detailed map (or a visit to ⊚lamountains.com), you can make the attempt by following Franklin Canyon Drive north into the parkland until you hit a fork in the road. The lake route, to the left, takes you to the upper reservoir, around which you can take a gentle walk amid ducks and old concrete abutments; the ranch route, to the right, leads to hiking trails and a central lawn, popular throughout the year. This side of the park also contains several amphitheaters and the **Sooky Goldman Nature Center**, 2600 Franklin Canyon Drive (☎310/858-7272 ext 31), where you can learn all about the park's ecosystem and geology.

Further west, in the verdant canyons and foothills above Sunset Boulevard, a number of palatial estates lie hidden away behind security gates. **Benedict Canyon Drive** climbs from the *Beverly Hills Hotel* past many of them, including Harold Lloyd's 1928 **Green Acres**, 1040 Angelo Drive, where he lived for forty years. Although the secret passageways and a large private screening room are still intact (and off-limits to the public), the grounds, which once contained a waterfall and a nine-hole golf course, have since been broken up into smaller lots. Apart from the Period Revival houses that dominate the area, a smattering of other styles can be found off Benedict Canyon, best among them the **Anthony House**, 910 Bedford Drive, a terrific Craftsman work by Charles and Henry Greene designed for the head of Packard Automobiles. The house, with its rugged wooden frame and elegant garden, bears more than passing resemblance to the brothers' larger and better-known Gamble House in Pasadena – though this one isn't open to the public.

Century City and around

CENTURY CITY, along with Bunker Hill, is LA's most egregious example of building for the automobile, and one of its least pedestrian-friendly areas, overrun by giant boulevards and dominated by bland, boxy skyscrapers. It is, however, something of a landmark for West LA, its huge, triangular **Century Plaza Towers** visible from far across the Westside. Originally part of the 20th Century-Fox studio lot, Century City began taking shape in the early 1960s during the height of glass-and-steel corporate modernism and remains flash-frozen in that era, though the relocation of Creative Artists Agency to new digs, with a promised four-story atrium, may offer a splash of modern color to enliven the dullness. If you're not here to stay at the grand *Century Plaza* hotel (see p.251), the only real reason to visit is the **Century City Shopping Center**, 10250 Santa Monica Blvd, a single-level, open-air mall loaded with pricey boutiques and department stores.

Perhaps due to its overall lack of charm, Century City has appeared in several dystopic Hollywood movies, most memorably in *Conquest of the Planet of the Apes* and in *Die Hard*, where Bruce Willis saved the day while holed up in the postmodern **Fox Plaza**, 2121 Avenue of the Stars. Just south at 10201 Pico Blvd, the current home of **20th Century-Fox** occupies much smaller digs than it used to, with much of its former 225 acres having been sold to make way for Century City. Now owned by Rupert Murdoch's News Corporation the company still has plenty of offices and movie sets on the premises, but the public is kept firmly out.

Around Century City

East of Century City, below Beverly Hills, an unassuming building houses the **Simon Wiesenthal Center for Holocaust Studies**, 9786 Pico Blvd. The US headquarters of the organization dedicated to prosecuting former Nazis, the center has an extensive library of Holocaust-related documents and photographs. The main draw for visitors, however, is the affecting **Beit HaShoa Museum of Tolerance** (April–Oct Mon–Thurs 11.30am–6.30pm, Fri 11.30am–5pm, Sun 11am–7.30pm; Nov–March Fri 11.30–3pm; $10, students $7; ❸www.wiesenthal.com/mot), an extraordinary interactive resource center that uses videotaped interviews to provide LA's frankest examination of the 1992 riots, and leads the visitor through multimedia re-enactments outlining the rise of Nazism to a harrowing conclusion in a replica gas chamber.

Apart from the **Westside Pavilion**, another of LA's multilevel shopping mall complexes west at Pico and Westwood boulevards, the area's only other sight of note is the colossal **Mormon Temple**, located on a hilltop some blocks to the north at 10777 Santa Monica Blvd. Visible throughout the mostly flat Westside, the local headquarters of the church is easily recognized by its 257-foot tower crowned by the angel Moroni. Although the main part of the building isn't open to non-Mormons, you can enter the **visitor center** (daily 9am–9pm; free), and steal a peek at a 12ft marble sculpture of Jesus.

Westwood and UCLA

Just west of Beverly Hills and Century City along Wilshire Boulevard, **WEST-WOOD** is divided between the pleasant, low-rise neighborhood of **Westwood Village** – crowded with students, shoppers, and theater-goers – and the adjacent traffic corridor loaded with some of LA's tallest buildings. In earlier days, nearly all of Westwood resembled the Village, but during the 1970s and 1980s, the zone around Wilshire exploded with high-rises, where penthouse condos with private heliports sold for upwards of $12 million. Even now, after the boom has faded somewhat, the intersection of Wilshire and Westwood boulevards continues to be choked with overflowing traffic, with some of LA's longest waits for a green light.

At this corner, the **UCLA Hammer Museum**, 10899 Wilshire Blvd (Tues–Sat 11am–7pm, Thurs 11am–9pm, Sun 11am–5pm; $5, kids free, Thurs free to all; ⓦwww.hammer.ucla.edu), comprises a sizable art stash amassed over seven decades by the flamboyant oil-tycoon **Armand Hammer**. Art critic Robert Hughes called the paintings here "a mishmash of second- or third-rate works by famous names," but while the Rembrandts and Rubenses may be less than stunning, the nineteenth-century pieces like Van Gogh's intense and radiant *Hospital at Saint Remy* more than make amends. There are some impressive American works as well, such as a Gilbert Stuart regal portrait of George Washington; Thomas Eakins' painting of *Sebastiano Cardinal Martinelli*, depicted with blunt, penetrating realism; and John Singer Sargent's *Dr Pozzi at Home*, another of the artist's skilled character studies. Just as compelling, some of the museum's exhibitions are drawn from the marvelous **Grunwald Center for the Graphic Arts**, which has some 35,000 drawings, photographs, and prints from the Renaissance on, with some exceptional Expressionist works by Emil Nolde and Käthe Kollwitz, Impressionist etchings from Paul Cezanne, and more current drawings and prints by Jasper Johns. Now under the management of neighboring UCLA, the Hammer has become acclaimed for its insightful, sometimes risk-taking contemporary and avant-garde exhibits – quite a leap from what the conservative Hammer had in mind when he built the art enclave.

Across from the museum, at the end of the driveway behind the Avco cinema, 1218 Glendon Ave, you'll find Armand Hammer's speckled marble tomb, sharing the cemetery of **Westwood Memorial Park** with the likes of movie stars Peter Lorre and Natalie Wood, wildman jazz drummer Buddy Rich, and the alleged (unmarked) graves of Roy Orbison and Frank Zappa. To the left of the entrance in the far northeast corner, a lipstick-covered plaque marks the resting place of **Marilyn Monroe**. You can also spot some of these stars on the radiant mural inside the **Crest Theater**, 1262 Westwood Blvd, also notable for its brash neon marquee.

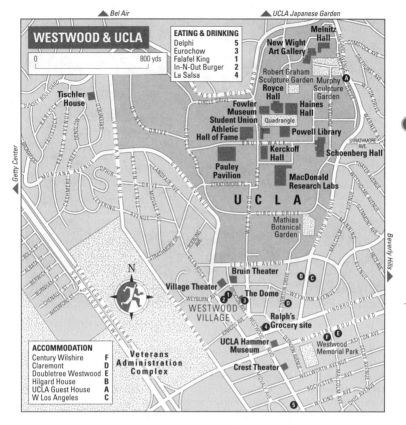

The map contains the following labels:

▲ Bel Air   ▲ UCLA Japanese Garden

WESTWOOD & UCLA

0   800 yds

EATING & DRINKING
Delphi	5
Eurochow	3
Falafel King	1
In-N-Out Burger	2
La Salsa	4

Melnitz Hall
New Wight Art Gallery
Robert Graham Sculpture Garden
Royce Hall
Murphy Sculpture Garden
Tischler House
Fowler Museum
Haines Hall
Student Union
Quadrangle
Athletic Hall of Fame
Powell Library
Kerckoff Hall
Schoenberg Hall
Pauley Pavilion
MacDonald Research Labs
U C L A
Mathias Botanical Garden
Getty Center
Bruin Theater
Village Theater
The Dome
WESTWOOD VILLAGE
Ralph's Grocery site
UCLA Hammer Museum
Westwood-Ashton Memorial Park
Veterans Administration Complex
Crest Theater

ACCOMMODATION
Century Wilshire	F
Claremont	D
Doubletree Westwood	E
Hilgard House	B
UCLA Guest House	A
W Los Angeles	C

Westwood Village

North of Wilshire, **Westwood Village** is one of LA's more walkable neighborhoods, a cluster of low-slung brick buildings that went up in the late 1920s, along with the campus of UCLA, which had just relocated from East Hollywood. Much of the original Spanish Colonial Revival design has survived the years, though most of the neighborhood businesses have been replaced by fancy boutiques and fast-food joints. It's an area that's easily explored on foot – street **parking** is nightmarish, so if you're driving, leave your car at one of the parking lots before beginning your wanderings. Even if you find a spot, keep in mind that the area features some of LA's most zealous parking enforcement, and you'll pay $35 if you're even a minute overtime.

    Broxton Avenue, the Village's main strip, is crowded with record stores, moviehouses, and diners, but its focal point is the great Zigzag spire atop the 1931 **Fox Westwood Village** at 961 Broxton Ave, which, together with the neon-signed **Bruin** across the street, are impressive Moderne designs. Both are used occasionally by movie studios for flashy movie premieres, as well as sneak previews for test audiences; this is a big movie-going district, with thirty or so cinema screens within a quarter-mile radius. Another familiar Westwood image is **The Dome**, 1099 Westwood Blvd, now an upscale pan-Asian

△ The Fox Westwood Village theater

restaurant called *Eurochow* (see p.286), but formerly the offices of the developer who created the surrounding Westwood tract and many other districts. Nowhere is its design signature more evident than at the one-time **Ralph's Grocery Store**, 1150 Westwood Blvd, a Spanish Romanesque design with a red-tile roof and cylindrical corner tower that's now a restaurant. Among several historic structures west of UCLA, the best is R.M. Schindler's private **Tischler House**, 175 Greenfield Ave, which resembles a highly abstract boat: thick white rectangles jut out from the house's base, while the wooden-gabled living space on top recalls a ship's upper deck.

UCLA

The University of California at Los Angeles, or **UCLA**, is one of the country's most prominent academic and athletic institutions, and the dominant feature in Westwood, a group of lovely Romanesque buildings spread generously over well-landscaped grounds. It's worth a wander if you've time to kill, particularly for a couple of good exhibition spaces.

The campus originally occupied the site of the Downtown Library, later moving to Los Feliz, and by the mid-1920s relocated to Westwood, where it became a model of Northern Italian–styled Romanesque design: intended by architect **George Kelham** to resemble the redbrick structures of Milan and Genoa, the buildings around the central quadrangle, such as the library and science halls, seem to be plucked straight from a Lombard blueprint, giving the campus a classic "collegiate" look. This pristine quality was, however, diminished by the concrete and steel of the 1960s and 70s, but recent years have seen creative experimentation by the likes of Frank Gehry and Robert Venturi, with more regard for visual continuity.

The campus and around

A good place to start touring the campus is the **Mathias Botanical Garden**, 405 Hilgard Ave (daily 8am–4pm, summer Mon–Fri closes at 5pm; free; @www .botgard.ucla.edu), a bucolic glade on the east side of the university where you can pick your way along sloping paths through the redwoods and fern groves, past small waterfalls splashing into lily-covered ponds. Just north, **Schoenberg Hall** pays homage to the twelve-tone composer, Arnold Schoenberg, who taught at the campus from 1936 to 1944.

Around the corner is the campus hub of the central **quadrangle**, a greenspace bordered by UCLA's most graceful buildings. The most visually appealing structures here include **Royce Hall**, modeled on Milan's Church of St Ambrosio, with high bell-towers, rib vaulting, and grand archways; and the **Powell Library** (Mon–Thurs 7.30am–11pm, Fri 7.30am–6pm, Sat 9am–5pm, Sun 1–10pm; @www.library.ucla.edu), featuring a spellbinding interior with lovely Romanesque arches, columns, and stairwell. The highlight is the dome above the **reading room**, where Renaissance printers' marks are inscribed, among them icons representing such pioneers as Johann Fust and William Caxton. Further south, one of UCLA's best contemporary structures, Robert Venturi's **MacDonald Research Labs**, is well worth seeking out for its postmodern take on the greatest hits of classical architecture, featuring off-color, brick upper stories with irregular windows, a concrete base, and quasi-Egyptian colonnade.

Further north, the **Fowler Museum of Cultural History**, Bruin Walk at West-wood Plaza (Wed–Sun noon–5pm, Thurs closes 8pm; free; @www.fmch.ucla.edu), exhibits an immense range of multicultural art. The museum's highlights include an extensive collection of African and Polynesian art, and an arresting display of pre-Columbian headdresses. To the northeast, the **Franklin Murphy Sculpture Garden** is LA's best outdoor display of modern sculpture, including pieces by such big names as Jean Arp, Henry Moore, Joan Miró, Henri Matisse, and Isamu Noguchi. Other notable works include Auguste Rodin's *Walking Man*, a stark nude composed of only a torso and legs, and George Tsutakawa's *OBOS-69*, a fountain resembling a stack of TV sets. If you really like the pieces on display here, you can take an informative free **tour** of the garden as well (reserve at ☎310/443-7041).

Just north of the Murphy Garden, the **New Wight Art Gallery**, 11000 Kinross Ave (Mon–Fri 9am–4.30pm; free; @www.art.ucla.edu/gallery.html), has a less intriguing collection of contemporary art on display, and houses the **Center for Digital Arts**, which occasionally shows interesting multimedia works. East of the Wight Gallery, in **Melnitz Hall**, UCLA's **film school** has produced offbeat filmmakers like Francis Ford Coppola, Alison Anders, and Alex Cox, the more independent-oriented rival to USC's studio-dominated media school. Here, you'll also find the massive storehouse of the **UCLA Film and Television Archive**, a treasure-trove holding classic, foreign, and art movies, and a wide range of old TV shows, state journalism footage, and even an assortment of Hearst newsreels from the turn of the twentieth century. The premises are open for research or viewing by making an appointment at 46 Powell Library, or by calling ☎310/206-5388 (Mon–Fri 9am–5pm). Melnitz Hall also presents regular screenings of films, many drawn from the archives, in its **James Bridges Theater** (screenings Wed & Fri–Sun, tickets $8; ☎310/206-FILM, @www .cinema.ucla.edu).

UCLA is also well known for its athletic prowess, winning more NCAA basketball championships – eleven – than any other team. Some of this history is on display at the **Athletic Hall of Fame** (Mon–Fri 8am–5pm; free) near the center of campus, where you can check out the school's awards in basketball, football, and volleyball, among other sports. UCLA's basketball team plays just west of here, at **Pauley Pavilion**, along with its volleyball and gymnastics squads, while the football team's home is the Rose Bowl (see p.202).

For a more contemplative experience, travel just north of campus to UCLA's **Hannah Carter Japanese Garden**, 10619 Bellagio Rd (Tues,Wed & Fri 10am–3pm; free; by appointment only at ☎310/825-4574 or ⍟www.japanesegarden .ucla.edu), an idyllic spot featuring magnolias and Japanese maples, and traditional structures and river rocks brought directly from Japan – though four hundred tons of dark-brown rocks were also hauled in from Ventura County to lend the right aesthetic touch. Adding to the calming Zen feel are a pagoda, teahouse, quaint bridges, and assorted gold and stone Buddhas.

The Sepulveda Pass and around

The gap through the Santa Monica Mountains known as the **Sepulveda Pass** runs alongside some of LA's most exclusive residential neighborhoods, as well as the **Getty Center**, and often gives tourists their first views of central LA as they travel south on the 405 freeway into town. The pass was, like the eponymous boulevard and district, named for Mexican soldier **Francisco Sepúlveda**, whose family controlled over fifty thousand acres of land in the LA region, and who gained ownership in 1839 of the Rancho San Vicente y Santa Monica, which once encompassed the surrounding area. The former rancho contains both the freeway and part of Sepulveda Boulevard – the longest road in LA County, leading from Long Beach into the north San Fernando Valley.

Bel Air and Brentwood

BEL AIR, just northwest of UCLA and east of the 405 freeway, is an elite subdivision – home to just under eight thousand swells – with opulent black gates fronting Sunset Boulevard and security guards driving about to catch interlopers. Despite the area's famous name and reputation, very little goes on here, as the only business is the well-known, luxurious **Bel Air Hotel** (see p.252) and the residential architecture is near impossible to see, typically hidden behind thick foliage.

For a closer look at the well-heeled, **BRENTWOOD** to the west is a much better bet. Known for its most famous former resident, O.J. Simpson (his Tudor mansion has since been razed), Brentwood also has an upscale shopping strip along **San Vicente Boulevard**, with a good range of boutiques and restaurants. The neighborhood also contains several residences of architectural interest, such as Frank Gehry's **Schnabel House**, 526 N Carmelina Ave, a chunky collection of metal cubes connected to an incongruous Moorish dome, partially visible from the sidewalk; Eric Owen Moss's striking **Lawson–Westen House**, with its jagged gray facade, tilted windows, and truly odd sense of proportion; and Frank Lloyd Wright's **Sturges House**, 449 Skyeway Rd, looking like a giant wooden shingle cantilevered off a hillside and hovering over the street below it, one of Wright's few LA experiments in contemporary, rather than pre-Columbian, housing design. Further north at 16221 Mulholland Drive, Charles Moore's enjoyable exercise in ecclesiastical postmodernism, the **Bel Air Presbyterian Church** (⍟www.belairpres.org), contains playful Gothic touches amid its asymmetrical contemporary style, and is one of several of the architect's churches in LA.

Skirball Cultural Center

Back along Sepulveda Boulevard, near the crest of the Santa Monica Mountains, the compelling **Skirball Cultural Center**, 2701 N Sepulveda Blvd (Tues–Sat noon–5pm, Sun 11am–5pm; $8, students $6; ⊛www.skirball.org), is housed in a striking modern complex by architect Moshe Safdie, and has several missions. One, its original purpose, is to focus on the history, beliefs, and rituals of Judaism, concentrating on the more mystical elements of the faith and offering a broad overview of Judaic treasures, from Hanukkah lamps to a Holy Ark from a German synagogue. The second goal of the Skirball is to be a modern center for Jewish expression in science, art, philosophy, and popular culture – including occasional musical and comedy performances. Thus, you may see a wide range of events and exhibits in its galleries, everything from the illustrated theories of Albert Einstein to dramatic photography shot in Israel. Moreover, the center looks at the American diaspora in stark photographs of c.1900 immigrants and written mementos of their arduous travel and assimilation, and among assorted other artifacts are an early copy of the Declaration of Independence and one of Abe Lincoln's stovepipe hats.

The Getty Center

Off Sepulveda and west of the 405 freeway, Getty Center Drive leads up to the monumental **Getty Center** (Sun & Tues–Thurs 10am–6pm, Fri & Sat 10am–9pm; free, parking $7; ⊛www.getty.edu; MTA line #761 from UCLA). The gleaming 110-acre museum and research complex towering over the city was built over fifteen years at a cost of $1 billion to hold the vast art holdings of oil mogul **J. Paul Getty**. The Center's architect, **Richard Meier**, originally planned for the whole complex to be wrapped in white metallic panels – his signature modern style – but protests from the Brentwood neighbors over sun glare forced him to redesign part of the Center in travertine: a good choice, since it combines the ancient roughness of fossil-bearing sandstone with the

△ The Getty Center

Taking a break at the Getty

If you spend a full day here – and many do – you'll want to grab a bite in one of the Getty's two central eateries. The **restaurant** (Tues–Fri 11.30am–2.30pm, Fri & Sat also 5–9pm, Sun 11am–3pm; reservations suggested at ☎310/440-6810) serves California cuisine and attracts locals who don't mind dropping a few extra dollars for an elegant setting and salads, pasta, crab cakes, and the like. Most visitors, however, head to the lower level for the massive **café** (Sun, Tues & Thurs 11.30am–3pm, Fri & Sat 11.30am–8.30pm), which has a broad and adequate sampling of international cuisines laid out in the style of a cafeteria, though a bit pricier. There are also **seasonal cafés** around the terrace and courtyard, though these are oriented more toward providing simple snacks and coffee.

austere geometry of high-modernism, ultimately leading some to dub the site the "American Acropolis."

Getty started building his massive collection in the 1930s, storing much of it in his own house until the first **Getty Museum** opened in 1974 on an ocean bluff near Malibu. That site, which has been closed for years, is reopening as a showcase for the foundation's antiquities by 2006 (see p.220), while the museum itself has moved to the grounds of the Center, which also includes facilities for art research, conservation, and acquisition, though none of these are open to the public. Despite the huge investment, the Getty Foundation still has billions in reserve and must, by law, spend hundreds of millions each year from its endowment. Thus, it plays an elephantine role on the international art scene and can freely outbid its competitors for anything it wants.

A good place to begin exploring the museum is outside in its **Central Garden**, a concentric array of leafy terraces designed by conceptual artist Robert Irwin. Occupying the middle ground of the complex, the garden is a stunning arrangement leading crowds along sloping paths through azaleas, bougainvilleas, and other plants and flowers, while the austere pavilions loom imperiously in the background. Though the garden provides a glorious centerpiece, Meier didn't much care for it and fought a number of public battles with its designer. More in the style of Meier, perhaps, is the topiary formalism of the **Desert Garden**, on the south end of the complex, where a low-scaled set of hardy plants sits in tight, circular confinement above a cliff of the Santa Monica Mountains.

The museum itself consists of five two-story structures that are landscaped around open plazas and shallow fountains, with the collection spread throughout the buildings. No matter where you start, you'll find the artworks still heavily influenced by Getty's tastes, long after the oil baron's death. One of his greatest enthusiasms was his formidable array of ornate **furniture** and **decorative arts**, with clocks, chandeliers, tapestries, and gilt-edged commodes, designed for the French nobility from the reign of Louis XIV, filling several overwhelmingly opulent rooms. The museum even stages an ongoing presentation of video and on-site **reproductions** of such classic items of furniture, showing in full detail the painstaking steps that went into creating cabinets, bureaus, and commodes for the elite. This collection is certainly fascinating, perhaps more so to design historians, but it's the museum's paintings, sculpture, and photographs that will really overwhelm you.

Painting

In **painting**, the European art is principally from the post-Renaissance era, but there are a few notable exceptions, including several from the **early to high**

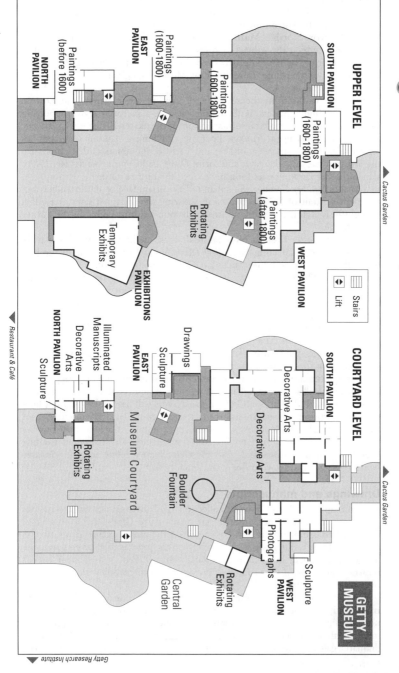

GETTY MUSEUM

UPPER LEVEL

SOUTH PAVILION

EAST PAVILION

NORTH PAVILION

Paintings (before 1600)

Paintings (1600-1800)

Paintings (1600-1800)

Paintings (1600-1800)

Paintings (after 1800)

WEST PAVILION

Rotating Exhibits

Temporary Exhibits

EXHIBITIONS PAVILION

▶ Cactus Garden

Stairs

◀▶ Lift

COURTYARD LEVEL

NORTH PAVILION

Sculpture

Illuminated Manuscripts

Decorative Arts

Rotating Exhibits

EAST PAVILION

Drawings

Sculpture

Museum Courtyard

SOUTH PAVILION

Decorative Arts

Decorative Arts

Boulder Fountain

Photographs

Sculpture

WEST PAVILION

Rotating Exhibits

Central Garden

▶ Cactus Garden

◀ Restaurant & Café

◀ Getty Research Institute

137

Renaissance. Among these are Andrea Mantegna's stoic but affecting *Adoration of the Magi*, Correggio's *Head of Christ*, a rich portrait that rivals Rembrandt's work for emotional expression, and Titian's *Venus and Adonis*, depicting in muted colors the last moments between the lovers before the latter is gored by a wild boar. Notable **Mannerist** works include Pontormo's *Portrait of a Halberdier*, in which the subject's expression has been variously interpreted as arrogant, morose, or contemplative, and Veronese's richly detailed *Portrait of a Man*, perhaps of the painter himself – a sword-bearing nobleman gazing proudly down at the viewer.

The finest works from the seventeenth century are **Flemish** and **Dutch**. Among the highlights are Rubens' *Entombment*, a pictorial essay supporting the Catholic doctrine of transubstantiation; Hendrik ter Brugghen's *Bacchante with an Ape*, showing a drunken libertine clutching a handful of grapes, an action mirrored by his pet monkey; and a trio of Rembrandts that emphasize the artist's interest in character and form: *Daniel and Cyrus before the Idol Bel*, in which the Persian king tries foolishly to feed the bronze statue he worships; *An Old Man in Military Costume*, the exhausted, uncertain face of an old soldier; and the great portrait of *Saint Bartholomew*, showing the martyred saint as a quiet, thoughtful Dutchman – the knife that will soon kill him visible in the corner of the frame.

While some lesser **French Neoclassical** works are included, notably David's overly slick and unaffecting *Farewell of Telemachus and Eucharis*, one of the best works from the period is Gericault's later *Portrait Study*, a sensitive portrait of an African man. The Getty Center is also known for bidding on **Impressionist** works; as such, these acquisitions read like a laundry list of late nineteenth-century French art: a portrait of *Albert Cahen d'Anvers* by Renoir, the inevitable Monet haystacks, and one of Degas' ballet dancers. Van Gogh's *Irises* was the object of a bruising 1980s bidding war, in which an Australian financier beat out other competitors (at a price of more than $50 million), but later defaulted on his payments; the painting languished in legal limbo before the Getty Trust snatched it up for an unknown price.

Other significant works from the **nineteenth century** include *Bullfight* by Goya, in which the bull stares triumphantly at a group of unsuccessful matadors; J.M.W. Turner's frenzied *Ships at Sea, Getting a Good Wetting*, all hazy colors and soft lines that look surprisingly modern and abstract; and Caspar David Friedrich's elegant and understated *A Walk at Dusk*, a Romantic painting of a lone man bowing before a stone cairn during twilight. Not surprisingly, the museum's painting collection continues to expand, with the Getty Trust recently acquiring notable works by such figures as Murillo, Titian, and Courbet.

Drawings and manuscripts

The museum also boasts a wide collection of **drawings**, among the best of which are Albrecht Dürer's meticulous *Study of the Good Thief*, a portrait of the crucified criminal who was converted on the cross; his *Stag Beetle*, precise enough to look as if the bug were crawling on the page itself; Piranesi's dramatic image of a ruined, but still monumental, *Ancient Port*; and William Blake's bizarre watercolor of *Satan Exalting over Eve*, an expressionless devil hovering over his prone captive.

Also fascinating is the museum's excellent collection of medieval **illuminated manuscripts**, depicting Biblical scenes such as the Passion cycle, as well as notable saints. Exquisitely drawn letters introduce chapters from Scripture and maintain their radiance to this day, especially when lit from behind in a dark, dramatic gallery. One of the most interesting volumes is the *Apocalypse with*

Commentary by Berengaudus, an English Gothic tome that shows the Book of Revelation in all its fiery detail, including an image of the Four Horsemen of the Apocalypse looking more like medieval knights.

Sculpture, photography, and other arts

As for **sculpture**, the most memorable are Benvenuto Cellini's *Hercules Pendant*, a small, finely rendered piece of jewelry that shows the ancient hero in shock, mouth agape; Antonio Canova's gracefully Neoclassical rendering of the god *Apollo*; and Gian Lorenzo Bernini's much smaller *Boy with a Dragon* – done when he was only 16 – depicting a plump toddler bending back the jaw of a dragon with surprising ease, either a playful putto or Jesus himself, depending on your view. The work of the great French classical sculptor Jean-Antoine Houdon also makes a few appearances, especially with the recent acquisition of a bust of stately, proud royal bureaucrat *Marie-Sebastien-Charles-Francois Fontaine de Bire*.

Some of the Getty's excellent array of **photographs** includes renowned works by Stieglitz, Strand, Weston, Adams, Arbus, and others, but again, it's the museum's less familiar works that are the most intriguing: an 1849 *Portrait of Edgar Allan Poe*, by an unknown photographer, has the writer staring at the camera with manic intensity; Thomas Eakins' photo study *Students at the Site for "The Swimming Hole"*, which the painter used as a dry run for his famous painting, showing his pupils jumping naked from a flat rock into a muddy pond; Civil War photographer Timothy O'Sullivan's seemingly doomed wagon train grinding on through the *Desert Sand Hills*; and August Sander's feral *Frau Peter Abelen*, an androgynous woman with slicked-back hair, white culottes, business shirt and tie, holding an unlit cigarette between gritted teeth.

Beyond all this, the museum hosts **temporary exhibitions** of classical and modern work (often with accompanying art films on the same themes, in the Williams Auditorium), everything from medieval tapestries and religious icons to old-fashioned lithographs and avant-garde photography. Displays that relate to recently conserved works are also on view in the lobby of the neighboring **Getty Research Institute**, just west of the main museum entrance (also free; same hours), which allows a brief glimpse into the workings of the rest of this sizable organization – though unfortunately, no tours are offered.

Culver City

Several miles south of Beverly Hills and Westwood, triangular **CULVER CITY** is one of the Westside's lesser-known gems, its past rich with movie lore and its current face shaped by groundbreaking architectural experiments. An extensive facelift since the 1990s has resulted in more parks and footpaths, streets lined with historic lampposts and jacaranda trees, and fewer drab streets and buildings. Although wedged between unappealing Venice Boulevard and the 405 freeway, it's one of LA's most ethnically diverse cities, with a harmonious mix of whites, blacks, Hispanics, and Asians.

The most impressive of the classic Culver City buildings is the **Ivy Substation**, at Culver and Venice boulevards, a 1907 power station for the old Red Car public transit line, which ended service in 1953. Located in a palm-tree-filled park, the Mission Revival building has been reborn as a 99-seat performing arts venue, though one that's irregularly open (call for details at ☎310/253-5762).

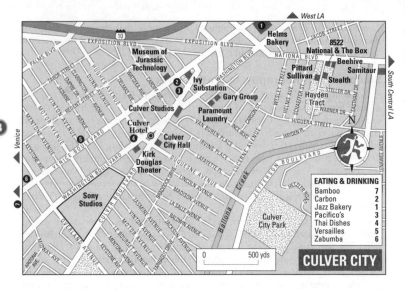

Helms Bakery

8522 National & The Box

Museum of Jurassic Technology

Pittard Sullivan

Beehive

Samitaur

Ivy Substation

Stealth

Gary Group

Hayden Tract

Culver Studios

Paramount Laundry

Culver Hotel

Culver City Hall

Kirk Douglas Theater

Sony Studios

Culver City Park

N

EATING & DRINKING

Bamboo	7
Carbon	2
Jazz Bakery	1
Pacifico's	3
Thai Dishes	4
Versailles	5
Zabumba	6

0   500 yds

CULVER CITY

Other major structures can be found nearby, including the **Helms Bakery**, 8800 Venice Blvd, a WPA landmark with its original iron lamps, grand sign and fixtures, which is now home to local furniture-dealers and craft shops, as well as the *Jazz Bakery* (a music venue reviewed on p.314). To the west, the old Culver Theater, 9820 Washington Blvd at Duquesne Ave, is a striking 1947 moviehouse with a streamlined marquee and sparkling neon pylon that has been newly reborn as the **Kirk Douglas Theater** (☎213/628-2772, ⓦwww.taperahmanson .com), named after the star of *Paths of Glory* and *Spartacus*.

Culver City movie studios

Without a doubt, Culver City's most significant historic structures are its movie studios, many of which still function, though in different guises. The man responsible for creating the two greatest studio complexes was **Thomas Ince**, a film pioneer and producer who was a major film-industry figure until he was mysteriously killed on William Randolph Hearst's yacht. Fans of *Gone With the Wind* may recognize the producer's former Ince Studios at **9336 Washington Blvd**, now Culver Studios – predictably, this Colonial Revival "mansion" is no more than a facade.

Ince's later, bigger creation was **Triangle Pictures**, 10202 Washington Blvd, which he helped build with the financial aid of Harry Culver, a journalist and realtor who founded the city specifically for the movie business. Triangle became **MGM** by the 1920s, helmed by legend Louis B. Mayer, and was the home of some of Hollywood's biggest productions during the Golden Age of Movies. The bloom faded in the 1950s and 60s, though, and sections of the lot were sold off to developers and what was left was swallowed up by **Sony** in the 1980s. You can still stroll past the fine old colonnade, but unfortunately, most of the glorious MGM backlot was torn down, so if you go on a **tour** of the Sony facility (for which call ☎323/520-TOUR; Mon–Fri 9am–3pm; $20), you'll have to be content with sauntering by massive, often empty soundstages and sets for such TV shows as *Jeopardy!*

Culver Hotel and around

A few blocks east, on a triangle of land formed by Duquesne Avenue and Culver and Washington boulevards, the early twentieth-century **Culver Hotel** has been restored to its original splendor, replete with checkered marble flooring, red-and-black interior, and intricate iron railings. Plenty of Hollywood history took place inside the hotel, which started as Harry Culver's office space, was later purchased by John Wayne, and was often a favorite spot to stay for stars like Greta Garbo and Clark Gable. However, stories of drunken debauchery by the midget cast of the *Wizard of Oz* – who apparently stayed here during

Eric Owen Moss and the Hayden Tract

Most small towns, even in LA, are known for their conservatism in design and architecture. Culver City is a major exception. With architect/artist **Eric Owen Moss** (director of Downtown's trailblazing Sci-Arc school; see p.67), this city has not only welcomed some bizarre buildings, it has also helped subsidize the business sites for many of his clients and prominently advertised his groundbreaking work. The **Hayden Tract**, one such city-subsidized business strip, has excellent examples of contemporary architecture ranging from austere modernism to cockeyed deconstructivism – indeed, Moss has tagged the entire area, a former industrial zone, as **The New City**, and the city has charged him with the task of redesigning it over the course of many years.

In the Tract, you can find a whole series of Moss's designs, including the 1997 **Pittard Sullivan** building, 3535 Hayden Ave, a giant gray box with massive wooden ribs poking out of its sides, somewhat like flying buttresses. Thanks to its architect, the company even got around a Culver City building code – that one percent of any structure's budget must be used for public art – when the building itself was declared art. Nearby, **8522 National**, also known as the IRS Building (1990), features a jangled-up facade with a white staircase leading to nowhere. Adjacent to this is **The Box**, with a cubic window riveted to one of its corners, which looks ready to come off its hinges and tumble down onto the street below. One of the best Moss works in the Tract is the 1995 **Samitaur** building, 3457 S La Cienega Ave, massive, gray warehouse-like offices with skewed lines, sharp points, and a freakish sense of proportion. A recent marvel, **The Pterodactyl** (2002), unfortunately lies hidden in a private parking lot, but another, the overwhelming **Stealth** (2001), 3530 Hayden Ave, is fronted by a massive, dark wall of projecting angles that seems more like the setting for a science-fiction film than a business complex, and with its arch geometry even suggests the sleek design of the eponymous bomber. Perhaps strangest of all, the **Beehive** (2001), 8520 National Blvd, is a bulbous take on the concept of the (business) hive, with curving bands and rooftop stairway, and grassy landscaping so undulating it looks ready to twist the knee of the unwary.

A pocket of his earlier works, from 1987 to 1989, sits near Ince Boulevard and Lindblade Street. The **Gary Group** building offers a fragmented white-and-red sign with – again – a ladder leading to nowhere, while the side of the structure is a concrete wall ornamented with jutting brick cubes and an array of metal chains. The adjoining **Paramount Laundry** is no more conventional: a series of fat red columns supports a metal awning, with one column sitting several feet out of place, but leaning desperately to give a hand to the others.

Proof that all this is not merely one town's quirky obsession with an LA iconoclast, Moss was recently tapped to redesign the courtyard of the **Smithsonian**'s National Portrait Gallery/American Art Museum in Washington, DC – which he's doing with a series of hanging glass rods. To learn more about this pioneering modern architect, head to ⓦ www.ericowenmoss.com.

the filming – are more Hollywood myth than reality. Not far away, **City Hall**, 9770 Culver Blvd (Mon–Fri 7.30am–5.30pm), is notable for its huge detached facade – a re-creation of the entryway to the previous City Hall. Between the facade's freestanding archway and the actual building, you'll find a pleasant park with a peek-through movie camera detailing the city's film history. For more eye-catching architecture, head a mile east to the **Hayden Tract**, a stretch of Hayden Avenue that, apart from being a city business district, is also one of LA's most fertile spots for wild modern designs (see box, overleaf).

The Museum of Jurassic Technology

If movie history and weird architecture aren't enough for you, top off your trip with a visit to the bizarre **Museum of Jurassic Technology**, 9341 Venice Blvd (Thurs 2–8pm, Fri–Sun noon–6pm; $6; ⊛www.mjt.org), on the northern edge of Culver City. As much an art museum as a science center, this institution has little to do with distant history or roving dinosaurs. Rather, it features a great range of oddities from the pseudo-scientific to the paranormal to the just plain creepy, including trailer-park artworks, showing junk collections next to tiny model RVs and mobile homes about to be swallowed up by the earth; exhibitions of folk superstitions, most memorably the image of dead mice on toast used as a cure for bedwetting; written and oral narratives of crank scientists and researchers, many of whom have reputedly disappeared under strange circumstances or gone mad; a strange re-creation of a Baroque-era museum run by a Jesuit scholar; and a series of unearthly insects, like an Amazonian bug that kills its prey through the use of a giant head-spike. The ultimate effect is quite unnerving, as these vivid exhibits are shown in dark rooms without windows or sunlight. However, if you assume the museum is merely the work of a local crank, consider that its creator David Wilson was the winner of a MacArthur "Genius" Award in 2001, due largely to his enterprising work for this quirky institution.

5

Santa Monica and Venice

L ocated on the western edge of LA, the contiguous beach districts of **SANTA MONICA** and **VENICE** supposedly represent two different sides of LA: Santa Monica, the trendy, well-heeled liberal enclave with its chic galleries, shops, and coffeehouses; and Venice, the offbeat, anarchic focus of dive bars, junk emporia, and fringe galleries. This is more of a false stereotype than reality, since the beachside blocks of each city are increasingly similar, lined as they are with upscale condos and expensive hotels, and driving north on Main Street, it can be hard to discern exactly where Venice stops and Santa Monica starts. Both places also have in common moderate temperatures – they're colder than the rest of the basin, with average midsummer temperatures sitting comfortably around 66°F. Perhaps for this reason, these areas have become home to at least one-quarter of LA's population of British and Irish expatriates, many of whom can be spotted in the local Euro-friendly pubs, clubs, and diners.

As the epitome of Southern California's sun-and-surf culture, the two cities contain some of the region's most enjoyable spots, with little of the pretension of Beverly Hills and West LA, and much in the way of laid-back attitudes and pleasantly low-scale development. Santa Monica's population is relatively stagnant due to the city's rent-control policies and the steep price of new housing and, like other parts of the Westside, is still fairly WASPy. Multiculturalism, however, has been long established in Venice, which was one of the few coastal cities not to use restrictive covenants to keep blacks from living there. The district continues to be home to a much wider range of classes and races than Santa Monica, and nowhere are these contrasts more apparent than near **Abbot Kinney Boulevard**, where upscale boutiques sit just a few short blocks from one of LA's bleakest ghettos, Oakwood.

Further south, the colorless real-estate tract of **MARINA DEL REY** offers few spots of interest, but the adjacent **Ballona Wetlands** have much natural appeal and **PLAYA DEL REY** maintains a certain faded charm, which takes an eerie turn near the airport, around the site of LA's only urban ghost town.

5

Healing the Bay

Although Los Angeles has a well-deserved reputation for having noxious air, its **water pollution** is less well-known to the nation, though is in many ways worse: while the city's air pollution has actually tailed off considerably in recent decades, the **Santa Monica Bay** continues to suffer from all kinds of problems, only slowly getting better.

Cities and districts from Santa Monica to Palos Verdes have the bad luck of being trapped next to nearly all of LA's outlets for wastewater and sewage, with streetside **storm drains** emptying the runoff of a 5000-mile network of LA urban sprawl and a single treatment center – **Hyperion**, near LAX – handling the task of cleaning up the collective filth. The periodic storms that LA receives, often driven by El Niño currents in the Pacific Ocean, make matters exponentially worse, forcing torrents of raw, untreated sewage directly into the bay and making any bodily contact with the seawater potentially hazardous, leading to anything from conjunctivitis to skin rashes.

You can see the pollution problem in full color just by walking past one of Santa Monica's storm drains, such as the ones near Pico Boulevard or Ashland Avenue, and seeing the rainbow slick of detritus floating along with the flecks of garbage. Just one look, or a sniff of the air, should be more than enough to keep you from bathing in Santa Monica Bay or from eating anything you might catch while fishing off the pier.

Still, there have been improvements to the bay in the last fifteen years since **Heal the Bay** and other such environmental groups were formed: Hyperion no longer freely dumps sewage as it once did, and chemical companies have stopped flushing DDT offshore. If you really feel the need to catch the California waves, make sure to do so well away from city piers – often the most polluted zones – and don't wade within one hundred yards of a beachside drain or venture into the water within three days after a storm, when runoff, sewage, bacteria, and algae combine to form a repellent aquatic poison.

To check out the sands beforehand, visit the Heal the Bay website at ⓦwww .healthebay.org and click on the color-coded beach map detailing which areas are fine for swimming or fishing.

Santa Monica

As a low-slung, oceanside burg with rent-controlled apartments and a relaxed air, and easy access to the rest of the city, **SANTA MONICA**'s attributes tend to keep it exclusive – a mix of expensive historic-revival bungalows and out-of-reach "apartments-for-life," coveted zealously by their lucky tenants. However frustrating the place is to move into, Santa Monica is a great spot to visit, a compact, accessible, and friendly bastion of breezy charm.

As little as a century ago, most of the land between Santa Monica and what was then Los Angeles was covered by ranch lands and citrus groves, interrupted by the outposts of Hollywood and Beverly Hills. Like so much of the state, the land was owned by the **Southern Pacific Railroad**, whose chief Collis Huntington tried to make Santa Monica into the port of Los Angeles, losing out to Phineas Banning and other interests in San Pedro and Wilmington – a blessing in disguise for Santa Monica. The linking of the beachfront with the rest of Los Angeles by the suburban streetcar system, known as the **Red Cars**, meant the town instead grew into one of LA's premier getaways – a giant funfair city that was the inspiration for Raymond Chandler's anything-goes "Bay City," memorably described in *Farewell My Lovely*. While working- and middle-class residents flocked to the Santa Monica Pier for its thrillrides and freewheeling

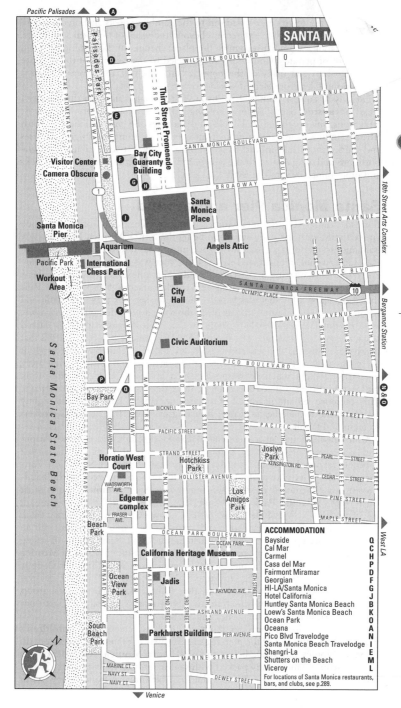

Pacific Palisades ▲ ▲ Ⓐ

SANTA M...

WILSHIRE BOULEVARD

0

ARIZONA AVENUE

SANTA MONICA BOULEVARD

Third Street Promenade

Ⓑ Ⓒ

Ⓓ

Ⓔ

Bay City
Guaranty
Building

Visitor Center
Camera Obscura

Ⓕ

Ⓖ Ⓗ

BROADWAY

Santa
Monica
Place

Ⓘ

COLORADO AVENUE

Santa Monica
Pier

Aquarium

Angels Attic

Pacific Park

International
Chess Park

Workout
Area

OLYMPIC BLVD

SANTA MONICA FREEWAY
OLYMPIC PLACE

10

MICHIGAN AVENUE

Ⓙ

Ⓚ

City
Hall

Civic Auditorium

Ⓜ

Ⓛ

PICO BOULEVARD

Ⓟ

Ⓠ

Bay Park

BAY STREET

BAY STREET

GRANT STREET

BICKNELL ST.

PACIFIC STREET

PACIFIC STREET

STRAND STREET

Joslyn
Park
KENSINGTON RD.

Horatio West
Court

Hotchkiss
Park

HOLLISTER AVENUE

WADSWORTH
AVE.

Edgemar
complex

FRASER
AVE.

Los
Amigos
Park

PEARL STREET

CEDAR STREET

PINE STREET

MAPLE STREET

Beach
Park

OCEAN PARK BOULEVARD

OCEAN PARK

California Heritage Museum

HILL STREET

Ocean
View
Park

Jadis

RAYMOND AVE.

South
Beach
Park

Parkhurst Building

PIER AVENUE

ASHLAND AVENUE

MARINE STREET

MARINE CT.
NAVY ST.
NAVY CT.

DEWEY STREET

▼ Venice

Santa Monica State Beach

THE PROMENADE

N

18th Street Arts Complex ►

Bergamot Station ►

Ⓝ & Ⓞ ►

West LA ►

145

...nosphere, the town's elite sailed out to the gambling boats anchored offshore to indulge in a bit of illicit excitement beyond the reach of the local authorities. Today Chandler wouldn't recognize the place: changes in the gaming laws and the advent of private swimming pools have led to the removal of the offshore gambling ships and many of the popular bathing clubs, and Santa Monica is now among LA's more elegant seaside towns.

The city lies across Bundy Drive from West LA, and splits into three general areas: **oceanside** Santa Monica, holding a fair bit of its history and tourist attractions, sits on the coastal bluffs and includes the pier and beach; **Main Street**, running south from the pier into Venice, is home to designer eateries and quirky shops; and **inland** Santa Monica is split between exclusive neighborhoods and art galleries, to the north, and acres of grungy apartment blocks and quiet bungalows, to the south.

Santa Monica Pier and around

For most casual visitors Santa Monica is worthwhile mainly for its oceanside amusements, with the main attraction being the **Santa Monica Pier** (ⓦwww .santamonicapier.org), a busy tourist zone jutting out into the bay at the foot of Colorado Avenue. Constructed in 1874, the pier was once one of LA's prime entertainments, offering nerve-jangling rides and a heady carnival atmosphere, while remaining fairly tame compared to the raucous Pacific Ocean Park that took shape a few decades later to the south (see box p.148). Rebuilt and reconstructed several times, it was often threatened with demolition, narrowly averting this fate on several occasions in the 1970s (thanks largely to citizen advocacy groups). The pier was also pounded by merciless storms in 1982 that nearly drove it into the sea, and it later developed a reputation as a hangout for gangs and petty thugs from outside the area. Many visitors stayed away, especially at night when skirmishes between hoodlums and cops often took place, and business suffered accordingly. Since then, the local police have made their presence felt and nearly all of the violent crime is long gone, and nightly tourist traffic is once again visible, attracting everyone from business workers to teens and families.

Although featuring an assortment of fast-food stands, video-game parlors, and watering holes, the pier's most obvious appeal is its restored 1922 wooden **carousel** (March–Sept Mon–Thurs 11am–5pm, Fri–Sun 11am–7pm; Oct–March Thurs–Mon only; 50¢ a ride), with more than forty colorful hand-carved horses, featured in the 1973 movie *The Sting*. Although the familiar thrill rides of **Pacific Park** (June–Aug daily 11am–11pm, Sat & Sun closes at 12.30am; $20–22, kids $11; ☎310/260-8744, ⓦwww.pacpark.com) may catch your eye, featuring a rollercoaster and various other amusements, it's still an overpriced attempt to lure back suburban families, and you're better off saving your money for a real theme park. Instead, consider visiting the **Santa Monica Pier Aquarium**, below the pier at 1600 Ocean Front Walk (Tues–Fri 2–5pm, Sat & Sun 12.30–5pm; $5, kids under 12 free; ☎310/393-6149, ⓦwww .healthebay.org/smpa), which is run by the Heal the Bay environmental group, offering a spot where you can find out about marine biology and get your fingers wet touching sea anemones and starfish.

To the south, kids can clamber about on the stone sculptures of a **children's park**, and near the end of the pier, anglers cast their lines into the murky depths of Santa Monica Bay, while below the pier, **Santa Monica State Beach** is a popular strip of sand, tightly packed with visitors on summer weekends. Swimming (or fishing) here is a gamble due to contaminants from nearby storm

△ The Santa Monica Pier

drains, but the threat of water-borne infections doesn't keep some locals from venturing out into the waters.

Just south of the pier, Santa Monica features LA's original "Muscle Beach" that predates Venice's own, more famous version, though it's a bit on the small side. Still, there are enough rings, bars, and other athletic equipment here to make it suitable for would-be bodybuilders and fitness fans. If you'd rather match wits than compare biceps, visit the adjacent **International Chess Park**, a fancy

147

Swept away by the tide

As with so much of LA, the **early days** of Santa Monica are visible here and there in pieces, but have in large measure been razed to make way for new development. The strip of sand around the Santa Monica Pier was once the site of some of LA's swankiest hotels, none more impressive than the Queen Anne colossus of the **Arcadia**, named after the wife of sheep-rancher and real-estate bigwig Robert S. Baker. He purchased much of the land that would become Santa Monica from the Sepulveda family, one of LA's old Spanish landowners (who also had dealings in West LA; see p.134), and the huge hotel, finished in 1887, became an icon of the Southern California coast.

Pumped up by the burgeoning development symbolized by the *Arcadia*, realtors of the era tried to call the town the "**Zenith City by the Sunset Sea**," which predictably didn't catch on – though the 1890s brought more people as Santa Monica continued to grow as a resort town. In later decades the boom continued, as the great beach houses just north of the pier were known as the "**Gold Coast**," because of the Hollywood personalities who lived there. The largest still standing, the **North Guest House**, 415 Palisades Beach Rd, was built as the servants' quarters of a massive 120-room house, now demolished, which William Randolph Hearst built for his mistress, actress Marion Davies. MGM boss Louis B. Mayer owned the adjacent Mediterranean-style villa, which was later rumored to be the place where the Kennedy brothers had their secret liaisons with Marilyn Monroe. Later rechristened as the **Sand and Sea** beach club, the old Hearst complex was closed after the 1994 Northridge earthquake, but in late 2004 the state announced plans to spend $21 million to redevelop the five-acre site for public use.

Further south, **Ocean Park Boulevard** was one of the main routes to the coast via the old streetcars of the **Pacific Electric**, and the entire beachfront between here and the Venice border, now overshadowed by massive gray condominiums, used to be the site of a resort community developed by Abbot Kinney, the man behind the design of Venice itself. Along with vacation bungalows, a wharf, and a colorful boardwalk, the neighborhood also featured the largest and wildest of the old amusement piers: the fantastic **Pacific Ocean Park**, or "P-O-P" as it was known, which had a huge rollercoaster, a giant funhouse, and a boisterous midway arcade, which architectural historian Reyner Banham once described as a "fantasy in stucco and every known style of architecture and human ecology." Against the sanitized fun zones like Disneyland, though, the old piers began to look faded and depressing, and despite a late-1950s refurbishment, P-O-P went steadily downhill, languishing for a time as a makeshift obstacle course for daredevil surfers before being demolished in the mid-1970s.

name for a serviceable collection of chessboards that attracts a range of players from rank amateurs to slumming pros. An odd sidelight is the park's human-sized chessboard, more of a novelty item than a place to spend your afternoon, unless you can find 32 "living pieces" to stand at rigid attention for a few hours. Finally, a **bike path** begins at the pier and heads twenty miles south to Palos Verdes, a stretch that ranks as one of the area's top choices for cycling. You can rent bicycles, surfboards, or rollerblades at equipment-rental shacks by the pier, or just stroll along taking in the local color.

Palisades Park

North of the pier across Ocean Avenue, **Palisades Park** is a palm- and cypress-tree-lined strip that affords stunning views stretching from Malibu to Palos Verdes – all the while sitting precariously atop high bluffs that are constantly being eroded. At least half of the **cliffside sidewalk** around the edge is usually fenced off, as it has a tendency to tumble down the bluffs, especially after heavy rains. Inside the park, you may want to stop by the **visitors information office** (daily 10am–4pm; ☎310/393-7593, ⊛www.santamonica.com), in a kiosk just south of Santa Monica Boulevard at 1400 Ocean Ave. The center's handy map shows the layout of the town and the routes of the Santa Monica Big Blue Bus transit system, a useful Westside complement to the MTA network (☎310/451-5444, ⊛www.bigbluebus.com).

Nearby, the **Camera Obscura**, 1450 Ocean Ave (Mon–Fri 9am–4pm, Sat & Sun 11am–4pm; free), provides unique entertainment by way of an old-fashioned device that prefigures modern photography. Inside a darkened room, you can view images of the outside world projected onto a circular screen by a rotating mirror on the roof – the sort of tool artists like Jan Vermeer once used as a visual aid for painting. On clear days, the clarity of the images can be startling. The camera is located within a social center for the elderly (with "Camera Obscura" clearly written on the facade), so make sure to ask one of the seniors inside for a key to this upstairs room.

The Third Street Promenade

Two blocks east of Ocean Boulevard, between Wilshire and Broadway, the **Third Street Promenade** is a pedestrian stretch attracting a lively crowd of characters. It's fun simply to hang out in the cafés, bars, and nightclubs, or play a game of pool, though chain retailers have virtually conquered the strip. It's especially busy on weekends, when huge numbers of tourists and locals jostle for space with sidewalk poets, swinging jazz bands, and street lunatics, under the watchful eyes of water-spewing **dinosaur sculptures** draped in ivy. The mall is anchored at its southern end by the expensive **Santa Monica Place**, a white stucco pile that's among architect Frank Gehry's less inspired work. It has the usual assortment of chain stores and a mandatory food court. Just to the north, towering over the shopping strip, is the **Bay City Guaranty Building**, Third Street at Santa Monica Boulevard, a Zigzag Moderne marvel topped by a colorful clock that was for years Santa Monica's tallest building. Recently designated a historic landmark, restoration plans for this mostly empty 1929 landmark are in the works.

A little further north, the 1939 **Shangri-La apartments**, now a hotel at Ocean and Arizona avenues (see "Accommodation," p.255), is perhaps the city's finest example of the 1930s Streamline Moderne style, which used nautical motifs to great effect, making this structure look like a giant, landlocked ocean liner. Finally, just one block away on Ocean Avenue in Palisades Park, stands the austere statue of the city's namesake, **Santa Monica**, the mother of St Augustine, a serene white pillar at the edge of the Pacific Ocean.

Main Street

The completion of the Santa Monica Freeway in 1965 bridged a deep arroyo and brought the city's beachfront homes within a fifteen-minute drive of Downtown (barring traffic gridlock), while isolating the north side of town from **Main Street**, five minutes' walk from the pier. Here, the collection of novelty shops, kite stores, and classy restaurants makes it one of the most popular shopping districts on the Westside. Beyond shopping, eating, and drinking, though, there's not much to do.

The big chain stores have arrived on the street, but there are still enough quirky local operations to make a visit here worthwhile, notably **Jadis**, 2701 Main St (☎310/396-3477), a prop-rental operation that, while not open to the general public, does offer LA's best display window: a collection of mannequins posed in various demented dioramas from 1930s horror films, such as a mad scientist's lab, and surrounded by all sorts of antiquated technical junk and contraptions. To make for a more comprehensive day of consumerism, you can travel between Main Street and the Santa Monica Promenade on the **Tide Shuttle** (every 15min; Sun–Thurs noon–8pm, Fri & Sat noon–10pm; ☎310/451-5444), ponying up a mere quarter to hit all the shopping highlights, as well as travel along the sands south of the pier.

One of the few actual sights, the **California Heritage Museum**, no. 2612 (Wed–Sun 11am–4pm; $5; ⊛www.californiaheritagemuseum.org), is the city's effort to preserve some of its architectural past. Two houses were moved here to escape demolition: one house – the museum itself – hosts temporary displays on California cultural topics like old-time amusement parks, and has permanent exhibits on regional pottery, furniture, and decorative arts, while the other house is known as the *Victorian Restaurant* (☎310/392-4956, ⊛www.thevictorian .com) and serves tea on its patio at weekends. There are also several noteworthy buildings on and around Main Street, including the angular gray volumes and strange geometry of Frank Gehry's **Edgemar** shopping development, no. 2415, a deliberately awkward construction that rewards closer inspection, especially on its second floor, where Gehry's chain-link fencing and sheet-metal design bring to mind an abstract sculpture. The more traditional **Parkhurst Building**, south on Main Street at Pier Avenue, is a 1927 Spanish Colonial Revival gem; while the cool white arches and simple boxlike shapes of Irving Gill's **Horatio West Court** (1919), north of Edgemar at 140 Hollister Ave, prefigured the rise of local modernism by about twenty years – it's also one of the few surviving works by the under-appreciated architectural pioneer.

Inland Santa Monica

Although **inland Santa Monica** is generally marked by quiet, well-off neighborhoods, fast-food diners, and entertainment-industry office parks, there are a handful of interesting attractions that make a visit here worthwhile.

Wilshire Boulevard is the main commercial axis of this area – less engaging than elsewhere in town – but further north, near the city border, **San Vicente Boulevard** is a more appealing diversion, a grassy tree-lined strip and a joggers' freeway that leads east to the wealthier confines of Brentwood. LA's true health-mania is visible just two blocks north of San Vicente, along Adelaide Drive between First and Seventh streets. Here an entire stair-climbing culture has evolved along the giant **stairways** that connect Santa Monica with Pacific Palisades. On any given morning, crowds of locals trot up and down the street, just waiting for a chance to descend down the bluffs and charge back up again, red-faced and gasping for air. You, too, may wish to descend the steps, to get a glimpse of the tonier confines of Pacific Palisades, Santa Monica's even more well-heeled neighbor to the north (see p.217).

Two blocks south of San Vicente, the pricey restaurants and boutiques of **Montana Avenue** mark the upward mobility of the area, but offer little you haven't seen elsewhere in West LA. The area does have one piece of world-class architecture in the wild **Gehry House**, 22nd St at Washington Ave, a fitting reflection of architect Frank Gehry's early taste for the perverse and unusual. Now partially hidden by foliage and remodeled for the worse, the house shattered conventional notions of architecture upon its completion in 1978: not a unified design at all, but what appears to be random ideas thrown together helter-skelter and bundled up with concrete walls and metal fencing.

Back toward the 10 freeway is **Angels Attic**, 516 Colorado Ave (Thurs–Sun 12.30–4.30pm; $6.50, kids $3.50; ☎310/394-8331, ⊛www.internetimpact .com/angelsattic), a slice of Victoriana in an elegant 1895 Queen Anne that serves as a museum. Apart from the large collection of oversized dolls, c.1900 arts and crafts, and assorted wooden and tin toys, you'll find a number of finely detailed miniatures, all exquisitely rendered, particularly the dwarf palace of Versailles, though it's actually a more contemporary work. After peering inside the junior palaces and mini-houses, take a seat on the veranda for the museum's afternoon tea service.

Bergamot Station and around

Inland Santa Monica has many fine **galleries** with works by emerging local and international artists. **Bergamot Station**, the city's aesthetic hub, is a collection of former tramcar sheds at 2525 Michigan Ave, near the intersection of 26th and Cloverfield, which houses a multitude of small art galleries (most open Tues–Fri 10am–6pm; free). Many of LA's latest generation of artists have shown here, and the highlight is the **Santa Monica Museum of Art**, in Building G-1 (Tues–Sat 11am–6pm; $3; ⊛www.smmoa.org). This is a good space to see some of the most engaging and curious work on the local scene. Among the regular displays, don't miss the **Gallery of Functional Art**, Building E-3 (free; ⊛www.galleryoffunctionalart.com), offering an array of mechanical gizmos and eccentric furniture like cubist lamps and neon-lit chairs. If you want to check out more adventurous art, the **Side Street Projects**, further inland at 1629 18th St (Wed–Sat noon–6pm; free; information at ☎310/829-0779), is another of the town's ambitious young art spaces and a part of the **18th Street Arts Complex** (⊛www.18thstreet.org), a hip and modern center for various types of art, much of it experimental. The performance space **Highways**, 1651 18th St (☎310/315-1459, ⊛www.highwaysperformance.org), is one such example in the complex (see p.320), showcasing edgy political and gender-based work.

Venice

South of Santa Monica, **Venice** was laid out in the marshes of Ballona Creek in 1905 by developer Abbot Kinney as a fantasy replica of the north Italian city (see box, p.154). While most of the architecture and canals have long since disappeared, the lingering pseudo-European atmosphere has since proved just right for pulling in the artsy crowd he was aiming at, making Venice one of the coast's better spots to check out the underground arts scene and its grubby bohemian charm. Not only are artists' studios and galleries vital to the town, even the mainstream commercial enterprises get into the spirit. Main Street, for instance, is home to the offices of advertising firm **Chiat/Day/Mojo**, just south of Rose Street. Marked by Claes Oldenburg's huge pair of binoculars that overshadow the entrance, the Frank Gehry–designed offices are one of LA's visual icons. A block north is the grotesque **Ballerina Clown**, an enormous sculpture by Jonathan Borofsky perched above the intersection of Rose Avenue and Main Street, its lithe body and stubbly clown head making for a disturbing combination. Elsewhere, a strong alternative arts scene centers around the **Beyond Baroque** literary center and bookshop in the old City Hall, 681 Venice Blvd (Feb–July & Oct–Dec Mon–Fri 11am–6pm; ☎310/822-3006, ⊛www.beyondbaroque.org), a good place to get a flavor of the work of local

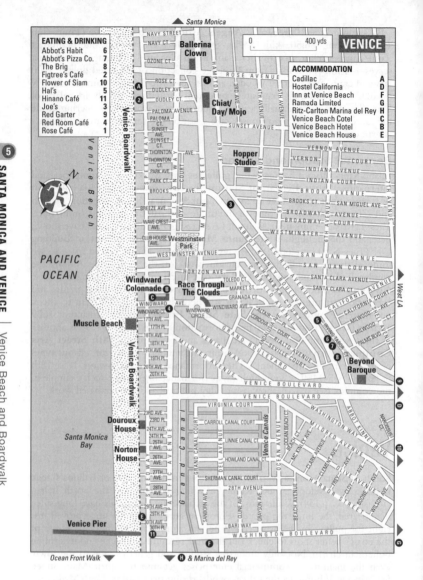

▲ Santa Monica

EATING & DRINKING

Abbot's Habit	6
Abbot's Pizza Co.	7
The Brig	8
Figtree's Café	2
Flower of Siam	10
Hal's	5
Hinano Café	11
Joe's	3
Red Garter	9
Red Room Café	4
Rose Café	1

VENICE

0 .... 400 yds

ACCOMMODATION

Cadillac	A
Hostel California	D
Inn at Venice Beach	F
Ramada Limited	G
Ritz-Carlton Marina del Rey	H
Venice Beach Cotel	C
Venice Beach Hotel	B
Venice Beach House	E

PACIFIC OCEAN

Santa Monica Bay

Ballerina Clown

Chiat/ Day/ Mojo

Hopper Studio

Westminster Park

Windward Colonnade

Race Through The Clouds

Muscle Beach

Douroux House

Norton House

Venice Pier

Beyond Baroque

Ocean Front Walk ▼   ▼ & Marina del Rey

artists and the city's latest cultural trends, catch one of the regular book readings, or sign up for a workshop in poetry, prose, or drama. Next door, SPARC offers tours of some of the more remarkable murals around town (see p.40).

Venice Beach and Boardwalk

Venice Beach draws most visitors to the district, and nowhere else does LA parade itself quite so conspicuously as it does along the **Venice Boardwalk**, a wide pathway tracking alongside the sands that's packed on weekends and all

SANTA MONICA AND VENICE | Venice Beach and Boardwalk

152

summer long with jugglers, fire-eaters, Hare Krishnas, and roller-skating guitar players. You'll have no difficulty picking up your choice of cheap sunglasses, T-shirts, personal stereos, sandals, and whatever else you need for a day at the beach. South of Windward Avenue along the Boardwalk is **Muscle Beach**, a legendary outdoor weightlifting center where stern-looking, would-be Schwarzeneggers

△ Jonathan Borofsky's Ballerina Clown

American Venice

As with various other parts of LA, such as Beverly Hills and San Marino, the development of **Venice** owed much to the desire to copy European models; however, if it weren't for a lucky coin flip, this Old World simulation would never have existed. When **Abbot Kinney**, winner of the fabled toss with his former real-estate partners, gained control of the area in 1904, he set about on a quixotic quest to build a paragon of learning, art, and culture from scratch. After deciding to base his ideal burg on the great Renaissance city-state, and once this area was linked up to the rest of LA by the Red Car mass transit line, Kinney began construction of the town – then labeled "**Venice-by-the-Sea**" – by first draining the land's marshes and developing an extensive network of canals and roads, then creating theaters, performance venues, and sites for restaurants and cafés, and even a think-tank for the liberal arts. He put much of his own money into the effort, investing about $1.5 million, and the initial payoff seemed great. Visitors were smitten by the new arts center's bungalows and hotel rooms, its gondoliers (some from Italy) to navigate the waterways, and its pleasant pier for seaside relaxation.

Culture alone, however, did not pay the bills, and soon the crowds were demanding more thrills and less thinking. In response, Venice shifted its focus to providing amusement for its seasonal vacationers and daily visitors, and Kinney oversaw the formation of what would become LA's greatest **boardwalk**. Minaret-topped palaces, rollercoasters, a Ferris wheel, giant balloons, freak shows, and all manner of carnival attractions were soon found along Venice's once-austere oceanfront, and by 1911, against competition from his Ocean Park neighbors to the north, Kinney engineered the town's incorporation, even though it scarcely resembled his original notion for the community (aside from certain visual motifs like the canals). The city thrived for about a decade, until the **oil industry** moved in next door: when the derricks started their crude production, water pollution became a major threat to the beloved canals, and before long the central lagoon and outlying channels became fetid sites for waste disposal and seeping filth. Although the boardwalk was still attracting tourists, the decaying canals sullied the town's image, leading to a significant fall-off in visitors. Without any solution in sight, Venice's city leaders (which at that point did not include Kinney, who died in 1920) allowed the growing metropolis of LA to take over. Before long, the larger city paved over most of the canals and the main lagoon around Windward Circle. Later decades would bring Depression-era economic convulsions, the demise of the boardwalk, and the severing of the Red Car line, all of which turned Venice into a shadow of its former self. The town's nadir may have come in 1958, when Orson Welles used it as a location in his film *Touch of Evil*, remaking it into a shabby Mexican border town rife with corruption and murder.

In the 1960s and 70s, Venice witnessed a renewed **arts scene** (with painters and poets moving into the cheaper apartments on Venice's oceanside blocks) and a redesigned boardwalk offering a hint of the old carnival atmosphere. But as soon as Venice re-established its bohemian bona fides once more, the rest of the city and the property developers began paying attention. By the 1980s many of the old residents of the quaint seaside buildings were driven out by gentrification, rents went up accordingly, and the place began to resemble just another funky but pricey LA arts zone. These days, little remains of Kinney's original plan, although vestiges, such as the fading colonnade and five renovated canals, are still visible here and there.

pump serious iron, high-flying gymnasts swing on the adjacent rings and bars, and intense games of basketball take place on the concrete courts. Contact the Venice Beach Recreation Center, 1800 Ocean Front Walk (☏310/399-2775), for information on the various activities and contests that occur here, including the Bench Press Championships held in July. Rollerbladers, skateboarders, volleyball players and bicyclists are ubiquitous throughout the year, and there are **rental shacks** along the beach for picking up skates, surfboards, or bikes.

Beyond the beach, the rather basic **Venice Pier** stretches into the ocean off of Washington Street, but don't expect much in the way of carnival fun or thrill rides – the pier doesn't offer a great deal of entertainment value these days, since it's used mostly for fishing in the often-polluted bay, and is a far cry from the wild amusement of old. Incidentally, be warned that Venice Beach at night can be a **dangerous** place. Walking on the beach after dark is illegal, but you should have no problem supping at a beachside café or browsing at a record store.

Windward Avenue and around

Windward Avenue is Venice's main artery, running from the beach into what was the Grand Circle of the canal system, now paved over and ringed by a number of galleries and the Venice **post office**, where you can peek at a mural of the early city layout. On the west side of the circle, the curvaceous roller-coaster facade of the postmodern 1987 **Race Through the Clouds** building pays tribute to the old theme park with a sweeping neon track and metal grid-work. Closer to the beach, colorful giant **murals** – depicting everything from a ruined freeway overpass cut short in midair to Botticelli's Venus in rollerskates – cover the walls of the original structures; while a Renaissance-style **arcade**, around Windward's intersection with Pacific Avenue, is alive with health-food shops, used-record stores, and rollerblade-rental stands. Of the remaining classical columns, several are painted in Day-Glo colors that Kinney would no doubt have gasped at, while others retain their original black-and-white coloring. Look closely at some of the columns and you'll see an odd touch: on their Ionic capitals are engraved the faces of local businessmen – a pointed reminder of Venice's entrepreneurial roots, and its early hubris.

This area has also become home to some of LA's most inventive artists and designers, whose offices are scattered around Windward Avenue and the traffic circle. You'll see the fruits of their labors in the small boutiques and far-out houses throughout the district, but especially to the south, along Ocean Front Walk (see overleaf). Lovers of **experimental architecture** may also want to visit the section of town between California Avenue and Venice Boulevard, around Superba and Amorosa courts, where the **Morphosis** architecture firm has created numerous colorful, bizarre structures around several notoriously narrow and hard-to-navigate streets.

Just a few blocks south from Windward, the five remaining **canals** are still crossed by their original 1904 bridges – quaint wooden structures that are among LA's few touches of Americana – and you can also sit and watch ducks paddle around in the still waters. It's a great place to walk around, though if you're in a car and wish to avoid the tiny, mazelike streets between the canals, there's only one way to see the area. Head north on Dell Avenue between Washington and Venice boulevards – a route that often draws a procession of slow-moving motorized gawkers. Whether you walk or drive, you'll get an eyeful of eclectic residential styles, modernist cubes and Tudor piles mixed in with Colonial bungalows and postmodern sheds. Keep in mind there's no organized way to take a boat trip through the canals; if you happen to get friendly with a resident, you may be able to talk him or her into giving you a **rowboat ride** around the canals – many homes have the skiffs docked right next to their back yards.

To the north, running diagonally between Venice Boulevard and Main Street, the shopping strip of **Abbot Kinney Boulevard** features a range of fine restaurants, funky clothing stores, and arty boutiques. However, wandering away from the strip at night is strongly discouraged, as this street is the southern border of Venice's notorious Oakwood ghetto. Even here, however, you can find the home of the odd celebrity – Dennis Hopper's **Hopper Studio**, 326 Indiana Ave, the ultimate in maximum-security architecture: a slanted, corrugated-steel box with no windows, incongruously surrounded by a quaint, white picket fence.

Ocean Front Walk

Between Marina del Rey and the ocean lies narrow Pacific Avenue, home to some of LA's finest contemporary architecture. Park either at the channel-side lot on the south side, near Via Marina street, or curbside on the north side, and follow **Ocean Front Walk** (actually the same route as the Venice Boardwalk further north) for a pleasant stroll by the sands and the colorful modern houses. From Venice Pier, the intersecting streets are named alphabetically – from Anchorage Street to Yawl Court – in keeping with the nautical theme.

From the north, you'll first hit Antoine Predock's groundbreaking **Douroux House**, 2315 Ocean Front Walk, frequently captured in TV commercials. Atop the heavy concrete frame are rooftop bleachers and a big red window that pivots toward the sea, allowing the ocean breezes to easily sweep through the cubic structure. Not far away is Frank Gehry's **Norton House**, 2509 Ocean Front Walk, a big yellow box with jagged wooden window-frames and a tiny metal staircase on the facade. Further south is the blue-and-white **Yacht House**, 3900 Pacific Ave, just a block east of Ocean Front Walk, an Art Deco–inspired "boat" whose bow is firmly stuck in the concrete sidewalk. Finally, the **Doumani House**, Ocean Front Walk at Yawl Court, is an angular white cube with stepped windows, metallic tracery, and a vaguely exotic character. Since new and off-kilter houses are being built here all the time (often by movie-industry owners), bring a copy of the latest LA architecture guide to find out which big name designed which eye-opening curiosity.

South of Venice

At its nadir in the 1950s and 1960s, Venice was confronted with a new and unwelcome neighbor to the south: **Marina del Rey**, a massive real-estate tract that blotted out the old city's coastal views with high-rises. As with the colossal towers plunked down along Wilshire Boulevard in Westwood, investment capital proved irresistible to the indifferent county commissioners who controlled the unincorporated land, and Marina del Rey has since grown in big, ugly spasms without any restraint whatsoever. Unless you own a yacht and are free to tool around the area's upscale marina (or stay in one of its handful of fancy hotels), you're unlikely to get too close to the water; the whole area is ringed by dreary chain restaurants, giant office complexes, and ugly apartment superstructures – closer in look with the tenements of the East Coast than any notion of luxury living.

Still, despite its utter lack of charm, many visitors often find themselves in Marina del Rey for one reason or another: the nearness of LAX, an attempted short-cut past the congestion of Lincoln Boulevard, or just plain bad luck. Along the south end of the area, at the end of Fiji Way, **Fisherman's Village** is Marina del Rey's top visitor attraction, though it's hard to see why, consisting as it does of low-end seafood joints and endless trinket and T-shirt shops. More appealing is the channel-side walking and biking **path** that stretches from the end of Fiji Way out to the end of the spit. Not only is this the place where the Christmas **regatta** takes place, but it's also a good spot to watch everyday yachts and speedboats make a leisurely sail into the marina. The end of the spit is a short distance from the channel **bridge** over Ballona Creek, which allows you to leave Marina del Rey and cross the "creek," really a storm drain, into the marginally more interesting district of **Playa del Rey**.

Ballona Wetlands

Further south down Lincoln Boulevard, Marina del Rey gives way to the wide expanse of the three-hundred-acre **Ballona** (pronounced *by-OH-na*) **Wetlands**, encompassing bodies of fresh and salt water that are home to two hundred major bird species and a host of other creatures, though their ecosystem has been disrupted in recent years by a rising number of foxes, which roam freely. Although off limits to humans, this natural preserve can be toured at a distance, starting by heading west on Jefferson Boulevard (off Lincoln) and taking a left onto Culver Boulevard. While you might not see conspicuous wildlife, you will get a sense of the uniqueness of this terrain in the heavily urbanized LA basin.

Before Abbot Kinney created what is now Venice, the wetlands of this mid-coastal area stretched all the way to the border of the community of Ocean Park, just one of several in the region. In the 1940s, though, with the area's proximity to the LA airport (then called "Mines Field"), **Howard Hughes** located his airplane-manufacturing facility on the eastern side of the site, which at its peak had countless huge hangars and engineering facilities, as well as the nation's longest private runway; it was also the place where the notorious **Spruce Goose** was built. Hughes Aviation lasted a half-century here, several decades after its founder's death, but in 1994 relocated elsewhere. That's when the preservation battles for the wetlands began in earnest. For well over a decade developers and environmentalists have battled for permanent control of this prime real estate, with the old aviation site (and parcels around it) turning into an 1100-acre tract of new condos and commercial structures called **Playa Vista**, and activists putting up a fierce rearguard action to protect what's left over. Although the planned site of the Dreamworks SKG movie studio was successfully scuttled after adverse publicity, "Phase Two" of the monumental development is proceeding apace, even if it means building over an ancient Indian burial ground. In the last twenty years there have been no fewer than nineteen lawsuits to stop "progress" in the wetlands. Several hundreds acres have been preserved as a concession (most west of Lincoln Blvd), but this conflict shows no sign of abating; for the latest news on this seemingly endless saga, check out ⊛www.ballona.org.

Playa del Rey

To the west from the wetlands, Culver Boulevard leads to the former resort community of **Playa del Rey**, once an essential link in the Red Car transit line and the site of grand hotels, restaurants, and a funicular railway, but since reduced to a faded collection of commercial shacks and unattractive condos. The peaceful **lagoon**, nestled near the beach along Pacific Street, is a popular spot for children's activities and dog-walking, but you're better off heading up to a high bluff above the main part of Playa del Rey, to the neighborhood of **Palisades del Rey**, which makes for a pleasant, hilly hike past some fine views of the ocean. There used to be more to this neighborhood (including historic houses by the likes of R.M. Schindler), and to Playa del Rey overall, but the need for a sound barrier between LAX and the ocean did much to ruin its idyllic setting. When the county condemned the property here in the 1960s, hundreds of homes were destroyed and an entire neighborhood all but disappeared. The result was one of LA's strangest attractions: a modern-day **ghost town** stretching for several miles from Waterview Street to Imperial Highway along Vista del Mar. Chain-link fences guard the empty streets, now lined by crumbling housing foundations and defunct street lights. The only residents these days are some 50,000 **butterflies** that have moved in since the south end of the area was turned into an ecological preserve. Head to Sandpiper Street to survey the surreal scene close up, or at least until the next blaring takeoff of a jumbo jet makes you jump back in your car.

6

South Central and East LA

S outh Central and East LA are far removed from the tourist circuit, and avoided by most visitors and almost all Westsiders, many of them believing any venture south of the I-10 freeway to be an open invitation to murder, mugging, or some other threat. In truth, while these places can be dicey and should be avoided at night, the ghetto stereotypes are blown out of proportion in selected districts, and a number of interesting museums and historic-revival homes can be found here, especially on the northern side of South Central around Exposition Park.

Contained mostly within the boundaries of the 405, 605, and 10 freeways, South Central and East LA make up a large portion of the LA basin, encompassing diverse cultures, with neighboring communities often separated by major differences in language, ethnicity, and religion. Hispanic population growth is a constant throughout these areas, as it is throughout the rest of LA, but otherwise, sweeping racial categorizing is simply not possible for most of these parts.

South Central LA

Lacking the scenic splendor of the coast, the glamour of West LA or the movie history of Hollywood, **SOUTH CENTRAL LA** hardly ranks on the city's list of prime attractions. However, it makes up a considerable part of the city: a big oval chunk bordered by Alameda Street and the 10 and 405 freeways. Though once mostly black, the population is increasingly Hispanic and Asian, interspersed here and there with a few whites. Typically made up of detached bungalows enjoying their own patch of palm-shaded lawn, South Central still has some of the worst poverty in the area, especially the closer you go toward districts like Watts and Compton, and most residents have little chance to move up the social ladder – a situation that fosters large, pervasive youth gangs, which have only been getting bigger and more violent in the last few years.

Not surprisingly, throughout much of the district, every block for miles looks much like the last, peppered with fast-food outlets, dingy liquor stores, and abandoned factories, with the occasional outdoor market to brighten the

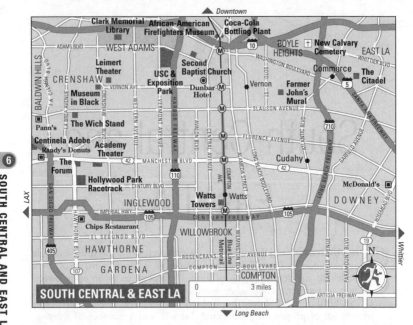

gloom. Most commuters zip through the area on the Harbor Freeway (I-110), which is largely confined to its own walled-off channel. Nonetheless, there are compelling sights to be found, including the historic homes of **West Adams**, several museums in **Exposition Park**, and the folk-art masterpiece of the **Watts Towers** – all best seen in daylight.

Some history

Like other parts of the city, much of South Central LA was settled in the nineteenth century by **Mexican immigrants** when the area was still governed by Mexico, and its large land tracts divided up as ranchos. Later, after the US took control of the land and California became the 31st state in 1850, **white Protestants** began migrating from the Midwest, drawn by the sunny weather, low cost of living, and favorable job market, continuing into the early twentieth century.

Although LA had the largest African-American settlement on the West Coast in the 1930s, it was World War II that brought blacks in great numbers from the South and the East Coast to work in defense-related industries, especially aerospace. Born or raised in LA were such notables as jazz musicians Dexter Gordon, Charles Mingus, and Eric Dolphy, United Nations undersecretary Ralph Bunche, dance choreographer Alvin Ailey, and Hollywood actress Dorothy Dandridge. (Even in the nineteenth century, when their population was significantly lower, black Angelenos were visible throughout the city, including such prominent figures as Robert Owens, a former slave who became the wealthiest and most prominent African-American in Southern California in the 1850s.)

Most of the new residents were unpleasantly surprised to experience a taste of the Old South in new LA. The rampant, blatant discrimination of the time ensured the widespread presence of **color bars** and **restrictive covenants** – social codes and housing bylaws that kept blacks out of white neighborhoods. African-Americans were hemmed in by avenues like Western and Slauson for their home-buying, and faced extreme hostility from whites whenever they ventured out of their neighborhoods to buy groceries, meet with friends, or watch movies. Because of this, areas like Central Avenue and West Adams became segregated, though culturally rich, enclaves for blacks, with a thriving entertainment scene in the former and excellent architecture in the latter.

The **Civil Rights Era** and changing demographics put an official end to the old ways of segregation, and LA's southern neighborhoods have become a diverse blend of blacks, Hispanics, and Asians, with many districts changing character in just a few decades. However, many problems persist, and what was formerly political and social apartheid has instead become de facto **economic segregation**. Poor and working-class blacks, even up to the middle class, are still stuck in South Central LA – largely to the western side – with Latinos increasingly settling in Watts and many other neighborhoods across the southern basin.

Inglewood

Bordered by the San Diego Freeway on the western edge of South Central, **INGLEWOOD** is, as the home to LAX, the first area most air travelers experience in LA. It's also well known for the **Hollywood Park Racetrack** (☏310/419-1500, ⓦwww.hollywoodpark.com), a landscaped track with lagoons and a state-of-the-art wide screen that shows the otherwise obscured back straight. Next door are the white pillars that ring **The Forum**, the 17,000-seat arena that was the former headquarters of LA's Lakers (basketball) and Kings (hockey). These days it's been converted into one of the country's biggest megachurches, owned by Faithful Central Bible Church, though concerts are still occasionally held here during the week (see p.311).

Unless you're here to play the horses, Inglewood's best attraction is its **pop architecture**. The grand but faded **Academy Theater**, 3100 Manchester Blvd, now a church, was built in 1939 to house the Oscars ceremony (it never did), and features a giant Moderne spire and spiky neon globe that beckon to worshippers, while further west, the **Loyola Theater**, at Sepulveda and Manchester boulevards, is a late Streamline Moderne design with a sweeping, red goose-neck curve on its facade, which now serves as office space. Not far away at 805 Manchester Blvd, **Randy's Donuts** (ⓦwww.randysdonuts.com) is one of LA's more surreal icons, a 1954 fast-food shack topped by a giant brown donut; while **Pann's** (ⓦwww.panns.com), a mile north at La Tijera Boulevard and Centinela Avenue, is perhaps the greatest "Googie" diner of all, which still serves classic comfort food, with a big neon sign, pitched and gabled roof, exotic plants, gravel roof, and a wealth of primary colors. Other classic diners are in fairly shopworn condition, except for the striking **Chips Restaurant**, a few miles south at 11908 Hawthorne Blvd, showcasing one of LA's great signs, three aquamarine columns supporting a sparkling set of letters, and the former **Wich Stand**, 4508 Slauson Ave, graced with a towering pastel pylon, though it no longer serves greasy burgers and fries – it's now a health-food store.

The Centinela Adobe

Just south of *Pann's*, the historic **Centinela Adobe**, 7636 Midfield Ave (Wed & Sun 2–4pm; free; private tours by appointment at ☏310/649-6272), was once home to Ignacio Machado, an heir to one of the Mexican founders of

Los Angeles. It's the oldest building in the area, dating from 1834 and furnished with antiques and replicas, including a good array of Victorian clothing and furniture, and offering details on Machado's life and his surrounding Aguaje de Centinela rancho, a 2200-acre land parcel granted him by the Mexican government. Also on site is the **Daniel Freeman Land Office**, built in 1887, a center for historic preservation, and a storehouse of curios and memorabilia of Inglewood city history and culture.

Crenshaw

Just to the north, **CRENSHAW** and adjacent **Leimert Park** form the contemporary center of African-American social activity in LA. Where once the nucleus of black culture was along Central Avenue, south of Downtown, it's now along **Crenshaw Boulevard**, a busy stretch of restaurants and book and record stores, as well as the Baldwin Hills Crenshaw Plaza, a multimillion-dollar shopping mall. The stunning **Leimert Theater**, 3300 43rd Place, an Art Deco gem by architects Morgan, Walls and Clements (see p.88), features a towering oil-derrick sign with neon accents, and is in occasional use as a performing-arts center. It lies in the heart of **Leimert Park Village**, several blocks of lively shops and decent restaurants.

The main cultural attraction here is the compelling **Museum in Black**, 4331 Degnan Blvd (Tues–Sat 11.30am–6pm; donation; ☎323/292-9528), which traces African and African-American art and history with roughly one thousand pieces in its collection, from knives, cooking utensils, and totemic statuary of the Old World to racist advertising and political propaganda of the New. Particularly disturbing are the papers on display that document the purchase and transport of slaves from West Africa, some of which date back nearly three hundred years.

Above Crenshaw and Leimert Park, the black upper-middle class resides in pleasant **Baldwin Hills**, named after Wall Street gambler and Santa Anita racetrack-builder E.J. "Lucky" Baldwin. Just before he died in 1909, Baldwin acquired the old Rancho La Cienega, which encompassed the hills and was named after the misspelled Spanish word for "marsh." (He also built an estate east of Pasadena that's now home to the LA County Arboretum; see p.206.) Later, the area would host the Olympic Village for LA's 1932 summer games and become the site of a catastrophic 1963 dam burst and flood. This was due in no small part to environmental damage from oil drilling, which continues to this day and is most visible here along La Cienega Boulevard, giving a hint of what much of petroleum-obsessed LA looked like in the 1920s.

West Adams

The charming, but faded, **West Adams** neighborhood, along Adams Boulevard from Crenshaw Boulevard to Hoover Street, was one of LA's few racially mixed neighborhoods in the early part of the twentieth century. Here, restrictive covenants were not as common as elsewhere in the city – and outlawed altogether in 1948. It was also one of the spots where movie stars tended to live, known in the 1920s and 30s as "**Sugar Hill**" and full of notable celebrities such as movie-musical director Busby Berkeley, and silent-film heavyweights Fatty Arbuckle and Theda Bara. Unfortunately, the 1960s took their toll on the neighborhood, partly because of the construction of the **Santa Monica Freeway** (I-10), which slashed the area in half. In the last decade, though, the district has experienced a small revival, with new homeowners of all colors arriving after being priced out of other parts of LA, raising the specter of gentrification in future years.

These days, many of the grand houses and mansions have become religious institutions. Berkeley's estate, the 1910 **Guasti Villa**, 3500 W Adams Blvd, is a graceful Renaissance Revival creation that might fit nicely in Italy but is now home to a New Age spiritual institute. However, you can still pop in at least once a year to experience the Da Camera Society's chamber music (see p.316). Nearby, the **Lindsay House**, no. 3424, a terracotta curiosity with a heavy stone facade and unique tilework (the first owner was a tile manufacturer), has become Our Lady of Bright Mount, a Polish Catholic church (☎323/734-5249); and the **Walker House**, no. 3300 (☎323/733-6260), a mishmash of Craftsman bulk, Tudor half-timbering, and a Mission-style tile roof, has turned into a Korean Seventh-Day Adventist church.

The finest building in the area is the French Renaissance **William Clark Memorial Library**, 2520 Cimarron St (Mon–Fri 9am–4.45pm; free; tours Mon–Fri 10am–2pm by reservation only, at ☎323/735-7605, ⊛www.humnet .ucla.edu/humnet/clarklib), with its elegant symmetry, yellow-brick walls, formal gardens, and grand entrance hall – a splash of Continental elegance in an unexpected LA setting. As millionaire heir to a copper fortune, founder of the LA Philharmonic, and a US Senator from Montana, Clark amassed this great collection before donating it to UCLA, which continues to oversee it. Besides rare volumes by Pope, Fielding, and Milton, plus a huge set of letters and manuscripts by Oscar Wilde, the library includes four Shakespeare folios, a group of works by Chaucer, and copies of key documents in American history. Four annual **exhibitions** are usually given of selected works from the collection.

USC

The **USC** (University of Southern California) campus, a few miles south of Downtown and east of West Adams, is a wealthy enclave in one of the city's poorer neighborhoods. For many years a breeding ground for political and economic fat cats, the university was well known for hatching LA's shadow rulers for the secretive "**Committee of 25**," supplying Richard Nixon with gung-ho advisers like H.R. Haldeman, and generally acting as the reactionary force in the local academic scene,

Today, USC, or the "University of Spoiled Children," is among the most expensive universities in the country, its undergraduates thought of as more likely to have rich parents than fertile brains. Indeed, the stereotype seems often borne out, both by their easygoing, beach-bumming stereotype, and by USC's being more famous for its sporting prowess than its academic achievements. Within fifteen years of the school's 1874 founding, it already had a **football** team, becoming the first university in Southern California to play the game. They remain a dominant force today, having won back-to-back national championships in 2003–4, and famous alumni include O.J. Simpson, who collected college football's highest honor, the Heisman Trophy, when he played here.

Though largely white and conservative, the university hasn't escaped to the suburbs (unlike its right-wing counterpart, Pepperdine), and there have even been a few small steps to integrate the **campus** more closely with the local, mainly black and Hispanic, community. Based on an Italian Romanesque style similar to that of UCLA, USC's 1920s buildings exhibit much nice detail and ornament, but the lack of greenspace gives the campus the appearance of a concrete desert at times, and the austere character of its modern buildings can, in places, look like something out of a de Chirico painting.

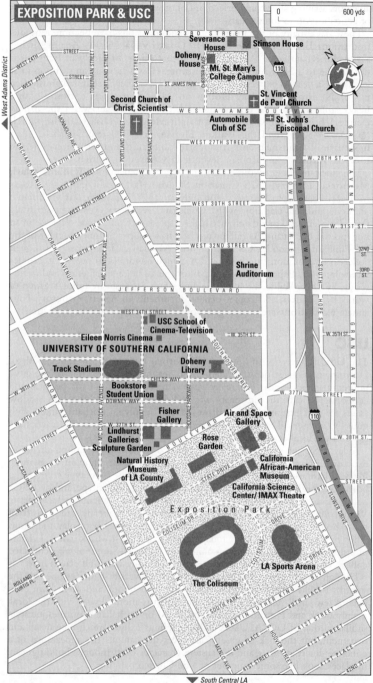

EXPOSITION PARK & USC

0   600 yds

N

West Adams District ◀

WEST 23RD STREET

Severance House

Stimson House

WEST 24TH STREET

WEST 25TH STREET

Doheny House

Mt. St. Mary's College Campus

St. Vincent de Paul Church

Second Church of Christ, Scientist

ST. JAMES PARK

WEST ADAMS BOULEVARD

Automobile Club of SC

St. John's Episcopal Church

WEST 27TH STREET

WEST 27TH STREET

W. 28TH ST.

WEST 28TH STREET

WEST 28TH STREET

WEST 29TH STREET

WEST 30TH STREET

W. 31ST ST.

WEST 30TH PL AVE

WEST 32ND STREET

32ND ST.

Shrine Auditorium

33RD ST.

JEFFERSON BOULEVARD

WEST 34TH STREET

USC School of Cinema-Television

W. 35TH ST.

W. 35TH ST.

Eileen Norris Cinema

UNIVERSITY OF SOUTHERN CALIFORNIA

W. 36TH ST.

Track Stadium

Doheny Library

W. 37TH STREET

Bookstore Student Union

CHILDS WAY

DOWNEY WAY

Fisher Gallery

Air and Space Gallery

W. 38TH ST.

Lindhurst Galleries

Rose Garden

Sculpture Garden

California African-American Museum

Natural History Museum of LA County

California Science Center/ IMAX Theater

39TH STREET

WEST 37TH DRIVE

STATE DRIVE

Exposition Park

WEST 38TH STREET

COLISEUM DR.

WEST 39TH STREET

The Coliseum

LA Sports Arena

ROLLAND CURTIS PL.

W. 39TH PLACE

SOUTH PARK DRIVE

MARTIN LUTHER KING JR. BLVD

40TH PLACE

LEIGHTON AVENUE

41ST STREET

BROWNING BLVD

41ST STREET

41ST PLACE

42ND ST.

▼ South Central LA

The campus

While sizable, USC's campus is reasonably easy to get around. You might find it easiest, however, to take the free fifty-minute **walking tour** (leaving on the hour Mon–Fri 10am–3pm; by reservation at ☎213/740-6605, ⓦwww .usc.edu), leaving on the hour from the USC Admissions Center, near Gate 2. Without a guide, a good place to start is the **Doheny Library** (Mon–Thurs 8am–midnight, Fri 8am–5pm, Sat 9am–5pm, Sun 1–10pm), an inviting Romanesque pile named after the famous LA oil baron, where you can pick up a campus map and investigate the large stock of overseas newspapers and magazines on the second floor. Another good place for general information is the **Student Union** building, just across from the library. Among the generally unremarkable eateries found here, a **café** under the Wolfgang Puck banner, featuring nouveau pizzas and salads, provides some respite.

Of things to see, USC's art collection is housed in the **Fisher Gallery**, 823 Exposition Blvd (Tues–Sat noon–5pm; free; ⓦwww.usc.edu/org/fishergallery), which stages several major international exhibitions each year and has a broad permanent collection, best for its nineteenth-century American works, including Thomas Cole's *The Woodchopper*, a Hudson River School painting, and Albert Bierstadt's landscape of *A Stream in the Rocky Mountains*, a grand Romantic vista. Elsewhere, you can see smaller shows of students' creative efforts, as well as retrospective shows featuring the models, blueprints, and sketches of internationally famous architects, in the **Helen Lindhurst Architecture Gallery**, in the USC School of Architecture, 850 W 37th St (Mon–Fri 10am–6pm; free), while the **Helen Lindhurst Fine Arts Gallery**, room 103 in the same complex (Mon–Fri 9am–4pm; free), focuses on contemporary and experimental works from student and regional artists. The structure itself is quite creative, too, with porch-level glass boxes doubling as skylights for the underground library.

One of the few compelling public artworks on campus is Jenny Holzer's **First Amendment**, in the **sculpture garden** around Harris Hall – a work commemorating the Hollywood Ten, those writers and directors blacklisted for refusing to rat out their colleagues as Communists in the McCarthy era. Steps of stone slabs lead to ten circular benches, all of which are inscribed with the names and writings of the persecuted filmmakers.

Finally, the campus is also home to the **School of Cinema-Television**, a mainstream rival to the UCLA film school in Westwood. Ironically, **Steven Spielberg** couldn't get in to USC when he applied, but nowadays his name is hallowed here, and writ large on the wall of the large and expensive sound-mixing center he later funded. You can sometimes catch a good classic or foreign flick at the nearby **Eileen Norris Cinema**, just south of the Cinema School at 3507 Trousdale Parkway; drop by for a look at the monthly schedule of screenings (or call ☎213/740-3332 for information).

Exposition Park

Once known as Agricultural Park because of its produce vendors and farming exhibits, **Exposition Park** is, given the bleak nature of the surrounding area, one of the better parks in LA, incorporating lush gardens and several modest museums. Although this area just south of USC – along with the residential quarters north of the school – was once home to LA's elite, subsequent white flight and economic downturns have taken their toll, an effect visible in the countless drab strip malls and liquor stores that have set up shop on the surrounding blocks.

△ The California Science Center and Air and Space Gallery

Along with being a favorite lunchtime picnic spot for school kids, the park's big draw is the **California Science Center**, one of a cluster of **museums** off Figueroa Street at 700 State Drive (daily 10am–5pm; free, parking $6; ☎323/724-3623, ⓦwww.casciencectr.org), a multimillion-dollar showcase for scientific education. The museum's highlights include a walk-in microscope and a giant talking robot – keep in mind, though, that three of the museum's attractions, including a "high-wire" bicycle, motion simulator, and rock-climbing wall, cost an extra $7 each. In the same complex, an **IMAX Theater** (tickets

$7.50, kids $4.50; information at ☎213/744-2015) plays a range of eye-popping documentaries on a gigantic curved screen.

Nearby, the **Air and Space Gallery** (Mon–Fri 10am–1pm, Sat & Sun 11am–4pm; same admission with Center) is marked by a jet stuck to its facade, offering a series of satellites and telescopes, a slew of airplanes and rockets, and the menacing presence of an LAPD helicopter "air ship" – to complement their constant drone in the skies above. The building itself is a white cubic mass designed by Frank Gehry, prefiguring some of his later, better, work. The close by **California African-American Museum**, 600 State Drive (Wed–Sat 10am–4pm; free; ☻www.caamuseum.org), has diverse temporary exhibitions on the history and culture of black people in the Americas, including musical instruments from Africa and the Caribbean, shows devoted to the life and legacy of performers like Ella Fitzgerald, and painting and sculpture by local artists.

On a sunny day, take a stroll through the park's **Rose Garden** (daily 10am –5pm; free). The flowers are at their most fragrant in April and May, which is when the bulk of the 45,000 annual visitors come by to admire the 16,000 rose bushes and the charm of their setting. Finally, near the center of the park, the grand **Coliseum**, 3939 S Figueroa St, was the site of the 1932 and 1984 Olympic Games. More recently, though, it's seen its glory days fade, with the Raiders pro-football team long gone and possible deals to land a new NFL franchise repeatedly failing. However, USC home games are still played here, if you can ever get a ticket (tickets $40 minimum; ☎213/740-GOSC), and the imposing grand arch on the facade and muscular, headless commemorative statues make the place worth a look.

Natural History Museum of Los Angeles County

The **Natural History Museum of Los Angeles County** (daily 10am–5pm; $9; ☎213/763-3466, ☻www.nhm.org), an explosion of Spanish Revival architecture in the northwest corner of the park, is the park's most striking building and best museum. Foremost among the exhibits is a tremendous stock of dinosaur bones and fossils, and some imposing skeletons (usually casts), including the crested "duck-billed" dinosaur, the skull of a Tyrannosaurus rex, and the astonishing frame of a Diatryma – a huge, flightless prehistoric bird. Exhibits on rare sharks, the combustible native plant chaparral, and a spellbinding insect zoo – centered around a sizable ant farm – add to the appeal, but there's a lot here beyond strict natural history, so you should allow several hours at least for a comprehensive look around. In the fascinating Pre-Columbian Hall, you'll find Mayan pyramid murals and the complete, reconstructed contents of a Mexican tomb, while the Californian history sections document the early (white) settlement of the region during the Gold Rush era and after, with some evocative photos of LA in the 1920s. Topping everything off is the breathtaking gem collection: several roomfuls of crystals, and a tempting display of three hundred pounds of gold, safely behind glass.

North of USC

Just to the **north of USC** and Exposition Park, around Adams Boulevard and Figueroa Street, is a pocket of some of LA's most important early twentieth-century architecture, much of which reflects the power of the district's most famous resident, oil magnate **Edward Doheny** (see box, p.128). The intersection of Adams and Figueroa itself features three of LA's best period-revival designs from the 1920s: **St John's Episcopal Church**, 514 W Adams

Blvd, an architectural competition's winning Italian Romanesque entry that now features the modern image of Martin Luther King Jr in stained glass; the church-like **Automobile Club of Southern California**, 2601 S Figueroa St, a Spanish Baroque structure with a high octagonal tower; and the grand **St Vincent de Paul Church**, catercorner to St John's, Doheny's own donation to the faith, an even more ornamental Spanish Baroque creation with a sparkling, tiled dome and richly detailed steeple. Nearby, the **Stimson House**, 2421 S Figueroa St, matches the spirit of the area, as a Romanesque castle-home, made in 1891 of red sandstone, that appears ready for a Crusader battle.

One long block to the west, **Chester Place** and **St James Park** are pedestrian-friendly zones loaded with the opulent residences of some of LA's most prominent citizens of the early twentieth century. The area's centerpiece is the palatial **Doheny House**, 10 Chester Place, a triumph of the Spanish Gothic style, where you can dawdle in the palm conservatory and immense dining hall built to seat one hundred guests. After the 1958 death of Edward Doheny's wife Estelle, this and the surrounding property were given to **Mount St Mary's College**, and the house is now one of several elegant buildings on campus. Periodically, the college offers "Doheny Soirees" Friday evenings at 8pm (see p.316), in which chamber music is played under the mansion's beautiful, reverberant dome. Right by here are more intriguing period-revival creations, including the **Severance House**, 650 W 23rd St, a 1904 Mission Revival structure with some Victorian detailing in back (and now a resource center for Vincentian Catholic priests); and the **Second Church of Christ, Scientist**, 948 W Adams

LA cops and riots

Los Angeles has had a longstanding reputation as having one of the most brutal police forces in the nation – the **LAPD** – whose paramilitary tactics were developed under 1950s super-cop William Parker. In reaction to the longstanding mistreatment of local blacks, the district of Watts first achieved notoriety as the scene of the six-day **Watts Riots** of August 1965. The arrest of a 21-year-old African-American man, **Marquette Frye**, on suspicion of drunken driving, gave rise to charges of police brutality and led to bricks, bottles, and slabs of concrete being hurled at police and passing motorists during the night of the 11th. The situation had calmed by the next morning, but by the following evening both young and old were on the streets, venting an anger generated by years of abuse by the police and other white-dominated institutions. Weapons were looted from stores and many buildings set afire (though few residential buildings, black-owned businesses, or community services, such as libraries and schools, were torched); street barricades were erected, and the events then took a more serious turn. By the fifth day the insurgents were approaching Downtown, which led to the call-out of the **National Guard**: 13,000 troops arrived, set up machine-gun placements and road blocks, and imposed a curfew, causing the rebellion to subside. In the aftermath of the uprising, which left 36 dead, one German reporter said of Watts, "It looks like Germany during the last months of World War II."

Watts hit the headlines for a second time in 1975, when members of the **Symbionese Liberation Army** (SLA), who had kidnapped publishing heiress Patti Hearst, fought a lengthy – and televised – gun battle with police until the house they were trapped in burned to the ground. The site of the battle, at 1466 E 54th St, is now a vacant lot, though the surrounding houses are still riddled with bullet holes.

Despite all the violence, nothing had changed by the 1980s when **Daryl Gates** hit the headlines for his new and disturbing LAPD tactics: the department's own tank bashed down the walls of alleged (often innocent) drug suspects, its helicopter gunships patrolled the skies over South Central LA, and its chief himself proudly

Blvd (☎213-749-3761), a Neoclassical jewel with forty-foot-high Corinthian columns and a copper dome that seats a thousand souls.

Just across the street from USC lies the most exotic piece of architecture in the area, the **Shrine Auditorium**, 665 W Jefferson Blvd (tickets and info ☎213/ 749-5123), best known as the former venue of the Oscars ceremony, which was presented here biannually from 1986 to 2001, before moving on to the Kodak Theater in Hollywood. Looking like a vestige of D.W. Griffith's *Intolerance* set in Hollywood, this 1920s Islamic-inspired fantasy, with its onion domes and streetside colonnade, is frequently a venue for traveling religious revival meetings, concerts by pop stars, and various award shows.

Central Avenue

Once the focus of African-American commerce and culture during the interwar years, **Central Avenue** had a vigor that has never been recaptured. Because pre-1960s segregation and restrictive housing covenants prohibited blacks from living in most of LA, this avenue from Eighth Street to Vernon Avenue became the hub for numerous restaurants, nightclubs, and jazz halls – including such hot spots as the *Down Beat Club* and *Last Word* – and attracted a broad mix of blacks, from blue-collar workers to celebrities, and a few white liberals from the Westside as well.

With the end of official segregation, Central Avenue inevitably declined, but there are still several appealing sights amid the abandoned lots and strip malls. A superb example of Streamline Moderne architecture lies at the north end of the

argued, in front of Congress, that casual drug-users should be taken out and shot. Gates was allowed to get away with these quasi-fascist antics only for so long, though, before he was forced out. In the **riots of 1992**, three white Los Angeles police officers were unexpectedly acquitted after being charged with using excessive force after they were videotaped kicking and beating African-American motorist **Rodney King**. What few predicted was the scale and intensity of the response to the verdict, which was partly fueled, ironically enough, by the almost total lack of a police presence during the first evening's bloodshed. Beginning in South Central LA, where motorists were pulled from their cars and attacked, the situation quickly escalated into a tumult of arson, shooting, and looting that spread from Long Beach to Hollywood. It took the imposition of a four-day dusk-to-dawn curfew, and the presence on LA's streets of several thousand well-armed National Guard troops, to restore calm – whereupon the full extent of the rioting became known. The **worst urban violence** seen in the US since the bloody, Civil War–era New York draft riots had left 58 dead, nearly 2000 injured, and caused an estimated $1 billion worth of damage.

Prompted by the Rodney King case, the **Christopher Commission** was set up to investigate racial prejudice within the LAPD. Sadly, its recommendations had all too blatantly not been implemented by the time of the **Rampart police scandal** in 2000, when evidence of possible hit-squad tactics and other vigilante actions by members of the LAPD confirmed people's worst fears of the cops being beyond civilian control. While politicians and Westsiders expressed shock at such charges, no one in South Central was very surprised. Since then, even though New York's trailblazing former police chief **William Bratton** has been brought in to turn things around, almost nothing has changed. **Gang violence** in 2005 is again on an upswing, this time with more Latino suspects than before. However, since much of South Central is well off the radar screen of upscale white Los Angeles, the problems continue to fester and worsen – waiting for the next spark to send LA up in flames once more.

△ South Central's Coca-Cola Bottling Plant

street: the **Coca-Cola Bottling Plant**, 1334 S Central Ave, looking like a huge, landlocked ocean liner, complete with rounded corners, porthole windows, and ships' doors. Besides being in excellent condition, the plant is still churning out bottles for the soft-drink giant. Built in 1937, this was the second ground-breaking building in LA created by Robert Derrah, after his Crossroads of the World (see p.112). Nearby at 1401 S Central Ave, the **African-American Firefighters Museum** (Tues & Thurs 10am–2pm, Sun 1–4pm; donation; ⓦwww.lafd.org/aafm.htm) is housed in Engine Company #30, LA's first all-black fire station, which protected the area from 1913 to 1980, and now displays a modest collection of historic equipment and memorabilia.

Eleven blocks south, pioneering black architect Paul R. Williams' first major building, the **Second Baptist Church**, 2412 Griffith Ave (☎213/748-0318, ⓦwww.sbcla.org), is a striking Romanesque Revival church built in 1924 for a congregation dating from 1885, making it LA's oldest black religious institu-tion; while further south, the **Dunbar Hotel**, 4225 S Central Ave, was the first US hotel built specifically for blacks and patronized by many prominent African-Americans – W.E.B. DuBois and Duke Ellington among them – during the 1930s through the 1950s. The hotel is only visible in its restored lobby and facade, as it is now a home for the elderly (information through the OASIS senior center; Mon–Fri 9am–5pm; ☎323/231-6220). It does, however, feature occasional art exhibits open to the public, and hosts the Central Avenue Jazz Festival in August (more details at ☎213/847-3169), which gives a hint of the area's swing and vigor in the old days.

Watts and Compton

Few neighborhoods inspire more fear in white LA than Watts and Compton, known mostly for their street crime and rap music. It is true that these spots can be dangerous, especially at night, and are best explored by those familiar with the area or in the company of a local.

The abandoned Art Deco campus of **Pepperdine University**, Vermont Avenue and 80th Street, is one of LA's most visible emblems of white flight, marking the spot where the Church of Christ–affiliated school was located from 1937 to 1972, after which it left for a bluff in Malibu. Further south from here, South Central becomes grittier and much more dicey. Now more Hispanic than black, **WATTS** provides only one compelling reason to visit (and only during the day), the Gaudí-esque **Watts Towers**, sometimes called the Rodia Towers, at 1765 E 107th St, a half-mile north off the 105 freeway on Wilmington Avenue. Constructed from iron, stainless steel, old bedframes, and cement, and adorned with bottle fragments and some 70,000 crushed seashells, these striking pieces of folk art are shrouded in mystery. Their maker, Italian immigrant **Simon Rodia**, had no artistic background or training, but labored over the towers' construction from 1921 to 1954, refusing offers of help and unable to explain their meaning or why he was building them. Once finished, Rodia left the area, refused to talk about them, and faded into obscurity. The towers, the tallest standing at almost 100 feet, managed to stave off bureaucratic hostility and structural condemnation for many decades, before finally being declared a cultural landmark. The site is open by appointment only, typically

The gangs of LA

South Central LA is the heartland of the city's infamous **gangs**, said to number one hundred thousand members among them, which have existed for more than forty years and often encompass several generations of a family. The black gangs known as **Crips** and **Bloods** are the most famous, but there are many huge Hispanic gangs as well, most prominently the **18th Street Gang** who, despite their name, operate all over the LA basin, as well as the US and Mexico. The characteristic violence associated with these groups often stems from territorial fights over drug-dealing, with many gangs staking claim to certain neighborhoods through their monikers. The larger gangs employ rather sophisticated schemes involving protection rackets, money laundering, and expansion into legitimate businesses from small retail operations to, it is rumored, the music industry – all tactics reminiscent not of common street thugs, but of old-style Italian mobsters.

The old stereotype of LA gangs is increasingly outdated, though. Gang life used to be fairly contained within the city, and could be broken down into simple black-on-black violence, which occasionally spilled into other neighborhoods (such as Westwood in the 1980s), making white Westsiders increasingly paranoid and supportive of all manner of hamfisted police tactics. Nowadays, though, local gangs are increasingly **international**, with chapters not only reaching other cities throughout the western US, but also strongly linked to Mexican gangs and organized-crime syndicates. Indeed, LA serves as a training ground for budding gangsters from Central America who, after their deportation, return to their home countries schooled in the high-tech ways of first-world killing, inflicting more misery on a region already awash in violence and poverty.

That said, with all the different ethnic gangs in the city, don't try to decipher the **graffiti** you see on the wall of an inner-city liquor store, or wrongly assume that a gang member must be an obvious hoodlum in the "bad part of town." This sort of crime is intrinsic to the city as a whole, from Downtown to the Westside, and is only at its most violent and visible in ghettos like South Central or Pico Union. By sticking to familiar areas in the day and well-policed districts at night, tourists should have few problems with gangs.

to small groups of five or so people; call or visit the adjacent **Watts Tower Arts Center**, 1727 E 107th St (Tues–Sat 10am–4pm, Sun noon–4pm; free; ☎323/860-9964, ⌨www.wattstowers.net), for more information. One good time to come is during the September Day of the Drums Festival, or the October Watts Towers Jazz Festival, both signature events in the city, which take place at an adjoining amphitheater.

Compton

Between Watts and the LA Harbor, the few districts are of passing interest. Despite its fame as the home of many of LA's rappers, as well as tennis champs Serena and Venus Williams, **COMPTON** is not a place where strangers should attempt to sniff out the local music scene. Oddly enough, the town's most famous resident was none other than former president George Bush (Sr), who lived here when the city was still known for its oil wells, and when whites were still in power. With the white flight of the 1950s and 1960s, though, investment capital dried up and Compton hasn't recovered. History buffs secure in their cars can stop at the **Dominguez Ranch Adobe**, just off the 91 freeway at 18127 S Alameda St (Sun & Wed 1, 2 & 3pm; ☎310/631-5981), which chronicles the social ascent of the adobe's founder, Juan Jose Dominguez, one of the soldiers who left Mexico with Padre Junípero Serra's expedition to found the California missions, and whose long military service was acknowledged in 1782 by the granting of these 75,000 acres of land. The six main rooms of the 1826 adobe are on display and are worth a look for anyone intrigued by pre-American California.

East LA

You can't visit LA without becoming aware of the Hispanic influence on the city's demography and culture, whether through the thousands of Mexican restaurants, the innumerable street names in Español or, most obviously, the preponderance of Spanish spoken on the streets in dialects from Tijuana to Oaxaca, from Guatemala to Peru. Of the many Hispanic neighborhoods all over the city, the most long-standing is **EAST LA**, which begins two miles east of Downtown, across the concrete flood-control channel of the LA River. There was a Mexican population here long before the white settlers came, and from the late nineteenth century onward millions more arrived, chiefly to work as agricultural laborers in orchards and citrus groves. As the white inhabitants gradually moved west towards the coast, the Mexicans stayed, creating a vast Spanish-speaking community that's one of the most historic in the country, as well as one of the most insular and unfamiliar to outsiders.

Activity in East LA (commonly abbreviated to "ELA" or "East Los") tends to be outdoors, in cluttered markets and busy shops. Non-Hispanic visitors are thin on the ground, but you are unlikely to meet any hostility on the streets during the day – though you should steer clear of the rough and very male-dominated bars, and avoid the whole area after dark. **Guadalupe**, the Mexican depiction of the Virgin Mary, appears in mural art all over East LA, nowhere more strikingly than at the junction of Mednik and Cesar Chavez avenues. Lined with blue tile, the mural serves as an unofficial shrine where worshippers place fresh flowers and candles.

Other than the street life and murals, there are few specific "sights" in East LA other than the mausoleum of **New Calvary Cemetery**, 4201 E Whittier Ave (daily 8am–5pm, spring & summer closes 6pm; ☎323/261-3106). Rivaling City Hall for sheer audacity, the monumental tomb piles on the styles, with Corinthian columns and pilasters, an Egyptian-pyramid roof and a few Byzantine domes, plus some sculpted angels thrown in for good measure. Beyond its exterior panache, the mausoleum is also the resting place of old-time Angelenos like Edward Doheny and movie stars like Lionel and Ethel Barrymore, and Lou Costello.

For a more animated scene, stroll along **Cesar Chavez Avenue**, going eastward from Indiana Street and check out the wild-pet shops for their free-roaming parrots and cases of boa constrictors, and the **botánicas**, which cater to practitioners of santéria – a religion that is equal parts voodoo and Catholicism. Browse among the shark's teeth, dried devil fish, and plastic statuettes of Catholic saints, or explain to the shopkeeper (in Spanish) what ails you, then pick out remedies from a wide selection of magical herbs, ointments, and candles. Only slightly less exotic fare can be found in **El Mercado de Los Angeles**, 3425 E first St (daily 10am–8pm; ☎323/268-3451), a market not unlike Downtown's Olvera Street, but much more authentic.

The heart of Southeast LA

Following the path of Interstate 5 between South Central and East LA, **Southeast LA** is generally made up of low-grade industrial sites and their dingy bedroom communities, along with large expanses of postindustrial concrete desert. In the years following World War II, Southeast LA was a center for auto manufacture and tire-making, but the subsequent loss of blue-collar jobs led to the disappearance of much of the white and black population. They were replaced by Mexican and Central American immigrant laborers, many of whom would work at or below the minimum wage in sweatshops. Because this is one of the main US centers for new arrivals, population density in some places has become overwhelming – the tiny town of **Cudahy** packs nearly 25,000 people on one square mile of land, and not surprisingly has one of the country's highest poverty rates – while in other industrial towns, residential zones are practically forbidden, and sweatshops evade labor laws through lack of local oversight.

If, for some reason, you should wind up here, there are a few things worth checking out, starting in **Vernon**, an inhospitable burg whose only highlight is the **Farmer John's Mural**, 3049 E Vernon Ave, a bucolic trompe l'oeil on a meat-packing plant, showing a team of little pigs scampering about a farm and managing to scale the building walls – an amusing scene that almost makes you forget the ugly business inside. Further east, in Commerce, is **The Citadel**, right off I-5 at 5675 Telegraph Rd (ⓦwww.citadeloutlets.com), modeled on the ancient Assyrian architecture of Khorsabad in the Middle East; note the massive battlements and carvings of priests and warriors on the huge facade. Built by the architecture firm of Morgan, Walls and Clements (see box, p.88), this structure started life as the Samson Tyre and Rubber Company, was a backdrop for the 1950s spectacular *Ben Hur*, only later to be abandoned, then finally restored and turned into a fashion outlet.

To the south, the community of **Downey** is uneventful in itself, but does feature a true pop-architecture icon – the country's original **McDonald's** fast-food restaurant, 10207 Lakewood Blvd, opened in 1953, a year before the chain officially started. Boasting a much more exuberant, colorful design than the mansard-roofed clones of today, this *McDonald's* also features big yellow-neon arches that stretch over, and into, the building itself, plus a winking chef named "Speedee" atop its 60-foot-high sign. More than just an old burger joint, the restaurant is also listed as a cultural monument by the National Trust for Historic Preservation and even has its own museum and gift shop.

Of the nearby districts, the only one of conceivable interest is **MONTEREY PARK**, northeast of East LA, a reasonably safe area that has the highest percentage of Asian residents of any city in the nation (40 percent) and is a major gateway for Taiwanese and mainland Chinese immigrants arriving in the US. It's also home to a number of excellent authentic Chinese restaurants, as well as many nightclubs, ethnic grocers, and theaters, on its main drag, **Atlantic Boulevard**.

Whittier and around

Well to the south of East LA, and almost to the border of Orange County, the small town of **WHITTIER**, originally founded by Quakers and named after Quaker poet John Greenleaf Whittier, offers a handful of interesting sights. It was here that **Richard Nixon** – a Quaker himself – was raised, went to law school, and started his first law office. (His birthplace and library is in the Orange County town of Yorba Linda; see p.235.) You can find out more at the engaging **Whittier Museum**, 6755 Newlin Ave (Tues–Fri 10am–4pm; $4; ☎562/945-3871, ⊛www.whittiermuseum.org), a treasure-trove of historic city artifacts and assorted gizmos ranging from a working model of an oil derrick to replicas of a Pacific Electric Red Car. Other highlights include an old-fashioned barn and Victorian cottage, a rebuilt version of a Quaker meeting hall, and the desk Tricky Dick used in his first law office.

For a look at another politician who had an even harder time of it, there's the engaging **Pio Pico State Historic Park**, 6003 Pioneer Blvd (Wed–Sun 10am–5pm; free; ☎562/695-1217), a nine-thousand-acre tract that used to be the ranch of **Pio Pico**, the last Mexican governor of California, and centered around an **adobe** full of Victorian furnishings and artifacts tracing his life. Constructed in 1842, the house saw Pico lose his governorship, re-emerge on the LA City Council, make a fortune in real estate and finally go bankrupt, eventually dying penniless. All this history is on display during one of the regular adobe tours (on the hour Wed–Sun 1–3pm, also Sat & Sun 10–11am).

Several miles south, at 10211 S Pioneer Blvd, the **Clarke Estate** (Tues & Fri 11am–2pm; free; ☎562/863-4896) is a popular wedding spot, with elegantly landscaped grounds. It's also another of Irving Gill's Mission Revival and early-modern melds, with Mediterranean balconies and Tuscan columns used to offset a number of pre-Columbian reliefs and icons – giving a hint of what LA would have looked like if it had been colonized by Italians and Mayans, instead of Spaniards. Neighboring **Heritage Park**, 12100 Mora Drive (daily 7am–10pm; free), is also worth a look for its collection of re-created, local historic buildings, including a windmill, aviary, and carriage barn, accompanied by a pretty English garden and an eighty-ton locomotive. Less refined is the **LA County Sheriffs Museum**, 11515 S Colima Rd (Mon–Fri 9am–4pm; free; ☎562/946-7859), where you can examine a replica of an early jail and a sizable set of law-enforcement antiques – from classic tommy-guns to razor-sharp ice picks. Look, too, for the menacing meat hooks and crude knives that were popular tools in LA's mid-nineteenth-century "Hell Town" days.

Workman-Temple Homestead Museum

If you've already ventured this far for historic attractions, you might as well head north to the **Workman-Temple Homestead Museum**, 15415 E Don Julian Rd (Wed–Sun 1–4pm; free; ☎626/968-8492, ⊛www.homesteadmuseum .org), a historic estate that's the lone point of interest in the drab **CITY OF INDUSTRY**. Here, an early emigrant party first staked a regional land claim

6

and constructed this historic Spanish Colonial house around an 1840 adobe, complete with expansive grounds. There's a smokehouse and water tower, as well as a cemetery that contains the graves of many figures from regional history, including that of Pio Pico. The house itself is striking, full of carved wooden details, wrought-iron railings, and tiled stairways, and the glimmering centerpiece – stained-glass windows depicting steadfast family members on their westward trek to Southern California.

The South Bay and LA Harbor

Stretching south of LAX to the edge of Orange County, the oceanside cities of the **South Bay** and the **LA Harbor** share little in common except their proximity to the sea and insularity from the rest of the metropolis. While the bluffs around the beaches are the province of wealthy whites, poorer whites, blacks and Latinos reside many miles inland, in bland suburbs like Carson and Hawthorne, and in bleak districts like North Long Beach. Overall, though, the area's balmy climate and windswept scenery make this one of the city's most visually appealing regions, at least by the shore.

The South Bay begins south of the airport, with three **south beach cities** that are smaller and more suburban than LA's other seaside towns. Further south, and visible all along this stretch of the coast, the **Palos Verdes Peninsula** occupies a wild, craggy stretch of coastline, with some rustic parks and pricey real estate – much of it behind locked gates – while rough-hewn **San Pedro** is a gritty, working-class community that forms part of the site for the LA Harbor. Its counterpart, **Long Beach**, is best known as the home of the *Queen Mary*, even though it is also the region's second-largest city, with nearly half-a-million people. Hardly a major draw for visitors, the **harbor** itself is a massive complex divided between San Pedro and Long Beach, consisting of so many ship passages, trucking routes, and artificial islands that the huge Vincent Thomas Bridge had to be built to carry travelers over the entire works.

Perhaps the most enticing place in the area is **Santa Catalina Island**, located twenty miles offshore and easily reached by ferry. Little visited, the interior of the island remains largely a wilderness, with many unique forms of plant and animal life, and there's just one significant center of population, **Avalon**, a charming city in which the main form of motorized transport is the golf cart.

South beach cities

South of LAX along the coast, you'll find few interesting sights, just the candy-striped stacks of the Scattergood steam plant, a few oil refineries, and LA's only sewage-treatment center – Hyperion, a major cause of water pollution in Santa Monica Bay (see box, p.144). Soon after, though, the main access route, **Vista**

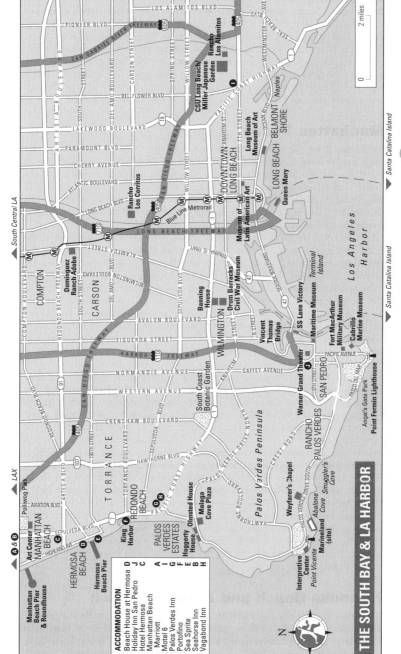

THE SOUTH BAY & LA HARBOR

ACCOMMODATION

Beach House at Hermosa	D
Holiday Inn San Pedro	J
Hotel Hermosa	C
Manhattan Beach Marriott	A
Motel 6	I
Palos Verdes Inn	G
Portofino	F
Sea Sprite	E
Seahorse Inn	B
Vagabond Inn	H

South beach cities

del Mar, rises up a bluff as it hugs the coastline, and an eight-mile strip of beach towns begins. Sitting on small, gently sloped hills, these **south beach cities** can make for a refreshing break if you like your beaches without trendy packaging. Along their shared beach boardwalk known as **The Strand** (which ends at Redondo Beach), the joggers and roller skaters are more likely to be locals than outsiders, and each city has at least one municipal pier and a beckoning strip of white sand, with most oceanside locations equipped for surfing and beach volleyball. These little towns are also well connected to the rest of the city, within easy reach of LAX, and linked by bus #439 to Downtown LA.

Manhattan Beach

Accessible along the bike path from Venice, or by car via PCH (Pacific Coast Highway) or Vista del Mar, **MANHATTAN BEACH** is the most northern of the three towns, a likeable place with a well-to-do air, home mainly to white-collar workers whose stucco houses sit near the beach, along the main drag of **Highland Avenue**. In recent years, it's also become the home of one of LA's smaller TV and film production facilities, Manhattan Beach Studios, so you might spot the occasional actor walking around as well.

Like its counterparts to the south, Manhattan Beach was first linked to the rest of LA by the Pacific Electric Railway's **Red Cars** at the beginning of the twentieth century, and before long this stretch was a favorite spot for pleasure -seekers of all types. While not as chaotic or thrilling as Venice, the city did provide a day's amusement along its sands and pier, though without many of the carnival games and working-class visitors of that more northerly town. These days, there's not much to do on Manhattan Beach's **pier**, save for visiting the aptly named **Roundhouse**. The **aquarium** (Mon–Fri 3pm–dusk, Sat & Sun 10am–dusk; $2) inside is a mildly interesting spot where you can peer at sharks and lobsters, and fiddle around with the helpless creatures in a tide-pool "touch tank."

The **beach** itself is the main reason to visit, with generally cleaner water than at Santa Monica and Venice beaches (except around the piers); **surfing** is a major local pastime – a two-week international surf festival occurs each August – along with beach volleyball. To play, just rent a ball at one of the many rental shacks found along the beach. The mildly diverting **Historical Center**, a mile from the beach in the post office at 1601 Manhattan Beach Blvd (Sat & Sun noon–3pm; donation; ⊛history90266.org), exhibits locally crafted pottery from the early part of the twentieth century and an illuminating collection of photos, tracing the city's history, from when it was known as Shore Acres right up to the present. Nearby, the **Manhattan Beach Art Center**, 1560 Manhattan Beach Blvd (Tues & Sat 1–5pm, Wed 2–8pm, Thurs 2–6pm; free), presents contemporary work from regional artisans. The art center lies across from **Polliwog Park**, which in the summer is one of the sites that hosts "**Shakespeare by the Sea**" (periodically Thurs–Sun 6, 7 & 8pm; free; ⊛www.shakespearebythesea.org), a series of local performances at South Bay parks, including this and Point Fermin in San Pedro, among others.

Hermosa Beach and Redondo Beach

To the south, the houses of **HERMOSA BEACH**, across Longfellow Avenue, are smaller and less showy than those of Manhattan Beach, but the town is in many ways more enjoyable, with a hint of a bohemian feel. It also has a lively beachside strip, which is most energetic near the foot of the **pier** on Twelfth

Street. Packed with restaurants and clubs (among them one of the South Bay's best-known nightspots, *The Lighthouse*; see p.314), the area has long been a major hangout for revelers of all stripes, and a good time to come is during the **Fiesta Hermosa** (@www.fiestahermosa.com), a three-day event held over Memorial Day that's good for music (including surf rock), tasty food, and displays of regional arts and crafts. Apart from ocean-based activities, the town boasts a lush **green belt** – a long, grassy median running between Valley Drive and Ardmore Avenue, which connects to Manhattan Beach and makes a good place for a workout on any of several bike and jogging paths.

Further south, despite its familiar name and fine views of Palos Verdes' stunning greenery, **REDONDO BEACH**, across Herondo Street, is less inviting than its relaxed neighbor, with hardly any noteworthy sights. Condos and hotels line the beachfront, and the yacht-lined King's Harbor is off limits to curious visitors.

The Palos Verdes Peninsula

South of the beach cities, the **PALOS VERDES PENINSULA**, a great green hump marking LA's southwest corner, is known for its rugged beaches and secluded coves, sweeping views of the coastline, and some of the most expensive real estate in Southern California. Originally intended as a "millionaires' colony" by 1920s developers, Palos Verdes has more or less worked out according to plan, with several gated communities like **Rolling Hills**, numerous multimillion-dollar estates, and an armada of private security guards. Despite this, the Palos Verdes Peninsula is one of the best spots for experiencing nature in the area (especially along Palos Verdes Drive), with sea cliffs and tide pools, and its oceanside scenery is nothing less than awe-inspiring.

North Palos Verdes

The north section of the peninsula is largely ungated and accessible, with most attractions located near the coast of **PALOS VERDES ESTATES**, the first city founded on the peninsula, in 1939, and the one with by far the most significant architecture and public greenspace. The area was first laid out by **John Olmsted** and **Frederick Law Olmsted Jr** – sons of the famed designer of New York's Central Park – who came here in the early twentieth century to design upscale neighborhoods and advise on the future direction of urban planning in LA (suggestions that were ahead of their time and were, predictably, ignored). Palos Verdes Estates amounts to a small-scaled version of what

---

Hiking tours of Palos Verdes

The Palos Verdes Peninsula Land Conservancy offers periodic monthly **hiking tours** of some of the most invigorating spots on Palos Verdes, from Abalone Cove to San Pedro's Sunken City, including marshes, canyons, cliffs, and other dramatic vistas. The treks typically take place the second Saturday of the month, are free, and last two to three hours, sometimes in rather rugged environs, and focus on the ecological, historical, or cultural value of a given area – information you're not likely to discover very easily otherwise (information at ☎310/541-7613, @www.pvplc.com).

might have been had the Olmsted brothers had their way. Nearly one-third of its space is preserved as parkland (on which you may come across a roaming herd of peacocks), while the town itself has a pseudo-European air, threaded by circuitous streets that overlook the ocean, its commercial development tightly controlled. Indeed, the town's early overseers were so committed to the period-revival aesthetic that all new designs, housing or otherwise, had to be reviewed and approved by an officially sanctioned "**art jury**" – surely the only time this has ever happened in LA.

The best place to soak in this "Old World" atmosphere is at **Malaga Cove Plaza**, Palos Verdes Drive at Via Corta, a Spanish Revival–flavored commercial and civic center with a central plaza and arcaded buildings, which the Olmsteds planned as a prototype for four other such areas in the city, none of which was ever built. The main draw here is the **Neptune Fountain**, a smaller replica of a 1563 structure in Bologna, Italy, of the same name, featuring a bronze sculpture and mock-late-Renaissance design. Elsewhere, much of the city's seaside architecture has a strong Mediterranean flair, good examples of which are the **Olmsted House**, Paseo del Mar at Via Arroyo, an elegant Spanish Colonial estate with a walled garden that was built for Frederick Law Olmsted Jr, and the **Haggerty House**, 415 Paseo del Mar, an Italian-style villa that was built by the Olmsteds themselves, since reincarnated as the Neighborhood Church.

South Coast Botanic Garden

Inland on the north peninsula, there are few compelling sights save the **South Coast Botanic Garden**, 26300 Crenshaw Blvd (daily 9am–5pm; $7; ⓦwww.palosverdes.com/botanicgardens), a relaxing spot that was first home to a diatomite mine for 37 years and then to a giant landfill. In the 1950s and 1960s, LA dumped 3.5 million tons of its trash here, creating one of the bigger eyesores in the region, but since 1961, the turf has been covered by layers of soil and successfully reclaimed as a garden, filled with exotic bromeliads, an expansive cactus garden, various palm trees, ferns, and flowering plants, and even a small French-style garden. The only sign of its former life is the terrain itself, which, thanks to the subsiding of the garbage below, has a weirdly undulating landscape, peppered here and there with "exhaust" pipes that allow for the release of carbon dioxide and methane from the chemical stew underground.

South Palos Verdes

South of Palos Verdes Estates along Palos Verdes Drive, the beaches are more easily visited, and worthwhile for their significant natural attractions, one of which is the promontory of **Point Vicente**, sitting on high cliff walls above the Pacific Ocean. An **interpretive center** (Mon–Fri 10am–1pm, Sat & Sun 10am–5pm; donation) here provides displays on the native and Spanish history of the region, the area's biology and geology, and especially the presence of **whales** – which you might see from the point during their seasonal migrations (heaviest Dec–Jan and March–April), when they occasionally get close enough to photograph. Nearby, a **lighthouse**, 31550 Palos Verdes Drive (second Sat of month 10am–3pm; free; ⓦwww.palosverdes.com/pvlight), dates from 1926 and towers nearly two hundred feet above sea level in a dramatic cliffside setting.

A bit further south, at Long Point, the abandoned **Marineland** theme park, 6610 Palos Verdes Drive South, used to be one of the prime draws to this part of the city, and even predates Disneyland. Like the northern piers, however, it's now just a part of LA's amusement-park history, and you can dimly see the old concrete sign, marine tanks, and crumbling buildings from the park's still-accessible parking lot (Mon–Fri 8.30am–4pm). More importantly for undersea explorers, Long Point offers some of LA's best **diving**, which you can get to from the park's lower gate near the parking lot. A golf course and resort are planned for the site, though this development has been in the works for a decade already and frequently been delayed.

Continuing south on Palos Verdes Drive, **Abalone Cove**, reached from a parking lot on Barkentine Road via a quarter-mile walk, boasts a cobblestoned beach, rock and tide pools, and, offshore, kelp beds alive with sea urchins, rock scallops, and the increasingly rare abalone.

The Wayfarer's Chapel and around

While you're in the area, don't miss one of the peninsula's signature sights, **Wayfarer's Chapel**, 5755 Palos Verdes Drive, a masterpiece of pitched glass and wood that was designed by Frank Lloyd Wright's son, Lloyd. A tribute to the eighteenth-century Swedish scientist and mystic Emanuel Swedenborg, and funded by the Swedenborgian Church, the ultimate aim is for the redwood grove around the chapel to grow and entangle itself in the glass-framed structure – a symbolic fusing of human handiwork with the forces of nature. Unsurprisingly, the place is one of LA's top choices for weddings. A recently built **visitor center** (daily 10am–5pm; free; ⑩www.wayfarerschapel.org) lays out the history and architecture of the site, and can send you on your way with a self-guided walk through the dramatic site. A half-mile south, the coast at **Portuguese Bend** provides another striking ocean vista (though it's also prone to landslides), and was once the place where Portuguese whalers hunted gray whales for their blubber, which was harvested for its oil. Their trade came to an end due to a lack of firewood to run their operation, and the only trace of their activity is the place name they inspired.

△ Inside the Wayfarer's Chapel

San Pedro

Forming part of the site of the LA Harbor, scruffy **SAN PEDRO**, at the south-eastern edge of the Palos Verdes Peninsula, is a diverse blue-collar town settled by immigrants from Portugal, Greece, and Yugoslavia. As one of several places along the West Coast where labor strife erupted during the Depression, the city has a long tradition of populism and a nagging antipathy toward the city of Los Angeles, which annexed it in 1909, despite local opposition. That distaste remains, though a recent drive for secession failed. For better or worse, everything about San Pedro, from its low-rise, old-time buildings to its maritime atmosphere, gives it little in common with any place else in the metropolis.

Downtown San Pedro

San Pedro's harbor abuts the city's **downtown** and forms part of the massive Port of Los Angeles – the biggest in the world outside of China. The focus of all shipping activity is an industrial zone known as **Terminal Island**, a man-made island across the harbor's main channel that offers nothing but bleak industrial vistas of endless stacks of shipping containers. While you'll have to keep your

The Port of San Pedro

First called the "**Bay of Smokes**" for the many fires set by Tongva natives along its shoreline, this formerly Spanish-controlled city was named in 1603 after **St Peter** and consolidated in 1784 into the territory owned by **Juan Domínguez**, whose ranch house is still standing in Compton. Later, around the time it was usurped by the US in the Mexican–American War, San Pedro became a major center for the maritime trade of animal skins and beef tallow, and, by taking advantage of the Wilmington-to-Downtown LA **rail lines** of entrepreneur **Phineas Banning**, later became linked to cities throughout the region in the 1870s. A decade later, the city was incorporated and began maturing as a port, with the action centered on **Timms Landing**. Although little physical evidence remains, you can get a sense of the place during this period by reading Richard Henry Dana's classic maritime book *Two Years Before the Mast*.

Around this time, **Collis Huntington** of the Southern Pacific Railroad was threatening to develop Santa Monica as the chief harbor of the region, clashing with many LA bigwigs as he did so, especially Harrison Gray Otis of the *Los Angeles Times*, whose newspaper did much to excite passions for a "free" harbor. In the end, Huntington's battle was unsuccessful, and by the end of the century, construction on a massive two-mile breakwater had begun in San Pedro and was completed a decade later. Shortly thereafter, Los Angeles mounted its annexation drive and the military base **Fort MacArthur** was built next to the harbor. The world wars and a booming maritime economy further helped San Pedro to attract shipbuilding industries and commercial canneries, and by the 1950s, despite occasional labor conflicts, the district hit its peak.

The industrialization of the harbor took its toll on the environment, however, resulting on one occasion in smog so thick that the airport had to be shut down. Even worse, for many decades corporations pumped **DDT** directly into the sea near Palos Verdes, and today the contaminant sits in a giant deadly "bubble" offshore. Along with this, economic **recessions** and industrial retrenchment contributed to San Pedro's decline, and by the 1980s the city was decayed, full of boarded-up businesses and postindustrial eyesores. In the last decade, though, redevelopment money, some ecological clean-up, and the opening of new museums have helped revitalize the city, though it's still well off the itinerary of most casual visitors.

distance from the docks and machinery, there are some points along the channel worth investigating.

Although it's heavily promoted, don't bother with downtown's overrated **Ports o' Call Village** – a dismal batch of wooden and corrugated-iron huts supposedly capturing the flavor of seaports around the world by way of its T-shirt and junk-food vendors.

Exploring downtown

To get a better sense of the harbor's history, a good place to start is the **SS Lane Victory**, in Berth 94, off Swinford Street, across from the shipyard (daily 9am–4pm; $3; @www.lanevictory.org). The huge, ten-thousand-ton cargo ship was built in the shipyard in 1945 for World War II, also operated in Korea and Vietnam, and today is maintained by the Merchant Marine. Tours lead through its many cramped spaces, including the engine and radio rooms, crew quarters, galley, and bridge. If you're after a ride, the ship offers all-day summertime **cruises** to Santa Catalina Island (one weekend per month July–Sept; $100, kids $60; ☎310/519-9545), involving onboard meals, historical re-enactments with captured stowaway spies, and dogfights with old-fashioned biplanes and Japanese and American air squadrons. Overhead is the towering **Vincent Thomas Bridge**, California's third-longest suspension bridge, completed in 1963 to take over the work of transporting sailors and fishermen to and from Terminal Island.

There's more nautical history at the **Maritime Museum**, further south at Sampson Way at Sixth Street (Tues–Sat 10am–5pm, Sun noon–5pm; $3; @www.lamaritimemuseum.org). Occupying the old ferry tower, the museum is a storehouse for artifacts from the glory days of San Pedro's fishing industries, focusing on everything from old-fashioned clipper-ship voyages to contemporary diving expeditions. Besides plenty of model ships, the museum has interesting exhibits on Native American seacraft, navigation devices, and artful scrimshaw from the whaling era. Behind the museum, full-sized boats are displayed, including an old-fashioned schooner and a racing yacht. Next door, at Berth 86, the museum houses **Fireboat 2** in its own large, red building. Nearly one hundred feet long, this restored 1925 floating fire station has served the LA Fire Department for decades, spraying over ten thousand gallons a minute to put out naval fires around the harbor. West of here, the austere **Bloody Thursday Monument**, Sixth Street at Beacon Street, is another reminder of the city's gritty past. Marking the 1934 strike by local waterfront workers, many of them new immigrants, it commemorates the two who were killed when police and guards opened fire.

Four blocks west of the Maritime Museum, old downtown San Pedro has been refurbished in recent years, thanks in part to the restoration of the opulent **Warner Grand Theater**, 478 W Sixth St (☎310/548-7672, @www.warnergrand.org), a terrific 1931 Zigzag Moderne moviehouse and performing-arts center with dark geometric details, grand columns, and sunburst motifs, a style that almost looks pre-Columbian. Also part of the clean-up effort is the **San Pedro Trolley** (Fri–Mon 10am–6pm; $1), a collection of three classic 1908 Pacific Electric Red Cars (two replicas, one restored) linking most of the city's major attractions, paralleling Harbor Boulevard and connecting the SS *Lane Victory* with the Cabrillo Marina at 22nd Street.

The Fort MacArthur Military Museum

To the south, the **Fort MacArthur Military Museum** (Tues, Thurs, Sat & Sun noon–5pm; free; @www.ftmac.org) is sited on the former Battery Osgood,

THE SOUTH BAY AND LA HARBOR

Downtown San Pedro

a gun emplacement at the original **Fort MacArthur**, a military post built in the late nineteenth century and named after General Arthur MacArthur – Douglas's dad. During the Cold War, the fort became a launch site for the early Nike-Ajax and later nuclear-warhead-equipped Hercules missiles, one of sixteen such sites in LA (the only other one now open to the public can be found in the Santa Monica Mountains; see "San Vicente Mountain Park," p.225). Reflecting its history, the fort's museum displays a clutch of military outfits and old photographs, as well as assorted disarmed bombs, mines, and missiles.

Point Fermin

At the tip of San Pedro, about a mile south of the trolley terminus, is **Point Fermin**, a cape that, at the end of the eighteenth century, explorer George Vancouver named for an early Franciscan missionary, Padre Fermín Lasuén. On the cape's far end, across Paseo del Mar, **Point Fermin Park** is a verdant strip of land sitting atop ocean bluffs that mark LA's southernmost point. Hidden on the seaward edge of the bluffs, blocked off by chain-link fences, sits what's left of an early twentieth-century resort known as **Sunken City**, where the crumbling streets and housing foundations are officially off-limits to the public. If you'd like to visit without trespassing, the Palos Verdes Peninsula Land Conservancy offers periodic **tours** of this and other interesting spots on the peninsula (see box, p.179).

Inland, **Point Fermin Lighthouse**, 807 Paseo del Mar (Tues–Sun 1–4pm, tours on the hour 1–3pm; donation; ⊛www.pointferminlighthouse.org), once contained a 6600-candlepower light and beamed it 22 miles out to sea. Ending its service during World War II, the lighthouse fell into disrepair until it was renovated in the 1970s; in 2004, it was spruced up again and reopened to the public. Now you can get a sense of its quaint old Victorian style and take a peek from the chamber where the light used to beam; there's also an outdoor whale-watching station where you can read up on the winter migrations. Bottle-nosed dolphins can often be seen during their fall departure and spring return as well.

Just north is **Angel's Gate Park**, at 3601 Gaffey St, on a windswept hill overlooking the Pacific. At the top of the hill, a central pagoda contains the **Korean Bell of Friendship**, a 17-ton copper-and-tin gift to the city from South Korea. Inscribed with Korean characters and twelve lines representing the signs of the zodiac, the bell has no clapper; instead, a hefty log strikes the instrument only on three key days of the year: Korean and American independence days, and New Year's Eve.

The Cabrillo Marine Aquarium and around

Below the bluffs, a beachside path winds around the cape and reaches the excellent **Cabrillo Marine Aquarium**, 3720 Stephen White Drive (Tues–Fri noon–5pm, Sat & Sun 10am–5pm; $5, parking $7; ⊛www.cabrilloaq.org), where a diverse collection of marine life has been imaginatively assembled into tanks and assorted displays: everything from predator snails and sea urchins to larger displays on otters, seals, and whales, plus the rare "sarcastic fringehead" (a peculiar fish whose name makes sense once you see it). Fully visible from the aquarium, a short jetty extends to a 1913 **breakwater** that is over 9000 feet long and marks the harbor entrance. At the end of the breakwater sits the **Angel's Gate Lighthouse**, a 75-foot-tall Romanesque-styled monolith that blasts its automated foghorn twice per minute, using a rotating green light to direct ships into the protected harbor and helping them avoid the breakwater's three-million-ton rock seawall.

Wilmington

North of San Pedro, **WILMINGTON** is the center of LA's petroleum industry, and holds the third-largest oil field in the entire US, extending from the Palos Verdes Peninsula to the bay outside Long Beach. The city's stark industrial landscape, dotted with derricks and refineries, massive towers spurting jets of flame and cargo trucks barreling down the bleak Terminal Island Expressway, was used to great effect as the dystopic backdrop for the *Terminator* movies.

It's startling that such a grim setting could be the home of several key structures from LA history. The first, the grand **Banning House**, 401 E Main St (guided tours hourly Tues–Thurs 12.30–2.30pm; Sat & Sun 12.30–3.30pm; $3; ⓦwww.banningmuseum.org), is an 1864 Greek-Revival estate that was the residence of mid-nineteenth-century entrepreneur **Phineas Banning**, who made his fortune when the value of his land increased astronomically as the harbor was developed. Through his promotion of the rail link between Wilmington and Downtown LA, he also became known as "the father of Los Angeles transportation" (at a time when the local transit system was one of the best in the world), and helped push for the creation of a breakwater and lighthouse as well. However, in his final years, he argued against extending the rail line to San Pedro, which ultimately led to his own city's gradual decline, which was reversed only in the 1930s with the discovery of oil. The 23-room house remains an engaging spot to visit, full of opulent Victorian touches (chandeliers, elegant place settings, and the like) and several restored carriages and stagecoaches kept in an outside barn.

Several blocks south is the **Drum Barracks Civil War Museum**, 1052 Banning Blvd (hourly tours Tues–Thurs 10am–1pm, Sat & Sun 11.30am –2.30pm; $3; ⓦwww.drumbarracks.org), originally part of a military base called Camp Drum and named for its commander, Richard Drum. Today, the only building remaining is the rickety barracks, housing a hodgepodge of nineteenth-century military antiques and artifacts, notably a 34-star US flag and an early version of a machine gun. In the 1860s, this base was the Southwest headquarters for the US Army, which processed volunteers here before sending them to fight in the battles in the East, and a staging point for attacks on nearby Confederate troops in neighboring Arizona and New Mexico. In later decades it became a base for federal soldiers fighting the native tribes of the Southwest.

Long Beach

Along with San Pedro, **LONG BEACH** is the home of the LA Harbor – or, as it likes to call itself, **Worldport LA** – and a sizable Southern California city in itself, with many acres of tract homes and flat, sprawling development. Not surprisingly, almost all of its interesting sights are grouped near the water, away from the port to the west, as are the tourist-oriented attractions around **Shoreline Drive** and the historic architecture of **downtown**.

Once the stomping ground of off-duty naval personnel, Long Beach's porn shops and sleazy bars lasted until the 1980s, when a billion-dollar cash infusion led to glossy office buildings and hotels, as well as a convention center, shopping mall, and the restoration of some of the best c.1900 buildings on the

DOWNTOWN LONG BEACH

Key locations shown on map: Rowan Building, Masonic Temple, First National Bank Building, Blue Line Light Rail Terminus, World Trade Center, Breakers Hotel (Site), Villa Riviera, Tichenor House, Catalina Cruise Center, Long Beach Convention Center, Marina Green Park, Shoreline Lagoon, Shoreline Village, Queensway Bridge, Aquarium of the Pacific, Tallship American Pride, Downtown Long Beach Marina, Island Grissom (Oil drilling island), Catalina Express, Scorpion submarine, Queen Mary.

Terminal Island, San Pedro
Belmont Shore, Naples
Queensway Bay
Santa Catalina Island

EATING & DRINKING

Alegria Cocina Latina	6
Blue Café	4
Cha Cha Cha	1
Club Samba	2
King's Fish House	5
L'Opera	7
Taco Beach	3

ACCOMMODATION

Hilton Long Beach	B
Long Beach Travelodge	A
Rodeway Inn	D
Westin Long Beach	C

0   800 yds

coast. Inland from downtown, however, it's a different story – bleak housing projects on the edge of impoverished South Central LA – and the only real point of interest is **Rancho Los Cerritos**, 4600 Virginia Rd, northeast of the junction of the 405 and 710 freeways (Tues–Sat 1–5pm, tours Sat on the hour; free; ⊛www.rancholoscerritos.org), the center of what was once a 27,000-acre Spanish land grant. This U-shaped adobe sits on five leafy acres with a number of cypress and black locust trees, a delightful garden of roses, herbs, and exotic plants, and an antiquated water tower. The restored orchard features the kind of citrus fruits, avocados, macadamia nuts, and cherimoyas that once flourished here. Fortunately, the site is easily accessible, via the 710, to Long Beach's more prominent attractions near the harbor.

Shoreline Drive and around

Since the early 1900s, Long Beach has sold itself as a splashy resort and, while it's difficult to imagine any romantic getaway nestled behind an industrial port basin, the city keeps trying. Its major seaside amusements now sit close to the curving strip of **Shoreline Drive**, an area that was more of an entertainment center a century ago than it is today.

Around 1910, Long Beach developed its municipal pier, known as "**The Pike**," teeming with street vendors and throngs of tourists queuing up for such thrilling rides as the Cyclone Racer and Salt Water Plunge. The highlight was the legendary artwork of the **Looff Carousel**, designed in 1911 by master builder Charles Looff. After the carousel burned in 1943, the pier began its decline, and today it's long gone; these days, the focus of attention is **Shoreline Village**, just south of Shoreline Drive, a ragtag collection of middling shops and restaurants. The only real draw is the **Tallship American Pride**, a 130ft cutter which is a simulation of an 1848 vessel, offering tourists the chance for three-hour whale-watching outings (Sat 10am–1pm & 1.30–4.30pm; $30) or brunch and dinner cruises around the harbor (Sat 6–9pm, $49; Sun 10am–1pm, $42); all trips are by reservation at ☎714/970-8800, ⊛www.americanpride.org.

North of Shoreline Village, along Ocean Boulevard, a row dominated by upscale corporate hotels has become the most visible symbol of Long Beach's renovation. Among them stands the appealing 1926 **Breakers Hotel**, 200 E Ocean Blvd, twelve sandstone-clad stories of Spanish Baroque Revival design topped by a green copper roof. Although the hotel itself now serves as senior housing, the top-floor *Sky Room* bar and restaurant (☎562/983-2703) is still a good spot for a drink in 1930s Art Deco surroundings. Two blocks south, Seaside Way connects with Shoreline Drive to create the circuit for the **Long Beach Grand Prix** (tickets at ☎1-888/82-SPEED, ⊛www.longbeachgp.com), an Indy car race that attracts several hundred thousand spectators in mid-April for a three-day event.

Around a lagoon south of Shoreline Drive, the intriguing, if pricey, **Aquarium of the Pacific** (daily 9am–6pm; $19, kids $11; ⊛www.aquariumofpacific.org) exhibits the aquatic flora and fauna of three distinct regions, namely the local Southern Pacific, Northern Pacific, and tropical zones. There are more than ten thousand species here, from the familiar sea lions and otters, tide-pool creatures and assorted ocean flora, to the more exotic leopard sharks and giant Japanese spider crabs. Between November and March, more than fifteen thousand whales cruise the "**Whale Freeway**" past Long Beach on their annual migration to and from winter breeding and berthing grounds in Baja California. Of several tour operators in the area, Spirit Cruises, 429 Shoreline Village Drive (☎562/548-8080, ⊛www.spiritmarine.com), and Harbor Breeze, Dock 2, Rainbow Harbor (☎562/432-4900, ⊛www.longbeachcruises.com), operate good two- to three-hour whale-watching trips for $15–20.

Along Ocean Boulevard, the four pastel "**islands**" visible offshore are not resort colonies, but rather oil-drilling platforms painted in soothing colors – Long Beach's attempt to beautify its harbor, which has over four hundred oil and gas wells operating at any one time.

The Queen Mary and Scorpion submarine

Long Beach's most famous attraction is the mighty ocean liner **Queen Mary**, moored on Pier H at the end of Queens Highway South (daily 10am–6pm; $28 guided tours, kids $17; ⊛www.queenmary.com), acquired by the city in 1964 with the sole aim of boosting tourism, which it has succeeded in doing, well beyond expectations. The ship lies across the bay, opposite Shoreline Village, and is accessible either by a lengthy walk or the free Long Beach Transit **shuttle** from downtown (information at ☎562/591-2301, ⊛www.lbtransit.org). Now a luxury hotel, the ship's exhibits suggest that all who sailed on the vessel – the flagship of the Cunard Line from the 1930s until the 1960s – enjoyed the extravagantly furnished lounges and luxurious cabins, all carefully restored

△ The Scropion submarine

and kept sparkling. But a glance at the spartan third-class cabins reveals the real story: the tough conditions experienced by the impoverished migrants who left Europe hoping to start a new life in the USA. The red British telephone kiosks around the decks and the hammy displays in the engine room and wheelhouse – closer to *Star Trek* than anything nautical – don't help, but it's nonetheless a marvelous ship. Apart from the wealth of gorgeous Art Deco details (glasswork, geometric decor, and streamlining), there are also stores and restaurants, and even a wedding chapel.

The latest addition to the *Queen Mary* site, the **Scorpion submarine** (same hours and admission as *Queen Mary*, otherwise $10), was used in the service of the Soviet, and then Russian, navy until 1994, carrying a payload of 22 nuclear weapons and powered by diesel engines – a rather creaky means of locomotion for a craft built in 1972. It's worth a look for its antiquated technology and cramped crew quarters, and makes for an especially bracing experience after taking a sanitized tour of the *Queen Mary*.

Downtown Long Beach

Running from Magnolia Avenue to Alamitos Boulevard and Ocean Boulevard to Tenth Street, **downtown Long Beach** offers a wide array of boutiques, antique dealers, and bookstores, many of them around a three-block strip known as **The Promenade**, lined with touristy restaurants that can get quite busy on weekend nights. Two blocks west of the Promenade, at the terminus of the Blue Line light rail to Downtown LA, **Pine Avenue** has some of the city's best-preserved architecture – historic-revival buildings that have since been reborn as hotels, artists' lofts, galleries, and nightclubs. For a closer look at Long Beach's historic and architectural gems, the preservation society Long Beach Heritage runs a bimonthly **tour** that begins at 315 W Third St, just a few blocks to the west (first & third Sat of month 10am–12.30pm; $5; reserve at ☏562/493-7019, ⊛www.lbheritage.org). Highlights include the **First National Bank Building**, 115 Pine Ave, a 1900 Beaux Arts structure with a resplendent clock tower; the 1903 **Masonic Temple**, no. 230, a triple-gabled building with a brilliant sun mural inside on its second story; and, best of all, the **Rowan Building**, no. 201, a vibrant 1931 Art Deco creation with detailed terracotta decor.

Further east is the striking **Villa Riviera**, 800 E Ocean Blvd, a fourteen-story Gothic Revival apartment block, recognizable by the high dormers on its pitched copper roof, pointed octagonal turret, and narrow ground-level archways. Curved to accommodate the bend in Ocean Boulevard, the Villa was the second-tallest building in all of LA when built in 1929. Just down the block, the 1905 **Tichenor House**, 852 E Ocean Blvd, a private, U-shaped Craftsman-style residence with Japanese touches and an imposing setting, was designed by the firm of Greene & Greene (see Pasadena's Gamble House, p.201) for an early Long Beach civic leader. Several blocks north, the **Museum of Latin American Art**, 628 Alamitos Ave (Tues–Fri 11.30am–7pm, Sat 11am–7pm, Sun 11am–6pm; $5; ⊛www.molaa.com), is devoted to the broad subject of Hispanic art. Showcasing artists from Mexico to South America, the absorbing collection includes big names like Diego Rivera and José Orozco, as well as lesser-known newcomers working in styles that range from social criticism to magical realism. Four blocks west, **St Anthony Roman Catholic Church**, 600 Olive Ave (☏562/590-9229), is one of LA's most colorful churches, an appealing mishmash of historic styles constructed in 1933 and remodeled two decades later. Note the eye-catching neo-Gothic stained glass and hexagonal turrets, along with the facade's sizable Byzantine golden mosaic, depicting the Virgin Mary amid flocks of angels.

East Long Beach

A mile east from the Villa Riviera, the **Long Beach Museum of Art**, 2300 E Ocean Blvd (Tues–Sun 11am–5pm, Thurs closes 8pm; $5; ⊛www .lbma.org), is housed in a stately 1912 Craftsman home, fringed by an abstract

sculpture garden and featuring a modest collection of early modernism, folk art, and Southern Californian art. The museum is notable for its horde of video art – one of the country's biggest collections – much of which is on display in the **video annex**, where you can stare at the thin white lines broadcast on Nam June Paik's television sets, or ponder the meaning of Bill Viola's enigmatic projections. Another mile further, the affluent **Belmont Shore** district is full of designer shops and yuppified cafés, though there's really not much to see.

From here, Second Street crosses man-made Alamitos Bay to reach the island community of **Naples**, supposedly designed after the Italian city, if that city was loaded with rows of T-shirt and trinket vendors. While the thin, circular **canal** may give you a romantic thrill during hour-long boat rides with picnic meals and serenading gondoliers (11am–11pm; $65 for two people; call Gondola Getaway for details ☎562/433-9595, ⊛www.gondolagetawayinc.com), the place is still little more than a tacky aquatic suburb thronged with tourists.

Two miles north, **Rancho Los Alamitos**, 6400 Bixby Hill Rd (Wed–Sun 1–5pm, tours every half-hour; free), is a grand version of the typical nineteenth-century adobe, with six historic buildings and plenty of antiques and relics from the Spanish and Mexican eras. Built in 1806, the renovated ranch house is noteworthy for its four acres of gardens, where you can wander amid herbs, roses, cacti, jacaranda, and oleander planted along the terraces and landscaped walks. Nearby, the campus of California State University at Long Beach is best known for its towering pyramid-shaped athletic complex, but is mainly worth visiting for the **Earl Burns Miller Japanese Garden**, 1250 Bellflower Blvd (Tues–Fri 8am–3.30pm, Sun noon–4pm; free; ☎562/985-8885, ⊛www.csulb.edu/~jgarden), providing a peaceful spot amid weeping willows, bamboo, and Japanese maples.

Santa Catalina Island

Though overlooked by many visitors, **SANTA CATALINA ISLAND** is an inviting mix of uncluttered beaches and wild hills twenty miles off the coast. Claimed by the Portuguese in 1542 as San Salvador, and renamed by the Spanish in 1602, it has stayed firmly outside the historical mainstream. Since 1811, when the indigenous Tongva Indians were forced to resettle on the mainland, the island has been in private ownership, and has over the years grown to be something of a resort – a process hastened by businessman **William Wrigley Jr** (part of the chewing-gum dynasty), who financed the Art Deco–styled **Avalon Casino**, the island's major landmark, in the 1920s, and used the island as a spring-training site for his baseball team, the Chicago Cubs, until the early 1950s.

Since 1975 the island has been almost entirely owned by the **Catalina Island Conservancy**, which maintains a sizable nature preserve here, and in more recent years Catalina has become a popular destination for boaters and nature lovers, and its small marina swells with luxury yachts and cruise ships in summer. Even so, the elegant hotels are unobtrusive among the whimsical architecture, and cars are rare – there's a ten-year waiting list to ferry one over. Consequently, most of the three thousand islanders walk, ride bikes, or drive electrically powered golf carts.

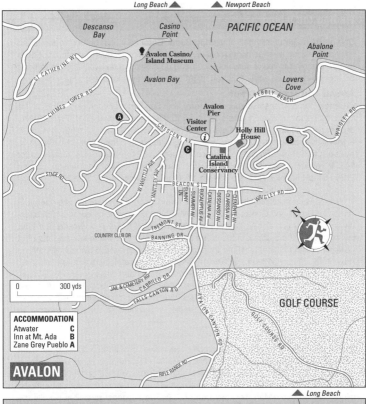

AVALON

Long Beach ▲   ▲ Newport Beach

PACIFIC OCEAN

Descanso
Bay

Casino
Point

Abalone
Point

ST CATHERINE WY

Avalon Casino/
Island Museum

Avalon Bay

Lovers
Cove

PEBBLY BEACH

CHIMES TOWER RD

WRIGLEY RD

A

CRESCENT AV

Avalon
Pier

Visitor
Center
ⓘ

Holly Hill
House

B

STAGE RD

C

Catalina
Island
Conservancy

W WHITLEY AVE

E WHITLEY AVE

BEACON ST

SUNNY
INN

SUMMER AV

EUCALYPTUS AV

CATALINA AV

DESCANSO AV

CLARISSA AV

CLEMENTE AV

WRIGLEY RD

COUNTRY CLUB DR

TREMONT ST

BANNING DR

JAIL & CEMETERY RD

CABRILLO DR

FALLS CANYON RD

AVALON CANYON RD

GOLF COURSE RD

GOLF COURSE

0   300 yds

ACCOMMODATION
Atwater   C
Inn at Mt. Ada   B
Zane Grey Pueblo   A

RIFLE RANGE RD

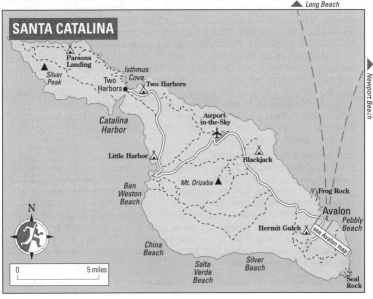

SANTA CATALINA

Long Beach ▲

Newport Beach ▶

Parsons
Landing

Silver
Peak

Isthmus
Cove

Two
Harbors

Two Harbors

Catalina
Harbor

Airport-
in-the-Sky

Little Harbor

Blackjack

Ben
Weston
Beach

Mt. Orizaba ▲

Frog Rock

Avalon

Pebbly
Beach

Hermit Gulch

see Avalon map

China
Beach

Salta
Verde
Beach

Silver
Beach

N

0   5 miles

Seal
Rock

Visiting the island

One of the major challenges of **visiting Santa Catalina** is just getting to the island itself and making arrangements for your stay. It's not difficult by any means, but does require planning to make sure you don't end up staying in an overpriced resort and paying top-dollar for a tour that you might otherwise take for cheap.

Arrival and transportation

Depending on the season, a round-trip **ferry** from San Pedro or Long Beach to Catalina Island's one town, **Avalon**, costs around $40. Catalina Explorer (☎1-877/432-6276, Ⓦwww.catalinaferry.com) and Catalina Express (☎310/519-1212 or 1-800/315-3967, Ⓦwww.catalinaexpress.com) run several services daily. From Newport Beach to Avalon, the Catalina Passenger Service (☎949/673-5245) runs a daily round-trip for $44. If you get seasick or feel extravagant, **helicopter** services to Avalon, costing $136 round-trip (plus tax), are offered by Island Express (☎310/510-2525, Ⓦwww.islandexpress.com) from Long Beach and San Pedro.

If you're interested in taking a **tour** of the island, one of the more reliable operators is the Catalina Island Company (☎1-800/446-0266, Ⓦwww.scico.com), which offers tours of the Avalon Casino or downtown area (each $13.50) and two- to four-hour jaunts through the outback of the island ($29–79) – the only way to see the interior of Catalina without hiking. Cheaper tours of the same terrain are provided by Catalina Adventure Tours ($13–35; ☎310/510-2888, Ⓦwww.catalinaadventuretours.com), which also offers combination trips with harbor cruises and glass-bottom-boat rides. **Golf carts**, for which you need a driver's license, and **bikes** (both banned from the rough roads outside Avalon) can be rented from stands throughout the island. Bikes run $20–35 per day, depending on the model, while golf carts are much steeper, at $35–40 per hour only.

Accommodation and eating

The cost of **accommodation** in Avalon hovers upwards of $100, and most beds are booked up throughout the summer and at weekends. The most interesting **hotel** is the *Zane Grey Pueblo*, 199 Chimes Tower Rd (☎310/510-0966 or 1-800/446-0271; $135), which has sixteen rooms overlooking the bay or mountains, with an enticing winter-season (Nov–Mar) weekday rate of $59. The cheapest overall is usually the *Atwater*, 125 Sumner Ave (☎310/510-2500 or 1-800/626-1496; $75), though there are also units here that reach $370. If you really have a bundle to spend, the *Inn on Mt. Ada*, 398 Wrigley Rd (☎310/510-2030, Ⓦwww.catalina.com/mtada; $340), is the final word in hilltop hotel luxury. The only true budget option is **camping** ($12 per person, kids $6). *Hermit Gulch* (☎310/510-8368) is the closest site to Avalon and thus the busiest. Four other sites – *Blackjack*, *Little Harbor*, *Parsons Landing*, and *Two Harbors* – in Catalina's interior (all bookable at ☎310/510-8368, Ⓦwww.scico.com/camping) are usually roomier; see p. 262 for more information.

For **eating**, *Catalina Cantina*, 313 Crescent Ave (☎310/510-0100), is among the best, offering tasty and affordable Mexican staples washed down with margaritas, with live music on weekends.

Sports and outdoor activities

The waters around Catalina are rich in yellowtail, calico bass, barracuda, and sharks. Catalina Island Sportfishing, 114 Claressa St (☎310/510-2420), runs **fishing trips** for around $100–120 an hour (though you can fish for free from the pier). EZ Ocean Charters (☎310/306-3006, Ⓦwww.e-zoceancharters.com) has a sliding scale ($70–120 per hour), depending on the number in your party, and also offers cheaper sightseeing trips ($30 per hour). **Snorkel** and **scuba** gear is available for rent at *Catalina Divers Supply*, on the pier and at the Casino (☎310/510-0330 or 1-800/353-0330, Ⓦwww.catalinadiverssupply.com), for $27 per day for a complete snorkel set, and $50 for the full scuba package.

Avalon and Two Harbors

The main city on the island, **AVALON**, can be fully explored on foot in an hour or two; pick up a map from the **Chamber of Commerce** at the foot of the ferry pier (☎310/510-1520, ⊛www.visitcatalina.org). The town itself offers the usual assortment of T-shirt vendors, restaurants, and boat operators, but the undeniable highlight is the resplendent **Avalon Casino**, on a promontory north of downtown at 1 Casino Way. Built as a dance hall and moviehouse, this 1920s structure still features an Art Deco ballroom and lavishly decorated auditorium: painted wild horses and unicorns roam through a forest on the side wall, while a sleek superhero rides a wave on the front screen and, above it all, a waif-like Botticelli Venus stands atop a seashell over the heads of two thunderbolt-clutching gods. Perhaps not surprisingly, the muralist for the theater, John Beckman, also helped design the equally fanciful Chinese Theatre in Hollywood, and you can still see Hollywood movies here on evenings throughout the year – an absolute must for any movie buffs who venture out this far. Much more subdued, a small **museum** (daily 10am–4pm, Jan–Mar closed Thurs; $2.50; ⊛www.catalina.com/museum.html) on the same premises displays Native American artifacts from Catalina's past, as well as tiles from local potters, and old photographs and biology exhibits on the surrounding area.

To the south, the **Zane Grey Pueblo Hotel**, 199 Chimes Tower Rd, is the former home of the Western author, who visited Catalina with a film crew to shoot *The Vanishing American* and liked the place so much that he stayed, building for himself this "Hopi pueblo" house, complete with beamed ceiling, stark white walls, and thick wooden front door. The hotel rooms (see box, opposite) are themed after his books, and the pool is shaped like an arrowhead. Similarly, the **Inn on Mt. Ada**, at 398 Wrigley Terrace Rd on the south hillside of Avalon, was the 1921 Colonial Revival home of William Wrigley and is now an elegant hotel (see box, opposite), with sweeping ocean views and a fine garden. Also striking is the **Holly Hill House**, 718 Crescent Ave (tours periodically offered; call ☎310/510-2414 for details), an 1890 Queen Anne cottage on a high bluff overlooking the bay, with an elegant conical tower and wraparound verandas.

Several miles southwest of Avalon, the **Wrigley Memorial and Botanical Garden**, 1400 Avalon Canyon Rd (daily 8am–5pm; $5), administered by the Catalina Island Conservancy, displays all manner of natural delights on forty acres, but is especially strong on native, endangered plants, such as indigenous varieties of manzanita, ironwood mahogany, and the wild tomato – a poisonous member of the nightshade family. Also fascinating is the Wrigley memorial, where a striking **cenotaph**, made from Georgia marble, blue flagstone, and red roof-tiles, honors the chewing-gum baron. A grand tiled staircase leads to an imposing Art Deco mausoleum, where Wrigley was to have been interred – though he's buried elsewhere.

Northwest of Avalon, the small, isolated resort town of **TWO HARBORS** sits on a small strip of land that connects Cherry Cove and Catalina Harbor. With a large marina and campground, the town is suitable enough for outdoor activities like kayaking, snorkeling, and scuba diving, but otherwise there's little to see.

The Santa Catalina interior

If you have the opportunity and a few days spare to explore it, venture into the rugged **Santa Catalina interior**, comprising 42,000 acres of largely untouched wilderness, home to many indigenous creatures and plants, and more than one hundred types of native bird. You can take a **bus tour** if time is short (see box, p.192); if it isn't, get a map and a free **wilderness permit**, which allows you to hike and camp, from the Chamber of Commerce or the Parks an0d Recreation Office (☎310/510-0688), both in Avalon. You can also get permits from the **Catalina Island Conservancy**, 125 Claressa Ave (daily 9am–5pm; ☎310/510-2595), which owns and manages 88 percent of the island's land; mountain biking requires a $60 permit, or $85 per family, from the same place.

There are some unique **animals** roaming about the wildlands, among them the Catalina Shrew, so rare it's only been sighted twice, and the Catalina Mouse, bigger and healthier than its mainland counterpart thanks to abundant food and lack of natural enemies. There are also foxes, ground squirrels, pigs, bald eagles, and quail, along with buffalo, descended from a group of fourteen left behind by a Hollywood film crew and now a sizable herd wandering about the island.

8

The San Gabriel and San Fernando valleys

R unning north of central LA, below the crests of their respective mountain ranges, lie the expansive **SAN GABRIEL** and **SAN FERN-ANDO VALLEYS**, which start close to one another a few miles north of Downtown and span outwards in opposite directions – east to the deserts around Palm Springs for the sloped foothills of the San Gabriel, west to Ventura on the California coast for the relatively flat San Fernando.

In the San Gabriel Valley, on the east side of the Verdugo Mountains, **Pasadena** is a cultural counterweight of sorts to the city of LA, a small, patrician town full of great architecture and diligent historic preservation. The neighboring cities of **South Pasadena** and **San Marino** also have their charms, particularly the latter's Huntington Library and Gardens, though the rest of the San Gabriel Valley holds more dispersed pleasures – including the LA Arboretum and San Gabriel Mission – worth a look only if you're staying in the LA region for at least a week.

North of the Hollywood Hills, the San Fernando Valley offers a more sprawling landscape, stitched together by seemingly endless ribbons of asphalt. The upper-middle-class suburb of **Glendale** is home to the famous cemetery Forest Lawn; while **Burbank**, further west, is studio central, accommodating the likes of Disney, Warner Bros, NBC, and, in its own municipal enclave, Universal. Further west are the bulk of LA's suburbs, known collectively as "**the Valley**," with historic attractions here and there, but mostly known for their sweltering temperatures and copious minimalls. At the apex of the triangular San Fernando Valley, places like **San Fernando** have a rich heritage, while further north, exciting **Magic Mountain** easily outdoes Disneyland for death-defying rides.

The San Gabriel Valley

Set at the foothills of the San Gabriel Mountains, the **San Gabriel Valley** escapes the derision that Angelenos pile upon the San Fernando Valley. However, though it has genuine cultural cachet in many places, it contains just as many dreary expanses as anywhere in the region – especially the eastern side, where you can breathe in some of the basin's worst smog, blown this way from central LA.

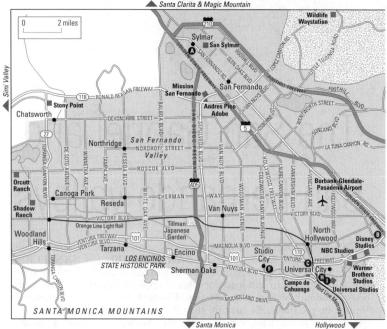

After its early settlement by native Tongva tribes and the later arrival of Spanish soldiers and missionaries, the San Gabriel Valley had become by the beginning of the twentieth century a choice region for American agriculture, growing predominantly grapes and citrus crops. Railroads brought new migrants, and by the 1950s, the foothills of the San Gabriel Mountains developed into another populous arm of LA, with suburban ranch-houses and swimming pools taking the place of ranches and orange groves. One thing that has not changed, however, is the torrential flooding. Thanks to its specific climate and geography, the Valley has always been a prime spot for **winter deluges**: great cascades of water sweep down the hillsides, turning into mudslides by the time they reach the foothills, and then charging through the canyons and destroying all in their wake – including encroaching suburban homes (memorably described by John McPhee in *Control of Nature*). This problem has been an occasional impediment to hillside growth, but with the creation of huge "**catch basins**" to contain the mudslides, real-estate developers have been able to push growth further up into the mountains.

Pasadena

At the western edge of the San Gabriel Valley, **PASADENA** is a mix of old-fashioned charm and contemporary popular appeal. Located ten miles northeast of Downtown LA, and connected to it by the rickety Pasadena Freeway (110 north), Pasadena was, like much of LA, settled by Midwesterners (in this case from Indiana) and even today retains a measure of its old style and genteel habits. The **Rose Parade**, an event dating back to 1890 that takes place every New Year's Day, is one reflection of this heritage, as are the grand estates of the **Arroyo Seco** neighborhood and the stylish Spanish Revival architecture

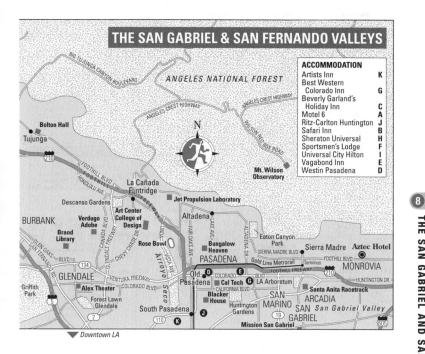

THE SAN GABRIEL & SAN FERNANDO VALLEYS

▼ Downtown LA

ACCOMMODATION

Artists Inn	K
Best Western Colorado Inn	G
Beverly Garland's Holiday Inn	C
Motel 6	A
Ritz-Carlton Huntington	J
Safari Inn	B
Sheraton Universal	H
Sportsmen's Lodge	F
Universal City Hilton	I
Vagabond Inn	E
Westin Pasadena	D

of downtown Pasadena. In the 1970s and 1980s, Pasadena was in a slump, but once urban-renewal dollars began flowing in the 1990s, tourists rediscovered the town, especially its **Old Pasadena** commercial strip and architectural treasures like the **Gamble House**. Not surprisingly, most of the city's appeal can be found either in the blocks surrounding Old Pasadena or in Arroyo Seco; while the burg stretches miles eastward, there's little reason to venture in that direction unless you're searching for cheap accommodation.

If in need of information, the **Pasadena Visitors Bureau**, 171 S Los Robles Ave (Mon–Fri 8am–5pm, Sat 10am–4pm; ☎626/795-9311, ⊛www.pasadenacal .com), provides **maps** and booklets detailing self-guided tours of city architecture and museums.

Downtown Pasadena

Bordered by Lake Avenue, California Boulevard, and the 210 and 710 freeways, **downtown Pasadena** is one of LA's few traditional downtowns, with fine municipal architecture, and worthwhile restaurants and shops. It's easily navigable on foot as well: most places of interest are located near **Colorado Boulevard**, the city's commercial axis. On and around this boulevard, between Fair Oaks and Euclid avenues, is **Old Pasadena** (⊛www.oldpasadena.org), a mix of antique sellers, used book and record stores, cafés, clothing boutiques, and theaters that gets quite crowded on weekends, especially with the recent construction of the **Gold Line** light rail linking directly to Downtown LA. Although there are few official sights on the strip – other than elegant architecture, such as the Italianate **White Block**, Fair Oaks Avenue at Union Street, and the 1894 **Venetian Revival Building**, 17 S Raymond Ave – Old Pasadena does feature decent museums and attractions within several blocks.

▲ Rose Bowl   ▲ Angeles National Forest

0   400 yds

DOWNTOWN PASADENA

EATING & DRINKING							
Arirang	5	Domenico's	2	La Luna Negra	10	The Muse	8
Beadle's	13	The Hat	1	Market City Caffé	7	Rose Tree Cottage	17
Burger Continental	14	Kingston Café	11	McMurphey's	4	Saladang	15
Café Santorini	6	Kuala Lumpur	9	Monty's Steakhouse	16	Xiomaratt	3
						Zona Rosa	12

Just south is the fascinating **Castle Green**, also known as "Hotel Green," 99 S Raymond St, formerly a 1903 resort that centered around a now-demolished hotel across the street. Later additions included the apartments that remain today, plus a **bridge** that crossed Raymond Avenue to link the structures. Although the walkway, which was billed as the "Bridge of Sighs" after the Venetian version, has been sliced in half and now stops in mid-air, its design still fascinates, with everything from Spanish-tiled domes and turrets to curvaceous arches – a short, glorious trip to nowhere. The Castle itself offers periodic tours of this evocative site (inquire at ☎626/577-6765, ⊛www.castlegreen.com), which is understandably popular for film shoots and weddings. Moreover, the local preservation society, **Pasadena Heritage**, offers regular tours of this and other area landmarks – including an excellent overview of Old Pasadena on the second Saturday of the month (Nov–June & Aug–Sept only; $10; reserve at ☎626/441-6333, ⊛www.pasadenaheritage.org).

North of Colorado Boulevard, the **ruins** of the old Romanesque city library, located in what is now **Pasadena Memorial Park**, Walnut Street and

198

△ Pasadena City Hall

Raymond Avenue, hint at the building's grandeur when it was open from the 1880s to the 1930s, before being demolished in 1954. The current **Public Library**, three blocks away at 285 E Walnut St, is a Spanish Renaissance gem with Corinthian columns, arched windows, Spanish tiling, and an elegant courtyard and atrium.

Across from the Memorial Park, the **Armory Center** (Wed–Sun noon–5pm, Fri closes 8pm; free; ⊛www.armoryarts.org), 145 N Raymond Ave, is a good place to get a glimpse of the local art scene, showing a mix of community folk art and professional avant-garde and modernist creations. More of the latter is on display in the center's annex, **Armory Northwest**, a mile north at 284 E Orange Grove Blvd (Fri–Sun noon–5pm; free), where edgier installation art and various other experiments are on display. Further east, on Garfield Avenue at Union Street, you'll find two nine-foot bronze sculptures of the great baseball pioneer **Jackie Robinson** and his brother, **Frank**, winner of a silver medal at the 1936 summer Olympics in Berlin. The Robinsons were raised in town and Jackie went to junior college here before transferring to UCLA.

In the immediate vicinity of the statues, Pasadena's old-world trappings are evident in its early municipal buildings, such as the city's centerpiece, **Pasadena City Hall**, 100 N Garfield Ave, one of several city buildings in Mediterranean Revival styles – in this case Spanish Baroque. Set on a wide city plaza, the structure has a large, tiled dome and an imposing facade with grand arches and columns, and an elegant garden with a patio and fountain, all of which make it more impressive than LA's City Hall – though it's under renovation until 2007, so tours have been temporarily suspended. You can, however, still get an excellent view by wandering around the complex, which seems to have a real Spanish flair – though it's only been here since the 1920s.

The Pacific Asia Museum and around

Across Euclid Avenue from City Hall, **Plaza de las Fuentes** is Lawrence Halprin's postmodern public square, with colorful tile work and a blocky pastel design, that suffers in comparison to its elegant neighbor.

The engaging **Pacific Asia Museum**, diagonally southeast at 46 N Los Robles Ave (Wed–Sun 10am–5pm, Fri closes 8pm; $7; @www.pacificasiamuseum.org), is modeled after a Chinese imperial palace, with a sloping tiled roof topped with ceramic-dog decorations, inset balconies, and dragon-emblazoned front gates. For twenty-five years, until 1948, this was the home of collector Grace Nicholson, who came to Pasadena around the beginning of the twentieth century and started amassing the expansive collection, which now includes thousands of historical treasures and everyday objects from Korea, China, and Japan, including decorative jade and porcelain, various swords and spears, and a large cache of paintings and drawings. In the museum's peaceful **courtyard garden**, koi fish rest in pools beneath marble statues and a variety of trees native to the Far East. Just around the corner, the three-story **Pasadena Museum of California Art**, 490 E Union St (Wed–Sun noon–5pm; $6; @www.pmcaonline.org), offers an eye-opening focus on the many aspects of the state's art world since it became part of the Union in 1850, in all kinds of media from painting to photography to digital art.

Bungalow Heaven and CalTech

Two miles northeast of Old Pasadena, the **Bungalow Heaven** historic district, bordered by Washington and Orange Grove boulevards and Hill and Catalina avenues, features a cache of quaint Craftsman bungalows that offer a glimpse of what much of the city looked like in the early 1900s. For Arts and Crafts enthusiasts, the neighborhood association puts on a yearly **tour** on the last Sunday in April ($15–18; information at ☎626/585-2172), peeking into several of the classic structures. Further south, the commercial strip of **South Lake Avenue** (@www.southlakeavenue.com) pulls in its share of visitors for its seven hundred or so retailers, but should be avoided unless you're in the mood for a cheek-to-jowl encounter with hordes of shoppers.

Much more appealing is the **California Institute of Technology**, or **CalTech**, campus, a few blocks east of Lake Avenue, best known for its "cool nerd" students and media-friendly seismologists who inevitably pop up on the local news every time a major temblor rumbles through the region. However, CalTech is worth visiting for its splendid assortment of pre-WWII architecture, notably the Spanish Baroque–flavored buildings of LA Central Library–designer **Bertram Goodhue** and the Islamic-styled work of Edward Stone; the campus makes for a fascinating jaunt if you have even the slightest interest in historic buildings. **Architecture tours** depart from the Spanish Colonial–style Atheneum, 551 S Hill Ave (Sept–Oct & Jan–June fourth Thurs of month, Nov third Thurs; 11am only; free; reserve at ☎626/395-6327), while for your own, self-guided campus tour, get a brochure from the visitor center at 315 S Hill Ave (Mon–Fri 9am–5pm).

The Norton Simon Museum

Just across the 710 freeway from downtown Pasadena, the collections of the **Norton Simon Museum**, 411 W Colorado Blvd (Wed–Mon noon–6pm, Fri closes 9pm; $6, students free; @www.nortonsimon.org), are at least as good as those of the LA County or Getty museums, though this museum is little known outside of the art world. The reason is because the institution sidesteps the hype of the local arts scene to concentrate on the quality of its presentation. You could easily spend a whole day wandering through the dark, intimate galleries, as well as a sculpture garden inspired by Monet's own Giverny.

The museum's focus is **Western European painting** from the Renaissance to early modernism. It's a massive collection, much of it rotated, but most of the major pieces are usually on view. Highlights include Dutch paintings of the seventeenth century – notably Rembrandt's vivacious *Titus, Portrait of a Boy* and Frans Hals' austerely aggressive *Portrait of a Man* – and Italian Renaissance work from the likes of Botticelli, Raphael, Giorgione, and Bellini. There's a good sprinkling of French Impressionists and post-Impressionists: Monet's light-dappled *Mouth of the Seine at Honfleur*; Manet's plaintive *Ragpicker*; and Degas' *The Ironers*, capturing the extended yawn of a washerwoman; plus works by Cézanne, Gauguin, and Van Gogh.

Unlike the Getty, the Norton Simon also boasts a solid collection of modernist greats, from Georges Braque and Pablo Picasso to Roy Lichtenstein and Andy Warhol. There are also some appealing, but less-heralded works from different eras, including Zurbaran's *Still Life with Lemons, Oranges and a Rose*; Jan Steen's *Wine is a Mocker*, an image of rural peasants assisting a drunken bourgeoise as she lies pitifully in the dirt; and Tiepolo's *The Triumph of Virtue and Nobility over Ignorance*, in which the winged, angelic victors gloat over their symbolic conquest of the wretched, troll-like figure of Ignorance. As a counterpoint to the Western art, the museum has a fine collection of **Asian art**, including highly polished Buddhist and Hindu figures, some inlaid with precious stones, and many drawings and prints – the highlight being Hiroshige's masterful series of colored woodblock prints, showing nature in quiet, dusky hues.

The Arroyo Seco

The isolated pocket northwest of the junction of the 134 and 210 freeways, known as **Arroyo Seco**, or "dry riverbed" in Spanish, is home to some of LA's best residential architecture. Orange Grove Avenue leads you into the neighborhood from central Pasadena and takes you to the **Pasadena Historical Society**, 470 W Walnut St at Orange Grove (Wed–Sun noon–5pm; $5, kids free; @www.pasadenahistory.org), which has fine displays on Pasadena's history and tasteful surrounding gardens, but is most interesting for the on-site **Feynes Mansion** (tours Wed–Sun 1.30 & 3pm; free with admission), designed by Robert Farquhar, also famous for his Clark Memorial Library, in South Central's West Adams neighborhood, and Downtown LA's California Club. Decorated with its original 1905 furnishings and paintings, this elegant Beaux Arts mansion was once the home of the Finnish Consulate, and much of the folk art on display comes from Pasadena's "twin town" of Jarvenpää in Finland.

But it's the **Gamble House**, 4 Westmoreland Place (60min tours Thurs–Sun noon–3pm; $8, students $5; @www.gamblehouse.org), that really brings people out here, the crown jewel in the rich architectural legacy of the brothers **Charles and Henry Greene**. Built in 1908 for David Gamble, of the consumer-products giant Proctor & Gamble, this masterpiece of Southern Californian Craftsman architecture helped give rise to a style that's replicated all over the state, freely combining elements from Swiss chalets and Japanese temples in a romantically sprawling, shingled mansion. Broad eaves shelter outdoor sleeping-porches, which in turn shade terraces on the ground floor, leading out to the spacious lawn. The interior was crafted with the same attention to detail, and all the carpets, cabinetry, and lighting fixtures were designed specifically for the house. In 2004, a major renovation was completed, repairing nearly a century of decay to its wooden beams and shakes, giving the house back the full splendor of its original rough-hewn look. The area around the Gamble House has at least eleven other private homes by the two brothers, including **Charles Greene's own house**, 368 Arroyo Terrace, and the picturesque **Duncan–Irwin House**, around the corner at 240 N Grand Ave, a perfect two-story Craftsman with stone lanterns and a rustic stone wall out front.

Arroyo Culture

The neighborhood around the **Arroyo Seco** has shifted somewhat through the years, first by geography, later by culture. Orange Grove Boulevard, several blocks east of the Arroyo proper, was originally lined with a series of grand estates, tagged **"Millionaires' Row,"** with the local gentry using the Arroyo itself as a source of wood and a place to picnic. The palaces went into decline in the early part of the twentieth century, to be replaced eventually by the apartment blocks visible today. Meanwhile, the Arroyo Seco was being built up by numerous **Arts and Crafts**–movement intellectuals, many from the East Coast and inspired by the English example of William Morris, and preaching a return-to-nature philosophy that reacted against the early-modern design aesthetic taking shape, along with industrialized culture in general. Built in the Arroyo's wooded lots amid craggy rocks and rugged cliffsides, the resulting Swiss chalets, Tudor mansions, and Craftsman monuments were manifestations of a new **Arroyo Culture**, its artisan practitioners prized for working with wood, clay, and stone. Not surprisingly, one of their heroes was Charles Lummis, famed for his eponymous boulder house in Highland Park (see p.78), and an equally prominent intellectual of the time, as well as an ardent booster for the new style, working as the first city editor of the *Los Angeles Times* when it was especially powerful in local affairs. Architects Charles and Henry Greene and Frank Lloyd Wright were all attracted by the Arroyo too, if not full believers in its attendant ideology. The culture faded, however, as much of the area was bought up by wealthy Angelenos, though fortunately, the architecture has been largely preserved – even as prices on the homes have predictably skyrocketed.

A quarter of a mile north of here is Frank Lloyd Wright's "La Miniatura," also known as the **Millard House**, which you can glimpse through the gate around 585 Rosemont Ave, a small, concrete-block house supposedly designed to look like a jungle ruin, with thick foliage growing over Mayan-style architecture. Also in the vicinity are works by noted architects Gregory Ain, Richard Neutra, and Craig Ellwood, including the latter's **Art Center College of Design**, several miles north at 1700 Lida St, a monumental steel-and-glass span crossing a natural ravine and home to one of the area's best schools for groundbreaking modern design. For a few examples, check out the eye-catching, often experimental modern sculptures and installations in the school's **Williamson Gallery** (Tues–Sun noon–5pm, Fri closes 9pm; free; ⊕www.artcenter.edu/williamson).

The Rose Bowl

North of the arroyo, the 104,000-seat **Rose Bowl** is just off Arroyo Boulevard and out of use most of the year, but is home to a popular monthly **flea market** (second Sun of month; $7, reserve tickets at ⊕323/560-7469) and, in the autumn, the place where the UCLA football team plays its home games (⊕310/825-2101, ⊕uclabruins.collegesports.com). It's also where one of college football's four Bowl Championship Series games is played in early January, meaning every fourth year the Rose Bowl officially gets to decide the champion. To the south on Arroyo Boulevard, pass under the monumental spans of the **Colorado Street Bridge**, one of the area's structural wonders – a 1467-foot monolith of curving concrete, built in 1913 – to reach the **Tournament House**, 391 S Orange Grove Blvd (tours Feb–Aug 2–4pm; free; ⊕626/449-4100, ⊕www.tournamentofroses.com), the administrative headquarters of the annual **Rose Parade**, which began in 1890 to publicize the mild Southern California winters, and now attracts over a million visitors every year to watch its marching bands and elaborate flower-emblazoned floats. The mansion itself is a pink 1914 Renaissance Revival gem, once owned by gum king William Wrigley, and well worth a look for its grand manor and surrounding gardens – containing up to 1500 types of rose.

South Pasadena

For all its historic architecture and small-town appeal, the separate city of **SOUTH PASADENA** only exists as it is today because of a series of lawsuits over the past thirty years fighting the completion of the **710 freeway**, which would divide the town in half and wipe out a thousand homes and seventy-odd historic sites. In 2004 the Federal Highway Administration (perhaps temporarily) withdrew funding for this dubious endeavor, but it's a subject that keeps residents understandably alarmed.

One reason for their concern is South Pasadena's wealth of fine buildings and historical legacy. The city's main strip, **Fair Oaks Avenue**, used to be part of the famous **Route 66**, and it's here where you can find such eye-catching sights as the landmark **Rialto Theater**, no. 1023 (☎626/799-9567), a 1925 movie palace that's also been a theatrical stage and vaudeville venue. The faded splendor inside is a treat, adorned with Moorish organ screens, Egyptian columns, winged harpies, and a central Medusa head, while above the screen lurks a gargoyle whose eyes continue to glow, even as films show below it. Just east, off nearby Monterey Road, is Irving Gill's **Miltimore House**, 1301 Chelten Way, a modular white structure with green trim that combines Mission Revival and modern styles. What's really interesting, though, is the weird street layout of the neighborhood, in which ancient **live oaks** jut out at random spots in the road – the trees used to be part of a long-forgotten city park.

Meridian Avenue, which parallels Fair Oaks Avenue several blocks west, takes you through the quaint Victorian-era homes south of the 110 freeway and into the larger residences north of it. On the southern end, the **Meridian Iron Works**, 913 Meridian Ave (Thurs 3–8pm, Sat 1–4pm; free; ⊛www.sppreservation.org), is a sturdy old pile from 1887 that houses the South Pasadena Preservation Foundation Museum, where exhibits and photographs cover the history of the ironworks (and its former lives as a hotel, blacksmith's and bicycle dealer's), as well as the city itself, including assorted curios from a local ostrich farm.

To the north, Meridian Avenue runs into posh **Buena Vista Street**, notable for two grand dwellings by Charles and Henry Greene: the **Garfield House**, no. 1001, a fairly well-preserved 1904 Swiss chalet with numerous Craftsman elements that was once the home of murdered US President James Garfield's widow; and the adjacent **Longley House**, no. 1005, the brothers' first commission, an eclectic 1897 mix of revival styles from Romanesque to Moorish to Georgian. A few blocks east, at the end of Oaklawn Avenue, the Greene's 1906 **Oaklawn Bridge**, a restored concrete relic draped in vines, spans the railway gully of the former Southern Pacific and Santa Fe line, which has been recently reincarnated for use by the Metrorail **Gold Line**, connecting Pasadena with Downtown LA.

San Marino

East of South Pasadena, uneventful **SAN MARINO** is marked by some of LA's most privileged residents and widest neighborhood streets. One of the most notable structures is the **Blacker House**, 1177 Hillcrest Ave, Charles and Henry Greene's Craftsman marvel, with dark wooden beams, rustic appearance, and Asian-influenced details. Unlike the larger Gamble House, you can't get into this one for regular tours, but you can drop in for periodic **chamber-music concerts**, courtesy of Pacific Serenades (tickets $50; ☎213/534-3434, ⓦpacser.org).

Beyond architecture, there's little of interest in town beyond the legacy of railway and real-estate magnate **Henry Huntington**, preserved in his museum and gardens. Before hitting the museum, you may want to check out **El Molino Viejo**, 1120 Old Mill Rd (Tues–Sun 1–4pm; free), a weathered adobe built as a flourmill in 1816 by Spanish missionaries from Mission San Gabriel. Nowadays the old mill presents a few historical exhibits and photographs, plus diagrams of how water generated the power to make flour. Just to the west, the towering **Ritz-Carlton Huntington Hotel**, atop a hill at 1401 S Oak Knoll Ave (see "Accommodation," p.257), began life as the *Wentworth Hotel* in 1906, later to be taken over by Huntington. The very definition of palatial accommodation, the hotel's Mediterranean-style main building boasts attractive gardens out back, and, further away, small bungalow-style residences for its swankiest guests – the only part of the hotel off limits to the general public.

The Huntington Library and Gardens

San Marino's most redeeming feature is the **Huntington Library, Art Collections and Botanical Gardens**, just off Huntington Drive at 1151 Oxford Rd (Tues–Fri noon–4.30pm, Sat & Sun 10.30am–4.30pm; $15, students $10; ⓦwww.huntington.org). Part of this cache of art is based on the collections of Henry Huntington, the nephew of childless multimillionaire Collis P. Huntington, who owned and operated the Southern Pacific Railroad – which in the late nineteenth century had a virtual monopoly on transportation in California. Henry, groomed to take over the railroad from his uncle, was dethroned by the board of directors and took his sizable inheritance to LA. Once there, he bought up the existing streetcar routes and combined them as the Pacific Electric Railway Company, which in turn controlled the Red Car line that soon became the largest transit network in the world, and helped make Huntington the largest landowner in the state. He retired in 1910, moving to the manor house he had built in San Marino, devoting himself full time to buying rare books and manuscripts, and marrying his uncle's widow Arabella and acquiring her collection of English portraits.

You can pick up a self-guided walking **tour** of each of the three main sections from the bookstore and information desk in the entry pavilion. The **library**, right off the main entrance, is a good first stop, its two-story exhibition hall containing numerous manuscripts and rare books, among them a Gutenberg Bible, a folio of Shakespeare's plays, Thoreau's manuscript for *Walden*, Thomas Jefferson's architectural plans, and the **Ellesmere Chaucer**, a c.1410 illuminated version of *The Canterbury Tales*. Displays around the walls trace the history of printing and of the English language from medieval manuscripts to a King James Bible, from Milton's *Paradise Lost* and Blake's *Songs of Innocence and Experience* to first editions of Swift, Coleridge, Dickens, Woolf, and Joyce.

To decorate the **main house**, a grand mansion done out in Louis XIV carpets and later French tapestries, the Huntingtons traveled to England and returned with the finest art money could buy. Unless you're passionate about eighteenth-century English portraiture, head through to the back extension, which displays important works by Van Dyck and Constable, as well as the stars of the collection: Gainsborough's ever-popular *Blue Boy*, Lawrence's *Pinkie*, and Reynolds' grandiose *Mrs Siddons as the Tragic Muse*. A bit less familiar, but perhaps more compelling, are colorful paintings by Turner, whose radiant *Grand Canal, Venice* is a vibrant, hazily sunlit image of gondolas on the water; and Blake, whose mystical *Satan Comes to the Gates of Hell* is the most stunning work in the collection, showing the ghostly, bearded figure of Death facing off with spears against a very human Satan and a serpentine Eve. Nearby, the **Scott Gallery for American Art** displays paintings by Edward Hopper and Mary Cassatt, and Wild West drawings and sculpture, and also features work by the architects Greene & Greene.

For all the art and literature, though, it's the grounds that make the Hunting-ton truly worthwhile. The acres of beautiful themed **gardens** surrounding the buildings include a Zen Rock Garden, complete with authentically constructed Buddhist Temple and Tea House, and a Desert Garden with the world's largest collection of desert plants, including twelve acres of cacti. Also here are two lush rose gardens, a sculpture garden full of Baroque statues, and a Japanese garden dotted with koi ponds, cherry trees, and "moon bridges." While strolling through these botanical splendors, you might also visit the Huntingtons themselves, buried in a neo-Palladian **mausoleum** at the northwest corner of the estate, beyond the rows of an orange grove, built as a marble Greek temple and claimed to be the inspiration for the later 1930s Jefferson Memorial in Washington, DC.

North of Pasadena

The cities and districts **north of Pasadena**, such as **Altadena** and **La Cañada Flintridge**, sit on hillsides that lead into the **Angeles National Forest**, a fifty-mile wilderness in the San Gabriel Mountains that is a favorite weekend spot for locals. Threatened by flood during heavy rains, these are also some of the more precarious places to live in LA, and you can see part of their elaborate flood-control system just off Oak Grove Drive, where the **Hahamongna Watershed Park** and Devils Gate Reservoir are dramatic testaments to the power of water: a huge green slope and massive catch basin designed specifically to contain water, mud, rocks, housing debris, and assorted other elements in the event of catastrophic flooding.

The Jet Propulsion Laboratory and around

Immediately north of the park and reservoir is one of the cornerstones of America's military-industrial complex: the **Jet Propulsion Laboratory**, 4800 Oak Grove Drive in La Cañada Flintridge (tours alternate by week, Mon & Wed 1pm; free; by reservation at ☎818/354-9314, ⊛www.jpl.nasa.gov), devoted to the development of space-related machinery such as orbiting satellites, long-range missiles and rockets, and secretive government projects. The two hour public tours (free) are very popular, and you'll have to reserve at least six months in advance and bring some form of ID – a visa or passport if you're a foreigner. Despite the JPL's obvious military mission, the lab chooses to focus on more PR-friendly displays, including replicas of the solar-system-exploring *Voyager* craft and the *Magellan* and *Galileo* vehicles that mapped Venus and Mars; photos from the Saturn-bound *Cassini* craft; and exhibits on the Hubble telescope, killer asteroids, and Hollywood's version of outer space.

Nearby, just a mile east of the reservoir, you can find one of LA's most unusual attractions, the **Mountain View Mausoleum and Art Gallery**, 2300 N Marengo Ave (daily 10am–4pm; free), the unexpected home to a variety of contemporary artworks by local California artists. The highlight is the ethereal **Arbor of Light Radiance Corridor**, a dark room illuminated with stained-glass skylights, which cast radiant reflections of plants and flowers across the walls as the sun moves across the sky.

West off Foothill Boulevard, **Descanso Gardens**, 1418 Descanso Drive, La Cañada Flintridge (daily 9am–5pm; $5, kids $1; ⊕www.descansogardens.org), squeezes all the plants you might see in the mountains into 155 acres of landscaped park, especially brilliant in spring when the wildflowers are in bloom. The centerpiece is a live-oak forest loaded with camellias, and there's also a Japanese tea house and garden, with a narrow red footbridge, and a tranquil bird sanctuary for migrating waterfowl.

Angeles National Forest and around

North from the 210 freeway, the **Angeles Crest Highway** (Hwy-2) heads into the mountains above Pasadena, through an area once dotted with resorts and wilderness camps. Today, a hike up any of the nearby canyons will bring you past the ruins of old lodges that either burned down or were washed away toward the end of the 1930s, when automobiles became popular. One of the most scenic of these trails, a rugged five-mile round-trip, follows the route of the **Mount Lowe Scenic Railway**, once one of LA's biggest tourist attractions, a funicular that hauled tourists 1500 feet up to Echo Mountain, to the remains of "**White City**" – formerly a mountaintop resort of two hotels, a zoo, and an observatory. Today, you'll see little more than crumbling walls, but the trail's expansive views of the basin can be striking when smog isn't a problem. To follow the old route of the railway (which ended service in 1937), drive north on Lake Avenue until it ends at the intersection of Loma Alta Drive. Find a parking spot and head east along the trailhead. More fine hiking can be found further east in **Eaton Canyon Park**, 1750 N Altadena Drive, a natural refuge on 190 acres, and the on-site **nature center** (daily 9am–5pm; free; ☎626/398-5420, ⊕www.ecnca.org) provides more information on the region's geology, flora, and fauna.

Further north, the Crest Highway passes through the **Angeles National Forest** – an increasingly crowded recreation zone where you can hike, camp most of the year, and ski (Mount Baldy; see p.338) in winter – to Mount Wilson, high enough to be a major site for TV broadcast antennae. At the peak, the **Mount Wilson Observatory** has a small **museum** (April–Nov 10am–4pm; $1; ⊕www.mtwilson.edu) where you can browse astronomical displays detailing the work of Edwin Hubble, who, aside from having a famous telescope named after him, developed the theory of cosmological expansion. The observatory was built by the Carnegie Institution in 1904, and although the last century of growth has added much light pollution, Carnegie researchers still find it useful, even if most of their groundbreaking discoveries are made in the Andes mountains.

East of Pasadena

East of Pasadena, the San Gabriel Valley becomes a patchwork of small cities with a few appealing sights scattered across large distances. The one feature these places share is Foothill Boulevard, which, before it was displaced by the Foothill Freeway (Hwy-210), was famously known as **Route 66**. Formerly the main route across the US, "from Chicago to LA, more than three thousand miles all the way," the strip has declined in recent decades, though sections of the road have been smartened up with fresh neon and retro-flavored building renovations (for copious info on the road's preservation and highlights, visit ⊕www.cart66pf.org).

Arcadia, Sierra Madre, and San Gabriel

If you follow Foothill Boulevard out of Pasadena, you'll come to **ARCADIA**, a colorless suburb whose **LA County Arboretum**, 310 N Baldwin Ave (daily

9am–4.30pm; $5; ⊛www.arboretum.org), contains many impressive gardens and waterfalls, flocks of peacocks and, of course, a great assortment of trees, arranged by their native continents. This was the 127-acre home of Elias "Lucky" Baldwin, who made his millions in the silver mines of Nevada's Comstock in the 1870s, settled here in 1875, and built a fanciful white mansion along a palm-tree-lined lagoon (later used in the TV show *Fantasy Island*) on the site of the 1839 Rancho Santa Anita. He also bred horses and raced them on a neighboring track that has since grown into the **Santa Anita Racetrack** (racing Oct to early Nov & late Dec to late April Wed–Sun, post time 12.30pm or 1pm; $5; ⊛www.santaanita.com), still the most famous racetrack in California, with a Depression-era steel frieze along the grandstand.

The foothill district of **SIERRA MADRE**, on the northern edge of Arcadia, lies directly beneath Mount Wilson and is worth a visit if you're a hiker. A seven-mile round-trip trail up to the summit makes for an excellent, if tiring, trek; to find the route, take Baldwin Avenue north from the 210 freeway until it becomes Mount Wilson Trail and ends at the trailhead. South of Sierra Madre stands the valley's original settlement, the church and grounds of **Mission San Gabriel Arcangel**, 428 S Mission Drive (daily 9am–4pm; $5; ⊛sangabrielmission.org), in the heart of the small town of **SAN GABRIEL**. The mission was established here in 1771 by Junípero Serra and the current building finished in 1812. Despite decades of damage by earthquakes and the elements, the church and grounds have been repaired and reopened, their old winery, cistern, kitchens, gardens, and antique-filled rooms giving some sense of mission-era life.

Monrovia

The attractions further east are even more isolated. The lone draw out in **MONROVIA**, east of Sierra Madre, is the zany **Aztec Hotel**, 311 W Foothill Blvd, a 1925 pre-Columbian creation from Mayan revivalist Robert Stacy-Judd that is still maintained as a boarding house, bar, and restaurant. Its faux-ancient carvings and designs, monumental appearance, and stunning facade encase a lobby that displays antiques like the original gas pumps found along Route 66. Beyond here, the only reason most Angelenos venture further east is to take a splash at **Raging Waters**, in the suburb of San Dimas at 111 Raging Waters Drive (May & early Sept Sat & Sun 10am–5pm; June–Aug Mon–Fri 10am–8pm; $28, kids $17, or $15/12 for entry after 4pm; parking $7; ⊛www.ragingwaters.com), an aquatic theme park with plenty of tubes and slides for cooling off in the summer heat, and plenty of summer smog as well – the area has some of the region's worst air pollution, thanks to unfavorable winds blowing in from central LA.

The San Fernando Valley

Home to acres of asphalt, countless minimalls, and nonstop tract housing, the **San Fernando Valley** is often derided by Westsiders as the epitome of dull, faceless suburbia. While there's some truth to this, the Valley has also become known for its rabid **secessionist movement**, which blames all difficulties – from crime to potholes to crummy schools – on Downtown LA bureaucrats, though so far little progress has been made.

The Valley's 1769 Spanish discovery predated the settlement of Los Angeles, and it was first named after **St Catherine**, only later acquiring its present

LA's aqueducts

Just beyond Mission San Fernando, I-5 runs past two of LA's main reservoirs, the water carried by the **California Aqueduct**, traveling from the Sacramento Delta, and the **LA Aqueduct**, coming from the Owens Valley and Mono Lake on the eastern slopes of the Sierra Nevada Mountains.

How LA came into the latter water source, however, is a shady matter indeed. Acting on behalf of water czar **William Mulholland**, agents of the city, masquerading as rich cattle-barons interested in establishing ranches in the Owens Valley, bought up most of the land along the Owens River in the first years of the twentieth century before selling it, at great personal profit, to the City of Los Angeles. Tellingly, when the first rush of water was brought to the city with great fanfare, Mulholland publicly pronounced his triumph with the memorable command, "There is it! Take it!" The Owens Valley farmers didn't take this subterfuge lying down, however, and resorted to **dynamiting** sections of the aqueduct in later years. The violent tactics proved of little use, though, for as soon as the water began flowing, LA's San Fernando Valley **suburbs** began to blossom, along with the profits of their new Downtown property owners – bankers and developers who, as with Mulholland's agents up north, tricked the local valley farmers into selling their land for a fraction of its potential value.

There is little doubt that the LA Aqueduct has served the interests of the city well, bringing water to two million people, but the morality and legality of such a distant supply of water is still disputed. After much controversy, even the conservative state supreme court ruled that the endangered Mono Lake area – the salty home of fascinating tufa (gnarled limestone) columns – must finally be removed from the clutches of LA's water empire. This result (along with California's losing its grip on a generous portion of the Colorado River's water) has resulted in the city finally getting down to serious **water-management** policies, controlling the amount of the precious fluid used to water people's lawns and fill their swimming pools.

moniker with the development of Mission San Fernando at its northern tip. After the US took possession of California and the Southern Pacific Railroad cut through it, the Valley rapidly transformed, going from a nineteenth-century tract of wheat fields and ranchos to an early twentieth-century expanse of citrus groves to a post–World War II dynamo of industry, media, and, above all, suburban housing. The spark that made all this development possible was the 1913 construction of the LA Aqueduct (see box, above). Today, the agricultural ghosts are apparent only in streets with idyllic names like Orange Grove, Walnut, and Magnolia.

Glendale

West of Pasadena, beyond the Verdugo Mountains, **GLENDALE** is an upper-middle-class suburb that extends from Griffith Park all the way past the northern reaches of foothill cities like La Cañada Flintridge. At least its downtown is compact, south of the 134 freeway along Brand Boulevard, where, apart from a handful of restaurants and boutiques, you'll find the **Alex Theater**, 268 N Brand Blvd, a striking piece of green-and-yellow Art Deco with a towering pylon; it now serves as a performing-arts venue and one of the sites for the annual Last Remaining Seats festival (see p.343 or ⓦwww.alextheatre.org).

North of the 134, the city has a smattering of noteworthy sites, such as the **Verdugo Adobe**, 2211 Bonita Drive (grounds daily dawn–dusk; free), displaying antiques and artifacts from the early nineteenth century; though the adobe itself is not open to the public, the gardens contain the **Oak of Peace**, a tree said to be more than five hundred years old, allegedly the place where in 1847 Mexican leaders decided to surrender to US troops in the Mexican–American War. To the northwest, the **Brand Library**, or "El Miradero," 1601 W Mountain St (Tues & Thurs 1–9pm, Wed 1–6pm, Fri & Sat 1–5pm; free), looks nothing remotely like anything else in LA. This white oddity from 1902 is said to be modeled on the East India Pavilion at Chicago's 1893 Columbian Exposition, and features a striking Islamic design of domes and minarets containing art books from the main Glendale Library. The site also contains an art gallery and hosts monthly talks by members of the LA Opera, when it's in season (usually second Thurs 7.30pm; free). Also located in Brand Park is the so-called **Doctors House** (tours Sun 2–4pm; free), a charming Eastlake residence from 1888, named for three physicians who lived there successively, with period decor, a projecting roofline and dormers, and latticed white porches.

Forest Lawn Glendale

For most visitors, the main reason to come to Glendale is to visit the city's branch of **Forest Lawn Cemetery**, 1712 S Glendale Ave (daily 9am–5pm; free; ⊛ www.forestlawn.org), at the vanguard of the American way of death for nearly a century. Founded in 1917 by one Dr Hubert Eaton, this soon became *the* place to be buried, its pompous landscaping and pious artworks attracting celebrities by the dozen to buy their own little piece of heaven. The graveyard's success has allowed it to expand throughout the LA region, notably with a branch near Griffith Park, in the Hollywood Hills (see p.104), though the others – in places like Covina Hills, Cypress Beach, and Long Beach – are best avoided.

It's best to climb the hill and see the cemetery in reverse from the **Forest Lawn Museum** (open during park hours; free), whose hodgepodge of worldly artifacts includes coins from ancient Rome, Viking relics, medieval armor, and a mysterious, sculpted Easter Island figure, discovered being used as ballast in a fishing boat in the days when the statues could still be swiped from the island. How it ended up here is another mystery, but it is the only one on view in the US. Next door to the museum, the **Resurrection and Crucifixion Hall** houses the colossal *Crucifixion* by Jan Styka – an oil painting nearly 200 feet tall and 50 feet wide, showing Jesus standing by a fallen cross, not being crucified as the title would suggest. In any case, you're only allowed to see it during the ceremonial unveiling every hour on the hour – and be charged $1 to boot. Besides this, Eaton owned a stained-glass "re-creation" of Leonardo da Vinci's *Last Supper* and, realizing that he only needed one piece to complete his trio of "the three greatest moments in the life of Christ," he commissioned Robert Clark to produce *The Resurrection* – which is unveiled every half-hour, appropriate since it's only half the size of the Styka. If you can't stick around for the ceremonial showings (with both, in any case, the size is the only aspect that's impressive), you can check out the scaled-down replicas just inside the entrance.

From the museum, walk down through the terrace gardens – loaded with sculptures modeled on the greats of classical European art, along with an ungainly 13-foot rendering of George Washington – to the **Freedom Mausoleum**, where you'll find a handful of the cemetery's better-known graves. Just outside the mausoleum's doors, Errol Flynn lies in an unspectacular plot (unmarked until 1979), rumored to have been buried with six bottles of whiskey at his side, while a few strides away is the grave of Walt Disney, who is not in the deep freeze as urban legend would have it. Inside the mausoleum you'll find Clara Bow, Nat King Cole, Jeanette MacDonald, and Alan Ladd placed close to each other on the first floor. Downstairs are Chico Marx and his brother Gummo, the Marx Brothers' agent and business manager. Back down the hill, the **Great Mausoleum** is chiefly noted for the tombs of Clark Gable (next to Carole Lombard, who died in a plane crash just three years after marrying him), and Jean Harlow, in a marble-lined room that cost over $25,000, paid for by fiancé William Powell. Amid all this morbid glamour, the cemetery has actually been the site of thousands of **weddings**, not least being Ronald Reagan's starcrossed wedlock with Jane Wyman in 1940.

Tujunga

Seven miles north of Glendale, **TUJUNGA** is mainly notable for its remarkable collection of boulder houses and bungalows built in the 1910s and 1920s, the inspiration of a small community of Socialists who, like the dwellers in Pasadena's Arroyo Seco, believed earthy materials like wood and stone made for the best, and most moral, forms of construction. Their restored 1913 clubhouse, **Bolton Hall**, 10116 Commerce Ave (Tues & Sun 1–4pm; free; ☎818/352-3420), hints at their aims, with a rocky central tower and interior with exposed wooden beams, which were supposed to recall, according to the building's architect George Harris, "the dense foliage of a great tree to the blue sky." Not surprisingly, this striking creation was the second historic monument ever declared by LA, and displays a good selection of antiques from its rich and varied history – it has also doubled as the town's city hall, and its jail. Curiously enough, the structure's name actually honors an author named "Bolton Hall," a friend of the developer who gave rise to the surrounding town.

Burbank

Although Hollywood's name is synonymous with the movies, in reality many of the big studios moved out of Tinseltown long ago, and much of the business of making films (and TV shows) is located over the hills in otherwise boring **BURBANK**. Hot, smoggy, and ugly, Burbank nonetheless has an official "Media District" bustling with activity, thanks to the explosion in demand from overseas markets, cable TV, and broadcast networks (to sit in an audience for a TV show, notably at a studio such as Disney that would otherwise be off-limits, see the box on p.115).

Disney is probably the most visible of the studios, with Robert A.M. Stern's starry wizard-hat building, visible from the 101 freeway, housing over seven hundred animators. Less appealing is Disney's other public face, its **Studio Office Building**, 500 S Buena Vista St, a clumsy effort from Michael Graves that has five of the Seven Dwarfs propping up the building's roof. As for touring the studio, forget it – the secretive company would rather have you plunk down your cash in Disneyland.

Nearby, **NBC**, or the National Broadcasting Company, 3000 W Alameda St (box office open Mon–Fri 9am–4pm; $7; reserve at ☎818/840-3537), offers an engaging ninety-minute tour of the largest production facility in the US, even though only a handful of shows currently tape there. The studio also gives you the chance to be in the audience for the taping of a TV program (phone ahead for free tickets), such as Jay Leno's *Tonight Show*. The **Warner Bros Studio**, 4000 Warner Blvd at Hollywood Way, offers tours of its facilities (May–Sept Mon–Fri 9am–4pm, Oct–April last tour 3pm; $35; reserve at ☎818/846-1403, ◉www.wbstudiotour.com) that take you past the sound

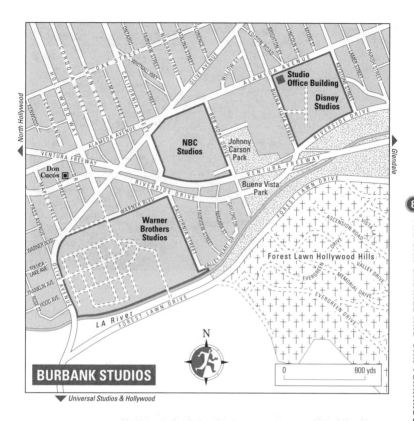

Burbank Studios

0   800 yds

Universal Studios & Hollywood

stages, around the production offices, and to the outdoor sets for movies and TV shows. Ultimately, you won't get to see any actual filming, but if you want to see a studio's actual working environment, it's worth the money.

Beyond the studios, Burbank's greatest attraction is the oldest **Bob's Big Boy** in existence, 4211 Riverside Drive, a well-preserved "Googie" coffee shop from 1949, used for a host of Hollywood flicks, and for good reason: the 70-foot-tall pink-and-white neon sign is a knockout. Occasionally on Friday nights, the restaurant hosts stylish hot-rod shows in the parking lot (6–10pm), and every Saturday night, you can chow down on your burgers and fries with old-fashioned car-hop service (6–10pm).

Universal Studios

Just to the south along the 101 freeway, the largest of the backlots belongs to **Universal Studios** (summer daily 8am–10pm; rest of year 10am–6pm; $50, kids $40; ☎818/508-9600, ⌨www.universalstudioshollywood.com), where the four-hour-long "tours" are more like a trip around an amusement park than a film studio, with the first half featuring a tram ride through a make-believe set where you can experience the fading magic of the Red Sea parting and a "collapsing" bridge, the second taking place inside the corny Entertainment Center, where unemployed actors engage in Wild West shootouts and stunt shows based on the studio's movies. The theme rides are based on the studio's more popular films,

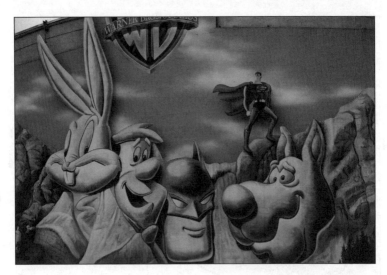

△ Warner Bros Studio mural

including *Back to the Future* (a jerky trip on a motion simulator) and *Spiderman Rocks!* (a musical version of the blockbuster franchise). You never actually get to see any filming, though.

Also part of the complex is **Universal CityWalk**, an outdoor mall that's free to all who pay the parking fee, where rock bands churn out MOR covers, street performers warble syrupy ballads, and giant TV screens run ads for the latest Universal releases.

The western San Fernando Valley

Beyond Burbank, the **western San Fernando Valley** suburbs of Los Angeles – some of the more well-known of which are **North Hollywood**, **Sherman Oaks**, **Van Nuys**, and **Reseda** – are often collectively called "the Valley," immediately bringing to mind strip malls, fast-food joints, and endless asphalt, but also host a handful of interesting, though widely separated, sights. The Valley is also the capital of America's **porn industry**, with home videotape sales and Internet demand making the low-rent video studios and distribution warehouses here an integral part of the local economy – cranking out more acres of photographed flesh than just about any spot on the planet. However, this is one aspect of the Valley's movie industry that, not surprisingly, is kept discreetly behind the closed doors of unmarked concrete warehouses and strip-mall office suites.

The first of the Valley's isolated points of interest is **Campo de Cahuenga**, across from Universal Studios – and a Red Line subway stop – at 3919 Lankershim Blvd, in North Hollywood (Sat & Sun 10am–2pm; donation; ☎818/763 -7651). Perhaps LA's most important historical site, this is where generals John Frémont and Andres Pico signed the 1847 Treaty of Cahuenga between the US and Mexico – which led to the more famous Treaty of Guadalupe Hidalgo – thus ending the Mexican–American War, and later allowing the US to officially acquire California and the rest of the Southwest. The adobe on the grounds is only a replica of an original 1840s structure, but every January you can watch a historical re-enactment of the events that made the site famous.

Several miles north on Lankershim Boulevard, the **North Hollywood Arts District** (⊛www.nohoartsdistrict.com), located around Magnolia Boulevard between Burbank and the western San Fernando Valley (and accessible by the Metrorail Red Line), was named "NoHo" by county bureaucrats as a play on New York's SoHo. While the name is a transparent ploy to drum up the tourist trade, it's still a lively enough spot, with no less than thirty live theaters and plenty of coffee shops, galleries, bookstores, restaurants, and odd boutiques to attract your interest. There are even flashes of the anarchic spirit that once flourished on Melrose Avenue, despite the fact that the district has almost nothing to do with Hollywood proper.

About six miles west in Van Nuys, the **Tillman Japanese Garden**, 6100 Woodley Ave, near the 405 freeway (grounds Mon–Thurs noon–4pm, Sun 10am–3.30pm, tours by reservation only Mon–Thurs; $3; ☏818/751-8166, ⊛www.thejapanesegarden.com), is a pleasant spot adorned with stone lanterns, bonsai trees, low bridges, a tea house, and artful streams and pools; surprisingly, the site uses reclaimed water from a nearby treatment plant and sits in the giant flood plain behind the Sepulveda Dam.

Due southwest off Ventura Boulevard, the district of **Encino** sits near **Los Encinos State Historic Park**, 16756 Moorpark St (Wed–Sun 10am–5pm; free; ☏818/784-4849, ⊛www.lahacal.org/losencinos.html), which includes all that remains of an original Native American settlement and later Mexican hacienda, along with an extensive cattle and sheep farm. In addition to a blacksmith's shop and lake fed by a natural spring, the main attraction is an 1849 adobe house, featuring high-ceilinged rooms that open out onto porches, shaded by oak trees (in Spanish, *encinos*) and kept cool by the two-foot-thick walls.

The Shadow and Orcutt ranches

At the western end of the Valley, in **West Hills**, are a few minor historic points of interest, including the **Shadow Ranch**, 22633 Vanowen St (Mon–Fri 10am–5pm, Sat 9am–5pm, Sun noon–5pm; free; ☏818/883-3637), the center of a 23,000-acre rancho that was controlled by land moguls I.N. Van Nuys and Isaac Lankershim. These days, it's mainly notable for its great stand of eucalyptus trees imported from Australia over 120 years ago, along with a main ranch home that retains its historic allure and hosts occasional arts-and-crafts shows. To the northwest is the **Orcutt Ranch**, 23600 Roscoe Blvd (daily 8am–5pm; free; ☏818/346-7449), also known as "Rancho Sombre del Roble," or Ranch Shaded by the Oak. Indeed, there's an impressive plot of ancient oaks here, some five hundred rose bushes, and citrus trees and bamboo too, alongside a traditional Spanish Colonial ranch house with a romantic grotto and a large sundial. Dating from 1921, the ranch first belonged to William Orcutt, the oil geologist who first found fossils in the La Brea Tar Pits, and initially spread out over two hundred acres – about ten times its current size.

The northern San Fernando Valley

A few miles east of Orcutt Ranch, Topanga Canyon Boulevard heads into the far northwest reaches of the Valley to **Stony Point**, a bizarre sandstone outcrop that has been used for countless Westerns, and in recent decades as a venue for LA's contingent of rock climbers. The area, though crossed by both Amtrak and Metrorail trains, has a desolate spookiness about it; it was used as a hideout by the legendary late-nineteenth-century bandit Joaquin Murrieta and it comes as little surprise to learn that during the late 1960s the Manson family lived for a

THE SAN GABRIEL AND SAN FERNANDO VALLEYS | Northern San Fernando Valley

Earthquake central: the San Fernando Valley

The devastating 6.7 magnitude **earthquake** that shook LA on the morning of January 17, 1994, was one of the most destructive disasters in US history. Fifty-five people were killed, two hundred more suffered critical injuries, and the economic cost is estimated at $8 billion. One can only guess how much higher these totals would have been had the quake hit during the day, when the many collapsed stores would have been crowded with shoppers, and the roads and freeways full of commuters. As it was, the tremor toppled chimneys and shattered windows all over Southern California, with the worst damage concentrated at the epicenter in the San Fernando Valley community of **Northridge**, where a dozen people were killed when an apartment building collapsed. At the northern edge of the Valley, the I-5/Hwy-14 interchange was destroyed, killing one motorist and snarling traffic for at least a year; while in West LA, the Santa Monica Freeway overpass collapsed onto La Cienega Boulevard at one of LA's busiest intersections. The Northridge event followed a quake in the eastern desert around **Landers** a few years earlier, and just eclipsed LA's previous worst earthquake in modern times, the 6.6 magnitude temblor of February 9, 1971, which had its epicenter in **Sylmar** – also in the Valley.

Small earthquakes happen all the time in LA, but in the unlikely event a sizable one strikes when you're in LA, protect yourself under something sturdy, such as a heavy table or a door frame, and well away from windows or anything made of glass. In theory, all the city's new buildings are "quake-safe"; the extent of the crisis in January 1994, however, forced the city to re-examine and reinforce buildings – though as the quake recedes in memory, the job seems to diminish in perceived importance. So when the inevitable **"Big One,"** a quake in the 8+ range, arrives, no one knows exactly what will be left standing.

time at the **Spahn Ranch**, just west at 12000 Santa Susana Pass, but off-limits to the public.

West of Stony Point, at the end of Santa Susana Pass Road, the little town of **Simi Valley** is the home of the **Ronald Reagan Presidential Library** (daily 10am–5pm; $7; ⊛www.reaganlibrary.com/pma), containing all the papers pertaining to the eight-year reign of the Gipper, as well as his memorial site, following on his death in 2004; worth a look is the graffiti-covered chunk of the Berlin Wall on display. More captivating is the bizarre folk-art shrine of **Grandma Prisbrey's Bottle Village**, 4595 Cochran St (by appointment only; ☎805/584-0572, ⊛echomatic.home.mindspring.com/bv), where assorted buildings – from the Leaning Tower of Pisa to simple shacks – are constructed from colorful bits of junk. Auto parts, broken lightbulbs, pencils, glass bottles, and other detritus all show up in the design, the highlight of which is the "Doll Head Shrine," a thoroughly disturbing array of antique plastic doll-heads stuck on poles. Although the site was damaged in the Northridge earthquake (and nearly torn down), slow work is being done to restore it.

San Fernando

At the northern tip of the Valley, the San Diego, Golden State, and Foothill freeways join together at I-5, the quickest route north to San Francisco. Standing near the junction, at 15151 San Fernando Mission Blvd in the small town of **SAN FERNANDO**, the church and many of the historic buildings of **Mission San Fernando Rey de España** (daily 9am–5pm; $5) had to be completely rebuilt following the 1971 Sylmar earthquake. It's hard to imagine now, walking through the nicely landscaped courtyards and gardens, but eighty-odd years ago, director D.W. Griffith used the then-dilapidated mission as a film site for *Our Silent Paths*, his tale of the Gold Rush. Nowadays, there's a good collection of pottery, furniture, and saddles, along with an old-time blacksmith's shop.

Also in the vicinity, another key nineteenth-century site can be found at 10940 Sepulveda Blvd, the **Andres Pico Adobe** (Mon & third Sun of month 10am–3pm; free; @www.sfvhs.com), the well-preserved estate and grounds of the eponymous Mexican general who fought off American troops, at least for a while, in the 1840s. This lovely, two-story brick adobe was built in 1834, with an upper story added in 1873 – which is the year to which the adobe has been restored. It's crammed with period furnishings and historical bric-a-brac, and makes a good spot for a stroll in an idyllic setting.

Sylmar and around

Up the road in nearby **SYLMAR** – famous mainly as the site of the 1971 earthquake – the wondrous **San Sylmar**, 15180 Bledsoe St (Tues–Sat 9am–4.30pm; tours by reservation 10am & 1.30pm; free; ☎818/367-2251, @www .nethercuttcollection.org), is a storehouse for all kinds of Wurlitzer organs, antique player-pianos, cosmetic paraphernalia, Tiffany stained glass, and classic French furniture. Most worthwhile, however, is its **Nethercutt Collection**, a stunning showroom filled with the finest collectors' automobiles imaginable. Packard, Mercedes, and Bugatti are all represented with classic models, but the eye-popping highlights are the Duesenbergs, splendid machines driven by movie stars in the Jazz Age, including a 1933 Arlington Torpedo model: a stunning silver roadster with curvaceous lines, sinuous bumpers, antique headlights, and an array of exposed chrome pipes.

A few miles east of the city of San Fernando, nature lovers can take a winding journey into the Angeles National Forest to see the **Wildlife Waystation**, 14831 Little Tujunga Canyon Rd (call for tours at ☎818/899-5201, @www .wildlifewaystation.org), which rehabilitates wild or unusual animals that have been injured in nature, abused in zoos, or kept (temporarily) as exotic pets by foolish owners – about four hundred at any one time. You'll see everything from foxes and coyotes to ocelots, chimps, and alligators, but especially numerous are big cats, including the likes of lions, jaguars, ocelots, lynxes, and even the lion-tiger hybrid of ligers.

North of the valleys

The thriving communities **north of the valleys** offer several compelling historical and cultural sights, along with one of LA's best theme parks. Most of these sights lie along or near the I-14 freeway, which leaves the San Fernando Valley to make a harsh trek into the periphery of the Mojave Desert – still part of the huge County of Los Angeles. To the far north of San Fernando, the remains of the former company town of **Mentryville**, three miles west of I-5 at 27201 W Pico Canyon Rd (grounds daily 9am–dusk; guided tours noon–4pm first & third Sun of month; donation; @www.mentryville.org), are where California's very first oil well was dug, in 1876. The boom only lasted a few decades and, despite the original well pumping until 1990 (making it the longest-operating oil well in history, at 114 years), the site was a ghost town for many years, until the state bought it from Chevron Oil. Saved from further decay, the preserved red-and-white barn, one-room 1880s schoolhouse, and

Victorian house of town-founder Charles Alexander Mentry evoke some of the city's old character.

To the east, in the town of **SANTA CLARITA**, the **William S. Hart Ranch and Museum**, 24151 San Fernando Rd (Wed–Fri 10am–1pm, Sat & Sun 11am–4pm; June–Aug Wed–Sun 11am–4pm; free; ⍟www.hartmuseum .org), holds a fine assemblage of native artworks, Remington sculptures, displays of spurs, guns, and lariats, Hollywood costumes, and authentic cowhand duds, housed in a Spanish Colonial mansion. The estate was constructed by silent-movie star Hart, who made 65 westerns and is still considered one of the all-time cowboy greats – playing many more complex and often troubled characters than his main cinematic rival, the smiling, white-hatted Tom Mix.

Conveniently, a trip to the Hart Museum may be combined with a trip to nearby **Magic Mountain**, Magic Mountain Parkway at I-5 (summer daily 10am–10pm; rest of year Sat & Sun only 10am–8pm; $47, kids $30, $8 parking; ⍟www.sixflags.com/parks/magicmountain), a three-hundred-acre complex that has some of the wildest roller coasters and rides in the world – a hundred times more thrilling than anything at Disneyland. Highlights include the Viper, a huge orange monster with seven loops; the appropriately named Goliath, full of harrowing 85mph dips; and Déjà Vu, a high-speed gut-wrencher that twists and jerks you in several different directions at once. The adjacent water park, **Hurricane Harbor** (same hours; $24, kids $17, or $57 for both parks; ⍟www .sixflags.com/parks/hurricaneharborla), provides plenty of aquatic fun if you don't mind getting splashed by throngs of giddy pre-adolescents.

The I-14 freeway, also called the Antelope Valley Freeway, branches off from I-5 into an extension of the Mojave Desert and takes you to **Vasquez Rocks Park**, off Agua Dulce Canyon Road at 10700 W Escondido Canyon Rd (☎661/268-0840), where acres of jagged, rocky outcroppings and an undulating terrain make for one of Hollywood's favorite film locations: everything from *The Flintstones* to *Dracula* to *Star Trek* has been shot here. Even more mythically, the illicit treasure of bandit Tiburcio Vásquez – one of LA's legendary figures, something like a Hispanic Jesse James – is supposedly buried in the vicinity. Further up I-14, near the remote desert burg of **LANCASTER**, the awe-inspiring **Antelope Valley Poppy Reserve**, on Lancaster Drive, spreads over 1800 acres. The reserve comes alive in April as the site of the annual **California Poppy Festival** (⍟www.poppyfestival.com), when the eye-blinding, fiery blooms appear in a sea of fluorescent orange.

Malibu and the Santa Monica Mountains

H ome to some of LA's most expensive real estate, **MALIBU** and the **SANTA MONICA MOUNTAINS** comprise a sweeping terrain relatively free from smog and violent crime, representing the contemporary good life in Southern California. Ironically, they are also under constant threat from natural dangers: built on eroding cliffs forever sliding into the ocean, the area faces considerable trouble from summer hillside fires, which blacken the landscape and leave a slick residue of burnt chaparral – a perfect surface for the catastrophic floods and mudslides that come just a few months later. The periodic arrival of El Niño–driven wet weather only makes the situation more dire, with watery calamities a constant, inescapable threat, most recently in 2005, when a **winter deluge** made for countless mudslides and street closures, and even (just up the coast in Ventura) a whole neighborhood being washed away.

Nonetheless, Malibu and the mountains feature some of LA's most picturesque scenery, their canyons, valleys, and forests making up a surprisingly large, pristine wilderness amid the surrounding urban development. From **Pacific Palisades**, a chic district just northwest of Santa Monica, to rustic **Topanga Canyon**, a wooded neighborhood with an artistic flair, to beautiful **Point Dume**, a whale-watching promontory, these seaside and mountainous areas are best navigated by car on the popular beachside motorway, the Pacific Coast Highway (also known as "PCH" or Highway 1). North of PCH, **Mulholland Highway** provides an alternative trip through the area, winding through the Santa Monica Mountains and skipping Malibu entirely, instead reaching the ocean less than a mile from LA County's distant northwest boundary – at one of its prime spots for surfing.

Pacific Palisades

Driving north on PCH beyond the bluffs of Santa Monica, you reach the sandy crescent of **Will Rogers State Beach** and, on the other side of the road, **PACIFIC PALISADES**, once an upper-crust community of artists and writers, but now the home of media-industry millionaires. No amount of wealth,

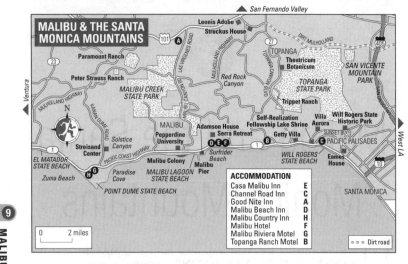

however, has been able to keep the district's hillsides from slowly falling into the ocean, most noticeably at the point above Chautauqua Boulevard and PCH. With each winter's storms, more of the place gets washed down to the street below by simple erosion or mudslides, blocking traffic on PCH and shrinking the backyards of the clifftop homes.

The Eames House and around

There are a few spots of interest among the suburban ranch houses, notably the **Eames House**, just off PCH at 203 Chautauqua Blvd, perhaps the most influential building of postwar LA. Fashioned out of prefabricated industrial parts in 1947 as part of the influential Case Study Program (see box, p.119), the compound boasts a main residential unit and an adjacent studio building, both resembling large, colored metal-and-glass boxes. Charles and Ray Eames (his wife) were one of the city's most creative couples in the 1950s, contributing thoughtful designs for art and architecture, furniture (especially the famous molded bucket chairs), and cinema – their short film *House: after 5 years* celebrates their residence with no less than three hundred evocative photographs. Although the property is off limits much of the time, and accessible only on a private drive, the grounds and exterior of the house are viewable, though strictly by appointment (call Mon–Fri 10am–4pm; entry $5; ☎310/459-9663, ⓦwww.eamesoffice.com).

The neighboring **Entenza House**, at no. 205, isn't quite up to the standard of the landmark next door, but this steel-framed structure was nonetheless built by the same architect, Charles Eames, with help from Eero Saarinen; also in this pocket of modern architecture is Richard Neutra's wood, glass, and steel marvel, the **Bailey House**, no. 219, part of the Case Study Program and recently up for sale if you have $4 million to spare. Best of the more contemporary buildings in Pacific Palisades is the **Schwartz House**, 444 Sycamore Ave, designed in 1994 by Pierre Koenig, more famous for his late-1950s Case Study House #22 (see box, p.119). His unique design includes a black-steel frame and foundation pivoted at a 30-degree angle from the rest of the boxy gray house, making for an unusual Rubik's Cube effect, which also has the function of keeping the living room and bedrooms out of the full glare of the rising sun.

Unexpected among all the sleek designs is a collection of **log cabins**, along Haldeman Road east of Rustic Canyon Recreation Center, sitting in the wooded hills that rise from Chautauqua Boulevard. These self-consciously quaint houses were the product of the **"Uplifters Club,"** a branch of the LA Athletic Club led by *Wizard of Oz* author L. Frank Baum, designed to "uplift art, promote good fellowship and build a closer acquaintance," but mainly serving as an excuse for having booze-soaked fun during Prohibition – giving it the nickname of the "Cuplifters Club." The rural charms of the houses, too, are somewhat deceptive – like Hollywood sets, many of the "cabins" have log facades that are merely glued on.

Will Rogers State Historic Park

To the north along Sunset Boulevard is **Will Rogers State Historic Park** (summer daily 8am–dusk; rest of year daily 8am–6pm; free; ☎310/454-8212), a steep climb from the MTA bus (#2, #302) stop. This was the home and ranch of Depression-era cowboy philosopher and journalist **Will Rogers**, one of America's most popular figures of the time, and renowned for saying that he "never met a man he didn't like" – though it's less well-known that he was a socialist who was also, ironically, mayor of Beverly Hills. After his death in a plane crash in 1935, there was a nationwide thirty-minute silence. The overgrown ranch-style house serves as an informal **museum**, though it's closed for renovation until 2006; when it reopens, it will likely be filled once more with cowboy gear and Native-American art. The still-open 200-acre park has miles of foot and bridle paths, including **polo grounds** where matches take place during the spring and summer (Apr–Oct Sat 2–4pm, Sun 10am–noon; free).

Castellammare

The western side of Pacific Palisades, **Castellammare** was named after a Latin port known as the "castle by the sea," its 1920s design mimicking Italian villas

△ The Santa Monica Mountains

MALIBU AND THE SANTA MONICA MOUNTAINS | Castellammare

and Spanish Colonial estates. Although it's now just another rich suburb, it does hold some appeal, mainly in structures whose settings are just as dramatic as their architecture.

Just before the street reaches PCH, the Pacific end of Sunset Boulevard reaches the most conspicuous sight in the area: the **Self-Realization Fellowship Lake Shrine**, 17190 Sunset Blvd (Tues–Sat 9am–4.30pm, Sun 12.30–4.30pm; free; ☎310/454-4114, ⊛www.yogananda-srf.org/temples/lakeshrine), a religious monument like no other, created in 1950 by Paramahansa Yogananda, whose life and works are recounted in an on-site **museum** (Tues–Sat 10am–4pm, Sun 10–10.30am & noon–4pm; free). The ten-acre lake shrine is an ecumenical ode to world faiths, featuring symbols and credos of the major religions. Visitors are invited to circle the lake on a literal path of spiritual enlightenment, pausing to view such sights as the **windmill chapel** (Tues–Sun 1–4.30pm; free), a church built as a replica of a sixteenth-century Dutch windmill, along with a massive archway topped with copper lotus flowers, a houseboat that the shrine's Indian founder once used, a bird refuge, gardens with religious symbols, and plaques and signs quoting the Bible, the Koran, and such. Unfortunately, the giant, gold-domed temple looming above on the hilltop is strictly for monks.

Up the bluffs from Sunset, the **Villa Aurora**, 520 Paseo Miramar, is an idyllic 1927 Spanish Colonial structure that was conceived as a public-relations project by the *LA Times*, which devoted a series of articles to the construction of the house and all its modern amenities – dishwasher, electric fridge, gas range – and stunning Mediterranean style, carried through in the Spanish tile, wrought-iron balconies, and alluring gardens. Readers were encouraged to tour the house and, it was hoped, be inspired to buy their own suburban dream home. Later, as the home of writer Lion Feuchtwanger, it became the focus of German emigres, hosting salons attended by Bertolt Brecht, Thomas Mann, Kurt Weill, Arnold Schoenberg, and Fritz Lang, and has since been reborn as a nonprofit organization that presents lectures, poetry readings, film screenings, and music recitals of contemporary artists from the Continent (usually free; ☎310/454-4231, ⊛www.villa-aurora.org).

The Getty Villa

North of Sunset Boulevard's intersection with PCH, the **Getty Villa** sits on a picturesque bluff overlooking the ocean. Once the site of the Getty Museum (now in West LA; see p.135), the villa will be reopening in 2006 as a center for the Getty's considerable cache of antiquities – a sizable horde of sculptures, vases, amphorae, and friezes displayed in galleries by theme, instead of chronology. The grounds have been remodeled to effect the look of a stylish hillside villa from the world of ancient Rome. Luckily, as with other facilities administered by this multibillion-dollar trust, the entrance should be free, though parking could be a problem (call for an update at ☎310/440-7300 or visit ⊛www.getty.edu).

Topanga Canyon

Around Topanga Canyon Boulevard north of PCH, **Topanga Canyon** is a stunning natural preserve. With hillsides covered in golden poppies and wildflowers, one hundred and fifty thousand acres of these mountains and adjacent seashore have been protected as the **Santa Monica Mountains National Recreation Area** (⊛www.lamountains.org). Boasting fine views and fresh air, the area is wilderness in many places, and you can still spot a variety of deer, coyote, and even the odd mountain lion. Like LA itself, the mountains are not without an element of danger, especially in winter and early spring, when mudslides threaten houses and waterfalls cascade down the cliffs. Most of the time, these hazards are of little concern to visitors, though the resultant damage can prevent you from traversing certain trails. Otherwise, rangers offer free guided hikes throughout the mountains most weekends (information and reservations at ☎818/597-9192). There are also self-guided trails through the canyon's **Topanga State Park**, off Old Topanga Canyon Boulevard at the crest of the mountains, with spectacular views over the Pacific. A good starting point for visitors is **Trippet Ranch**, north off Entrada Road, where trails like the Musch Trail – an easygoing trek through prime wildflower country – thread through terrain less rugged than other parts of the park. The local Audubon Society offers monthly birdwatching hikes through this and other LA-area nature zones (for Topanga State Park, first Sun of month 8am; reserve at ☎323/874-1318, ⓦwww.laaudubon.org). If you'd like to find out more, the Santa Monica Mountains **visitor center** in neighboring Thousand Oaks, 401 W Hillcrest Drive (daily 9am–5pm; ☎805/370-2301, ⓦwww.nps.gov/samo), has maps and information.

The nearby community of **TOPANGA**, further up Topanga Canyon Boulevard, was a proving ground for West Coast rock music in the 1960s and 70s, when Neil Young, the Byrds, and other (rich) artists moved here and held all-night jam sessions in the sycamore groves along Topanga Creek. The neighborhood still has an air of this history, although few real bohemians are left. If you'd like to revisit a bit of the old musical spirit, the **Topanga Community House**, 1440 Topanga Canyon Blvd (info at ☎310/455-1980), hosts occasional classical and pop concerts, along with children's puppet shows and storytelling hours. More enjoyable is the **Theatricum Botanicum**, close by at no. 1419, a wooded outdoor amphitheater known for its classical and modern plays, plus good summer performances of Shakespeare ($15–25, kids $8; information and tickets at ☎310/455-3723, ⓦwww.theatricum.com). Originally founded by Will Geer, known best as TV's Grandpa Walton, the theater is still very much a family affair, with daughter Ellen now directing the plays. If you're around for Memorial Day weekend, drop by the area for **Topanga Days** ($10; ⓦwww.topangacommunityclub.org), a country-flavored fair with art and craft booths, music, and vegetarian-oriented cuisine.

Before leaving the area, don't miss **Red Rock Canyon**, off Old Topanga Canyon Road via Red Rock Road, a stunning red-banded sandstone gorge that was formerly a Boy Scout retreat. Now a state park, the colorful rock formations, surrounding gardens, and riparian wildlife give you a good reason to leave your car behind and go exploring on foot.

Malibu

Further up PCH, past a long stretch of gated beachfront homes, lies **MALIBU**, the very name of which conjures up images of beautiful people sunbathing on palm-fringed beaches and lazily consuming cocktails. As you enter the small town, the succession of tourist-oriented surf shops and unassuming restaurants around **Malibu Pier** (primarily for fishing, at 23000 PCH), don't exactly reek of big money, but the secluded estates just inland are as valuable as any in the entire US, even though many are vulnerable to hillside wildfires and mudslides that are notoriously difficult to control.

Malibu Lagoon State Beach and around

Adjacent to the pier, **Surfrider Beach** was the surfing capital of the world in the early 1960s. Before that time, Southern California had been a hotspot for killer waves for a number of years, but, for better or worse, it took the *Gidget* and *Beach Blanket Bingo* movies (starring the likes of Sandra Dee, Annette Funicello, and Frankie Avalon) to really draw the masses. The waves are best in late summer, when storms off Mexico cause them to reach upwards of eight feet. Just to the west is **Malibu Lagoon State Beach** (daily 8am–dusk), a nature reserve where birdwatching walks around the lagoon are offered on occasional weekends, along with seasonal guided tours that showcase, among other things, the sea life in the marshes and tide pools. A small **museum**, 23200 PCH (Wed–Sat 11am–3pm; donation), gives you the historical rundown, from the Chumash era up to the arrival of Hollywood movie stars, with special emphasis on the long-running "Rindge saga" that informs much of Malibu's modern history.

Getting to the sands in Malibu

Visitors to Malibu commonly believe that all **beaches** in the area, aside from the officially marked state or county variety, are off-limits to interlopers – not surprising considering the sands are located in the very backyards of the gated communities that hug the Malibu shoreline. In reality, the sand along Santa Monica Bay is **open to visitors** below the high-tide mark, which means that as long as you stay off the private beachside territory above that mark (ie sticking to where the sand is wet and matted, instead of dry and hilly), you can go anywhere you please, peering into the guarded domains of the rich and famous – of which there are many, as any guide to stars' homes will tell you. The challenge, however, is in finding the **pedestrian rights-of-way** that give access to the beach. Space is at such a premium along PCH that there are hardly any public routes that lead to the public beaches. However, you can get around this situation with just a little effort. To begin with, there are no rights-of-way around the Malibu Colony, that gated and well-guarded celebrity province in the center of town, but if you don't mind walking a mile and a half along the ocean to get to the beaches behind these homes, you can park your car along the 22700 block of PCH (public parking lots are rare around here) and then take the unmarked stairway down to the sands. If for some reason you're thwarted at that entrance, or your *Map to the Stars' Oceanside Houses* simply directs you elsewhere, other access points can be found at 19900, 20300, and several between 24300 and 25100 PCH – admittedly farther from where the glitzy action is. Keep in mind also that these public-access points have been the subject of a number of **lawsuits** in recent years, with the elite sometimes putting up barriers to the less well-heeled, and aggrieved beach lovers seeking their revenge in court. Thus, if one public right-of-way is blocked, just keep trying.

While you may choose to head to the sands behind the Malibu Colony, there are almost as many celebs located to the east of Malibu Pier, around Carbon Beach. Even better, what decent works of architecture there are in Malibu can be spotted in full glory along this beach. There are few better than Richard Meier's stunning **Ackerberg House**, 22466 PCH, which looks like a nondescript wall of cement and white tile from the street, but from the beach looks exactly as its architect intended: a 1986 practice run for the Getty Center, rendered small, with the same rigidly geometric form clad in white-steel paneling and wraparound windows.

The story involves one **May K. Rindge** (widow of entrepreneur Frederick Rindge), who, up until the 1920s, owned all of Malibu – considered at the time to be the single most valuable real-estate parcel in the US. Employing armed guards and dynamiting roads to keep travelers from crossing her land on their way to and from Santa Monica, Rindge operated her own roads and private railroad and fought for years to prevent the Southern Pacific Railroad from laying down track through her property, as well as the state of California from building the Pacific Coast Highway across her land. She ultimately lost her legal battle in the state supreme court, and her money in the Depression; the road was built in 1928.

Before her mother went broke, Rindge's daughter and her husband hired architect Stiles O. Clements, of the legendary firm of Morgan, Walls and Clements (see box, p.88), to design the magnificent **Adamson House** (grounds 8am–sunset, house Wed–Sat 11am–pm; donation; ☎310/456-8432), on the grounds of the Malibu Lagoon museum. One of LA's finest pieces of Spanish Colonial architecture, the house features Mission Revival and Moorish elements, such as individually carved teak doors, glazed ceramic tiles, detailed ironwork, and Spanish and Middle Eastern furnishings, as well as expansive gardens and a pool and fountain.

The Malibu Colony and downtown

After May Rindge's mischief finally ceased, her son took over the ranch and quickly sold much of the land, establishing the **Malibu Colony**, along Malibu Colony Drive off of Malibu Road, as a haven for movie stars. Unless you take a long oceanside trek (see box, opposite) to see the estates of the glitterati from the sands, there's very little to see here because the public is barred admittance. For a celluloid look inside, check out Robert Altman's *The Long Goodbye*, in which the colony plays home to washed-up artists and blasé murder suspects. If you're after a glimpse of the stars, visit the **Malibu Colony Plaza**, near the area's gated entrance, good for star-spotting and stocking up on food and drink before a day on the sands, or **Malibu Country Mart**, 3835 Cross Creek Rd, where celebrities are regularly seen munching on veggies or sipping espressos.

To the north, spiritual relaxation can be found at the **Serra Retreat**, 3401 Serra Rd (☎310/456-6631, ⓦwww.serraretreat.com), a nondenominational religious haven named for Franciscan friar and missionary Junípero Serra, one of several such retreats operated by the friars throughout the West. You can enjoy a weekend getaway here in one of the hundred rooms, wander the flower gardens or get a fantastic hilltop view of the Pacific. The retreat was originally the site of the **Rindge Mansion**, but construction was mothballed during the Depression and the half-built property given over to the Franciscans, who finished the mansion and established their retreat here in 1943, only to see it burn down in 1970 and rebuilt after the missions of old.

Downtown Malibu, further up the coast, doesn't have much to grab your attention other than the **Malibu Castle**, a bizarre mock-medieval Scottish castle – with arched windows, stone tower, and crenellated walls and battlements – that sits on a hilltop and is a frequent film and TV shooting location. Your best bet is seeing it from Civic Center Way, well below its battlements.

North of downtown

Pepperdine University, 24255 PCH, moved north of downtown Malibu after hastily abandoning its Art Deco digs in South Central LA in 1971, and is mainly notable for its sloping green lawns and gigantic white cross, though the campus's

Frederick R. Weisman Museum of Art (Tues–Sun 11am–5pm; free; @ www .pepperdine.edu/arts/museum) sometimes puts on engaging shows of modern abstraction and Southern California art.

Across from Pepperdine, the hilltop **Malibu Bluffs State Park**, 24250 PCH, is a prime local spot for whale watching in the winter months, when you may spot orcas or baleen whales, depending on the time and weather. Further up, the less crowded shoreline of **Dan Blocker County Beach** – dedicated to the actor who played Hoss in TV's *Bonanza* – is the most appealing sight before you get to Corral Canyon Road, which leads you into **Solstice Canyon Park**, one of LA's hidden treasures and also one of its most peculiar. A mile down placid Solstice Canyon Creek is a rustic **cabin** from 1865 sitting in a state of arrested dilapidation – supposedly the oldest stone structure in Malibu. Past the cabin are the atmospheric remains of a modern estate known as **Tropical Terrace**, built in 1952 by master architect Paul Williams (more famous for the MCA Building in Beverly Hills, p.126), which was once surrounded by a ranch stocked with buffalo, camels, giraffes, and African deer. Burned down in 1982, the basic structure of the house is still standing, as are its surrounding brick steps, garden terraces – with inlaid horseshoes and bits of colored glass – and partially visible bomb shelter, with trees sprouting through the concrete and vines covering the brickwork. Beyond this, part of the estate was also leased by the technology firm TRW to test satellite and medical equipment, and you can still spot several structures for this research (done here because of the acoustic quirks of the canyon) along the TRW Trail.

Point Dume and beyond

Several miles northwards up the coast from downtown Malibu, **Point Dume**, named after the Franciscan padre Francisco Dumetz in 1793, is the tip of a great seaward promontory built on lava extruded from an ancient volcano, offering stunning vistas of Santa Monica Bay. Along with being a popular whale-watching spot from November to March, it also features some excellent strips of sand, including **Zuma Beach**, north at 30000 PCH (parking $8 for most beaches), the largest of the LA County beaches, where the surprise ending of the original *Planet of the Apes* was filmed; and **Point Dume State Beach**, a relaxed spot below the bluffs. Just east, **Paradise Cove** is a secluded stretch that makes for a fine walk, with superb views of fancy cliffside houses getting ready to fall into the surf from their high perches.

Given Malibu's walled-off security and privacy, the **Barbra Streisand Center**, north of Point Dume and PCH at 5750 Ramirez Canyon Rd, in Ramirez Canyon Park (individual tours Wed 1–4pm, groups Tues & Thurs 1–4pm; $35; by reservation only at @310/589-2850, @www.lamountains .com), comes as a bit of a shock: a 22-acre complex of houses and gardens that "Babs" donated to the Santa Monica Mountains Conservancy in 1993. Amid extensive flower, herb, and fruit gardens, you can get a glimpse into her former properties: the stained-glass windows and river-rock fireplace of the quaint "Barn," the Mediterranean and Art Nouveau stylings of the "Peach House," the Craftsman splendor of the singer's one-time production company building, the "Barwood," and the finest building on the site, the "Deco House," with its red-and-black colors, geometric decor, and stainless-steel panels taken from Downtown's Richfield Building, before that Art Deco monument was sadly destroyed in 1968.

Several miles up the coast from Point Dume, at 32100 PCH, **El Matador State Beach** was where the opening shots of the movie musical *Grease* were filmed, and still has the flair of a secluded private beach, thanks mostly to its entrance being at an easily missable turn off PCH – look for it on the south side of the road about a half-mile east of the junction with Encinal Canyon Drive. Another five miles north, where Mulholland Drive reaches the ocean, **Leo Carrillo** ("ca-REE-oh") **State Beach Park**, 35000 PCH, marks the northwestern border of LA County and the end of the MTA bus system (on route #434). The mile-long sandy beach is divided by Sequit Point, a bluff with underwater caves and a tunnel you can pass through at low tide, and is also one of LA's best campgrounds (see p.262). The beach has also starred in quite a few Hollywood flicks (including several in the *Gidget* series), much like its namesake: Carrillo was an actor who appeared in nearly one hundred films and was best known as Pancho in the 1950s TV show *The Cisco Kid*.

Mulholland Highway

Most familiar as the road running along the crest of the Hollywood Hills, Mulholland Drive continues west of the 405 freeway and takes drivers through the heart of the Santa Monica Mountains, where it becomes **Mulholland Highway**, a lengthy, winding route that can easily take several hours to traverse because of its alternatively rutted terrain and hair-raising curves. Keep in mind that the highway is completely off-limits when winter rains reduce these hillsides to mud-choked slurry. Nonetheless, in the dry season it's an excellent introduction to LA's unheralded natural environment; just make sure to bring a sturdy vehicle that can handle the initial leg of the trip.

For most of its first seven miles westward, from Encino Hills Drive to Topanga Canyon Boulevard, Mulholland is a bumpy dirt road strewn with broken rocks, fallen trees, and sizable mudholes, truly earning its nickname, "**Dirt Mulholland**" – though the awe-inspiring vistas and abundant greenery are reward enough. While in the area, don't miss the towering ten-acre hilltop of **San Vicente Mountain Park**, 17500 Mulholland Hwy, less than three miles west of the 405 freeway, a decommissioned military site that was used between 1956 and 1968 as a radar center and launching pad for Nike anti-aircraft missiles, to be fired in the event of a Soviet bomber run over LA. This unusual state park offers you the chance to climb a zigzagging stairway up to a hexagonal viewing platform on top of the command tower, where you can ponder the Cold War while staring down at striking vistas of the San Fernando Valley.

The Struckus House and Leonis Adobe

The paved portion of Mulholland Highway can be picked up from either the end of Dirt Mulholland, roughly around Canoga Avenue in the suburb of Woodland Hills, or from the Mulholland Drive exit off the 101 freeway. Just to the north, the **Struckus House**, Canoga Avenue at Saltillo Street, is one of LA's most unusual homes, designed by quirky architect Bruce Goff (see also LACMA's Pavilion for Japanese Art, p.93). Looking somewhat like an alien landing pod, it features a four-story redwood cylinder decorated with four vertically stacked, convex "eyes," a wooden roof with flywheel spokes, and a square door that pivots on a single ball-bearing. For a close-up look at another of the area's notable buildings, head north toward the 101, west of Mulholland Drive, to the **Leonis Adobe**, 23537 Calabasas Rd (Wed–Sun 1–4pm, Sat opens 10am; $4; ☏818/222-6511, ⊛www.leonisadobemuseum .com), an 1844 ranch and adobe. The grounds of this lovely Spanish estate include a blacksmith, windmill, barn, and restored carriage, as well as the engaging **Plummer House**, a Victorian-era home relocated from Holly-wood and now the rancho's visitor center, where you can see exhibits on the estate's history.

Malibu Creek State Park and Paramount Ranch

To the south, Mulholland Highway takes you through the forest, brush, and scattered dwellings of the Santa Monica Mountains, at times via dizzying switchbacks and narrow cliffside passages. There are many excellent state and regional parks here (get a sense of their size and splendor at ⊛lamountains .com) and plenty of movie history, too. Perhaps the most notable site is **Malibu Creek State Park**, just south of Mulholland Highway on Las Virgenes Road, a scenic 4000-acre park that once belonged to 20th Century-Fox studios, which filmed many Tarzan pictures here, as well as the original *Planet of the Apes*, and used the chaparral-covered hillsides to simulate South Korea for the TV show *M*A*S*H*. Pick up a map at the visitor center (Sat & Sun noon–4pm) to avoid getting lost on its nearly fifteen miles of hiking trails, or make a reservation beforehand to pitch your tent and camp (see p.262).

Further west on Mulholland, **Paramount Ranch**, 2813 Cornell Rd (☏818/222-6511, ⊛www.nps.gov/samo/maps/para.htm), is another old studio lot dating from 1927, with an intact Western movie set used in films starring Gary Cooper, W.C. Fields, and Hopalong Cassidy, and TV programs like *The Rifleman*, *The Cisco Kid*, and *Dr. Quinn Medicine Woman*. Film and TV crews still occasionally shoot here on weekdays, though generally without public notice. Oddly, visitors often mistake the phony rail station and tracks behind the set and the dummy cemetery for the real thing.

△ Filming on location at Paramount Ranch

West to the ocean

A few miles west of Cornell Road, at 30000 Mulholland Hwy, the charming **Peter Strauss Ranch** was once the site of the **Lake Enchanto Resort**, a top LA amusement spot from the 1930s through the 1950s, until a nearby dam burst and washed it away. Resurrected variously as a resort and a nudist colony, the property passed into the hands of actor and producer Peter Strauss, who, after yet another dam burst, turned it over to the Santa Monica Mountains Conservancy. Although a few hints of the old days remain – such as a disused swimming pool and terrazzo patio – the park is a pretty low-key attraction, laced with plenty of hiking trails and hosting occasional art exhibitions, as well as blues and classical concerts on Sunday afternoons in summer (call ☎805/370-2301 for details, ◉www.nps.gov/samo/maps/peter.htm).

Mulholland continues westward until it reaches the Pacific Ocean near Leo Carrillo State Beach Park (see p.225), passing a number of excellent parks and striking vistas along the way, most of them controlled and protected by the Santa Monica Mountains Conservancy. Other than these natural delights, the last point of interest on Mulholland is the **Arch Oboler House**, a little-known Frank Lloyd Wright structure near Westlake Boulevard and the LA County line at 32436 Mulholland Hwy. The unfinished studio and gatehouse, angular curiosities built of wood and stone, were meant to be part of an expansive hillside complex for the now-forgotten film director Oboler, creator of such works as *Bwana Devil*, the first movie in 3-D, and *Five*, about the survivors of a nuclear holocaust – which the director filmed here at his own residence.

10

Orange County

N ow that the abundant citrus groves that provided its name are long gone, **ORANGE COUNTY** is more synonymous with insular, suburban conservatism than it is with fruit. The longstanding stereotype has painted the place as a West Coast version of Levittown – where tract homes and asphalt stretched to the horizon and anyone not fitting into the rigid sense of bourgeois conformity was shunned, ridiculed, or forced into exile in LA proper. These days, though, Orange County is no more bland and homogenous than any other part of metropolitan LA. In fact, the county has in the last two decades become multicultural, with rising numbers of Latino immigrants transforming the character of cities like Santa Ana, and other newcomers from Southeast Asia, India, and Eastern Europe developing their own urban communities as well. The fractured social landscape of libertarian beach cities, reactionary old-line suburbs, burgeoning immigrant districts, and hordes of itinerant tourists is bound together by the ubiquitous freeway system.

Although there is no simple way of splitting up the place, two general divisions are useful. The original heart of the 1940s and 1950s suburbs, **inland Orange County** is the famous domain of Mickey Mouse and Knott's Berry Farm. The area's become just as notable, though, for its rapid cultural changes, as white-bread suburbia has been in retreat for some time. More appealing for visitors without a yen for theme parks, the **Orange County coast** is a collection of relaxed seaside towns with both easygoing "surfer-dude" attitudes and upscale, beach-condo snootiness. Keep in mind, though, that the coastal cities never really stop, but just blend into even more housing colonies as you head further south – a seemingly endless exurban stretch between LA and San Diego – where the insularity and fear of change can resemble the Orange County of old.

Inland Orange County

Located in the heart of **INLAND ORANGE COUNTY**, the first modern theme park, **Disneyland**, was opened in 1955 by Walt Disney, who correctly divined that the area around the seminal theme park – the bland burg of **Anaheim** – would become the next great center of population growth in Southern California. It did, but not as he intended: for miles around the park stretch nothing but tacky strip malls, chain motels, and knick-knack shops. Nonetheless, this suburb and those around it continue to grow rapidly, drawing immigrants by the thousands. **Westminster**, for example, is now the site

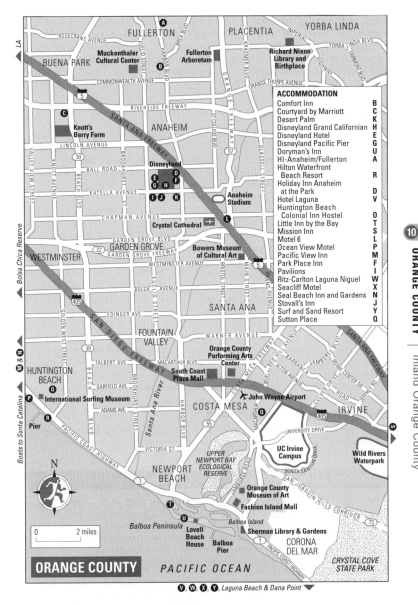

ACCOMMODATION

Comfort Inn	**B**
Courtyard by Marriott	**C**
Desert Palm	**K**
Disneyland Grand Californian	**H**
Disneyland Hotel	**E**
Disneyland Pacific Pier	**G**
Doryman's Inn	**U**
HI-Anaheim/Fullerton	**A**
Hilton Waterfront Beach Resort	**R**
Holiday Inn Anaheim at the Park	**D**
Hotel Laguna	**V**
Huntington Beach Colonial Inn Hostel	**O**
Little Inn by the Bay	**T**
Mission Inn	**S**
Motel 6	**L**
Ocean View Motel	**P**
Pacific View Inn	**M**
Park Place Inn	**F**
Pavilions	**I**
Ritz-Carlton Laguna Niguel	**W**
Seacliff Motel	**X**
Seal Beach Inn and Gardens	**N**
Stovall's Inn	**J**
Surf and Sand Resort	**Y**
Sutton Place	**Q**

ORANGE COUNTY

PACIFIC OCEAN

V, **W**, **X**, **Y**, *Laguna Beach & Dana Point* ▼

of Little Saigon, a center for Vietnamese expatriates, and is the most fervent bastion of anti-Communism in Southern California, long after the end of the Cold War.

One thing hasn't changed, though: Disneyland, or the presumed allure of it, still dominates the area. Elsewhere, the thrill rides at **Knott's Berry Farm** go some way to restoring antique notions of what amusement parks used to be like, the **Crystal Cathedral** is an imposing reminder of the potency of the evangelical movement, and the **Richard Nixon Library and Birthplace** is a good spot to find out about the illustrious life and career of Tricky Dick. Isolated spots of cultural and entertainment interest can even be found in places like **Santa Ana** and **Fullerton** – places usually well off the well-beaten tourist trail.

Disneyland

In the minds of many tourists, the sole reason to visit Orange County, perhaps LA itself, is to experience the colossal theme park of **Disneyland**, 1313 Harbor Blvd at Katella Avenue, Anaheim (summer daily 8am–1am; rest of year Mon–Fri 10am–6pm, Sat 9am–midnight, Sun 9am–10pm; $50, $40 kids, parking $8; ☏714/781-4565, ☖disneyland.com), known the world over as one of the defining bulwarks of American culture (with some intellectual wags like Jean Baudrillard claiming *this* as the real America, and everything else as fake). Since its opening fifty years ago, Walt Disney's fun zone has long been the most famous, most carefully constructed, most influential theme park anywhere.

For such a culturally powerful place, Disneyland occupies less than one square mile of Anaheim (unlike Disneyworld in Florida, which sits on 46 square miles of Disney-owned turf), and is hemmed in by the low-end developments surrounding it, making the park a hermetically sealed world unto itself. Even within such rigid boundaries, it remains corporate America's ultimate fantasy, with the emphasis strongly on family fun.

Even if you only have a (rather expensive) one-day pass to Disneyland, you will not see everything in the park, no matter how hard you try: the lines are lengthy and unavoidable. As such, it's wisest to choose a few of the top rides – which during peak periods may have lines with two-hour waiting periods – alongside a larger range of less popular ones. The admission price includes them all, except for **California Adventure**, which will cost you quite a bit more.

Main Street and Adventureland

From the front gates, **Main Street** leads through a scaled-down, camped-up replica of a c.1900 Midwestern town, filled with souvenir shops, food

---

Planning a trip to Disneyland

Depending on traffic, Disneyland is about 45 minutes by **car** from Downtown LA on the Santa Ana Freeway (I-5). By **train** from Downtown (there are ten a day), it's a thirty-minute journey to Fullerton, from where OCTD buses will drop you at Disneyland or Knott's Berry Farm. By **bus**, MTA #460 from Downtown takes about ninety minutes, and Greyhound runs twelve-to-fourteen buses a day and takes 45 minutes to get to Anaheim, from where it's an easy walk to the park.

As for **accommodation**, most people try to visit Disneyland just for the day and spend the night somewhere else, or at home. If you must stay, we've listed some reasonable options on p.258; alternately, the *HI-Anaheim/Fullerton* hostel is the cheapest bet in the area (see p.260). Your culinary options in Disneyland are more limited: a massive central kitchen produces all the **food** that's eaten in the park (you're not permitted to bring your own), unloading popcorn, hot dogs, hamburgers, and other all-American junk food from the many stands by the ton. For anything healthier, you'll need to leave the park and travel a fair way. The "Eating" listings on p.272 and p.296 suggest some of the more palatable options.

stands, and penny arcades, directly to **Sleeping Beauty's Castle**, a pseudo-Rhineland palace at the heart of the park that looks inviting, but in reality isn't much more than a walk-through prop – the official Disneyland logo, writ large.

Radiating out clockwise from Main Street, **Adventureland** was built near the height of the Tiki craze in the 1950s and 1960s, and could make for a swinging, retro-kitsch experience, if Disneyland ever bothered to renovate it. As it is, the old-time centerpiece, the Jungle Cruise, looks pretty anti-quated these days, offering "tour guides" making crude puns about the fake animatronic beasts creaking amid the trees. Tarzan's Treehouse isn't much better, little more than a movie tie-in taking up the space once occupied by the Swiss Family Robinson Treehouse – catwalks in the branches, rustic rooms with assorted playthings, and an 8-year-old target audience. Ultimately, if you're going to spend any time at all in this section, then get in line for the **Indiana Jones Adventure**, which more than four hundred "imagineers" (the cutesy Disney term for ride engineers) worked to create. Two hours of waiting in line are built into the ride, with an interactive archeological dig and 1930s-style newsreel show leading up to the main feature – a speedy journey along 2500ft of skull-encrusted corridors, loosely based on the *Indiana Jones* trilogy, in which you face fireballs, burning rubble, venomous snakes, and a rolling-boulder finale.

The nearby **New Orleans Square**, clockwise to the northwest, is the site of **Club 33**, Walt's ultra-exclusive dinner club for his chums in the corporate and political elite, which even today offers membership by invitation at a (last-reported) entry cost of $5000, and once featured microphones surreptitiously hidden in the chandeliers to record the comments of dinner guests – it's also the only place in the park where alcohol is served. Although you definitely can't get in, you can spot the club's door, marked with a "33." The door is located next to the facade of the *Blue Bayou* restaurant, which, despite its jaw-dropping prices for steak and seafood, has some of the best dining ambience in Orange County: a darkly romantic waterfront scene with dim lighting, old-fashioned Southern decor, and imitation crickets chirping in the distance. (Reserve early at ☏714/956-6755, the reservation line for all Disneyland restaurants, or ☏714/781-3463 for priority seating.)

From your table, you'll be able to see crowds lining up for the park's best ride, the **Pirates of the Caribbean**, a renowned boat-trip through underground caverns, singing along with drunken pirates, laughing skeletons, and all manner of ruddy-cheeked yokels hooting and bellowing for your amusement. Nearby, another of Disneyland's legendary rides, the **Haunted Mansion**, features a riotous "doom buggy" tour in the company of the house ghouls, with a night-marish elevator ride to start the trip off in skin-crawling fashion and plenty of creepy portraits to stare at along the way, culminating with a ghost hitching a ride in your buggy.

Frontierland and Fantasyland

Less fun is **Frontierland**, the smallest of the various themelands, located further clockwise around the park. Supposedly the area takes its cues from the Wild West and the tales of Mark Twain, but any unsavory and complex elements have been carefully deleted; still, Tom Sawyer Island offers an elaborate playground for tots, with treehouses, caves, and canoes. The centerpiece of Frontierland, Thunder Mountain Railroad, despite being a slow-moving roller coaster, was the site of a fatal accident in 2003 when one of its cars derailed. Apart from this fluke, the ride isn't dangerous, and takes you through a rocky landscape resembling a cartoon version of a Hollywood Western. Nearby, the focus of **Critter Country** is Splash Mountain, a fun log-flume ride in which you can expect to get drenched.

Across the drawbridge from Main Street, **Fantasyland** shows off the cleverest and most sentimental aspects of the Disney mind. The highlight, Mr Toad's Wild Ride, is a jerky funhouse trip through Victorian England featuring an actual trip into hell. The other rides are much tamer, such as those involving Peter Pan flying over London and Snow White being tormented by the wicked witch. It's a Small World gets the most extreme reactions, with children delighting in this boat tour of the world's continents – in which animated dolls sing the same cloying song over and over again – and adults finding it a slow, gurgling torture test. Distract yourself by trying to spot the sole non-smiling character on the entire ride, a frowning clown in the final room. Lastly, the one Fantasyland roller coaster, the Matterhorn, is somewhat entertaining for its phony cement mountain and goofy abominable snowman appearing when you round a corner, though the dips and curves are rather bland compared with most coasters these days.

Tomorrowland and Toontown

On the park's northern end, **Toontown**, a cartoon village with goofy sound effects and Day-Glo colors, is aimed only for the under-10 set and generally unbearable for older, thrill-seeking visitors.

On the eastern side of the park, **Tomorrowland** is Disney's vision of the future, where theme-park regulars know to go first when the place opens. Here, the Space Mountain roller coaster zips through the pitch-blackness of "outer space," bumbling scientists dabble with 3-D trickery in Honey, I Shrunk the Audience, and a runaway space cruiser blasts through the Moon of Endor (home of the Ewoks) in George Lucas's Star Tours. This idea of the future occasionally looks like a hangover from the past – note rides such as Autopia, where you drive a miniature car at a glacial pace – but this fun zone has been updated somewhat in recent years, with new rides like the Jules Verne–inspired Astro Orbiter taking the place of old ones like the torpid PeopleMover and its failed replacement, Rocket Rods. One of the more interesting additions is Innoventions, which comes with a lot of futurist babble but is really a fun opportunity to look at, and play with, the latest special effects. In addition to these attractions, **firework displays** explode every summer night, and **parades** and special events celebrate important occasions – such as Mickey Mouse's birthday.

California Adventure

The latest part of Disneyland is **California Adventure**, technically a separate park but connected to the main one in architecture, style, and spirit. It does for California's history and culture what Epcot Center in Florida does to the world's – remove all the rough edges and make it digestible for even the youngest children. Aside from its slightly better food, California Adventure is really just another "land" to visit, albeit a much more expensive one. You cannot get access to both parks with a single-day admission ticket, so if you want to visit, you'll instead have to shell out another $50 or plunk down $98 for a two-day pass that covers both (kids $70). Such high prices and the comparative lack of thrills have really served to puncture the hype that Disneyland built up for this park, so unless you're hopelessly obsessed by all things Disney, you're better off avoiding the place.

There are a handful of highlights if you do visit: Grizzly River Run is a fun giant-inner-tube ride, splashing through plunges and "caverns"; Soarin' Over California is an exciting trip on a mock-experimental aircraft that buzzes through hairpin turns and steep dives; and the **Pacific Pier** zone has a slew of old-fashioned carnival rides that only faintly recall the wilder, harder-edged midways of California's past. There's also a rather tame zone devoted to Tinseltown, the **Hollywood Pictures Backlot** which, aside from a few theaters, special-effects displays, and the Twilight Zone Tower of Terror (a shock-drop ride in a haunted hotel), is mainly notable for its loose borrowing of the set design from D.W. Griffith's 1916 failure *Intolerance* – exotic columns, squatting elephants, and so on (a design also used in the Hollywood and Highland mall; see p.109.)

Knott's Berry Farm

It's hard to escape the clutches of Disneyland even when you leave: everything in the surrounding area is built around it, from diners to dive bars. Some prefer the more down-to-earth **Knott's Berry Farm**, four miles northwest, off the Santa Ana Freeway at 8039 Beach Blvd (summer Mon & Sun–Thurs 9am–11pm, Fri & Sat 9am–midnight; rest of year Mon–Fri 10am–6pm, Sat 10am–10pm, Sun 10am–7pm; $45, kids $30; ⊛www.knotts .com), a relaxed, though still pricey, park born during the Depression when people began lining up for the fried-chicken dinners prepared by Mrs Knott, a local farmer's wife. To amuse the children while they waited for their food, Mr Knott reconstructed a Wild West ghost town and added amusements until the park had grown into the sprawling sideshow of roller coasters and carnival rides standing today.

Unlike Disneyland, this park can easily be seen in one day, as long as you concentrate on the roller coasters, which now make Knott's second only to

△ Thrill rides at Knott's Berry Farm

Magic Mountain (see p.216) on the West Coast for number of thrill rides per acre. Although there are ostensibly six themed lands here, several of them, namely the **Ghost Town** and **Indian Lands**, consist only of familiar carnival rides, fast-food stands, and dodgy versions of history. **Camp Snoopy** is the Knott's version of Disney's Toontown, and just as tiresome, while the **Wild Water Wilderness** isn't really a theme area at all, but simply the site of the moderately exciting Bigfoot Rapids giant-inner-tube ride.

Simply put, you should spend most or all of your time in just two areas: **Fiesta Village**, home to Montezooma's Revenge, the original one-loop coaster, and Jaguar, a high-flying coaster that spins you around the park concourse; and the **Boardwalk**, which is all about heart-thumping thrill rides. There's the Boomerang, a forward-and-back coaster that can easily induce nausea; WindJammer, two racing coasters looping and dipping around each other; Supreme Scream, a delightfully terrifying freefall drop; Xcelerator, a 1950s-themed roller coaster; and the Perilous Plunge, a hellish drop at a 75-degree angle that's far more exciting than any old log-flume ride. Similarly, this Boardwalk, Knott's version of a carnival midway, with its death-defying rides and vomit-inducing thrills, easily puts Disney's Pacific Pier to shame. The adjacent Knott's water park, **Soak City U.S.A.** (May–Sept only, hours vary but generally 10am–8pm; $25, kids $13, $15 for entry after 3pm; ⓦwww.knotts.com/soakcity), offers 21 rides of various heights and speeds, almost all of them involving the familiar water slides – either with or without an inner tube – that can really bring out the sweltering masses on a hot summer day.

Around Disneyland

South of Disneyland just off the Santa Ana Freeway, in otherwise uneventful **GARDEN GROVE**, the giant **Crystal Cathedral**, 12141 Lewis St (tours Mon–Sat 9am–3.30pm; free; ⓦwww.crystalcathedral.org), is a hugely garish Philip Johnson design of tubular space-frames and plate-glass walls that forms part of the vision of televangelist Robert Schuller. Not content with owning the world's first drive-in church next door, Schuller commissioned this dramatic prop to boost the ratings of his Sunday sermons, raising $1.5 million for its construction during one service alone. These sermon-spectacles reach their climax with the special Christmas production, using live animals in biblical roles and people disguised as angels suspended on ropes.

A more worthwhile attraction lies in the nearby burg of **SANTA ANA**, where the splendid **Bowers Museum of Cultural Art**, 2002 N Main St (Tues–Sun 11am–4pm; $14, kids $8; ⓦwww.bowers.org), features anthropological treasures from early Asian, African, Native-American, and pre-Columbian civilizations. Showcasing artifacts as diverse as ceramic Mayan icons, hand-crafted baskets from native Californians and highly detailed Chinese funerary sculpture, the museum is an essential stop for anyone interested in the art and history of non-Western civilizations. Same-day visitors can, for the same entry ticket, take their children to the adjacent **Kidseum** (Sat & Sun 11am–4pm), a less invigorating look at the same subject, made easily digestible for bored youngsters.

Fullerton

North of Disneyland, unimposing **FULLERTON** also has a few interesting sights, among them the **Fullerton Arboretum**, in the northeast corner of the

California State campus at 1900 Associated Rd (daily 8am–4.45pm; $2; @www
.arboretum.fullerton.edu), which provides relief from theme-park overload
with its own themed gardens, including cycads, palms, cacti, rare fruits, and even
the kind of citrus groves that used to grow in abundance in Orange County.
In the middle of the arboretum stands the **Heritage House** (tours Sat & Sun
2–4pm; free), an 1894 Eastlake Victorian that, with its historic displays and
vintage decor, harkens back to a more bucolic time.

Much more surprising is the presence of an esteemed institution in
such a little-known hamlet like Fullerton, the **Muckenthaler Cultural
Center**, 1201 W Malvern Ave (Wed–Sun noon–4pm; $5, kids free; @www
.muckenthaler.org), located in an attractive 1924 Renaissance Revival
mansion and hosting a wide range of cultural events and exhibits. The
emphasis here is strongly on international multicultural art, with Native-
American art and textiles, African craftwork and jewelry, and contemporary
Korean ceramics only a few of the highlights. There are also countless examples of decorative arts, drawings, and textiles from around the world – not
to mention displays of local artists, and, this being Southern California, an
annual display of "automotive art" in the spring, with many colorful car-
related illustrations and designs.

The Richard Nixon Library and Birthplace

Mickey Mouse may be its most famous resident, but Orange County's favorite
son was 37th US president Richard Milhous Nixon, born in 1913 in what is
now freeway-caged **YORBA LINDA**, eight miles northeast of Disneyland.
Here, the **Richard Nixon Library and Birthplace**, 18001 Yorba Linda Blvd
(Mon–Sat 10am–5pm, Sun 11am–5pm; $8, kids $3; @www.nixonfoundation
.org), is a hagiographic library, museum, and memorial that features oversized
gifts from world leaders, amusing campaign relics, and obsequious letters written by and to Nixon. However, it's in the constantly running archive of TV
recordings that the distinctive Nixon persona – shaking his head and glowering
– really shines through.

After viewing a few of these recordings, such as the famous "Checkers"
speech (see box, overleaf), take a walk through the **World Leaders Gallery**
of Nixon's heyday, with Mao, Brezhnev, and de Gaulle among them, cast in
metal and arranged in rigid, pompous poses. Throughout the museum, Nixon's
face leers down in Orwellian fashion from almost every wall, but only inside
the **Presidential Auditorium** (at the end of the corridor packed with notes
attesting to the president's innocence in Watergate) do you get the chance to
ask him a question. After making your selection, Nixon's gaunt features will fill
the overlarge screen and provide the stock reply – though "I am not a crook"
is never one of the correct answers.

In 2004, the new **Loker Center** opened on the premises, the high points of
which are a miniature, 70ft replica of the White House and the re-creation of
the **East Room** of the executive mansion, replicated in architecture and decor.
It's an odd tribute, given that Nixon was always uncomfortable in Washington
and did all he could to escape it. Even in death, he avoided lying in state (unlike
Ronald Reagan) and made provision for his memorial service to take place
here, where he's buried.

On your way out, stop by the **gift shop** to see its most popular item, a picture
of Nixon greeting a zonked-out Elvis in the Oval Office, on the occasion of
the president's granting the King – ironically, as it turned out – honorary status
as a federal agent in the war on drugs.

Richard Nixon: a life in politics

Qualified as a lawyer from the town of Whittier (see p.174) and fresh from wartime, non-combat service in the Navy, **Richard Milhous Nixon** entered politics as a Republican congressman in 1946, smearing his incumbent rival Jerry Voorhees as a closet Communist and later running for the Senate, calling his opponent Helen Gahagan Douglas the "Pink Lady... right down to her underwear." For all his venom, Douglas gave him the name that stuck throughout his career – **Tricky Dick**.

Shortly after arriving in Washington, Nixon joined the **House Un-American Activities Committee (HUAC)**, a legendary group of red-baiters led by the infamous Joseph McCarthy, which wrecked the lives and careers of many Americans. Although these hearings eventually backfired on McCarthy (he was later censured by Congress), they launched Nixon to national prominence, culminating in his becoming Dwight Eisenhower's **vice-president** in 1953, at only 39 years old. It almost didn't happen, though: just before the election, the discovery of undeclared income precipitated the "funds crisis," which cast doubts over Nixon's honesty. Incredibly, his **"Checkers speech"** convinced 58 million TV viewers of his integrity, his performance climaxing with the statement that, regardless of the damage it may do to his career, he would not be returning the cocker spaniel (Checkers) given to him as a gift and now a family pet.

Eight years later, Nixon was defeated in his own bid for the presidency by John F. Kennedy, due in no small part to his sweaty, nervous appearance during their 1960s live **TV debates**, and – some allege – by the cattle voting in Texas and the dead in Chicago. This loss led him into his **"wilderness years"**: avoiding the spotlight, except to raise money for fellow Republicans, he took several lucrative corporate posts and wrote *Six Crises*, a book of deep introspection and some degree of paranoia. Seeking a power base for the next presidential campaign, Nixon ran for the governorship of California in 1962. His humiliating defeat to Pat Brown ended with a memorable jibe at the press ("You won't have Nixon to kick around anymore") and prompted a short-lived "retirement," which did nothing to suggest that six years later he would beat Ronald Reagan to the Republican nomination and be **elected president** in 1968.

The country Nixon inherited was more divided than at any time since the Civil War. The **Vietnam War** was at its height, and in time his large-scale illegal bombing of Cambodia earned him worldwide opprobrium. Nonetheless, facing a weak opponent in George McGovern, Nixon was decisively re-elected in 1972, winning 49 states.

Despite his victory, Nixon's second term ended prematurely over the **Watergate Scandal**. In January 1973, seven men were tried for breaking into and bugging the headquarters of the Democratic Party in Washington's Watergate building, an act discovered to have been financed with money allocated to the Committee to Re-elect the President (CREEP). Ironically, Nixon's insistence on taping all White House conversations in order to ease the future writing of his memoirs was to be the major stumbling block to his surviving the crisis. Upon the revelation of a "smoking gun" tape proving his complicity in obstructing justice, Nixon **resigned** in 1974 under threat of impeachment.

The full **pardon** granted to Nixon by his successor, Gerald Ford, did little to arrest widespread public disillusionment with the country's political machine. Remarkably, Nixon's post-presidency saw him quietly seek to establish elder-statesman credentials, opining on world affairs through books and newspaper columns, and waging a seemingly endless legal battle to keep control of the notorious audiotapes (which have only recently become available to the public). He died in 1994 and was buried at Yorba Linda.

The Orange County coast

A string of towns stretching from the edge of the LA Harbor to San Diego County 35 miles south, the **ORANGE COUNTY COAST** is chic suburbia with a shoreline: swanky beachside houses line the sands, and the general ambience is easygoing, affluent, and conservative or libertarian, depending on the area. As the names of the main towns suggest – **Huntington Beach**, **Newport Beach**, and **Laguna Beach** – most of the good reasons to come here involve sea and sand, though a handful of museums and festivals can also make for an interesting excursion as well. To the far south, **San Juan Capistrano** merits a stop as the site of the best-kept of all the Californian missions, and **San Clemente** is a surfing hotspot and one-time stomping ground for Richard Nixon.

The fastest way to **travel** from LA to San Diego skips the coast by passing through Orange County on the inland San Diego Freeway, the 405. The coastal cities, though, are linked by the more appealing **Pacific Coast Highway (PCH)**, part of Hwy-1, which you can pick up from Long Beach (or from the end of Beach Boulevard in Anaheim), though it's often busy in the summer. OCTD bus #1 rumbles along PCH roughly hourly during the day, though Greyhound connections aren't so good: San Clemente gets ten buses a day and San Juan Capistrano gets two in the early morning, but there are none to Huntington, Laguna, or Newport beaches. **Amtrak** connects Downtown LA (or Disneyland) to San Juan Capistrano, though you can travel all the way along the coast from LA to San Diego using local buses for about $5 – but allow a full day for the trip. A pricier, but more worthwhile, transit option is the Metrolink commuter train line (see p.37), which not only connects Downtown LA with Orange County down to San Clemente, but continues on to Oceanside in San Diego County, from where you can pick up that region's Coaster and connect to downtown San Diego.

Huntington Beach

Starting on the north Orange County coast, **HUNTINGTON BEACH** is the most free-spirited of the beach communities and one that you don't need a fortune to enjoy. It's a compact place composed of single-story cafés and beach shops grouped around the foot of a long **pier**, off PCH at Main Street. Here, you can find the **Surfers Walk of Fame**, appropriately honoring the greats of the sport – this is where California **surfing** began in 1907, imported from Hawaii to encourage curious day-trippers to visit on the Pacific Electric Railway, whose chief, Henry Huntington, the town was named after. Top surfers still flock here for the **Pro Surfing Championship**, an internationally televised event held each June. Even more of this culture can be found at the **International Surfing Museum**, 411 Olive Ave (Oct–May Thurs–Mon noon–5pm; June–Sept open daily; $3; ⊛www.surfingmuseum.org), with exhibits on such legendary figures as Corky Carroll and Duke Kahanamoku, historic posters from various contests, and an array of traditional, contemporary, and far-out boards, including one shaped like a Swiss Army knife.

In October, the largely blond and suntanned locals celebrate a fun **Oktoberfest**, with German food and music. Otherwise, there's not much else to see, though it does have Orange County's cheapest beds in the **youth hostel** near the pier (see "Accommodation," p.261). Several miles north, nature lovers won't want to miss the **Bolsa Chica State Ecological Reserve**, PCH at Warner

△ Body-boarders on on Huntington Beach

Avenue, a sizable wetland preserve that's been kept out of the hands of local developers by state regulation. Taking a one-and-a-half-mile loop tour will get you acquainted with some of the current avian residents of this salt marsh, including a fair number of herons, egrets, and grebes, and even a few peregrine falcons and endangered snowy plovers. Self-tours are free, and guided tours are available on the first Saturday of the month (9–10.30am; $2; groups by reservation at ☎714/840-1575, ⓦwww.amigosdebolsachica.org).

Newport Beach and around

Ten miles south from Huntington Beach, **NEWPORT BEACH** could hardly provide a greater contrast: an upmarket enclave with no less than ten yacht clubs, where the image-conscious residents work to acquire a deep tan they can show off on the long stretches of sand or in the singles bars nearby. You'll need a pocketful of credit cards and a presentable physique to join them properly, but the sheer exclusivity of the place may be an attraction in and of itself.

Newport Beach is spread around a natural bay that cuts several miles inland, and although there are hardly any conventional "sights" in town, the obvious place to hang out is on the thin **Balboa Peninsula**, located along Balboa Boulevard, which runs parallel to the three-mile-long beach. The most colorful and boisterous section is about halfway along, around **Newport Pier** at the end of 20th Street. To the north, beachfront homes restrict access; to the south, around **Balboa Pier** (the second of the city's piers), there's a marina from which you can hop on the *Catalina Flyer*, which leaves for Santa Catalina Island (1hr 15min trip, leaves daily 9am, returns 4.30pm; $44 total; ☎949/673-5245, ⓦwww.catalinainfo.com).

On the peninsula itself, the highlight is the modernist **Lovell Beach House**, 1242 Ocean Ave, a private home designed by Rudolph Schindler and finished in 1926. Raised on five concrete legs, its living quarters jutting out toward the sidewalk, the house formed the basis of the architect's international reputation (though it has since been altered for the worse by errant renovations). On

very rare occasions, it's even open for tours (contact ☎323/651-1510, ⓦwww
.makcenter.org to check).

Across the main harbor channel from the peninsula, the Newport Beach
district of **Corona Del Mar** is mainly worth a stop for its **Sherman Library
and Gardens**, 2647 E Pacific Coast Highway (daily 10.30am–4pm; $3; ⓦwww
.slgardens.org), devoted to the horticulture of the American Southwest and raising many vivid blooms in its botanical gardens, including cacti, orchids, roses,
and an array of different herbs.

Due north from the gardens, Newport Beach is home to the **Orange
County Museum of Art**, 850 San Clemente Drive (Tues–Sun 11am–5pm,
Thurs closes 8pm; $7, free Tues; ⓦwww.ocma.net), a fine institution that
focuses on contemporary work from LA artists like Lari Pittman, Edward
Ruscha, and Ed Kienholz, and also periodically exhibits the work of video
pioneers like Nancy Thater and Bill Viola. A short distance west, San
Joaquin Hills Road leads you to Backbay Drive, which provides a marvelous trip around the edge of one of Orange County's natural wonders, the
Upper Newport Bay Ecological Reserve, 2301 University Drive (daily
7am–dusk; free; ☎949/923-2290, ⓦwww.ocparks.com/uppernewportbay), an
idyllic 750-acre preserve and renowned bird-watching spot, from which you
can see a great range of birds, including falcons, pelicans, terns, and rails, some
of them endangered. The preserve – and its hills, wetlands, and inlets – also
presents excellent opportunities for hiking, kayaking, horseback riding, and
cycling. There's also an **interpretive center** (Tues–Sun 10am–4pm; free),
which gives an overview of the area's ecology and geology.

On the eastern side of the north end of the reserve, University Drive
crosses into the bland city of **IRVINE** to a branch of the University of
California, **UC Irvine**, which is only interesting if you're a student or fan of
contemporary architecture – the campus features a slew of buildings by such
famous names as Frank Gehry, Robert Venturi, Charles Moore, and Robert
A.M. Stern. A one-hour **tour** can give you some sense of the campus and
its assorted visual highlights (Mon–Fri noon; free; reserve at ☎949/824-4636,
ⓦwww.campustours.uci.edu).

Crystal Cove State Park

Back along PCH, the area between Newport and Laguna beaches offers an
inviting, unspoiled three-mile chunk of coastline, **Crystal Cove State Park**
(ⓦwww.crystalcovestatepark.com). Far from the tourist crowd, the park's two
thousand acres feature some rugged inland terrain around El Moro canyon that's
good for hiking and biking, threaded as it is with trails crossing hilly peaks and
ravines. Also fascinating is a twelve-acre, federally protected "Historic District"
featuring 46 shambling beachside bungalows and cottages providing an eerie
hint of the old rustic character of the shoreline when they were constructed
in the 1920s and 30s (they're slowly being restored as well). Crystal Cove also
has some excellent stretches for surfing, diving, and snorkeling, exploring the
aquaculture of the offshore "underwater park," or just poking around on the
beach among the evocative coves and tide pools.

Laguna Beach

Six miles south of Crystal Cove, nestled among the crags around a small
sandy beach, **LAGUNA BEACH** grew up late in the nineteenth century as
a community of artists drawn by the beauty of the location. You need a few
million dollars to live here nowadays, but there's a relaxed and tolerant feel

The festivals of Laguna Beach

Laguna Beach hosts a number of large summer **art festivals** over six weeks in July and August. The best-known – and most bizarre – is the **Pageant of the Masters**, in which the participants pose in front of a painted backdrop to portray a famous work of art (or in some cases, a famous movie poster). It might sound ridiculous, but it's actually quite impressive and takes a great deal of preparation – something reflected in the prices: $20–75 for shows that sell out months in advance. You may, however, be able to pick up cancellations on the night (shows begin at 8.30pm; ☏949/494-1145 or 1-800/487-3378, ⊛www.foapom.com). The idea for the pageant was hatched during the Depression as a way to raise money for local artists, and the action takes place at the Irving Bowl, close to where Broadway meets Laguna Canyon Road, a walkable distance from the bus station. The pageant is combined with the **Festival of the Arts** (daily 10am–11.30pm; $5; information as above) held at the same venue, featuring the work of 150 local artists.

The excitement of both festivals waned in the 1960s, when a group of hippies created the alternative **Sawdust Festival**, 935 Laguna Canyon Rd (July–Aug 10am–10pm; $6.50, season pass $12; ☏949/494-3030, ⊛www.sawdustartfestival.org), and stole some of the thunder from the other events; these days, it's just as established as the other two, but easier to get into, featuring artists setting up makeshift studios to demonstrate their skills.

among the inhabitants, who range from millionaires to upper-middle-class gays and lesbians. The scenery is still the great attraction, and despite the upswell in population, Laguna remains relatively unspoiled with a still-flourishing arts scene in the many streetside galleries.

PCH passes through the center of Laguna, a few steps from the small main **beach**, which is less snooty than Newport Beach, and less crowded than LA's sand strips. From the beach's north side, an elevated wooden walkway twists around the coastline above a protected **ecological area**, enabling you to peer down on the ocean and, when the tide's out, scamper over the rocks to observe the tide-pool activity. From the end of the walkway, make your way through the legions of posh beachside homes and head down the hill back to the center. You'll pass the **Laguna Beach Museum of Art**, 307 Cliff Drive (daily 11am–5pm; $9; ⊛lagunaartmuseum.org), which has changing exhibitions from its stock of Southern California art from the 1900s to the present. A few miles south is relaxed **South Laguna**, where the secluded **Victoria** and **Aliso beaches** are among several below the bluffs.

About two-and-a-half miles inland from downtown Laguna Beach is one sight not to be missed by lovers of sea life, the **Friends of the Sea Lion Marine Mammal Center**, 20612 Laguna Canyon Rd (daily 10am–4pm; free; ☏949/494-3050), a rehabilitation center that lets you watch as underweight, injured, or otherwise threatened seals and sea lions are nursed back to health.

Dana Point

From South Laguna, it's possible to see **DANA POINT**, a town and promontory jutting into the ocean about four miles south. It was named after sailor and author Richard Henry Dana Jr, whose *Two Years Before the Mast* described how cattle hides were flung over these cliffs to trading ships waiting below, and did much to romanticize the California coast while still viewing it with a wary eye. He ended his voyaging career here in 1830, and there's a statue of him and a replica of his vessel, *The Pilgrim*, at the edge of the harbor. This is also the site of the **Ocean Institute**, 24200 Dana Point Harbor Drive (Sat & Sun 10am–4.30pm; $5.50; ⊕www.ocean-institute.org), which offers marine-biology cruises and public visits during which you can view oceanic wildlife, from lobsters to anemones, in glass-enclosed tanks.

San Juan Capistrano and San Clemente

Three miles inland from Dana Point along the I-5 freeway, most of the small suburb of **SAN JUAN CAPISTRANO** is built in a Spanish Colonial style derived from the **Mission San Juan Capistrano**, right in the center of town at Ortega Highway and Camino Capistrano (daily 8.30am–5pm; $6; ⊕949/234-1300, ⊕www.missionsjc.com), a short walk from the Amtrak stop. The seventh of California's missions, founded by Junípero Serra in 1776, the mission was within three years so well populated that it outgrew the original chapel. Soon after, the **Great Stone Church** was erected, the ruins of which are the first thing you see as you walk in. The huge structure had seven domes and a bell tower, but was destroyed by an earthquake soon after its 1812 completion, and the ruins themselves are now decaying rapidly, requiring up to $20 million in projected restoration. For an idea of how it might have looked, see the full-sized replica – now a church – just northwest of the mission.

Meanwhile, the mission's main **chapel** is small and narrow, decorated with Indian drawings and Spanish artifacts from its earliest days, and set off by a sixteenth-century altar from Barcelona. In a side room is the chapel of **St Pereguin**, a tiny room kept warm by the heat from the dozens of candles lit by hopeful pilgrims who arrive here from all over the US and Mexico.

Other restored buildings include the kitchen, smelter, and workshops for dyeing, weaving, and candlemaking. There's also a rather predictable **museum** (open during mission hours; free), giving a history of Spanish California and displaying odds and ends from the mission's past. The complex is also noted for its **swallows**, popularly thought to return here from their winter migration on March 19. They sometimes do arrive on schedule – along with flocks of tourists – but the birds are more likely to show up as soon as the weather is warm enough, and when there are enough insects on the ground to provide a decent homecoming banquet.

San Clemente

Five miles south of San Juan Capistrano down I-5, the sleepy town of **SAN CLEMENTE** is a pretty little place, its streets contoured around the hills, effecting an almost Mediterranean air. Because of its proximity to one of the largest military bases in the state, **Camp Pendleton**, it's a popular weekend retreat for military personnel. It's also home to some of Orange County's better surfing beaches, especially toward the south end of town, and a reasonable campground, too (see "Accommodation," p.262). Around the city's southern tip, San Clemente had a brief glimmer of fame when President Richard Nixon convened his **Western White House** here from 1969 to 1974, regularly meeting with cronies and political allies. The 25-acre estate is located off Avenida del Presidente and visible from the beach, but off-limits to interlopers.

Listings

Listings

11

Accommodation

F inding **accommodation** in Los Angeles is easy, and whether you seek budget motels or world-class resorts, the city has plenty of options. Finding somewhere that's good value *and* well located can be trickier, but it's far from impossible; you can often find worthwhile deals by shopping around or booking online. If driving, you needn't worry as much about staying in a less than ideal location – a freeway is never far away. Otherwise you'll need to be more choosy about the district you pick, as getting across town can be a time-consuming business.

Motels and low-end **hotels** start at $50 for a double, and if you're comfortable in the familiar two-story, neon-lit 1960s motel built around a shallow swimming pool, you'll find many options. For pricier accommodations, LA has a seemingly limitless collection of mid-level to high-end **hotels** and **resorts** that rival the best in the world for views, comfort, and amenities – and you can expect to pay a small fortune for some of them. **Bed-and-breakfasts** are slowly becoming more common in LA (typically based on a Victorian-architecture or country-cottage theme), but the few that do exist tend to be expensive.

For those on a tight budget, **hostels** are dotted all over the city, many in good locations with desirable amenities – though at some, stays are limited to a few nights, and at others, the nonstop party atmosphere can be grating. **Camping** is also an option – from the beach north of Malibu, throughout Orange County, and in the San Gabriel Mountains – but you'll need a car to get to the campgrounds. Clean, reasonably inexpensive **college rooms** are also sometimes available for rent during student vacation time: contact **UCLA**'s Interfraternity Council (☎310/825-7878) or **USC**'s off-campus housing office (☎1-800 /USC-4632, ⓦhousing.usc.edu) for information.

Since there are few booking agencies, and visitor centers don't make hotel reservations (though they will offer information and advice), you can only **book a room** through a travel agent, by phoning the hotel directly or through its online Web page – if it has one – or by using an Internet reservations site (see p.19 for a list of options).

Where to stay

LA is so big that if you want to avoid constantly having to cross huge expanses, it makes sense to divide your stay between several districts. Prices and options vary by area, and except for the most desirable spots – Beverly Hills, West Hollywood, Malibu – you can find standard chain hotels that are reasonably affordable. **Downtown** has both swank hotels and drab, basic dives, with cheaper accommodations west of Downtown, across the 110 freeway, in much dicier neighborhoods. **Hollywood** provides a good range of choices, a few of them historic hotels and many more classic old roadside motels, along Hollywood and Sunset boulevards, while **West Hollywood** has some of the most chic and trendy accommodations in town, with predictably high prices. **West LA** and **Beverly Hills** are predominantly upper-range territory, with very expensive establishments in Century City and the relatively few bargains around the Westwood campus of UCLA. Staying in **Santa Monica** can be costly near the ocean and inexpensive further inland, while just south, **Venice** offers a cheaper alternative, with quite a few decent hostels and the occasional funky hotel, though higher-ticket properties are making headway in recent years. Although not a destination by itself, **Marina del Rey** to the south has a number of clean chain hotels, if all else fails.

Among options further out from central LA, the **South Bay** has a fair selection of low- to mid-range hotels strung along the Pacific Coast Highway, with higher-end hotels sitting by the bay in **Long Beach**. The upscale choices in the **San Gabriel** and **San Fernando valleys** are around Universal City and Pasadena, although basic chain alternatives can be found everywhere else, including North Hollywood, Burbank, and further out in places like Canoga Park and Sherman Oaks. The limited selections in **Malibu** are almost all upper-end resorts or inns (worth the trip if you have the money), except for several roadside motels along Pacific Coast Highway – located well out of town. Finally, the dreariest accommodations in **Orange County** tend to be around Disneyland, where an array of faded motels competes for tourist dollars, while the county coast has many more appealing choices, from luxury hotels to quirky motels to inexpensive youth hostels.

Hotels and motels

Hotels and **motels** are listed by neighborhood, with specific accommodation options for gay and lesbian travelers listed in Chapter 16, "Gay and lesbian LA"– though most LA hotels are gay friendly. We've also listed a few affordable places to stay near the airport should you be arriving late or leaving early (see box, p.253).

On the whole, you can comfortably stay throughout LA by **spending** around $120 a night, though there are plenty of bare-bones spots charging far less. Paying $200–250 will get you an elegant, entry-level room in a swank hotel, and beyond that anything is possible, with suites often going for $350 and up – though many affordable chain hoteliers offer basic suites for around $150. Prices increase at tourist-oriented establishments during peak travel periods, typically over the summer and on weekends, especially those near major attractions like Disneyland and Universal Studios. Conversely, weekend rates at business-oriented hotels can be much cheaper than weekday prices, often to the tune of $80–100.

Listed **amenities** include features that are not always standard to hotel rooms in the area, such as hot tubs, fireplaces, kitchenettes, on-site gyms, spas, and other features. More common in-room amenities – the likes of ironing boards, hairdryers, cable TV, free parking, etc – are not listed, except in truly low-end accommodations where their presence comes as a surprise.

Downtown

Cecil 640 S Main St ☎ 213/624-4545. Grand old 1920s hotel that's been refurbished as a nice, low-budget property; rooms are basic, but have more style than you'd expect, and there's also Internet acess. $40 shared bathrooms, $50 private.

Downtown LA Standard 550 S Flower St ☎ 213/892-8080, ⊛ www.standardhotel.com. Located in a former oil-company building, the most recent branch of LA's self-consciously trendy chain features sleek, modern furnishings and quirky decor, though is best for its rooftop bar (see p.299). While billed as a business hotel, the party scene is pretty much constant. $165.

Figueroa 939 S Figueroa St at Olympic Blvd ☎ 213/627-8971 or 1-800/421-9092, ⊛ www.figueroahotel.com. Well renovated, mid-range hotel south of Bunker Hill, with a Southwestern flavor, cheery, sizable pastel rooms, pool and hot tub, 24-hour coffee shop, and even a few scattered statues of saints. $125.

Hilton Checkers 535 S Grand ☎ 213/624-0000 or 1-800/HILTONS, ⊛ www.hiltoncheckers.com. One of the great LA hotels, with sleek modern appointments in historic 1920s architecture, and nicely furnished rooms, rooftop pool and spa. Terrific Downtown views, too. $250 weekdays, $150 weekends.

Holiday Inn City Center 1020 S Figueroa St ☎ 213/748-1291, ⊛ www.holiday-inn.com. Located south of Downtown near the Harbor Freeway, this blocky chain hotel is part of the Staples Center–Convention Center complex, and provides an affordable stay with pool, gym, and Internet access, as well as easy access to most Downtown sights. Rooms start at $120.

Hyatt Regency 711 S Hope St ☎ 213/683-1234 or 1-800/233-1234, ⊛ losangelesregency.hyatt.com. A block from the Metrorail line, this chain hotel offers smart but standard rooms just south of Bunker Hill, with a spa and health club on site, and Internet access. $170 weekdays, $140 weekends.

Kawada 200 S Hill St at Second St ☎ 213/621-4455 or 1-800/752-9232, ⊛ www.kawadahotel.com. Comfortable and clean rooms in a somewhat bland hotel near the Civic Center; popular with value-oriented business travelers. $90.

Los Angeles Athletic Club 431 W Seventh St ☎ 213/625-2211, ⊛ www.laac.com. Beaux Arts brick-and-terracotta charmer that's home to an exclusive club, but the top three floors make up a hotel with 72 nicely furnished rooms and nine expensive suites; a real plus is free use of the club's track, pool, exercise equipment, and handball and basketball courts. $195.

Marriott Downtown 333 S Figueroa St ☎ 213/617-1133, ⊛ www.marriott.com. Palm-tree-laden pool area, spacious rooms and health club add some charm to this chain hotel, centrally located near the 110 and 101 freeways, and Bunker Hill sights such as Disney Hall and MOCA. $180.

Millennium Biltmore 506 S Grand Ave at Fifth St ☎ 213/624-1011 or 1-800/222-8888, ⊛ www.thebiltmore.com. Renaissance Revival architecture from 1923, combined with modern luxury: a health club modeled on a Roman bathhouse, cherub and angel decor, and a view overlooking Pershing Square. The well-appointed rooms match the stateliness of the design. $200, with cheaper rates on weekends.

Miyako Inn and Spa 328 E First St ☎ 213/617-2000, ⊛ www.miyakoinn.com. Despite the grim, concrete-box exterior, this mid-price hotel remains a good bet in the heart of Little Tokyo. Modest but pleasant rooms include refrigerators and Internet access, and hotel has a spa and karaoke bar as well. $125 without breakfast, $145 with.

New Otani 120 S Los Angeles St ☎ 213/629-1200 or 1-800/421-8795, ⊛ www.newotani.com. Business hotel featuring spacious suites but unexciting rooms, a good restaurant with Asian cuisine (see p.275), and the small Japanese Garden in the Sky, which uses the traditional technique of "borrowed scenery" to incorporate existing views into the design. $150, with weekend rates as low as $110.

Omni Los Angeles 251 S Olive St at Fourth St ☎213/617-3300 or 1-800/327-0200, ⊛www .omnilosangeles.com. Fancy Bunker Hill hotel with plush, elegant rooms, swimming pool and weight room. Adjacent to MOCA and the Music Center. $230; good weekend deals available.

Ritz Milner 813 S Flower St ☎213/627-6981, ⊛www.milner-hotels.com. Somewhat bare-bones rooms at this restored old building south of Bunker Hill, but still cheap and clean, and in a prime location. Larger suites also available. $80.

Westin Bonaventure 404 S Figueroa St, between Fourth and Fifth sts ☎213/624-1000 or 1-800/228-3000, ⊛www.westin.com. Modernist luxury hotel with five glass towers that resemble cocktail shakers, a six-story atrium with a "lake," and elegantly remodelled, curved rooms. A breathtaking exterior elevator ride ascends to the rotating *Top of Five* cocktail lounge. $250, with suites up to $2000.

▽ Westin Bonaventure

Wilshire Grand 930 Wilshire Blvd ☎213/688-7777 or 1-800/695-8284, ⊛www.wilshiregrand .com. Large Bunker Hill hotel with health club and pool. Mainly geared toward business travelers heading to the nearby convention center; rack rate is overpriced for rather bland rooms, but special discounts can knock up to $100 off the price. $225.

Around Downtown

Best Western Mayfair 1256 W Seventh St ☎213/484-9789 or 1-800/528-1234, ⊛www .mayfairla.com. Grand 1920s building with classical arches and pillars in the lobby and predictably clean rooms and suites, with sundeck and exercise room – but edgy neighborhood. Wide range of rates, depending on size and amenities, starting from $90.

City Center Motel 1135 W Seventh St at Lucas ☎213/628-7141. Basic bargain accommodation with 1960s-style decor, free continental breakfast, and airport shuttle bus. Walking not recommended, however, in dicey surroundings. $55.

Vagabond Inn 3101 S Figueroa St ☎213/746-1531 or 1-800/522-1555, ⊛www.vagabondinn .com. The best place to stay near USC and the Shrine Auditorium, a few miles south of Downtown. Clean and basic chain-motel rooms, with an on-site pool. $100.

Mid-Wilshire

Beverly Laurel 8018 Beverly Blvd at Laurel Ave ☎323/651-2441. While the coffee shop here, *Swingers*, attracts most of the attention, the motel has nice retro-1960s touches albeit plain rooms. Good location, not far from the Fairfax District and Beverly Hills. $95.

Bevonshire Lodge 7575 Beverly Blvd at Curson Ave ☎323/936-6154. Well situated for both West LA and Hollywood, across from Pan Pacific Park and the black cube of CBS Studios. All the basic rooms come with a fridge; for a few dollars more you can have a kitchenette. $60.

Farmer's Daughter 115 S Fairfax Ave ☎323/937-3930, ⊛www.farmersdaughterhotel.com. A fun monument of motel kitsch conveniently located across from, naturally, the Farmers Market; the simple rooms feature lots of wood – chairs, floors, even TV cabinets – with gingham accents and cornpone art and murals. The no-frills swimming pool sometimes attracts B-list celebs and would-be bohemians. $130.

Guesthouse International 1904 W Olympic Blvd ☎213/380-9393, ⊛www.guesthouse.net. Solid lower-end chain motel with agreeable rooms and a swimming pool. Good value, not far from Koreatown. $70.

Orlando 8384 W Third St ☎323/658-6600, ⊛www.theorlando.com. Elegant, well-appointed rooms make this renovated spot one of the area's better boutique hotels, with swimming pool, hot tub, and fitness center. Good location for accessing the Beverly Center mall. $225, but special rates drop to as low as $170.

Oxford Palace 745 S Oxford Ave ☎213/389-8000, ⊛www.oxfordhotel.com. Solid choice for business travelers with nicely furnished lobby, 86 serviceable rooms and a few suites. Located near the heart of Koreatown, just around the corner from the Wiltern Theater. Rooms $120, suites $340.

Radisson Wilshire Plaza 3515 Wilshire Blvd ☎ 213/381-7411 or 1-800/777-7800, ⓦ www .radwilshire.com. Friendly chain accommodations, located in Koreatown, with modern Californian design, adequate rooms, pool, and fitness center. Business-class rooms have complimentary breakfast and Internet access. $150.

Wilshire Crest 6301 Orange St ☎ 323/936-5131, ⓦ www.wilshirecrestinn.com. Small hotel with plain rooms in a charming, period-revival residential area, conveniently located just north of Wilshire Blvd and west of Fairfax Ave and Museum Row. $110.

Wilshire Orange 6060 W 8th Ave ☎ 323/931-9533 ⓦ www.hoteldelflores.com. A block south and east of Museum Row, one of the cheapest alternatives in the area, with bare-bones amenities, but clean and functional rooms that have fridges. Having shared bath knocks another $15 off the price. $85.

Hollywood

Best Western Hollywood Hills 6141 Franklin Ave between Gower and Vine ☎ 323/464-5181, ⓦ www.bestwesterncalifornia.com. Reliable and recently remodelled chain hotel, with Internet access and heated pool, at the foot of the Hollywood Hills. $110.

Comfort Inn and Suites 2010 N Highland Ave ☎ 323/874-4300, ⓦ www.cisuiteshollywood .com. One of the better deals in town, offering chain-motel rooms but with microwaves, fridges, complimentary breakfast, and heated pool. Just three blocks north of the center of Hollywood. $150 weekends, weekdays as low as $90.

Dunes Sunset 5625 Sunset Blvd ☎ 323/467-5171. On the dingy eastern side of Hollywood, but far enough away from the weirdness of Hollywood Boulevard to feel safe; adequate motel rooms and good access to Downtown. $75.

Hollywood Hills Magic Hotel 7025 Franklin Ave ☎ 323/851-0800, ⓦ www.magiccastlehotel.com. One of the unheralded deals in these parts, a hotel with suites with a kitchen, sofa, and two TVs per room, plus continental breakfast. An added plus is being able to buy tickets to the adjacent Magic Castle (see p.111) – otherwise off-limits to the general public. Rooms $140, suites $170.

Holiday Inn Hollywood 2005 N Highland Ave ☎ 323/876-8600 or 1-800/465-4329, ⓦ www .holiday-inn.com. Massive and perfectly placed, near the heart of Hollywood Boulevard and the Chinese Theatre. Basic rooms, but amenities include pool, spa, gym, and Internet access. The highlight is the top-floor revolving nightclub, which affords a great view of Tinseltown. $130.

Hollywood Metropolitan 5825 Sunset Blvd ☎ 323/962-5800 or 1-800/962-5800, ⓦ www .metropolitanhotel.com. Sleek high-rise in central Hollywood, featuring a flashy exterior elevator, good views, and spacious rooms. Good value for the area, though a bit south of major attractions. $90.

Hollywood Roosevelt 7000 Hollywood Blvd ☎ 323/466-7000, ⓦ www.hollywoodroosevelt .com. The first hotel built for the movie greats in 1927. The rooms are standard, but the Corinthian-columned lobby reeks of Hollywood atmosphere and the hotel features a hot tub, fitness room, swimming pool, and a "History of Hollywood" exhibit on the second floor. The popular *Cinegrill* cabaret (p.322) entertains on the ground level. $170.

Hollywood Towne House 6055 Sunset Blvd at Gower St ☎ 323/462-3221. Motel with decayed exterior and 1920s-era phones that connect to the front desk only. Yet the place itself is comfortable enough, with decent rooms and simple furnishings. $75.

Orchid Suites 1753 Orchid Ave ☎ 323/874-9678 or 1-800/537-3052, ⓦ www.orchidsuites.com. Roomy, if basic, suites with kitchenettes, and heated pool; central to the most popular parts of Hollywood – and adjacent to the massive Hollywood & Highland mall. $100.

Ramada Inn Hollywood 1160 N Vermont Ave ☎ 323/660-1788, ⓦ www.westhollywoodramada .com. The best place to stay in a somewhat dicey, though increasingly hip, part of Hollywood, featuring comfortable rooms with microwaves and fridges, along with a pool, spa, bar, restaurant, fitness center, and free continental breakfast. $80.

Renaissance Hollywood 1755 N Highland Blvd ☎ 323/856-1200, ⓦ www.renaissancehollywood .com. The hotel centerpiece of the Hollywood & Highland mall complex, with upscale rooms and suites, and prime location in the heart of Tinseltown. $210, with executive suites (seating areas and oversize bathrooms included) at $230.

Saharan 7212 Sunset Blvd at Poinsettia Place
☎ 323/874-6700, ⓦ www.saharanmotel.com.
A classic 1950s-style motel: double-decker
layout with standard rooms built around a
pool, plus cheesy neon sign and brash color
scheme. Comparatively good value, and
some rooms have kitchenettes and fridges.
$65.

Sunset–La Brea Travelodge 7051 Sunset Blvd
☎ 323/462-0905, ⓦ www.travelodge.com. A
safe, cheap bet south of Hollywood's major
sights, with adequate rooms, sundeck, and
pool. There's another *Travelodge* with similar
amenities at 1401 N Vermont St ☎ 323/665-
5735, on the opposite side of the area in
lower-rent East Hollywood, near Barnsdall
Park and a Metrorail stop. Both $75.

West Hollywood

Argyle 8358 Sunset Blvd ☎ 323/654-7100,
ⓦ www.argylehotel.com. An Art Deco landmark now converted into an upper-end
luxury hotel, featuring automotive radiator-
grill decor and 1930s Zigzag Moderne style,
but also modern amenities like stereos and
VCRs, along with marble-floored bathrooms
and prime views of the Sunset Strip. $250.

▽ The Argyle Hotel

Chamberlain 1000 Westmount Drive ☎ 310/657-
7400, ⓦ www.chamberlainwesthollywood.com.
Sumptuous hotel just off the Strip, within
easy walking distance of major clubs and
attractions, but just far enough away from
the chaos and noise. The impressive,
recently redesigned suites include sunken
living rooms, DVD players, fireplaces, balconies, and refrigerators. $190.

**Chateau Marmont 8221 Sunset Blvd at Crescent
Heights Blvd** ☎ 323/626-1010, ⓦ www
.chateaumarmont.com. Exclusive Norman
Revival hotel, which resembles a dark castle
or Hollywood fortress as it hovers over the
Sunset Strip. The hotel has welcomed the
likes of Boris Karloff, Greta Garbo, Errol
Flynn, Jean Harlow, John Belushi (who
died in one of its elite bungalows), and Jim
Morrison, who broke two ribs falling off a
balcony. Rates start at $315.

Elan Hotel Modern 8435 Beverly Blvd
☎ 323/658-6663, ⓦ www.elanhotel.com. Semi-
upscale boutique hotel, located in a busy
shopping zone just north of the Beverly
Center mall. Rooms are nicely appointed,
and there's also an on-site fitness center
and spa. $140.

Grafton 8462 Sunset Blvd ☎ 323/654-6470,
ⓦ www.graftononsunset.com. Mid-level
boutique hotel with attractive furnishings, in-
room stereos and VCRs, plus a pool, fitness
center, and complimentary shuttle to nearby
malls and businesses. $170.

Hyatt West Hollywood 8401 Sunset Blvd
☎ 323/656-4101, ⓦ westhollywood.hyatt
.com. Big and boxy on the outside, but also
the legendary site of outlandish rock-star
antics, from Led Zeppelin to the Who to
Guns N' Roses. It's now a tastefully upscale
business hotel, with nice, spacious rooms
that offer Stripside balconies, but sadly (or
perhaps luckily) without the same hip edge
as before. $205.

Le Montrose 900 Hammond St ☎ 310/855-1115,
ⓦ www.lemontrose.com. Excellent spot with
Art Nouveau stylings, featuring upscale
restaurant and rooftop tennis courts, pool,
and hot tub. Most rooms are suites with
full amenities such as stereos, sunken living
rooms, dual televisions, refrigerators, and
expansive views. Located just below the
main part of the Sunset Strip. $190.

Le Parc 733 N West Knoll Drive ☎ 310/855-8888
or 1-800/578-4837, ⓦ www.leparcsuites.com.
Graceful apartment hotel in a residential
area not far from major sights (including the

Beverly Center mall), with simple studios, more spacious one- and two-bedroom suites, stereos, refrigerators, and rooftop pool and hot tub with views of the hills. $250.

Mondrian 8440 Sunset Blvd ☎ 323/650-8999, ⓦ www.mondrianhotel.com. Like other Strip hotels, this place oozes art and luxury from every orifice, though with a much heavier dose of pretension – especially in the celebrity-bootlicking *SkyBar* up top. Spacious rooms are stylish and chic, if not quite enough to justify the snooty attitudes. $340.

Standard West Hollywood 8300 Sunset Blvd ☎ 323/654-2800, ⓦ www.standardhotel.com. Amazing style, but not much substance, at this famed hipster "party hotel" offering extra-spartan rooms furnished with beanbags, swinging outdoor pool and bar, and a goofball design with Astroturf floors and other self-consciously bizarre decor. The smallest rooms start at $100.

Sunset Marquis 1200 N Alta Loma Rd ☎ 310/657-1333 or 1-800/858-9758, ⓦ www .sunsetmarquishotel.com. A hangout for musicians (featuring an on-site recording studio and "Whisky bar"), with two pools with private cabanas, hot tub, sauna, weight room, and outside gardens surrounding very pricey villas; most rooms are smart suites with kitchens, balconies, and patios. Prices start at $300 and can top out over $2000.

Wyndham Bel Age 1020 N San Vicente Blvd ☎ 310/854-1111, ⓦ www.wyndham.com. Solid chain hotel stuffed with art (some of it kitsch), plus lovely rooms with nice decor, balconies and kitchens, and an exquisite lobby. Also with pool and gym. $220.

Beverly Hills and Century City

Avalon 9400 W Olympic Blvd ☎ 310/277-5221, ⓦ www.avalonbeverlyhills.com. Located in south Beverly Hills, three long blocks from the Golden Triangle, this hipster hotel boasts cozy rooms and modern furnishings, along with in-room CD players, fax machines, VCRs, and fitness club. The poolside bar is where the young elite pose in their black togs. $220.

Beverly Hills Hotel 9641 Sunset Blvd ☎ 310/276-2251 or 1-800/283-8885, ⓦ www .beverlyhillshotel.com. The pinnacle of hotels in LA and the classic Hollywood resort, with a bold pink-and-green color scheme and Mission-style design, surrounded by its own exotic gardens. Rooms feature marbled bathrooms, VCRs, hot tubs, and other such luxuries, and the famed *Polo Lounge* restaurant is also on site. Along with W.C. Fields, John Barrymore, and countless other celebrities, Marilyn Monroe also stayed here, and one of the fancy bungalows is decorated in her honor. $305.

Beverly Hills Reeves 120 S Reeves Drive ☎ 310/271-3006. Housed in a former apartment building south of Wilshire Boulevard, this inexpensive hotel is an obvious choice if you're in LA on a tight budget. Simple and clean rooms include microwaves, refrigerators, and complimentary breakfast, along with a rooftop sundeck. Weekly and monthly discounts available. $80.

Beverly Hilton 9876 Wilshire Blvd ☎ 310/274-7777 or 1-800/922-5432, ⓦ www.hilton.com. Prominent white, geometric hotel at the corner of Wilshire and Santa Monica boulevards, and site of the famed *Trader Vic's* restaurant. Elegant rooms and decor, refurbished in recent years. Rates start at $300 but can go as low as $220 on weekends.

Beverly Pavilion 9360 Wilshire Blvd ☎ 310/273-1400, ⓦ www.beverlypavilion.com. Boxy, though remodeled, *Best Western* hotel that has good rates for the area, better-looking furnishings than you'd expect, and Internet access, rooftop pool, and spa. Located not too far from Rodeo Drive. $150.

Beverly Terrace 469 N Doheny Drive ☎ 310/274-8141, ⓦ www.beverlyterracehotel.com. A good, clean motel with complimentary breakfast and some balconies. Central location on the border between Beverly Hills and West Hollywood. $120.

Century Plaza 2025 Avenue of the Stars ☎ 310/277-2000 or 1-800/WESTIN-1, ⓦ www .centuryplazala.com. In the middle of Century City, a huge, crescent-shaped hotel offering stylish rooms with outstanding views from Beverly Hills to the ocean. Amenities include multiple pools, health club, business center, rental car outlets, and so on. The corridors are decorated with photos of visiting celebrities and politicians. $300, with promotional weekend rates dipping to $210.

Crescent 403 N Crescent Drive ☎ 310/247-0505 or 1-800/451-1566, ⓦ www.crescentbh.com. Adjacent to Beverly Hills City Hall and *Hotel del Flores*, a formerly low-priced property that's been smartened up in recent years, and now offers an upscale restaurant and lounge, swank furnishings, in-room iPods and Internet access, and on-site DVD library. Prices are predictably steeper than before, too. $175.

Four Seasons Beverly Hills 300 S Doheny Drive ☎310/273-2222 or 1-800/332-3442, ⓦwww .fourseasons.com/losangeles. One of the most famous luxury hotels in Beverly Hills, featuring well-furnished rooms with balconies, elegant decor and decent artworks, along with pool and health-club facilities. Ultra-high prices attract A-list celebs in droves. Weekdays $455, weekends $380.

Hotel del Flores 409 N Crescent Drive at Little Santa Monica Blvd ☎310/274-5115, ⓦwww .hoteldelflores.com. Three blocks from Rodeo Drive, one of the better deals around. Modest, pleasant, and surprisingly good value for the area, with faded old period-revival look from 1926 and quaint rooms. Shared baths bring down the cost by $20. $95.

Le Meridien 465 S La Cienega Blvd ☎310/247-0400, ⓦwww.lemeridien.com. Luxury hotel in an exclusive chain that offers three hundred elegantly furnished rooms, swimming pool, spa, and health club, with 55 ultra-chic suites providing boundless comfort for movie-industry bigshots. $220.

Maison 140 140 S Lasky Drive ☎310/281-4000, ⓦwww.maison140.com. High-profile entry for hipsters, featuring rooms with CD players and nice appointments, plus salon, bar, fitness room, and complimentary breakfast. $190.

Mosaic 125 S Spalding Drive ☎310/278-0303, ⓦwww.innatbeverlyhills.com. A 1958 building that's been remodelled many times, the latest round turning it into a boutique hotel featuring rooms with CD players, Internet access, fridges, and pool, sauna and fitness room, along with complimentary breakfast. Located near the Golden Triangle shopping zone, but far enough away to sit in its own quiet, leafy setting. $250.

Park Hyatt 2151 Avenue of the Stars ☎310/277-1234 or 1-800/233-1234, ⓦwww.hyatt.com. Century City stalwart with access to sights in West LA and Beverly Hills. Decent rooms with balconies and on-site pool and spa. Weekdays $300, weekends $225.

Peninsula Beverly Hills 9882 Little Santa Monica Blvd ☎310/551-2888 or 1-800/462-7899, ⓦwww.peninsula.com. Pricey luxury item featuring chic rooms, suites and villas thick with graceful furnishings and decor, along with pool, sundeck, cabanas, rooftop gardens, whirlpool, and weight room. $475.

Regent Beverly Wilshire 9500 Wilshire Blvd ☎310/275-5200, ⓦwww.fourseasons.com. Located near the heart of Rodeo Drive, amid countless boutiques and chic department stores, this 1928 hotel has stylish modern rooms, three restaurants, palatial designs, and views overlooking Beverly Hills. Now part of the *Four Seasons* chain, which has made it even more palatial, if that's possible. $425, with reduced weekend rates available.

West LA

Bel Air 701 Stone Canyon Rd ☎310/472-1211 or 1-800/648-1097, ⓦwww.hotelbelair.com. Perhaps LA's poshest hotel, and the only commercial business in Bel Air, located in a thickly overgrown canyon, with lush gardens and waterfall. Go for a beautiful brunch by the Swan Pond if you can't afford the rooms, which will cost you at least $400 for their exquisite decor, spaciousness, and the like.

Best Western Royal Palace 2528 S Sepulveda Blvd ☎310/477-9066, ⓦwww .bestwesternroyalpalace.com. The name overstates it more than a little, but if you want good, cheap accommodation and don't mind staying near the junction of the 405 and 10 freeways, this is the place: with in-room microwaves, and a pool, hot tub, fitness center, and Westside Pavilion shopping mall a mile away. $100.

Brentwood Inn 12200 Sunset Blvd ☎310/476-9981. Unassuming little spot that's been around since 1947, and still has some of the area's more affordable rates, for modernized units that have complimentary breakfast and Internet access. Decor is basic, but rooms are nice. $165.

Carlyle Inn 1119 S Robertson Blvd ☎310/275-4445, ⓦwww.carlyle-inn.com. Just north of Pico Boulevard, a hotel close enough to Beverly Hills to make an affordable visit worthwhile; basic rooms include fridges, and there's also complimentary breakfast and a smallish gym. $130.

Culver Hotel 9400 Culver Blvd ☎310/838-7963 or 1-800/888-3-CULVER, ⓦwww.culverhotel.com. A lovely, restored historic landmark, once the offices of town founder Harry Culver and hotel of the midget cast during filming of *The Wizard of Oz*, today featuring red-and-black decor, checkered marble floors and old-time iron railings in the lobby, and cozy rooms with good views of the city. $110.

Econo Lodge 11933 W Washington Blvd ☎310/398-1651, 🖰www.econolodge.com. Basic chain motel with small, clean rooms and complimentary breakfast; some rooms with microwaves and refrigerators. Located in dreary district of Mar Vista, but close enough to West LA and, further west, Venice. $70.

Holiday Inn Brentwood 170 N Church Lane at Sunset Blvd and 405 freeway ☎310/476-6411, 🖰www.hibrentwood.com. Cylindrical concrete eyesore that pokes out of a hillside below the Getty Center, but with good comfort and decent furnishings, plus pool, spa, weight room, and rooftop restaurant. All rooms have balconies, some with terrific views across the Westside. $105.

Holiday Inn Express West LA 10330 W Olympic Blvd ☎310/553-1000, 🖰www.holiday-inn .com. Located between Century City and the Westside Pavilion mall, offering adequate rooms with VCRs and fridges, and suites with lofts and spiral stairways. $140.

Luxe Sunset Boulevard 11461 Sunset Blvd ☎310/476-6571 or 1-800/HOTEL-411, 🖰www .luxehotels.com. Upper-end spot with impeccable, smartly designed rooms with marble bathtubs, Internet access, and refrigerators, and there are two on-site pools, tennis courts, health club, and free shuttle to nearby Getty Center. $160.

Westwood and UCLA

Century Wilshire 10776 Wilshire Blvd ☎310/474-4506 or 1-800/421-7223, 🖰www .centurywilshirehotel.com. Renovated old hotel, located along a prime section of Wilshire near Westwood Village. Kitchens and complimentary breakfast are standard; some rooms have balconies. $110.

Claremont 1044 Tiverton Ave ☎310/208-5957. An amazingly good deal for the area, this cheerful and inexpensive little hotel sits very close to UCLA and Westwood Village. The 53 rooms are fairly basic and only have double beds, but the main issue is the lack of parking. $65.

Airport hotels

If you're catching an early-morning flight and want to beat the traffic, or just getting into town late, you may want to stay at a **hotel near LAX**. The most conspicuous choices are arrayed along and around Century Boulevard east of the airport, but there are also pockets of motels and hotels in the suburb of El Segundo to the south, and in the dodgier turf of Inglewood a mile northeast (mostly bland motels). The following represent some of the better values in the immediate airport area.

Clarion LAX 5249 W Century Blvd, just east of LAX ☎310/645-2200 or 1-800/228-5151, 🖰www.qualityinn.com. Newly renovated chain choice featuring ten floors of comfortable and well-equipped rooms, plus pool, gym, laundry room, two restaurants, a bar, and free 24hr LAX shuttles. $100.

Courtyard Marriott El Segundo/LAX 2000 E Mariposa Ave, El Segundo, just south of LAX ☎310/322-0700, 🖰www. courtyard.com/laxca. Given the surrounding area – industrial beachside suburbia best known for its oil refineries – this is one of the better options; a chain hotel offering nice rooms with microwaves, refrigerators, and Internet access. Amenities include spa, pool, weight room, and airport shuttle. $180.

Embassy Suites LAX North 9801 Airport Blvd, just east of LAX ☎310/215-1000 or 1-800/695-8284, 🖰www.embassysuites.com. Affordable luxury from this hotel giant, offering in-room wet bars, refrigerators, Internet access, and microwaves in spacious, two-room suites; other features include spa, weight room, sauna, pool, and airport shuttle. $170. There's another good branch a bit further from LAX to the south, at 1440 Imperial Ave, El Segundo (☎310/640-3600). $150.

Renaissance 9620 Airport Blvd ☎310/337-2800 or 1-800/228-9898, 🖰www.renaissancehotels.com. If you feel compelled to splurge near the airport, this is one of the best of the LAX-area hotels: swanky wood-and-marble decor, ample rooms, and pool, spa, and health club. $190. For an extra $10–30, elegant suites are available with tasteful appointments and good views.

ACCOMMODATION | Hotels and motels

Doubletree Westwood 10740 Wilshire Blvd ☎ 310/475-8711, ⓦ www.doubletreelawestwood .com. Centrally located near Westwood Village, this big, blocky chain hotel offers standard, clean, if unexciting rooms (and a handful of more expensive suites), with pool, sauna, gym, and daily shuttle to the Getty Center. $170.

Hilgard House 927 Hilgard Ave ☎ 310/208-3945 or 1-800/826-3934, ⓦ www.hilgardhouse.com. Positioned just beyond UCLA's southern boundary, this ivy-covered charmer draws the visiting-parent crowd for its nicely designed rooms, covered parking, fridges, continental breakfast, and some rooms with hot tubs and refrigerators. $150.

UCLA Guest House 330 Young Drive E ☎ 310/825-2923, ⓦ www.hotels.ucla.edu. Excellent choice for anyone visiting the UCLA campus, with rooms offering basic amenities (including complimentary breakfast), use of nearby university recreation center, and kitchenettes available for only $5 extra. Parking nearby for $7 per day. $110.

W Los Angeles 930 Hilgard Ave ☎ 310/208-8765 or 1-800/421-2317, ⓦ www.whotels.com. Chain luxury in Westwood, featuring well-decorated – though not huge – suites with CD players and Internet access, plus on-site pool, spa, health club, and ample parking. Popular with parents visiting kids at adjacent UCLA. $300.

Santa Monica and Venice

Bayside 2001 Ocean Ave at Bay St, Santa Monica ☎ 310/396-6000, ⓦ www.baysidehotel .com. Just a block from the beach and Main Street. Outside of the colorful bathroom tiles, the rooms are fairly bland, but some have fridges, Internet access, and kitchenettes. Generally comfortable, with ocean views from the more expensive rooms. $125, with weekday rates $20 lower.

Cadillac 8 Dudley Ave at Rose Ave, Venice ☎ 310/399-8876, ⓦ www.thecadillachotel.com. Stylish Art Deco hotel on the Venice Boardwalk. Although the suites are nice, some of the lower-end rooms are spartan and have few amenities; given the location and price, though, there are few better deals around. On-site sundeck, pool, gym, and sauna. Also with hostel facilities. Dorms $25, hotel rooms start at $90.

Cal Mar 220 California St, Santa Monica ☎ 310/395-5555, ⓦ www.calmarhotel.com. One of the more unheralded choices in the area, but excellent for its central location (two blocks from the beach, one from the Promenade), garden suites with dining rooms, kitchens, and balconies, plus heated kidney-shaped pool, fitness room, and airport shuttle. $140.

Carmel 201 Broadway at Second St, Santa Monica ☎ 310/451-2469, ⓦ www.hotelcarmel .com. The solid bet for lodging if location is the central issue: near Santa Monica beach and Third Street Promenade, with the ocean two blocks away. Good, basic accommodation with limited appeal, other than the placement. $140.

Casa del Mar 1910 Ocean Way, Santa Monica ☎ 310/581-5503 ⓦ www.hotelcasadelmar.com. Another luxury item on a crowded beach-side strip for upscale hotels, not far from the pier and Promenade. Tasteful rooms feature stylish decor and Internet access, and there's an on-site pool, spa, and garden. Gloriously restored from an old landmark building. For all this, rates start at $400.

Fairmont Miramar 101 Wilshire Blvd, Santa Monica ☎ 310/576-7777, ⓦ www.fairmont .com. Upscale even for this area, this swanky hotel is a classic fixture near the north end of the Promenade, with nicely appointed suites and tropical-flavored bungalows near the pool, and health club, salon, spa, fitness center, and fine views over the Pacific. One of the best luxury choices in town, and not packed cheek-to-jowl with the other elite choices to the south. $340.

Georgian 1415 Ocean Ave, Santa Monica ☎ 310/395-9945 or 1-800/538-8147, ⓦ www .georgianhotel.com. A stunning blue-and-gold Art Deco gem, renovated with an airy Cali-fornian interior design. Rooms are elegant if small, though pricier suites offer more space and better views, from Malibu to Palos Verdes. Some rooms feature VHS players and Internet access. $205.

Hotel California 1670 Ocean Ave, Santa Monica ☎ 310/393-2363, ⓦ www.hotelca.com. Near *Loew's* (see below), but somewhat cheaper, with a central location not far from the pier. Rooms are modest but elegant, with hard-wood flooring and tasteful furnishings, and there's a pool, spa, gym, and sauna. $190.

Huntley Santa Monica Beach 1111 Second St, Santa Monica ☎ 310/394-5454, ⓦ www .preferredhotels.com. Attractive, newly rede-signed rooms with Internet access, DVD players, and superb vistas, plus a flashy exterior elevator that brings you up twenty stories to a lounge on top. Even if you don't stay here, the views over Santa Monica and the rest of the city and ocean are worth the price of a drink or two. $250.

Inn at Venice Beach 327 Washington Blvd, Venice ☎310/821-2557 or 1-800/828-0688, ⓦwww.innatvenicebeach.com. A good choice for visiting the beach and the Venice canals, with simple, tasteful rooms with balconies and refrigerators. Other choices in the area are mostly chain-oriented. $130.

Loew's Santa Monica Beach 1700 Ocean Ave at Pico Blvd, Santa Monica ☎310/458-6700, ⓦwww.loewshotels.com. One of the city's biggest hotels: a deluxe, pink pile overlooking the ocean and the pier, and occasionally in demand as a film set. The finest rooms top $450, with lesser rooms being adequate, if a bit cramped and overpriced. You're paying plenty for the location. $300.

Ocean Park 2680 32nd St, Santa Monica ☎310/452-1469. Decent alternative to the higher-priced hotels nearby, with weekly rates only ($250 and up) and clean, basic rooms with fridges, cable TV, and shared bathrooms. Several miles from the beach, not far from the Santa Monica Airport.

Oceana 849 Ocean Ave, Santa Monica ☎310/393-0486 or 1-800/777-0758, ⓦwww.hoteloceanasantamonica.com. An all-suite hotel with courtyard, good oceanside views, pool, spa, fitness room, in-room kitchens, and CD players. Located at the base of trendy Montana Avenue, giving some explanation for the overly steep prices. Rates start at $360, with occasional promo rates at $300.

Ramada Limited 3130 Washington Blvd, Venice ☎310/821-5086, ⓦwww.ramada.com. Located between Venice and Marina del Rey, a good budget choice with basic, clean rooms and pool, spa, weight room, and complimentary breakfast – a much better option than the grubby, low-end motels littering nearby Lincoln Boulevard. $90, with weekend rates $20 more.

Ritz-Carlton Marina del Rey 4375 Admiralty Way ☎310/823-1700, ⓦwww.ritzcarlton.com. One of the few good reasons to come to this unappealing district, a beautiful luxury hotel with all the high-end accoutrements, including nicely furnished rooms with balconies, swimming pool, spa, weight room, and garden terrace overlooking the marina. Weekdays $300, weekends $230.

Santa Monica Beach Travelodge 1525 Ocean Ave, Santa Monica ☎310/451-0761, ⓦwww.travelodge.com. Basic chain lodging, excellent for its beach proximity. To save $10, try the less appealing units on the eastern edge of town, in a grim, colorless building, 3102 Pico Blvd (☎310/450-5766). $150 weekdays, weekends $10 more.

Shangri-La 1301 Ocean Ave, Santa Monica ☎310/394-2791 or 1-800/345-STAY, ⓦwww.shangrila-hotel.com. Formerly the Shangri-La Apartments, a terrific, 1930s Art Deco structure with wraparound Streamline Moderne windows and railings, and alluring white-and-black design, with some original fixtures. Rooms are unexceptional but furnished with Deco motifs and art, and offer excellent views of the ocean and Third Street Promenade. $170.

Shutters on the Beach 1 Pico Blvd at Appian Way, Santa Monica ☎310/458-0030 or 1-800/334-9000, ⓦwww.shuttersonthebeach.com. The seafront home to the stars, a white-shuttered luxury resort south of the pier. Amenities include hot tubs (with shuttered screens), pool, spa, sundeck, ground-floor shopping, and ocean views. Rooms start at $445.

Venice Beach 1515 Pacific Ave, Venice ☎310/452-3052, ⓦwww.caprica.com/~vbh. Built over one of the last remaining colonnades, this hotel/hostel offers cheap and basic private rooms, cable TV with VCRs, and close access to the beach. Shared hostel rooms for $15–20; private rooms for $50.

Venice Beach House 15 30th Ave, Venice ☎310/823-1966, ⓦwww.venicebeachhouse.com. A quaint bed-and-breakfast in a 1915 Craftsman house, with nine comfortable rooms and suites finished with lush period appointments and named for famous guests – Charlie Chaplin, Abbot Kinney, etc. – and, true to the name, right next to the beach. $130 for a shared bath, $170 for a suite.

Viceroy 1819 Ocean Ave, Santa Monica ☎310/451-8711, ⓦwww.viceroysantamonica.com. Luxury accommodation with great bay views and nicely appointed rooms with CD players, on-site pool, and lounge. The high-end rooms reach $600. Rooms start at $340.

The South Bay and LA Harbor

Beach House at Hermosa 1300 Strand, Hermosa Beach ☎310/374-3001, ⓦwww.Beach-House.com. The height of luxury in the South Bay, offering two-room suites with fireplaces, wet bars, balconies, hot tubs, stereos, and refrigerators, with many rooms overlooking the ocean. On the beachside concourse of the Strand. $225.

Hilton Long Beach 710 W Ocean Blvd
☎562/983-3400, 🌐www.hilton.com. Corporate-oriented property, home to clean rooms with the usual style and amenities, though with the added plus of prime location near many Downtown sights; also with gym and business center. $190.

Holiday Inn San Pedro 111 S Gaffey St, San Pedro
☎310/514-1414, 🌐www.holidayinnsanpedro .com. While not in an ideal spot – several blocks from the end of the 110 freeway – the cheap rates, quaint decor, antique furnishings, and nicely appointed rooms and suites (all with fridges and some with kitchens) make this chain hotel worth considering. $90.

Hotel Hermosa 2515 PCH, Hermosa Beach
☎310/318-6000, 🌐www.hotelhermosa.com. In a bustling part of town, off a busy stretch of PCH between Hermosa and Manhattan beaches, a plush hotel with rooms starting at moderate prices and rising up to $350 suites. A short downhill walk to the beach. $90.

Long Beach Travelodge 80 Atlantic Ave, Long Beach ☎562/435-2471, 🌐www .travelodgelongbeach.com. A decent bargain in a central location, with the simple, spare rooms familiar to budget travelers, but also with refrigerators and coffeemakers and good access to major area sights. $80.

Manhattan Beach Marriott 1400 Parkview Ave
☎310/546-7511, 🌐www.marriott.com. One of the biggest hotels along the coast, with some four hundred rooms and suites at a variety of price levels. Many of the units have Internet access, and there's a pool, gym, hot tub, and nine-hole golf course for visiting duffers. $200.

Motel 6 5665 E 7th St, Long Beach ☎562/597-1311, 🌐www.motel6.com. Solid, basic rooms at cheap prices; good mainly for travelers motoring on their way south to Orange County or San Diego. $60.

Palos Verdes Inn 1700 S PCH, Redondo Beach
☎310/316-4211, 🌐www.palosverdesinn.com. Affordable accommodation on the edge of Redondo Beach, on a busy highway near Torrance and Palos Verdes, but just a half-mile from the water. Clean and simple rooms, with pool, spa, and gym. $85.

Portofino Hotel and Yacht Club 260 Portofino Way, Redondo Beach ☎310/379-8481,

🌐www.hotelportofino.com. One of the few good reasons to come to Redondo Beach is to stay at this elegant suite-hotel by the ocean. Although smaller single rooms are available, the best choices are the well-furnished, comfortable two-room suites with hot tubs and nice vistas, which look out over the elite playground of King Harbor. $170.

Rodeway Inn 50 Atlantic Ave at Ocean Blvd, Long Beach ☎562/435-8369, 🌐www.rodewayinn .com. Inoffensive chain-motel, a block from the beach and a serviceable base for exploring Long Beach and its downtown and harbor areas. Also with Internet access. $85.

Sea Sprite Motel 1016 Strand, Hermosa Beach
☎310/376-6933, 🌐www.seaspritemotel.com. Right next to the beach along a popular strip. Several different room options come with varying prices, including weekly rates for longer stays, plus units with kitchenettes and balconies. $105.

Seahorse Inn 233 N Sepulveda Blvd, Manhattan Beach ☎310/376-7951 or 1-800/233-8050. Typical roadside motel with faded pastel exterior and clean rooms. Further from the beach than others, but with a pool and parking. $65.

Vagabond Inn 150 Alamitos, Long Beach
☎562/435-7621, 🌐www.vagabondinn.com. One of the cheapest, most reliable of the chain lodging options in the area, with a pool, located just a few blocks west of the main downtown action. $50.

Westin Long Beach 333 E Ocean Blvd, Long Beach ☎562/436-3000, 🌐www.westin.com. A solid bet for bayside luxury at surprisingly affordable prices (cheaper when ordered online), right by the convention center, with spa, fitness center, pool, and nicely designed rooms. $220.

The San Gabriel and San Fernando valleys

Artists' Inn 1038 Magnolia St, South Pasadena
☎626/799-5668 or 1-888/799-5668, 🌐www .artistsinns.com. Themed B&B with ten rooms and suites (some with spas) honoring famous painters and styles. Best of all is the Italian Suite, with an antique tub and sun porch. Located just two blocks from the nearest stop on the Gold Line Metro. $125.

Best Western Colorado Inn 2156 E Colorado Blvd, Pasadena ☎626/793-9339, 🌐www .bestwesterncalifornia.com. Comfortable chain lodging just north of San Marino's

Huntington Museum, with clean rooms, pool, spa, Internet access, and fridges. $75.

Beverly Garland's Holiday Inn 4222 Vineland Ave, North Hollywood ☎818/980-8000 or 1-800/BEVERLY, ⊛www.beverlygarland.com. Two-tower complex with standard chain-style rooms (some with balconies), but also with pool, tennis courts, gym, sauna, and screening room, and close to Universal Studios CityWalk. The proprietor played maternal roles on TV. $110.

Graciela Burbank 322 N Pass Ave ☎818/842-8887, ⊛www.thegraciela.com. Ultra-modern boutique accommodations to enliven the drab Valley scene. Entry-level King rooms ($240) have fridges, DVD and CD players, and Internet access, while more comfy and spacious suites ($425) also feature hot tubs and kitchenettes, with about twice the room. Other amenities include pool, gym, sauna, and rooftop sundeck with hot tub.

Motel 6 12775 Encinitas Ave, Sylmar ☎818/362-9491, ⊛www.motel6.com. On the northern tip of the Valley near the 5 freeway, a budget chain motel with small, clean rooms, but best for providing good access to sights near San Fernando and, further north, to Magic Mountain. $55.

Ritz-Carlton Huntington 1401 S Oak Knoll Ave, Pasadena ☎626/568-3900, ⊛www.ritzcarlton .com. Utterly luxurious landmark 1906 hotel, located in residential Pasadena on an imposing hilltop. Palatial grounds, ponds, and courtyards, three restaurants, expansive rear lawn, and terrific San Gabriel Valley views. The elegant rooms with marble and wood are a bit on the small side (though they cost $345), and suites can run well over $500. For even bigger bucks, inquire about the private bungalows.

Safari Inn 1911 W Olive St, Burbank ☎818/845-8586, ⊛www.safariburbank.com. A classic mid-century motel, renovated but still loaded with Pop-architecture touches (Tiki and Googie styles). Features a pool, fitness room, Burbank airport shuttle, and in-room fridges, with some suites also available. $125.

Sheraton Universal 333 Universal Terrace, Universal City ☎818/980-1212 or 1-800/325-3535, ⊛www.starwood.com/sheraton. A large and luxurious high-rise hotel on the south end of the Universal Studios lot, with health club, spa, pool, and good restaurant, and well-designed rooms with superior valley views. Easily accessible off the 101 freeway. $190.

Sportsmen's Lodge 12825 Ventura Blvd, Studio City ☎818/769-4700, ⊛www.slhotel.com. Old-time multistory motel remodelled for a new era and built around a pool, with hot tub, quaint gardens, exercise room, on-site restaurant, thirteen suites, and hundreds of more basic rooms. The units also have fridges and Internet access. $130.

Universal City Hilton 555 Universal Terrace, Universal City ☎818/506-2500, ⊛www.hilton .com. A sleek high-rise neighbor to the *Sheraton Universal*, with similar appointments and amenities – pool, spa, and health club – though a much better-looking, sparkling steel-and-glass edifice. Rooms are nicely furnished within an easy stroll of CityWalk. $190.

Vagabond Inn 1203 E Colorado Blvd at Michigan Ave, Pasadena ☎626/449-3170, ⊛www .vagabondinn.com. Friendly budget chain-motel, well placed for exploring Pasadena, with clean rooms though limited amenities. $70. A similar *Vagabond Inn* is located at 120 W Colorado St in nearby Glendale ☎818/240-1700, for $80.

Westin Pasadena 191 N Los Robles Ave, Pasadena ☎626/792-2727, ⊛www.westin.com. Located in the cheesy, postmodern Plaza de las Fuentes, an imposing pastel creation with Spanish Revival touches like Mission-style arches and bright, fancy tiling. Luxury rooms have decent amenities such as Internet access and stylish decor, but location is the best feature, near Old Pasadena and grand buildings like City Hall. $190.

Malibu and the Santa Monica Mountains

Casa Malibu Inn 22752 PCH ☎310/456-2219. Located opposite Carbon Beach and featuring superb, well-appointed rooms – facing a courtyard garden ($110) or right on the beach ($230) – with great modern design and some in-room fireplaces and balconies.

Channel Road Inn 219 W Channel Rd at PCH ☎310/459-1920, ⊛www.channelroadinn.com. B&B rooms in a romantic getaway nestled in lower Santa Monica Canyon (northwest of the city of Santa Monica), with ocean views, a hot tub, and free bike rental. Eat free grapes and sip champagne in the sumptuous rooms, each priced according to its view. $185.

Good Nite Inn 26557 Agoura Rd, Calabasas ☎818/880-6000 or 1-800/NITE-INN, ⊛www .good-nite.com/calabasas.html. Perhaps the best deal in the area if you don't mind driving, this double-decker chain motel boasts a pool and spa, and offers clean rooms at affordable rates in a rustic suburb on the north side of the Santa Monica Mountains. A fifteen-minute drive to the ocean. $65.

Malibu Beach Inn 22878 PCH ☎310/456-6445 or 1-800/4-MALIBU, ⓦwww.malibubeachinn .com. Sunny pink Spanish Colonial resort by the Malibu Pier, with in-room fireplaces, tiled bathtubs, seaward balconies, DVD players, continental breakfast, and oceanside hotel deck. Wooden ceilings and quaint period-revival touches add to the charm. $195.

Malibu Country Inn 6506 Westward Beach Rd ☎310/457-9622, ⓦwww.malibucountryinn .com. Near Zuma Beach and Point Dume, a B&B in an old-fashioned 1943 structure, with nicely renovated rooms, hot tubs, and fridges, and each unit having a different style and views of either the ocean, on-site gardens, or Santa Monica Mountains. Weekday rates drop by about $40, otherwise $190.

Malibu Hotel 22541 PCH, Malibu ☎310/456-6169, ⓦwww.the-malibu-motel.com. King-sized beds and refrigerators make this roadside motel one of the more affordable choices in the area (though still not cheap), with swimming pool and DSL connections. $120.

Malibu Riviera Motel 28920 PCH ☎310/457-9503. Quiet place outside town, less than a mile from the beach, with clean and basic rooms, a sundeck and hot tub. Fairly isolated from the rest of the city. $95.

Topanga Ranch Motel 18711 PCH ☎310/456-5486, ⓦmalibubusiness.com/topangaranch.html. Thirty old-fashioned cottages painted red and white, with crude, no-frills decor; located a few blocks from the beach, not far from the intersection of PCH and Topanga Canyon Blvd. Aimed at surfers and budget travelers who don't mind the scarce amenities. $70.

Anaheim around Disneyland

Comfort Inn 1251 N Harbor Blvd ☎714/635-6461, ⓦwww.comfortinn.com. One of the more worthwhile options in town, offering rooms with continental breakfast, Internet access, fridges and microwaves, on-site pool and spa, and shuttle to Disneyland, about three miles away. $70.

Courtyard by Marriott 7621 Beach Blvd, Buena Park ☎714/670-6600, ⓦwww.courtyard .com/snabp. The best bet for visiting Knott's

Berry Farm, and a good choice for its business-oriented accommodations, with in-room fridges and Internet access, plus free parking, pool, spa, bar, and restaurant. $100.

Desert Palms 631 W Katella Ave ☎1-800/635-5423, ⓦwww.desertpalmshotel.com. Restful rooms and suites with fridges, microwaves, high-speed Net access, VCRs, and continental breakfast – and suites also with kitchenettes. Conventions in town make prices jump, but the hotel usually offers good amenities at agreeable rates, and is more stylish after a recent renovation. Rooms $90, suites start at $120.

Disneyland Grand Californian 1600 S Disneyland Drive ☎714/956-6425, ⓦdisneyland .com/resort. Massive resort supposedly built in the spirit of Craftsman design, but mostly a lot of pseudo-rustic brown-and-green kitsch. Still, a pool, fitness room, and day-care center offer some temptation for parents, along with the comfortable, well-furnished rooms (some with balconies overlooking California Adventure) beginning at $265; an entry-level suite will cost you at least $665.

Disneyland Hotel 1150 W Cerritos Ave at West St ☎714/956-6400, ⓦdisneyland.com/resort. A thousand crude, cookie-cutter rooms in a huge, monolithic establishment without much charm – but still, an irresistible stop for many. Also with pools, faux beach, and interior shopping outlets, and the place to go for a pricey wedding with Mickey in attendance. The Disneyland monorail stops outside – though park admission is separate. Ultra-basic rooms begin at $205, simple one-bedroom suites at $460.

Disneyland Pacific Pier 1717 S Disneyland Drive ☎714/956-6425, ⓦdisneyland.com/resort. Renovated concrete complex turned into overflow lodging for park visitors; location is further from the main theme park than its counterpart on Cerritos Avenue, but shuttles are available and rooms are slightly cheaper (beginning at $160), with the same amenities and massive scale.

Holiday Inn Anaheim at the Park 1221 S Harbor Blvd ☎714/758-0900, ⓦwww.holiday-inn.com. Safe, clean lodging not far from the Magic Kingdom, offering standard rooms with limited amenities, but much cheaper rates than the Disney equivalent. $75.

Motel 6 2920 W Chapman Ave ☎714/634-2441, ⓦwww.motel6.com. Unexciting chain-motel rooms (though some have microwaves and fridges), but given the surrounding options, the best bargain in the area – and located right off I-5. On-site pool, too. $50.

Park Place Inn 1544 S Harbor Blvd ☎714/776-4800, ⓦwww.parkplaceinnandminisuites.com. Recently upgraded *Best Western* chain hotel across from Disneyland, with the customary clean rooms with fridges and microwaves, plus pool, sauna, hot tub, and continental breakfast. $140.

Pavilions 1176 W Katella Ave ☎714/776-0140, ⓦwww.pavilionshotel.com. Convenient chain hotel offering basic rooms with fridges for $8 extra, as well as a pool, spa, sauna, and shuttle to Disneyland. $90.

Stovall's Inn 1110 W Katella Ave ☎714/778-1880, ⓦwww.stovallsinn.com. Tasteful, clean chain accommodation near Disneyland, with fitness center, pools, and spa, and in-room fridges and microwaves for extra. $95.

The Orange County coast

Doryman's Inn 2102 W Ocean Front, Newport Beach ☎714/675-7300, ⓦwww.dorymansinn .com. Lovely historic B&B built in 1921 and located near the tip of Balboa Peninsula, overlooking the sands and offering eleven rooms, some with fireplaces and old-fashioned tubs (and a few hot tubs), plus a rooftop patio. Room costs vary widely, depending on amenities, anywhere from $195 to $365.

Hilton Waterfront Beach Resort 21100 PCH, Huntington Beach ☎714/960-7873, ⓦwww .waterfrontbeachresort.hilton.com. A towering high-rise with nicely furnished rooms and the added attractions of private balconies, serpentine pool, spa, and rentals of everything from surfboards to rollerblades; rooms have views of gardens or ocean. $220.

Hotel Laguna 425 S Coast Hwy, Laguna Beach ☎949/494-1151, ⓦwww.hotellaguna.com. Atmospheric and comfortable, with luxurious appointments and location in the center of Laguna Beach. Nearly every room looks out at the ocean, though price depends on quality of view. Basic rooms for $100 (or $30 more in high season), and suites begin at $225 (or $325 peak).

Little Inn by the Bay 2627 Newport Blvd, Newport Beach ☎949/673-8800, ⓦwww .littleinnbythebay.com. Eighteen nice rooms near Newport Beach in a renovated complex; the cheapest accommodation in

the area, with in-room fridges, microwaves, and complimentary breakfast. Close to Balboa Peninsula. $100.

Mission Inn 26891 Ortega Hwy at I-5, San Juan Capistrano ☎949/493-1151, ⓦwww .missioninnsjc.com. Stylishly updated rooms come with CD players and fridges, plus continental breakfast and use of hot tub and pool. Located in a distant Orange County city, but close enough to the main draw, the old Spanish Mission. $145.

Ocean View Motel 16196 PCH, Huntington Beach ☎562/592-2700, ⓦwww.oceanviewmotel-hb .com. Family-run roadside establishment with clean and comfy rooms for $65, just off the main drag. As a bonus, get a hot tub in your room for an extra $20.

Pacific View Inn 16220 PCH, Huntington Beach ☎562/592-4959, ⓦwww.pacificviewinn.com. Located several miles northwest of town, the *Pacific View* offers twenty beachside rooms with tasteful decor in a comfortable establishment; free continental breakfast, and some rooms with ocean views and hot tub. $60.

Ritz-Carlton Laguna Niguel PCH at One Ritz-Carlton Drive ☎949/240-2000, ⓦwww .ritzcarlton.com/resorts/laguna_niguel. Another stunning *Ritz-Carlton*, this one perhaps the best in town for its oceanside beauty (on the cliffs overlooking the sea around Dana Point) and rooms and suites chock full of luxury. The high-end amenities – swank decor, pool, spa, racquet club, etc – are everything you'd expect if paying $390 a night.

Seacliff Motel 1661 S Coast Hwy, Laguna Beach ☎714/494-9717, ⓦwww.seaclifflaguna.com. Renovated motel with close ocean access, heated pool, and complimentary breakfast. Rates start at $65, but jump if you want a room with a sea view or a balcony ($140–220, depending on the season).

Seal Beach Inn and Gardens 212 Fifth St, Seal Beach ☎562/493-2416, ⓦwww.sealbeachinn .com. Although located in an uneventful burg, a fine B&B offering cottages, villas, and suites, with sumptuous appointments two blocks from the sands. Rooms on lower level have fetching antiques ($140), but the best room, the Penthouse, is up top overlooking the ocean ($400).

Surf and Sand Resort 1555 S Coast Hwy, Laguna Beach ☎949/497-4477 or 1-800/524-8621, ⓦwww.surfandsandresort.com. Among the best of the coast's hotels, with terrific

oceanside views, easy beach access, and luxurious rooms and suites with many features, including balconies. Rates begin at $300, but three penthouses are available to the true swells ($800–1100).
Sutton Place 4500 MacArthur Blvd, Newport Beach ☎949/476-2001 or 1-800/810-6888, ⓦ**www.suttonplacenb.com.** Rather forbidding-looking hotel that features good amenities – pool, spa, tennis courts, restaurant, bar, shuttle to John Wayne Airport – and attractive, spacious rooms. $170.

Hostels

As you might expect, **hostels** are found at the bottom of the price scale, offering dorm rooms and beds going for somewhere around $15–20, depending on whether you're a member of their organization. Many hostels also offer cut-rate single and double rooms. You can expect little more from your stay than a clean, safe bed, somewhere to lock your valuables, and a typically colorful crowd of visitors – sometimes making for quite the party atmosphere. Some hostels also offer tours of surrounding areas (mostly theme parks, shopping malls, and stars' homes), while others organize social events – volleyball, pizza parties, and the like. There's often a three-to-five-night maximum stay, though this is generally enforced only when demand outstrips supply.

Adventure Hostel 527 Knickerbocker Rd, Big Bear Lake ☎1-866/866-5255, ⓦ**www.adventurehostel .com.** One of the region's best bets if you've got a car, a recently remodelled mountainside spot with plenty of activities, from skiing and snowboarding in winter to jet-skiing, hiking, and parasailing in summer. Two-hour drive from LA; the only public buses run from San Bernardino (☎909/808-5465). Dorm rooms $20–25, private rooms $60 and up.
Banana Bungalow 2775 Cahuenga Blvd W, in the Cahuenga Pass ☎323/851-1129 or 1-800/446-7835, ⓦ**www.bananabungalow.com.** Popular hostel near Universal City and US-101, with free airport shuttles, city tours to Venice Beach and Magic Mountain, and a relaxed atmosphere. Outdoor pool, free parking, and as much beer as you can drink every second night for $3. Dorms $18–21, and pricier private doubles $64.
HI-Anaheim/Fullerton 1700 N Harbor Blvd at Brea, Fullerton ☎714/738-3721, ⓦ**www.hihostels.com.** Convenient and comfortable, five miles north of Disneyland on the site of a former dairy farm. The hostel's excellent facilities include a grass volleyball court, golf driving range, and picnic area. There are only twenty dorm beds, so reservations are a must. Summer check-in 5–11pm; rest of year 4–11pm. Mornings open 7.10am–noon. OCTA bus #43 stops outside. Members $17, others $20.

HI-LA/Santa Monica 1436 Second St, Santa Monica ☎310/393-9913, ⓦ**www.hihostels .com.** A few blocks from the beach and pier, the building was LA's Town Hall from 1887 to 1889, and retains its historic charm, with inner courtyard, ivy-covered walls, and a skylight – and 224 beds. Members $27, others $30; private rooms for $70 or more. All prices include laundry machines and kitchen use. Smoking and drinking prohibited. Reservations essential in summer. Open 24 hours.
HI-LA/South Bay 3601 S Gaffey St, Bldg #613, San Pedro ☎310/831-8109, ⓦ**www.hihostels .com.** Sixty beds in old US Army barracks, with a panoramic view of the Pacific Ocean. Ideal for seeing San Pedro, Palos Verdes, and the whole LA Harbor area. Open 7am–midnight. $17 members, $20 others; private rooms $38 per person. MTA bus #446 passes close by, but it's a two-hour journey from Downtown. You can also take the SuperShuttle from LAX. During Oct–Apr only open to groups of 15 or more.
Hollywood International Hostel 6820 Hollywood Blvd ☎323/463-0797 or 1-800/750-6561, ⓦ**www.hollywoodhostels.com.** One of three good-value locations in the area, this one in the heart of Hollywood, with free tea and coffee, game room, gymnasium, barbecues, patio garden, kitchen, and laundry. Tours of Hollywood offered, as well as tours beyond the immediate area to theme parks, Las Vegas, and Tijuana.

Shared rooms start at $17 and reach $40 and over for private rooms.

Hostel California 2221 Lincoln Blvd at Venice Blvd, Venice ☎310/305-0250, ⓦhostelcalifornia .net. LA's first hostel, several miles from Venice Beach in a somewhat seedy commercial section of town. Accommodations run from private rooms ($40 for two) and six-bed male/female dorms ($16) to a 30-bed mixed dorm ($13). Amenities include kitchens, pool table, big-screen TV, linen, and parking. Shuttle bus to and from LAX.

Huntington Beach Colonial Inn Hostel 421 Eighth St at Pecan, Huntington Beach ☎714/536-3315, ⓦwww.huntingtonbeachhostel .com. Four blocks from the beach and mostly double rooms. Easy access to Disneyland and Knott's Berry Farm. Sleeping bags allowed. Open 8am–11pm. Key rental after 1pm, $1 (plus $20 deposit). Dorms $21, private rooms $50; weekly rates $130.

Orange Drive Manor 1764 N Orange Drive, Hollywood ☎323/850-0350, ⓦorangedrivehostel .com. Centrally located hostel (right behind the Chinese Theatre) offering tours of film studios, theme parks, and houses of the stars. Members $20, others $24, private rooms $40–55.

Orbit Hotel and Hostel 7950 Melrose Ave ☎323/655-1510 or 1-877/ORBIT-US, ⓦwww .orbithotel.com. Retro-1960s complex with sleek Day-Glo furnishings and ultra-hip modern decor, offering complimentary breakfast, movie screening room, patio, café, private baths in all rooms, shuttle tours, and $20-per-day car rental. Located just west of the most frenetic and colorful part of Melrose. Dorms $18–21, private rooms $55–70.

Surf City Hostel 26 Pier Ave, Hermosa Beach ☎310/798-2323 or 1-800/305-2901, ⓦwww .surfcityhostel.ws. Good location near popular beachside strip, the Strand, and numerous restaurants, clubs, and bars. Shared rooms from $19 or private doubles from $48. Also with kitchen, laundry, and shuttles to Disneyland and other major theme parks and shopping zones.

USA Hostels – Hollywood 1624 Schrader Ave ☎323/462-3777 or 1-800/LA-HOSTEL, ⓦwww .usahostels.com. A block south of the center of Hollywood Boulevard, near major attractions and with game room, private baths, main bar, Internet access, area tours ($5–7), and garden patio, as well as airport and train shuttles. Shared rooms $16–20, private rooms from $40.

Venice Beach Cotel 25 Windward Ave, Venice ☎310/399-7649, ⓦwww.venicebeachcotel.com. Occupying what's left of the old colonnade, with trompe l'oeil Venetian-style windows and painted-on people peering out, this is one of the stranger-looking hostels in LA. Directly near the Venice Boardwalk and Muscle Beach, with dorm rooms for around $16–18, and private rooms $35–50. Also with door-to-door trips to major theme parks, homes of the stars, and Getty Center, plus complimentary boogie boards.

Campgrounds

Reserve America (☎1-800/444-7275, ⓦwww.reserveamerica.com) processes reservations at many of the **campgrounds** listed below and can help you find an alternative if your chosen site is full. It charges a $7 fee per reservation per night up to a maximum of eight people per site, including one vehicle.

Mainland

Bolsa Chica Huntington Beach ☎714/846-3460. Facing the ocean near a thousand-acre wildlife sanctuary and bird-watchers' paradise, with fishing opportunities as well. $25–30 for campers with a self-contained vehicle. No tent camping. Add $9 to the rate for sites near the ocean.

Chilao Flat on Hwy-2 twenty miles northeast of Pasadena ☎818/899-1900, ⓦwww.fs.fed .us/r5/angeles. The only campground in the San Gabriel Mountains reachable by car, though there are others accessible on foot. For details contact the Angeles National Forest Ranger Station at 701 N Santa Anita Ave, Arcadia (☎626/574-1613). $12, with $5 vehicle pass; may be periodically closed due to bear activity.

Crystal Cove State Park Orange County coast ☎1-800/444-7275. With two thousand woodland acres and nearly four miles of beach, a distant outpost in Orange County with much natural appeal; recreational activities include scuba diving, bicycling, swimming, and exploring the tide pools or craggy beachside coves throughout the park. $15–20.

Dockweiler Beach County Park 8255 Vista del Mar ☎310/322-4951 or 1-800/950-7275, Ⓦbeaches.co.la.ca.us. On a noisy coastal strip, almost at the western end of LAX. Mainly for RVs, tent sites by reservation only. A popular urban beach, which can get a little dicey on weekends. $25–32.

Doheny State Beach Dana Point ☎949/496-6171 or 1-800/444-7275. Located at south end of Orange County, not far from Dana Point Harbor, and often packed with families on weekends. $16–21, add $10 for beach-front sites.

Leo Carrillo State Beach Park northern Malibu ☎818/706-1310 or 1-800/444-7275. Pronounced "Ca-REE-oh," near one of LA's best surfing beaches, 25 miles northwest of Santa Monica on Pacific Coast Highway, and served twice an hour in summer by MTA bus #434. Not far from the end of Mulholland Highway. $15–20.

Malibu Creek State Park 1925 Las Virgenes Rd, in the Santa Monica Mountains ☎818/706-8809 or 1-800/444-7275. Rustic campground with sixty sites in the shade of huge oak trees, almost all with fire pits, solar-heated show-ers, and flush toilets. One-time filming loca-tion for *M*A*S*H* and *Planet of the Apes*, among other things. $15–20.

San Clemente State Beach 3030 Avenida del Presidente, two miles south of San Clemente ☎949/492-3156 or 1-800/444-7275. A prime spot for hiking, diving, and surfing, around an area that was once home to Richard Nixon's "Western White House." $16–21, add $9 for beachfront sites.

Santa Catalina Island

Campgrounds on **Santa Catalina Island** are all processed through the Catalina Island Company (☎310/510-8368, Ⓦ www.scico.com/camping), which charges $12 for adult use, $6 for kids, and usually requires reserva-tions. Island transportation by boat or bus is not included; see box on p.192 for more details on getting around the area.

Blackjack Not for the timid – an isolated site high in the trees near the island's center, a rugged nine-mile trek from the nearest town, Avalon (which has its own, much tamer *Hermit Gulch*, below), with limited facilities except for barbecues, fire pits, toilets, and showers.

Hermit Gulch Only a mile and a half from the boat launch at Avalon, this camp-ground is popular and easy to access, with barbecues, picnic tables, and even a microwave and a few tepees. Provides a good jumping-off point for exploring the island.

Little Harbor Sited on the island's south side, you can get here by hiking or by bus, and fire rings are available, too. The main draw, though, is the pair of sandy beaches, good for swimming in a relaxed, isolated setting.

Parsons Landing Remote site on the island's northern tip; eight camp sites with no show-ers or fresh water, but offering fire rings, picnic tables, and, for a fee from a lockbox, firewood and bottled water. Boating is the obvious choice for arrival, though the site is accessible on foot. Seven miles from Two Harbors.

Two Harbors Located on a lovely isthmus near the island's center, a tourist-oriented campground offering standard tent sites, along with "Catalina Cabins" for around $35 (Nov–May only), which provide amenities like fridges and heaters.

(12)

Eating

S ince the arrival of California cuisine in the 1980s (based both out of Northern and Southern California), LA has been one of the major nodes on the country's dining map, its **restaurants** and **cafés** attracting high-profile chefs and generating national culinary buzz. Even twenty years later, the city's gastronomic trendsetters are still going strong, from old favorites such as *Michael's* and *Spago* that helped get the tide rolling, to newcomers specializing in a variety of Cal-cuisine hybrids, from Northern Italian to pan-Asian. The range of cuisines in LA stretches far beyond the influence of California-style dishes like salmon glazed with saffron and shiitake mushrooms, however, with everywhere from exclusive supper clubs to the dingiest burger shacks doling out delicious meals. Beside the fast-food drive-ins that were invented here, LA is the birthplace of such enduring favorites as the cheeseburger, hot fudge sundae, French dip sandwich, and Caesar salad.

For many of the restaurants listed, you won't need to **reserve** ahead, though you should make the effort on weekends, during major holidays, and at the most expensive or trendy places. For **dinner**, expect to pay $5–10 per person for simple fast food, $15–20 for most ethnic and old-fashioned, steak-and-potatoes American restaurants, and $30–60 for the latest hot spots of any sort (and this doesn't include wine or cocktails). To sample great food without paying a bundle, go for **lunch** at those upscale eateries that offer it, where you can typically eat for about half of what you might shell out at dinner. The price breaks do not, however, continue downward at those establishments that offer **breakfast**, and unless you're going for a rock-bottom meal at *Denny's* or at *Norm's* diners, you'll end up paying $10–15 for any sort of edible morning repast.

No matter where you choose to eat, though, don't reach for a cigarette – health-conscious LA banned **smoking** in 1993, and the state of California then followed with a blanket tobacco prohibition in restaurants and most bars.

Cuisines

Budget food is plentiful in LA, ranging from good sit-down meals in street-corner coffee shops to burger chains – so much so that we've included a special section that leads off the reviews. Almost as common, and just as cheap, is **Mexican food**, the closest thing you'll get to an indigenous LA cuisine. Mexican burrito stands and lunch-trucks are often the city's best deals, serving tasty and filling food for as little as $5 per person; they're at their most authentic in East LA, although there's a good selection of more Americanized examples all over the city. The cuisines of the rest of **Latin America** have made plenty of inroads, too, from the flavors of Honduras and Nicaragua and the blending of Peruvian cuisine with local seafood (aka "Peruvian seafood"), to the hot, garlicky platters of Argentine beef available throughout the Westside.

The city lacks a wide selection of **African** restaurants, other than those based on the cuisines of North Africa. Those that do exist are mainly found in Hollywood and Mid-Wilshire. **Moroccan** food is typically good, though not concentrated in any one neighborhood, while the best **Ethiopian** restaurants are in a small pocket around Olympic Boulevard in Mid-Wilshire, and are fairly inexpensive. Aside from such singular cuisines, pan-African hybrids have made some headway on the menus of adventurous restaurants, mixing the grains, spices, and vegetables of Africa with the foods of the Caribbean, Europe, and the American South.

Old-fashioned **American** cuisine, with its steaks, baked potatoes, and mountainous salads, doesn't ride the wave of LA food trendiness, but does attract the broadest swath of the city's chow-hounds – everyone from Armani-wearing executives to the most benighted tourists likes a good prime rib. The fare is available across LA, costing as little as $10 for a gut-busting blowout in a roadside diner, to well over $70 for a choice porterhouse served amid chandeliers in a luxury steakhouse. Much more conspicuous, and trendier, is the juggernaut of **California cuisine**, which not only adds bold new twists to American cooking, but often combines with other cuisines (Japanese, Indian, etc) to produce some unusual entrees. In its original form, "Cal-cuisine" uses fresh, locally available ingredients, more likely grilled than fried, and is stylishly presented with a nod to French *nouvelle cuisine*. In its more recent and decadent incarnation, it's an excuse to mix-and-match discordant flavors on the same plate, with varying results – there's only so much apple-cinnamon-glazed beef heart one can stand. As a side avenue of American cuisine, spicy **Cajun** food is affordable as well as enjoyable, and there are a number of fine establishments sprinkled throughout the region.

Unlike many ethnic cuisines in LA, those from the **Caribbean** – namely Jamaican – are more visible in West LA and Santa Monica than in Hollywood. With few exceptions, local Caribbean restaurants leave subtlety behind in exchange for sweat-inducing flavors and spices, added to staples like plantains, yucca root, and jerked chicken; however, **Cuban** restaurants (and bakeries, where you can find them) offer more complex flavors, and number among the city's finest restaurants.

LA's most fashionable districts offer many delicious **Chinese** and dim sum restaurants, which can easily set you back $30. More authentic and less pricey outlets tend to be located Downtown, notably in Chinatown, where you can get a good-sized meal for around $15 – though the more jade-and-bamboo kitsch you see, the less authentic and more tourist-centric the place is. **Vietnamese** food is catching on quickly in LA restaurants, both in its authentic variety – namely in the Orange County suburbs of Santa Ana or Westminster – and in its Cal-cuisine incarnation, often employed as a hybrid with *nouvelle* French fare.

French restaurants proper are among LA's fanciest; look to those on the Westside for the most expensive prices, and unexpected spots in the San Gabriel Valley and Downtown for cheaper fare. On the other hand, LA's **Greek** restaurants provide fairly traditional entrees for inexpensive prices, but are fairly thin on the ground, sometimes better known for their spirited nightly singing and dancing than for their menus.

Indian restaurants are growing in popularity, with restaurant menus embracing Californian dishes to create hybrids like curry polenta and duck tandoori, though more traditional meals are almost always offered as well. Most of the

Indian restaurants in Hollywood or West LA charge $15–20 for a full meal, less for a vegetarian dish. **Pakistani** variants on Indian cuisine can be equally delicious, though of course without pork ingredients (or alcohol), and are located in roughly the same areas as Indian eateries.

After decades of having nothing more exotic than takeout pizza chains, LA in the 1980s became home to some of the country's best regional **Italian** restaurants, with those specializing in Northern Italian food usually being the most expensive. That said, as common as it is, Italian food can also be quite variable in quality, often little more than bland, mealy piles of pasta. A more appealing phenomenon is the **designer pizza**, invented at Hollywood's (now Beverly Hills') *Spago* restaurant by celebrity chef Wolfgang Puck, and topped with duck, shiitake mushrooms, or whatever comes to mind. None of this comes cheap, however: the least elaborate designer pizza will set you back around $15. On the other hand, LA's **traditional pizza** joints are generally good and affordable.

Japanese cuisine is available throughout LA in a wide range of styles and settings. Not surprisingly, Little Tokyo is a good place for sushi, with *udon* and *soba* spots more noticeable as you head further west, and more authentic fare concentrated in the drab immigrant center of Gardena. Along with French cooking, Japanese cuisine is one of the favorites used by California-cuisine chefs for their culinary experiments, making many "Japanese" restaurants more international in style, and good representatives of the city's latest cultural trends.

Outside the giant minimalls and diners of Koreatown, **Korean** cuisine tends to be limited to isolated pockets in the Westside and the northern suburbs. Spicy barbecued ribs and *kim chee* (pickled cabbage) are among the more traditional dishes; expect to pay under $20 per person for a good-sized meal.

LA's various **Middle Eastern** restaurants can be affordably good. Aside from citywide falafel and pita chains, excellent examples of this cuisine are found in strip-mall eateries, and in health-food or vegetarian restaurants, where the old-style Levantine cooking becomes all but unrecognizable, containing ingredients such as avocado, bean sprouts, tofu, and kasha.

Russian and **Eastern European** restaurants are uncommon in LA outside of isolated ethnic enclaves – particularly present in Mid-Wilshire, the eastern side of West Hollywood, and in the San Fernando Valley around Ventura Boulevard. For the most part, you can expect authentic dishes, though prices tend to vary, depending on the neighborhood and the type of restaurant.

Although **seafood** is offered throughout LA in a variety of styles, there are plenty of worthwhile seafood-only restaurants, predominantly along the coast, with a strong concentration near Malibu and Newport Beach. However, some oceanside restaurants are better for their views than their food, and by venturing just a mile or so inland, you can find a better meal than you might at a restaurant located within sight of whales and seagulls – *Gladstone's* is the most conspicuous example of this, where you really end up paying for the view.

Spanish cooking, along with **tapas bars**, has made an increasingly large dent in LA's culinary culture. While the classic form of such restaurants are good spots for a pitcher of sangría and savory seafood and pork dishes, the latest variety use tapas as an excuse to offer "little plates" of anything that comes to mind – meatballs, sushi, garlic fries – hardly Spanish, but definitely expensive, once you finish counting all the plates you need to make you full.

Considering all of LA's options for Asian cuisines, authentic **Thai** food might be the best deal, both for its spicy flavors and reasonable prices. Thai food is at its best and least pretentious in the less trendy sections of town, such as mini-malls in Hollywood and run-down storefronts in Mid-Wilshire. If you don't

EATING | Cuisines

mind sacrificing atmosphere for delicious food, a trip to such environs is usually well rewarded.

Mind- and body-fixated LA has a wide variety of **vegetarian** and **wholefood** restaurants, the bulk of them on the Westside and many along the coast as well. Some vegetarian places can be very good value ($5–10 or so), but watch out for those that flaunt themselves as a New Age experience and include soporific music and a gift shop selling crystals and pyramids – these can be three times as costly.

Rough Guide favorites

Burgers
The Apple Pan p.270
Cassell's Hamburgers p.268
Hamburger Haven p.269
Jay's Jayburgers p.268
Tommy's p.269

California cuisine
Michael's p.290
Patina p.273
Spago p.286
vermont p.280
Water Grill p.273

Chinese
Chung King p.286
Hong Kong Deli p.280
Mandarin Deli p.274
Ocean Seafood p.274
Ocean Star p.295

Diners
Du-Par's p.268
Fred 62 p.268
Original Pantry p.267
Pann's p.271
Rae's Diner p.270

French
Angelique Café p.275
Café des Artistes p.281
Café Pinot p.275
Fenix p.282
L'Orangerie p.282

Indian
Bombay Café p.286
The Clay Pit p.286
Electric Lotus p.281
New East India Grill p.277
Surya p.277

Italian
Ca' Brea p.276
Campanile p.277
Il Pastaio p.286
Locanda Veneta p.287
Valentino p.290

Japanese
Matsuhisa p.287
Mishima p.278
Mori Sushi p.287
Shiro p.295
Sushi Ryo p.281

Korean
Arirang p.278
Dong Il Jang p.278
In Chon Won p.297
Monsoon Café p.291
Soot Bull Jeep p.278

Mexican and Latin American
Border Grill p.291
El Taurino p.275
El Tepayac p.292
Guelaguetza p.278
Luminarias p.292

Pizza
Abbot's Pizza Company p.290
Frankie and Johnny's p.283
Jacopo's p.286
Palermo p.281
Wildflour Pizza p.291

Seafood
Claes Seafood p.297
I Cugini p.291
Kincaid's Bay House p.294
Mario's Peruvian Seafood p.278
Neptune's Net p.292

Steakhouses
Arnie Morton's p.285
Engine Co. No. 28 p.273
Jar p.282
Pacific Dining Car p.273
Taylor's p.276

Thai and Southeast Asian
Blue Bamboo p.284
Chan Darae p.282
Saladang p.296
Sanamluang Café p.296
Talesai p.288

If you'd rather have a picnic than visit a restaurant, try the Trader Joe's chain – which started as a liquor store with a sideline in unusual food, but now sells imported cheeses, breads, and canned foods – or the area's frequent **farmers markets**, loaded with organic produce and frequently advertised in the press.

Finally, LA is littered with **celebrity-owned** outfits, but the food is usually so unremarkable we haven't listed them. For chowing down, celebrity-watching, or just enjoying a nice view, you're better off practically anywhere else.

Coffee shops, delis, and diners

At its best, budget food in LA is doled out in the many small **coffee shops**, **delis**, and **diners** that offer soups, omelets, sandwiches, and a slew of comfort food. It's easy to eat this way and never have to spend much more than $10 for a full meal. There are, of course, the usual fast-food franchises on every street; better are the local chains of **hamburger stands**, most open 24 hours a day, providing filling meals as well as abundant local color. Some, such as *Fatburger*, originally at San Vicente and La Cienega boulevards on the border of Beverly Hills, and *In-N-Out Burger*, are now extending their reach across the US; others, like the ever-popular *Tommy's*, are only-in-LA favorites.

Sadly, the best of the 1950s **drive-ins** have either been torn down or remodelled beyond recognition, such as *The Wich Stand*, now a health-food store. However, some spots, including *Pann's* near Inglewood, continue to cater to fans of old-fashioned formica diners, with their neon signs, boomerang roofs, and classic steak-and-eggs breakfasts.

Downtown

Clifton's Cafeteria 648 S Broadway ☎213/627-1673. Classic 1930s cafeteria, the last remaining in a chain of six quirky eateries, with plenty of bizarre decor: redwood trees, a waterfall, even a mini-chapel. The food is less daring – traditional meat-and-potatoes American – and cheap, too. Mon–Fri 6.30am–7.30pm, Sat & Sun 6.30am–8pm.

Cole's Pacific Electric Buffet 118 E Sixth St ☎213/622-4090. LA's oldest surviving restaurant, here since 1908 when the old Red Car transit floot woo otill operating. The decor and food haven't changed much, with the dark-wood paneling, sawdust-covered floors, and ancient-looking fixtures mirroring the rich, hearty French dip sandwiches – loaded with steak, pastrami, or brisket – a dish invented at this very spot. Daily 8.30am–7pm.

Emerson's 606 S Olive St ☎213/623-3006, **862 S Los Angeles St** ☎213/623-8807. Solid breakfast-and-lunch spot where you can knock back some of the city's best cheap sandwiches, with the *croque monsieur* and chicken-salad baguette among the highlights. Sip espresso and munch on a regular salad, too, or sample the clam chowder or

jambalaya, for less than $10 each. Mon–Fri 7.30am–5pm.

Grand Central Market 317 S Broadway ☎213/624-9496. Selling plenty of tacos, deli sandwiches, and Chinese food, plus a few more exotic items, like pigs' ears and lamb sweetbreads. A fun, cheap place to eat. Daily 9am–6pm.

Langer's Deli 704 S Alvarado St ☎213/483-8050. "When in doubt, eat hot pastrami" says the sign. Helpful, but you still have to choose from over twenty ways of eating what is easily LA's best pastrami sandwich. Located in a dicey spot, but curbside pick-up available. Mon–Sat 8am–4pm.

Mitsuru Café 117 Japanese Village Plaza ☎213/613-1028. On a hot day nothing beats the snow cones at *Mitsuru*, which come in such exotic flavors as *kintoki* (adzuki-bean paste) or milk *kintoki* (sweet custard). In colder weather, try the *imagawayaki* – adzuki beans baked in a bun. Located in a popular mall. Mon 11am–7.30pm, Tues–Sun 11am–9pm.

Original Pantry 877 S Figueroa St ☎213/972-9279. Generous portions of meaty American cooking – chops and steaks, mostly – in this legendary 24-hour diner owned by former mayor Richard Riordan. The quirky old-fashioned brochures are worth a look while you wait.

Original Texas Barbeque King 867 W Sunset Blvd ☎213/972-1928. Delicious and heaping platters of ribs and chicken served up Lone Star State–style, with smoked, goopy sauce and more napkins than you can shake a drumstick at. Just west of Chinatown. Mon–Sat 8.30am–5.30pm.

Philippe the Original French Dip 1001 N Alameda St, Chinatown ☎213/628-3781. Renowned sawdust café, a block north of Union Station, where you can tuck into juicy, artery-clogging French dips – loaded with turkey, pork, beef, or lamb – at one of the long communal tables. An amazingly good and filling treat for less than $5. Daily 6am–10pm.

The Yorkshire Grill 610 W Sixth St ☎213/623-3362. New York–style deli and neighborhood fave since 1947, with big sandwiches and friendly service for under $10. Lunchtime is crowded with yuppies and locals. Mon–Fri 6.30am–4pm, Sat 7am–2pm.

Mid-Wilshire

Canter's Deli 419 N Fairfax Ave ☎323/651-2030. Iconic LA deli with huge sandwiches for around $8 and excellent kosher soups served by famously aggressive waitresses in pink uniforms and running shoes. Live music on Tuesday nights in Canter's adjoining "Kibitz Room." Open 24 hours.

Cassell's Hamburgers 3266 W Sixth St ☎213/480-8668. No-frills takeout hamburger stand that some swear by, serving up nearly two-thirds of a pound of beef per bun. Mon–Sat 11am–4pm.

Du-Par's 6333 W Third St ☎323/933-8446. A long-standing LA institution, located in the Farmers Market, which draws a whole host of grizzled old-timers for its greasy breakfasts and heavy-duty cheeseburgers. Make sure to sample a piece of pie – they come in a full range of bright colors and flavors. Sun–Thurs 6.30am–1am, Fri & Sat 6.30am–4am.

Hard Rock Café in the Beverly Center mall, Beverly Blvd at San Vicente Blvd ☎310/276-7605. Almost unavoidable for some visitors, highlighted by rock'n'roll memorabilia and loud music. The fancy merchandise is the focus; the bland, greasy food is an afterthought. Sun–Thurs 11.30am–11pm, Fri & Sat 11.30am–midnight.

Maurice's Snack 'n Chat 5549 W Pico Blvd ☎323/931-3877. Everything here is cooked to order: spoon bread or baked chicken requires a call two hours ahead, though you could just drop in for fried chicken, pork chops, grits, or salmon croquettes. Mon–Thurs noon–11pm, Fri noon–11pm, Sat noon–4pm, Sun 2–8pm.

Oki Dog 5056 W Pico Blvd ☎323/938-4369. Along with *Pink's* (see opposite), this low-rent shack is an essential stop for lovers of "red hots," in this case wieners wrapped in tortillas and stuffed with all manner of gooey, super-caloric ingredients – from cheese to chili. Daily 10am–10pm. Also a branch closer to Hollywood at 860 N Fairfax Ave (☎323/655-4166); Mon–Sat 7.30am–2am.

Picholine 3360 W First St ☎213/252-8722. A good selection of sandwiches stuffed with gourmet ingredients – pesto, sun-dried tomato, etc – along with mouthwatering sides of pasta, all for under $8. Tues–Sat 10am–7pm.

Swingers in the Beverly Laurel Motor Lodge, 8018 Beverly Blvd at Laurel Ave ☎323/653-5858. Affordable American comfort food – with a few eclectic vegan and pan-Asian offerings – served in a strangely trendy motel environment, luring a large crowd of hipsters and poseurs, as well as a few movie-star wannabes. Sun–Thurs 6am–2pm, Fri & Sat 9.30am–4am.

Hollywood

Back Door Bakery 1710 Silver Lake Blvd ☎323/662-7927. Popular for its breakfasts of pancakes and French toast, this Silver Lake favorite also serves standard lunch fare (soups, sandwiches), along with its unique variations on junk-food treats like cupcakes and Twinkies – served here home-made and doused in rich chocolate cream. Daily 7am–6pm.

Fred 62 1854 N Vermont Ave, Los Feliz ☎323/667-0062. Designed like something out of the 1950s – with a soda fountain, streamlined booths, and 24hr operation – this restaurant offers stylish, affordable California-cuisine twists on familiar staples like salads, burgers and fries, and a tempting array of pancakes and omelets, too.

Jay's Jayburgers 4481 Santa Monica Blvd ☎323/666-5204. A gutbusting favorite for nearly forty years, doling out savory burgers and hot dogs – at their best, with chili and a side of potato chips – in modest sub-diner surroundings in a grim part of town. Sun–Thurs 6am–midnight, 24hr on weekends.

KFC 340 N Western Ave ☎323/467-7421. Chain-food chicken meals are generic as ever, but the postmodern architecture is striking: a giant, 40-foot-high "bucket" and a little white cube, featuring the Colonel's face, balancing precariously on top. The towering interior ceiling and spiral staircases inside are well worth a look. Daily 10am–11pm.

Pink's Hot Dogs 709 N La Brea Ave ☎323/931-4223. One of LA's quintessential diners, making legendary chili dogs served with all kinds of messy toppings. Depending on your taste, these monsters are either gut bombs or lifesavers. Sun–Thurs 9.30am–2am, Fri & Sat 9.30am–3am.

▽ Pink's Hot Dogs

Roscoe's Chicken and Waffles 1514 N Gower St ☎323/466-7453. An unlikely spot for Hollywood's elite, this diner attracts all sorts for its fried chicken, greens, goopy gravy, and thick waffles. Listen to the ringing pagers and cell phones as you wait in line for breakfast with movie-industry big shots. One of four area locations. Daily 9am–midnight, weekends closes at 4am.

Tommy's 5873 Hollywood Blvd ☎323/467-3792. One of the prime LA spots for big, greasy, mouthwatering burgers – and, many would say, the best. Located right off the 101 freeway through Hollywood. 24hr.

West Hollywood

Astro Burger 7475 Santa Monica Blvd ☎323/874-8041. Not just burgers, but sandwiches and even veggie meals are the appeal of this diner – along with the late hours: daily 7am–3am, weekends closes at 4am.

Barney's Beanery 8447 Santa Mo. ☎323/654-2287. Two hundred be . beers and hot dogs, hamburgers, a. bowls of chili served in a hip, grungy e ronment, which used to be a haunt of Jir Morrison, among others. Daily 11am–2am.

Duke's 8909 Sunset Blvd ☎310/652-3100. A favorite of visiting rock musicians (the *Roxy* and *Whisky-a-Go-Go* clubs are nearby), this basic coffee shop also attracts a motley crew of night owls and bleary-eyed locals who've managed to hang on 'til daybreak. Mon–Fri 7.30am–8.30pm, Sat & Sun 8am–3pm.

Griddle Café 7916 Sunset Blvd ☎323/874-0377. The postmodern Hollywoodized version of a diner, where the pancakes, chili, and omelets come with various outlandish toppings, and the real point is to be seen by slumming producers and casting directors. Daily 7.30am–3pm.

Hamburger Haven 8954 Santa Monica Blvd at Robertson Blvd ☎310/659-8796. A classic burger shack serving up rich, greasy fare in its cramped dining room and at outdoor patio tables (with a view of traffic whipping by at full volume). Especially busy on weekend nights. Daily 7.30am–1am.

Mel's Drive In 8585 Sunset Blvd ☎310/854-7200. Calorie-packing milkshakes, fries, and, of course, burgers make this classic 24-hour diner a must if you've got the late-night munchies.

Tail o' the Pup 329 N San Vicente Blvd ☎310/652-4517. Worth a visit for the roadside Pop architecture alone (a squat little wiener trapped in a massive concrete bun), though the hot dogs and hamburgers are also good. Outdoor seating only. Mon–Sat 7am–5pm, Sun 8am–4pm.

Topz 8693 Santa Monica Blvd ☎310/659-8843. One in a local chain of fast-food joints that focuses, somehow, on the healthier side of eating burgers, hot dogs, and french fries, with lo-cal cooking oils and lean meats on the culinary agenda. Mon–Thurs 11am–9pm, Fri–Sun 11am–10pm.

Yukon Mining Co 7328 Santa Monica Blvd ☎323/851-8833. Excellent coffee shop, best known for its tasty omelets, with a diverse clientele – don't be surprised to see a crowd of newly arrived Russians, neighborhood pensioners, and glammed-up drag queens. Open 24hr.

...ico Blvd, West LA ...spot at the coun- ...ed apple pie and ...s from the impos- ...l. An old-time joint ...ld War II. Tues– ...kends closes 1am.

....o's Taco Shop 11614 Santa Monica Blvd, West LA ☎310/442-9924. Tacos rolled up in a flour tortilla and served with beef, pork, or fish, and for just a few bucks. Most combos are also under $5, making this a good spot to gulp and run. One in a chain of four 24hr diners.

Brighton Coffee Shop 9600 Brighton Way, Beverly Hills ☎310/276-7732. This simple coffee joint provides welcome relief from the smugness of the district – it's located right in the middle of the Golden Triangle – by offering solid diner food, with especially good omelets, quesadillas, and sandwiches. Mon–Sat 7am–5pm, Sun 10am–3pm.

In-N-Out Burger 922 Gayley Ave, Westwood ☎1-800/786-1000. The best-looking fast-food place in town, selling wonderfully greasy hamburgers in an award-winning Pop Art building – a red-and-white modern box with zingy yellow boomerang signs and an oversized interior logo looming behind the diners. Daily 10.30am–1am.

Jerry's Famous Deli 8701 Beverly Blvd, Beverly Hills ☎310/289-1811. The most engaging of the many *Jerry's* locations in LA, featuring a sizable deli menu and open 24hr. Occasionally, celebrities stop in to nosh.

John o' Groats 10516 W Pico Blvd, West LA ☎310/204-0692. Excellent cheap breakfasts and lunches (mostly staples like bacon and eggs), but come at an off-hour; the morning crowd can give you a headache. Mon & Tues 7am–3pm, Wed–Fri 7am–3pm & 6–9pm, Sat & Sun 7am–2pm & 6–9pm.

Johnnie's Pastrami 4017 S Sepulveda Blvd, Culver City ☎310/397-6654. A wonderful 1950s diner where fans line up for the massive pastrami sandwiches, which cost around $7 and are prepared before your eyes in all their dripping, steaming glory. Sun & Mon 10am–1am, Tues–Thurs 10am–2am, Fri & Sat 10am–3am.

Nate 'n' Al's 414 N Beverly Drive ☎310/274-0101. The best-known deli in Beverly Hills, popular with movie people and one of the few reasonable places for dining in the vicinity. Get there early (opens 7am) to grab a booth. Daily 7.30am–8.30pm.

The Nosh of Beverly Hills 9689 Little Santa Monica Blvd, Beverly Hills ☎310/271-3730. Filling breakfasts and home-made bagels, pies, and deli fare are the favorites at this unassuming diner, a quiet hangout of movie-industry lawyers and producers. Mon–Fri 7am–5pm, weekends closes at 4pm.

Santa Monica, Venice, and Malibu

Bagel Nosh 1629 Wilshire Blvd, Santa Monica ☎310/451-8771. With an ambience straight out of the 1960s, this is a neighborhood favorite for its sizable breakfasts of omelets and bagel sandwiches, picked up from an old-fashioned short-order counter. Daily 6am–7.30pm.

Café 50's 838 Lincoln Blvd, Venice ☎310/399-1955. A favorite retro-styled diner with Ritchie Valens on the jukebox, and juicy burgers on the tables. One of several Westside locations. Daily 7am–11pm.

Café Montana 1534 Montana Ave, Santa Monica ☎310/829-3990. The eclectic menu is highlighted by solid breakfasts, excellent salads, and tasty grilled fish, in an upmarket section of Santa Monica. Daily 8am–3pm & 5.30–9pm.

Norm's 1601 Lincoln Blvd, Santa Monica ☎310/450-0074. One of the last of the classic diners, this local chain has nine other branches and serves breakfasts and lunches for around $5. Great Googie architecture, too. Daily 6.30am–4pm.

Rae's Diner 2901 Pico Blvd, Santa Monica ☎310/828-7937. Small 1950s diner doling out heavy comfort food, especially popular with the late-night crowd. Its turquoise-blue facade and interior have been seen in many films, notably *True Romance*. Daily 6am–10.30pm.

Reel Inn 18661 PCH, Malibu ☎310/456-8221. Seafood diner by the beach, with unsurprising food, but cheap prices and a fun atmosphere. Also at 1220 W Third St, Santa Monica ☎310/395-5538. Daily 11am–10pm.

The Sidewalk Café 1401 Ocean Front Walk, Venice ☎310/399-5547. Though the food is only adequate, this café is a prime spot for watching the daily parade of beach people as you dine outside. Daily 8am–10pm, until midnight on weekends.

South Central and East LA

B & B Bar-B-Que Connection 5403 S Vermont Ave, a mile and a half south of Exposition Park ☎323/778-6070. Barbecue aficionados may wish to venture into this dicey area to sample slabs of LA's best ribs, smothered in barbecue sauce, and served with baked beans and a sweet-potato tart. Daily 11am–8pm, weekends open until 10pm.

Chips 11908 Hawthorne Blvd, south of Inglewood ☎310/679-2947. A solid array of comfort food from sandwiches to burgers, served in a classic diner with a fabulous neon sign. Daily 7am–5pm.

The Donut Hole 15300 Amar Rd, La Puente ☎626/968-2912. Pop architecture fans will definitely want to make the twenty-mile drive east from Downtown LA to see this eye-popping favorite which, like *Randy's Donuts* (see below), is shaped like a giant donut – except this one you can actually drive through, picking up a hot sack of fried, sugared dough from deep inside a tunnel of comfort food. Daily 8am–5.30pm.

Pann's 6710 La Tijera Blvd, Inglewood ☎323/776-3770. One of the all-time great Googie diners, where you can't go wrong with the classic burgers or biscuits and gravy – and you can always jog off the calories amid the oil wells of Baldwin Hills, just to the north. Daily 7am–10.30pm.

Randy's Donuts 805 W Manchester Ave, Inglewood ☎310/645-4707. This Pop Art fixture is hard to miss, thanks to the colossal donut sitting on the roof. Excellent for its piping-hot treats, which you can pick up at the drive-through on your way to or from LAX. One of four South Central locations, though the only one with a giant donut on top. 24hr.

▽ Randy's Donuts

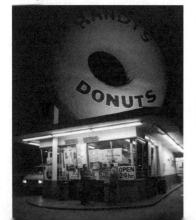

The South Bay and LA Harbor

Blueberry Hill 2667 E 28th St, near Long Beach in Signal Hill ☎562/981-8300. Hefty helpings of good, old-fashioned comfort food, where the burgers are chunky, the onion rings are stacked high, and the fries come coated in thick gravy. Mon–Sat 8am–5.30pm.

East Coast Bagels 5753 E PCH, Long Beach ☎562/985-0933. Located in a dreary mini-mall, but with an excellent selection of bagels, ranging from New York staples to hybrids like the jalapeño-cheddar bagel stuffed with cream cheese. One of several branches in a local chain. Daily 7am–5.30pm.

Hof's Hut 6257 E 2nd St, Long Beach ☎562/598-4070. One bite of the *Hut's* juicy Hofburger and you know you've found the real deal. Three other Long Beach locations, and seven in Orange County. Daily 6am–midnight.

Johnny Reb's 4663 N Long Beach Blvd ☎562/423-7327. The waft of barbecued ribs, catfish, and hushpuppies alone may draw you to this prime Southern spot, where the portions are hefty and the price is cheap. Daily 7am–9pm, weekends closes at 10pm.

The Local Yolk 3414 Highland Ave, Manhattan Beach ☎310/546-4407. As the name suggests, everything here is made with eggs, and there are airy muffins and pancakes, too. Breakfast and lunch only. Daily 6.30am–2pm.

Ocean View Café 229 13th St, Manhattan Beach ☎310/545-6770. Enjoyably light breakfasts, and soup and baguettes for under $10, in a pleasant hillside setting on a quiet pedestrian path overlooking the Pacific. Mon–Thurs 10.30am–4pm, Fri & Sat 9am–5pm, Sun 10am–5pm.

Pier Bakery 100-M Fisherman's Wharf, Redondo Beach ☎310/376-9582. A small but satisfying menu, featuring the likes of jalapeño-cheese bread and cinnamon rolls. Probably the best food around in this touristy area. Daily 8am–7pm.

The San Gabriel and San Fernando valleys

Art's Deli 12224 Ventura Blvd, Studio City ☎818/762-1221. Long-time film-industry favorite (mainly for old-timers, not for the nubile), with a good range of hefty, scrumptious sandwiches and soups. Daily 7am–9pm, weekends closes at 10pm.

Bob's Big Boy 4211 W Riverside Drive, Burbank ☎818/843-9334. The classic chain diner, fronted by the plump burger lad, was saved from demolition through the efforts of "Googie" preservationists. Car-hop service on Saturdays (5–10pm) and regular car shows on Fridays (6–10pm). 24hr.

Carney's 12601 Ventura Blvd, Studio City ☎818/761-8300. The place to come if you really want to get your fill of burgers and hot dogs in an old railway car. A neighborhood institution, as is the branch on the Sunset Strip at 8351 Sunset Blvd ☎323/654-8300. Daily 11am–10pm, weekends until midnight.

Conrad's 861 E Walnut St, Pasadena ☎626/577-7603. Diner that's best for its burgers and sandwiches, though the old-time restaurant throws in a little Italian and Mexican cooking into the mix as well. Daily 5am–1am, weekends 24hr.

Coral Café 3321 W Burbank Blvd ☎818/566-9725. A few miles north of Burbank's studios, this 24hr diner draws a mix of movie-crew workers and locals with its filling breakfasts and lunchtime burgers and steaks.

Dr Hogly-Wogly's Tyler Texas Bar-B-Q 8136 Sepulveda Blvd, Van Nuys ☎818/780-6701. Long lines snake out the door here for some of the best chicken, sausages, ribs, and beans in LA, despite the depressing surroundings in the middle of nowhere. Daily 11.30am–10pm.

Fair Oaks Pharmacy and Soda Fountain 1526 Mission St, South Pasadena ☎626/799-1414. A fabulously restored soda fountain, with many old-fashioned drinks, from lime rickeys to egg creams – a historic 1915 highlight along the former Route 66. Daily 11am–8pm, Sun closes 7pm.

The Hat 491 N Lake Ave, Pasadena ☎626/449-1844. Very popular spot selling good burgers, "world-famous pastrami" and French dip sandwiches at this and five other Valley locations. Daily 8am–5.30pm.

Lamplighter 5043 Van Nuys Blvd, San Fernando Valley t818/788-5110. A funky, old-style diner serving tasty, good-sized portions that bring in assorted colorful characters. Daily 6am–11pm.

Law Dogs 14114 Sherman Way, Van Nuys ☎818/908-3234. Another of those only-in-LA establishments, this one serving

up adequate hot dogs from a basic food stand, but with the added attraction of free legal advice (Wed 7pm) dished out by the attorney-proprietor. Mon–Sat 8am–5.30pm.

Pie 'n' Burger 913 E California Blvd, Pasadena ☎626/795-1123. Classic coffee shop, with primo cheeseburgers and excellent fresh fruit pies, served fresh and hot to your gullet. Mon–Sat 6am–10pm, Sun 7am–9pm.

Portos Bakery 315 N Brand Blvd, Glendale ☎818/956-5996. Popular and cheap café serving flaky Cuban pastries, scrumptious sandwiches, cheesecakes soaked in rum, croissants, tarts and tortes, and cappuccino. Mon–Sat 6.30am–6pm, Sun 7am–2pm.

Rose Tree Cottage 395 E California Blvd, Pasadena ☎626/793-3337. Scones, shortbread, and high tea in a country-home setting so thoroughly English that it's the West Coast HQ of the British Tourist Board. Reservations are essential. Daily 10am–6pm.

Wolfe Burgers 46 N Lake St, Pasadena ☎626/792-7292. Longtime Valley favorite with mouthwatering burgers, chili, and tamales, plus good gyros and breakfasts, including splendid *huevos rancheros*. Daily 7am–10pm, weekends opens at 8am.

Orange County

Angelo's 511 S State College Blvd, Anaheim ☎714/533-1401. Straight out of TV's *Happy Days*, a drive-in complete with roller-skating car-hops, neon signs, vintage cars, and good burgers. Daily 11am–midnight, until 2am on weekends.

Duke's 317 PCH, Huntington Beach ☎714/374-6446. Best to stick to staples like steak and salad at this frenetic beachside favorite, known more for its prime location near the pier. Mon–Sat 11.30am–2.30pm & 3.30–10.30pm, Sun 11am–10pm.

Harbor House Café 34157 PCH, Dana Point ☎949/496-9270. Worth seeking out for its excellent breakfasts, and particularly for its overstuffed omelets – a slew of them, with a veritable laundry list of options. Daily 8am–5.30pm.

Heroes 125 W Sante Fe Ave, Fullerton ☎714/738-4356. The place to come if you're starving after hitting the theme parks, with countless beers available and meaty dishes including hamburgers, beef stroganoff, and meatloaf. Daily 11am–11.30pm, weekends closes at 1am.

Knott's Chicken Dinner Restaurant just outside Knott's Berry Farm at 8039 Beach Blvd, Buena Park ☎714/220-5080. Serving cheap and tasty meals for more than 65 years. People have been flocking here for delicious fried-chicken dinners long before Disneyland was around, and still do. Don't miss the delectable boysenberry pies. Daily 7am–8pm.

Mimi's Cafe 18342 Imperial Hwy, Yorba Linda ☎714/996-3650. Huge servings, low prices, and a relaxing atmosphere down the street from the Nixon Library. Part of a sizable

chain in Los Angeles and Orange counties, and popular in both. Daily 7am–11pm.

Ruby's 1 Balboa Pier, Newport Beach ☎949/675-RUBY. The first and finest of the retro-streamline 1940s diners that have popped up all over LA – in a great location at the end of Newport's popular pier. Mostly offers the standard burgers, fries, and soda fare. Daily 7am–10pm, weekends open until 11pm.

Zinc Café 350 Ocean Ave, Laguna Beach ☎949/494-2791. A popular breakfast counter offering simple soup-and-salad meals and other light fare. Good for a day on the sands. Daily 7am–4pm.

Restaurants

The listings below generally follow the chapter divisions of our guide, grouping **restaurants** first by neighborhood, then by cuisine. A number of specialty categories (late-night, expense-account, etc) appear in boxes.

⑫

Downtown

American, Californian, and Cajun

Café Metropol 923 E Third St ☎213/613-1537. One of several restaurants attempting to bring eateries (and people) back to a formerly grim part of town. The area may still be industrial, but this artsy, affordable spot is worth a visit for its hearty sandwiches, salads, pizza, and pasta. Mon–Sat 8am–6pm, Sun 10am–4pm.

Checkers in the Hilton Checkers hotel, 535 S Grand Ave ☎213/624-0519. One of the most elegant Downtown restaurants, serving top-rated California cuisine, with rack of lamb and sea bass among the better offerings. If you're lucky, you and a companion can escape with a bill under $100. Daily 5.30–9pm, also Mon–Fri 6.30am–2.30pm, Sat 7am–2pm, Sun 8am–2pm.

Engine Co. No. 28 644 S Figueroa St ☎213/624-6996. Longtime favorite for all-American fare, featuring expensive grilled steaks and seafood, served with great fries in a renovated 1912 fire station. A solid wine list rounds out this classic eatery. Mon–Fri 11.30am–9pm, Sat & Sun 5–9pm.

L.A. Prime inside the Westin Bonaventure hotel, 404 S Figueroa St ☎213/612-4743. Plump slabs of tender Midwestern beef are the draw at this pricey New York–style steakhouse, while the side orders and Strawberries Romanoff dessert hold their

own. Fine views from the hotel's 35th floor. Daily 5.30–10pm, weekends closes at 11pm.

New Moon 102 W Ninth St ☎213/624-0186. Good mainly for its location near the Garment District and its reasonably priced mix of American cooking – salads, soups, steaks, and the like – and Chinese dishes. Mon–Fri 11am–5pm, Sat 11am–2pm.

Pacific Dining Car 1310 W Sixth St ☎213/483-6000. One of LA's oldest eateries, a would-be English supper club housed inside an old railroad carriage with excellent, though highly expensive, steaks. Breakfast is better value. Open 24 hours.

Patina 141 S Grand Ave ☎213/972-3331. One of LA's signature eateries, a fancy, ultra-swank spot that's now relocated to Disney Hall. Here you can devour pheasant in apple-champagne sauce, pork loin medallions, and other rotating items on the menu if you're prepared to drop a wad of cash. Daily 11.30am–2pm & 5–10pm, weekends closes at 11pm.

Water Grill 544 S Grand Ave ☎213/891-0900. One of the top-notch spots for munching on California cuisine in LA, with the focus on seafood, prepared in all manner of colorful and ever-changing ways. Wear your silkiest power-tie to fit in with the other high-powered diners. Mon–Fri 11.30am–9.30pm, Sat 4.30–10pm, Sun 5–9pm.

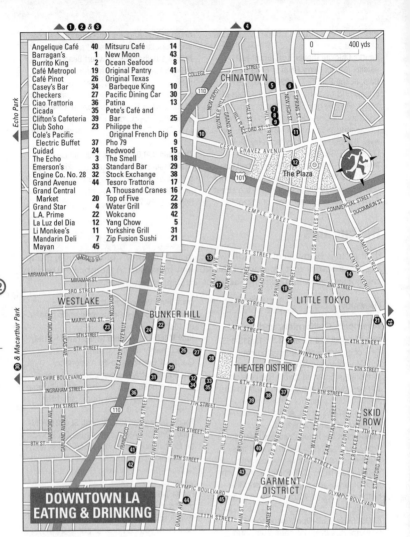

Angelique Café	40	Mitsuru Café	14
Barragan's	1	New Moon	43
Burrito King	2	Ocean Seafood	8
Café Metropol	19	Original Pantry	41
Café Pinot	26	Original Texas	
Casey's Bar	34	Barbeque King	10
Checkers	27	Pacific Dining Car	30
Ciao Trattoria	36	Patina	13
Cicada	35	Pete's Café and	
Clifton's Cafeteria	39	Bar	25
Club Soho	23	Philippe the	
Cole's Pacific		Original French Dip	6
Electric Buffet	37	Pho 79	9
Cuidad	24	Redwood	15
The Echo	3	The Smell	18
Emerson's	33	Standard Bar	29
Engine Co. No. 28	32	Stock Exchange	38
Grand Avenue	44	Tesoro Trattoria	17
Grand Central		A Thousand Cranes	16
Market	20	Top of Five	22
Grand Star	4	Water Grill	28
L.A. Prime	22	Wokcano	42
La Luz del Dia	12	Yang Chow	5
Li Monkee's	11	Yorkshire Grill	31
Mandarin Deli	7	Zip Fusion Sushi	21
Mayan	45		

DOWNTOWN LA EATING & DRINKING

Chinese and Vietnamese

Grand Star 934 Sun Mun Way ☎213/626-2285. While the traditional soups and meat dishes at this moderately priced eatery are flavorful and authentic, the real appeal is the video karaoke on Sun, Tues, and Wed. Also offers takeout. Daily 5pm–midnight, weekends closes 2am.

Li Monkee's 679 N Spring St ☎213/628-6717. Long-standing favorite for affordable fresh fish and rich, hearty seafood soups. Daily 11.30am–8pm.

Mandarin Deli 727 N Broadway #109 ☎213/623-6054. Delectable and cheap noodles, pork and fish dumplings, and other hearty staples in the middle of Broadway's riot of activity. Also at 356 E Second St, Little Tokyo ☎213/617-0231. Daily 11am–7.30pm, closed Thurs.

Ocean Seafood 747 N Broadway ☎213/687-3088. Cavernous but busy restaurant serving inexpensive and excellent food – abalone, crab, shrimp, and duck are among many standout choices. Daily 9am–10pm.

Pho 79 727 N Broadway #120 ☎213/625-7026.
Great spot for noodles and authentic soups:
the original location of a Vietnamese chain
without too many frills, but with low prices
and excellent flavors. Daily 8.30am–7pm.

Yang Chow 819 N Broadway ☎213/625-0811.
Solid, affordable Chinese restaurant, where
you can't go wrong with the Szechuan beef
or any shrimp dish. Mon–Thurs 11.30am–
9.30pm, weekends closes at 10.30pm.

French

Angelique Café 840 S Spring St ☎213/623-8698.
A marvelous and affordable Continental
eatery in the middle of the Garment District,
where you can sit on the quaint patio and
dine on well-crafted pastries for breakfast or
savory sandwiches, rich casseroles, and fine
salads for lunch. Mon–Sat 8am–3pm.

Café Pinot 700 W Fifth St ☎213/239-6500.
Located next to the LA Public Library, this
elegant restaurant offers a touch of French
cooking for its *nouvelle* California cuisine
– one of the best known in LA for that style.
Daily 2.30–9.30pm, weekends opens at
5pm.

Italian and pizza

Ciao Trattoria 815 W Seventh St ☎213/624-
2244. Housed in a striking Romanesque
building, full of lovely historic-revival decor,
and a solid choice for upscale Northern Italian cuisine. Daily 11am–9pm.

Cicada 617 S Olive St ☎213/488-9488. Lodged
in the stunning Art Deco Oviatt Building
(see p.72), this Northern Italian restaurant
offers fine pasta for half the price of its fish
and steak entrees – but still very expensive.
Mon–Sat 11.30am–2.30pm & 5.30–9.30pm,
Sat opens at 5.30pm.

Tesoro Trattoria 300 S Grand Ave ☎213/680-
0000. Convenient for visiting MOCA, this
swank but comfortable Italian spot has
the usual pastas, salads, and sandwiches,
but is particularly tasty for its *calamari* and
salsiccia pizza. Lunch is a better value than
dinner. Mon–Fri 11.30am–8.30pm, Sat
5–9pm.

Japanese

Shibucho 3114 Beverly Blvd ☎213/387-8498.
Seriously tasty, affordable sushi bar west
of Downtown. The squid and eel are quite
fine, along with the famed *toro*, an expensive but delicious tuna delicacy. Mon–Sat
5.30pm–midnight.

**A Thousand Cranes 120 S Los Angeles St,
Little Tokyo** ☎213/253-9255. Also known as
"Senbazuru," and located beside the Japa-
nese Garden in the Sky of the *New Otani
Hotel* (see p.247), this is dining at its most
refined, with pleasant views of the water
and greenery, and multiple courses – nota-
bly tempura – served in an elegant setting.
Daily 7–10am & 11.30am–2pm & 6–9pm,
Sun opens 11am.

Wokcano 913 S Figueroa St ☎213/892-8999.
Full-tilt pan-Asian dining, heavy on sushi
and sashimi. The Volcano and Red Dragon
rolls are best for those ready for a spicy
spin, while others may be content with the
pad Thai or Chinese fare like the Shanghai
noodles. Three other citywide locations, all
moderately priced. Daily 11am–midnight,
weekends closes at 2am.

Zip Fusion Sushi 744 E Third St ☎213/680-
3770. Bringing color back to a former dead
zone, this affordable Cal-cuisine-styled sushi
bar has inventive takes on the usual fish
staples, plus an arty vibe and occasional live
music and DJs. Mon–Fri 11.30am–2.30pm
& 5–10pm, Fri closes at 11.30pm, Sat
5–11pm.

Mexican and Latin American

**Burrito King 2109 W Sunset Blvd at Alvarado,
Echo Park** ☎213/484-9859. Excellent, cheap
burritos and tasty tostadas from this small
stand. Also nearby at 2827 Hyperion Ave
☎323/663-9378. Daily 9.30am–3am.

El Taurino 1104 S Hoover St, Westlake
☎213/738-9197. One of Downtown's top
Mexican eateries, doling out stout portions
of stomach-filling food to locals in the know
– everything from fat beef ribs to succulent
roasted lamb and spicy tostadas – all for an
ultra-cheap price under the watchful eyes of
giant steer-heads. Daily 11am–4am, weekends open 24hr.

King Taco 2904 N Broadway ☎323/222-8500.
The most centrally located diner in a chain
of the many around Downtown (this one
north of Chinatown), with many varieties
of inexpensive, savory tacos. Mon–Sat
11am–8pm.

La Luz del Día 107 Paseo de la Plaza
☎213/628-7495. Amid the throngs of trinket
vendors on Olvera Street, this authentic
Mexican eatery is worth seeking out for its
fiery burritos, enchiladas, and stews, served
in sizable portions that won't bleed your
wallet. Mon–Fri 11.30am–9pm.

Spanish

Ciudad 445 S Figueroa St ☎213/486-5171.
Roast chicken and quinoa fritters are
some of the highlights at this colorful, if
pricey, Mexican-influenced spot, where the
live Latin music competes with the delicious food for your attention. Mon–Thurs
11.30am–9pm, Fri 11.30am–10pm, Sat
5–11pm, Sun 5–9pm.

Mid-Wilshire

African

Nyala 1076 S Fairfax Ave ☎323/936-5918.
One of several reasonably priced Ethiopian
favorites along Fairfax, serving staples like
doro wat (marinated chicken) and *kitfo*
(chopped beef with butter and cheese)
with spongy *injera* bread. Daily 11.30am–
10.30pm.
Rosalind's 1044 S Fairfax Ave ☎323/936-2486.
Spicy goat meat and pepper chicken are
among the highlights at this moderate Ethiopian spot, a neighborhood favorite for many
years. Daily 11am–11pm, weekends closes
at 2am.

American, California cuisine, and Cajun

Ca' Brea 346 S La Brea Ave ☎323/938-2863.
One of LA's top, and priciest, choices for
the mix of California and Italian cuisines
– especially good for *osso bucco* and risotto
– making this a difficult spot to get in to.
Daily 11.30–2.30pm & 5.30–10.30pm.
Flora Kitchen 460 S La Brea Ave ☎323/931-
9900. Connected to a flower shop, this
eclectic, al fresco eatery is best for its
California cuisine–style sandwiches, made
with a host of deliciously fresh ingredients.
Mon–Sat 8am–8pm.

The Gumbo Pot 6333 W Third St, in the Farmers
Market ☎323/933-0358. Ever-popular, delicious and dirt-cheap Cajun cooking. Try the
full-flavored gumbo yaya of chicken, shrimp,
and sausage, along with the fruit-and-
potato salad. Daily 9am–9pm, Sun closes
at 7.30pm.
Luna Park 672 S La Brea Ave ☎323/934-
2110. The latest in California food hybrid-
izing, matching mid-priced Continental fare
with Latin and pan-Asian borrowings, and
ending up with dishes like mushroom risotto
with tomatillo sauce, Hawaiian tuna with
wonton chips, and goat cheese fondue.
Daily 11.30am–2.30pm & 5.30–10.30pm,
Sun closes at 9.30pm.
Sabor Too 3221 Pico Blvd ☎310/829-3781.
Mid-level Cal-cuisine with the occasional
nod to Cajun cooking, best for its molas-
ses-and-ginger salmon, chili-spiced lamb
chops, and tart cactus salad. Be wary in
this dicey part of town. Mon–Fri 11.30am–
2pm & 5.30–10pm, Sat 5.30–10pm, Sun
5–9pm.
Taylor's 3361 W Eighth St ☎213/382-8449.
Good old-fashioned American meat in a
darkly lit, old-school steakhouse ambience,
priced a bit more reasonably than at similar
Westside spots. Daily 11.30am–10pm,
weekends opens at 4pm.

Caribbean

Prado 244 N Larchmont Blvd ☎323/467-3871.
A stylish, affordable spot in the Larchmont
Village shopping zone, better than the
standard Caribbean offerings in LA,
using a wealth of tropical fruits and
seafood – especially the pepper shrimp
– to brighten up the cuisine. Daily
11.30am–3pm & 5.30–10pm, weekends
opens at 4.30pm.

Rough Guides favorites

Fine dining

At the following restaurants – good for business dinners or impressing your loved
one – you'll need to book ahead and, likely, dress up too. Meals can easily run about
$100 per head, including drinks.

Checkers p.273	**L'Orangerie** p.282
Chinois on Main p.290	**Maple Drive** p.285
Citrine p.282	**Matsuhisa** p.287
Diaghilev p.284	**Pacific Dining Car** p.273
Geoffrey's p.291	**Valentino** p.290
Granita p.290	**Water Grill** p.273

Chinese and Vietnamese

Genghis Cohen 740 N Fairfax Ave ☎323/653-0640. Familiar, cheap Chinese dishes with a Yiddish touch: the menu abounds with culinary puns, much like the restaurant's name. The Szechuan beef and kung pao chicken are good, as are the chicken wings served for lunch. Sun–Thurs noon–11pm, weekends noon–midnight.

Pho 2000 215 N Western Ave ☎323/461-5845. The first in a chain of three Koreatown restaurants specializing in hot, spicy bowls of the Vietnamese soup *pho*: cheap and authentic, drawing a loyal crowd of regulars. Also at 667 S Western Ave (☎213/368-0710) and 2897 W Olympic Blvd (☎213/480-8485). Mon–Sat 11am–7.30pm.

Pho Western 425 S Western Ave ☎213/387-9100. You won't have to look hard in Koreatown to find solid Vietnamese eateries, and this one's no different – offering the spicy soup *pho*, along with rice-noodle bowls and other authentic entrees – and cheap, too. Mon–Fri 10am–8pm.

French

Mimosa 8009 Beverly Blvd ☎323/655-8895. Expensive French bistro cooking with an accent on pasta, with savory offerings like seafood risotto, beef bourguignon, and tagliatelle, and macaroni with prosciutto au gratin. Tues–Sat 6–10.30pm.

Greek

Le Petit Greek 127 N Larchmont Blvd ☎323/464-5160. Sizable, mid-priced servings of Greek staples in a quiet Larchmont Village location. Stick to the lamb and fish dishes for maximum pleasure. Daily 11.30am–10.30pm.

Papa Cristos 2771 W Pico Blvd ☎323/737-2970. Consider venturing to this grim neighborhood near the 10 freeway to sample the authentic delights at this Greek joint, including delicious gyros, Greek sausage, caviar, and hefty portions of lamb chops or roast chicken for under $10. Tues–Sat 9am–8pm, Sun 9am–4pm.

Sofi 8030 W Third St ☎323/651-0346. A pleasant, comfortable place near the Farmers Market, serving classic Greek items like stuffed grape leaves and moussaka to a loyal crowd. Daily 11.30am–3pm & 5.30–10.30pm, Sun opens at 5.30pm.

Indian

India's Oven 7231 Beverly Blvd ☎323/936-1000. Friendly, inexpensive Indian restaurant where you'll get large, delicious portions of old favorites like stuffed naan and vindaloo. Daily 10.30am–10pm.

New East India Grill 345 N La Brea Ave ☎323/936-8844. Affordable southern Indian cuisine with a touch of the California treatment: specialties include spinach curry, ginger chicken, curried noodles, and "parmesan naan." Daily 10.30am–10.30pm, weekends closes at 11pm.

Surya 8048 W Third St ☎323/653-5151. A scrumptious array of Indian flavors matched with borrowings from Japanese and California cuisines, where the tandooris and vindaloos come with the familiar curry sauces and less predictable ingredients like duck and sashimi. Mon–Fri 11.30am–2pm & 5.30pm–9.30pm, Sat 5.30–9.30pm, Sun 5.30–8.30pm.

Italian and pizza

Angeli 7274 Melrose Ave ☎323/936-9086. Refreshingly basic pizza styles – baked in a wood-burning oven – make this a worthwhile, affordable stop, as do the tasty frittatas and croquettes. Fixed-price, family-style dinners ($28 per person) on Thursdays are worth considering. Tues–Fri 11.30am–10pm, Sat & Sun 5–11pm.

Campanile 624 S La Brea Ave ☎323/938-1447. Rather pricey but tremendous Northern Italian dishes – the likes of rosemary-infused lamb and butternut squash ravioli. If you can't afford a full dinner, just try the dessert or pick up some of the city's best bread at La Brea Bakery nearby (see p.364). Mon–Fri 11.30am–2.30pm & 5.30–11pm, Sat 9.30am–1.30pm & 5.30–11pm, Sun 9.30am–1.30pm.

Chianti Cucina 7383 Melrose Ave ☎323/653-8333. Old-fashioned, somewhat pricey 1930s restaurant on Melrose's shopping strip south of Hollywood. Try the delicious raviolis or chicken and lamb entrees. Mon–Thurs 5.30–11.30pm, Fri & Sat 5.30pm–midnight, Sun 5–11pm.

Japanese

Ita-Cho 7311 Beverly Blvd ☎323/938-9009. Not the most authentic fare around, but still worth it for the tasty and affordable sashimi, sushi, and eggplant dishes,

served in a chic Westside setting. Tues–
Sat 6–10.30pm.

Mishima 8474 W Third St ☎ 323/782-0181.
Great miso soup, and delicious *udon* and
soba noodles, at very cheap prices are the
hallmarks of this popular Westside eatery.
Daily 11.30am–10pm.

Sushi Roku 8445 W Third St ☎ 323/655-6767.
This upscale, slightly stuffy eatery is worth
visiting for its fine Spanish mackerel sushi,
octopus sashimi, and crab rolls. One
of several Westside locations. Mon–Fri
11.30am–2.30pm & 5.30–11.30pm, weekends 5.30–11pm.

Korean

Arirang 954 S Norton Ave, Koreatown
☎ 323/937-7343. Fine eatery where the
scrumptious meat and seafood are barbecued before your eyes, and you'll have to
split each sizable platter with a companion. If you don't like barbecue, there's
always sushi – with most items moderately
priced. Daily 11am–9.30pm, weekends
until 10pm.

Busan 203 N Western Ave ☎ 323/871-0703.
Classy spot just north of Koreatown, with
authentic and delicious spicy entrees,
and fresh fish that goes from the tank to
your stomach in a jiffy. Daily 11.30am–
10pm.

Dong Il Jang 3455 W Eighth St, Koreatown
☎ 213/383-5757. Cozy little mid-priced
restaurant where the meat is cooked at your
table and the food is consistently good,
especially the grilled chicken and BBQ beef.
Tempura dishes and a sushi bar are an
added draw. Daily 11am–10pm.

Soot Bull Jeep 3136 W Eighth St, Koreatown
☎ 213/387-3865. A genuine Korean BBQ
joint, where you'll appreciate just how delicious slow-cooked, heavily spiced slabs
of chicken, pork, and steak really are, for
moderate prices. Fans of this type of cooking will rejoice. Daily 11am–10.30pm.

Mexican and Latin American

Casa Carnitas 4067 Beverly Blvd ☎ 323/667-
9953. Delicious and cheap Mexican food
from the Yucatán, inspired by Cuban and
Caribbean cooking, and including lots of fine
seafood, too. Tues–Sun 11am–10pm.

El Cholo 1121 S Western Ave ☎ 323/734-2773.
One of LA's first big Mexican restaurants
and still one of the best – offering a solid
array of staples like enchiladas and tamales

– despite the frequent presence of drunken
frat-rats from nearby USC. Daily 11am–
10pm, Sun closes 9pm.

El Coyote 7312 Beverly Blvd ☎ 323/939-2255.
Labyrinthine restaurant serving heavy but
succulent Mexican fare, almost more than
you can stand. But cheap and lethal margaritas are the primary draw to the gloomy
setting. Daily 11am–10pm, weekends until
11pm.

Guelaguetza 3014 Olympic Blvd, Koreatown
☎ 213/427-0608. Primo eatery that appeals
for its cheap, authentic Mexican fare from
the Oaxacan region – delicious *moles*,
savory stews and soups, and all manner
of south-of-the-border staples whipped
up with tongue-twisting spices and exotic
ingredients (including a few with insects).
Daily 9.30am–10pm.

Mario's Peruvian Seafood 5786 Melrose Ave
☎ 323/466-4181. Good and authentic Peruvian fare: supremely tender squid, rich and
flavorful mussels, with a hint of soy sauce
in some dishes. Inexpensive too. Daily
11.30am–8pm.

Middle Eastern

Eat A Pita 465 N Fairfax Ave ☎ 323/651-0188.
Open-air stand serving cheap and sizable
falafel, shawarma, and hummus plates, as
well as thirst-quenching vegetable-juice
drinks. Daily 11am–10pm, weekends until
11pm.

Haifa 8717 W Pico Blvd ☎ 310/888-7700.
Located south of Wilshire, this affordable
Mediterranean spot rewards a visit if you
love good falafel, kabobs, and shawarma,
and can drive a car to get there. Daily
11.30am–9.30pm.

Shah-Abbas 400 S San Vicente Blvd ☎ 310/659-
3242. Solid Iranian dining south of the
Beverly Center, where you can get your
fill of rich and savory kabobs, salads, and
other staples for reasonable prices. Daily
11.30am–2.30pm & 4–9.30pm.

Russian and Eastern European

Csardas 5820 Melrose Ave ☎ 323/962-6434.
Located a few blocks from the Paramount
Studios gate, this funky and fairly priced
little Hungarian restaurant serves up
spicy old-world flavors, with its hearty
stews, stuffed cabbage rolls, and
roasted chicken and pork. Daily noon–
9.30pm.

Spanish

Cobras and Matadors 7615 Beverly Blvd
T 323/932-6178. A fine, mid-priced tapas restaurant just down the street from Pan Pacific Park, where you can sample all your favorite Castilian delights, like flavorful bites of spiced pork loin and game hen, in a hushed, intimate setting. Daily 6–11pm, weekends until midnight.

Thai and Southeast Asian

Singapore's Banana Leaf 6333 W Third St, in the Farmers Market T 323/933-4627. A fine hole in the wall where you can sample Malaysian cuisine at its spiciest and most savory, with the curry soups, satay, and tandoori dishes providing a good over-view of Southeast Asian dining. Daily 9.30am–9pm.
Vim 831 S Vermont Ave T 213/386-2338. Authentic Thai and Chinese food at low prices; the seafood soup and pad Thai are especially good. Daily 9am–11pm, until midnight on weekends.

Vegetarian and wholefood

Erewhon 7660 Beverly Blvd T 323/937-0777. A good old-fashioned juice bar and deli in a natural-foods market, where you can gulp down your choice of wheatgrass concoctions and bee-pollen smoothies. Mon–Sat 8am–10pm, Sun 9am–9pm.
Fountain of Health 3606 W Sixth St T 213/387-6621. Vegetarian chili and non-meat burgers are the highlights at this affordable eatery just south of Hollywood. Mon–Fri 8am–2.30pm.
Inaka Natural Foods 131 S La Brea Ave T 323/936-9353. Located in the trendy La Brea district and featuring vegetarian and macrobiotic food with a strong Japanese theme. Live music on weekends. Tues–Fri noon–2.30pm & 6–10pm, Sat 5.30–10pm, Sun 5.30–9pm.

Hollywood

African

Dar Maghreb 7651 Sunset Blvd T 323/876-7651. Set in a faux-African palace, done up in ogee arches and antique decor, this eatery's rich (and slightly pricey) Moroccan dishes, including b'stilla (a pastry stuffed with chicken, chickpeas and spices), almost take a backseat to the belly-dancing. Daily 6–11pm, Sun closes 10.30pm.

Moun of Tunis 7445 Sunset Blvd T 323/874-3333. Lemon chicken, spicy crêpes, and other mouthwatering, mid-priced Tunisian dishes presented in huge, multiple courses, heavy on the spices and rich with exotic flavors – plus regular belly-dancing. Daily 5.30–11pm.

American, Californian, and Cajun

Hollywood Canteen 1006 N Seward St T 323/465-0961. A dark club scene with fish, steak, and clam chowder – just the right ambience to make you feel like a Tinseltown big shot. Not as pricey as similar joints in the area. Mon–Fri 11.30am–3pm & 7pm–2am, Sat 6pm–2am.
Musso and Frank Grill 6667 Hollywood Blvd T 323/467-7788. A 1919 classic, loaded with authentic atmosphere and history in a dark-paneled dining room. The drinks (see p.300) are better than the costly, mostly upscale diner food. Tues–Sat 11am–11pm.

▽ Musso and Frank Grill

Off Vine 6263 Leland Way T 323/962-1900. Dine on eclectic, expensive Cal cuisine – pecan chicken, duck sausage, and Grand Marnier soufflé – in a renovated but still funky Craftsman bungalow. Daily 11.30am–2.30pm & 5.30–11pm, weekends opens at 5.30pm.
Pig 'n Whistle 6714 Hollywood Blvd T 323/463-0000. Historic 1927 eatery refurbished as a posey Cal-cuisine restaurant, with the emphasis on all things porcine, from ribs to pork roast to bacon. Although much of the old spirit and decor are the same, the prices are not: no diner has food this pricey. Sun–Thurs 11.30am–10.30pm, weekends until 11pm.
Pinot Hollywood 1448 Gower St T 323/461-8800. Upmarket American food crossed with nouvelle French, in a spacious environment with 24 types of martini and Polish potato vodka. You may even spot

EATING | Restaurants

WHITLEY
HEIGHTS

Paramount Studios ▼

1650	23	Café des Artistes	29	Hollywood Canteen	41	Pig 'n Whistle	15
All-Star Theatre		Cat 'n Fiddle	34	Hotel Café	26	Pinot Hollywood	37
Café	11	Catalina Bar		King King	10	Power House	8
American		and Grill	20	The Knitting Factory	35	The Room	27
Legion Hall	1	Chan Darae	31	Lava Lounge	28	Roscoe's Chicken	
Arena	44	Cyber Java	16	Little Hong		and Waffles	32
Avalon	5	Dar Maghreb	38	Kong Deli	21	The Ruby	14
Bar Sinister	22	El Floridita	42	Miceli's	17	Sushi Ryo	43
Beauty Bar	25	Frolic Room	12	Moun of Tunis	39	Taipan	30
Blue	19	Goldfinger's	4	Musso and Frank		Tommy's	13
Boardners	18	Hampton's		Grill	9	Uzbekistan	7
Bourgeois Pig	2	Havana on Sunset	33	Off Vine	36	Yamashiro	3
Burgundy Room	24	Highlands	6				

a celebrity or two, lurking in the shadows. Mon–Fri 11.30am–1am, Sat 5.30pm–1am.

vermont 1714 N Vermont Ave ☎ 323/661-6163. Pretentious lower-case letters aside, this is one of the best upper-end Cal-cuisine spots to open in recent years. The entrees may be predictable – roasted chicken, crab cakes, ravioli, etc – but the culinary presentation can be inspired. Tues–Sun 5.30–10.30pm, also Tues–Fri 11.30am–3pm.

Vida 1930 Hillhurst Ave, Los Feliz ☎ 213/660-4446. Despite the cringe-inducing puns on the menu – Thai Cobb Salad and the like – this is ground zero for LA's culinary hipster set, with a dark, Polynesian-style bar and succulent, mid-level Cal-cuisine like *calamari* (served in a paper bag) and organic, hormone-free meat and chicken dishes. Daily 5.30pm–midnight.

Caribbean

El Floridita 1253 N Vine St ☎ 323/871-8612. Lively Cuban restaurant where the dance floor swings on the weekends and there's regular live music throughout the week. The menu features solid standards like plantains, croquetas, and yucca, all affordably priced. Restaurant 11am–10pm, live music 8pm–1am.

Havana on Sunset 5825 Sunset Blvd #105 ☎ 323/464-1800. Like the name says, everything is Cuban at this festive, mid-priced eatery, from the lively music to the rich, authentic meals of soups, seafood, and garlic-heavy entrees. Daily 11.30am–10pm, weekends until midnight.

Chinese and Vietnamese

Hong Kong Deli 1645 N Cahuenga Blvd ☎ 323/957-1998. Appealing for its traditional

Szechuan and Mandarin entrees, but also worth trying for specials like succulent lemon scallops and walnut shrimp. Located just south of Hollywood Boulevard. Also at 8474 Third St, Mid-Wilshire (☏323/658-8288). Both 11.30am–10pm.

Pho Café 2841 Sunset Blvd ☏213/413-0888. Traditional Vietnamese food transformed by Silver Lake trendiness into a hipster hangout, with the usual *pho* soup and egg rolls, plus a decent selection of rice-noodle dishes. It's cheap, but cash only. Daily 11am–midnight.

Taipan 7075 Sunset Blvd ☏323/464-2989. A good, affordable neighborhood eatery offering appetizing shrimp and chicken entrees, plus a few surprises like black-bean catfish. Daily 11am–10pm.

French

Café des Artistes 1534 N McCadden Place ☏323/469-7300. With a French chef at the helm and French customers at the tables, this cozy, pricey spot is as authentically Gallic a place as you'll find in LA, highlighted by such treats as plum-garnished pork roast, *coq au vin*, and an array of good seafood dishes. Daily 5.30pm-midnight, also Mon–Fri 11.30am–3pm, closes at 2am Thurs–Sat.

Indian

Electric Lotus 4656 Franklin Ave, Los Feliz ☏323/953-0040. While somewhat cramped and located in a minimall, an excellent choice for traditional staples – pakoras, vindaloo, curries, etc – at affordable prices. Daily 11.30am–midnight, weekends until 2am.

Tantra 3705 Sunset Blvd ☏323/663-8268. Popular and reasonably priced Silver Lake eatery where you can dig into favorites like lamb curry and vindaloo, chicken tikka, and much more. There's a mild hipster vibe, so try to grab a seat before it fills up. Tues–Sun 11.30am–2.30pm & 6–11pm.

Italian and pizza

Louise's Trattoria 4500 Los Feliz Blvd ☏323/667-0777. Everybody in LA knows this chain: some love it for its good mid-priced pizzas, while others hate it for its over-cooked, uninspired pasta. You decide. Daily 11.30am–11pm.

Miceli's 1646 N Las Palmas St ☏323/466-3438. Hefty, old-style pizzas that come laden with

gooey cheese and plenty of tomato sauce. It's hardly *nouvelle cuisine*, but you'll be too busy scarfing it down to notice. Mon–Thurs 11.30am–midnight, Fri 11.30am–1am, Sat 5pm–1am, Sun 5–11pm.

Palermo 1858 N Vermont Ave ☏323/663-1178. As old as Hollywood itself, and with as many devoted fans, who flock here for the rich pizzas, cheesy decor, and gallons of affordable red wine. If you like huge platefuls of spaghetti in chunky red sauce, this is the place. Wed–Mon 11am–midnight.

Japanese

Sushi Ryo 6779 Santa Monica Blvd ☏323/462-7200. One of the best sushi restaurants in town, specializing in fresh fish and delicacies such as eel, squid, and monkfish, and much cheaper than comparable eateries on the Westside. Mon–Sat 6–11pm, also Tues–Fri 11.30am–2pm.

Yamashiro 1999 N Sycamore Ave ☏323/466-5125. Although the food can be an over-priced letdown, this place is still a must-see for its outstanding gardens, koi ponds, palatial design, and outstanding view of LA from the Hollywood Hills – making it a perfectly romantic attraction. Daily 5.30–10pm, weekends until 11pm.

Mexican and Latin American

Mexico City 2121 N Hillhurst Ave ☏323/661-7227. Spinach enchiladas and other Californian versions of Mexican standards, including a mean *pollo verde* chicken dish, with prices that are easy to stomach. Daily 5–11pm, also Wed–Sun noon–3pm.

Yuca's Hut 2056 N Hillhurst Ave ☏323/662-1214. A small, hidden jewel serving good al fresco burritos and other cheap and authentic staples, opposite the more popular *Mexico City* (above). Daily 11am–6pm.

Zumaya's 5722 Melrose Ave ☏323/464-0624. Worth a stop if you're in this Paramount-dominated neighborhood, with tasty staples such as burritos and *rellenos*, and a crowd of movie-industry laborers chowing down for lunch and dinner. Daily 11.30am–10pm, weekends opens at 4pm.

Middle Eastern

Marouch 4905 Santa Monica Blvd ☏323/662-9325. Located in a nondescript part of town, this excellent Lebanese restaurant provides flavorful and very affordable kebabs and shawarma. Tues–Sun 11.30am–11pm.

Zankou Chicken 5065 Sunset Blvd ☎323/665-7845. Easily the best-value Middle Eastern option in town (in this case, with a bent toward Armenian), with delicious, garlicky chicken cooked on a rotisserie and tucked into a sandwich, plus all the traditional salads – tabouli, hummus, and the like. Daily 10am–midnight.

Russian and Eastern European
Uzbekistan 7077 Sunset Blvd ☎323/464-3663. Savory, though heavy, servings of mostly lamb-based Uzbekistani food, especially heavy on dumplings. Affordable and authentic. Daily 11am–11pm.

Thai and Southeast Asian
Chan Darae 1511 N Cahuenga Blvd ☎323/464-8585. Terrific Thai food, and the locals know it, with a mid-priced range of scrumptious staples such as *tom yum* soup and pad Thai. Daily 11am–11pm, weekends opens at 5pm.
Jitlada 5233 Sunset Blvd ☎323/667-9809. In a dreary minimall, but the spicy chicken, squid, and seafood curries more than make up for the setting. Affordable prices, too. Tues–Sun 11.30am–10pm.
Palms Thai 5273 Hollywood Blvd ☎323/461-7053. A popular only-in-LA locale, swamped nightly not due to the dishes served – though the fairly priced Thai standards are terrific – but for the kitschy entertainment, namely "Thai Elvis," a surprisingly winning impersonator of the King. Daily 11am–midnight, until 1.30am Fri and Sat.
Thai Seafood 5615 Hollywood Blvd ☎323/461-7053. Egg rolls, noodles, and seafood are the tasty, fairly authentic highlights of this small, mid-priced joint in a busy section of Hollywood. Daily 11.30am–11pm.

West Hollywood

American, Californian, and Cajun
Café La Boheme 8400 Santa Monica Blvd ☎323/848-2360. The dark, somewhat spooky decor is matched by the indulgent (and expensive) melange of Cal-cuisine flavors mixed with pan-Asian cooking, for a truly memorable experience. Daily 5.30pm–midnight, weekends until 1am.
Citrine 8360 Melrose Ave ☎323/655-1690. Be prepared to drop a load when you saunter into this delicious, if ultra-trendy, Cal-cuisine eatery, where the menu changes regularly, but may include the likes of sauteed duck,

Kobe beef, and sea bass. The crowd is self-consciously chic and clad in black, so try not to smile too much. Daily 6–10pm, weekends until 11pm.
Jar 8225 Beverly Blvd ☎323/655-6566. An upper-end steakhouse featuring all the usual red-meat fare – prime rib, T-bone, even a pot roast – with an inspired Cal-cuisine flair, throwing in different spices and exotic flavors to create an unusual, yet traditional, result. Daily 5.30–11pm.
Lucques 8474 Melrose Ave ☎323/655-6277. Expensive but tasty eatery that doles out comfort food for the culinary elite – ribs, chicken, and pork dishes that have an all-American flavor but also feature exotic sauces and ingredients. Tues–Sat 11.30am–2.30pm & 6pm–midnight, Sun 5.30–10pm.
Tangerine 8788 Sunset Blvd ☎310/360-0274. Arriving a little late on the retro meat-and-potatoes scene, this glossy steakhouse still appeals for its swank ambience, hearty entrees such as filet mignon and lamb chops, and prime Stripside location. You might want to wear a tie, too. Daily 6pm–10.30pm.

Chinese and Vietnamese
Chin Chin 8618 Sunset Blvd ☎310/652-1818. Flashy but affordable dim sum café, a long-standing favorite and one of several around town. Open until midnight. Daily 11.30am–11pm.
Joss 9255 Sunset Blvd ☎310/276-1886. Sitting at the west end of the Sunset Strip, the Westside's version of Chinese cuisine: pricey meals with rich, complex flavors and a minimum of excessive color and style – which, of course, makes it all very hip. Mon–Fri noon–3pm & 6–10.30pm, Sat 6–11.30pm, Sun 6–10pm.

French
Fenix 8358 Sunset Blvd, in the Argyle Hotel ☎323/848-6677. Elite French cooking on the Sunset Strip, in an exclusive establishment popular with culinary trendsetters. Fenix offers up terrific steaks and seafood prepared with both local and exotic ingredients. Daily 7am–10pm.
L'Orangerie 903 N La Cienega Blvd ☎310/652-9770. The closest Francophiles can get to Escoffier in LA, though the stylish French food has more than a dash of California cuisine as well. If you haven't got the $150

WEST HOLLYWOOD EATING & DRINKING

7969	24	El Compadre	3	L'Orangerie	34	Rainbow Bar and Grill	14
Angeli	43	The Factory	52	Lucques	46	Real Food Daily	56
Astro Burger	22	Fat Fish	55	Marix Tex-Mex Playa	12	Red Rock	37
Barney's Beanery	20	Fenix	6	Mark's	35	Roxy	15
Café La Boheme	29	Frankie and Johnnie's	16	Mel's Drive-In	11	Shelter	1
Cajun Bistro	5	French Quarter	21	Mickey's	38	Spanish Kitchen	36
Carlitos Gardel	41	Griddle Café	4	Miyagi's	2	Swingers	62
Cat Club	19	Hamburger Haven	51	Mother Lode	42	Tail 'o the Pup	57
Champagne French Bakery	40	House of Blues	8	Normandie Room	32	Todai	61
Chianti Cucina	44	Jar	60	Noura Café	49	Topz	30
Chin Chin	10	Jerry's Famous Deli	58	Numbers	33	Ultra Suede	54
Citrine	47	Jones	23	The Palms	31	Urth Caffé	50
Diaghilev	27	Joss	26	Pearl	48	Viper Room	28
Doug Weston's Troubadour	53	Katana	7	Poquito Mas	9	Whisky-a-Go-Go	18
Duke's	17	Key Club	13	Prey	45	Yukon Mining Co.	25
		King's Road Espresso House	59	Rage	39		

it takes to sit down, or a fancy enough suit to wear, then enjoy the view from the bar. Tues–Sun 6–11pm.

Italian and pizza

Frankie & Johnnie's 8947 Sunset Blvd ☎310/275-7770. Amid all the big rock clubs, an old favorite for its sizable pizzas loaded with greasy and healthy ingredients alike.

Check out the ink-scrawled messages on the walls, which include praise from famous regulars, from Don Knotts to Fred Durst. Mon–Fri 11am–2am, Sat noon–2am, Sun noon–midnight.

Japanese

Katana 8439 Sunset Blvd ☎323/650-8585. A good example of a prototypical Westside sushi house – stunning ambience with high production values, fine and tasty sashimi, rolls, and sushi, and a killer price tag. Worth going east to Hollywood for similar fare at a cheaper price, but the swank atmosphere here is hard to beat. Daily 5.30pm–1am, weekends until 2am.

Miyagi's 8225 Sunset Blvd ☎323/650-3524. A hip, affordable sushi complex with a mid-priced menu of traditional and hybrid raw-fish offerings, served on three floors to piped-in dance music. Also a major pick-up joint for the area. Restaurant 5.30–11.30pm, bar until 2am.

Todai 8612 Beverly Blvd #157 ☎310/659-1375. Tourist-oriented chain diner where the sushi and other Asian cuisine are cheaper than at similar spots in the vicinity. Mon–Sat 11.30am–2.30pm & 5.30–9.30pm, Sun 11.30am–2.30pm & 5–9pm.

Mexican and Latin American

Carlitos Gardel 7963 Melrose Ave ☎323/655-0891. Rich, affordable, and delectable Argentine cuisine – ie, heavy on the beef and spices – with sausages and garlic adding to the potent kick. Mon–Fri 11.30am–2.30pm & 6–11pm, Sat 6–11pm, Sun 5–10pm.

El Compadre 7408 W Sunset Blvd ☎323/874-7924. With potent margaritas, live mariachi bands, and cheap Mexican standards, this is a music-loving gourmand's delight. One of several locations, most in more distant parts of the metropolis. Daily 11.30am–2am.

Poquito Mas 8555 Sunset Blvd ☎310/652-7008. Grab a chicken enchilada or burrito, the top choices at this popular low-priced chain, one of seven in the LA region. Daily 11am–10pm.

Spanish Kitchen 826 N La Cienega Blvd ☎310/659-4794. Swank but fun Mexican eatery that doles out a rib-stuffing selection of tamales, quesadillas, tortilla soup, and other staples – sometimes authentic, sometimes tweaking the fare with European and Cal-cuisine items such as sea bass and risotto. Daily 6–11pm, weekends until 1:30am.

Middle Eastern

Noura Café 8479 Melrose Ave ☎323/651-4581. Moderately priced Middle Eastern specialties. For beginners, the "taster's delight"– hummus, baba ganoush, tabouli, falafel, fried eggplant zucchini and stuffed

grape leaves – is a good, filling bet. Daily 11am–11pm, weekends until midnight.

Russian and Eastern European

Diaghilev in the Wyndham Bel Age hotel, 1020 N San Vicente Blvd ☎310/854-1111. Exquisite establishment with classic Russian fare – caviar, Chicken Kiev, borscht, and such – that's quite delicious, but comes at rather ungodly prices, at least $70 a head. Tues–Sat 6–9.30pm.

Thai and Southeast Asian

Blue Bamboo 359 N La Cienega Blvd ☎310/854-0622. Successful Westside take on the Thai restaurant, with the mid-priced curries, satays, and soups presented with dash, and more unexpected treats such as Thai ribs and Chinese and Malaysian dishes adding to the flavor palate. Mon–Thurs 10am–10pm, Fri & Sat 10am–11pm, Sun 5–10pm.

Michelia 8738 Third St ☎310/276-8288. Located between Beverly Hills and West Hollywood, *Michelia* is something of a *nouveau* Southeast Asian eatery, with Cal-cuisine versions of spicy salads and fish dishes. Prices are mid-to-high, but the menu does include numerous veggie offerings. Daily 11am–10.30pm, Sun opens at 5pm.

Vegetarian and wholefood

Mason Jar Café 8928 Santa Monica Blvd ☎310/659-9111. Sizable sandwiches and refreshing smoothies are the highlights of this central WeHo eatery, where you can chow down for lunch and dinner without dropping a wad. Daily 8am–10pm, weekends until 11pm.

Real Food Daily 414 N La Cienega Blvd ☎310/289-9910. Avocado rolls, beet bisque, and salads draw a good crowd at this fine, mid-level vegan restaurant, which also operates branches at 514 Santa Monica Blvd, Santa Monica (☎310/451-7544), and 242 S Beverly Drive, Beverly Hills (☎310/858-0880). Daily 11.30am–11pm.

Beverly Hills and West LA

African

Koutoubia 2116 Westwood Blvd, West LA ☎310/475-0729. Good, authentic Moroccan lamb, couscous, and seafood, served in comfortable surroundings with a touch of the North African style. Can be expensive, though. Daily 11.30am–10pm.

American, Californian, and Cajun

Arnie Morton's 435 N La Cienega Blvd, Beverly Hills ☎310/246-1501. A 1950s-style homage to the old days of American eats, where hefty steaks and scrumptious sides of creamed spinach and baked potatoes pull in grizzled veterans of Tinseltown. Part of the upper-end *Morton's* chain. Daily 11.30am–2.30pm & 5.30–11pm, weekends opens at 5.30pm.

Cheesecake Factory 364 N Beverly Drive, Beverly Hills ☎310/278-7270. For many visitors, this provides comfort in the busy world of LA dining: the flagship branch of what's now a national chain of cheesecake houses, which serves up agreeable all-American fare. Come at an off-hour if you want a table. Mon–Thurs 11am–11pm, Fri & Sat 11am–12.30am, Sun 10pm–11pm.

Daily Grill 11677 San Vicente Blvd, Brentwood ☎310/442-0044. Beef, chicken, and fish are the main staples of this popular Westside chain, one of the few affordable restaurants around this upscale zone. Mon–Thurs 11.30am–10pm, Fri & Sat 11.30am–11pm, Sun 10am–10pm.

The Farm of Beverly Hills 439 N Beverly Drive ☎310/273-5578. The name and decor are, of course, ironic, since there's hardly anything relaxed or bucolic about this Beverly Hills Cal-cuisine power diner, where the rotating menu may feature items such as steak, braised duck, and ham, at predictably steep prices. Also in the Grove shopping mall, Third St at Fairfax Ave (☎323/525-0663). Daily 9am–11pm.

Kate Mantilini 9101 Wilshire Blvd, Beverly Hills ☎310/278-3699. Tasty, upscale versions of classic American diner food, served up in a stylish interior designed by edgy architectural firm Morphosis. Mon–Thurs 7.30am–1am, Fri 7.30am–2am, Sat 11am–2am, Sun 10am–midnight.

Maple Drive 345 N Maple Drive, Beverly Hills ☎310/274-9800. Fine upmarket fare drawn from a large culinary palette that includes foie gras, meatloaf, and pork chops. If you're lucky, you might spot local celebs sneaking in for an oyster or two. Mon–Fri 11.30am–2.30pm & 6–10pm, Sat 6–10pm.

A Votre Santé	31	Chaya Brasserie	4	Kate Mantilini	25
Arnie Morton's	15	The Cheesecake		Locanda Veneta	9
Backstage		Factory	20	Lulu's Alibi	6
Café	19	The Farm of Beverly		Maple Drive	5
Baja Fresh	13	Hills	14	Matsuhisa	30
Bar Noir	27	Hard Rock Café	3	McCormick and	
Barefoot	8	Il Pastaio	16	Schmick's	21
Brighton Coffee		Jacopo's	12	Mishima	10
Shop	22	Jerry's Famous		Mr. Chow	23
Century Club	28	Deli	1	Nate 'n Al's	17

Newsroom	
Café	26
The Nosh of	
Beverly Hills	18
Shah-Abbas	2
Spago	24
St. Nick's	11
Sushi Roku	7
Talesai	32
Trader Vic's	29

Spago 176 N Cañon Drive, Beverly Hills
⊤310/385-0880. Now that the original
Sunset Strip branch of LA's most famous
restaurant has closed, you'll have to go
to this stuffy Beverly Hills location to get a
taste of Wolfgang Puck's latest (and priciest) Cal-cuisine concoctions, among them
designer pizzas. Daily 11.30am–2.30pm &
6–10.30pm, Sun opens at 6pm.

Caribbean

Bamboo 10835 Venice Blvd, Culver City
⊤310/287-0668. In a section of West LA
full of enticing ethnic restaurants, *Bamboo*
stands out for its chicken dishes and spicy
Caribbean flavors, as well as its reasonable
prices. Daily 11am–10.30pm.
Versailles 10319 Venice Blvd, Culver City
⊤310/558-3168. Bustling authentic Cuban
restaurant with hearty dishes, including excellent and affordable fried plantains, paella, and black beans and rice.
Also nearby at 1415 S La Cienega Blvd
⊤310/289-0392. Daily 11am–10pm.
Zabumba 10717 Venice Blvd, Culver City
⊤310/841-6525. In a colorful building amid
drab surroundings, this venue is a Brazilian favorite for its bossa nova music, Latin
American–inflected pizzas, tasty seafood,
cheap prices, and convivial atmosphere.
Tues–Sun 5.30pm–2am.

Chinese and Vietnamese

Chung King 11538 W Pico Blvd, West LA
⊤310/477-4917. The best neighborhood
Chinese restaurant in LA, serving spicy,
mid-priced Szechuan food: don't miss out
on the *bum-bum* chicken and other house
specialties. Daily 11am–10pm, weekends
until 11pm.
Eurochow 1099 Westwood Blvd, Westwood
⊤310/209-0066. Located in the historic
Dome building (see p.131), this stylish
restaurant offers a melange of Chinese and
European flavors, with a heavy dash of California cuisine: dumplings, pastas, shrimp
rolls, seafood, and even designer pizzas.
Daily 6–11pm.
Mr Chow 344 N Camden Drive, Beverly Hills
⊤310/278-9911. An ultra-pricey hangout
where delicious Chinese food comes in a
wide variety of flavors and spices, extravagantly blended with a panoply of world
cuisines. Good for star-spotting, too. Daily
noon–2pm & 6–11.30pm, weekends opens
at 6pm.

Pho Bac Huynh 11819 Wilshire Blvd, West LA
⊤310/477-9379. The authentic Vietnamese
soup *pho* is the focus of this excellent,
affordable Westside eatery, served as an
entree with spices and exotic flavorings.
Daily 11.30am–10pm.

Greek

Delphi 1383 Westwood Blvd ⊤310/478-2900.
The place to come in West LA for authentic
Greek cooking, from flavorful *dolmas* and
tabouli to the hearty pitas and *souvlaki* – an
unpretentious joint that offers plenty of food
for a reasonable price. Mon–Sat 11.30am–
2.30pm & 5–9.30pm, Sat opens 5pm.

Indian

Bombay Café 12021 Pico Blvd, West LA
⊤310/473-3388. One of LA's finest Indian
restaurants, with terrific traditional and
nouveau offerings, a helpful, friendly staff,
and fair prices. Mon–Fri 11.30am–3pm &
5–11pm, Sat 5–11pm, Sun 5–10pm.
Clay Pit 145 S Barrington Ave, West LA
⊤310/476-4700. Some of LA's best Indian
food, featuring delights like lamb-stuffed
keema naan and a fine tandoori chicken
– for mid-to-high prices. Daily 11.30am–
2.30pm & 5–10pm, Sat opens 5pm.
Nizam 10871 W Pico Blvd, West LA ⊤310/470-
1441. Small Indian haunt, where hefty
portions of curried lamb and tandoori
chicken go for fairly cheap prices. Daily
11.30am–2.30pm & 5–9.30pm, weekends
opens at 5pm.

Italian and pizza

Barefoot 8722 W Third St, Beverly Hills
⊤310/276-6223. Good pasta, pizza and
seafood between Beverly Hills and the
Beverly Center. Affordable prices, considering the upscale location. Daily 11am–11pm,
weekends until midnight.
Il Pastaio 400 N Canon Drive ⊤310/205-5444.
Ever-popular Beverly Hills fave, which,
unlike similar restaurants with a big culinary
buzz, actually serves fine, affordable food
– tasty Northern Italian offerings such as
risotto (prepared in a range of ways), traditional pastas, and veal, pork, and seafood
entrees. Mon–Sat 11.30am–11pm, Sun
5.30–10pm.
Jacopo's 490 N Beverly Drive, Beverly Hills
⊤310/858-6446. Dumpy little brickhouse
that surprisingly has some of LA's best
pizza, served piping hot and fairly cheap.

If you're less interested in eating fine cuisine and would rather catch glimpses of your favorite film and TV stars, there are a number of places where you can watch **celebrities** go through their paces of alternately hiding from, and then mugging for, the public. While practically any upper-end eatery is a likely spot to find the stars – especially in Beverly Hills, Santa Monica, and Malibu – some places have that special cachet. Note that the few restaurants listed below without page references are recommended for their star-spotting potential, not their overpriced food, and are not reviewed in the Guide.

Chinois on Main p.290
Citrine p.282
Drago p.290
Eurochow p.286
The Farm of Beverly Hills p.285
Frankie & Johnnie's p.283
Geoffrey's p.291
Granita p.290
The Ivy 113 N Robertson Blvd, Beverly Hills ☎310/274-8303
Jerry's Famous Deli p.270
Koi 730 N La Cienega Blvd, West Hollywood ☎310/659-9449.
LA Farm p.290
Le Dôme 8720 Sunset Blvd, West Hollywood ☎310/659-6919
Maple Drive p.285

Matsuhisa p.287
Mr Chow p.286
Morton's 8764 Melrose Ave, West Hollywood ☎310/276-5205
Musso and Frank Grill p.279
Nate 'n' Al's p.270
The Palm 9001 Santa Monica Blvd, Beverly Hills ☎310/550-8811
Patina p.273
Patrick's Roadhouse 106 Entrada Drive, Pacific Palisades ☎310/459-4544
Pig 'n Whistle p.279
Roscoe's Chicken and Waffles p.269
Spago p.286
Sunset Room 1430 N Cahuenga Blvd, Hollywood ☎323/463-0004
Valentino p.290

Also at 8166 Sunset Blvd, West Hollywood (☎323/650-8128), and 11676 W Olympic Blvd, in West LA (☎310/477-2111). Daily 11.30am–midnight.

Locanda Veneta 8638 W Third St, Beverly Hills ☎310/274-1893. Whether it's the scrumptious ravioli, risotto, veal or carpaccio, you can't go wrong at one of LA's culinary joys (near the Beverly Center). Expensive, but not unreasonably so. Mon–Fri 11.30am–2.30pm & 5.30–11pm, Sat 5.30–11pm, Sun 5–10pm.

Japanese

Matsuhisa 129 N La Cienega Blvd, Beverly Hills ☎310/659-9639. The biggest name in town for sushi, charging the highest prices. Essential if you're a raw-fish aficionado with a wad of cash; otherwise, you can dine two or three times at other fine, and much cheaper, Japanese restaurants. Daily 5.30–10pm, also Mon–Fri 11.30am–2pm.

Mori Sushi 11500 W Pico Blvd, West LA ☎323/479-3939. A subtly stylish spot that resists trendiness, offering up superb sushi in spare and elegant arrangements.

Mon–Fri 11.30am–2pm & 5.30–9.30pm, Sat 6–9.30pm.

The Sushi House 12013 Pico Blvd, West LA ☎310/479-1507. Reggae and sushi coalesce in a hole-in-the-wall bar with limited seating and reasonable prices. Try the "Superman," an appealing rainbow-colored roll of salmon, yellowtail, whitefish, and avocado. Mon–Fri 11.30am–2.30pm & 5.30–10pm, Sat & Sun 5.30–10pm.

Mexican and Latin American

Baja Fresh 475 N Beverly Drive, Beverly Hills ☎310/858-6690. Cheap and enjoyable Mexican food served to a hungry crowd of window-shoppers and movie-industry wannabes – thus the emphasis on "healthy" eating. Many other area locations. Daily 11am–10pm.

Casa Antigua 12217 Wilshire Blvd, West LA ☎310/820-2540. Upscale *nuevo*-Mexican dining served in an atmosphere that borders on kitsch – still, the *mole* chicken, spicy seafood soups and crêpes, and rich pork and chicken dishes make this a spot to visit. Daily 11.30am–10:30pm, Sun opens at noon.

La Salsa 1154 Westwood Blvd ℡310/208-7083. The place to come for fresh, delicious soft tacos and burritos, on the lower end of the price scale. One of many Westside branches. Daily 11am–8pm.

Monte Alban 11927 Santa Monica Blvd, West LA ℡310/444-7736. Forget the tacky minimall setting and focus on the fine, affordable selection of *mole* sauces and Mexican staples that make any trip here worthwhile. Daily 9am–midnight.

Middle Eastern

Falafel King 1059 Broxton Ave, Westwood ℡310/208-4444. Falafel is the house special here, and you can get a lot of it for only a few dollars. Daily 11.30am–11pm.

Magic Carpet 8566 W Pico Blvd, West LA ℡310/652-8507. Unexpected treats like fried pancakes and more traditional falafel – both in generous portions for fair prices – bring loyal crowds to this excellent Yemeni restaurant. Mon–Thurs 11am–10pm, Fri 11am–2.30pm, Sun 9am–10pm.

Shamshiry 1916 Westwood Blvd, West LA ℡310/474-1410. Top Iranian restaurant in the area, offering delicious kebabs, pilafs, and exotic sauces for moderate cost. Mon–Thurs 11.30am–10pm, Fri 11.30am–11pm, Sat noon–11pm, Sun noon–10pm.

Seafood

J.R. Seafood 11901 Santa Monica Blvd ℡310/268-2468. West LA seafood with a Chinese flair; without dropping a wad, you can chow down on platefuls of spicy shrimp, lobster, mussels, and fish, with the added boost of lip-smacking soups. Daily 11am–3pm & 5–10pm.

McCormick and Schmick's 206 N Rodeo Drive, Beverly Hills ℡310/859-0434. Swank seafood joint for business types known for great weekend dinner specials; part of an esteemed national chain. Daily 11.30am–11pm.

Pacifico's 9341 Culver Blvd, Culver City ℡310/883-3197. Good spot for Latin-flavored seafood, with affordable dishes of *ceviche*, and staples such as fish tacos, red snapper, and the like. Daily 11.30am–9pm, weekends until 10pm.

Thai and Southeast Asian

Chaya Brasserie 8741 Alden Drive, Beverly Hills ℡310/859-8833. Pan-Asian bistro with moderate-to-expensive prices and a chic clientele that lurches in to munch on fancy presentations of noodle, curry, and fish dishes. Worth a splurge if you like your Asian fare with LA trendiness. Daily 6–10.30pm, weekends until 11pm.

Talesai 9198 Olympic Blvd, Beverly Hills ℡310/271-9345. Excellent and affordable curried seafood and Cal-cuisine–style noodle dishes served to in-the-know gourmets inside a drab strip mall. Daily 5.30–10.30pm, also Mon–Fri 11.30am–2.30pm.

Thai Dishes 9901 Washington Blvd, Culver City ℡310/559-0987. Basic but good Thai fare, with the usual noodle dishes and soups presented in a no-frills manner. Westside chain that makes for an excellent stop if you don't have the time to hunt down more authentic eateries. Daily 11am–10pm.

Vegetarian and wholefood

À Votre Santé 242 S Beverly Drive, Beverly Hills ℡310/860-9441. Scrambled tofu and fried vegetables are on tap – along with veggie and turkey burgers – at this mid-priced Westside chain. Mon–Fri 8am–9.30pm, Sat & Sun 9am–9pm.

Newsroom Café 120 N Robertson Blvd, Beverly Hills ℡310/652-4444. A prime spot to see B-list celebrities with A-list attitudes eating (reasonably priced) veggie burgers and drinking wheatgrass "shooters." Also offers magazine racks (thus the name) and Internet terminals. Mon–Thurs 8am–9.30pm, Fri 8am–10pm, Sat 9am–10pm, Sun 9am–9.30pm.

Rough Guide favorites

Round-the-clock dining

Bob's Big Boy p.272
Canter's Deli p.268
Coral Café p.272
Fred 62 p.268
Jerry's Famous Deli p.270

Original Pantry p.267
Pacific Dining Car p.273
Randy's Donuts p.271
Tommy's p.269
Yukon Mining Co p.269

Santa Monica, Venice, and Malibu

American, Californian, and Cajun

17th Street Café 1610 Montana Ave, Santa Monica ☎310/453-2771. Seafood, pasta, sandwiches, and burgers at moderate prices in a casual, unpretentious atmosphere in a chic part of town. Daily 8am–9.30pm.

Aunt Kizzy's Back Porch 4325 Glencoe Ave, Marina del Rey ☎310/578-1005. Serving up

the likes of hushpuppies, chicken, and collard greens, this is one of the few places to get decent soul food in this part of LA – though the prices are cheaper and the quality better in South Central. Daily 11am–9pm, weekends until 11pm.

Crocodile Café 101 Santa Monica Blvd, Santa Monica ☎310/394-4783. Pizzas, sandwiches, and burgers are the dining allure at this inexpensive *nouveau* fast-food spot, part of

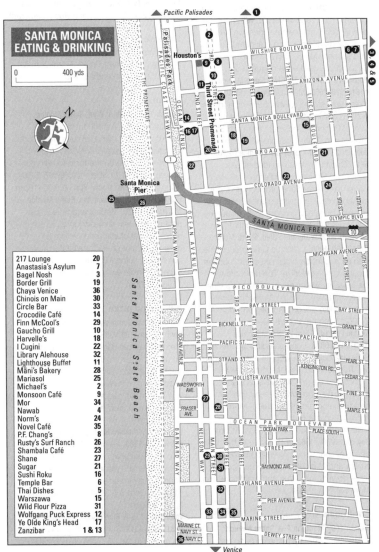

217 Lounge	20
Anastasia's Asylum	7
Bagel Nosh	3
Border Grill	19
Chaya Venice	36
Chinois on Main	30
Circle Bar	33
Crocodile Café	14
Finn McCool's	29
Gaucho Grill	10
Harvelle's	18
I Cugini	22
Library Alehouse	32
Lighthouse Buffet	11
Màni's Bakery	28
Mariasol	25
Michael's	2
Monsoon Café	9
Mor	34
Nawab	4
Norm's	24
Novel Café	35
P.F. Chang's	8
Rusty's Surf Ranch	26
Shambala Café	23
Shane	27
Sugar	21
Sushi Roku	16
Temple Bar	6
Thai Dishes	5
Warszawa	15
Wild Flour Pizza	31
Wolfgang Puck Express	12
Ye Olde King's Head	17
Zanzibar	1 & 13

SANTA MONICA EATING & DRINKING

0   400 yds

12 **EATING** | Restaurants

a local chain. Sun–Thurs 11am–10pm, Fri & Sat 11am–midnight.

Granita 23725 W Malibu Rd, Malibu ☎310/456-0488. If you can't get enough of Wolfgang Puck (see *Spago*, p.286), check out his Malibu entry – a heady mix of Cal-cuisine and Italian flavors. Delicious and pricey, and good for spotting a few names here and there. Tues–Sun 6–10.30pm, weekends also 11am–2.30pm.

Hal's 1349 Abbot Kinney Blvd, Venice ☎310/396-3105. Popular restaurant along a hip shopping zone in Venice, with a range of well-done, somewhat expensive American standards, including marinated steaks and salmon dishes. Daily 11.30am–3pm & 6–10.30pm, weekends opens 10am.

Houston's 202 Wilshire Blvd, Santa Monica ☎310/576-7558. Mid- to upper-end chain dining with savory salads, burgers, and international cuisine, but especially good for its prime location a block from the Third Street Promenade. Daily 11.30am–10.30pm.

Joe's 1023 Abbot Kinney Blvd, Venice ☎310/399-5811. One of the less heralded of LA's better upscale eateries, offering appealing California-cuisine dishes (mixed with a dash of French cookery) using staples like crispy chicken, pork, and salmon. Daily 11.30am–2.30pm & 6–10pm, weekends until 11pm.

LA Farm 3000 W Olympic Blvd, Santa Monica ☎310/449-4000. Delicious California cuisine, with an accent on crab cakes and lobsters, though very expensive. The main draw is the celebrity-watching: here the stars dine in peace, away from the flashier confines of places like *Spago*. Mon–Fri 11.30am–2.30pm, also Fri & Sat 5.30–10pm.

Michael's 1147 Third St, Santa Monica ☎310/451-0843. Long-standing favorite for California cuisine, served here amid modern art. This venerable establishment always attracts the crowds with its succulent steak, pasta, and fowl. Reservations are essential, and prices are steep. Mon–Sat noon–2.30pm & 6–10.30pm.

Uncle Darrow's 2560 S Lincoln Blvd, Marina del Rey ☎310/306-4862. A bit south of the main beach action, but worth a stop if you like savory and affordable catfish, gumbos, and other downhome Cajun and creole cooking. Mon–Sat 11am–8pm.

Caribbean

Babalu 1002 Montana Ave, Santa Monica ☎310/395-2500. The pumpkin pancakes at this pan-ethnic, mid-priced Caribbean restaurant are delightful, as are the fried Havana eggs – fried eggs in a salsa-and-bean tortilla – and the smiling image of Carmen Miranda above the front door. Mon–Thurs 11am–9.30pm, Fri 11am–10.30pm, Sat 8am–10.30pm, Sun 8am–9.30pm.

Chinese and Vietnamese

Chinois on Main 2709 Main St, Santa Monica ☎310/392-9025. A Wolfgang Puck restaurant mixing *nouvelle* French and Chinese cuisine for a ravenous crowd of yuppie diners and self-appointed food critics willing to pay the top-flight cost. Wed–Fri 11.30am–2pm & 6–10.30pm, weekends 6–10pm.

Indian

Nawab 1621 Wilshire Blvd, Santa Monica ☎310/829-1106. Though there are few surprises on the menu, pleasing renditions of Indian standards like chicken vindaloo and *tikka masala* do the trick, for affordable prices. Mon–Fri 11.30am–2.30pm & 5.30–10pm, Sat & Sun noon–3pm & 5.30–10pm.

Pradeep's 1405 Montana Ave, Santa Monica ☎310/395-6675. Modest and reasonable spot on a swank shopping strip, which serves up vegetarian-oriented Indian cuisine (without ghee) to rail-thin diners; not exactly authentic, but tastier than you'd expect in these well-heeled parts. Daily 11am–9.30pm.

Italian and pizza

Abbot's Pizza Company 1407 Abbot Kinney Blvd, Venice ☎310/396-7334. Named after the old-time founder of the district, this home of the scrumptious (and inexpensive) bagel-crust pizza allows your choice of seeds, tangy citrus sauce, or shiitake and wild mushroom sauce. Also at 1811 Pico Blvd, Santa Monica ☎310/314-2777. Daily 11am–11pm.

Drago 2628 Wilshire Blvd, Santa Monica ☎310/828-1585. Among LA's better super-chic Italian eateries, serving various Cal-cuisine–oriented dishes and pastas in an appropriately pretentious setting. Daily 11.30am–3pm & 5.30–11pm, weekends opens 5.30pm.

Valentino 3115 W Pico Blvd, Santa Monica ☎310/829-4313. Some call this the best Italian cuisine in the US, served up in classy

⑫

EATING | Restaurants

surroundings with great flair. The listed specials, especially veal, duck, and venison, are sure to please, though your pocketbook won't be quite so lucky. Reservations and formal wear are mandatory. Mon–Thurs 5.30–10.30pm, Fri & Sat 5.30–11pm.

Wildflour Pizza 2807 Main St, Santa Monica ☎310/392-3300. Serving up a great and cheap thin-crust pizza, this cozy little spot often draws large crowds. Sun–Thurs 11.30am–10.30pm, Fri & Sat 11am–11.30pm.

Wolfgang Puck Express 1315 Third Street Promenade, Santa Monica ☎310/576-4770. On the second floor of a food mall, watch Promenade tourists below while munching on great mid-priced pizzas and salads. One of a national chain. Daily 11am–9.30pm, weekends until 11pm.

Japanese

Chaya Venice 110 Navy St, Venice ☎310/396-1179. Elegant mix of Japanese and Mediterranean foods in an arty sushi bar, with a suitably snazzy clientele. Mon–Fri 11.30am–midnight, Sat 5pm–midnight, Sun 5–10pm.

Lighthouse Buffet 201 Arizona Ave, Santa Monica ☎310/451-2076. All-you-can-eat sushi buffet; indulge to your heart's content for around $10 at lunchtime or $20 in the evening. Not always great, but good and filling if you're hungry, and in a prime location. Daily 11.30am–2.30pm & 5.30–9pm.

Sushi Roku 1401 Ocean Ave, Santa Monica ☎310/458-4771. While the ambience here can be a bit on the stuffy side, this upscale eatery is worth visiting for its fine Spanish mackerel sushi, monkfish, octopus sashimi, and crab rolls. Mon–Fri 11.30am–2.30pm & 5.30–11.30pm, Sat noon–11.30pm, Sun 5.30–10.30pm.

Korean

Monsoon Café 1212 Third St, Santa Monica ☎310/576-9996. Stylish space offering a mid-priced mix of Pacific Rim cuisines: expect anything from sushi to Szechuan to Malaysian to Korean barbecued beef. Mon–Thurs 11.30am–10.30pm, Fri & Sat 11.30am–11.30pm, Sun 2–9.30pm.

Mexican and Latin American

Border Grill 1445 Fourth St, Santa Monica ☎310/451-1655. Good place to sup on delicious shrimp, pork, plaintains, and other *nuevo* Latin American–flavored fixings,

with excellent desserts, too. Prices are on the expensive side, but the ambience is always swinging. Sun & Tues–Thurs 11.30am–10pm, Mon 5.30–10pm, Fri & Sat 11.30am–11pm.

Gaucho Grill 1251 Third St, Santa Monica ☎310/394-4966. One in a fine local chain of mid-level Argentine beef-houses, where the steaks come rich and garlicky, and the spices can bowl you over. Located along the Third Street Promenade. Daily 11.30am–10pm, weekends until 11pm.

Mariasol 401 Santa Monica Pier, Santa Monica ☎310/917-5050. Cervezas with a view, hidden away at the end of the pier, with good, straightforward Mexican staples. On weekend afternoons, the small rooftop deck affords a sweeping panorama from Malibu to Venice. Mon–Thurs 10am–10pm, Fri & Sat 9am–11pm, Sun 9am–10pm.

Marix Tex-Mex Playa 118 Entrada Drive, Pacific Palisades ☎310/459-8596. Flavorful fajitas and big margaritas are the best picks at this rowdy beachfront cantina. A popular and affordable choice. Also at 1108 N Flores St, West Hollywood ☎323/656-8800. Daily 11.30am–midnight, weekends until 2am.

Russian and Eastern European

Warszawa 1414 Lincoln Blvd, Santa Monica ☎310/393-8831. Pleasant, if a bit pricey, establishment with fine Polish cuisine. Don't miss the hearty potato pancakes, pierogi, and borscht. Tues–Sat 6–11pm, Sun 5–10pm.

Seafood

Geoffrey's 27400 PCH, Malibu ☎310/457-1519. One of Malibu's most upscale spots for steak, seafood, and sunset-watching. The Cal-cuisine–inspired menu is almost secondary to watching the Tinseltown luminaries drop in. Mon–Fri noon–9.30pm, Sat 11.30am–10.30pm, Sun 11am–10pm.

Gladstone's 4 Fish 17300 PCH, Pacific Palisades ☎310/454-3474. An inevitable tourist stop at the junction of Sunset Boulevard, known best for its prime beachfront location – not for the heavily fried and breaded seafood or steep prices. Daily 8am–10pm, weekends until 11pm.

I Cugini 1501 Ocean Ave, Santa Monica ☎310/451-4595. One of the city's more prominent seafood restaurants is also, luckily, one of its best – offering delectable Italian-influenced dishes such as seafood risotto and seared salmon (with the usual complement of pastas), and not quite as pricey as some of its counterparts in Malibu. Mon–Thurs 11.30am–10pm, Fri & Sat 11.30am–11pm, Sun 10.30am–10pm.

Killer Shrimp 523 Washington St, Marina del Rey ☎310/578-2293. When all you want is shrimp, and lots of it, this popular, somewhat dreary-looking spot is the place to come. For a pretty cheap price, you can happily stuff your maw with fistfuls of crustaceans. Daily 11.30am–11pm.

Neptune's Net 42505 PCH, Malibu ☎310/457-3095. It's worth a trip to the far reaches of LA County's northwestern border to gorge on clams, shrimp, oysters, and lobster at basic picnic tables for low-end prices. Daily 10.30am–8pm, weekends closes at 7pm.

Thai and Southeast Asian

Flower of Siam 2553 Lincoln Blvd, Venice ☎310/827-0050. Some swear by the authentic Thai food served here, guaranteed to set your tastebuds on fire and your eyes watering. The chicken satay and noodles are highlights of this moderately priced spot. Daily 11.30am–9.30pm.

Thai Dishes 1910 Wilshire Blvd, Santa Monica ☎310/828-5634. Very basic Thai meals geared toward diners unfamiliar with the spicier, more extreme versions of the cuisine. Part of a citywide chain. Daily 11am–10.30pm, weekends opens at noon.

Vegetarian and wholefood

Figtree's Café 429 Ocean Front Walk, Venice ☎310/392-4937. Tasty veggie food and grilled fresh fish on a sunny patio just off the Boardwalk. Health-conscious yuppies come in droves for inexpensive breakfasts. Daily 9am–9pm.

Inn of the Seventh Ray 128 Old Topanga Rd, Topanga Canyon ☎310/455-1311. The ultimate New Age restaurant in a supremely New Age area, serving expensive vegetarian and other wholefood meals in a relatively secluded environment. Excellent desserts, too. Daily 11.30am–3pm & 5.30–10pm, Sun opens at 9.30am.

Mäni's Bakery 2507 Main St, Santa Monica ☎310/396-7700. An array of veggie treats – from sugarless brownies to meatless sandwiches – may draw you to this coffeehouse and bakery for breakfast or lunch. You might even see a weight-obsessed celebrity darting in. Also a good bakery and coffeehouse at

519 S Fairfax Ave, Mid-Wilshire (☎323/938-8800). Daily 7.30am–8pm.

Shambala Café 607 Colorado Ave, Santa Monica ☎310/395-2160. Apart from organic chicken, the mid-priced menu is good and meat-free, with shrimp, pasta, tofu, eggplant, and some very interesting seaweed dishes. Daily 11.30am–8pm.

South Central and East LA

American, Californian, and Cajun

Harold and Belle's 2920 Jefferson Blvd, South Central ☎323/735-9023. One of the most authentic and affordable of the Cajun-cuisine restaurants in town, with a rich gumbo, excellent po' boy sandwiches, and heaping portions of crayfish, catfish, and shrimp, alongside standards like corn on the cob. Daily 11.30am–9.30pm, weekends until 10.30pm.

Phillips 4307 Leimert Blvd ☎323/292-7613. One of several excellent, and cheap, Southern barbeque joints that appeal for their authentic smoky sauces and spicy marinades (over beef or pork ribs), and full set of sides like potato salads and fine desserts. Well worth a trip to Leimert Park for a taste. Mon–Thurs 11am–10pm, Fri & Sat 11am–midnight.

Woody's 3446 W Slauson Ave ☎323/294-9443. What some claim as LA's best barbeque is, unfortunately, located in one of its grimmer corners – but still, if you come during the day, you can get your fill of some rich beef ribs and gut-stuffing pork sausages. Pretty inexpensive, too. Daily 11am–11pm.

Mexican and Latin American

Ciro's 705 N Evergreen Ave, East LA ☎323/267-8637. A split-level cave of a dining room, serving enormous platters of shrimp and *mole* specials for decent prices, along with *flautas* – the main draw. They also offer takeout. Tues–Sun 7am–9pm.

El Tepayac 812 N Evergreen Ave, East LA ☎323/267-8668. Huge, luscious burritos and hot salsa bring true lovers of (inexpensive) Mexican food out to this rather removed section of the San Gabriel Valley. Mon & Wed–Thurs 6am–9.30pm, Fri & Sat 6am–11pm, Sun 6am–10pm.

Luminarias 3500 Ramona Blvd, Monterey Park ☎323/268-4177. Dance to salsa and merengue between bites of seafood-heavy, mid-priced Mexican food, surprisingly good for an area best known for its Chinese cuisine. The Spanish name refers to honorary candles in brown paper bags. Mon–Thurs 11am–3pm & 4–10pm, Fri & Sat 11am–3pm & 4–11pm, Sun 9.30am–3pm & 4–10pm.

Paco's Tacos 6212 W Manchester Ave, West chester ☎310/645-8692. Potent margaritas and good, filling burritos are the highlights at this affordable local chain. Daily 11am–10pm, weekends until 11pm.

The South Bay and LA Harbor

American, Californian, and Cajun

Avenue 1141 Manhattan Ave, Manhattan Beach ☎310/802-1973. A cozy, upscale "new American" hangout where the rotating menu offers delicious, impeccably made variants on familiar diner fare such as meatloaf, mac 'n cheese, and apple pie – though for about ten times what you would pay in an actual diner. Wed–Sun 6–10pm, weekends closes at 11pm.

New Orleans 140 Pier Ave, Hermosa Beach ☎310/372-8970. Not the kind of place where you'd expect to find deep-South Cajun cuisine, but a welcome respite anyway – a lip-smacking, authentic diner serving up jambalaya, gumbo, po' boy sandwiches, and fried oysters, all of them plenty tasty and cheap. Daily 11.30am–2.30pm & 5–9pm, weekends until 10.30pm.

Rock 'n Fish 120 Manhattan Beach Blvd, Manhattan Beach ☎310/379-9900. Whether you're in the mood for halibut, sea bass, blackened shrimp, or just a good old prime rib, this cozy surf 'n turf eatery is a good, affordable spot to indulge. Just make sure to reserve ahead. Daily 11.30am–10pm, weekends until 11pm.

Caribbean

Cha Cha Cha 762 Pacific Ave, Long Beach ☎562/436-3900. Paella, black-pepper shrimp, and jerk chicken are all highly recommended here, one of Long Beach's better and more colorful mid-priced restaurants. Also in Hollywood at 656 N Virgil Ave ☎323/664-7723. Mon–Thurs 11.30am–10pm, Fri & Sat 11.30am–11pm, Sun 10am–10pm.

Greek

Mykonos 5374 E Second St, Long Beach ☎562/434-1856. Authentic dishes and spirited nightly dancing at this unpretentious,

affordable Greek eatery, where the gyros, *souvlaki*, and other favorites are served with a deft culinary flair. Sun–Thurs 11.30am–10pm, Fri & Sat 11am–11pm.

Italian and pizza

L'Opera 101 Pine Ave, Long Beach ☎562/491-0066. Very swank Italian dining – mixed with a fair bit of California-cuisine style – in a historic old building near the center of Long Beach's downtown activity. Mon–Thurs 11.30am–10.30pm, Fri & Sat 5pm–midnight, Sun 5–11pm.

Mangiamo 128 Manhattan Beach Blvd, Manhattan Beach ☎310/318-3434. Fairly pricey but worth it for the tasty Northern Italian seafood – and right off the beach, too. Mon–Thurs 11.30am–9.30pm, Fri & Sat 11.30am–10.30pm, Sun 11am–8pm.

Mexican and Latin American

By Brazil 1615 Cabrillo Ave, Torrance ☎310/787-7520. Hearty and affordable Brazilian fare, mostly grilled chicken and beef dishes; worth a visit to inland Torrance for a taste. Tues–Sun 11.30am–9.30pm, weekends until 10pm.

El Pollo Inka 1100 PCH, Hermosa Beach ☎310/372-1433. Good, cheap Peruvian-style chicken, catfish, and hot and spicy soups to make your mouth water. For a closer visit to central LA, try the one at 11701 Wilshire Blvd, Westwood ☎310/571-3334. Daily 11am–11pm.

Pancho's 3615 Highland Ave, Manhattan Beach ☎310/545-6670. Big portions of old favorites like tacos and burritos, and fairly cheap for the area. One of the few serviceable Mexican eateries down this way. Daily 11am–10pm, weekends until 11pm.

Taco Beach 211 Pine Ave, Long Beach ☎562/983-1337. As you might guess, fish tacos are the main draw here, though the rest of the eatery's low-priced south-of-the-border fare is also quite palatable. Sun–Thurs 11am–10pm, Fri & Sat 11am–midnight.

Russian and Eastern European

Czech Point 1981 Artesia Blvd, Redondo Beach ☎310/374-7791. One of the few good reasons to venture down here, a relaxed, inexpensive, and unfussy diner presenting the cuisine of the Czech Republic, with tasty and filling goulash, schnitzel, dumplings, and spicy, roasted meats. Wed–Sat 5–10pm, Sun 5–9pm.

Seafood

Bluewater Grill 665 N Harbor Drive, Redondo Beach ☎310/318-3474. The South Bay outpost of an Orange County favorite (see p.297), featuring a slew of mid-priced fresh fish – salmon and catfish to crabs and oysters – though a few more tourists than the other branch. Mon–Thurs 11.30am–10pm, Fri & Sat 11.30am–11pm, Sun 10am–10pm.

Kincaid's Bay House 500 Fishermans Wharf, Redondo Beach ☎310/318-6080. The epitome of South Bay seafood swank, a dramatically placed fishhouse serving some of the best crab, lobster, and prawns in the area, and drawing equal numbers of locals and tourists. Mon–Fri 11.30am–10pm, Sat 11.30am–11pm, Sun 11am–9pm.

King's Fish House 100 W Broadway, Long Beach ☎562/432-7463. Esteemed seafood restaurant with a full selection of predictable, but well-prepared, entrees – including salmon, tuna, oysters, and sea bass. One in a local chain of six upmarket restaurants. Sun & Mon 11.30am–9pm, Tues–Thurs 11.30am–10pm, Fri & Sat 11.30am–11pm.

Spanish

Alegria Cocina Latina 115 Pine Ave, Long Beach ☎562/436-3388. Prime tapas and gazpacho served with plenty of sangría on the patio, and to the beat of live flamenco every night. In a good location in downtown Long Beach. Mon–Thurs 11.30am–11pm, Fri 11.30am–2am, Sat noon–2am, Sun noon–11pm.

Vegetarian and wholefood

Good Stuff 1300 Highland Ave, Manhattan Beach ☎310/545-4775. Healthy eating, vegetarian or otherwise, is the goal at this popular spot, with a range of cheap and filling sandwiches and fruit plates. One of five South Bay locations. Daily 7am–9pm.

Papa Jon's 5006 E Second St, Long Beach ☎562/439-1059. Meatless Mexican entrees and garden burgers are the highlights at this quiet, mid-priced Belmont Shores eatery, which has totally vegan meals as well as an on-site market. Sun–Thurs 9am–9pm, Fri & Sat 9am–9.30pm.

The Spot 110 Second St, Hermosa Beach ☎310/376-2355. A staggering selection of inexpensive vegetarian dishes, based on Mexican and other international cuisines and free of refined sugar or any animal products. Daily 11.30am–7pm.

The San Gabriel and San Fernando valleys

African

Langano 14838 Burbank Blvd, Sherman Oaks ☎818/786-2670. One of the few places in the Valley to fill up on Ethiopian food, but a solid, inexpensive choice nonetheless for its delicious *injera* bread and *wat* soups and stews, with some vegetarian options as well. Tues–Thurs 11am–10pm, Fri–Sun 11am–11pm.

Marrakesh 13003 Ventura Blvd, Studio City ☎818/788-6354. Moroccan restaurant in the Valley, where good, filling couscous and lamb dishes are served amid lush furnishings and belly dancing, for mid- to expensive cost. Daily 5–10pm, weekends until 11pm.

American, Californian, and Cajun

Beadle's 825 E Green St, Pasadena ☎626/796-3618. An old-fashioned cafeteria doling out stews, burgers, salads, ribs, and macaroni; the culinary effect isn't subtle – some of the dishes glow with artificial colors and even Jello is on the menu – but for hefty platters of comfort food at a cheap price, the place has few equals. Mon–Fri 7am–7.30pm, Sat & Sun 11am–7.30pm.

Monty's Steakhouse 592 S Fair Oaks Ave, Pasadena ☎626/792-7776. Long-standing favorite, dating from 1947, where thick and pricey servings of juicy meat and hearty potatoes appeal to a loyal, graying crowd. Daily 9am–10pm, weekends until 11pm.

Saddle Peak Lodge 419 Cold Canyon Rd, Calabasas ☎818/222-3888. On the San Fernando Valley side of the Santa Monica Mountains, this is elite LA's nod to rustic hunting lodges, where exquisite California cuisine is presented below mounted game-heads, and you can elegantly devour anything from venison to boar to antelope. Sun & Wed–Fri 6–9pm, Sat 5–9:30pm, Sun also 11am–2pm.

Caribbean

Kingston Café 333 S Fair Oaks Ave, Pasadena ☎626/405-8080. All the Caribbean favorites make an appearance here, including oxtail, plantains, jerk chicken, beans and rice, and other traditional specialties of Jamaica and other islands. Mon–Sat 11am–2pm & 4.30–9pm.

Xiomara 69 N Raymond Ave, Pasadena
☎626/796-2520. An upscale Old Pasadena restaurant serving delicious Cuban and Latin American meals, mainly beef, pork, and fish entrees, plus a solid range of stews and colorful sauces. Daily 11.30am–11pm, Sat & Sun opens at 5pm.

Chinese and Vietnamese

City Wok 10949 Ventura Blvd, Studio City
☎818/506-4050. A fine little establishment selling Chinese food without frills or attitude; the dishes are flavorful, the prices are cheap. Mon–Sat 11am–10pm, Sun 5–9.30pm.

Lee's Garden 1428 S Atlantic Blvd, Alhambra
☎626/284-0320. As with many of the Chinese restaurants in the vicinity, a fine neighborhood eatery that has a good range of staples – pork dumplings, *kung pao* dishes, etc – at affordable prices. Daily 11.30am–10pm.

Ocean Star 145 N Atlantic Blvd, Monterey Park
☎626/308-2128. One of the prime names in a city bursting with excellent Chinese restaurants, in this case specializing in dim sum, with the fried shrimp, dumplings, and salty chicken among the highlights. Very popular and affordable, too. Daily 10am–2.30pm & 5–10pm.

French

Café Bizou 14016 Ventura Blvd, San Fernando Valley ☎818/788-3536. Bringing affordable French cuisine to the northern valleys, this delightful, busy restaurant serves succulent pork tenderloin and salmon salads. Also at 91 N Raymond Ave, Pasadena ☎626/792-9923. Daily 11.30am–2pm & 5–10pm, weekends until 11pm.

Julienne 2649 Mission St, San Marino
☎626/441-2299. While the pâté and apricot chicken are good, the chicken salad, sandwiches, and rich desserts are even better at this excellent, well-priced French restaurant. Mon–Fri 7am–3.30pm, Sat 8am–4pm.

Greek

Café Santorini 70 W Union St, Pasadena
☎626/564-4200. A fine mix of mid-range Greek and Italian food – *capellini*, *souvlaki*, risotto, and the like – with a little Armenian sausage thrown in as well. Located in a relaxed plaza and offering some patio dining. Daily 11am–11pm, weekends until midnight.

Great Greek 13362 Ventura Blvd, Sherman Oaks
☎818/905-5250. A busy, mid-range old-world enterprise serving delicious *dolmas*, kebabs, and moussaka to ethnic music beats and fervent dancing. Daily 11.30am–11pm, weekends until midnight.

Indian

Passage to India 14062 Burbank Blvd, Van Nuys ☎818/787-8488. Savory and affordable Indian cooking with a British flair, covering South Asian staples such as spicy vindaloos, tandoori chicken, stuffed naan, and beef and lamb kebabs. Daily 11.30am–2pm & 5–10pm.

Italian and pizza

Market City Caffè 36 W Colorado Blvd #300, Pasadena ☎626/568-2303. Excellent Southern Italian pizza and seafood, along with a superb antipasto bar at this moderately priced spot. Also at 164 E Palm Ave, Burbank ☎818/840-7036. Daily 11.30am–10pm, weekends until midnight.

Panzanella 14928 Ventura Blvd, Sherman Oaks
☎818/784-4400. Some of the best Italian cuisine in LA, with a dash of California creativity, but staying true to the simple, delicious character of traditional pasta, rice, and beef dishes. A bit on the expensive side. Mon–Sat 11.30am–2.30pm & 5.30–10pm, weekends until 11pm.

Japanese

Genmai-Sushi 4454 Van Nuys Blvd, Sherman Oaks ☎818/986-7060. *Genmai* is Japanese for brown rice, which you can sample alongside soft-shell crabs in *ponzu* sauce, regular sushi, and seasonal macrobiotic dishes. Good food for moderate cost. Mon–Sat noon–2.30pm & 5.30–10.30pm, Sun 5–10pm.

Shiro 1505 Mission St, South Pasadena
☎626/799-4774. One of LA's few top-notch restaurants in South Pasadena. The seafood – particularly the grilled catfish and smoked salmon – is best here, prepared in rich, tangy flavors. Tues–Sun 6–9pm, weekends until 10pm.

Sushi Nozawa 11288 Ventura Blvd, Studio City
☎818/508-7017. Excellent, if expensive, sushi dishes served to trendy regulars who don't mind being berated by the imperious chef: if you sit at the bar, he will decide what you'll eat. Period. Mon–Fri noon–2pm & 5.30–10pm.

Tama Sushi 11920 Ventura Blvd, Studio City ☎818/760-4585. Presents a formidable array of sushi, sashimi, rolls and soups, and a price that won't leave you gasping. Daily 11.30am– 2.30pm & 5–10pm, weekends until 11pm.

Mexican and Latin American

Don Cuco's 3911 W Riverside Drive, Burbank ☎818/842-1123. Good food, mainly familiar Mexican staples, with a great Sunday brunch. One of several in a Valley chain. Daily 11.30am–10pm.

El Tepeyac 800 S Palm Ave, Alhambra ☎626/281-3366. Huge burritos and hot salsa bring fans of Mexican food out to this section of the San Gabriel Valley. Several other Eastside locations, most conveniently at 812 N Evergreen Ave, East LA ☎323/268-1960. Sun, Mon & Wed–Thurs 6am–9.30pm, Fri & Sat 6am–11pm.

Izalco 10729 Burbank Blvd, North Hollywood ☎818/760-0396. Salvadoran cuisine presented with style, from plantains and pork ribs to corn cakes and *pupusas* – a pleasant surprise for the area, and not too pricey, either. Daily 10am–10pm.

Señor Fish 618 Mission St, South Pasadena ☎626/403-0145. Drab-looking joint with great fish tacos and charbroiled halibut for under $10. Daily 11.30am–9pm.

Middle Eastern

Burger Continental 535 S Lake Ave, Pasadena ☎626/792-6634. Although it sounds like a fast-food joint, this is actually one of LA's better Middle Eastern restaurants, where you can get mounds of chicken and lamb kebabs for no more than a few bucks. Daily 7am–11pm.

Carousel 304 N Brand Ave, Glendale ☎818/246-7775. A Lebanese charmer in downtown Glendale, chock full of Levantine cultural artifacts and deliciously authentic food, from roasted chicken and quail to several different kinds of kebab – all for affordable cost. Daily 11am–9pm, weekends until 12.30am.

Russian and Eastern European

Hortobagy 11138 Ventura Blvd, Studio City ☎818/980-2273. Roasted pork and sausage, schnitzel and cabbage rolls are but a few of the appealing offerings available at this Hungarian restaurant in the Valley. Plenty of spicy, paprika-laden satisfaction for a fair price. Tues–Sun 11.30am–2pm & 5–9.30pm, weekends until 10pm.

Spanish

La Luna Negra 44 W Green St, Pasadena ☎626/844-4331. An affordable spot for mouthwatering tapas, including classic croquetas, paellas, and spicy seafood dishes – prepared mostly in a traditional fashion. Daily 11am–10pm, weekends until midnight.

Thai and Southeast Asian

Kuala Lumpur 69 W Green St, Pasadena ☎626/577-5175. Curried soups and tangy salads are a few of the highlights at this Malaysian eatery, along with coconut rice and spicy chicken, plus other delectable Southeast Asian dishes for inexpensive cost. Daily 11.30am–2.30pm & 5.30– 9.30pm.

Saladang 363 S Fair Oaks Ave, Pasadena ☎626/793-8123. Don't miss out on the pad Thai, curry, and salmon at this chic and delicious (but reasonable) spot. The more recent *Saladang Song* annex offers spicier noodles and concoctions of a more traditional bent from different regions of Thailand. Daily 10am–10pm.

Sanamluang Café 12980 Sherman Way, North Hollywood ☎818/764-1180. The cheap, plentiful noodles at this nearly all-night Thai eatery are unbeatably good. Daily 11am–4am.

Orange County

American, Californian, and Cajun

Aubergine 508 29th St, Newport Beach ☎949/723-4150. Cal-cuisine versions of quail, pâté, and other French delicacies, served with a noticeable lack of attitude – though still very expensive. Tues–Sat 5.30–10pm, Sun 4.30–9.30pm.

Bistro 201 3333 W PCH, Newport Beach ☎949/631-1551. The salmon and lamb are among the better *nouveau* American cuisine offerings at this pleasant, upmarket Orange County–coast restaurant. Mon–Fri 11.30am–10pm, Sat 5–10pm, Sun 10.30am–2.30pm & 5–10pm.

The Cottage 308 N Coast Hwy, Laguna Beach ☎949/494-3023. Filling American breakfasts and affordable seafood, pasta, and chicken dishes for lunch and dinner. Mon–Fri 8am–9.30pm, Sat 4.30–10.30pm, Sun 7am–9.30pm.

Five Crowns 3801 E Coast Hwy, Corona del Mar ☎949/760-0331. Aside from the rather diverse menu, most locals come for the thick, juicy steaks and quality ribs – not to mention the mildly kitschy Olde English decor and fancy club style. Mon–Thurs 5–10pm, Fri & Sat 5–11pm, Sun 10am–2.30pm & 5–10pm.

Jack Shrimp 2400 W Coast Hwy, Newport Beach ☎949/650-5577. One in a chain of Cajun dinner establishments in various spots along the Orange County coast, offering an appealing assortment of spicy seafood and Louisiana staples for fair prices. Mon–Sat 5–10pm, Sun 3.30–9pm.

Chinese and Vietnamese

Anh Hong 10195 Westminster Ave, Garden Grove ☎714/537-5230. Terrific Vietnamese restaurant known for its slew of traditional, affordable favorites (including broiled pork with vermicelli noodles) and "seven courses of beef," a multi-course meal of red meat in all its glory. Mon–Thurs 4.30–9.30pm, Fri & Sat 11am–10pm, Sun 11am–9.30pm.

Favori 3502 W First St, Santa Ana ☎714/531-6838. Worth the long drive out for what may be LA's best Vietnamese food, including delicious garlic shrimp, curried chicken with lemon grass and savory noodles, all for decent prices. Sun–Thurs 11.30am–9.30pm, Fri & Sat 11.30am–10pm.

Italian

Antonello 3800 Plaza Drive, Costa Mesa ☎714/751-7153. Although Orange County is hardly prime turf for quality Italian fare, this is one of the exceptions – a fine, upper-crust eatery where the ravioli and fettuccini (among other pastas) are always well-cooked, and the beef and salmon entrees rarely disappoint. Mon–Fri 11.30am–2pm & 5–9.30pm, Sat 5–10pm.

Villa Nova 3131 W Coast Hwy, Nowport Bcach ☎949/642-7880. Old-time Italian seafood presented in a classy setting for locals and out-of-towners alike; the pastas and seafood risotto draw the crowds, so reserve ahead. Nightly live music at 8pm. Daily 5pm–midnight, Sun opens at 4pm.

Korean

In Chon Won 13321 Brookhurst St, Garden Grove ☎714/539-8989. One of the best spots outside of LA's Koreatown for rich, tasty barbecue – from pork and chicken to wild boar – prepared before your very eyes, for reasonable cost. Sun–Thurs 11am–9.30pm, Fri & Sat 11am–10pm.

Mexican and Latin American

Don Jose's 15101 Goldenwest St, Huntington Beach ☎714/894-5519. A Mexican eatery doling out the usual staples – *rellenos*, burritos, and the like – with fresh ingredients and cheap prices. One of several in this Orange County chain. Daily 11am–9.30pm.

Las Brisas 361 Cliff Drive, Laguna Beach ☎949/497-5434. Enjoy sweeping ocean views while dining on the patio of this upscale eatery; the spicy Mexican seafood entrees are almost as good as the scenery. Mon–Sat 8am–3.30pm & 5–10pm, Sun 9am–3pm & 4.30–10pm.

Taco Mesa 647 W 19th St, Costa Mesa ☎949/642-0629. Cheap, tasty burritos, quesadillas, and tacos, as well as more unexpected choices like lobster bisque and *calamari*, at this always reliable Orange County chain. Daily 7am–11pm.

Middle Eastern

Zena's 294 N Tustin St, city of Orange ☎714/279-9511. A friendly Lebanese spot offering a good selection of gyros, kebabs, stuffed grape leaves, shawarma, and other traditional, inexpensive favorites. Daily 11am–10pm, Sun closes at 8pm.

Seafood

Bluewater Grill 630 Lido Park Drive, Newport Beach ☎949/675-3474. Delectable, surprisingly affordable seafood standards – *ahi* tuna, salmon, and the like – accompanied by appealing ocean views from the patio. Mon–Thurs 11.30am–10pm, Fri & Sat 11.30am–11pm, Sun 10am–10pm.

Claes Seafood in the Hotel Laguna, 425 S Coast Hwy, Laguna Beach ☎949/376-9283. Sample pricey and delicious *ahi* tuna and halibut, plus Cal-cuisine spins on the same fare, with fine views of the Pacific from indoors. Tues–Sat 7am–2pm & 5.30–9.30pm, Sun 9am–2pm & 5.30–9.30pm.

Crab Cooker 2200 Newport Blvd, Newport Beach ☎949/673-0100. The hefty plates of crab legs and steaming bowls of chowder at this affordable diner make the long lines here a bit more bearable. Daily 11am–10pm.

Oysters 2515 E Coast Hwy, Corona del Mar ☎949/675-7411. Another Orange County stab at California cuisine–style seafood; not quite as expensive as *Claes Seafood* (see above), further up the road, but in taste and looks the food here is almost as good. Mon–Thurs 5–10pm, Fri & Sat 5–11pm, Sun 4–9pm.

Drinking

N **ightlife** in LA can be among the best and most frenetic in the country, with options for serious drinking and partying available throughout the metropolis. Weekend nights are the busiest at the various bars and clubs, but during the week things are cheaper and often just as enjoyable. For uninterrupted drinking, there are **bars** and lounges on seemingly every other corner, especially in Hollywood, with many of the lower-end dives seeing a mixed crowd of grizzled old-timers and slumming hipsters. However, **smoking is banned** in most establishments under California law (though some proprietors and customers still manage to puff away furtively).

In any case, bar styles tend to go in and out of fashion quickly, changing from month to month, often according to music and showbiz trends. What follows are descriptions of some of the more established bars in LA, generally those that have been around for at least a year or two; the trendiest joints sometimes only last a few months, disappearing once they lose their buzz and their exorbitant overhead finally catches up with them.

If you want something of the bar atmosphere without the alcohol, visit one of LA's many **coffeehouses**, which can be relaxed and fun, but sometimes carry a bit of the attitude associated with self-consciously hip domains. Given the West Coast's taste for expensive coffee concoctions, they can also make for a refreshing break from the usual bars, especially if you want some culture with your coffee – alternative music and performing art provide the entertainment at many java joints.

LA's many **clubs** often double as live music venues (for which, see p.309), but we've tried to focus on what the dominant entertainment is from night to night, and especially on weekends. When big-name touring DJs pull up, door charges can be as much as going to a regular rock concert; more often, however, such big names are the exception and the usual scene will be based around a series of local DJs. There will often be an attached bar to the club (allowing for overlap with that category), but unless the lounge itself is the reason people come, we've tried to focus on the beats.

Bars

As you'd expect, LA's **bars** reflect their locality: a clash of artists and financial whiz kids Downtown; serious hedonists and leather-clad rock fans in Hollywood; movie-star wannabes and self-styled producers in West Hollywood and West LA; a batch of jukebox- and dartboard-furnished bars in Santa Monica (evidence of British expats) and the more oddball selection in Venice; and the random assortment of interesting, out-of-the-way spots in the valleys. A few hard-bitten bars are open the legal maximum hours (from 6am until 2am daily), though the busiest hours are between 9pm and midnight. During **happy hour**, usually from 5–7pm, drinks are cheap and there'll be a selection of snacks like taco dips, chips, buffalo wings, and sometimes more substantial appetizers.

Downtown

Barragan's 1538 W Sunset Blvd, Echo Park ☎213/250-4256. Actually a Mexican restaurant with reasonably palatable food, but allegedly producing the most alcoholic margarita in LA. Be alert for the dicey neighborhood, though.

Casey's Bar 613 S Grand Ave ☎213/629-2353. White floors, dark wood-paneled walls, and piano music on Wed and Thurs nights – something of a local institution in entertainment-starved Downtown.

Mr T's Bowl 5621 N Figueroa Ave, Highland Park ☎323/256-7561. Formerly a bowling alley, this quirky bar north of Downtown draws a regular crowd of hipsters and local characters. On weekends, there's eclectic live music, with a strong punk-surfer bent.

Pete's Café and Bar 400 S Main St ☎213/617-1000. Stylish effort to bring a dash of class back to a tough part of town – a retro-flavored Deco bar (with upscale diner food) located in an old bank building, which despite the dicey environs draws a regular crowd of business types and a few artsy loft-occupiers.

Redwood 316 W Second St ☎213/617-2867. Not overly flashy or eventful, but a solid Downtown choice for serious drinking and cheap all-American grub since 1943, attracting a mix of office workers, newspaper hacks, and only a few outsiders.

Standard Hotel Bar 550 S Flower St ☎213/892-8080. LA's poseur pinnacle: a rooftop, alcohol-fueled playpen where the black-leather-pants crowd goes to hang out in red metallic "pods" with waterbeds and sprawl out on an Astroturf lawn, against a backdrop of modern corporate towers. You'll have to navigate the velvet-rope scene and $20 cover charge if staying at the hotel.

Top of Five at the Westin Bonaventure hotel, 404 S Figueroa St ☎213/624-1000. Thirty-five floors up, this constantly rotating cocktail lounge spins faster after a few of the expensive drinks, and offers an unparalleled view of the sun setting over the city.

Mid-Wilshire

Bungalow Club 7174 Melrose Ave ☎323/964-9494. Because it's located in the still-hip

Melrose zone (between Hollywood and Mid-Wilshire), this moody cocktail lounge isn't as posey as those on the Westside. The ambience is dark and evocative, but the real draws are the private bungalows out back – reserve ahead if you want to have any chance of getting one.

El Carmen 8138 W Third St ☎323/852-1552. Groovy faux dive-bar with a south-of-the-border theme, pushed to the extreme, with black-velvet pictures of Mexican wrestlers, steer horns, stuffed snakes, and much tongue-in-cheek grunge, as well as signature margaritas.

H.M.S. Bounty 3357 Wilshire Blvd ☎213/385-7275. An authentic dive experience. Advertising "Food and Grog," a scruffy bar that's a hot spot for hipsters and grizzled old-timers – who come for the dark ambience, cheap drinks, and nautical kitsch, dating from 1937.

Lucy's El Adobe Café 5536 Melrose Ave ☎323/462-9421. Something of a celebrity hot-spot in the 1970s for figures such as then-Governor Jerry Brown, this Mexican restaurant serves only adequate food, but the house specialty is worth a try: lethal and cheap margaritas.

Molly Malone's Irish Pub 575 S Fairfax Ave ☎323/935-1577. One of LA's drinking staples: an authentic, self-consciously Irish bar, with a crowd of regulars who look like they've been there for ages, plus nightly music, shamrock decor, and the requisite pints of thick Guinness. See also "Live music," p.313.

St. Nick's 8450 W Third St ☎323/655-6917. A few blocks from the colossal Beverly Center mall sits this relaxed and unassuming neighborhood bar, with a decent selection of brews and a formidable jukebox.

Snake Pit 7529 Melrose Ave ☎323/852-9390. One of the better bars along the Melrose shopping strip, and not too showy, with a mix of jaded locals and inquisitive tourists.

Tom Bergin's 840 S Fairfax Ave ☎323/936-7151. Old-time drinking joint from 1936, and a great place for Irish coffee. You can spot the regulars from the pictures on the walls.

Hollywood

4100 4100 Sunset Blvd, Silver Lake ☎323/666-4460. Although it continues the annoying LA

(13)

DRINKING | Bars

trend of naming itself after its street address, this darkly colorful bar does boast inventive pan-Asian decor, moody lighting, and a mix of gays, straights, and imbibing tourists.

Akbar 4356 Sunset Blvd ☎ 323/665-6810. A diverse crowd – manual laborers and bohemians, gays and straights, old-timers and newbies – frequents this cozy, unpretentious Silver Lake watering hole. Also presents occasional comedy and fringe theater events.

Beauty Bar 1638 N Cahuenga Blvd ☎ 323/464-7676. A drinking spot devoted to hair, nails, and cosmetics, featuring a welter of 1950s-style salon gadgets and retro-decor, and a cocktail list to match, emphasizing colorful and well-groomed concoctions. One of three in a national mini-chain. See also "Shopping," p.359.

Boardners 1652 N Cherokee Ave ☎ 323/462-9621. A likably unkempt neighborhood bar in the middle of Hollywood's tourist central, attracting salty old-timers and curious youngsters alike, with a history dating back to World War II. Occasional guitarists provide the soundtrack.

Burgundy Room 1621 Cahuenga Blvd ☎ 323/465-7530. A classic place to get down and dirty with the old Hollywood dive-bar vibe, with minimal decor, stiff drinks, a growling crowd of regulars, decent DJs, and a rocking jukebox.

Cat n' Fiddle Pub 6530 Sunset Blvd ☎ 323/468-3800. A boisterous but comfortable pub with darts, British food (served until midnight on weekends), expensive English beers on tap, and live jazz on Sundays (7–11pm) in the leafy courtyard. See also "Live music," p.313.

Cheetah's 4600 Hollywood Blvd ☎ 323/660-6733. One of LA's biggest underground attractions, with strong drinks, topless entertainment, and a crowd of both men and women.

The Dresden Room 1760 N Vermont Ave ☎ 323/665-4298. One of the neighborhood's classic bars, best known perhaps for its nightly entertainment (except Sun), in which the husband-and-wife lounge act of Marty and Elayne takes requests from the crowd of old-timers and goateed hipsters.

Formosa Café 7156 Santa Monica Blvd ☎ 323/850-9050. Started during Prohibition, this tiny bar is said to be alive with the ghosts of Bogie and Marilyn. Indulge in the potent spirits (not the insipid food) and soak in a true Hollywood institution.

Frolic Room 6245 Hollywood Blvd ☎ 323/462-5890. Classic LA bar featured in the film *LA Confidential*, decorated with Hirschfeld celebrity cartoons and steeped in a dark, old-time ambience. Right by the Pantages Theater.

Goldfingers 6423 Yucca St, north of Hollywood Blvd ☎ 323/962-2913. Fascinating 1960s-kitsch decor, with striking black-and-gold lamé touches. Drinks aren't bad, either, and nightly music is a mix of dance and acoustic stylings.

Good Luck Bar 1514 Hillhurst Ave ☎ 323/666-3524. A hip Los Feliz retro-dive, this hangout is popular for its cheesy Chinese decor and tropical drinks straight from the heyday of *Trader Vic's*. Located near the intersection of Sunset and Hollywood blvds.

Highlands 6801 Hollywood Blvd ☎ 323/461-9800. On the fourth floor of the Hollywood & Highland mall, this restaurant, bar, and club mixes passable *nouveau*-American food, a solid range of cocktails, and weekend dance beats. The view is excellent, but the emphasis on posing and preening can get irritating.

Lava Lounge 1533 N La Brea Ave ☎ 323/876-6612. Wallow in the cheesy retro decor and slurp down a glowing cocktail to the sounds of pounding rockabilly and freewheeling surf music. Especially fun is "Kinky Karaoke" on Sunday nights.

Musso and Frank Grill 6667 Hollywood Blvd ☎ 323/467-7788. Simply put, if you haven't had a drink in this landmark 1919 bar, you haven't been to Hollywood. You can also have a pricey bite to eat. For more details, see p.107.

Pinot Hollywood 1448 Gower St ☎ 323/461-8800. Nearly thirty types of martini and Polish potato vodka, served in airy surroundings with an upscale crowd. See also "Eating," p.279.

Power House 1714 N Highland Ave ☎ 323/463-9438. Enjoyable, long-standing hard-rockers' watering hole just off Hollywood Blvd. Few people get here much before midnight.

The Room 1626 N Cahuenga Blvd ☎ 323/462-7196. Small, intense bar with acceptably stiff drinks and a decent music selection, mostly funk and soul tunes. Nightly DJs and an ongoing buzz make the place increasingly crowded, especially on weekends.

Smog Cutter 864 N Virgil Ave ☎ 323/667-9832. Dive bar that attracts a mix of boozers and smirking Gen-Xers. Don't miss the Tuesday night karaoke, which, like the liquor, can be pleasantly mind-numbing.

Tiki Ti 4427 W Sunset Blvd ☏323/669-9381. Tiny grass-skirted cocktail bar straight out of *Hawaii-Five-O*, packed with kitschy pseudo-Polynesian decor, on the edge of Hollywood. Powerful cheap cocktails include mai tais, zombies, and the like.

West Hollywood

Barney's Beanery 8447 Santa Monica Blvd ☏310/654-2287. Well-worn poolroom/bar, stocking over 200 beers, with a solid, rock'n'roll-hedonist history. It also serves all-American food; see p.269.

Jones 7205 Santa Monica Blvd ☏323/850-1726. Groovy, youthful scene with a colorful atmosphere and decent American cuisine, though the main draw is the head-spinning drinks named after rock stars.

The Palms 8572 Santa Monica Blvd ☏310/652-6188. Comfortable mixed, leaning toward lesbian-oriented, scene (see p.328), with pool tables and a patio making for a relaxed vibe; also has dance music most nights of the week.

Parlour Club 7702 Santa Monica Blvd ☏323/650-7968. Located in WeHo's grimmer eastern side, a strange and stylish bar with an eclectic musical selection (from metal and rap to disco and electro) playing nightly and the occasional dose of creepy performance art.

Rainbow Bar & Grill 9015 Sunset Blvd ☏310/278-4232. A down-and-dirty lounge that's been catering to the rock-and-thrash scene on the Sunset Strip for decades – it's a lot more authentic (and potent with its drinks) than the posier lounges to the east.

Red Rock 8782 Sunset Blvd ☏310/854-0710. Energetic watering hole with a wide array of drafts on tap and a similarly broad assortment of customers, everyone from bleary-eyed club kids to preppies.

Shelter 8117 Sunset Blvd ☏323/654-0030. If you've come to the Sunset Strip to pose in your black-silk suit or dress, this is the place to show it off: a pricey and snooty spot with airy, big-ticket art decoration and overpriced cocktails, sitting right in the middle of the Strip.

Beverly Hills and West LA

Bar Noir in the Maison 140 hotel, 140 S Lasky Drive, Beverly Hills ☏310/271-2145. A swank lounge with much effort spent on the self-consciously dark and atmospheric "set design," and less so on the bartender's knowledge of mixology. Still, worth a look to see how the beautiful people imbibe.

Century Club 10131 Constellation Blvd, Century City ☏310/553-6000. Exemplifies the West LA version of a "cool" watering hole, thick with lawyers and agents attempting to shake their suit-clad behinds, but with some decent weekend beats, too (of the electronica and salsa variety), and predictably high cover and cocktail prices.

The Joint 8771 Pico Blvd, West LA ☏310/275-2619. Something of an antidote to the stuffier attitudes found in Beverly Hills, further north, this "joint" is good for both its affordable, old-school cocktails and regular indie bands, who perform in a cramped but relaxed setting.

Liquid Kitty 11780 Pico Blvd, West LA ☏310/473-3707. As its quirky name might suggest, this bar is aimed solidly at the hipster contingent, with a fine selection of cocktails and nightly lounge and dance music to set the mood, with live music on Sunday nights.

Q's Billiards 11835 Wilshire Blvd, Brentwood ☏310/477-7550. Not completely free of the pretension that plagues West LA bars, but close enough – a good spot to knock back a brew in a packed, college atmosphere, play a game of pool, and listen to DJs spin retro-favorites.

Trader Vic's 9876 Wilshire Blvd, Beverly Hills ☏310/276-6345. Long-standing favorite for Tiki style and Polynesian-themed cocktails, this is a great old spot with a broad mix of customers, and a place where you can finally get that Zombie or Blue Hawaiian mixed just as you like it.

Santa Monica and Venice

217 Lounge 217 Broadway, Santa Monica ☏310/394-6336. A little slice of West LA by the bay, complete with upscale dress code, smart decor, well-balanced cocktails, and, of course, trendy regulars.

The Brig 1515 Abbot Kinney Blvd, Venice ☏310/399-7537. One of the more conspicuous lounges along this stretch of interior Venice, not a bad place to stop in to soak up the stylish decor and decent cocktails, though other bars around town have a more authentic vibe.

Circle Bar 2926 Main St, Santa Monica
☎310/392-4898. Old-fashioned dive bar that
in recent years has lurched toward drawing
in fashionable out-of-towners. If you get
plastered on the pricey drinks, Venice is well
within staggering distance.

Encounter 209 World Way, at LAX ☎310/215-
5151. A Space Age–themed bar, inside
architect Eero Saarinen's futuristic Theme
Building, overlooking the LAX parking lot.
Well worth a visit to sample the potent Day-
Glo drinks while watching the jets land.

Finn McCool's 2700 Main St, Santa Monica
☎310/452-1734. Despite the dubious-sound-
ing name, this worthwhile Irish pub has a
savory selection of Emerald Isle brews and
Celtic artwork on the walls, plus hefty platters
of traditional food (cabbage, liver, beef stew,
and the like) that require an accompanying
pint of Guinness for proper consumption.

Hinano Café 15 Washington Blvd, Venice
☎310/822-3902. Low-attitude chill bar by the
beach – a good place to drink without too
many tourists breathing down your neck,
with pool tables, shambling decor, and
crowd of mostly locals.

Library Alehouse 2911 Main St, Santa Monica
☎310/314-4855. Presenting the choicest
brews from West Coast microbreweries and
beyond, this is a good spot to select from
a nice range of well-known and obscure
labels while munching on salty bar food.

O'Brien's 2226 Wilshire Blvd, Santa Monica
☎310/396-4725. A fun, tub-thumping scene
serving Irish food and brews to a heady
crowd of locals and Irish expats.

Red Garter 2536 Lincoln Blvd, Venice
☎310/306-8300. To avoid the beachside
trendies, head inland a half-mile to this
old-time fave for boozing, where the drinks
are cheap (especially during happy hour,
4–7pm) and the local crowd comes to relax
and play pool in an unpretentious atmosphere.

Ye Olde King's Head 116 Santa Monica Blvd,
Santa Monica ☎310/451-1402. British-heavy
joint with jukebox, dartboards, and signed
photos of all your favorite rock dinosaurs;
don't miss the steak-and-kidney pie, afternoon tea, or the fish and chips.

The San Gabriel and San Fernando valleys

Amazon 14649 Ventura Blvd, San Fernando
Valley ☎818/986-7502. A small wonderland

of kitsch, in which you can knock back
Trader Vic's–type tropical concoctions
amid pseudo South American and
Polynesian decor: waterfalls, ferns, and
so on.

Aura 12215 Ventura Blvd, Studio City
☎818/487-1488. What passes for hip in the
San Fernando Valley: a trendy lounge/night-
club atop a strip mall, with an increasing
allure for its plush decor, DJs and live music,
and serviceable cocktails.

Clear 11916 Ventura Blvd, Studio City
☎818/980-4811. Another big name in the
attempt to draw Westsiders up to the
Valley: a chic lounge with the requisite
minimal-but-swanky decor, overpriced
cocktails, and preening crowd of beautiful
types. Worth a visit to see the Valley at its
maximum pose.

Clearman's North Woods 7247 N Rosemead
Blvd, San Gabriel ☎626/286-3579. A kitsch-
lover's delight with fake snow on the
outside and mooseheads mounted on the
walls inside; a great place to space out
while listening to moody, live torch singers and throwing your peanut shells on
the floor.

The Colorado 2640 E Colorado Blvd, Pasadena
☎626/449-3485. A bright spot along a bleak
Pasadena stretch. Salty bartenders, cheap
drinks, and a couple of pool tables amid
hunting-based decor.

Cozy's Bar & Grill 14048 Ventura Blvd, Sherman
Oaks ☎818/986-6000. Listen to blues on the
weekend, or come by any time to throw
darts, shoot pool, or knock back a few. A
friendly, laid-back San Fernando Valley spot
with a devoted clientele.

Gitana 260 E Magnolia Blvd, Burbank
☎818/846-4400. Giant entertainment
complex in the shadow of a mall, with
mixed drinks, pool tables, cigar bar,
and eclectic tunes on the dance floor.
Pulls in a mixed crowd of tourists and
locals.

Ireland's 32 13721 Burbank Blvd, Van Nuys
☎818/785-5200. One of the Valley's better
spots for quaffing Irish drafts, powering
down traditional stews and chops, and
soaking in a fair amount of traditional decor,
shamrocks and all.

McMurphy's 72 N Fair Oaks Ave, Pasadena
☎626/666-1445. A crowded Irish pub in Old
Pasadena, where you can get a taste of
lively Celtic folk and foamy Guinness at the
same time.

Coffeehouses

You can find **coffeehouses** throughout LA, from hole-in-th̶
sanitized yuppie magnets. Although straightforward java joints a̶
throughout the metropolis (along with chain-coffeehouses s̶
well-trafficked tourist routes like Melrose Avenue and Sant̶
Street Promenade are loaded with more inventive spots to̶
listings below go beyond java, focusing on unique establishm̶.....
serving coffee (and perhaps tea, food, and alcohol), also offer diversions like art,
music, poetry, or eye-popping decor. The areas to visit for these coffee joints are
Hollywood, West LA, Santa Monica, and the valleys – which have more appealing coffeehouses than you might expect.

Hollywood and West Hollywood

All-Star Theatre Café 6675 Hollywood Blvd
T323/962-8898. Antique store/café with a
1920s feel and overstuffed armchairs, now
inhabiting the historic 1936 Vogue moviehouse – very sleek and hip. Open until 3am
weekends.

Bourgeois Pig 5931 Franklin Ave, Los Feliz
T323/962-6366. Hip environment and
outrageously overpriced cappuccinos – you
really pay for the atmosphere of mirrors,
chandeliers, and loveseats – but the tasty
java, colorful clientele, and inviting decor
might make it worth your while.

Coffee Table 2930 Rowena Ave, Los Feliz
T323/644-8111. Casual, unpretentious
space with affordable coffees and relaxed
surroundings – a nice antidote for the
Bourgeois Pig (see above), further west.

CyberJava 7080 Hollywood Blvd T323/466-
5600. Located near the corner of La Brea
Avenue, this spot offers DSL Internet access
while selling Web surfers the usual range of
smoothies, java drinks and assorted sweets.

Highland Grounds 742 N Highland Ave
T323/466-1507. The posiest of LA's coffee
bars and something of a scene, serving iced
latte, pancakes, and even beer. At night
it's a club, with poetry and up-and-coming
bands.

**King's Road Espresso House 8361 Beverly Blvd,
West Hollywood** T323/655-9044. Sidewalk
café in the center of a busy shopping strip.
Popular with the hipster crowd as well as a
few interloping tourists.

Stir Crazy 6917 Melrose Ave T323/934-4656.
Cozy haunt that provides a glimpse of
what this stretch of Melrose used to be
like before the chain retailers moved in
– with mellow attitudes, decent java, and
Western-themed decor. Open til 1am
weekends.

Beverly Hills and West LA

**Cacao Coffee 11609 Santa Monica Blvd, West
LA** T310/473-7283. Fun and friendly joint
with all kinds of kitsch and retro-Tiki bric-a-
brac for decor, and good snacks and coffee
served to an amenable crowd of regulars.

Insomnia 7286 Beverly Blvd, north of Mid-Wilshire
T323/931-4943. A chic spot for chugging
cappuccinos while sitting on comfy sofas
and admiring the vivid art on the walls. The
people you see conspicuously writing on their
laptops are less likely to be budding poets or
novelists than would-be screenwriters plotting
bloody action flicks.

Lulu's Alibi 1640 Sawtelle Blvd, West LA
T310/479-6007. Restaurant/coffeehouse
that offers a full complement of traditional
foods (salads, sandwiches), quirky snacks
(deep-fried Twinkies), and nice array of
gourmet coffee beverages – plus a friendly,
colorful vibe.

**Nova Express 426 N Fairfax Ave, south of
West Hollywood** T323/658-7533. One of the
grooviest coffee joints around, designed
with retro-futuristic sci-fi decor, with weird
colors and lighting, and additional curiosities
like lava lamps and alien lounge and dance
music most nights. Open until 4am.

Urth Caffè 8565 Melrose Ave T310/659-0628.
Customers at this high-priced vendor tend
toward navel-gazing and celebrity-watching, but the coffees here are certainly tasty
enough, and the atmosphere is pleasant
and fairly well-scrubbed. Also at 267 S
Beverly Drive, Beverly Hills, and 2327 Main
St, Santa Monica.

Santa Monica and Venice

Abbot's Habit 1401 Abbot Kinney Blvd, Venice
T310/399-1171. Prototypical coffee house
for this part of Venice – rich, tasty coffee

DRINKING | Coffeehouses

j-made snacks and desserts, ud artwork on the walls, occasional ıc and spoken-word events, and a .endly neighborhood vibe.

Anastasia's Asylum 1028 Wilshire Blvd, Santa Monica ☎310/394-7113. Comfortable place with quirky decor and customers, and strong coffee and tea. Also with nightly entertainment, of eclectic character and varying quality.

Novel Café 212 Pier Ave, Santa Monica ☎310/396-8566. Used books and high-backed wooden chairs set the tone; good coffees, teas, and pastries, though with many self-consciously studious patrons. Located near the Venice border.

Red Room Café 1604 Pacific Ave, Venice ☎310/399-1785. A coffeehouse with acceptably good beverages and snacks, but best for the actual artworks displayed for your perusal, in forms ranging from painting to sculpture to multimedia installations.

Rose Café 220 Rose Ave, Venice ☎310/399-0711. A somewhat trendy, though not pretentious, place for coffee and pastries that also offers occasional blues and jazz music. A neighborhood favorite, conveniently located near the Santa Monica border.

Un-Urban Coffee House 3301 Pico Blvd, Santa Monica ☎310/315-0056. A combination coffee-house and performance space, worth a look for its alternative music and comedy acts.

The South Bay and LA Harbor

Coffee Cartel 1820 S Catalina Ave, Redondo Beach ☎310/316-6554. Somewhat unremarkable coffeehouse that nonetheless puts on interesting shows of acoustic music and poetry readings; worth a visit if you're in this town.

Java Man 157 Pier Ave, Hermosa Beach ☎310/379-7209. Tables lit by halogen lamps, plus a rotating display of work from local artists, adorn this coffeehouse not far from the beach. Also with sandwiches and decent desserts. Open until midnight on weekends.

The Library 3418 E Broadway, Long Beach ☎562/433-2393. Like the *Novel Café* (see above), this is a prime spot for reading and/or buying literature, looking studious with the rest of the java intellectuals, while gulping down hot and iced coffee drinks.

Portfolios 2400 E Fourth St, Long Beach ☎562/434-2486. The kind of place where

you're encouraged to browse the artworks for sale as you knock back your demi-tasse. Occasional open-mike nights, plus jazz on weekend evenings.

Sacred Grounds 399 W Sixth St, San Pedro ☎310/514-0800. Although located far from central LA, this combo coffeehouse and club offers a sizable stage for regional performers, with open-mike night, music jams, and even some marginal comedy acts.

San Gabriel and San Fernando valleys

Aroma Coffee and Tea 4360 Tujunga Ave, Studio City ☎818/508-6505. Housed in a remodelled house, this is an unfussy, mellow spot where you can enjoy beverages with cakes and scones, on the patio near the gardens, and in a redesigned living room with an old-fashioned fireplace.

Cobalt Café 22047 Sherman Way, Canoga Park ☎818/348-3789. Grungy but hip coffeehouse in the San Fernando Valley, with food and live music, and poetry readings, too.

Coffee Connection 4397 Tujunga Ave #B, Studio City ☎818/769-3622. Enjoyable joint that has nightly open-mike sessions around dinner-time, and weekend acoustic troubadours as well.

Coffee Gallery Backstage 2029 N Lake Ave, Altadena ☎626/398-7917. On the northern side of the San Gabriel Valley, an appealing spot to lounge on sofas, munch on pastries, browse artworks and various art and culture books while you sip your espresso. Periodically presents poetry and music in its spacious back room.

Coffee Junction 19221 Ventura Blvd, Tarzana ☎818/342-3405. If you end up trapped in this remote corner of the Valley, close to nothing particularly interesting, the tasty coffee and folk music here are worth a stop. Open-mike night on Sundays can also be entertaining.

Hallenbeck's General Store 5510 Cahuenga Blvd, North Hollywood ☎818/985-5916. A coffeehouse done up as an old-fashioned general store, serving treats like sarsaparilla along with the java, and presenting nightly shows that lean toward spoken-word, folk, and poetry.

Hotwired Café 11651 Riverside Drive, North Hollywood ☎818/753-9929. Ultra-caffeinated java in a Valley joint with a range of curious entertainment, from Monday-night blues jams to comics and acoustic strummers several nights of the week.

iBrowse Coffee and Internet 11 W Main St, Alhambra ☎626/588-2233. Browse the Web to the sounds of eclectic music (especially big on alternative rock) while sipping super-charged coffee, at this spot well off the main tourist path.

Kulak's Woodshed 5230 Laurel Canyon Blvd, North Hollywood ☎818/766-9913. Basic coffee shop putting on nightly shows in a cramped but colorful space, ranging from acoustic and spoken-word to performance art and poetry.

Lulu's Beehive 13203 Ventura Blvd, Studio City ☎818/986-2233. This quirky coffeehouse is good not only for a spot of java, but also for taking in some art work, along with regular performances of rock, folk, and jazz – not to mention comedy and poetry.

Zona Rosa 15 El Molino Ave, Pasadena ☎626/793-2334. One of the city's high points for rich, hearty java in a creative environ-ment, with excellent, inventive drinks (often using South American beans), an arty atmosphere, and periodic live music of the jazz and salsa variety.

Clubs

The **clubs** scene in LA is one of the finest in the country, ranging from posey hangouts to industrial noise cellars, with everybody claiming to be either a rock musician or in the movies. Many of the more interesting and unusual clubs are transient, especially those catering to the house/electronic-music scene. As a result, the trendier side of the club scene is hard to pin down, and you should always check the *LA Weekly* before setting out.

Weekend nights are predictably the busiest, but during the week things are often cheaper and just as fun, and the best time to turn up is between 11pm and midnight. Most of the **cover charges** range widely, depending on the night (anywhere from $4 to $20; call ahead). The **minimum age** is 21, and it's normal for ID to be checked, so bring your passport or other photo ID. (Some establishments that don't serve alcohol or separate the bar from the rest of the club admit patrons ages 18–21.) You should dress with some sensitivity to the club's style, but prohibitive dress codes are common only at those "velvet rope" clubs that supposedly cater to movie brats and starlets.

Most of the top clubs are either in Hollywood or along a ten-block stretch of West Hollywood. Beverly Hills is a lifeless yuppie desert, Downtown is home to a handful of itinerant clubs operating above and below board, and the San Fernando Valley's more rough-and-ready scene is usually confined to the week-ends. (For gay and lesbian clubs and discos, see p.328.)

DRINKING | Clubs

Downtown

Club Soho 333 S Boylston St ☎213/989-7979. The latest club in a space that has seen many in recent years, with this incarnation focusing on rap, soul, and dance music, and an upscale dress code to boot – but you might want to take a cab to the dicey location west of the 110 freeway.

The Echo 1822 Sunset Blvd ☎213/413-8200. Like the name says, an Echo Park scene with scrappy dance DJs spinning a range of old- and new-school favorites most nights, with rap on weekends, and rock and retro DJs on Sundays.

Grand Avenue 1024 S Grand Ave ☎213/747-0999. Based around salsa, hip-hop, and elec-tronica, this is a DJ-centric spot that draws

a steady crowd for its pounding, big-beat atmosphere and Westside club attitude.

Mayan 1038 S Hill St ☎213//46-4287. Formerly a pre-Columbian–styled movie palace, now hosting nonstop Latin rhythms and nonstop disco and house tunes on three dance floors. Fri and Sat only, no jeans or sneakers.

▽ The Mayan nightclub

305

Stock Exchange 618 S Spring St ☎213/489-3877. An attempt to broaden the Downtown club scene on a previously deserted stretch of road, spinning enough funk and disco tunes to make the yuppie crowd gyrate with abandon. Cover can reach $15.

Mid-Wilshire

Conga Room 5364 Wilshire Blvd ☎323/938-1696. A high-profile celebrity investment resulting in a surprisingly appealing feast of Cuban food and Latin music, with weekend DJs to stir the salsa soul – but the cover can run up to $20 or more.

El Rey Theater 5515 Wilshire Blvd ☎323/936-4790. Favorite old neighborhood movie palace turned into an itinerant club and performing-arts space; check listings for periodic dance-club nights and special events.

Jewel's Catch One 4067 W Pico Blvd ☎323/734-8849. Sweaty barn catering to a mixed crowd of gays and straights and covering two wild dance floors. A longtime favorite for club-hoppers of all sorts. Especially busy Fri–Mon, though located in the middle of nowhere.

Hollywood

1650 1650 Schrader Blvd ☎323/871-1650. Signature Hollywood dance club, which draws plenty of club-kids for its rap, house, reggae, and retro DJs, with several party scenes sometimes going on at once in the house, at full volume.

Arena 6655 Santa Monica Blvd ☎323/462-0714. Work up a sweat to funk, hip-hop, and house on a massive dance floor inside a former ice factory. The fervent crowd is diverse, but leans toward a mix of Hispanics and gays. Plays host to many different, ever-changing club nights.

Avalon 1735 N Vine St ☎323/462-3000. Formerly *The Palace*, now converted into a weekend dance club spinning old-school faves, along with a dash of rock and retro, with the occasional big-name DJ dropping in.

Bar Sinister 1652 N Cherokee ☎323/769-7070. A collection of sprightly dance beats most nights of the week, then memorably spooky Goth music and anemic-looking vampire types on Saturdays ($10 if in costume). Connected to *Boardner's* bar (see p.300).

Blue 1642 N Las Palmas Ave ☎323/462-7442. Goth, industrial, fetish freak-outs, and some retro-80s draw the pallid and neo-zombie contingent to this combo restaurant and club, nightly except Tuesdays and Thursdays.

The Derby 4500 Los Feliz Blvd ☎323/663-8979. Restored supper club on Hollywood's east side, with gorgeous high wooden ceilings and round bar; one of the originators of the retro-swing craze, thanks to the movie *Swingers*.

Dragonfly 6510 Santa Monica Blvd ☎323/466-6111. Unusual decor, two large dance rooms, and house and disco club nights that are continually buzzing on Thurs–Sun nights; live music at other times.

Florentine Gardens 5951 Hollywood Blvd ☎323/464-0706. Stuck between the Salvation Army and a porno theater, but popular with the LA dance crowd, especially the under-21 set, for weekend DJ nights.

The Ruby 7070 Hollywood Blvd ☎323/467-7070. A wide range of feverish dance nights take turns Thurs–Sun, covering everything from gothic and grinding industrial to perky house and garage.

Three Clubs 1123 N Vine St ☎323/462-6441. Dark, perennially trendy bar and club where the usual crowd of hipsters drops in for retro and funk music, and gets pleasingly plastered. Colorless exterior and lack of good signage makes the joint even hipper.

West Hollywood

7969 7969 Santa Monica Blvd ☎323/654-0280. Classic WeHo dance club – a landmark for its frenetic assortment of gay-themed (but straight-friendly) shows, from go-go girls to male strippers to drag queens. Always one of LA's most colorful spots for dancing and grinding.

The Factory 652 N La Peer Drive ☎310/659-4551. Mixed straight and gay crowd grooving to DJs spinning house and retro most nights of the week at what is still one of West Hollywood's more popular clubs.

Key Club 9039 Sunset Blvd ☎310/274-5800. A hot spot in the liveliest section of the west side of the Strip, attracting a young, hip group for its hip-hop, funk, and house music spinning nightly.

Pearl 665 N Robertson Blvd ☎310/358-9191. The latest twist on Strip nightlife, a dance club with a cabaret flair, featuring performing-arts pieces (often of the sex-oriented variety) mixed with dance nights, karaoke, and various peculiar entertainment offerings.

Prey 643 N La Cienega Blvd ℡310/652-2012. The most recent incarnation of what was once *The Gate*, now transformed into a pulse-pounding, ear-jangling hub of rap and electronica, with a frenetic crowd of dancers and, on the sidelines, arch-poseurs.

Tempest 7323 Santa Monica Blvd ℡323/850-5115. After 10pm on weekends, the eclectic grooves start to spin here, from retro-funk and disco to the latest hip-hop to 1960s Austin Powers–style sing-a-longs.

Ultra Suede 661 N Robertson Blvd ℡310/659-4551. The spot for superior retro-dancing on Wednesday and weekend nights, heavy on 1970s disco and 80s technopop. Neighbor to *The Factory* and draws much of the same mixed crowd.

The Viper Room 8852 Sunset Blvd ℡310/358-1880. Excellent live acts, with occasional DJs spinning an eclectic mix of dance and other styles. See also "Live music," p.312.

West LA

Backstage Café 9433 Brighton Way ℡310/777-0252. Epitomizing nightlife on the Westside, a Cal-cuisine bar and restaurant where the nice decor and well-made cocktails are offset by pretension, high prices, and a corporate feel (most evident in the gift shop).

Café Muse 11301 W Olympic Blvd ℡310/268-7855. House beats from the Far East collide nightly with varying sounds – dub, trance, rap, reggae and more – at this electronica-friendly club.

Carbon 9300 Venice Blvd ℡310/558-9302. Though hardly near anywhere central, a good spot for eclectic nightly DJs, whose turntables glow with Latin, retro, hip-hop, soul, garage, and rock beats, depending on the night.

El Dorado Cantina 11777 San Vicente Blvd, Brentwood ℡310/207-0150. A decent Mexican restaurant and bar – one of the few adequate nightspots on the notoriously stiff Westside – providing serviceable spirits and regular dance music.

Osteria Romana Orsini 9575 W Pico Blvd ℡310/277-6050. Funk, rap, and soul on weekends at this Italian restaurant, aka "Orsini's," where, despite the big beats, the crowd tends toward stuffy Beverly Hills attitudes.

Santa Monica a[...]

Mor 2941 Main St, [...] 6720. Nightly sel[...] house, and sor[...] club nights m[...] setting, and [...] new wave, [...]

Shane 2424 Main [...] 4122. Agreeable Morocc[...] later in the evening, turns into a r[...] with DJs spinning electronic and downbe[...] sounds; generally more crowded on weekends, drawing a mix of locals and out-of-towners.

The Space 2020 Wilshire Blvd, Santa Monica ℡310/829-1933. Ground zero for weekend retro vibes, a bar and lounge with backward-looking DJs massaging everything from 1980s electro, pop, and New Wave to spacey 1970s disco and funk to more contemporary breakbeats.

Sugar 814 Broadway, Santa Monica ℡310/899-1989. Hard-hitting electronica, from big beat to house to techno, served up in a shiny and gorgeous glass-and-steel interior. Cover ranges widely per night, from $5–20.

Temple Bar 1026 Wilshire Blvd, Santa Monica ℡310/392-1077. Popular, if chaotic, mix of different groove styles, from rap to R&B, with heavy doses of world beat thrown in as well. Always a fun, engaging scene.

Zanzibar 1301 Fifth St, Santa Monica ℡310/451-2221. Nightly DJs spinning sounds with a house, funk, and soul bent, but also with a bit of experimentation – anything from ragga to sci-fi techno.

San Gabriel and San Fernando valleys

Bigfoot Lodge 3172 Los Feliz Blvd, Atwater Village ℡323/662-9227. On the far side of East Hollywood in dreary Atwater, but a prime draw for its nightly DJs, who set feet to stomping with retro-rock and -punk tunes, and other glam, goth, thrash, and rockabilly sounds thrown in as well.

CIA 11334 Burbank Blvd, North Hollywood ℡818/506-6353. Or the "California Institute for Abnormal Arts," a truly odd venue where art and music collide, with curious visual installations (often based on circus clowns and freak shows) and sounds from punk to avant-garde.

Coda 5248 Van Nuys Blvd, Sherman Oaks ℡818/783-7518. Fairly hip for the Valley, with

...el, vaguely industrial decor;
...y as you might think, either,
...cals for its bouncy blend of rap,
...d electronica.

260 E Magnolia Blvd, Burbank
8/846-4400. Giant dance-and-dining
...mplex in the shadow of a mall, with pool
tables, cigar bar, and eclectic tunes on the
dance floor. Mixed crowd of tourists and
locals.

The Mix 2612 Honolulu Ave, Glendale
☏**818/248-3040.** Fairly safe sounds at this
dance club and restaurant (located on the
northern edge of Glendale), mainly country
and middle-of-the-road tunes with plenty of
retro-pop thrown in.

The Muse 54 E Colorado Blvd, Pasadena
☏**626/793-0608.** Old Town Pasadena is the
site where dance, funk, and hip-hop tunes
mingle in one tri-level club with nightly DJs
and no less than eleven pool tables.

**Sagebrush Cantina 23527 Calabasas Rd, Cala-
basas** ☏**818/222-6062.** About as close as the
western San Fernando Valley gets to having
a live-music scene, this Mexican restaurant
offers 1970s-leaning rock cover bands
several nights of the week to an appreciative crowd.

14

Live music

Los Angeles has an overwhelming choice of **live music** venues. Besides local acts, there are always plenty of big stateside and European names on tour, from major artists to independents, and an enormous number of venues. Most venues open at 8pm or 9pm; headline bands are usually onstage between 11pm and 1am. Cover ranges widely from $5 to $50, and you should phone ahead to check set times and whether the gig is sold out. You will often need to be 21 and will likely be asked for ID. As ever, *LA Weekly* and the "Calendar" section of the Sunday *Los Angeles Times* are the best sources of **listings**.

Seats for concerts or sports events are often purchased from Ticketmaster, which has branches in Tower Records stores, and charge-by-phone numbers (☏213/480-3232 or 714/740-2000). A quick way through the maze of LA's theaters is to phone the LA Stage Alliance (☏213/614-0556, ⊛www.lastagealliance.com) and ask for the availability of discount tickets for a given show, under its LA Stage Tix program.

The music scene

Just about any musical form can be heard in LA, whether on the biggest concert stages or in the dingiest bars. Since the nihilistic punk bands of nearly thirty years ago drew the city away from its spaced-out slacker image, LA's **rock** scene has been second to none, peaking in the 1980s with the Sunset Strip's own brand of "hair metal" and more recently having an alternative or indie tinge. The old **punk** scene has been revitalized with up-and-coming bands, and heavy metal can still be found here and there. The influence and popularity of **hip-hop** is also prevalent, whether mixed in dance music by Westside DJs or in its more authentic form in the inner city (best avoided by out-of-towners).

Surprisingly, **country music** is fairly common, at least away from trendy Hollywood, and the valleys are hotbeds of bluegrass and swing. There's also **jazz**, played in a few genuinely authentic downbeat dives, though more commonly found in diluted form in upscale restaurants. Latin **salsa** music is immensely popular among LA's Hispanics, and can be found in a few Westside clubs; and there's a small live **reggae** scene, occasionally featuring big names but more often sticking to local bands.

Concert halls and performance spaces

LA's **concert halls** and **performance spaces** are spread throughout the region, though most major rock and alternative clubs are in Hollywood or West Hollywood, with many right on the Sunset Strip.

A short history of popular music in LA

Although LA has been home to **rock'n'roll** since its birth in the 1950s, in part due to such homegrown talent as Ritchie Valens and The Platters, it was only with the rise of 1960s pop culture that LA's **rock** music scene really took off. The style was first defined by **surf rock**, with the pleasant harmonies of the Beach Boys and Jan and Dean, and pop vocalists like Frankie Avalon pushing the Southern California dream of cool muscle cars, bikini-clad chicks, and killer waves.

With even Brian Wilson's mood darkening and growing more complex (especially with such key records as *Pet Sounds* and the finally released *Smile*), the mid-1960s saw **psychedelic rock** take over; bands like The Doors, Buffalo Springfield, and Love were at the forefront of the LA scene, while lighter groups like The Mamas and the Papas added their own spin on "California Dreamin'." Up the road on the central California coast, the 1967 **Monterey Pop Festival** brought LA and San Francisco bands to prominence nationally, and resulted in a flood of record deals given to once obscure acid-rock bands.

By the early 1970s, after being awash in first LSD and then cocaine, LA's musicians gave rise to the laid-back, **country-rock** sound, defined by the Eagles, Jackson Browne, and Linda Ronstadt, who sang about the city as a spaced-out pleasure zone filtered through a druggy haze. This all came to an end around 1978, with the emergence of an energetic **punk** scene, first headed by "old-style" groups such as the Germs and X, later to be usurped by the **hardcore** thrash style out of Orange County, epitomized by Black Flag. Along with their penchant for youthful rebellion, LA punks recaptured some of rock's earlier, more freewheeling days, before the dominance of slicked-down corporate rock.

Perhaps the most popular movement of all, contemporary with both country-rock and punk, was **heavy metal**, its aggressive presence dating back to Led Zeppelin's first American tour at the dawn of the 1970s, and carried through the late 1970s and 1980s when Van Halen, Mötley Crüe, and Guns N' Roses leaped onto the national stage as soon as they hit it big on the Sunset Strip.

Beginning in the 1990s, and to some extent a reaction against turgid arena rock and heavy metal, **alternative rock** arose in Southern California on the heels of its emergence in Seattle, and still makes regular appearances on the local scene, with its introspective, downbeat lyrics and formal creativity. For the most part, though, LA has always been more of a follower on this musical trend, with most of the top acts imported from less sunny spots like the Pacific Northwest.

Far more influential in the last decade has been LA's own **hip-hop** or **rap music** scene, which in the 1990s was arguably the most vital force in popular music, though the style was largely imported from elsewhere – in this case, New York City. By the end of the 1980s, the city's rappers had created their own unique sound through the efforts of such rappers and producers as Snoop Dogg, Ice Cube, Ice T, and especially Dr Dre, who almost single-handedly elevated the **West Coast sound** to prominence: laid-back beats, an undertone of funk and soul, and above all, a lyrical emphasis on violence and hedonism. This was the prototypical **gangsta rap**, a style that fueled an intercoastal rivalry (now played out) that allegedly resulted in the murders of the West Coast's Tupac Shakur and the East Coast's Notorious B.I.G.

Major concert venues

Arrowhead Pond 2695 E Katella Blvd, Anaheim ☎714/704-2400, ⊛www.arrowheadpond.com. A 19,000-seat sports arena that draws the usual big-ticket events in music and entertainment, and also features a separate "Theatre" – about a third the size – for smaller-scaled rock groups.
Carpenter Performing Arts Center 6200 Atherton St, on the campus of Cal State Long Beach ☎562/985-7000, ⊛www.carpenterarts.org.

A major arts space in the South Bay, attracting mostly mid-level entertainers in pop, traditional rock, folk, jazz and country. **Cerritos Center for the Performing Arts** 12700 Center Court Drive ☎1-800/300-4345, ⊛www .cerritoscenter.com. North of downtown Long Beach, a top draw for mainstream country, gospel, classical, pop and jazz acts – usually nothing too quirky or adventurous. **The Forum** 3900 W Manchester Blvd, Inglewood ☎310/330-7300, ⊛www.laforum.com. Despite being converted into a mega-church for Sunday services, this huge venue with giant columns still hosts the occasional, sinning, rock band, usually about once a month. **Greek Theatre** 2700 N Vermont Ave, Griffith Park ☎323/665-1927 ⊛www.greektheatrela.com. A broad range of mainstream rock and pop acts stream through this outdoor, summer-only venue, which has seating for five thousand. Parking can be a mess, so arrive early. **Grove of Anaheim** 2200 E Katella Ave ☎714/712-2700, ⊛www.thegroveofanaheim .com. Orange County concert space show- casing old-time performers and mid-level entertainers in soul, country, pop, and jazz. **Hollywood Palladium** 6215 Sunset Blvd, Hollywood ☎323/962-7600, ⊛www .hollywoodpalladium.com. Once a big-band dance hall, with an authentic 1940s interior, now a home to all manner of hard rock, punk, and rap outfits. **Kodak Theatre** 6801 Hollywood Blvd, Hollywood ☎323/308-6363, ⊛www.kodaktheatre.com. Part of the colossal Hollywood & Highland mall, a media-ready theater partly designed to host the Oscars, which it will for many years, as well as top-name pop and rock acts. **Staples Center** 865 S Figueroa St, Downtown ☎213/624-3100, ⊛www.staplescenter.com. Big, glassy sports arena (home to the LA Lakers) with millions of municipal and corpo- rate dollars behind it. A good showcase for Top 40 rock and pop acts. **Universal Amphitheater** 100 Universal City Plaza ☎818/622-4440, ⊛www.hob.com/venues /concerts/universal. A huge but acoustically excellent auditorium putting on regular rock shows by headline groups. Located on the Universal Studios lot. **Wiltern Theater** 3790 Wilshire Blvd, Mid-Wilshire ☎323/388-1400, ⊛www.thewiltern.com. A striking blue Zigzag Art Deco movie palace, recently renovated and converted into a top

performing space for standard pop acts as well as edgy alternative groups.

Rock

14 Below 1348 14th St, Santa Monica ☎310/451-5040. At this casual bar, pool tables and a fireplace compete for your attention with rock, folk, and blues acts that perform nightly. **American Legion Hall** 2035 Highland Ave, Hollywood ☎323/851-3030. One of the more unexpected places to put on a punk show, this Art Deco marvel has occasional performances by head-thrashers and hard- rockers. **Cat Club** 8911 Sunset Blvd, West Hollywood ☎310/657-0888. Hard, meaty jams can be heard here every night of the week, mainly rock, punk, and rockabilly – which should come as no surprise, since the owner's a former Stray Cat. **Cobalt Café** 22047 Sherman Way, Canoga Way ☎818/348-3789. Valley outpost for all kinds of thrashing, head-banging, and behaving badly, with nightly bands and decent coffee drinks, too (see p.304). **Doug Weston's Troubadour** 9081 Santa Monica Blvd, West Hollywood ☎310/276-6168. An old 1960s mainstay that's been through a lot of incarnations. Used to be known for folk and country rock, then metal, now for alternative and acoustic line-ups. **El Rey Theater** 5515 Wilshire Blvd, Mid-Wilshire ☎323/936-4790. Although not as famous as its Sunset Strip counterparts, this rock and alternative venue is possibly the best spot to see explosive new bands and enduring oldsters. Also offers a variety of dance club nights. **Gabah** 4658 Melrose Ave, Hollywood ☎323/664- 8913. Eclectic, laid-back spot serving up a mix of reggae, funk, dub, and rock – even flamenco. The dicey neighborhood leaves much to be desired; always let the valet take charge of your car. **The Gig** 7302 Melrose Ave, north of Mid-Wilshire ☎323/936-4440. Central Melrose hot spot for hard-rocking and fist-shaking, with a regular line-up of spirited local groups and a good group of spirits, too. **Henry Fonda Music Box Theater** 6126 Holly- wood Blvd, Hollywood ☎323/464-0808, ⊛www.henryfondatheater.com. A charming, renovated old theater that began life in 1926 and still hosts theatrical productions, but more typically alternative rock and country acts.

The Joint 8771 Pico Blvd, West LA ☎310/275-2619. A dark, mirrored neighborhood venue with assorted punk screamers and occasionally decent rock and alternative groups.

Key Club 9039 Sunset Blvd, West Hollywood ☎310/274-5800. A hot spot in the most lively section of the Strip, attracting a young audience for its regular concerts in the rock, punk, and metal vein, with occasional lighter fare as well.

King King 6555 Hollywood Blvd ☎323/960-5765. A solid Hollywood bet for nightly concerts by chord-crunching rockers and for live dance music on weekends, with house, funk, rap, and retro-pop all on the DJ docket.

Largo 432 N Fairfax Ave, north of Mid-Wilshire ☎323/852-1073. Cozy cabaret that features some of LA's more unusual live bands, performing mostly jazz, rock, and pop.

The Lighthouse 30 Pier Ave, Hermosa Beach ☎310/376-9833. Adjacent to the beach, this old favorite has a broad booking policy, which spans rock, jazz, and reggae as well as Monday-night karaoke and occasional comedy.

Mr T's Bowl 5621 N Figueroa Ave, Highland Park ☎323/960-5693. Former bowling alley, since been remodelled into a quirky bar with a regular crowd of hipsters and local characters. On weekends, there's live music, with a strong punk-rock-surfer bent.

The Roxy 9009 Sunset Blvd, West Hollywood ☎310/276-2222. An intimate club showcasing the music industry's new signings and boasting a great sound system, too. On the western – but still frenetic – end of the strip.

▽ The Roxy

Silver Lake Lounge 2906 Sunset Blvd ☎323/666-2407. A hole in the wall, popular for its energetic punk and alternative shows, while some weekends feature drag and dance acts.

The Smell 247 S Main St, Downtown ☎213/625-4325. A funky space with cool art grunge, including strange decor, frenetic rock, and punk music, and a notoriously grim location.

Spaceland 1717 Silver Lake Blvd, Hollywood ☎213/833-2843. Excellent spot to catch up-and-coming local and national rockers and other acts, including punk and alternative musicians.

Temple Bar 1026 Wilshire Blvd, Santa Monica ☎310/392-1077. A popular, if chaotic, mix of styles can be heard here, from funk and soul to rap and R&B, as well as occasional forays into rock, pop, and world beat.

The Viper Room 8852 Sunset Blvd, West Hollywood ☎310/358-1880. Great live acts, plus a famous owner (Johnny Depp) and a headline-grabbing past have helped boost this club's hip aura. Expect almost any musician to show up onstage.

Whisky-a-Go-Go 8901 Sunset Blvd, West Hollywood ☎310/652-4202. Legendary spot, thanks mostly to The Doors, and important for LA's rising music stars. Mainly hard rock, though you might catch an alternative act now and then.

Country and folk

Boulevard Music 4136 Sepulveda Blvd, Culver City ☎310/398-2583. This unglamorous music store manages to host some fairly interesting folk acts on weekends, from roots country to delta blues, with international groups adding even more to the eclectic mix.

Celtic Arts Center 4843 Laurel Canyon Blvd, Studio City ☎818/760-8322. A celebration of all things Celtic and Gaelic (and not just Irish, either), offering monthly concerts, dance lessons and, best of all, free Sunday night Céili dances followed by traditional-music jam sessions.

Cowboy Country 3321 E South St, Long Beach ☎562/630-3007. Pull out your best line-dancing moves and your fanciest boots for this multi-story country club, which really draws the self-styled cowpokes for its weekend live performances.

Cowboy Palace Saloon 21635 Devonshire St, Chatsworth ☎818/341-0166. Worth a trip to this distant corner of the San Fernando Valley for the spirited down-home country concerts and free Sunday BBQ fixings.

CTMS Center 16953 Ventura Blvd, Encino ⊤818/817-7756. The home base for the California Traditional Music Society, which puts on periodic performances throughout the year of ancient and modern folk music, offering education and training, monthly jam sessions (open to the public), and occasional concerts by visiting musicians.

Finn McCool's 2702 Main St, Santa Monica ⊤310/452-1734. Along with being a serviceable spot for quaffing draughts, this Irish bar also offers twice-weekly performances of folk tunes from the Emerald Isle.

Hotel Café 1623 N Cahuenga Blvd, Hollywood ⊤323/461-2040. Comfortable spot for acoustic acts and earnest singer-songsmiths, with nightly tunes except on Sunday.

McCabe's 3103 W Pico Blvd, Santa Monica ⊤310/828-4497. LA's premier acoustic guitar shop; long the scene of some excellent and unusual folk and country shows, with the occasional alternative crooner thrown in as well.

Molly Malone's Irish Pub 575 S Fairfax Ave, Mid-Wilshire ⊤323/935-1577. Local favorite for its colorful clientele, and mix of traditional Irish music, American folk, rock, and R&B. See also p.299.

Oil Can Harry's 11502 Ventura Blvd, Studio City ⊤818/760-9749. Unassuming joint with a strong bent for country music, with occasional down-home performances, line-dancing, and a mildly cornpone atmosphere.

Rusty's Surf Ranch 256 Santa Monica Pier ⊤310/393-7437. Offers not only surf music – and displays of old-time long boards – but also rock, pop, folk, and even karaoke. Always a popular spot for tourists, near the end of the pier.

The Scene 806 E Colorado St, Glendale ⊤818/241-7029. Head-scratching booking policy features punks on some nights, country crooners on others, and rockabilly swingers on the next. Call ahead to find out what you're in for.

Viva Cantina 900 Riverside Drive, Burbank ⊤818/845-2425. A Mexican restaurant on the far side of Griffith Park, where you can hear some of LA's most engaging country, bluegrass, and honky-tonk artists performing nightly.

Jazz and blues

Babe and Ricky's Inn 4339 Leimert Blvd, South Central ⊤323/295-9112. Long a top spot for blues on Central Ave, this premier music hall continues to attract quality, nationally known acts at its more recent Leimert Park location.

The Baked Potato 3787 Cahuenga Blvd W, North Hollywood ⊤818/980-1615. A small but near-legendary contemporary jazz spot, where many reputations have been forged. Don't come looking for bland lounge jazz/muzak – instead, expect to be surprised.

BB King's Blues Club 1000 Universal Center Drive, Universal City ⊤818/6-BBKING. Ignore the garish CityWalk exterior and head to Lucille's, the club room inside (named after BB's guitar), for good acoustic blues on weekends.

Blue Café 210 Promenade, Long Beach ⊤562/983-7111. A range of nightly blues near the harbor, plus a slew of pool tables and an upstairs dance floor. No cover.

Café Boogaloo 1238 Hermosa Ave, Hermosa Beach ⊤310/318-2324. One of the better spots in the South Bay for seeking out nightly blues, with occasional New Orleans jazz and swing.

Cat n' Fiddle Pub 6530 Sunset Blvd, Hollywood ⊤323/468-3800. An English-style pub with worthwhile jazz performers on Sundays from 7pm until 11pm; no cover.

Catalina Bar and Grill 1640 N Cahuenga Blvd, Hollywood ⊤323/466-2210. This central Hollywood jazz institution offers traditional sounds and good acoustics, plus filling meals and potent drinks.

Cozy's Bar and Grill 14048 Ventura Blvd, Sherman Oaks ⊤818/986-6000. Listen to blues on the weekend, or periodically during the week, at this restaurant and lounge that also features karaoke, funk, and soul performances.

Harvelle's 1432 Fourth St, Santa Monica ⊤310/395-1676. Near the Third Street Promenade, a stellar blues joint for more than six decades, offering different performers nightly and a popular band showcase on Monday nights.

House of Blues 8430 Sunset Blvd, West Hollywood ⊤323/848-5100. Over-commercialized mock sugar-shack, with good but pricey live acts. Very popular with tourists (also a branch at Disneyland ⊤714/778-2583). Cover can reach $40 or more.

Jax 339 N Brand Blvd, Glendale ☎818/500-1604. A combination restaurant and performing stage where you can take in a good assortment of jazz, from traditional to contemporary. No cover.

Jazz Bakery 3233 Helms Ave, Culver City ☎310/271-9039. More performance space than club, and the brainchild of singer Ruth Price, where the best local musicians play alongside big-name visitors in a former bakery building.

Knitting Factory 7021 Hollywood Blvd, Hollywood ☎323/463-0204. West Coast branch of the landmark New York City club, featuring a wide range of eclectic interpretation, much of it experimental or avant-garde.

Lunaria 10351 Santa Monica Blvd, West LA ☎310/282-8870. This restaurant's intimate lounge hosts nightly jazz performers playing a good range of styles, from swing to bebop. No cover.

Spazio 14755 Ventura Blvd, 2nd Floor, Sherman Oaks ☎818/728-8400. Swank Italian eatery that's one of the bigger-name spots for mainstream jazz, hosting regular nightly performances.

Vibrato Grill and Jazz 2930 Beverly Glen Circle, West LA ☎310/474-9400. You're not going to find anything too challenging at this Bel Air club, but for traditional and smooth jazz sounds, this recent arrival fits the bill.

World Stage 4344 Degnan Blvd, South Central LA ☎323/293-2451. Informal, bare-bones rehearsal space that attracts top-name players like drummers Billy Higgins and Max Roach. Thursday jams, Friday and Saturday gigs.

Latin and salsa

Club Samba 701 Long Beach Blvd, Long Beach ☎562/435-6238. The first Saturday night of the month in winter and spring is the time for eye-opening samba performances, also taking place on Saturday nights in July. Also with Monday-night samba classes.

Conga Room 5364 Wilshire Blvd, Mid-Wilshire ☎323/938-1696. Live Cuban, salsa, and South American music throughout the week at this hip, lively club on the Miracle Mile, where the cover can sometimes be steep.

El Floridita 1253 N Vine St, Hollywood ☎323/871-8612. Decent Mexican and Cuban food complements a fine line-up of Cuban and salsa artists, who play on weekends and jam on other nights.

Luminarias 3500 Ramona Blvd, Monterey Park ☎323/268-4177. Hilltop restaurant with live salsa reckoned to be as good as its Mexican food. No cover.

Mama Juana's 3707 Cahuenga Blvd W, Studio City ☎818/505-8636. Spanish/Mexican restaurant that also serves up nightly helpings of live salsa, merengue, and other Latin-flavored tunes. Also salsa lessons on weekends before the shows begin.

Rio Lounge and Grill 15910 Ventura Blvd, Encino ☎818/205-9799. Weekend salsa, samba, and bossa nova set the scene for a fun, tub-thumping atmosphere in the San Fernando Valley, with salsa lessons also offered on Sunday before the music.

Zabumba 10717 Venice Blvd, West LA ☎310/841-6525. In a colorful building amid drab surroundings, this venue is more bossa nova Brazilian than straight salsa, but it's still great, and very lively.

Reggae

Club 49 49 S Pine Ave, Long Beach ☎562/493-9059. Depending on the night, a range of live music – including reggae – and DJs enlivens the surf'n'turf meals here.

Domenico's 82 N Fair Oaks Ave, Pasadena ☎626/449-1948. This Old Pasadena restaurant has reggae offerings several nights a week; call first for the current schedule.

Fais Do-Do 5247 W Adams Blvd, South Central ☎323/954-8080. Though it often hosts DJ nights of the dance, funk, and rap variety, also presents weekend concerts from regional reggae and R&B acts.

Golden Sails Hotel 6285 E PCH, Long Beach ☎562/596-1631. Some of the best reggae bands from LA and beyond show up at this hotel on Friday and Saturday nights.

Lighthouse Café 30 Pier Ave, Hermosa Beach ☎310/372-6911. Adjacent to the beach and the Strand, this club has a broad booking policy that spans reggae, rock, jazz, and more.

Malibu Inn 22969 PCH, Malibu ☎310/456-6060. Hardly the place you'd expect to find reggae acts, but this joint offers just that on the weekends, along with rock and rap stylings.

15

Performing arts and film

espite the countless stereotypes about Southern California being a
culture-free zone, in truth the city offers a wealth of **performing arts**
options scattered throughout the basin. While it's true that the city's
range of highbrow cultural offerings was at one time quite limited,
confined to art-house cinemas and a handful of mainstream playhouses, since
then LA has firmly established itself in the performing-arts field thanks to a
renewed push from old-money and corporate interests.

LA boasts a world-class classical-music **orchestra** and conductor, along
with several less-familiar entities like chamber-music groups. The fields of
opera and **dance** are also represented by several noteworthy companies.
Theater is always a growth industry here, with more than a thousand shows
annually (and more than one hundred running at any one time), plenty of
actors to draw from, and a burgeoning audience for both mainstream and
fringe productions. **Cabaret** caters to a select crowd of lounge-entertain-
ment fans, but **comedy** is always a big draw, and it comes as no surprise that
this is one of the prime entertainment options that first-time visitors usually
seek out. Not surprisingly, though, it's **film** that is still the chief cultural
staple of the region, and there is no shortage of excellent theaters in which
to catch a flick.

Classical music

Surprisingly, perhaps, LA's **classical-music** scene has in the last decade
become second to none in the US. Under the guidance of conductor Esa-
Pekka Salonen, and housed in the stunning Disney Hall, the **LA Philharmonic** has come into its own, and should be one of the first highbrow
options people with an interest in the performing arts should seek out. Less
well known, though still intriguing, are the city's smaller performing groups,
which tend to float from art centers to universities to church venues, drawing a loyal, though limited, audience. Your best bet for following the cultural
trends is to watch the press, especially the *LA Times*, for details. In any case,
you can expect to pay from $10 to $120 for most concerts, and more for
really big names.

PERFORMING ARTS AND FILM | Classical music

Classical-music companies

Da Camera Society rotating venues throughout LA ☎213/477-2929, ⓦwww.dacamera.org. This organization's "Chamber Music in Historic Sites" series provides a great opportunity to hear classical, Romantic, and modern chamber works in stunning settings, from grand churches to private homes, including such inspired sites as Doheny Mansion, the *Biltmore* hotel, and the beautiful Canfield-Moreno estate. Ticket prices vary widely, depending on the venue, and can run anywhere from $37 to $100.

Long Beach Symphony Terrace Theater, 300 E Ocean Blvd, Long Beach ☎562/436-3203, ⓦwww.lbso.org. Not quite up to the level of Long Beach Opera, but a light alternative to LA's heavier repertoire, playing mainstream favorites like Tchaikovsky and Beethoven, interspersed with crowd-pleasing pops selections. $12–57.

Los Angeles Chamber Orchestra rotating local venues ☎213/622-7001 ext 215, ⓦwww.laco.org. Appearing at UCLA's Royce Hall and Glendale's Alex Theater on one weekend per month, the orchestra presents a range of chamber works, not all strictly canonical, from different historical eras. Concerts vary widely by price and seating choices. $17–75. (For a monumental interpretation of the orchestra's musicians, check out Kent Twitchell's colossal *Harbor Freeway Overture* mural in Downtown LA; see p.75.)

Los Angeles Master Chorale Disney Hall, Downtown; also at rotating venues ☎1-800/787-LAMC, tickets through Ticketmaster at ☎213/365-3500, ⓦwww.lamc.org. Classic works, along with lighter madrigals and pops favorites, are showcased by this choral institution, now performing in Disney Hall. $20–79.

Los Angeles Philharmonic Disney Hall, Downtown ☎323/850-2000, ⓦwww.laphil.org. The one big name in the city performs regularly during the year at Disney Hall, and conductor Esa-Pekka Salonen always provides a diverse, challenging program, from powerful Romantic works to craggy modern pieces, with regular appearances by celebrity conductors and musicians. Not to be missed if you have even the slightest interest in "longhair" music. $17–120.

Pacific Serenades ☎213/534-3434, ⓦpacser.org. Chamber-music concerts taking place monthly in the LA area, usually at historic sites like the Blacker House in San Marino and Pasadena's Neighborhood Church. $50.

Pacific Symphony Orchestra Orange County Performing Arts Center, 600 Town Center Drive, Costa Mesa ☎714/755-5788 ⓦwww.pacificsymphony.org. Although not as groundbreaking or experimental as the LA Philharmonic, this suburban orchestra nonetheless draws big crowds for its excellent, stylish performances. $20–75.

Pasadena Symphony at Pasadena Civic Auditorium, 300 E Green St ☎626/584-8833, ⓦwww.pasadenasymphony.org. Veering between the standard repertoire and more contemporary pieces, this esteemed symphony provides plenty of artistic sustenance for its audience, performing once a month from October to May. $15–69, $12 for students.

Southwest Chamber Music ☎1-800/726-7147, ⓦwww.swmusic.org. A nationally recognized performing and recording troupe that offers a wide range of music, from medieval to modern. Venues include the wintertime (Oct–May) series at the Norton Simon Museum and Colburn School of Performing Arts, summer concerts at the Huntington Library, and regular open rehearsals at Pasadena's Armory Center. $25; students $10.

Classical-music venues

Alfred Newman Recital Hall on the USC campus, South Central ☎213/740-2584, ⓦwww.usc.edu/music. A fine venue for the Thornton School of Music, with most tickets less than $20 – and even cheaper for students, around $12. During the season (Sept–May), weekly concerts are broadcast on KUSC 91.5 FM and sometimes feature name guest conductors.

Bing Theater 5905 Wilshire Blvd, Mid-Wilshire ☎213/473-8493 or 213/473-0625, ⓦwww.lacma.org. When it isn't hosting movie revivals, this auditorium at the LA County Museum of Art provides a fine space for classical concerts, which occur periodically during the year.

Disney Hall First St at Grand Ave, Downtown ⓦwww.laphil.org/wdch. LA's most renowned cultural attraction (along with the Getty Center) and home of the LA Philharmonic. A striking Frank Gehry design that hosts a range of music and arts groups.

Dorothy Chandler Pavilion at the Music Center, 135 N Grand Ave, Downtown ☎213/972-7211, ⓦwww.musiccenter.org. Long-standing warhorse of the arts community, used by LA Opera and other top names, though no longer the LA Philharmonic.

The Hollywood Bowl 2301 N Highland Ave, Hollywood ☎323/850-2000, ⓦwww.hollywoodbowl .org. Hosts the LA Philharmonic and Hollywood Bowl Orchestra for open-air concerts, usually of the pops variety, Tuesday through Saturday evenings from July to September.

Orange County Performing Arts Center 600 Town Center Drive, Costa Mesa ☎714/556-ARTS, ⓦwww.ocpac.org. Home of the Pacific Symphony Orchestra and Opera Pacific, and also showcasing traveling pop and jazz acts.

Pasadena Civic Auditorium 300 E Green St, Pasadena ☎626/449-7360, ⓦwww.pasadenacal .com/civic.htm. A bit more appealing than it sounds, this 3000-seat municipal hall hosts award shows and the esteemed Pasadena Symphony.

Royce Hall on the UCLA campus in Westwood ☎310/825-9261 or 825-2101, ⓦwww .performingarts.ucla.edu. Classical concerts, often involving big names, occur at this splendid Historic Revival structure throughout the season (Sept–June).

Shrine Auditorium 665 W Jefferson Blvd, South Central ☎213/749-5123; box office at 655 S Hill St. Huge 1926 Moorish-domed curiosity that hosts touring pop acts, choral gospel groups, and countless award shows – though not the Oscars any more.

△ Shrine Auditorium

Topanga Community House 1440 Topanga Canyon Blvd, Santa Monica Mountains ☎818/999-5775, ⓦwww.topangasymphony.8k .com. This low-key concert venue – used also for rock and children's music performances – hosts symphonic and chamber works throughout the year by the Topanga Symphony, often for cheap prices or simply for free.

Opera and dance

Although not quite on the national map yet, **opera** and **dance** in LA can still be quite compelling. The few major opera companies in LA and Orange counties are divided between the old-line institutions that focus on the warhorses of the repertoire and newcomers that make more of an effort to cross artistic boundaries and program contemporary works. Dance performances tend to be grouped around major events, so check cultural listings or call the venues listed below for seasonal information. Otherwise, check for performances at universities like UCLA (☎310/825-4401, ⓦwww.performingarts.ucla.edu), where some of the most exciting names in dance have residencies.

Opera companies and venues

Casa Italiana Opera Company at St Peter's parish church, 1051 N Broadway, Downtown ☎310/451-6012, ⓦwww.casaitaliana.org. About four times during the year, this alternative company stages popular Romantic Italian operas,

from Puccini to Verdi and Mascagni, for very affordable prices. $30–40.

LA Opera at the Music Center, 135 N Grand Ave, Downtown ☎213/972-8001, ⓦwww .losangelesopera.com. With Plácido Domingo at the helm, this institution stages mainstream productions between September and June, from heavy *opera seria* to lighter operettas. The undisputed opera heavyweight in town. $30–190.

Long Beach Opera at the Carpenter Center, 6200 Atherton St ☎562/439-2580, ⓦwww .lbopera.com. Despite being eight years older than the LA Opera, this alternative company presents the freshest and edgiest work in the city, from old pieces by Monteverdi to newer works by modernists like Bartok. Even canonical pieces by Puccini get radically reworked, driving purists to distraction and pleasing most everyone else. $30–120.

Opera Pacific Orange County Performing Arts Center, 600 Town Center Drive, Costa Mesa ☎949/474-4488 or 1-800/34-OPERA, ⓦwww .operapacific.org. Performs mostly mainstream grand opera and tub-thumping operettas. $30–145.

Dance companies and venues

Carpenter Performing Arts Center 6200 Atherton St, on the campus of Cal State Long Beach ☎562/985-7000, ⓦwww.carpenterarts.org. The South Bay's major arts space, hosting the Long Beach Opera and mainstream pop concerts, as well as periodic dance performances and touring arts groups.

Cerritos Center for the Performing Arts 12700 Center Court Drive, Southeast LA ☎1-800/300-4345, ⓦwww.cerritoscenter.com. Located in distant Cerritos on the Orange County border, this is one of LA's better-known and-funded venues, home to mainstream classical, opera,

and dance performances, as well as big-name pop and jazz performers.

Dance Kaleidoscope at John Anson Ford Theatre, 2850 Cahuenga Blvd, Hollywood ☎323/343-5120, ⓦwww.fordamphitheatre.org. The year's major dance event is held over two weeks in July and is organized by the Los Angeles Area Dance Alliance (LAADA), a co-operative supported by LA's smaller dance companies that provides a central source of information on events. Prices vary.

Japan America Theater 244 S San Pedro St, Little Tokyo ☎213/680-3700, ⓦwww.jaccc.org. Intriguing theatrical, dance and performance works drawn from Japan and the Far East, mixing traditional and contemporary styles.

John Anson Ford Theatre 2850 Cahuenga Blvd, Hollywood ☎323/461-3673, ⓦwww .fordamphitheatre.org. Besides the summer "Dance Kaleidoscope," this open-air venue also presents eclectic productions by local groups, as well as summertime chamber music.

Pasadena Dance Theater 1985 Locust Ave, Pasadena ☎626/683-3459, ⓦwww .pasadenadance.org. One of the San Gabriel Valley's more prominent dance venues, hosting diverse groups throughout the year. $20–40.

UCLA Center for the Performing Arts office at 10920 Wilshire Blvd, Westwood ☎310/825-4401, ⓦwww.performingarts.ucla.edu. Features a broad range of touring companies, and runs an "Art of Dance" series between September and June, with an experimental bent.

Theater

LA has an active and energetic **theater** scene. You can expect to find most anything on any given night in one of the city's venues, including huge, Broadway juggernauts, hole-in-the-wall and avant-garde productions, edgy political melodramas, and even revivals of classic works by the likes of Shaw and Ibsen. Aside from the nationally touring megahits, some of the productions to attract the most attention are multicharacter one-person shows and irreverent stagings of canonical works, with Shakespeare often in the cross-hairs.

Since the region is home to a wealth of **film actors**, most of them unemployed in the movie biz, there is always a good pool of thespians for local productions. Depending on the play, you may even find semi-popular TV actors or big celebrity names like Dustin Hoffman on stage, their presence occasionally impromptu and unannounced. While the bigger venues host a predictable array of shopworn musicals and hidebound classics, there are over a hundred "Equity waiver" theaters with fewer than a hundred seats, enabling non-Equity cardholders·to perform. This means a lot of fringe performances take place, for which prices can be very low and the quality can vary greatly – but you may catch an electrifying surprise now and again.

Tickets are less expensive than you might expect: a big show will set you back at least $40, or up to $80 for some blockbusters (matinees are cheaper), with smaller shows around $10 to $25. A quick way through the maze of LA's **theaters** is to phone the **LA Stage Alliance** (☏213/614-0556, ⓦwww .lastagealliance.com) and ask for the availability of discount tickets for a given show, under its LA Stage Tix program.

Major theaters

Actors' Gang Theater 6209 Santa Monica Blvd, Hollywood ☏323/465-0566, ⓦwww .theactorsgang.com. A cross between a major and an alternative theater; having less than a hundred seats keeps it cozy, though it does host the odd spectacular production featuring semi-famous names from film or TV.

Ahmanson Theatre at the Music Center, 135 N Grand Ave, Downtown ☏213/628-2772, ⓦwww .taperahmanson.com. A two-thousand-seat theater hosting colossal traveling shows from Broadway. If you've seen a major production advertised on TV and on the sides of buses, it's probably playing here.

Alex Theatre 216 N Brand Blvd, Glendale ☏818/243-ALEX, ⓦwww.alextheatre.org. A gloriously restored movie palace – with a great neon spike and quasi-Egyptian forecourt – hosting a fine range of musical theater, dance, comedy, and film.

Coronet Theatre 366 N La Cienega Blvd, West Hollywood ☏310/657-7377, ⓦwww .coronet-theatre.com. Home of the LA Public Theater and the Youth Academy of Dramatic Arts; the spot where mid-level Hollywood actors come to test new material before crowds of supportive fans.

Freud Playhouse in MacGowan Hall on the UCLA campus, Westwood ☏310/825-2101, ⓦwww.performingarts.ucla.edu. A nearly six-hundred-seat venue that features a mix of mainstream and contemporary pieces – plus risk-taking experimental works – sometimes with Hollywood up-and-comers or familiar has-beens in the cast.

Geffen Playhouse 10886 Le Conte Ave, Westwood ☏310/208-5454, ⓦwww.geffenplayhouse.com. A 500-seat, Spanish Revival building that often hosts one-person shows. There's a decided Hollywood connection, evident in the crowd-pleasing nature of many of the productions.

International City Theatre 300 E Ocean Ave, Long Beach ☏562/436-4610, ⓦwww.ictlongbeach .com. Part of the Long Beach Performing Arts Center, this is an enjoyable, affordable spot for mainstream comedy and drama. Nothing too challenging, but makes for a reasonably fun night in the South Bay.

Mark Taper Forum at the Music Center, 135 N Grand Ave, Downtown ☏213/972-0700, ⓦwww.taperahmanson.com. Theater in the three-quarter round, with familiar classics and, less frequently, assorted new plays. Don't expect fringe-theater radicalism; this high-culture spot is mostly known for its conservatism and adherence to the mainstream repertoire.

Pantages Theater 6233 Hollywood Blvd, Hollywood ☏323/468-1770, ⓦwww.nederlander .com/wc. Quite the stunner: an exquisite, atmospheric Art Deco theater, in the heart of historic Hollywood, hosting major touring Broadway productions.

Pasadena Playhouse 39 S El Molino Ave, Pasadena ☏626/792-8672 or 356-PLAY, ⓦwww.pasadenaplayhouse.org. A grand old space – also known as the State Theatre of California – that has been refurbished to provide enjoyable mainstream entertainment. Actors are often a mix of youthful professionals and aging TV and movie stars.

Ricardo Montalbán Theatre 1615 N Vine St, Hollywood ☏323/462-6666, ⓦwww .ricardomontalbantheatre.org. The former James Doolittle Theatre now restored and renamed for the classic Latino actor best known as Mr. Roarke from *Fantasy Island*. Presents a range of productions dealing with social politics and ethnic identity, in a classic building in the heart of Hollywood.

South Coast Repertory 655 Town Center Drive, Costa Mesa ☏714/708-5555, ⓦwww .scr.org. Orange County's major entry for theater, where you can watch well-executed performances of the classics on the main stage, and edgier works by new writers on the smaller, 150-seat second stage. Adjacent to the Orange County Performing Arts Center (see p.317).

⑮

A Noise Within 234 S Brand Blvd, Glendale ⓣ818/240-0910, ⓦwww.anoisewithin.org. A very mainstream performance space in downtown Glendale, focusing heavily on the classics, with a strong emphasis on Shakespeare, Molière, and the like.

Actors Forum Theatre 10655 Magnolia Blvd, North Hollywood ⓣ818/506-0600, ⓦwww .actorsforumtheatre.org. Unpredictable venue that hosts a range of topical dramas, one-person shows, and the odd production from nontraditional actors and playwrights. Dramatic workshops are also offered.

The Complex 6476 Santa Monica Blvd, Hollywood ⓣ323/465-0383. A group of alternative theaters west of Cahuenga Blvd, revolving around a group of six small theaters, where you're likely to see any number of dynamic productions.

Evidence Room 2220 Beverly Blvd, Mid-Wilshire ⓣ213/381-7118, ⓦwww.evidenceroom.com. Edgy, startling works, alternated with more conventional modern dramas and comedies. Call to confirm listings and venue space.

Gascon Center Theater 8737 Washington Blvd, Culver City ⓣ310/204-3126. Comedy and satire are frequently on the bill at this venue in the former Helms Bakery; despite its location outside Hollywood, this theater offers as many interesting plays and skilled actors as anywhere in LA.

Highways 1651 18th St, Santa Monica ⓣ310/453-3711, ⓦwww.18thstreet.org. Located in the 18th Street Arts Complex, an adventurous performance space that offers a range of topical drama and politically charged productions, with a strong bent toward the angry, polemical, and subversive.

Hudson Mainstage Theatre 6539 Santa Monica Blvd, Hollywood ⓣ323/856-4252, ⓦwww .hudsontheatre.com. Socially conscious "message" plays alternate with more satiric, comedic works at this venue for upcoming actors. Complex consists of four stages, each with less than a hundred seats, plus a coffeehouse.

Knightsbridge Theatre 1944 Riverside Drive, Glendale ⓣ626/440-0821, ⓦwww .knightsbridgetheatre.com. On the edge of Griffith Park, Knightsbridge is a prime spot for classical theater, from Shakespeare to Molière. While you won't recognize most of the names in the cast, you'll likely enjoy the fresh spins on familiar standards.

Lee Strasberg Creative Center 7936 Santa Monica Blvd, West Hollywood ⓣ323/650-7777, ⓦwww.strasberg.com. Although Method acting as once taught by the master Strasberg is plentiful here – as well as a few stars in the crowd – all types of plays are performed.

Lonnie Chapman Group Repertory 10900 Burbank Blvd, North Hollywood ⓣ818/769-PLAY. A troupe that tends toward plays involving dark and heavy social themes – though some musicals and comedies are staged, too.

Los Angeles Theatre Center 514 S Spring St, Downtown ⓣ213/485-1681. A centerpiece of the Old Bank District that's had its ups and downs, and offers irregular performances of modern works in its four theaters. Check listings, as performances are only periodic.

Matrix Theater 7657 Melrose Ave ⓣ323/852-1445. Melrose theater offering excellent, uncompromising productions that often feature some of LA's better young actors and playwrights.

Odyssey Theater Ensemble 2055 S Sepulveda Blvd, West LA ⓣ310/477-2055, ⓦwww .odysseytheatre.com. Well-respected Westside theater company with a modernist bent, offering a range of quality productions on three stages for decent prices.

Open Fist Theatre 1625 N La Brea Ave, Hollywood ⓣ323/882-6912, ⓦwww.openfist.org. As you might expect from the name, biting and edgy works are often the focus at this small theater company, employing a limited cast of spirited unknowns – though sometimes with larger names dropping in.

Pacific Resident Theatre 703 Venice Blvd, Venice ⓣ310/822-8392, ⓦwww.pacificresidenttheatre .com. Good mix of productions, leaning toward the classics, at this compelling small venue. A ways from the center of the theater action, but worth a visit if you like old-fashioned drama.

Powerhouse Theatre 3116 Second St, Santa Monica ⓣ310/396-3680, ⓦwww .powerhousetheatre.com. On the border of Venice, this alternative theater presents risk-taking experimental shows; perhaps the best of its kind in town. Located in a former electrical station for the old Red Car transit line.

Stages Theatre Center 1540 N McCadden Place, Hollywood ⓣ323/465-1010, ⓦwww .stagestheatrecenter.com. With three stages offering twenty to one hundred seats, this is an excellent place to catch a wide range of comedies and dramas, including re-stagings of canonical works and contemporary productions.

Theatre West 3333 Cahuenga Blvd W, Hollywood ☎323/851-7977, ⊛www.theatrewest.org. A favorite venue that's always a good spot to see inventive, sometimes odd, productions, with a troupe of excellent young up-and-comers.

Theatricum Botanicum 1419 N Topanga Canyon Blvd, Topanga Canyon ☎310/455-3723, ⊛www.theatricum.com. Terrific spot showing a range of classic (often Shakespeare) and modern plays amid an idyllic outdoor setting. Founded by Will Geer – TV's Grandpa Walton.

Zephyr Theater 7456 Melrose Ave ☎323/653-4667. Although featuring a range of acting troupes and plays, shows here lean toward socially relevant, issue-related content, occasionally with a bit of irreverence.

Comedy

LA has a wide range of **comedy** clubs. While rising stars and beginners can be spotted on the "underground" open-mike scene, most of the famous comics, both stand-up and improv, appear at the more established clubs in Hollywood, West LA, or the valleys. These venues usually have a bar, charge a $10–15 cover, and put on two shows per evening, generally starting at 8pm and 10.30pm – the later one being more popular. The better-known places are open nightly, but are often solidly booked on weekends.

Acme Comedy Theater 135 N La Brea Ave, Mid-Wilshire ☎323/525-0202, ⊛www.acmecomedy.com. A fancy venue with mostly sketch and improv comedy, as well as variety shows. $10–15.

Bang Theater 457 N Fairfax Ave, Mid-Wilshire ☎323/653-6886, ⊛www.bangstudio.com. One-person shows and long-form improvisation are the specialties at this small theater/comedy club, with the popular shows running on weekends. Cover often around $10.

Comedy & Magic Club 1018 Hermosa Ave, Hermosa Beach ☎310/372-1193, ⊛www.comedyandmagicclub.info. Strange couplings of magic and comedy; Jay Leno sometimes tests material here. Tickets can run up to $25, depending on the performer.

Comedy Store 8433 W Sunset Blvd, West Hollywood ☎323/656-6225, ⊛www.thecomedystore.com. LA's premier comedy showcase and popular enough to be spread over three rooms – which means there's usually space, even at weekends. Run by Pauly Shore's mom. $10–20.

Empty Stage 2372 Veteran Ave, West LA ☎310/470-3560, ⊛www.emptystage.com. Sometimes funny, sometimes irritating sketch comedy that draws upon long improv routines, with the odd short comic play as well. Cast mainly with up-and-comers of varying hilarity. $8–15.

Groundlings Theater 7307 Melrose Ave ☎323/934-9700, ⊛www.groundlings.com. Another pioneering venue where only the

gifted survive, with furious improv events and high-wire comedy acts that can inspire greatness or groans. $12–20.

Ha Ha Café 5010 Lankershim Blvd, North Hollywood ☎818/508-4995, ⊛www.hahacafe.com. Amateur and even a few professional comedians face off for your amusement nightly, at this combination comedy club and café space around the NoHo Arts District. $15.

The Ice House 24 N Mentor Ave, Pasadena ☎626/577-1894, ⊛www.icehousecomedy.com. The comedy mainstay of the Valley, very established and fairly safe; often amusing, with plenty of old names and the occasional big name. $10–20 cover.

Improv Olympic West 6366 Santa Monica Blvd, Hollywood ☎323/962-7560, ⊛www.iowest.com. In the heart of old Hollywood, a spot for those who like their improv drawn out and elaborate, with comedy routines more like short theater pieces than a set of wacky one-liners. $10.

The Improvisation 8162 Melrose Ave, Mid-Wilshire ☎323/651-2583, ⊛www.improv.com. Long-standing brick-walled joint known for hosting some of the best acts working in the area in both stand-up and improv. One of LA's top comedy spots, and the fore runner of a national chain of such clubs – so book ahead. $10–20.

LA Connection 13442 Ventura Blvd, Sherman Oaks ☎818/784-1868, ⊛www.laconnectioncomedy.com. Cozy space for sketch comedy, group antics, and individual jokesters. Seldom less than memorable. $10.

LA TheatreSports 11050 Magnolia Blvd, North Hollywood ☏ 323/401-6162, ⓦ www .theatresports.com. As you might guess, comedy competitions here are arranged like sports contests, with plenty of feedback from the audience and all kinds of high-spirited theatrics. Operates a school of comedy and offers lessons in being funny. $8–10.

The Laugh Factory 8001 Sunset Blvd, West Hollywood ☏ 323/656-1336, ⓦ www .laughfactory.com. Nightly stand-ups of varying standards and reputation, with the odd big name. Features a variable open-mike night. $10–15.

Second City Studio Theatre 8156 Melrose Ave, Hollywood ☏ 323/651-2583 ext 176. Connected to the *Improv*, with nightly sketch comedy, sometimes built around lengthy routines and theme performances. Mostly up-and-comers.

Cabaret

LA's **cabaret** scene is a favorite hangout for some SoCal hipsters, with the rediscovery of lounge music attracting a young, trendy crowd (as well as the requisite grizzled old-timers and lounge lizards). The food at most of the venues leaves much to be desired, but it hardly matters to those who attend. Most of the best and biggest cabarets are in Hollywood.

Canter's Kibitz Room 419 N Fairfax Ave, Mid-Wilshire ☏ 323/651-2030. Located next to *Canter's Deli*, this is one of the more bizarre versions of cabaret in LA, featuring an assortment of pop, rock, and jazz artists – as well as audience members on open-mike nights – performing in a retro-1950s lounge space. Free.

Cinegrill 7000 Hollywood Blvd, Hollywood ☏ 323/466-7000, ⓦ www.hollywoodroosevelt .com. Housed in the beautifully restored landmark *Roosevelt Hotel* and still the biggest name in LA cabaret, offering an assortment of mostly mainstream jazz and cabaret acts. You'll pay for their reputation, though: $25–40, plus food-and-drink minimum of $10–25.

The Dresden Room 1760 N Vermont Ave, Hollywood ☏ 323/665-4294, ⓦ www.thedresden .com. Little-known singers doing your favorite easy-listening covers from Wayne Newton to Tom Jones on Tuesday nights (see "Bars," p.300), as well as a regular husband-and-wife lounge act the rest of the time. Another joint made popular by the film *Swingers*. Free cover, but two-drink minimum.

Gardenia Lounge 7066 Santa Monica Blvd, Hollywood ☏ 323/467-7444. Straight-up jazz and adult contemporary tunes presented to a gracious crowd nightly. The odd comedian provides some variation, but music is the real attraction. $10–15, plus two-drink minimum.

Largo 432 N Fairfax Ave, Mid-Wilshire ☏ 323/852-1073. Intimate cabaret venue

that features a colorful range of singers and acts on periodic nights, along with some of LA's more unusual live bands (though mostly jazz, rock, and pop). Cover varies.

Masquers Cabaret 8334 W Third St, Mid-Wilshire ☏ 323/653-4848, ⓦ www.masquerscabaret.com. Zany comedies, slap-dash variety acts, and energetic drag queens at this spirited nightly dinner theater near the Beverly Center mall. Although not always successful, the performers here rarely give up on trying to amuse the crowd. $7–15.

Parlour Club 7702 Santa Monica Blvd ☏ 323/650-7968. West Hollywood spot that offers music and performance art, plus bizarre weekend karaoke hosted by local crooners, drag queens, and anyone else with a yen for belting out tunes. $5.

San Gennaro 9543 Culver Blvd, Culver City ☏ 310/836-0400. On weekends, prepare yourself for loving tributes to Ol' Blue Eyes at this swinging "cigar lounge." Along with hearing Sinatra covers, listen to slick crooners belting out favorites from Dean Martin, Tom Jones, and other Vegas acts. $10; two drinks included.

vermont 1714 N Vermont Ave ☏ 323/661-6163. Chic Cal-cuisine restaurant plays host to Monday-night open-mike cabaret, with a mix of slumming pros and (more commonly) ear-jangling, would-be Streisands screeching to hit the high notes. $5.

Vitello's 4349 Tujunga Ave, Studio City ☏ 818/769-0905. Broadway toe-tappers and operatic showstoppers are the norm in this cozy lounge with decent singers, passable Italian food, and just the right sort of funky, downmarket atmosphere. Wed & Fri–Sun; $10 minimum food and drink purchase.

Film

Feature **films** are typically released in LA months (or years) before they play anywhere else in the world, sometimes only showing here and nowhere else. A huge number of cinemas focus on new releases, though there are also plenty of venues for silver-screen classics, independent or art-house films, and foreign movies. Tickets tend to be around $7–10, with cheaper prices for matinees and repertory screenings (around $5–7). **Drive-ins** are rare these days; the ones that still exist are littered with weeds and offer dilapidated sound systems, and are located in distant burgs miles from anywhere you might want to find yourself.

For **cheap** or **free films**, the USC campus often has interesting free screenings aimed at film students (announced on campus notice-boards), and UCLA's James Bridges Theater shows films drawn from the school's extensive archive (☎310/206-FILM or ✆www.cinema.ucla.edu).

Of the countless venues for **mainstream cinema**, the most notable are in Westwood and Hollywood. For **art houses** and **revival theaters**, there are a few worthwhile choices, some of them surprisingly sited in massive shopping complexes, but mostly scattered across the Westside. Finally, the grand **movie palaces** described elsewhere in this guide are here listed only as to their value as actual movie theaters, as many others have been converted into performing-arts venues, music halls, churches or, depressingly, swap meets and flea markets. The still-functional ones Downtown are still open, once a year in June, for the "Last Remaining Seats" festival (see p.343), run by the LA Conservancy, which you should catch if you have the chance.

Mainstream cinema

AMC Century 14 in the Century City mall, 10250 Santa Monica Blvd, Century City ☎310/553-8900. Never mind that it's in a mall – this is one of the best places to see new films in LA. The theaters are somewhat boxy, but if you're after crisp projection, booming sound, comfy seating, and a rapt crowd, there are few better choices.
Beverly Cineplex in the Beverly Center mall, Beverly and La Cienega blvds, Mid-Wilshire ☎310/777-FILM. An enterprisingly programmed venue, with fourteen small screens showing a mix of artsy, independent film programs and first-run blockbusters.
Bruin 948 Broxton Ave, Westwood ☎310/208-8998. While smaller than it used to be, thanks to aggressive remodelling, this 1930s moviehouse remains a city landmark for its wraparound marquee and sleek Moderne styling.
Cinerama Dome 6360 Sunset Blvd, Hollywood ☎323/466-3401 or 464-4226. This white hemisphere has the biggest screen in California, a giant curved panel with slight distortion at the corners. Now part of a larger complex of theaters and shops called ArcLight.
Crest 1262 Westwood Blvd, Westwood ☎310/474-7866. A riot of neon and flashing lights outside, with glowing murals of Old Hollywood inside. Typically shows Disney flicks.
Fairfax 7907 Beverly Blvd, Mid-Wilshire ☎323/655-4010. Three screens and great old decor, refurbished for independent and art films; located in the middle of the Fairfax District.
Fine Arts 8556 Wilshire Blvd, Beverly Hills ☎310/652-1330. Proof that modern moviehouses don't necessarily have to be ugly concrete boxes. The simple exterior and lobby give way to a grandly opulent 1936 theater showing a mix of mainstream and art-house films.
IMAX Theater 600 State Drive, at the California Science Center in Exposition Park ☎213/744-2015. Six-story, hemispheric screen showing short, eye-popping documentaries,

including the occasional 3-D presentation. Presents mostly science and nature films; though somewhat tedious, the monumental programs never fail to draw sizable crowds of kids and tourists.

National 10925 Lindbrook Drive, Westwood ⊤310/208-4366. In every way a period piece from the 1960s, this giant, curvaceous theater is another solid Westwood venue in the Mann theater chain.

One Colorado 42 Miller Alley, Pasadena ⊤626/744-1224. Comfortable Old Pasadena venue showing a mix of mainstream and independent productions; convenient for shopping and dining, too.

Regent 1045 Broxton Ave, Westwood ⊤310/208-3259. Recently restored by the Landmark chain, a fine old favorite for a mainstream flick, in the heart of a neighborhood teeming with great movie theaters.

Universal Cinemas end of Universal City Drive, Burbank ⊤818/508-0588. This eighteen-screen complex at Universal CityWalk is one of LA's better multiplexes, a plush complex that includes a pair of pseudo-Parisian cafés. Despite all the screens, though, only five or six films are typically shown, with multiple theaters reserved for each.

Village 961 Broxton Ave, Westwood ⊤310/208-5576. One of the most enjoyable places to watch a movie in LA, with a giant screen, fine seats, good balcony views, and a modern sound system; it's a frequent spot for Hollywood premieres. Come early and take a look at the marvelous 1931 exterior, particularly the white spire on top.

Arthouses and revival theaters

Aero 1328 Montana Ave, Santa Monica ⊤310/395-4990, ⊛www.aerotheatre.com. Thanks to the American Cinematheque film organization, you can watch classic and art-house movies in this fine old venue from 1940 (often the same fare playing at the organization's Egyptian; see opposite). The fare is eclectic and intelligently programmed.

Bing at the LA County Art Museum, 5905 Wilshire Blvd, Mid-Wilshire ⊤323/857-6010. Offers afternoon screenings of Warner Bros classics for just $3, as well as full-priced evening programs of classic, independent, foreign, art-house, and revival cinema.

Los Feliz 1822 N Vermont Ave, Hollywood ⊤323/664-2169. Having successfully avoided

a descent into the porn-movie market in the 1960s, this theater's three small screens now show international and low-budget American independent fare.

Monica 4-Plex 1332 Second St, Santa Monica ⊤310/394-9741. Although the Third Street Promenade has some big houses showing mainstream schlock, this is the closest nearby theater (a block away) where you're apt to see something decent, featuring a mix of indie and art-house fare.

New Beverly Cinema 7165 Beverly Blvd, Mid-Wilshire ⊤323/938-4038. Not a particularly attractive theater, but a worthwhile one for its excellent art films and revival screenings, with some imaginative double bills.

Nuart 11272 Santa Monica Blvd, West LA ⊤310/478-6379. Showing rarely seen classics, documentaries, and edgy foreign-language films, this is the main option for independent filmmakers testing their work, and sometimes offers brief December previews of Oscar contenders weeks or months before they're released nationwide. Be prepared to wait outside the theater in a lengthy line near the 405 freeway.

NuWilshire 1314 Wilshire Blvd, Santa Monica ⊤310/394-8099. With a solid booking policy, this is one of LA's better venues for art and foreign films, located a mile east of Palisades Park.

Old Town Music Hall 140 Richmond St, El Segundo ⊤310/322-2592, ⊛www.otmh.org. An old-fashioned spot to see historic movies, with accompanying organ or piano music on some nights, this quaint theater is unfortunately sited in a grim industrial location south of LAX.

Royal 11523 Santa Monica Blvd, West LA ⊤310/477-5581. Though it doesn't quite live up to its regal name, this is still a prime spot for independent fare, with one spacious, classically ornamented theater.

Silent Movie 611 N Fairfax Ave, Mid-Wilshire ⊤323/655-2520, ⊛www.silentmovietheatre .com. Offers an enjoyable mix of silent comedies and adventure flicks – Douglas Fairbanks swashbucklers and the like – along with darker fare like Fritz Lang's *Metropolis* and even the occasional talkie.

Sunset 5 8000 Sunset Blvd, West Hollywood ⊤323/848-3500. This arthouse complex sits on the second floor of the Sunset Plaza outdoor mall – former site of the legendary *Schwab's* drugstore – and shows a good assortment of edgy, independent flicks.

Vista 4473 Sunset Drive, Hollywood ☎ 323/660-6639. A nicely renovated moviehouse with very eclectic offerings – from mindless action flicks to micro-budgeted indie productions – located near the intersection of Sunset and Hollywood boulevards.

Westside Pavilion Cinemas in the Westside Pavilion mall, 10800 Pico Blvd, West LA ☎ 310/475-0202. Something of a surprise: one of the city's better art-houses located on the third floor of a huge mall. Four screens, plus free parking.

Movie palaces

Avalon 1 Casino Way, Santa Catalina Island ☎ 310/510-0179. Located in the stunning Casino building, this great old moviehouse is a riot of mermaid murals, gold-leaf motifs, and an overall design sometimes called "Aquarium Deco." Also presents a yearly silent-film fest.

Chinese 6925 Hollywood Blvd, Hollywood ☎ 323/464-8111. With its large main screen, six-track stereo sound, and wild chinoiserie design, this Hollywood icon shows relentlessly mainstream films, but is still worthy of all the postcard images. Has recently and unfortunately been incorporated into the design of a giant adjacent shopping mall.

Egyptian 6712 Hollywood Blvd, Hollywood ☎ 323/466-FILM, ⊛ www.americancinematheque .com. Thanks to the American Cinematheque film group, this historic 1922 moviehouse has nightly showings of revival, experimental and art films, and has been lovingly restored as a kitschy masterpiece of the Egyptian Revival – all grand columns, winged scarabs, and mythological gods. During the day, a PR film about Hollywood is shown to tourists.

El Capitan 6834 Hollywood Blvd, Hollywood ⓘ 323/467-7674. Whether or not you enjoy the typically kiddie-oriented fare offered here – thanks to its Disney ownership – the restored splendor of this classic Hollywood movie palace is bound to impress you.

Los Angeles 615 S Broadway, Downtown ☎ 213/623-CITY. Boasting an exquisite French Second Empire lobby, with triumphal arches lined by marble columns supporting an intricate mosaic ceiling, and an 1800-seat auditorium enveloped by

trompe l'oeil murals. One of the all-time great moviehouses in the country, though only periodically open to the public. You can get a glimpse inside on Los Angeles Conservancy tours (see "City tours," p.40) or during the Last Remaining Seats film festival in June (tickets $20 per film; call ☎ 213/623-CITY for details).

Orpheum 842 S Broadway, Downtown ☎ 213/239-0939. Recently renovated, a spellbinding mix of French Renaissance and Baroque decor, with a pipe organ, brazen chandeliers, ornamental grotesques, nude nymphs, and grand arches in gold-leaf. Visible during the Last Remaining Seats festival, but also for periodic film and performing-arts events.

Palace 630 S Broadway, Downtown ☎ 213/688-6166. Sports mock-Venetian architecture galore, with gilded Corinthian columns, splendid Baroque arches and ornament, and an imitation Tiepolo hanging near the movie screen. Slated for renovation at some point.

Rialto 1023 Fair Oaks Ave, South Pasadena ☎ 626/799-9567. A 1925 movie palace that also served as a theatrical stage and vaudeville locale, with Moorish organ screens, Egyptian columns, winged harpies, and a central Medusa-head. Having survived numerous demolition threats over the years, the theater is now a historic landmark.

State 703 S Broadway, Downtown ☎ 213/239-0962. Once the jewel of MGM's theaters, a colossus with nearly 2400 seats and a staggering display of Spanish Renaissance and Baroque designs with copious mythological ornament, intricate friezes, and two prominent pseudo-opera boxes on the sides. Now a church, though it hosts occasional films and public events.

Warner Grand 478 W Sixth St, San Pedro ☎ 310/548-7672, ⊛ www.warnergrand.org. Definitely worth a trip down to the LA Harbor to see the glory of this restored 1931 Zigzag Moderne masterpiece, with its dark geometric details, majestic columns, and sunburst motifs – a style that almost looks pre-Columbian. Having fallen into disuse for many years, the theater is now a repertory cinema and performing-arts hall.

⑮

PERFORMING ARTS AND FILM | Film

16

Gay and lesbian LA

A lthough nowhere near as nationally prominent as San Francisco's, LA's **gay and lesbian scene** is similarly well-established, and the city as a whole is generally quite welcoming in its urban core and inner suburbs (though the further into the exurbs you go, the less tolerance you'll find). The best known gay-friendly area is the city of **West Hollywood**, which has become synonymous with the (affluent, white) gay lifestyle, not just in LA but all over California. Santa Monica Boulevard, east of Doheny Drive, in particular has a wide range of restaurants, shops, and bars aimed at gay men, though less flashy lesbian-oriented businesses can also be found here and there. West Hollywood is also the site of the exuberant **Gay Pride Parade**, held annually in June. Another well-established gay and lesbian community is **Silver Lake**, home to the gay-oriented bars and restaurants of Hyperion Boulevard, and with more of a Hispanic feel along Sunset Boulevard. Even Orange County has its pockets of gay and lesbian culture, centered mainly around the coast, and especially the upscale confines of **Laguna Beach** and its trendy restaurants and bars.

Gay couples will find themselves readily accepted at most LA **hotels**, but there are a few that cater especially to gay travelers and can also be useful sources of information on the scene in general. Listed below, too, are **restaurants**, **bars**, and **clubs** that cater to gay men and lesbians.

The most-read local publication, though it's also distributed nationally, is *The Advocate* (@www.advocate.com), a bimonthly gay news magazine with features, general information, and classified ads. Other gay-oriented publications feature weekly club and event listings, community information and topical articles, and can be found at eateries and retailers around LA – often for free.

Accommodation

See the box on p.246 for information on accommodation pricing.

Coral Sands 1730 N Western Ave, Hollywood ☎1-800/467-5141, @www.coralsands-la.com. Cruisy spot exclusively geared towards gay men. All rooms face the inner courtyard pool. Also with on-site sauna, Jacuzzi, and gym. $80.
Holloway Motel 8465 Santa Monica Blvd, West Hollywood ☎323/654-2454, @www.hollowaymotel.com. Typical clean roadside motel, if rather dreary looking. Comes with

complimentary breakfast. Add $50 during key holidays like Halloween and Gay Pride. $95.
Hollywood Metropolitan 5825 Sunset Blvd ☎323/962-5800, @www.metropolitanhotel.com. Spanish-style hotel with a mix of small, comfortable rooms and larger suites, featuring the *Havana on Sunset* restaurant on site. Just off the 101 freeway. $90.

AIDS Project Los Angeles 611 S Kingsley Drive, Hollywood ☎213/201-1600, ⓦ www.apla.org. Sponsors fundraisers throughout the year and a well-attended annual walkathon. Office open Tues, Wed & Fri 10am–5pm.

A Different Light 8853 Santa Monica Blvd, West Hollywood ☎310/854-6601, ⓦ www.adlbooks .com. The city's best-known gay and lesbian bookstore, with monthly art shows, readings, music events, and comfortable chairs for lounging.

Gay and Lesbian Community Services Center 1625 N Schrader Blvd, Hollywood ☎323/993-7400, ⓦ www.laglc.org. Counseling, health-testing, and information. Publishes *The Center News*, a bimonthly magazine. Open Mon–Fri 9am–9pm, Sat 9am–1pm.

Gay Community Yellow Pages 1604 Vista Del Mar Ave, Hollywood 90028 ☎323/469-4454. Gay businesses, publications, and services are listed yearly. Available all over LA.

One Institute and Archives 909 W Adams Blvd, South Central LA ☎213/741-0094, ⓦ www.oneinstitute .org. The world's biggest library of rare books and magazines, literature, artworks, and related information on gay and lesbian culture, social issues and politics, with a collection of materials numbering in the thousands. Open Tues & Wed 3.30–9pm, Thurs & Fri 1.30–5.30pm, Sat 11am–3pm.

Ramada Inn 8585 Santa Monica Blvd, West Hollywood ☎310/652-6400 or 1-800/845-8585, ⓦ www.thegayhotel.com. The self-styled "Gay Hotel," a modern place with clean and comfortable rooms, plus pool and gym, in the center of the community. $120.

San Vicente Inn 854 N San Vicente Blvd, West Hollywood ☎310/854-6915, ⓦ www.gayresort .com/sanvicenteinn. Small and comfortable bed-and-breakfast located just north of Santa Monica Boulevard, with pool, spa, and sauna. $119 per night, $150 with private bath.

Restaurants and cafés

Champagne French Bakery 8917 Santa Monica Blvd, West Hollywood ☎310/657-4051. Convenient bakery and coffee shop with serviceable pastries and baked treats in a central location – good for an inexpensive breakfast or lunch on the main drag.

Coffee Table 2930 Rowena Ave, Los Feliz ☎323/644-8111. A neighborhood coffeehouse with low-fat sandwiches and health food, mixed with a smattering of tasty desserts.

Fat Fish 616 N Robertson Blvd, West Hollywood ☎310/659-3882. Housed in the former *Cobalt Cantina* space, an enjoyable and upscale pan-Asian and Cal-cuisine restaurant with inventive cocktails, good sushi, and better ribs than you'd expect.

French Quarter 7985 Santa Monica Blvd, West Hollywood ☎310/654-0898. Inside the French Market Place, a New Orleans–themed restaurant that can be at least as much fun as Disneyland, with food that's more tasty than it is authentic at moderate prices.

Golden Bull 170 W Channel Rd, Pacific Palisades ☎310/230-0402. Enjoyable and expensive steak-and-seafood restaurant and bar that makes for a relaxed atmosphere near the ocean, not far from Santa Monica.

Marix Tex-Mex Playa 118 Entrada Drive, Pacific Palisades ☎310/459-8596. Flavorful fajitas and big margaritas in this rowdy beachfront cantina, which attracts mixed gay and straight crowds. An even livelier branch at 1108 N Flores St, West Hollywood ☎323/656-8800.

Mark's 861 N La Cienega Blvd, West Hollywood ☎310/652-5252. High-end establishment serving Cal-cuisine, with especially good crab cakes, *osso bucco*, and Australian lamb chops.

Numbers 8741 Santa Monica Blvd, West Hollywood ☎320/652-7700. Second-story mid-priced bar and restaurant with Continental and California cuisines, with a nice view overlooking the city.

(16)

GAY AND LESBIAN LA | Restaurants and cafés

Woody's at the Beach 1305 S Coast Hwy, Laguna Beach ☎949/376-8809. Upscale bar and restaurant in Orange County serving quality California cuisine to a fairly well-heeled clientele.

Yukon Mining Co 7328 Santa Monica Blvd, West Hollywood ☎323/851-8833. Colorful 24hr coffee shop where you're likely to see local drag queens, newly arrived Russians, and neighborhood pensioners.

Bars and clubs

Mid-Wilshire

Faultline 4216 Melrose Ave ☎323/660-0889. Hardcore denim-and-leather scene with plenty of frenetic action inside, including driving house beats and testosterone-fueled mayhem.

Jewel's Catch One 4067 W Pico Blvd ☎323/734-8849. Longtime favorite on the local club scene, a sweaty barn catering to a mixed crowd and covering two wild dance floors.

The Plaza 739 N La Brea Ave ☎323/939-0703. Nondescript joint hosts wild, mind-blowing drag shows to a multiethnic, mostly gay crowd.

Silver Lake

Akbar 4356 Sunset Blvd ☎323/665-6810. A mellow and unpretentious Silver Lake watering hole that draws a diverse, bohemian crowd, including a loyal coterie of gay visitors. Also presents occasional comedy and fringe theater events. No cover.

Cobalt 4326 Sunset Blvd ☎323/953-9991. A low-key, elegant bar and restaurant where the stylish interior and well-scrubbed yuppie patrons contrast dramatically with the grungy neighborhood outside. Two-for-one drinks are available during the 5–7pm happy hour.

Cuffs 1941 Hyperion Ave ☎323/660-2649. As the name would suggest, the action here can get pretty heavy – which gives this gay-male-oriented spot quite a reputation. Friday nights bring "Hanky Panky," recalling the antique days of color-coded hankerchiefs.

Dragstrip 66 at the Echo, 1151 Glendale Blvd ☎323/969-2596. Every second Saturday of the month, it's time to "dress up, drag down" to this crazy crossdressing night, throbbing to the sound of dance tunes, euro-disco, and whatever else makes the pulse pound. $15.

Le Bar 2375 Glendale Blvd ☎323/660-7595. Quiet and welcoming bar in a bland section of Silver Lake. Not as much attitude as with some West Hollywood spots. No cover.

MJ's 2810 Hyperion Ave ☎323/660-1503. Favorite neighborhood hangout that has a diverse set of gay-male customers, along with a few bohemian straights from the neighborhood.

Hollywood and West Hollywood

7969 7969 Santa Monica Blvd ☎323/654-0280. Legendary club back in business after closing due to fire, and offering high-energy dance tunes, frenetic DJs, and colorful theme-party nights.

Arena 6655 Santa Monica Blvd ☎323/462-0714. A longtime gay hangout for its funk, trance, and house grooves, as well as the occasional live band. Also at the same address, *Circus* (☎323/462-1291) has electronica dance nights and eye-opening weekend drag shows. Cover can reach $20 or more.

The Factory 652 N La Peer Drive ☎310/659-4551. DJs spin house music most nights of the week at what is one of West Hollywood's more popular clubs.

Micky's 8857 Santa Monica Blvd ☎310/657-1176. Lively, pulsating scene with a full range of club nights, including the usual retro-70s and -80s dance-pop, thundering house and hip-hop beats, and twice-weekly drag shows. 18 and over.

Miyagi's 8225 Sunset Blvd ☎323/650-3524. Three-story dance club that also hosts a frenetic scene for its house and electronica sounds, free-spirited crowd, five liquor bars, and decent Japanese menu – served at seven sushi bars around this giant space.

Mother Lode 8944 Santa Monica Blvd ☎310/659-9700. Strong drinks, wild dancing to house and hi-NRG music, and periodic drag antics make this one of the more colorful area clubs.

Normandie Room 8737 Santa Monica Blvd, West Hollywood ☎310/659-6204. Long-standing, if smallish, lesbian hangout that draws a big weekend crowd for its stiff drinks, pool table, and relaxed neighborhood vibe.

The Palms 8572 Santa Monica Blvd ☎310/652-6188. Mostly house and pop-music dance nights at West Hollywood's most estab-lished lesbian bar, which increasingly caters to a mixed crowd.

Rage 8911 Santa Monica Blvd ☎310/652-7055. Very flashy gay-men's club playing the latest in house music. Also with drag comedy. Drinks are fairly cheap.

Ultra Suede 661 N Robertson Blvd ☎310/659-4551. Featuring various clubs where a mixed gay and straight crowd gyrates to new wave, rock, house, and retro-pop music. Hosts "Girl Bar" on Friday night for lesbians.

The valleys and Orange County

Apache 11608 Ventura Blvd, Studio City ☎818/506-0404. San Fernando Valley club that offers $2 well drinks during happy hour and hosts regular theme dance parties, with electronica, retro-disco, and garage among the musical offerings.

Boom Boom Room 1401 S Coast Hwy, Laguna Beach ☎949/494-7588. The pulse-pounding name says it all: house and disco tunes spun by local DJs on weekends, male strip shows, and all kinds of other colorful performances and spectacles.

Oil Can Harry's 11501 Ventura Blvd, Studio City ☎818/760-9749. Engaging San Fernando Valley club with a mix of theme nights, including country-and-western line dancing, 1970s disco, a leather scene, and more.

Ozz Supper Club 6231 Manchester Blvd, Buena Park ☎714/522-1542. A lively dance club with booming house, disco, and salsa music on the weekends and assorted drag shows, cabaret music, and lounge performers as well. A gay standout in this Orange County burg.

17

Sports and outdoor activities

enowned for its sun and surf, Los Angeles has plenty of **sports** and **outdoor activities** to keep you occupied, wherever your interests may lie. While LA doesn't have the same die-hard enthusiasm for its **spectator sports** as does, say, New York or Chicago, Angelenos still often make a good showing at basketball, baseball, and hockey games, as well as college football, with the hometown USC Trojans claiming back-to-back national titles for the 2003–4 seasons. If seeing games in person isn't your idea of fun, there are always **sports bars** where you can catch your favorite team on television and knock back a few brews as well.

Regardless of the local interest in team sports, it's obvious that participatory sports like **surfing** are what most often define LA to the rest of the world, along with more self-conscious pursuits like bodybuilding. Much of the stereotype of Southern California as a body-fixated culture can be depressingly accurate at times, but with the right pastime, you can usually enjoy yourself without concern for the correct clothes, attitude, or abs.

Water and **beach sports** are still the city's main claims to fame, be they swimming or surfing along the coast, snorkeling or scuba diving around Santa Catalina Island, or even kayaking and jet-skiing. If you'd rather not get wet, you can always try a bit of in-line skating, skateboarding, or bicycling along strips like the Venice Boardwalk, or simply suntanning at the beach – always a good choice for making an impression in the land of well-bronzed movie stars and celebrities. For less earthbound thrills, **airborne activities** include ballooning above the LA basin, hang gliding off precarious seaside cliffs, or just traveling safely in a helicopter tour. For more of a physical jump-start, there are many **fitness sports** to make you gasp and sweat, including jogging, rock climbing, and hiking – not to mention hanging out in one of the city's many fitness clubs. Just as strenuous, **skiing** and **snowboarding** are both possible in the mountains east of LA, especially around the Big Bear region, a favorite weekend getaway for many locals. If all this sounds like too much work, there are plenty of other **leisure activities**, like horseback riding, fishing, and bowling, to keep you amused.

Spectator sports

The first choice of a definite minority of visitors to LA, the city's **spectator sports** are just as worthwhile as anywhere else in the country – though you can expect less enthusiasm here for the home squad than you'd find on the East Coast. For most in the regions, team sports are a diversion, not a way of life.

Baseball

LA has two area major-league **baseball teams**, playing from April to October: the **Dodgers** (☎323/224-1-HIT, ⊛www.dodgers.com), who play at the top-notch setting of Dodger Stadium in Chavez Ravine, north of Downtown, and the **Angels** (☎714/663-9000 or 1-888/796-4256, ⊛www.angelsbaseball.com), who play at drab, ugly Anaheim Stadium out in Orange County, and were renamed for Los Angeles instead of Anaheim in the 2005 season, to satisfy their owner's desire.

The Dodgers are historically the more triumphant and beloved franchise, having relocated from Brooklyn in the late 1950s, though they've taken some hits in recent years for being consistently overpaid and underachieving. Whereas the Dodgers last won a world championship back in 1988, the Angels had their best season in 2002, winning the World Series for the first time. Tickets for both teams are easy to get, with Dodger games running $8–30 or more, and Angels games for $7–35.

Basketball

Basketball's flashy **LA Lakers** (☎213/480-3232, ⊛www.lakers.com) have boasted such luminaries through the years as Kareem Abdul-Jabbar, Magic Johnson, and Shaquille O'Neal, and won a total of thirteen championships, including three in a row through 2002. Led by Kobe Bryant after the departure of O'Neal, the current version of the team is not as stunning, but games are still a relative hot ticket. They play at the Staples Center in Downtown LA; tickets run from $25

to more than $250, but can be hard to come by.

The far lesser light in LA's basketball galaxy, the **LA Clippers** (☎213/742-7430, ⊛www.clippers.com), have a history of shocking ineptitude, and rarely make the playoffs; games are also held at the Staples Center, with seats running $10–220, and you should have no problem getting a ticket – unless the Lakers are the opponent. The NBA **season** runs from November through late April, not including the play-offs.

As an alternative, the WNBA women's basketball league has fourteen teams playing nationally, one of which is the **Los Angeles Sparks** (☎1-877/44-SPARKS, ⊛www.wnba.com/sparks). As with the other local basketball squads, the Sparks play their home games at the Staples Center, though on a summertime schedule (May–Aug).

Football

Los Angeles has had no professional **football** teams for the last decade, and few locally seem to care. However, college ball is another story: Pasadena's 102,000-seat **Rose Bowl** (☎626/577-3100, ⊛www.rosebowlstadium.com) hosts one of the four Bowl Championship Series games to decide the championship, and is also the home field for UCLA's respectable football team (tickets $15–45; ☎310/825-2101, ⊛uclabruins.ocsn.com). The top-notch USC squad also plays in historic digs, at the LA Coliseum in South Central (tickets $35–60; ☎213/740-GOSC, ⊛usctrojans.ocsn.com), site of the 1932 and 1984 Olympics. Ticket prices can vary widely depending on the opponent or, as in the case of

USC, whether the school has recently won a championship, and games are played on Saturdays throughout Fall.

Hockey

Hockey in LA didn't mean much until the late 1980s, when the **LA Kings** (☎1-888/KINGS-LA, ⓦwww.lakings.com) traded for superstar Wayne Gretzky from the champion Edmonton Oilers. Gretzky's long gone from these parts, and the Kings have since moved from the Forum to the Staples Center; seats are $25–100. The **Anaheim Mighty Ducks**, in Orange County, play at Arrowhead Pond in Anaheim (☎714/704-2500, ⓦwww.mightyducks.com); tickets $20–175. When not subject to crippling lockouts or strikes, the NHL season lasts throughout the winter and into early spring, when the play-offs take place.

Soccer

One of the more recent teams in town, the **LA Galaxy** (☎1-877/3-GALAXY, ⓦwww.lagalaxy.com) plays **soccer** in the MLS (Major League Soccer), and games take place at the Home Depot Center, in the city of Carson in the South Bay. The season runs much of the year, save winter; tickets $20–55.

Horse racing

Horse racing is a fairly popular spectator sport in the LA area, which has two main tracks. **Santa Anita**, in the San Gabriel Valley town of Arcadia at 285 W Huntington Drive, has a winter and spring season (☎626/574-7223, ⓦwww.santaanita.com); while **Hollywood Park**, 1050 S Prairie Ave in Inglewood, has a spring-to-autumn season (☎310/419-1500, ⓦwww.hollywoodpark.com).

Water and beach sports

Many visitors to LA head straight for the ocean. Along the sands from Malibu to Orange County, you can find any number of **water** and **beach sports** to keep you busy. However, for more passive pleasures at the seaside, **suntanning** with crowds of other locals and visitors is always a popular option.

Swimming, snorkeling, and scuba diving

Although you'd never believe it from watching TV, **swimming** in many coastal areas is definitely not recommended. As a rule, the further you go from most city piers, the better off you are. Piers, along with run-off pipes and channels, are sources for water-borne contamination, thanks to heavy-metal and chemical offshore dumping, and the nasty, unfiltered overflow from the city's streetside drains. The authorities, however, will only inform you of dangerous conditions when heavy rains make it absolutely off-limits for human activity. (For more on LA's waters, see ⓦwww.healthebay.org, or the box on p.144.)

The beaches closer to Malibu, Palos Verdes, and Orange County are usually less crowded and safer than those around Santa Monica and Venice, though any spots near the harbor are to be avoided. **Parking** at major strips of sand will cost you upwards of $8, even for a short time, but there are usually sufficient roadside spots to deposit your car if you want to take a dip along the rockier coves and crags. Similarly, **snorkeling** and **scuba diving** are better experienced well away from LA in places like Santa Catalina Island. Prices for excursions to see Catalina's astounding undersea life, kelp forest, and shipwrecks can vary widely, but expect to pay at least $80–120 for any trip. Lover's Cove, a marine preserve just east of Avalon, is the best spot to view the local sea life close-up, though only snorkeling is allowed.

Catalina Dive Shop at Lover's Cove, Santa Catalina Island ☎ 1-877/SNORKEL, ⓦ www .catalinadiveshop.com. Provides ecological tours, snorkeling equipment for rent (generally $35 per day for a decent package), and underwater cameras for sale.

Catalina Divers Supply Avalon Casino and pier, Avalon ☎ 310/510-0330 or 1-800/353-0330, ⓦ www.catalinadiverssupply.com. Leads undersea tours of Santa Catalina and rents scuba and snorkeling equipment; $27 per day for a complete snorkel set, and $50 for the full scuba package.

Catalina Island Kayak Expeditions PO Box 386, Avalon 90704 ☎ 310/510-1226, ⓦ www .kayakcatalinaisland.com. Offering kayaking and snorkeling trips and hourly, half-day, or two-day packages, running anywhere from $28 to $250 per person.

Scuba Luv 126 Catalina Ave, Avalon ☎ 1-800/262-DIVE or 310/510-2350, ⓦ www.scubaluv.com. Good for introductory dives for beginners, with basic, overnight trips to the island running $212–230 per person – though more elaborate versions are available, too.

Sundiver 106 N Marina Drive, Long Beach ☎ 562/493-0951 or 1-800/955-9446, ⓦ www .sundiver.net. Popular package deals include boating trips to area islands for one or two days of scuba diving; prices vary widely.

Surfing, windsurfing, kayaking, and jet-skiing

Since railroad magnate Henry Huntington first began importing Hawaiian talent to publicize his Red Car route in the South Bay, **surfing** has been big business in LA, having a big impact on the city's culture and image. If you want to give the sport a try, head to where the surfers are: along the Malibu section of the Pacific Coast Highway from Surfrider to Leo Carrillo beaches and around Point Dume; along the South Bay in towns like Manhattan Beach; and at ever-popular Orange County beaches from Huntington to San Clemente. Don't worry about buying equipment, though: **surfboards** are available for rent by the hour from rental shacks up and down the coast.

If you've never been **windsurfing**, a trip to LA might not be the ideal time to start, the success of the experience depending on your overall dexterity and the velocity of the wind. But if you feel confident, several coastal outlets rent windsurfers by the hour or day. The newer sport of **kiteboarding** may be even more challenging, letting an actual kite drag you along the waves on a windy day – lessons can be very expensive. Somewhat easier is **kayaking**, with ocean-going kayaks being more basic and manageable than river kayaks, as you simply sit atop the sea-going boat and row with another person. Finally, there's **jet-skiing**, a popular choice that will cost you around $100 to rent a machine for a half-day of splashing around Santa Monica Bay or elsewhere.

Alfredo's Beach Rentals 5411 Ocean Blvd, Long Beach ☎ 562/434-6121. Rents kayaks for around $10–20 per hour, as well as small boats for $40–50 per hour and up.

Catalina Ocean Rafting 103 Pebbly Beach Rd, Avalon ☎ 1-800/990-RAFT or 310/510-0211, ⓦ www.catalinaoceanrafting.com. Takes groups out in small, flat "ocean rafts" to tour the seaside world. Half-day trips for $158 per person.

Jet Ski Fun 1753 Ninth St, Suite 201, Santa Monica ☎ 310/822-1868. Well-established spot for renting jet skis, by appointment only. May cost upwards of $100, depending on the model and length of time you're using it.

Long Beach Windsurf Center 3850 E Ocean Blvd, Long Beach ☎ 562/433-1014, ⓦ www .windsurfcenter.com. Located near the Belmont Pier, this operator rents in-line skates and kayaks for $10–20 per hour; windsurfers themselves run upwards of $25–30 per hour. Kiteboarding lessons start at $100.

Southwind Kayak Center 17855 Sky Park Circle, Irvine ☎ 1-800/SOUTH-WIND, ⓦ www .southwindkayaks.com. Orange County operator with rental spots in Newport Beach and Dana Point (call for locations). Kayak rentals from $14–20 per hour, or $50–65 per day. Excellent for beaches further south.

West End Dive Center Santa Catalina Island, at Two Harbors ☎ 310/510-0303 ext 272 or 1-800/785-8425, ⓦ www.scico.com/twoharbors.

Water and beach

SPORTS AND OUTDOOR ACTIVITIES

⑰

s in kayak and scuba trips, with
package deals starting at $60
guided dive. Kayaks and bikes
22 per two hours, or $45 for a

﹍﹍ Jay Surfboards 22775 Pacific Coast Hwy,
Malibu ☎310/456-8044. Solid choice for
boards around some major waves. Expect
to pay $20–25 per day, or $10 for a wetsuit
in winter months.

△ Venice's beachside path

Rollerblading and bicycling

The popularity of **rollerblading**, or
in-line skating, cannot be overstated
along the Venice Boardwalk and other
beachside paths, or in certain urban
parks and recreation zones. These linear
skates are found on the feet of countless locals and visitors traveling along
the famed **cycling path** from Santa
Monica to Palos Verdes, a terrific route
for exploring the seaside edge of the
metropolis. If you're walking, avoid this
crowded path, as skaters and cyclists
race down the asphalt lanes like automobiles, giving little respect to the
painted yellow lines. The oceanside
path along this area is also the main
choice for **bicycling** in LA, even
though there are myriad bike paths
throughout the region, from the peaceful, leafy setting of the Arroyo Seco to
the post-apocalyptic landscape of the
LA River. Although you can rent a bike
for as little as $6 per hour off the beaten
trail, the beachfront is the only place
with a good selection of dealers, who
may charge $10–15 an hour for skates
or bikes, depending on the equipment.

Bikestation 105 Promenade North, Long Beach
☎562/436-BIKE, ⓦwww.bikestation.org. Offers
bicycle rental, repair, and storage, and even
valet bike-parking.

**California Association of Bicycling Organiza-
tions** ☎310/639-9348, ⓦwww.cabobike.org.
Good online source of maps and information, plus regular updates of California laws
and municipal strategies affecting cyclists.

**California Department of Transportation
(CalTrans)** LA office at 120 S Spring St, Downtown ☎213/897-3656, ⓦwww.dot.ca.gov.
Perhaps the most comprehensive source of
guides and maps for the LA urban area and
region, showing which commuter arterials
are best for cycling, and which should be
avoided.

Perry's Café and Rentals 2400 & 2600 Ocean
Front Walk, Venice ☎310/452-2399, ⓦwww
.perryscafe.com; 930 Pacific Coast Hwy, Santa
Monica ☎310/394-0086; and 1200 PCH, Santa
Monica ☎310/458-3975. A mini-chain of
oceanside rental spots where the bikes and
skates go for $20–25 per day or $7–9 per
hour.

Sea Mist 1619 Ocean Front Walk, Venice
☎310/395-7076. Located opposite the Venice
Pier, with affordable bike and skate rentals
for $5–7 per hour, or around $15 per day.

Spokes 'n' Stuff 4175 Admiralty Way, Marina del
Rey ☎310/306-3332; 1700 Ocean Ave, Santa
Monica ☎310/395-4748. Among the better
choices of many similar bike-rental agents
along the sands; $8–10 per hour minimum.
In Griffith Park, the outfit has a branch near
the LA Zoo, at 4400 Crystal Springs Drive
(☎323/662-6573).

Airborne activities

If you want to get above the smog, LA has several worthwhile **airborne activities** that may interest you. The most affordable is **hang gliding**, using a simple

glider to drift down from a hill, mountain, or cliff on air currents and slowly coming to a safe landing. If you've come to LA as a hang-gliding pro, bring your glider to the bluffs overlooking the Pacific near Point Fermin for a strikingly picturesque trip over the sea cliffs and toward the beach.

An appealing alternative is **soaring** in enclosed gliders. Again using air currents to rise and fall, these simple craft provide a memorable experience, if not quite as awe-inspiring as that of hang gliding. While most of your time will doubtless be spent watching from the back seat of the glider, you'll have a vivid experience that you, and your stomach, will not soon forget.

If the above ideas don't sound appealing, a **helicopter ride** may provide all the airborne excitement you need, allowing you to view some of LA's premier sights, like the Hollywood sign, from thousands of feet above the ground. There are a number of different packages and tours available, all at fairly steep prices. The most expensive, and most conventional, mode of flying is also available – an **airplane trip** in a single- or twin-engine craft, though unless you're well away from the central city, such operators are few and far between.

Blue Skies Aviation 7535 Valjean Ave #4, Van Nuys, San Fernando Valley ☏818/901-1489, ⊛www.blueskiesaviation.com. Charter airplane flights for $300 per hour or, for those already in possession of a student pilot's license, prop-plane rentals for $84–210 per hour.

Bravo Aviation 401 World Way at LAX ☏310/337-6701, ⊛www.bravoair.com. Short helicopter excursions to the South Bay for around $100 and hour-long overhead tours of LA's top sights for $309, or $200 for a half-hour tour – the latter two with a meal included.

Great Western Soaring 32810 165th St E, Llano, north of LA in the Antelope Valley ☏805/944-3341 or 1-800/801-GLIDE, ⊛www .greatwesternsoaring.com. Provides gliders

and lessons, at a cost of $85 for a basic lesson, up to $176 for a more involved ride.

Group 3 Aviation 16425 Hart St, Van Nuys Airport, San Fernando Valley ☏818/994-9376, ⊛www.group3aviation.com. Takes movie-oriented helicopter trips from central LA to various points along the coast (from $130–230).

Windsports Soaring Center 12623 Gridley St, Sylmar ☏818/367-2430, ⊛www.windsports .com. One of the more prominent of the hang-gliding tour and rental outlets throughout town. For around $120, they will give you the basic experience, but if you want a greater challenge, more expensive package deals are also available for $200.

Fitness activities and extreme sports

LA's preoccupation with tanned, muscular, and silicone-boosted bodies is most evident in the city's vigorous pursuit of **fitness activities**, which can veer from simply keeping one's body in shape to zealously worshipping it to testing the body's physical limits with **extreme sports**.

Fitness activities

For a taste of LA's health mania, **working out** at a fitness club or along the beach is an obvious place to start. Whether you've come to pump iron yourself or watch the weightlifters go through their paces, there are few better spots than **Muscle Beach** near the Venice Boardwalk – although having the right abs and biceps is

essential if you're in the mood to show off your physique. Contact the Venice Beach Recreation Center, 1800 Ocean Front Walk (☏310/399-2775), for more information on bench-pressing with the local iron-pumpers. If you're not quite there yet, the exercise and training equipment just south of the **Santa Monica Pier** should start you on your way, but for less conspicuous bodybuilding and training, LA's numerous **health clubs** are everywhere, with Gold's Gym among the most prominent.

For less social workouts, **jogging** is a popular choice, though you should stick to the safer Westside, and avoid anywhere Downtown or in Mid-Wilshire. Although Hollywood would at first seem like a dubious choice for exercising, the steeply inclined paths and fine views of Runyon Canyon Park make for an excellent workout (enter off Mulholland Drive or Fuller Avenue), as does the circuitous route around Lake Hollywood. Elsewhere, the best paths for joggers include the green median strip of San Vicente Boulevard from Brentwood to Santa Monica; Sunset Boulevard through Beverly Hills and Westwood (but not Hollywood); the Arroyo Seco in Pasadena; and most stretches along the beach – except anywhere near the LA Harbor.

Also along the beach, you may be able to join a **volleyball** game at any of the sandy courts from Santa Monica to Marina del Rey. Hermosa Beach is another good choice for volleyball (the city famously hosts competitions in the sport throughout the year), as are seaside Orange County towns like Huntington and Laguna beaches. **Tennis** is also played at courts across LA, with space available for visitors at city parks and universities. Call the city's Department of Recreation and Parks for more information on reserving a court (☎213/485-5555).

The best workout in town is also one of the cheapest. **Hiking** in LA doesn't have the same reputation as it does in other parts of California, but under no circumstances is it a token pursuit. Rather, the Santa Monica Mountains – a huge natural preserve west of LA and north of Malibu – have many different trails and routes for exploration, most of which feature jaw-dropping scenery, copious wildlife, and interesting rustic sights.

Audubon Society at Plummer Park, 7377 Santa Monica Blvd, West Hollywood ☎323/876-0202,

Ⓦwww.laaudubon.org. Provides periodic guided hikes through the Santa Monica Mountains and other LA-area nature zones, as well as information on their various chirping and warbling denizens. Operates a bookstore and library at its headquarters; Tues–Sat 9.30am–4pm.

California Department of Parks ☎818/880-0350, Ⓦwww.parks.ca.gov. Good source of information and maps, especially online, where you can get an overview of each state park and the resources available therein.

Hiking in LA 15206 Ventura Blvd, Sherman Oaks, San Fernando Valley 91403 ☎818/501-1005. A private group that offers treks through the Santa Monica Mountains in several foreign languages, as well as English. Part of JRT International.

Santa Monica Mountains Conservancy ☎310/589-3200, Ⓦlamountains.com. The leading name in preserving land in the mountains and ensuring public access to them (including weddings), with trail maintenance, property purchases, and other conservation activities. Also a good source of information about the region at five major park visitor centers.

Santa Monica Mountains Visitor Center 401 W Hillcrest Drive, Thousand Oaks ☎805/370-2301, Ⓦwww.nps.gov/samo. Offers maps and information on hiking trails and parks in the area. Located in a neighboring city just north. Daily 9am–5pm.

Sierra Club 3435 Wilshire Blvd #320, Mid-Wilshire ☎213/387-4287, Ⓦangeleschapter.org. Major political and environmental advocacy group that offers information on local natural areas, and conducts hikes and tours of key ecological zones.

Extreme sports

As elsewhere in the country, **extreme sports** have gained a strong following in Los Angeles, with many such pursuits originating in the city itself; if you're already an acolyte, there are few better ways to spend your vacation here.

Of course, any of the previously listed sports, such as hang gliding or kayaking, can with the right intensity level and risk-taking behavior be converted into an extreme activity. Beyond those pursuits, however, there are some edgy sports and activities that are also popular. The operators below only provide a hint of the range and possibility of such perilous endeavors.

The original "extreme sport" was arguably **skateboarding**, and in the 1970s LA quickly became a trailblazer for the high-flying version of this sport, establishing its dominance worldwide. Slightly more sedate, though potentially just as thrilling, **rock climbing** has gained in renown in recent years, and private rock "clubs" or "gyms" allow you to scale vertical surfaces to your heart's content, and equipment can also be rented for an additional fee. For a close-up look at the sport without paying a dime, turn up at Stony Point near Chatsworth, in the San Fernando Valley, to watch crowds of hardcore rock enthusiasts dangling by their fingertips.

For sheer terror, **bungee jumping** is hard to beat, though it's lost a little luster since its 1990s heyday, and there are far fewer operators in the business nowadays outside of amusement parks and traveling carnivals. For a different kind of thrill, powering a **motocross** dirtbike around desert washes and boulder-strewn valleys is good for heart-stopping sensation, though your balance must be excellent and you can't be scared of taking a nasty spill. If that isn't extreme enough for you, though, there's always **skydiving**, which you can experience in the desert north of Los Angeles.

Bungee America ☏310/322-8892, ⊛www .bungeeamerica.com. Long-standing bungee operator that usually supplies equipment to

amusement parks and Hollywood, but also offers thrilling weekend jumps from the so-called "Bridge to Nowhere" in the Angeles National Forest, an abandoned span; package deals start from $69 for one leap to $165 for five.

California City Skydive 22521 Airport Way, in California City in the Mojave Desert ☏1-800/2-JUMPHI, ⊛www.calcityskydive.com. A good introduction to the sport, at a cost of $169 if you jump yourself (with 4–5hr training), and $120 more if you need two assistants to help you on the way down. If you fall with one instructor (for $194), only a half-hour introductory session is required before you make your ten-thousand-foot airborne journey to the desert floor.

MotoVentures off Reed Valley Rd, Temecula ☏951/767-0991, ⊛www.motoventures.com. Motorcycle ranch two hours east of LA that offers instruction in motocross for novices and, for riders of all skill levels, thrilling two-wheeler tours of the surrounding mountains and desert. If you have your own dirtbike, day-long tours are $150, or about twice as much if you need a rental.

The Rock Gym 2599 E Willow St, near Long Beach ☏562/981-3200, ⊛www.therockgym .com. One of LA's top climbing venues, which provides a 12,000-square-foot space for scaling; one climb is $15, or kids for $12. Find other, similar operators around town by looking under "Rock Gyms" or "Rock and Mountain Climbing Instruction" in the Yellow Pages.

Skateboard Parks ⊛skateboardparks.com. Although you can certainly earn a daring reputation skateboarding illegally in city plazas and the like, to find a list of above-board skateboard parks in LA, visit this national website: it offers sites and features of skate parks across the country, with a special emphasis on LA and Southern California.

Skiing and snowboarding

The fringe of the LA region boasts some prime territory for **skiing** and **snowboarding** in the mountainside lake and hamlet of **Big Bear**, located about two hours east of Downtown LA, north of San Bernardino. Along with Mount Baldy and other such places in the general vicinity of the San Bernardino Mountains, Big Bear is deservedly a top winter draw for thousands of Angelenos, who drive out here (there are hardly any public transit options, except from San Bernardino itself) to experience the excellent ski and snowboard conditions from November through April, and similarly fine opportunities for hiking, boating, fishing, and jet-skiing in the summer. Located near state highways 18 and 38, Big Bear has several appealing resorts that provide plenty of outdoor activities, winter or summer, while the fine *Adventure Hostel* (see p.260) provides cheap accommodation.

Bear Mountain 43101 Goldmine Drive, Big Bear Lake ⊕909/585-2519, ⊛www.bearmtn .com. Major ski area with twelve chairlifts, plus the added attraction of some of the country's top terrains parks, as well as all the summer activities found elsewhere. Lift tickets $49, kids $19; also good for use at Snow Summit.
Mount Baldy off Mountain Avenue in the Angeles National Forest ⊕909/981-3344, ⊛www .mtbaldy.com. Located on the edge of LA County, with a nice assortment of straightforward skiing trails and routes, along with decent snowboarding opportunities. Lift tickets $45, kids $15; half-day tickets for $30 and $10.
Mountain High near Wrightwood at 24512 Hwy-2 ⊕760/249-5803, ⊛www.mthigh.com.

Caters to assertive winter athletes with two high-speed chairlifts (out of ten), plus night skiing every day of the week until 10pm. Also offers terrain parks for snowboarders. Lift tickets $45, kids $17.
Snow Summit 880 Summit Blvd, Big Bear Lake ⊕909/866-5766, ⊛www.snowsummit.com. One of the best ski areas, which has twelve chairlifts that operate in summer for hikers and mountain bikers. Lift tickets $49, kids $19; also good for use at Bear Mountain.
Snow Valley 35100 Hwy-18 near Running Springs ⊕909/867-2751, ⊛www.snow-valley .com. Located further from Big Bear Lake, a spot where besides the usual snow sports, you'll find a terrain park, along with twelve chairlifts. Lift tickets $44, kids $17.

Leisure activities

If you're interested in activities that don't require a lot of grunting and sweating, LA has numerous **leisure activities**, beyond simply watching TV in your hotel room.

Fishing

Fishing is encouraged at a few locations, like the northern beaches around Malibu. Elsewhere, however – especially the Santa Monica and Venice piers – you risk ingesting a lifetime's worth of mercury and cadmium from any fish you bite into. A better, though more costly, alternative is to charter a **sport-fishing cruise** out to sea and cast your line there, for one to two thousand dollars for a six-hour trip on a winter weekday, or three thousand or more for an eight-hour cruise during a summer weekend.

A California state **fishing license** is required for anything from pier casting to ocean fishing, and costs nonresidents $11, $17, or $33, for one, two, or ten days of fishing, with annual licenses running $90 ($33 for residents). **Special permits** are required for salmon ($1.60 extra),

bass ($5), and abalone ($16) fishing. Many cruise operators and fishing-supply dealers provide short-term fishing licenses. For more information, check ⊛www.dfg.ca.gov/licensing.
Catalina Island Sportfishing 114 Claressa St, Avalon ⊕310/510-2420. Runs charter fishing trips for $100–120 an hour in the waters off Santa Catalina Island – though you can always fish for free from the Avalon pier.
E-Z Ocean Charters at Avalon harbor ⊕310/510-2281, ⊛www.e-zoceancharters.com. Charter fishing expeditions around Santa Catalina Island, with rates from $80–130 per hour, depending on the number of people in your party (up to six allowed). Also offers sightseeing trips for $35/hr per person.
LA Harbor Sportfishing 1150 Nagoya Way, Berth 79, San Pedro ⊕310/547-9916, ⊛www .laharborsportfishing.com. Partial ($30 per person) or full-day ($45) trips to offshore waters are offered, along with overnight trips ($90), seasonal whale-watching cruises (2hr 30min; $16), and LA Harbor tours (45min; $10).

Long Beach Sportfishing 555 Pico Ave, Berth 55, Long Beach ☎562/432-8993, ⊛www .longbeachsportfishing.com. Organizing overnight ($125) and half-day ($30) fishing expeditions to deep-sea waters, as well as whale-watching trips ($12).

Marina del Rey Sportfishing 13759 Fiji Way, Marina del Rey ☎310/822-3625. Somewhat more touristy than the other operators, though the tour prices and packages are much the same (rental equipment, licenses, day or half-day trips for $40 and $30, etc).

Redondo Sportfishing 233 N Harbor Drive, Redondo Beach ☎310/372-2111, ⊛www .redondosportfishing.com. Half- and full-day trips are offered ($32–47), sailing to waters near Palos Verdes all the way out to more distant islands off the California coast. Also offers whale-watching cruises ($17).

Golf

Southern California is a prime spot for **golfing**, with links throughout the region. Unfortunately, the most notable and upscale of the courses in LA tend to be off-limits unless you're chummy with a member. By contrast, the courses listed below are all open to the public, and much more affordable than the big names but no less centrally located (with the exception, on both counts, of the course in Malibu). The fairways at these courses might not be as immaculate or the views as stunning, but for a relaxing day putting and driving in the California sun, there are few better, or cheaper, options. A full list of LA-area courses, public and private, can be found at ⊛thegolfcourses.net; for the thirteen operated by the City of Los Angeles, which supposedly runs more links than any other US city, call ☎818/246-1135 ext 227 or visit ⊛www.ci.la.ca.us/RAP.

Griffith Park 4730 Crystal Springs Drive, north of Hollywood ☎323/664-2255, ⊛www .griffithparkgolfshop.com. Set over four thousand acres in one of LA's best outdoor settings, the four courses of Griffith Park – Wilson, Harding, Roosevelt, and Los Feliz – mostly date from the eras of their respective presidents (with the latter from 1952), though all are kept in good shape and quite

busy throughout the week. Golf classes, with lessons from beginner to advanced, are held on weekend nights and throughout Saturday (30–60min; $35–90). Regular fees are $26–34 per eighteen holes at Wilson and Harding, or $13–17 for the nine-holers at Roosevelt and Los Feliz.

Malibu Country Club 901 Encinal Canyon Rd, Malibu t818/889-6680, ⊛www .malibucountryclub.net. If you have the money to spend on an upper-crust public course, this is the place to spend it: in the Santa Monica Mountains amid some of LA's best rustic scenery. Keep in mind that you must check in twenty minutes before your tee time and wear appropriate golf attire. Eighteen holes $60–85, nine for $35–50.

Rancho Park 10460 W Pico Blvd, West LA ☎310/839-4374. Set in one of the most convenient areas for visitors on the Westside, this inexpensive course, like Griffith Park and others operated by the city, requires an annual Los Angeles City Card ($35; call for information) if you want to reserve ahead. The layout is undulating and the greens are packed at peak hours on weekends, but it's still been a local favorite for almost sixty years. $26–34 for eighteen holes, $13–17 for the nine-hole course.

Bowling

Best exemplified by the crazy characters in the film *The Big Lebowski*, **bowling** in LA attracts a diehard crowd of local enthusiasts, and you can find bowling alleys at many spots in town, from old linoleum-and-formica lanes to newer bowl-o-ramas where flashy bowling nights feature glow-in-the-dark lanes and bowling balls. Costs start around $4–6 per game, with shoe rental a few bucks extra.

All Star Lanes 4459 Eagle Rock Blvd ☎323/254-2579. Located between Glendale and Pasadena in the little burg of Eagle Rock, this retro-styled alley features a bar, dance floor, video games, and pool tables to keep you busy when you're not prowling the lanes. Rockabilly bands provide the thumping live soundtrack.

Brunswick West Covina 675 S Glendora Ave, West Covina, San Gabriel Valley ☎626/960-3636. Lovers of Googie pop architecture will not want to miss this colorful, Polynesian-styled alley – with its own coffee shop and

⑰

cocktail lounge – though it's located out in the middle of nowhere.

Jewel City Bowl 135 S Glendale Ave, Glendale ☎818/243-1188. Bowling zealots may hate it, but casual fans will enjoy a trek out to this popular Valley spot, where glowing balls, heavy metal music, artificial fog, and headache-inducing lights all serve to distract you from hitting strikes.

Mar Vista Lanes 12125 Venice Blvd, West LA ☎310/391-5288. A set of funky old alleys east of Venice, which also features Mexican food and weekend karaoke. Appeals to the more hardcore league bowlers.

Pickwick Bowling 921 W Riverside Drive, Burbank ☎818/842-7188, ⓦwww.pickwickgardens.com. With twenty-four lanes and a mixed crowd of young and old, this colorful Valley spot has gimmicks like Friday dance-music nights and Saturday's "Electric Fog" bowling, featuring copious amounts of dry ice and wild lighting.

Pinz Bowling Center 12655 Ventura Blvd, Studio City ☎818/769-7600, ⓦwww.pinzbowlingcenter.com. A big-time renovation has made this the place to be seen for Valley bowling, with 32 lanes, plenty of arcade games, and a rock'n'roll atmosphere. Don't be surprised to see a B-list TV actor or recent Hollywood has-been in the lane next to you.

Regal Lanes 1485 N Tustin Ave, city of Orange ☎714/997-9901. Located in Orange County and supposedly the biggest bowling center on the West Coast, with an astounding 72 lanes, plus an accompanying German bar and restaurant.

Horseback riding

You can go **horseback riding** at several ranches and stables throughout the greater LA region, principally around the Santa Monica Mountains and the hills of Griffith Park. Most businesses give you a choice of packages that may include evening journeys, individual or group rides, easy or difficult routes, and various added amenities like dinners or barbecues. Costs can be anywhere from $15 to $50 per hour, depending on the location and package.

Bar S Stables 1850 Riverside Drive, Glendale ☎818/242-8443. A Griffith Park–area operator that provides guided equine tours during the daylight or evening hours, and occasionally under moonlight, starting at $20 per hour.

Catalina Stables 600 Avalon Canyon Rd, Avalon ☎310/510-0478, ⓦwww.bdaservices.com/catalinastables. Offers guided tours of gorgeous Santa Catalina Island, with simple half-hour tours starting around $30, two-hour treks for $64, and five-hour journeys costing $170.

Circle K Riding Stables 910 S Mariposa St, Burbank ☎818/843-9890. Located near the LA Equestrian Center, the Circle K provides affordable rides for $20 per person per hour.

Dude's Ranch Tarzana, San Fernando Valley ☎818/337-9921, ⓦwww.dudesranch.com. Many tours through varying terrain around the Santa Monica Mountains – from mountains and canyons to waterfalls and beaches – with most rides one to five hours long, at $50–65 per hour, per person. Includes rides at sunset and under moonlight for same cost. Lessons $45 per hour.

LA Equestrian Center 480 Riverside Drive, Burbank ☎818/840-8401, ⓦwww.la-equestriancenter.com. Across the LA River from Griffith Park, this outfit offers horse rentals for $20 an hour or evening rides for $40, with a tasty barbecue to boot.

Sunset Ranch 3400 N Beachwood Drive, Hollywood ☎323/469-5450, ⓦwww.sunsetranchhollywood.com. A Griffith Park operator providing 90min evening horse rides through the surrounding area, starting Friday at 4.30pm, on a first-come first-served basis; $50.

Will Rogers Trails 1501 Will Rogers State Park Rd, Pacific Palisades ☎310/455-2900. Watch a polo match on the park's front lawn (April–Oct Sat 2–4pm, Sun 10am–noon; free) before enjoying a horseback ride in the vicinity for $50.

Festivals and events

L os Angeles has a great number of **parades** and **festivals** to celebrate throughout the year, from proud displays of ethnic culture to internationally famous parades to oddball street fairs and quirky festivals. No matter when you come, you'll likely find some sort of event or celebration, especially in summer, when beach culture is in full bloom. This selective list concentrates on some of the more notable observances, along with smaller, local events that provide unusual or nontraditional festivities. For a list of national **public holidays**, see Basics, p.44.

January

Japanese New Year (1st) Art displays, ethnic cuisine, cultural exhibits, and more at this annual Little Tokyo festival, centered around the Japanese American Community and Cultural Center. ☎213/628-2725, ⓦwww.jaccc.org.

Tournament of Roses Parade (1st) Pasadena's famous procession of floral floats and marching bands along a five-mile stretch of Colorado Blvd, coinciding with the annual Rose Bowl game. ☎626/795-9311 or 449-ROSE, ⓦwww.tournamentofroses.com.

Martin Luther King Parade and Celebration (mid) The civil-rights hero is honored with activities at King Park, Baldwin Hills, Crenshaw, and many other city locations. ☎310/314-2188 in LA, ☎562/570-6816 in Long Beach.

Golden Globe Awards (mid to late) As the annual run-up to the Oscars, this awards show is held by the Hollywood Foreign Press Association, and attracts ever-increasing (some say undeserved) attention. Tourists are encouraged to watch the stars arrive, and gape accordingly. ☎310/657-1731, ⓦwww.hfpa.org.

February

Chinese New Year (early to mid) Three days of dragon-float street parades, tasty food, and various cultural programs, based in Chinatown, Alhambra, and Monterey Park. ☎213/617-0396, ⓦwww.lachinesechamber.org.

Mardi Gras (mid) Floats, parades, costumes, and lots of singing and dancing at this Brazilian fun fest: properly observed at Olvera Street, much more colorfully in West Hollywood. Throughout LA at ☎323/634-7811 or 310/289-2525.

Bob Marley Reggae Festival (mid to late) A two-day event that exalts the reggae legend with food, music, and plenty of spirit. At the Long Beach Convention and Entertainment Center. ☎562/436-3661, ⓦwww.bobmarleydayfestival.com.

Queen Mary Scottish Festival (mid to late) All the haggis you can stand at this two-day Long Beach celebration, along with peppy Highland dancing and bagpipes. ☎562/435-3511, ⓦwww.queenmary.com.

Camellia Festival (late) In Descanso Gardens in La Cañada-Flintridge, many different

341

varieties of camellias are on display to the public. ☎818/952-4401, 🌐www.descansogardens.org.

The Academy Awards (end) The top movie awards, presented at the Kodak Theater at the Hollywood & Highland mall. Bleacher seats are available to watch the limousines draw up and the stars emerge for the ceremony. ☎310/247-3000, 🌐www.oscars.org.

March

LA City Marathon (early) Cheer on the runners all around town, or sign up to participate in this 26-mile run, which covers a course from Downtown to the Westside and South Central LA. ☎310/444-5544, 🌐www.lamarathon.com.

Television Festival (early) Few things could be more appropriate to LA than this two-week celebration at the Directors' Guild honoring the idiot box. If you love TV, it's one event you shouldn't miss, honoring shows from the past and present with clips, cast reunions, lectures, and more. Each night's program focuses on a different show, but can be pricey at $29 each. ☎1-888/464-2468, 🌐www.mtr.org/festivals/paleyfest2005.

Route 66 Art Auction (mid) A good opportunity to get a look at the latest and most engaging artworks to come out of LA's vibrant gallery scene, northeast of Downtown; held at the Center for the Arts in Eagle Rock ☎323/226-1617, 🌐www.centerartseaglerock.org/route66.html.

St Patrick's Day (mid) No parade in LA, but freely flowing green beer in the "Irish" bars along Fairfax Ave in Mid-Wilshire. Parades along Colorado Blvd in Old Town Pasadena (☎626/796-5049), and in Hermosa Beach. ☎310/374-4972, 🌐www.stpatricksday.org.

Blessing of the Animals (late). A long-established ceremony, Mexican in origin, in which locals arrive on Olvera Street to have their pets blessed, then watch an accompanying parade. ☎213/625-5045, 🌐olvera-street.com/html/fiestas.html.

Spring Festival of Flowers (late) A floral explosion of color at Descanso Gardens, including different types of tulips, lilies and daffodils, among many others. ☎818/952-4401, 🌐www.descansogardens.org.

Cowboy Poetry and Music Festival (end) Folk music from the Old West and accompanying cowboy poems – some excellent, some cornpone – are the highlights of this three-day Santa Clarita celebration, just north of LA. ☎661/286-4078 or 1-800/305-0755.

April

California Poppy Festival (early) Although located in a bleak northern valley, Lancaster's 180-acre poppy reserve draws big crowds with its blinding orange colors each spring, while the town festival presents local foodstuffs, folk art and crafts to go with the blooms. ☎661/723-6077, 🌐www.poppyfestival.com.

Jimmy Stewart Relay (mid) The late great actor – and star of such classics as *Vertigo* and *Mr. Smith Goes to Washington* – is honored with a 26.2-mile marathon with five-person relay teams. It's fun to watch the runners charge through the hills and valleys, but if you want to participate, it'll cost your team $200. ☎310/829-8968.

Long Beach Grand Prix (mid) Some of auto-racing's best drivers and souped-up vehicles zoom around Shoreline Drive south of Downtown in the city's biggest annual event, taking place over three days. ☎562/752-9524 or 1-888/82-SPEED, 🌐www.longbeachgp.com.

Songkran Festival (Thai New Year) (mid) The Wat Thai Temple in North Hollywood is the focus for this cultural event, with spicy food and authentic music. ☎818/997-9657.

Antique Street Fair (mid to late) Dig out those treasured family heirlooms and see how much they're worth at this Whittier antique show, where nearly a hundred appraisers are available to assist you. ☎562/696-2662, 🌐www.whittieruptown.com.

Fiesta Broadway (late) Lively Hispanic pop singers and delicious Mexican food are the highlights of this street fair along Broadway in Downtown. ☎310/914-0015, 🌐www.fiestabroadway.la.

May

Cinco de Mayo (5th) A day-long party to commemorate the Mexican victory at the Battle of Puebla. Besides a spirited parade along Olvera Street, several blocks Downtown are blocked off for Latino music performances. There are also celebrations in most LA parks. ☎213/625-5045, ⊛olvera-street.com/html/fiestas.html.

LA Modernism (early) This annual show, at Santa Monica Civic Auditorium, is a fine opportunity to see a wealth of modernist art and design from the twentieth century. ☎310/455-2886, ⊛www.caskeylees.com/modernism.

NoHo Theater and Arts Festival (mid) Music, food, poetry, theatre, and dance fill the streets of this artsy district in North Hollywood in the San Fernando Valley. ☎818/508-5155, ⊛www.noho.org.

Venice Art Walk (mid) A great chance to peer into the private art studios in town, where you can see the work of both big-name local artists and lesser-known up-and-comers – though it will cost you $50. ☎310/664-7911.

Fiesta Hermosa (late) Memorial Day weekend is a great time to visit this fun-loving beach town, which puts on a spirited display with food vendors, music, oceanside sports, and other activities. ☎310/376-0951, ⊛www.fiestahermosa.com.

Strawberry Festival (late) Garden Grove in Orange County is the setting for this huge, old-fashioned display of carnival rides, games, parades, and other festivities – all in celebration of the humble strawberry. ☎714/638-0981, ⊛www.strawberryfestival.org.

UCLA Jazz and Reggae Festival (late) Two days of jazz and reggae concerts, plus heaps of food, on the UCLA campus. ☎310/825-9912, ⊛www.studentgroups.ucla.edu/jazzreggae.

Renaissance Pleasure Faire (weekends April-June, plus Memorial Day) Dress up in your Tudor best for this old-fashioned celebration, which includes dancing, theater, food, and the inevitable jousting. Held in distant San Bernardino. ☎909/880-0122, ⊛recfair.com/socal.

June

Beachfest (early) Rock, reggae, and blues bands, and a huge chili cook-off, are just some of the high points of this annual Long Beach party. ☎949/376-6942.

Irish Fair and Music Festival (2nd weekend) Sizable Irish music, food, and culture celebration held at Woodley Park in Encino, in the San Fernando Valley. ☎818/501-3781, ⊛www.irishfair.org.

Last Remaining Seats (mid) An excellent film festival that draws huge crowds to the grand Los Angeles and Orpheum movie palaces to watch revivals of classic Hollywood films. Also offers films at Glendale's eye-opening Alex Theatre. Tickets to each screening $20, often with live entertainment. ☎213/623-CITY, ⊛laconservancy.org.

Los Angeles Film Festival (mid) Although Hollywood is better for making generic films than honoring good ones, this ten-day festival is

an exception, screening notable independent and art-house films across West LA at a variety of venues. ☎1-866/FILMFEST, ⊛www.lafilmfest.com.

Playboy Jazz Festival (mid) Renowned event held at the Hollywood Bowl, with a line-up of traditional and not-so-traditional musicians. ☎213/480-3232 (tickets), ⊛www.playboy.com/arts-entertainment/features/jazzfest2005.

Bayou Festival (late) Heaps of Creole food, wild parades, and plenty of high-spirited Cajun and Zydeco music at this colorful Long Beach event. ☎562/427-3713, ⊛www.longbeachfestival.com.

Gay Pride Celebration (late) Raucous parade along Santa Monica Blvd in West Hollywood, with hundreds of vendors, an all-male drag football-cheerleading team and a heady, carnival atmosphere. ☎323/860-0701, ⊛www.lapride.org.

July

Festival of the Arts/Pageant of the Masters (early July to late Aug) Laguna Beach's

signature street festival, featuring the standard displays of food, arts, and dancing, but most memorable for its living tableaux, which re-create classic paintings – a unique Southern California spectacle (see box, p.240). ☏949/494-1145, ⓦwww.foapom.com.

Independence Day (4th) The *Queen Mary* in Long Beach hosts a particularly large fireworks display, as well as colorful entertainment (☏562/435-3511). Other fireworks displays throughout LA, including West Hollywood's Plummer Park (☏323/848-6530).

Lotus Festival (first weekend after 4th) An Echo Park celebration featuring dragon boats, ethnic food, pan-Pacific music and, of course, the resplendent lotus blooms around the lake. ☏213/485-1310.

Old Pasadena Jazz Festival (early to mid) In the historic Old Pasadena zone, a nice mix of mainstream jazz and appetizing foodstuffs. ☏818/771-5544, ⓦwww.omegaevents.com.

Festa Italia (mid) An enticing display of food, music, and culture in the otherwise dreary confines of Santa Monica's Civic Auditorium. ☏310/535-2416.

Greek Festival (mid) Three days of food and music at St Katherine Greek Orthodox Church in Redondo Beach, with arts and crafts displays and energetic dancing adding to the festivities. ☏310/540-2434, ⓦwww.sbgreekfestival.com.

LA Mariachi Festival (mid) Munch on Mexican food or take a music workshop, all to the sounds of nonstop mariachi bands; appropriately enough, held in Mariachi Plaza in Boyle Heights. ☏213/485-2437.

Central Avenue Jazz Festival (late) Jazz and blues concerts by big names and lesser-known performers, held in front of the historic *Dunbar Hotel* in South Central. ☏213/847-3169.

August

Festival of the Chariots (early) Three giant chariots, brightly painted and decorated with flowers, parade down Venice Boardwalk to the sound of lively music and the smell of ethnic food. Sponsored by the International Society for Krishna Consciousness. ☏310/839-1572, ⓦwww.festivalofchariots.com.

International Surf Festival (early) Newcomers and old-time fans alike will find this surfing tournament and festival in the South Bay an exciting three-day spectacle. Also includes volleyball, fishing, and sandcastle design. ☏310/305-9546, ⓦwww.surffestival.org.

Long Beach Jazz Festival (mid) Relax and enjoy famous and local performers at the Rainbow Lagoon park in downtown Long Beach. ☏562/436-7794, ⓦwww.long-beachjazzfestival.com.

Nisei Week (mid) A celebration of Japanese America, with martial arts demonstrations, karaoke, Japanese brush painting, baby shows, and performance. ☏213/687-7193, ⓦwww.niseiweek.org.

African Marketplace and Cultural Faire (late) Hundreds of arts and crafts booths and many different entertainers make up this annual celebration at Exposition Park in South Central LA. Runs to early Sept. ☏323/734-1164, ⓦwww.AfricanMarketplace.org.

Sunset Junction Street Fair (last weekend) A spirited neighborhood party, and one of LA's most enjoyable fêtes, along Sunset Boulevard in Silver Lake. The live music, ethnic food, and carnivalesque atmosphere draws a big crowd of locals in the know. ☏323/661-7771, ⓦwww.sunsetjunction.org.

September

Long Beach Blues Festival (early) Hear some of the country's top blues performers at this annual event at Cal State University at Long Beach. ☏562/985-7115, ⓦwww.kkjz.org/events.

LA's birthday (5th) A civic ceremony and assorted street entertainment around El Pueblo de Los Angeles to mark the founding of the original pueblo in 1781. ☏213/625-5045, ⓦolvera-street.com/html/fiestas.html.

Manhattan Beach Arts Festival (second Sunday) Colorful arts and crafts are on display at this South Bay event, along with food and music. ☏310/545-5621 or 802-5000.

Festival of Philippine Arts and Culture (mid) Good food, music, dancing, theater, and film at this annual Point Fermin event in San Pedro. ☏213/389-3050, ⓦfpac.filamarts.org.

Koreatown Multicultural Festival (mid) Dancing, parading, and tae kwon do exhibitions

△ Sunset Junction Street Fair

are the main events at this Mid-Wilshire event (☎213/730-1495). A similar event takes place in Pasadena around the same time (☎626/449-2742).

Los Angeles County Fair (last two weeks) In the San Gabriel Valley, Pomona hosts the biggest county fair in the US, with livestock shows, pie-eating contests, rodeos, and fairground rides. ☎909/623-3111, ⊛www.fairplex.com.

Oktoberfest (late Sept through Oct) Venture into Alpine Village, in the South Bay suburb of Torrance, to revel in Teutonic culture, from the hearty German food to music and dancing. ☎310/327-4384, ⊛www.alpinevillage.net. Also a spirited event in Huntington Beach, Orange County. ☎714/895-8020, ⊛www.oldworld.ws.

Watts Towers Day of the Drum/Jazz Festival (late) Two days of community spirit and free music – African, Asian, Cuban, and Brazilian – with the towers as the striking backdrop; taking place at the same time, and in the same location, the Jazz Festival is the most long-standing such event in LA. ☎213/847-4646.

October

Catalina Island Jazz Trax (first three weekends) A huge line-up of major and rising jazz stars performs in the beautiful Art Deco ballroom of the historic Avalon Casino. ☎1-888/330-5252, ⊛www.jazztrax.com.

Eagle Rock Music Festival (early) This funky district, due north of Downtown LA near Glendale, hosts a freewheeling festival of food, crafts, and a widely eclectic assortment of music – classical to karaoke, Cajun to cabaret. ☎323/226-1617, ⊛www.centerartseaglerock.org.

Scandinavian Festival (early) Folk dancing with assorted foods and art, along with vivid displays of ethnic costumes. Held at Grand Hope Park in Downtown LA. ☎213/661-4273, ⊛asfla.org.

Lithuanian Fair (early) Traditional music and food, and Easter egg painting, are some of the highlights of this Los Feliz fair, held at St Casimir's Church. ☎323/664-4660.

LA Street Fair and Carnival (second weekend) Free rock music, theater, and comedy on the streets of Sherman Oaks in the San Fernando Valley. At the same time as West Hollywood Street Festival, a display of handmade arts and crafts. ☎310/781-2020.

Los Angeles Bach Festival (mid) Revel in the Baroque master's music at the First Congregational Church, just north of Lafayette Park in Westlake. ☎213/385-1345, ⊛www.fccla.org.

Halloween (31st) A wild procession in West Hollywood, featuring all manner of bizarre and splashy outfits and characters (☎310/289-2525). There's also the Halloween Shipwreck on the *Queen Mary*, which spends one day as a "haunted" ocean liner filled with ghouls and demons. ☎562/435-3511.

November

Dia de Los Muertos (2nd) The "Day of the Dead," celebrated authentically throughout East LA and more blandly for tourists on Olvera Street and elsewhere. Mexican traditions, such as picnicking on the family burial spot and making skeleton puppets, are faithfully upheld. ℡213/625-5045, Ⓦolvera-street.com/html/fiestas.html.

Intertribal Marketplace (early) Jewelry, baskets, pottery, beads, and more, presented by Native American artists at Highland Park's Southwest Museum. ℡323/933-4510, Ⓦwww.southwestmuseum.org.

Doo-dah Parade (Sun before Thanksgiving) Absurdly costumed characters marching through Pasadena are the main attraction at this immensely popular LA event, which began as a spoof of the Tournament of Roses parade. ℡626/440-7379, Ⓦwww.pasadenadoodahparade.com.

Griffith Park Light Festival (late) Hugely popular spectacle stretching a mile along Crystal Springs Road, complete with drive-through tunnels of light, thematic displays, and representations of familiar LA sights like the Hollywood sign. ℡213/485-8743.

December

Hollywood Christmas Parade (1st) The biggest of LA's many Yuletide events, with a procession of mind-bogglingly elaborate floats, marching bands, and famous and semi-famous names from film and TV. ℡323/469-2337.

Belmont Shore Christmas Parade (early) Homemade floats and marching bands kick off the holiday season in the area at this East Long Beach event. ℡562/434-3066.

Christmas Boat Parade (mid) Marina del Rey is the site for this annual, ocean-going procession of brightly lit watercraft, supposedly the largest of its kind on the West Coast. ℡310/821-7614. A similar event takes

place along Shoreline Village in Long Beach. ℡562/435-4093.

Las Posadas (mid to late) An Olvera Street event that re-enacts the biblical tale of Mary and Joseph looking for a spot to rest on Christmas Eve, culminating with a piñata-breaking. ℡213/625-5045, Ⓦolvera-street.com/html/fiestas.html.

LA County Holiday Celebration (Christmas Eve) Thousands of people pack the Dorothy Chandler Pavilion in Downtown LA to catch this juggernaut of multicultural entertainment, including everything from Japanese dance to Jamaican reggae. ℡213/974-1396, Ⓦwww.lacountyarts.org/holiday.html.

Kids' LA

Although most of LA's attractions are geared for adults, the city does hold some appeal for **kids**, from popular **museums** and numerous **aquariums** to the natural attractions of the region's excellent **parks and beaches**. If these don't hold the kids' interest, there are always a number of **shops** in town where you can pick up something bright and shining that will. And many, if not most, kids will doubtless want to experience the thrills of major theme parks like **Disneyland**, **Knott's Berry Farm**, and **Magic Mountain**, but it only takes a couple of days – or even hours – of being jostled by massive crowds, waiting in interminable lines, and eating lackluster theme-park food for kids to grow tired of the experience. As such, it always helps to have contingency plans available, which may involve some of the selections below.

Museums

Perhaps the most obvious choice for children is the city's many **museums**, some of which feature kid-friendly exhibits and hands-on, interactive displays with lots of flashing lights and bright colors. Although the Children's Museum of Los Angeles is moving to a location in the San Fernando Valley (set to open in 2006), youngsters can have a similar experience at several solid museums. **Exposition Park** (see p.165), south of Downtown, has two such places where you can let the kids loose for a while: the **California Science Center** and the associated **Air and Space Gallery**. Meanwhile, all age groups should find the neighboring **Natural History Museum of Los Angeles County** to be a worthwhile experience; like the **George C. Page Museum** in Mid-Wilshire (p.89), it's a fine place to view the colossal dinosaur bones of extinct creatures. The Page Museum itself features mammoths, sloths, wolves, and saber-toothed cats dredged up from the adjacent La Brea Tar Pits.

For Western-tinged fun, **Will Rogers State Historic Park** (p.219), once it reopens, has a great ranch house loaded with lariats, cowboy gear, and even the mounted head of a Texas Longhorn. Kids with a taste for roping and riding may also warm to the **William S. Hart Ranch and Museum** (p.216), for its wide range of Western duds, cowboy equipment, and Tinseltown memorabilia, as well as the meatier exhibits at the **Museum of the American West** (p.104).

If all else fails, there are also a good number of offbeat museums in LA that may intrigue children. The least odd of these is **Angels Attic** (p.151), devoted to dolls and dollhouses of the Victorian and other eras. Older kids with a taste for the surreal may enjoy the **Museum of Jurassic Technology** (p.142), an institutional haunted house of sorts filled with all manner of bizarre displays, including creepy bugs.

△ Seal at the Aquarium of the Pacific

Aquatic attractions

The region's biggest and most comprehensive collection of marine life is kept at the **Aquarium of the Pacific** (p.187) in Long Beach, where there are plenty of sharks, tide-pool creatures, jellyfish, and many other specimens to tantalize kids. Less crowded is the smaller **Cabrillo Marine Aquarium** (p.184) in San Pedro, and the coast is also the site of the **Friends of the Sea Lion** (p.240) – where kids can watch injured animals being nursed back to life.

Just a few miles north, along the rugged coastline of Palos Verdes, the **Point Vicente Interpretive Center** has simple exhibits on local marine life (p.180), but is best for its **whalewatching** during the winter months. These massive creatures can also be spotted from other promontories along the Santa Monica Bay, but if you wish to take a **whale watching cruise**, there are plenty of tour-boat operators to assist you on Santa Catalina Island and in Long Beach.

Further north from Point Vicente, Manhattan Beach's **Roundhouse and Aquarium** (p.178) offers an inexpensive look at the region's ocean flora and fauna, but for a much more in-depth view, the **Santa Monica Pier Aquarium** (p.146) is another good choice, second only to the Aquarium of the Pacific. Here, at the base of the pier, kids can get good views of sea creatures and receive a good dose of marine-biology and -ecology education while they're at it.

Finally, if you're on your way south toward San Diego, bring the kids to the **Ocean Institute** (p.241) in Dana Point, where the highlight isn't any sea creature, but a full-sized replica of a tall ship anchored just offshore.

Parks

The most prominent of LA's natural attractions is **Griffith Park** (p.102), just north of Hollywood. Here you can find an excellent network of hiking, biking, and horse-riding trails, amid the rustic charm of a large, mountainous greenspace, not to mention prime views of the LA basin and even a glimpse of the Hollywood sign. The park has numerous attractions to pique children's interest, including a pleasant **bird sanctuary** and a peaceful **Fern Dell**, as well as the imposing profile of the **Griffith Observatory**, which is closed for renovation until 2006.

The observatory, and its attendant displays, will probably appeal to older children more than the **LA Zoo** on the other side of the park, where a standard array of animals is shown before the public in mostly outdated displays and cramped environments. Much more revealing is the **Wildlife Waystation** (p.215) in the northern San Fernando Valley, a rehabilitation center for abused animals where the public can get a close-up look at familiar and exotic species. Back in Griffith Park around the zoo, **Travel Town** is geared to smaller tots, who will appreciate walking around the disused old trains sitting near the LA River.

If you're not planning a stop at Griffith Park but still want a rustic experience for the kids, the **Santa Monica Mountains** are a good place to visit for the many hiking trails and buzzing wildlife. One sight in the mountains, **San Vicente Mountain Park** (p.225), a decommissioned missile base, is a fascinating excursion for older kids, who can get great views of LA by clambering atop a tower that used to cover a launch center.

Paramount Ranch (p.226) is equally interesting for kids and adults as the site of numerous Hollywood Westerns, just as the nearby **Peter Strauss Ranch** is an idyllic natural landscape that was once the site of a colorful resort. Not far away, **Malibu Creek State Park** (p.226) is a good choice for a half-day family outing into some of LA's more rugged, unspoiled terrain.

Both parents and kids may enjoy spending time in the city's **ecological reserves**, which offer fine opportunities for hiking, birdwatching, and sometimes horseback riding and bicycling. Although LA's own Ballona Wetlands are not readily explored, much of **Santa Catalina Island** (p.190) makes for a rewarding experience, whether hiking, camping, or taking a bus tour around the island's unspoiled interior. Orange County, too, has several worthwhile options, including **Crystal Cove State Park** (p.239) along the coast, and the **Bolsa Chica** (p.237) and **Upper Newport Bay** (p.239) ecological reserves, both worthwhile if the children have any interest in seeing nature in its sublime, undeveloped state.

Beaches and water parks

Finally, LA has, of course, a number of popular **beaches**, most of which will be fine for a supervised day of splashing around. The best, and least polluted, can be found around **Malibu** and along the **Orange County coast**. One beach area that's no good for swimming, but has a better slice of social activity for children (at least during the daytime), is the **Santa Monica Pier**, a fine place for cotton candy, video games, and carnival rides.

For freshwater amusement, the region has a quartet of **water parks** that are sure to delight kids with a yen for hydrotubes and splash pools. These include the excellent, and sometimes expensive, rides at Magic Mountain's **Hurricane Harbor** (p.216), Knott's Berry Farm's **Soak City U.S.A.** (p.234), **Raging Waters** in the eastern San Gabriel Valley (p.207), and **Wild Rivers** in the Orange County city of Irvine, at 8770 Irvine Center Drive (June–Aug hours vary, generally daily 10am–8pm; May & Sept Sat & Sun 10am–5pm; $28, kids $18; ☎949/788-0808, ⊛www.wildrivers.com), loaded with forty water tubes, pools, and flumes, and a short distance from the 405 freeway.

High Culture for kids

Bright, motivated children will not be disappointed by LA. Though the **Getty Center** and **Los Angeles County Museum of Art** are not specifically geared toward children, they both offer headphones and "listening tours" for kids on occasion, and also sell children's guidebooks to fine art in their bookstores. The Getty's **Central Garden** has attractive foliage and concentric paths for kids to walk off some of their excess energy.

One museum in the region, the **Bowers Museum of Cultural Art**, features a separate institution – the **Kidseum** (p.234) – geared for the little ones, with simplified displays on native and world cultures. Better, perhaps, is the **Muckenthaler Cultural Center** (p.235) in nearby Fullerton, a whole mansion loaded with international cultural treasures.

Children may find **functional art** to be of particular interest in several of the city's galleries. Bizarre clocks, chairs, and televisions are but a few of the novelties to look at, and perhaps even touch and tinker with, at places like the **Gallery of Functional Art** (p.151) in Santa Monica's Bergamot Station.

For art out in the open, away from confining museums and galleries, the **Franklin Murphy Sculpture Garden** is without peer (p.133). Not even the LA County Museum's **Cantor Sculpture Garden** (with its many Rodins; p.91) can beat UCLA's treasure-trove of twentieth-century abstract sculpture for its visual appeal, all set amid bright sunshine and grassy lawns. For a strange twist on "living art," reserve tickets for Laguna Beach's **Pageant of the Masters** (see p.240), in which people dress up and pose as characters from actual paintings and sculptures.

For a bit of musical edification, the **LA Philharmonic** (p.316) offers seasonal "youth symphonies" either at Disney Hall or the Hollywood Bowl, playing child-oriented staples like Prokofiev's *Peter and the Wolf*, Saint-Saëns' *Carnival of the Animals*, and accessible works from Bach, Mozart, and Vivaldi.

While in the neighborhood, a trip to Disney Hall can be combined with a visit to the **Bob Baker Marionette Theater**, 1345 W First St (shows Tues–Fri 10.30am, Sat 10.30am & 2.30pm, Sun 2.30pm; $10, toddlers free; by reservation only at ☎323/250-9995, ⓦ www.bobbakermarionettes.com), one of LA's best puppet shows for forty years running, performed by a classic puppeteer. The only downside is the theater's dicey location on the west side of the 110 freeway – don't linger in the area after dark. An alternative puppet experience in a more hospitable location is the tiny **Santa Monica Puppet and Magic Center**, 1255 Second St, which has displays of historic puppets and a performance space for the long-running spectacle of *Puppetolio!* (shows Wed 1pm, Sat & Sun 1pm & 3pm; $6.50; ☎310/656-0483, ⓦ www .puppetmagic.com), a one-man production featuring whimsical characters.

Toy and game shops

Dinosaur Farm 1510 Mission St, South Pasadena ☎1-888/658-2388, ⓦ www.dinosaurfarm.com. A paradise for little dino-lovers, chock full of games, puzzles, lunchboxes, and models relating to the giant reptiles – not to mention clothing, masks, and outfits for dressing like a T. Rex yourself.

Gregory's Toys and Adventures in the Encino Place mall, 16101 Ventura Blvd #135, Encino ☎818/906-2212. This San Fernando Valley retailer stocks a fine selection of action figures, puzzles, electric trains, old-fashioned blocks and more – all at competitive prices, typically lower than the big names.

Hollywood Toys and Costumes 6600 Hollywood Blvd, Hollywood ☎323/464-4444 or 1-888/760-3330, ⓦ www.hollywoodtoys.com. A classic, one-of-a-kind LA business, with not only an array of dolls and action figurines, but also dress-up treats – wigs, masks, Halloween outfits, costume jewelry, and all kinds of colorful trinkets and eye-catching junk.

Kip's Toyland in the Farmers' Market, 6333 W Third St, Mid-Wilshire ☎323/939-8334.

Venerable dealer in assorted toys, dolls, stuffed animals, puzzles, and games – not always the flashiest items around, but the store maintains a loyal following in a central location.

Robotoys in the Sherman Oaks Galleria, 15301 Ventura Blvd, Studio City ☎818/788-3344, ⓦwww.robotoys.com. You guessed it: nothing but robots to suit every taste, ranging from cheesy tin toys to slick Transformers-types, and even kit-sets that allow you to build your own mechanical man.

San Marino Toy and Book Shoppe 2424 Huntington Drive, San Marino ☎626/309-0222 or 1-888/895-0111, ⓦwww.toysandbooks.com. Excellent, but pricey, selection of puppets, dollhouses, and building blocks, along with more unusual items such as woolly-mammoth skeleton puzzles and children's "mood lamps."

Would You Believe? 1118 Fair Oaks Ave, South Pasadena ☎626/799-3828, ⓦwww.wyb.com. A terrific spot for magic supplies, novelty gifts, balloons, and juggling equipment, as well as toys. Kids and adults can also rent costumes and go around town dressed as a moose, a monk, or Darth Vader.

Wound & Wound Toy Company 7374 Melrose Ave ☎1-800/937-0561, ⓦwww .thewoundandwound.com. Something of a shopping institution, packed with all kinds of wind-up toys, from goofy aliens and tin trucks to burgers with feet. The display cases full of rare collectibles – *Star Wars* dolls prominent among them – are worth a look.

Shopping

Shopping in LA is an art, and the city is packed with virtuosos. The level of disposable income in the wealthy parts of the city is astronomical, and touring the more outrageous stores can offer some insight into LA life – revealing who's got the money and what they're capable of blowing it on. Besides the run-of-the-mill chain retailers you'll find anywhere, there are big, only-in-LA **department stores** and mega-sized **malls** where most of the serious shopping goes on; countless **clothing** stores, which sell everything from ritzy designer apparel to moth-eaten thriftwear; and upmarket **hair** and **make-up salons**, which give the fanciest dos and looks to the city's fashion elite, and anyone else who can afford them.

LA also has a good assortment of **book** and **record stores**, and whether you're in search of a cozy secondhand shop or a megastore with all the new releases, plus a café to boot, you won't have a hard time finding it, especially in the trendiest shopping zones. LA's diverse array of **food stores** includes everything from corner delis and supermarkets to exquisite cake shops and gourmet emporiums, and you'll also find **specialty stores** selling perfectly weird California souvenirs, from colorful wind-up toys to macabre beach towels.

If you have bags of money to spend, LA provides plenty of cultural shopping as well, in the form of trendy **galleries**, where you can spot the latest works from the city's hottest artists offered at jaw-dropping prices.

Shopping districts

While you can find souvenirs and touristy merchandise in most consumer quarters, there are a few stellar **shopping districts** worth seeking out. In Downtown, the main shopping area is the **Garment District**, where you can pick up a variety of fabrics and clothes, including designer knockoffs and markdowns – at some of the lowest prices on the West Coast. Although its signature Miracle Mile has seen better days, Mid-Wilshire has no less than four major shopping areas: **La Brea Avenue**, just north of Wilshire, a stretch of clothing, furniture, and antique stores; **Third Street**, a short strip of boutiques and restaurants east of the Beverly Center mall and west of the more recent Grove mall; **Larchmont Village**, a mix of small retailers and chain stores on the edge of Hancock Park; and the irrepressible **Melrose Avenue**, between Mid-Wilshire and Hollywood, LA's most conspicuously hip area, where the quirky shops are increasingly being displaced by high-end boutiques.

To the north, **Hollywood Boulevard** is one big cut-rate shopping zone, especially for movie memorabilia and discount T-shirts, with merchandisers concentrated between La Brea Avenue and Gower Street, and the giant Hollywood & Highland mall anchoring the whole scene. To the east is the **North Vermont Avenue** strip in Los Feliz, which attracts the city's alternative-minded buyers with its subversive bookstores, idiosyncratic boutiques, and good restaurants. By contrast, West Hollywood is more self-consciously chic, and you can expect to find small boutiques along the western end of **Santa Monica Boulevard**, and numerous music and bookstores (and more than a few sex shops) along the **Sunset Strip**. Beverly Hills is, of course, the pinnacle of upscale shopping, especially in the downtown core known as the **Golden Triangle**, highlighted by the stratospheric retailers of **Rodeo Drive**. West LA has fewer attractions for tourists, except perhaps for Brentwood's **San Vicente Boulevard**, another ritzy zone, and **Westwood Village**, a student haven full of inexpensive bookstores, clothing outlets, and used-record stores – not to mention the colossi of the Westside Pavilion and Century City malls. Out in Santa Monica, the **Third Street Promenade** is one of LA's most trafficked strips, with a mix of small retailers and, increasingly, mega-chain stores; linked from the Promenade by a free bus (in summer), Santa Monica's **Main Street** is popular for its book dealers, clothing stores, and trinket shops. The same types of retailers are also visible further south, around Venice's **Windward Arcade**, though of a funkier and more downmarket character.

In the outlying areas, there are countless malls, minimalls, and chain-store outlets, but only fewer truly interesting places to shop or browse. **Downtown Long Beach**, especially around Pine Avenue, is appealing for its used-book stores and scattered clothing shops; **Old Pasadena** – notably Colorado Boulevard – offers music stores, apparel merchandisers, and used-book sellers; **Ventura Boulevard**, running through Studio City in the San Fernando Valley, is a good place to buy new and used music, assorted souvenirs, colorful trinkets, and cheap clothing; the so-called **NoHo Arts District** in North Hollywood in the Valley has a clutch of eclectic boutiques and arty souvenir stores; and along Newport Beach's **Balboa Peninsula**, on the Orange County coast, you can pick up expensive designer duds and similarly pricey outfits at numerous boutiques. The South Bay, San Fernando Valley, and Orange County are also well-stocked with overgrown malls of the familiar variety. Oddly enough, the high-profile city of Malibu has relatively few unique shopping attractions that are open to the general public.

Department stores and shopping malls

You won't have to travel far to find LA's flagship **department stores**. Bloomingdale's, Macy's, Neiman–Marcus, Nordstrom, Robinsons–May, and Saks Fifth Avenue are all located in malls throughout the region. For mall addresses, refer to "Shopping malls" below.

Department stores

Barneys 9570 Wilshire Blvd, Beverly Hills ☎310/276-4400. At the base of the Golden Triangle, this high-end retailer offers five levels of dapper shoes and clothing – and a high-end restaurant and café, on the fifth floor; if you don't have the right look, expect the sales clerks to ignore you.

Bloomingdale's 10250 Santa Monica Blvd, in the Century City Marketplace, Century City ☎310/772-2100. This major chain features all the standard men's and women's apparel, kitchen items, and assorted jewelry and kidswear. Also in the Beverly Center, Sherman Oaks Fashion Square, and Newport Beach Fashion Island.

Macy's 8500 Beverly Blvd, in the Beverly Center mall ☎310/854-6655. A familiar figure in the LA department store scene, at the Century City Marketplace ☎310/556-1611; 750 W Seventh St, Downtown ☎213/628-9311; the Santa Monica Place mall ☎310/393-1441; Sherman Oaks Fashion Square ☎818/788-8350; Paseo Colorado mall ☎626/796-0411; 401 S Lake Ave, Pasadena ☎626/792-0211; 3400 Sepulveda Blvd, Manhattan Beach ☎310/546-5525; Del Amo Fashion Center, South Bay ☎310/542-8525; Glendale Galleria ☎818/240-8411; Newport Beach Fashion Island ☎714/640-8333; South Coast Plaza, Costa Mesa ☎714/556-0611; and five other Orange County locations.

Neiman-Marcus 9700 Wilshire Blvd, Beverly Hills ☎310/550-5900. With three fancy restaurants, opulent displays of jewelry, and a plethora of fur coats, this store is quintessential Beverly Hills, located at the base of the Golden Triangle. Also in Orange County at Newport Beach Fashion Island ☎949/759-1900.

Nordstrom 10830 Pico Blvd, in the Westside Pavilion mall, West LA ☎310/470-6155. Mostly clothing and accessories at this Westside department store. If you can't decide on the right party dress or power tie, a "personal shopper" can help you – for a steep price. Also at the Grove,

Mid-Wilshire ☎323/930-2230; Glendale Galleria ☎818/502-9922; 6602 Topanga Canyon Blvd, Canoga Park ☎818/884-7900; South Coast Plaza ☎714/549-8300; and many other branches in the valleys and Orange County. A cheaper option is the Nordstrom Rack at 901 S Coast Drive, Costa Mesa ☎714/751-5901; and 227 N Glendale Ave, Glendale ☎818/240-2404.

Robinsons-May 103 Santa Monica Place, in the Santa Monica Place mall ☎310/451-2411. Offers better prices than some of its competitors, along with a wide selection of clothing and housewares. Also at 920 Seventh St, Downtown ☎213/683-1144; 9900 Wilshire Blvd, Beverly Hills ☎310/275-5464; Westside Pavilion, 10730 W Pico Blvd ☎310/475-4911; 6050 Sepulveda Blvd, Culver City ☎310/390-8811; Glendale Galleria ☎818/247-2600; Del Amo Fashion Center ☎310/542-5941; South Coast Plaza ☎714/546-9321; Newport Beach Fashion Island ☎949/644-2800; and many other suburban locations.

Saks Fifth Avenue 9600 Wilshire Blvd, Beverly Hills ☎310/275-4211. A high-end chain with expensive perfume, eye-popping jewelry, and high fashion. Also at South Coast Plaza ☎714/540-3233; and in Palos Verdes at 550 Deep Valley Drive, Rolling Hills Estates ☎310/265-2600.

Shopping malls

Beverly Center 8500 Beverly Blvd, between Mid-Wilshire and West Hollywood ☎310/854-0070. Chic shopping for the masses, atop a multi-story parking garage: seven acres of boutiques, Macy's and Bloomingdale's department stores, a multiplex cinema, and a ground-level *Hard Rock Café*.

Burbank Town Center 201 E Magnolia Blvd at N San Fernando Rd, Burbank ☎818/566-8617. Branches of Sears, Mervyn's and the low-cost furniture retailer IKEA occupy this complex of buildings just outside the heart of old Burbank, right beside the I-5 freeway.

Century City Marketplace 10250 Santa Monica Blvd, Century City ☎310/553-5300. An outdoor mall, with Macy's and Bloomingdale's department stores, one hundred upscale shops, and a good food court. The place to see stars do their shopping or catch a first-run movie at the excellent AMC Century 14 Theater (see p.323).

Del Amo Fashion Center Hawthorne Blvd at Carson St, Torrance ☎310/542-8525. A huge mall in the South Bay, with Macy's and Robinsons-May stores, plus a convenient location just south of the 405 freeway.

Fashion Island 401 Newport Center Drive, Newport Beach ☎949/721-2000. A reasonable alternative to Orange County's South Coast Plaza, though not as large, with an appealing outdoor setting. The mall, anchored by Bloomingdale's, Macy's, Robinsons-May, and Neiman-Marcus, is close to the Orange County Museum of Art.

Glendale Galleria Central Ave at Colorado St, Glendale ☎818/240-9481. A sprawling downtown complex with Robinsons-May, Nordstrom, and Macy's, and a broad selection of clothiers.

The Grove 6301 W Third St, Mid-Wilshire ☎323/571-8830. Stylish, open-air complex next to the Farmers Market, with a Nordstrom and all the usual chain retailers and restaurants, plus mainstream movie theaters.

Hollywood & Highland at the same intersection in Hollywood ☎323/960-2331. A mega-mall modeled after an elaborate silent-film set, but offering the usual corporate boutiques and trendy shops, and a multiplex connected to the Chinese Theatre.

▽ Hollywood & Highland mall

Paseo Colorado E Colorado Blvd at S Los Robles Ave, Pasadena ☎626/795-8891. Two

levels of (mostly chain) stores, including Macy's, beneath several levels of housing, with street-front entrances and an open-air design that invites strolling.

Santa Monica Place Broadway at Second St, Santa Monica ☎310/394-5451. Sunny, skylit mall with three tiers of major chain stores, including Macy's, and outdated pastel decor.

Sherman Oaks Fashion Square 14006 Riverside Drive, San Fernando Valley ☎818/783-0550. The famed Galleria – the original Sherman Oaks home to the notorious "Valley girls" – no longer exists, so this nearby mall now suffices for Valley denizens. Macy's and Bloomingdale's are the anchors, with around 120 other chain stores vying for your attention.

Sherman Oaks Galleria 15301 Ventura Blvd, Sherman Oaks ☎818/990-4060. Sleek mall – and nothing like the original Galleria – with a handful of restaurants and shops, plus a multiplex; mildly worthwhile if you're in the neighborhood.

South Coast Plaza 3333 Bristol St, north of 405 freeway, Costa Mesa ☎714/435-2000. Orange County's main super-mall, where you'll get a good workout navigating around the nearly three hundred shops and huge crowds of locals and tourists. Includes seven anchor stores – among them Robinsons-May, Saks Fifth Avenue, and Nordstrom.

Third Street Promenade Third St between Broadway and Wilshire Blvd, Santa Monica. A rare successful attempt to lure back consumers to the heart of the city, packed on weekend evenings with mobs scurrying about the fashion outlets, restaurants, and cinemas amid throngs of itinerant musicians, homeless people, and gaping tourists. Chain retailers have replaced the independent businesses in recent years, though.

Westside Pavilion Pico and Westwood blvds, West LA ☎310/474-6255. The obligatory chain stores at this postmodern shopping complex centered around Nordstrom and Robinsons-May; the outdoor, western side of the mall is more engaging to stroll through, but has the same familiar retailers.

Clothes and fashion

LA's **clothing** stores are some of its most important cultural phenomena – where you can pick out a new personality to go with a freshly bought Hermès bag, velvet cape, or gold lamé dog collar. Apart from the usual chain-clothing stores, you'll find hordes of haughty designer boutiques along Rodeo Drive, on the western side of West Hollywood, and increasingly along Melrose Avenue. Much more relaxed are the funky clothing stores for which LA is famous, many of them located along La Brea and north Vermont avenues and Santa Monica and Sunset boulevards. If you're just looking for cheap duds, however, LA has a good selection of secondhand and vintage clothiers to choose from. Finally, for designer clothes, such as Chanel, on **consignment**, visit Rodeo Drive Resale, 11306 Ventura Blvd, Studio City in the San Fernando Valley (☎818/980-9990).

Upscale chain stores

Bernini 8500 Beverly Blvd, in the Beverly Center mall ☎310/855-1786. Any money you haven't spent elsewhere in the mall will quickly evaporate at this pricey Italian shop, which offers chic men's and women's clothing, notably fancy suits and tuxedos, plus colognes and perfumes. Also at 131 N La Cienega Blvd, West Hollywood ☎310/659-0228; 346 N Rodeo Drive, Beverly Hills ☎310/278-6287; and in the Century City Marketplace ☎310/551-1786.

Chanel 442 N Rodeo Drive, Beverly Hills ☎310/278-5500. As you'd expect, a pricey selection of swanky clothes and perfumes from Paris. You'll get a healthy dose of attitude, too, if you've only come to browse.

Christian Dior 309 N Rodeo Drive, Beverly Hills ☎310/859-4700. Top-flight high fashion for predictably high prices – but you knew that already. Show up wearing jeans and sneakers and expect to be shown the door. Also at South Coast Plaza ☎714/549-4700.

Façonnable 9680 Wilshire Blvd, Beverly Hills ☎310/247-8277. An upper-income clothing merchant at the base of the Golden Triangle, selling sleek casual and dress wear, and an assortment of colognes and fragrances; a shade less pretentious than some of its bigger-name neighbors. Also at South Coast Plaza ☎714/966-1140.

Fendi 355 N Rodeo Drive, Beverly Hills ☎310/276-8888. Ultra-chic designer shirts, sportswear, and watches for Americans who want to look vaguely European, but not be too showy about it. Also at South Coast Plaza ☎714/751-1111.

Giorgio Armani 436 N Rodeo Drive, Beverly Hills ☎310/271-5555. One of LA's most elite fashion dealers, featuring sleek, well-cut suits that are standard issue to movie agents, lawyers, and other self-anointed big shots. For slightly cheaper clothing, try Emporio Armani at 9533 Brighton Way ☎310/271-7823, or Armani Exchange, at 8700 Sunset Blvd, West Hollywood ☎310/659-0171; 131 N La Cienega Blvd, West Hollywood ☎310/289-3610; and 1215 E Colorado Blvd, Glendale ☎818/244-1456.

Gucci 347 N Rodeo Drive, Beverly Hills ☎310/278-3451. Aside from the outlandishly priced shoes, wallets and accessories that you can find here, there's also a fair assortment of men's and women's clothing. Also at South Coast Plaza ☎714/557-9600.

Hugo Boss 414 N Rodeo Drive, Beverly Hills ☎310/859-2888. The place to go if you're looking for a thousand-dollar suit. Also at 8625 Sunset Blvd, West Hollywood ☎310/360-6935; in the Beverly Center mall ☎310/659-6676; Century City Marketplace ☎310/553-5300; and South Coast Plaza ☎714/641-8661.

Kenneth Cole Broadway at Second Street, in the Santa Monica Place mall ☎310/458-6633. Leather jackets, tapered boots, sleek earrings, and hip-hugging pants – all in black – to help you get into the chic nightclubs in town. Also a branch in the Century City Marketplace ☎310/658-6633; and Newport Beach Fashion Island ☎949/219-0671.

Louis Vuitton 295 N Rodeo Drive, Beverly Hills ☎310/859-0457. Designer wallets and luggage, with plenty of expensive styles from which to choose. Also at the Beverly Center mall ☎310/360-1506; Century City Mall ☎310/551-0090; Hollywood & Highland mall ☎323/962-6216; Newport Beach Fashion Island ☎949/759-1900; and South Coast Plaza ☎714/662-6907.

Miu Miu 8025 Melrose Ave, West Hollywood ☎323/651-0072. Where the masses (and a few celebs) go when they don't want to drop a wad at Prada – this is a cheaper and more colorful offshoot of the same parent company, stocked with plenty of eye-catching clothes for men and women and a famously impressive array of shoes.

Prada 469 N Rodeo Drive, Beverly Hills
℡310/385-5959. The best place to gape at the stars: an incomparable clothier whose clients don't bat an eyelash at paying thousands for a shirt. Somewhat less stuffy is the branch at South Coast Plaza ℡714/979-3003, and there's a wholesale version in Downtown, 1125 Maple Ave ℡213/749-9696.

Ralph Lauren 444 N Rodeo Drive, Beverly Hills
℡310/281-7200. The top place to get yourself outfitted as a member of the English gentry. Pick up a gilded walking cane, finely tailored suit, and a smart tweed cap, all for a small fortune. Also at South Coast Plaza ℡714/556-7656.

Zegna 301 N Rodeo Drive, Beverly Hills
℡310/247-8827. Exclusive lines of menswear and the high-end men's ZegnaSport collection make this a popular spot for young celebrities and even old-money types. Also at South Coast Plaza ℡714/444-1534.

Designer boutiques

Betsey Johnson 8050 Melrose Ave, West Hollywood ℡323/852-1534. An upscale boutique where stiletto heels, micro-miniskirts, and fashionably dingy attire are all part of a funky look, for which you'll pay plenty. Other branches in the Sherman Oaks Fashion Square, 14006 Riverside Drive ℡818/783-0550; Beverly Center Mall, 8500 Beverly Blvd ℡310/854-0070; plus a wholesaler at 127 E 9th St, Downtown ℡213/489-2326.

Diavolina 334 S La Brea Ave, Mid-Wilshire
℡323/936-3000. Shoes to give you the look of a "little devil" and which you can really strike a pose with: killer stilettos, modest mules and funky boots, priced anywhere from around $100 to well over $500.

Fred Segal 8118 Melrose Ave, West Hollywood ℡323/655-3734. For those poseurs and party-hoppers who wouldn't be spotted dead in Beverly Hills, this Melrose complex of four Segal outlets – selling everything from stylish shoes and duds to make-up – provides just the right mix of designer gloss and funky edge. Also with many other citywide branches.

Frederick's of Hollywood 6606 Hollywood Blvd, Hollywood ℡323/466-8506. The pink-and-purple tower of Frederick's houses a panoply of frilly, lacy and leathery lingerie (prices vary), as well as a Hall of Fame devoted to famous celebrity undergarments. Many

other branches in and around LA, though none with the style and pizzazz of this one.

Giselle 1306 Montana Ave, Santa Monica
℡310/451-2140. Well-made designer women's clothing in a variety of styles, but with a strong emphasis on wispy, pre-Raphaelite designs aimed for size-2 waifs. Also at 3835 Cross Creek Rd, Malibu ℡310/456-0142.

Jimmy Choo 469 N Canon Drive, Beverly Hills
℡310/860-9045. Even if you're just looking, and can't afford the exorbitant prices, there are enough glam stilettos and stylish leather boots to give you warm memories on your trip home.

Kbond 7257 Beverly Blvd, Mid-Wilshire
℡323/939-8866. On the cutting edge of contemporary trendiness on the Westside, a cheeky high-end clothing merchant selling rotating labels amid artworks of varying quality and coffee-table books on upscale art and design.

Kendo 7218 Melrose Ave ℡323/934-9450. The self-proclaimed women's "sneaker boutique" that really is the height of conspicuous, almost absurd consumption – selling high-priced vintage running shoes from the 1970s and 80s, along with limited-edition designer footwear of the stylish and sporty varieties.

Maxfield 8825 Melrose Ave, West Hollywood ℡310/274-8800. One of LA's most exclusive (and haughty) boutiques, selling big-name and lesser-known labels, and displaying pricey classic and modern antiques, expensive baubles, and an eye-popping array of jewelry.

Paper Bag Princess 8700 Santa Monica Blvd, West Hollywood ℡310/358-1985. A cross between an elite boutique and a second-hand store: an upscale dealer in gently worn vintage designer fashions – from Chanel to Versace. Some items on the racks are on consignment from actual celebrities (who allegedly frequent the place).

Scala 153 S La Brea Ave, Mid-Wilshire
℡323/954-8204. Quirky but smart women's attire made by the owner herself. This trendy little boutique has lower prices than comparable stores to the west, though it's still far from cheap.

Funky clothing

Agent Provocateur 7961 Melrose Ave, West Hollywood ℡323/653-0229. If Victorian-style knickers and tasteful, yet racy, boudoir duds are what you're seeking, this is the spot – LA's own, quirkier spin on Victoria's Secret, with a lot more spark and imagination.

Don't Panic! 802 N San Vicente Blvd, West Hollywood ⓣ310/652-9689. The racy counterpart to the many bland T-shirt shops in LA, stocking more than a hundred styles bearing shocking, crude, or off-color slogans. Also at 1738 Cordova St, just off the I-10 freeway in Mid-Wilshire ⓣ323/373-1965.

Dream Dresser 8444 Santa Monica Blvd, West Hollywood ⓣ323/848-3480. A fetish-wear institution, with a selection of corsets, dresses, and lingerie made from rubber, leather, and vinyl, plus matching whips and harnesses for the S&M set. Custom-designed outfits can be tailored for women or men.

Ipso Facto 517 N Harbor Blvd, Fullerton ⓣ714/525-7865. Piercing supplies for serious punks, ultra-black goth clothing, and a full range of skull-emblazoned belts, rings, and boots at this retailer in, of all places, Orange County.

Necromance 7220 Melrose Ave, north of Mid-Wilshire ⓣ323/934-8684. A skeleton in the window invites you in to try on the latest ghoulish clothing at this morbidly themed shop, which sells outfits suitable for black-clad, cape-wearing goths and can make you look like a spooky specter before you know it.

Playmates of Hollywood 6438 Hollywood Blvd, Hollywood ⓣ323/464-7636. Despite the dubious name, not an escort service, but a risqué clothing emporium selling pasties, push-up bras, scanty bikinis, lacy and leathery underwear, and feather boas, among many other fashionable temptations of the flesh.

Red Balls 7365 Melrose Ave, north of Mid-Wilshire ⓣ323/655-3409. One of Melrose's signature retailers, and a bit longer-lasting than most have been, stocking fun and funky clubwear, leather belts and jackets, and various other sporty, sprightly duds.

Retail Slut 7308 Melrose Ave, north of Mid-Wilshire ⓣ323/934-1339. An essential Melrose stop for decades, where you can pick up all the vinyl dresses, skull necklaces, leather dog collars, bondage gear, and spiked wristbands you'll ever need.

Trashy Lingerie 402 N La Cienega Blvd, West Hollywood ⓣ310/659-4550. Not only can you find the sort of undergarments suggested by this store's name, you can also browse

through a wide selection of more traditional satin and silk bras, teddies, and bustiers. All of the revealing items are handmade, and you'll have to pay $5 for an annual "membership fee" to get in.

Uncle Jer's 4459 Sunset Blvd, Silver Lake ⓣ323/662-6710. Quirky shop crammed with colorful and inexpensive clothing from developing countries, much of it handmade, along with soaps and fragrances, incense and "magic potions," and assorted trinkets.

Secondhand and vintage clothing

Aardvark's Odd Ark 21434 Sherman Way, Canoga Park ⓣ818/999-3211. One of LA's best spots for buying used garments, whether wild psychedelic shirts, old leisure suits, goofy ball caps and frumpy pants, or more recent – and more fashionable – shirts, skirts, dresses, and suits. Also at 7579 Melrose Ave ⓣ323/655-6769.

American Rag 150 S La Brea Ave, Mid-Wilshire ⓣ323/935-3154. Not your typical second-hand clothing store; the beaten-up denim jackets, floral-print dresses, and retro shoes here are often high-end designer material, sometimes restyled into new forms. This is among the most prominent of LA's vintage dealers, so be prepared to shell out. Another branch at 5724 W Third St, Mid-Wilshire ⓣ323/965-8339.

Cheap Vintage 705 S Pacific Ave, San Pedro ⓣ310/547-1000. Worth a trip down to the harbor area for its bargain-basement coats, dresses, shoes, and skirts ($5–15). The secondhand garments vary in quality, but some are in surprisingly good condition.

Decades 8214 Melrose Ave, West Hollywood ⓣ323/655-0223. A reseller of elegant designer wear, but concentrating on mod retro-clothes from the 1960s, with occasional detours into stylish 1950s apparel and ungainly 1970s jumpsuits.

Golyester 136 S La Brea Ave, Mid-Wilshire ⓣ323/931-1339. A favorable LA seller of very vintage materials, with clothes dating as far back as the nineteenth century, in every sort of fabric imaginable. Also sells antiques.

It's a Wrap 3315 W Magnolia Blvd, Burbank ⓣ818/567-7366. Fans of fashion and Hollywood will squeal with delight at this Valley reseller of garments and wardrobes from recent movies and TV shows. The prices aren't too cheap, but if you can't go another minute without owning a jacket worn by one of the Desperate Housewives, this store is for you.

Jet Rag 825 N La Brea Ave, Hollywood
☎323/939-0528. Vintage dealer selling stylish club jackets from the old Hollywood days, as well as various garments from the early 1900s to the present. Another branch in the South Central district of Florence, at 1001 E 62nd St ☎323/232-1191.

Julian's 8366 W Third St, Mid-Wilshire
☎323/655-3011. No retro-kitsch here, only ultra-chic vintage clothing from the 1950s and earlier, including hats, furs, dinner jackets, dresses, and scarves, at somewhat higher prices than elsewhere.

Junk for Joy 3314 W Magnolia Blvd, Burbank
☎818/569-4903. A vintage dealer whose old-time clothing from the 1950s to the 1970s not only looks great, it's never been worn. The attire on display consists of ancient, discontinued items that have been over-looked by various fashion trends – but not by Hollywood, whose wardrobe designers sometimes use them for shoots.

Ozzie Dots 4637 Hollywood Blvd, Los Feliz
☎323/663-2867. A vintage store that offers a fine selection of colorful and eye-catching 1930s-through-1970s attire – but since this is East Hollywood, the place also has assorted offbeat theatrical costumes, props, and accessories like feather boas, Tiki cuff links, and soda-jerk hats.

Polkadots and Moonbeams 8367 Third St, Mid-Wilshire ☎323/651-1746. Dresses, swimsuits and sweaters from the pre-1970s era, most in fine condition and some quite affordable. If it's more modern clothing you crave, drift down to the pricier contemporary outlet at 8379 Third St ☎323/655-3880.

Reel Clothes 5525 Cahuenga Blvd, North Hollywood ☎818/508-7762. A San Fernando Valley store that sells all types of used clothing and props from movie and TV-show se the scarf, hat or dress – or even outfit – of a lead character in a of your fancy, with 40–90 percent on

Re-Mix 7605 1/2 Beverly Blvd, Mid-Wilshire
☎323/936-6210. Stylish men's and women's shoes from the supper-club 1940s up to the disco 1970s, all of them authentic and none of them ever worn before.

Squaresville 1800 N Vermont Ave, Los Feliz
☎323/669-8464. A bit off the beaten vintage path, but worth a trip for its cheap prices for mainly 1950s-through-80s wear and color-ful jewelry and accessories – plus a good selection of holiday (ie, Halloween) wear during the season.

Star Wares 5341 Derry Ave, Agoura Hills
☎818/881-9077. If you desperately want something previously owned by a celebrity, and find yourself on the western edge of LA County, this spot sells old duds from the closets of the stars. As with Reel Clothes, the prices are below retail.

Wasteland 7428 Melrose Ave, north of Mid-Wilshire ☎323/653-3028. Solid vintage and used designer wear for a variety of prices; not the flashiest store on the block, but one of the more reliable resellers on this busy strip.

▽ Wasteland on Melrose

Spas and beauty services

As the capital of self-worship and personal transformation, LA has a large array of **hair** and **make-up salons** where you can be teased, sprayed, and made up. While cheap spots for a haircut are everywhere, if you're really looking to get a fancy makeover, or a massage, manicure, or pedicure, there are a few top–notch **spas** and salons around, as well as some that charge affordable prices.

Ball Beauty Supply 416 N Fairfax Ave, north of Mid-Wilshire ☎323/655-2330. A great storehouse for inexpensive make-up, wigs, and other adornments, where the clientele is a mix of youthful male and female club-hoppers and old-timers who've been coming here for ages.

Beauty Bar 1638 N Cahuenga Blvd, Hollywood
☎323/464-7676. A fun watering-hole where you can choose from an array of beauty

services at affordable prices – plus knock back a neon-colored concoction and let your head swim. See also p.300.

Goodform 727 N Fairfax Ave, West Hollywood ☎323/658-8585. Whether you're going clubbing or to a power lunch, this colorful parlor will do the trick for around $50–100, using a variety of hair-styling and makeover techniques, along with more straightforward skin care and manicures.

Jessica's Nail Clinic 8627 Sunset Blvd, West Hollywood ☎310/659-9292. The place where the stars get their pedicures and manicures, and you can too, often starting at $40.

Larchmont Beauty Center 208 N Larchmont Blvd, Mid-Wilshire ☎323/461-0162. Features a comprehensive, and pricey, assortment of beauty-care treatments, from hair styling, manicures and pedicures, makeovers and skin care to Swedish massage and aromatherapy.

Ona Spa 7373 Beverly Blvd, north of mid-Wilshire ☎323/931-4442. Although not in Beverly Hills per se, this chic spa has much of the attitude and trendy atmosphere, with a vaguely Asian- (or at least feng shui-) inspired design, and such options as Indian-styled massage and "Ayurvedic vitality and detox treatments" for those in need of soul- as well as body-cleansing.

Raphaël 9020 Burton Way, Beverly Hills ☎310/275-5810. Watch this hair-care wizard do masterful things to your tangles and split ends; in the process, you might even glimpse a celebrity or two. By appointment only.

Robinson's Beautilities 12320 Venice Blvd, West LA ☎310/398-5757. A fun spot to get supplies for your own hair and facial design. Along with a good selection of hair-care products and make-up, this supply house stocks a fascinating assortment of designer

and fright wigs, facial glitter, and special-effects make-up for the movie biz.

Rudy's Barber Shop 4451 W Sunset Blvd, Los Feliz ☎323/661-6535. Idiosyncratic LA salon, a super-hip joint in a converted East Hollywood garage that draws the local rocker and actor crowd. Expect a long, but worthwhile, wait to re-imagine yourself in a spiked mohawk, feathered 1970s-dude look, trendy goatee, or devilish Vandyke.

Taka 2010 Sawtelle Blvd, West LA ☎310/575-6819. Hair styling with an Asian flair and a sharp modern edge that won't cost you a fortune (if it isn't entirely cheap, either), offering a full arsenal of perms, cuts, weaves, straightenings, kinks, and anything else you can dream up.

Umberto 452 N Camden Drive, Beverly Hills ☎310/274-0393. Another celebrity-friendly locale, with steep prices, but not quite as much pretension as some of its neighbors. While you wait, eat a sandwich, or sip a cappuccino from the in-house food service. Also at 416 N Canon Drive, Beverly Hills ☎310/274-6395.

Vidal Sassoon 9403 Little Santa Monica Blvd, Beverly Hills ☎310/274-8791. While the full-price haircuts may seem out of reach, assistants in training charge roughly half the cost ($60) – a very good deal considering the area. Cosmetology students can also tinker with your looks for even less (as little as $19) at Vidal Sassoon's own "hair academy," located at 321 Santa Monica Blvd, Santa Monica ☎310/255-0011.

Wax Poetic 3208 W Magnolia Blvd, Burbank ☎818/843-9469. A good choice for those who want to be pampered with a full range of treatments (waxings, hair styling, tints, chemical peels) in a welcoming atmosphere.

Drugstores and pharmacies

Horton & Converse 11600 Wilshire Blvd, West LA ☎310/478-0801. Open until 2am. Other locations are open regular business hours: 2001 Santa Monica Blvd, Santa Monica ☎310/829-1834; 7080 Hollywood Blvd ☎323/466-8187; 735 S Figueroa St, Downtown ☎213/623-2838; and 1127 Wilshire Blvd, Downtown ☎213/481-7030. Open seven days at 325 N Larchmont Blvd, Mid-Wilshire ☎323/466-7606; and 10250 Santa Monica Blvd, West LA ☎310/557-2332.

Longs Drugs 8490 Beverly Blvd, Mid-Wilshire ☎323/653-0880. Also at 9618 Pico Blvd, West LA ☎310/858-1070; and 11941 San Vicente Blvd, West LA ☎310/440-4160.

Mickey Fine 433 N Roxbury St, Beverly Hills ☎310/271-6123. You could have guessed it might exist: an only-in-LA pharmacy where the elite meet to pick up fancy European hair- and facial-care products, along with all the latest foreign creams, ointments, gels, and anything else you might want to smear on your body to make it more radiant.

Rite-Aid 226 N Larchmont Blvd, Mid-Wilshire
☎**323/467-1366.** Also at 300 N Canon Drive,
Beverly Hills ☎310/273-3561; 7900 Sunset
Blvd, Hollywood ☎323/876-4466; 1637 N
Vermont Ave, Hollywood ☎323/664-9854;
7900 W Sunset Blvd, West Hollywood
☎323/876-4466; 1101 Westwood Blvd,
West LA ☎310/209-0708; 1843 S La Cienega Blvd, West LA ☎310/559-1402. See
Ⓦwww.riteaid.com for more area branches.
Sav-On/Osco 201 N Los Angeles St, Downtown
☎**213/620-1491.** Also at 861 N Vine St,

Hollywood ☎323/466-7300; 5570 Wilshire
Blvd, Mid-Wilshire ☎323/936-6121; 5510
Sunset Blvd, Hollywood ☎323/464-2169;
8491 Santa Monica Blvd, West Hollywood
☎310/360-7303; 12315 Venice Blvd,
West LA ☎310/390-6296; 12015 Wilshire
Blvd, West LA ☎310/479-6500; 13171
Mindanao Way, Marina del Rey ☎310/821-
8908. See Ⓦwww.savon.com for more area
branches.

**West LA Medical Center 6041 Cadillac Ave, West
LA** ☎**323/857-2151.** Open 24 hours.

Food and drink

Since eating out in LA is so common, you may never have to shop for **food** and
drink at all. But if you're preparing a picnic, or want to indulge in a bit of home
cooking, there are plenty of places to stock up. **Delis** and **groceries**, many open
around the clock, can be found on many street corners, and supermarkets are
almost as common, with some open 24 hours or at least until 10pm – look in
the *Yellow Pages* for Albertson's, Vons, Pavilions, Ralph's, and Trader Joe's, and the
more gourmet-oriented Whole Foods and Wild Oats. There are also a number
of good **ethnic groceries** and **health–food stores**, as well as various fine
bakeries, mainly clustered in West LA.

Delis and groceries

Art's Deli 12224 Ventura Blvd, Studio City
☎818/762-1221. Long-standing film-industry favorite, and the one deli that rarely
provokes complaints among aficionados,
providing a good range of sandwiches,
soups, and breads.

Brent's Deli 19565 Parthenia Ave, Northridge
☎818/886-5679. This New York–style deli, in
a remote corner of the San Fernando Valley,
features a huge takeout selection of meat,
fish, desserts, salads, and sandwiches.
Easily the best of its kind in the Valley, some
would even say LA itself.

Bristol Farms 7880 W Sunset Blvd, Hollywood
☎323/874-6301. One of the region's best
grocers, with delicious meats, cheeses,
wine, and caviar, but prices can be rather
high. Also at 9039 Beverly Blvd, West
Hollywood ☎310/248-2804; 1515 Westwood Blvd, West LA ☎310/481-0100;
606 Fair Oaks Ave, South Pasadena
☎626/441-5450; and four South Bay locations. See Ⓦwww.bristolfarms.com for
details.

**Canter's Deli 419 N Fairfax Ave, north of Mid-
Wilshire** ☎323/651-2030. An LA institution,
next to its own unusual cabaret (see p.322),
with sandwiches, kosher soups, a good

selection of meat and fish, and assorted
sweets. Open 24 hours.

**Grand Central Market 317 S Broadway, Down-
town** ☎213/624-2378. One of the city's
prime culinary features, a warren of food
stalls and vendors of all sorts of produce,
meat, cheese, snacks, and pastries from
the region.

Izzy's Deli 1433 Wilshire Blvd, Santa Monica
☎310/394-1131. Long-standing favorite for
straightforward deli fare, and one of the few
good bets for authentic deli sandwiches
along the coast. Open 24 hours.

**Jerry's Famous Deli 8017 Beverly Blvd, West
Hollywood** ☎310/289-1811. This local institution has the standard array of takeout
soups, sandwiches, and meats, but is
best for its wide array of tempting cakes
and pies. This particular branch is open
24 hours, as is the one in Studio City at
12655 Ventura Blvd ☎818/980-4245.
Also at 10925 Weyburn Ave, Westwood
☎310/208-3354; and four suburban locations. See Ⓦwww.jerrysfamousdeli.com for
details.

Junior's 2379 Westwood Blvd, West LA
☎310/475-5771. This fine Westside deli and
restaurant features a good bakery and deli
counter that stocks all of the usual favorites
– including lox and egg dishes.

Langer's 704 S Alvarado St, Mid-Wilshire
☎213/483-8050. In the middle of the high-crime Westlake district, this is nevertheless one of LA's finest delis, with an excellent selection of takeout meats and baked goods, and twenty variations on LA's best pastrami sandwich. Open daylight hours only; curbside pick-up available.

Nate 'n' Al's 414 N Beverly Drive, Beverly Hills
☎310/274-0101. This superior deli, in the middle of Beverly Hills' Golden Triangle, has a good array of meat and bread offerings – not to mention terrific blintzes, lox, and matzo-ball soup. See also p.270.

Smart and Final 7720 Melrose Ave, north of Mid-Wilshire ☎323/655-2211. This bulk retail chain packs its stores with big, industrial-sized boxes of cereal, paper towels, fruit juice, and just about anything else you might need in massive quantities. Many locations around town.

Stan's Produce 9307 W Pico Blvd, West LA
☎310/274-1865. A popular neighborhood grocer with a fine selection of fruits, vegetables, and exotic produce. Just south of Beverly Hills.

Vicente Foods 12027 San Vicente Blvd, Brentwood ☎310/472-5215. If you're in this upscale neighborhood, this is a good place to stop for a terrific selection of quality foods, with breads, cheeses and meats to suit your fancy and worth the high prices.

Ethnic groceries

Alpine Village 833 W Torrance Blvd, Torrance
☎310/323-6520. Though quite a hike, and in a rather drab South Bay area, this place has all the bratwurst and schnitzel you'll ever need, and plays host to one of LA's more spirited Oktoberfest celebrations.

American Armenian Grocery 1442 E Washington Blvd, Pasadena ☎626/794-9220. The place to come if you want to sample a taste of authentic food from the Caucasus region of Asia; a store frequented by a few of the growing numbers of Armenian immigrants to the LA region.

Bang Luck Market 5170 Hollywood Blvd, Hollywood ☎323/660-8000. Thai grocer in Los Feliz, with meat, fish, sauces, and noodles to help you make a Southeast Asian feast, or a simple snack.

Bay Cities 1517 Lincoln Blvd, Santa Monica
☎310/395-8279. An excellent, centrally located deli and retailer that, with its Italian

focus, offers piles of fresh pasta and meat from the Old World, along with spices, sauces, and many French and Middle Eastern imports.

Bharat Bazaar 11510 Washington Blvd, Culver City ☎310/398-6766. One of several fine Indian grocers in this section of town, providing goods for making your own curries and vindaloo.

Claro's Italian Market 1003 E Valley Blvd, San Gabriel ☎626/288-2026. This compact but well-stocked spot has everything from Italian wines, chocolate, and crackers to store-brand frozen meals, plus a deli and a bakery offering some forty varieties of cookies. Worth the drive out to this section of the San Gabriel Valley – the closest of six rather distant stores.

Domingo's Italian Grocery 17548 Ventura Blvd, Encino ☎818/981-4466. A good reason for traveling to the San Fernando Valley: authentic Italian meats, pasta, and cheeses.

Elat Meat Market 8730 Pico Blvd, West LA
☎310/659-7070. Mainly Middle Eastern staples at this colorful kosher market, located near other ethnic grocers on Pico Blvd, just southeast of Beverly Hills.

Gastronom 7859 Santa Monica Blvd, West Hollywood ☎323/654-9456. Smoked fish and caviar are the highlights at this bustling market, a fixture in the area's burgeoning Russian community.

Mandarin Deli 727 N Broadway, Downtown
☎213/623-6054. Very tasty and cheap noodles, pork and fish dumplings, and other hearty staples in the middle of Chinatown. Also at 356 E Second St, Little Tokyo ☎213/617-0231.

Market World 3030 W Sepulveda Blvd, Torrance ☎310/539-8899. A good selection of prepared Asian meats, vegetables, and noodles at this South Bay grocery. Located off Crenshaw Blvd.

Nijiya Market 2130 Sawtelle Blvd, West LA
☎310/575-3300. Bentos – rice-and-meat combos served in a bowl – are some of the succulent takeout items available at this Japanese grocer. Also a branch in the South Bay at 2121 W 182nd St, Torrance ☎310/366-7200.

Olson's Deli 5560 Pico Blvd, Mid-Wilshire
☎323/938-0742. Herring, meatballs, and assorted sausages at this solid Swedish grocer, one of the few Scandinavian food stores in LA and definitely worth a try.

Standard Sweets and Snacks 18600 Pioneer Blvd, Artesia ☎562/860-6364. Good Indian finger-food joint selling vegetarian *dosas* (pancakes) and delicious desserts, along with other traditional fare. North of Long Beach.

Thailand Plaza 5321 Hollywood Blvd, Hollywood ☎323/993-9000. This Thai supermarket and eatery has an impressive selection of Southeast Asian dishes, including noodles, spices, and delicacies for very cheap prices.

Vallarta Supermarket 10950 Sherman Way, Burbank ☎818/846-1717. San Fernando Valley chain – whose Burbank store is the closest to central LA – focusing on food-stuffs from Latin America, including special chilis and spices for cuisine from the region. Find more stores at ⓦwww .vallartasupermarket.com.

United Poultry 742 N Broadway, Downtown LA ☎213/620-9948. This Chinatown food retailer stocks not only chicken, but an array of familiar and exotic meats, from pork to boar.

Health-food stores

Beverly Hills Juice Club 8382 Beverly Blvd, north of Mid-Wilshire ☎323/655-8300. Raw foods are the focus of this vegan-oriented takeout vendor and grocery, which supplies fruit, veggies, meatless sushi, sprout rolls, and, of course, ultra-healthy juices.

Co-Opportunity 1525 Broadway, Santa Monica ☎310/451-8902. A popular neighborhood store selling organic and vegetarian foods, with a coffee & juice bar, plenty of macro-biotic and other specialty foodstuffs, and herbs, vitamins, and oils meant to soothe the body and soul.

Erewhon 7660 Beverly Blvd, north of Mid-Wilshire ☎323/937-0777. The epitome of health-obsessed LA, selling pricey health food and all the wheat grass you can swal-low. Close to CBS Television City and Pan-Pacific Park.

Full o' Life 2515 W Magnolia Blvd, Burbank ☎818/845-8343. This mother of all health-food stores dates back to 1959 and offers an organic market, deli, dairy, restaurant, and book department, and there are nutri-tionists and a naturopath on the premises daily. The premises burned up in early 2004, but was rebuilt as a new and improved store six months later.

Mother's Market 225 E 17th St, Costa Mesa ☎949/631-4741. A large health-food retailer

in Orange County, the perfect place to stock up on bulk supplies of juice, vitamins, veggie cuisine, and even animal-friendly beauty supplies. Also at 19770 Beach Blvd, Huntington Beach ☎714/963-6667, and several other, more distant Orange County locations.

Nature Mart 2080 Hillhurst Ave, Hollywood ☎323/667-1677. A Los Feliz storehouse for organic produce, non-sugary sweets, and a wealth of vitamins and herbs. Somewhat cheaper than comparable Westside retailers.

One Life 3001 Main St, Santa Monica ☎310/392-4501. Healthy eating near the bay, courtesy of this neighborhood grocer for organic produce, bulk foods, herbs, brown rice, unprocessed bread, and all the rest.

Papa Jon's 5006 E Second St, Long Beach ☎562/439-1059. Long-standing restaurant and market catering to vegetarians and vegans, with a range of affordable breads and juices as well as meatless entrees and garden burgers.

VP Discount Health Food 11665 Santa Monica Blvd, West LA ☎310/444-7949. A chain retailer that has a following of hard-core acolytes and vegans willing to pay a bit more for clean, sanctified food. Also at 3002 S Sepulveda Blvd, West LA ☎310/478-9798, and many other branches in the San Gabriel and San Fernando valleys.

Whole Foods Market 239 N Crescent Drive, Beverly Hills ☎310/274-3360. One in a nationwide chain of health-food megastores, this small but central branch is located in the exclusive Golden Triangle shopping zone. For other LA branches see ⓦwww .wholefoods.com.

Wild Oats 500 Wilshire Blvd, Santa Monica t310/395-4510. Another of the big names in healthy eating, with organic produce, bulk foods, etc, and many citywide branches. See ⓦwww.wildoats for details.

Baked and dairy goods

Al Gelato 806 S Robertson Blvd, West LA ☎310/659-8069. That delectable Italian version of ice cream – *gelato* – is served here with American panache: delicious flavors doled out in sizable helpings. The espresso *gelato* is particularly mouthwater-ing.

Beverlywood Bakery 9128 Pico Blvd, West LA ☎310/278-0122. Old World desserts and baked goods, from heavy strudels to chewy, thick-crusted breads are on offer, along with premium prices that reflect the store's proximity to Beverly Hills, a block north.

The Cheese Store 419 N Beverly Drive, Beverly Hills ☎1-800/547-1515 or 310/278-2855. More than four hundred types of cheese from all over the world, including every kind produced in the US – many of them suspended invitingly over your head, plus typically high prices to match.

Cobbler Factory 33 N Catalina Ave, Pasadena ☎626/449-2152. Bakery selling a range of scrumptious, fruity cobblers from $5–35, depending on how huge you want them. Occupies a prime spot near Old Pasadena.

Diamond Bakery 335 N Fairfax Ave, north of Mid-Wilshire ☎323/655-0534. In the heart of the Fairfax District, this great old Jewish bakery provides a good number of traditional favorites, including cheesecake, rugelach, and a legendary pumpernickel bread.

Doughboys Café and Bakery 8136 W Third St, Mid-Wilshire ☎323/651-4202. Tasty and filling pizzas, scones, and sandwiches are available for midday meals, but the real highlight of this Westside bakery is the bread: rich, hearty loaves with interesting ingredients like walnuts, olives, and various cheeses.

Eiger Ice Cream 124 S Barrington Place, Brentwood ☎310/471-6955. Whether in cones, dishes, or pies, the ice cream at this Westside favorite is always good and rich – with a lip-smacking chocolate raspberry to make you smile.

Fair Oaks Pharmacy and Soda Fountain 1526 Mission St, South Pasadena ☎626/799-1414. A fabulously restored soda fountain along the former Route 66, with many classic soda drinks, such as egg creams, and good old-fashioned ice-cream treats like sundaes and banana splits.

Fosselman's 1824 W Main St, Alhambra ☎626/282-6533. Reason alone to visit this San Gabriel Valley town: what many, many Angelenos regard as the region's best ice cream, a very long-standing (70+ years) seller of rich, creamy concoctions, highlighted by a delicious macadamia crunch and burgundy cherry.

Gill's Old Fashioned 6333 W Third St, north of Mid-Wilshire ☎213/936-6786. The name says it – a longtime neighborhood fave with a convenient location in the Farmers Market and nice selection of rich ice creams, yogurts, ices, and frozen bananas.

Hansen Cakes 193 S Beverly Drive, Beverly Hills

☎310/273-3759. A local institution that sells resplendently decorated, and very tasty, cakes – though not by the slice.

LA Desserts 113 N Robertson Blvd, Beverly Hills ☎310/273-5537. If you don't mind a few snide looks from the Hollywood swells, step into this terrific bakery inside the swank *Ivy* restaurant and try the delicious cakes, cookies, and tarts, among the best on the Westside.

La Brea Bakery 624 S La Brea Ave, Mid-Wilshire ☎323/939-6813. This bakery (adjacent to the upscale *Campanile* restaurant; see p.277) is a serious treat for anyone with an interest in fine breads, from sourdough rolls to fancier olive- and cherry-laden loaves.

Mäni's Bakery 2507 Main St, Santa Monica ☎310/396-7700. This vegetarian- and vegan-oriented bakery provides sugarless brownies and meatless sandwiches to local bohemians and wholefood-oriented yuppies. Also at 519 S Fairfax Ave, Mid-Wilshire ☎323/938-8800.

Mousse Fantasy 2130 Sawtelle Blvd, West LA ☎310/479-6665. A Japanese version of a French patisserie, located in a crowded strip mall, where the range of tasty tarts and pastries includes the noteworthy Green Tea Mousse cake – an unusual-tasting concoction.

Portos Cuban Bakery 315 N Brand Blvd, Glendale ☎818/956-5996. In a town that used to be a major home of Cuban immigrants, this throwback to the old days offers tasty baked goods and desserts, along with flaky Cuban pastries, cheesecakes soaked in rum, muffins, Danishes, croissants, and tortes.

Röckenwagner 2435 Main St, Santa Monica ☎310/399-6504. A Westside culinary delight serving California cuisine and *nouveau* German food, including chocolate desserts, rich pastries and scones, and hearty breads. Located in the Edgemar shopping complex.

Say Cheese 2800 Hyperion Ave, Silver Lake ☎323/665-0545. A distinctive array of French and other international cheeses, priced from moderate to expensive. The delicious sandwiches may be your best bet.

Viktor Benes Continental Pastries 8718 W Third St, West LA ☎310/276-0488. The place to go for freshly baked bread, coffee cakes, Danish pastries and various chocolate-flavored treats, and appreciative local fans know it. Five other area locations as well.

Beer, wine, and spirits

Cañon Liquor and Deli 1586 E Chevy Chase Drive, Glendale ☎818/547-1764. Pick up a bottle of wine or a pound of Italian meat at this excellent local grocer.

Greenblatt's Deli & Fine Wine 8017 Sunset Blvd, West Hollywood ☎323/656-0606. A Sunset Strip deli and liquor mart that's a neighborhood favorite, and is most well known for its excellent sandwiches and wide assortment of wine, brandy, Champagne, and Scotch. Open until 2am.

Hi-Time Wine Cellars 250 Ogle St, Costa Mesa ☎1-800/331-3005, ⓦwww.hitimewine.com. Despite the unimpressive name, this is one of Southern California's finest spots for wine and spirits, and perhaps its best overall choice for buying microbrewed and European beers. Worth a trip down to Orange County if you want to pick up that specialty Dunkelweisen from the Old World that you thought didn't exist in the New.

Red Carpet Wine 400 E Glenoaks Blvd, Glendale ☎818/247-5544 or 1-800/339-0609. Besides having a comfortable in-store wine bar and a sizable stock of vino and beer, this store is also a fine spot to purchase spirits, cigars, Champagne, and chocolates.

Valley Beverage Company 14901 Ventura Blvd, Sherman Oaks ☎818/981-1566. Offering an excellent selection of local and international wines, many at discounted prices, with a special emphasis on kosher wines, Scotch, tequila, and brandy.

Wally's 2107 Westwood Blvd, West LA ☎310/475-0606. A gourmet grocery that has a good assortment of caviar, cheeses, and other fancy treats, and sells hard liquor and cigars, too.

Wine and Liquor Depot 16938 Saticoy St, Van Nuys ☎818/996-1414. Promising the lowest area prices on blended and single malt Scotch, this Valley dealer is also worth a look for its international wines, port, sherry, bourbon, and beer.

Bookstores

At times, it can seem like LA has almost as many **bookstores** as people, with enough variety to suit every taste, whether you want flagship **superstores**, cozy local bookstores, or **specialist** and **secondhand** places that may reward several hours' browsing along the miles of dusty shelves. Also, while not so common, there are a few good **travel** bookstores worth noting, too.

Chains and superstores

Barnes and Noble 1201 Third St, Santa Monica ☎310/260-9110. High-volume chain with three floors of general and specialty books overlooking the end of the Third Street Promenade. See ⓦwww.bn.com for other branches.

Borders 1360 Westwood Blvd, West LA ☎310/475-3444. Easily the top LA branch of this omnipresent retailer, and at one time the biggest Borders in the US, with two sprawling floors, an upper-level café with outside seating, and an expansive music area with listening stations. See ⓦwww.borders.com for other branches.

Brentano's 10250 Santa Monica Blvd, in the Century City Mall ☎310/785-0204. While this chain dealer has a voluminous general selection, it's also possibly the most crowded bookshop in LA – near a popular movie theater and mall food court – and the one that tourists usually find themselves in, one way or another. Less-packed branches

in the Beverly Center (☎310/652-8024) and Sherman Oaks Fashion Square (☎818/788-8661) malls.

Dutton's 11975 San Vicente Blvd, Brentwood ☎310/476-6263. LA city-chain bookstore, with a wide selection and devoted group of Westside readers – meaning the prices aren't cheap. Also at 447 N Canon Drive, Beverly Hills ☎310/281-0997; the San Fernando Valley at 5146 Laurel Canyon Blvd, North Hollywood ☎818/769-3866; and 3806 W Magnolia Blvd, Burbank ☎818/840-8003.

Tower Books 8844 W Sunset Blvd, West Hollywood ☎310/657-3344. Hip chain merchant across the street from the massive Tower Records on the Sunset Strip, with a broad selection of titles centered on youth culture, rock music, sexuality, and leftist politics.

General interest and new books

Book Baron 1236 S Magnolia Ave, Anaheim ☎714/527-7022. Large independent bookseller with stacks upon stacks of new and used books. Part of a complex that includes Magazine Baron and Music Baron, both selling a total of some half-million items.

Book Soup 8818 W Sunset Blvd, West Hollywood ☎310/659-3110. Great selection, right on Sunset Strip. Narrow, winding aisles stuffed pell-mell with books, strong in entertainment, travel, and photography. Celebs are sometimes known to come in, attempting to look studious.

Illiterature 452 S La Brea Ave, Mid-Wilshire ☎323/937-3505. Although this smallish bookstore has a limited, but well-chosen, selection of general-interest titles, it appeals for its quality soaps, candles, toys, and other gifts near the back of the store.

Midnight Special 1450 Second St, Santa Monica ☎310/393-2923. Moved out of its old Promenade digs by a rent hike, this lefty favorite has relocated and still attracts locals nearby with its eccentrically arranged shelves, and focus on liberal politics and social sciences.

Skylight Books 1818 N Vermont Ave, Hollywood ☎323/660-1175. Just north of Barnsdall Park in a trendy shopping zone, this Los Feliz bookseller has a broad range of mainstream and alternative literature, plus a fine selection of film books and regular author readings.

Small World Books 1407 Ocean Front Walk, Venice ☎310/399-2360. A modest neighborhood dealer by the beach that has many good choices for mystery novels and literature from local and national authors, including publications from small presses.

Vroman's 695 E Colorado Blvd, Pasadena ☎1-800/769-2665 or 626/449-5320. One of the San Gabriel Valley's largest retailers for new books, and a good place to browse, but don't expect to find any bargains. Also includes an in-store café.

Secondhand books

Acres of Books 240 Long Beach Blvd, Long Beach ☎526/437-6980. Worth a trip down the Blue Line Metrorail just to wallow in LA's largest, and most disorganized, secondhand collection. You may not be able to find the exact title you're looking for, but chances are you'll stumble across something good.

Aladdin Books 122 W Commonwealth Ave, Fullerton ☎714/738-6115. What may be the region's finest assortment of film and fantasy titles, both new and used – not to

be missed by visitors willing to drive to this distant Orange County burg.

Atlantis Book Shop 144 S San Fernando Rd, Burbank ☎818/845-6467. Just down the street from the huge Burbank Town Center mall, Atlantis specializes in history, fiction, politics, and – as the name might suggest – the paranormal, extraterrestrial, and mythological.

Berkelouw Books 830 N Highland Ave, Hollywood ☎323/466-3321. An easy-to-miss dealer with voluminous stacks of titles in fiction, biography, entertainment, and history – plus a knowledgeable owner who'll be glad to help you sift through his well-chosen collection.

Book Alley 611 E Colorado Blvd, Pasadena ☎626/683-8083. A handsomely designed bookstore with a large stock of affordable used books on a wide variety of subjects. You'll find a similar selection at the store's annex, Book Alley Too!, nearby at 696 E Colorado Blvd ☎626/795-0818.

Brand Book Shop 231 N Brand Blvd, Glendale ☎818/507-5943. Valley used-book seller with a broad range of liberal-arts titles and particular strengths in entertainment, history, and politics. Located in the pulsing heart of downtown Glendale.

Cliff's Books 630 E Colorado Blvd, Pasadena ☎626/449-9541. This long-standing used-bookseller, with narrow aisles stacked with titles on a wide assortment of subjects, has a bigger selection than some other bookstores in the vicinity, with slightly higher prices as well.

Cosmopolitan Book Shop 7017 Melrose Ave, north of Mid-Wilshire ☎323/938-7119. The cozier Westside equivalent to Acres of Books, a dealer loaded with thousands of titles stacked high on oversized bookcases, on a variety of subjects but especially strong on film and media.

Heritage Book Shop 8540 Melrose Ave, West Hollywood ☎310/659-3674. If you don't already know about this place, you're probably not a serious and committed antiquarian. For everyone else, the rare and antique editions and valuable autographs for sale are compelling to look at – but likely to be a little out of one's price range.

Wilshire Books 3018 Wilshire Blvd, Santa Monica ☎310/828-3115. An excellent used-bookstore for its size, which is quite small and cramped. Features a well-chosen collection of tomes on art, politics, religion, and music – all of them coherently organized and accessible.

Specialist bookstores

Bodhi Tree 8585 Melrose Ave, West Hollywood ☎310/659-1733. Ultra-trendy Westside book retailer in an ultra-chic part of Melrose, with a range of New Age, occult, and psychobabble titles, including plenty of information on the healing power of crystals, pyramids, and the like.

Circus of Books 4001 Sunset Blvd, Silver Lake ☎323/666-1304. Take a trip through LA's seamier side at this well-known (mainly magazine) dealer in weird murder tales, serial-killer exposés, S&M diaries, and assorted pornography. Also at 8230 Santa Monica Blvd, West Hollywood ☎323/656-6533.

Cooks Library 8373 W Third St, north of Mid-Wilshire ☎323/655-3141. It's all about eats at this top-notch dealer in culinary matters, from whipping up a mean steak tartare to hunting down that ancient 1950s recipe for apple brown betty; some seven-thousand titles altogether.

Creation Books 1228 W Seventh St, Downtown ☎213/623-6995. An edgy alternative dealer selling books on true crime, paranoid conspiracy rants, and a host of underground topics through its small store and large mail-order base.

Dawson's 535 N Larchmont Blvd, north of Mid-Wilshire ☎323/469-2186. Dating back a hundred years, supposedly the longest-lasting bookstore in LA (though at different sites), and known for its excellent stock of vintage books of California and Western US history, regular salons on social and city politics, and an attached photography gallery of some note.

A Different Light 8853 Santa Monica Blvd, West Hollywood ☎310/854-6601. The city's best-known gay and lesbian bookstore, in the heart of the city's gay district, with monthly art shows, readings, and women's music events. See also "Gay and lesbian LA," p.327.

Hennessey and Ingalls 214 Wilshire Blvd, Santa Monica ☎310/458-9074. An impressive range of coffee-table art and architecture books makes this Promenade bookstore among the best of its kind in LA. Rare posters, catalogs, and hard-to-find books are also in stock. While there are many cut-rate remainders, the books you'll likely want will be priced at premium.

Hollywood Book City 6627 Hollywood Blvd ☎323/466-2525. Located in the Hollywood & Highland complex, this is a high-profile dealer in classic movie books and memorabilia, along with autographs, scripts, film-related antiques, and the like. Also a nearby "Collectables" store at 6631 Hollywood Blvd (☎323/466-0120), and a branch in Burbank at 308 N San Fernando Blvd (☎818/848-4417).

Larry Edmunds Book Shop 6644 Hollywood Blvd, Hollywood ☎323/463-3273. Many stacks of books, a large number of them out of print, are offered on every aspect of film and theater, with movie stills and posters. Located at the center of tourist-oriented Hollywood.

Mitchell Books 1395 E Washington Blvd, Pasadena ☎626/798-4438. A favorite San Gabriel Valley dealer in detective and mystery novels, where you can grab a copy of Raymond Chandler, Walter Moseley, or James Ellroy to use as a fiction travel-guide to LA's dark side.

Norton Simon Museum Bookstore 411 W Colorado Blvd, Pasadena ☎626/449-6840. Prices in this museum store are lower than in many other art bookstores in LA, and the stock is, not surprisingly, superb. Includes numerous titles on museum specialties like Impressionism and early modern art, and biographies and monographs of the artists in the institution's collections.

Samuel French Theatre & Film Bookshop 7623 Sunset Blvd, Hollywood ☎323/876-0570. LA's broadest selection of theater books are found in this local institution, along with a good collection of movie and media-related titles. In the back room, you can sometimes find discounted or used titles.

Taschen 354 N Beverly Drive, Beverly Hills ☎310/274-4300. Fun, edifying, and weird titles that focus on everything from Renaissance art to Americana kitsch to fetish photography. Cheap volumes on both familiar and obscure subjects, and even the coffee-table books are occasionally affordable. Also features an art gallery, café, and performance space.

Travel bookstores

California Map and Travel Center 3312 Pico Blvd, Santa Monica ☎310/396-6277. You'll find

SHOPPING | Bookstores

20

atlases, maps, and books about outdoor activities – including hiking and biking – and other adventures at this bookshop near the 10 freeway, on the eastern edge of Santa Monica.

Distant Lands 56 S Raymond Ave, Pasadena ☎626/449-3220. Well-stocked travel bookstore in Old Pasadena, with some fairly hard-to-find titles, as well as maps and travel gear. Also hosts the occasional public speaker and globe-trotting slide show.

Geographia 4000 Riverside Dr, Burbank ☎818/848-1414. Solid San Fernando Valley choice for an array of travel items, from the basic guides to detailed maps and other publications.

Nations 500 Pier Ave, Hermosa Beach ☎310/318-9915. A South Bay travel-guide retailer that sells all the familiar publishers at reasonable prices and can book trips through an in-house agency; includes a decent selection of maps, globes, and travel accessories.

Rand McNally in the Century City Marketplace, 10250 Santa Monica Blvd, Century City ☎310/556-2202 or 1-800/333-0136. A cramped little store loaded with tourists and shoppers, featuring a wide range of travel books and maps, and even a good selection of globes. One of several regional branches, with most in Orange County.

Thomas Brothers Maps 521 W Sixth St, Downtown ☎213/627-4018 or 1-888/277-6277. The well-known mapmakers who produce highly detailed, spiral-bound city maps operate this Downtown store, which also carries a good assortment of local to international maps and travel publications. Also in Orange County at 17731 Cowan St, Irvine ☎949/863-1984.

Traveler's Bookcase 8375 W Third St, Mid-Wilshire ☎323/655-0575. A bookseller overflowing with travel guides, maps, and publications, along with a fine array of literary travel stories, wanderlust novels, trip diaries, and personal essays.

Music stores

Music lovers will be spoiled for choice when it comes to shopping for **music** in LA. The selection below leans toward the city's more one-of-a-kind stores, many of which still carry used LPs.

A-1 Record Finders 5639 Melrose Ave, Hollywood ☎323/RECORDS. One of the West Coast's top spots for tracking down classic and (not-so-classic) vinyl. By request, the staff hunts for LPs from its millionplatter inventory, whether it's an obscure 1960s garage-rock band or a legendary blues singer of the 1940s. Visit ⓦwww .aonerecordfinders.com to get started.

Amoeba Music 6400 W Sunset Blvd, Hollywood ☎323/245-6400. A vast selection of titles – supposedly numbering around half a million – on CD, tape, and vinyl, which you can freely hear at listening carrels throughout the store. Also presents occasional in-store live music.

Aron's Records 1150 N Highland Ave, Hollywood ☎323/469-4700. Secondhand discs – all styles, all prices, and a sizable stock, though nothing too out of the ordinary. Getting help can be a problem, as the place is often packed.

Backside Records 139 N San Fernando Rd, Burbank ☎818/559-7573. Though very much oriented toward the vinyl-minded, this two-level, DJ-oriented store stocks both LPs

and CDs with a broad range of electronica, plus some jazz, rap, and soul.

Counterpoint 5911 Franklin Ave, Hollywood ☎323/957-7965. Although not the highest-profile dealer in town, Counterpoint has a terrific smorgasbord of used vinyl, CDs, movies on cassette and DVD, books, and even antique 78 records. Also connected to its own underground art gallery.

Destroy All Music 3818 Sunset Blvd, Silver Lake ☎323/663-9300. The punk-rock antidote to the chain stores, selling recordings new and old from Southern California to Europe.

DMC Records 7619 Melrose Ave, north of Mid-Wilshire ☎323/651-3520. A prime spot to buy used CDs and, especially, vinyl. Local club-hoppers and DJs come here to stock up on the latest dance records and find more obscure tracks by little-known artists.

Fingerprints 4612 E Second St, Long Beach ☎562/433-4996. A formidable indie outfit in the South Bay, offering alternative-leaning CD and vinyl, plus in-store performances from local rockers, and a mellow, soft-sell attitude. Located in the Belmont Shore district.

Heavy Rotation 12354 Ventura Blvd, Studio City ☎818/769-8882. Cheap prices for used CDs, cassettes, laserdiscs, and video games are one big draw for this San Fernando Valley dealer; the other is the interesting assortment of music-industry promotional records.

Penny Lane 12 W Colorado Blvd, Pasadena ☎626/564-0161. New and used records at reasonable prices. Always crowded, this local chain features listening stations from which you can sample up to a hundred eclectic discs. Also at 7563 Melrose Ave (☎323/651-3000) and 10914 Kinross Ave, Westwood (☎310/208-5611).

Poo-Bah Records 1101 E Walnut Ave, Pasadena ☎626/449-3359. Plenty of American and imported New Wave sounds, along with 1980s technopop and various other genres.

Record Surplus 11609 W Pico Blvd, West LA ☎310/478-4217. A massive LP collection of surf music, early rock'n'roll, 1960s soundtracks, and unintentionally hilarious spoken-word recordings. Prices are excellent, with many CDs and cassettes offered at ridiculously low prices. Anyone with an interest in classic, alternative, or offbeat music knows this place.

Rhino Records 1720 Westwood Blvd, West LA ☎310/474-8685. The biggest selection of international independent releases, stocked with rock, punk, funk, and everything else, not to mention the countless records put out by Rhino Records itself.

Rockaway Records 2395 Glendale Blvd, Silver Lake ☎323/664-3232. Great place to come for both used CDs and LPs, as well as laserdiscs. Also offers old magazines, posters, and memorabilia. Located just east of the Silver Lake reservoir.

Tower Records 8801 W Sunset Blvd, West Hollywood ☎310/657-7300. The most visible of the many stores in this music chain, due mostly to its very prominent position in a bend in the Sunset Strip. Draws a cross-section of music buyers, more than it might if located elsewhere.

Vinyl Fetish 1614 N Cahuenga Blvd, Hollywood ☎323/957-2290. Loaded with punk, alternative, and indie sounds – plus plenty of vinyl for budding DJs – this is also a good place to discover what's new on the ever-changing LA music scene and even to buy a cheesy T-shirt or two.

Virgin Megastore 8000 Sunset Blvd, West Hollywood ☎323/650-8666. A Sunset Strip corporate-music giant with steep retail prices, but well worth a look for the extensive selection spread over two levels, including CDs, DVDs, books, and video games.

Specialty stores

The **specialty stores** below are some of the more colorful you'll find in LA.

Condomania 1001 Orange Drive, Hollywood ☎1-800/926-6366. Features a fun and vibrant assortment of prophylactics in a variety of colors, textures, and sizes, all inflated on a central rack, so you can see what they potentially look like when in use.

Freehand 8413 W Third St, north of Mid-Wilshire ☎323/655-2607. Great arts-and-crafts store showcasing the work of local designers, featuring stoneware bowls, porcelain teapots, hand-embroidered fabrics, colorful glasswear and jewelry, and carved bowls – some of it affordable, some not.

G.A.L.A.X.Y. Gallery 7224 Melrose Ave ☎323/938-6500. An LA original: an upscale head-shop with arty pipes and elaborate bongs, and tasteful paraphernalia aimed at the discriminating toker. The "wacky tabacky" is, of course, not available, but you're encouraged to smoke an alternative, legal drug (say, tobacco) at the store's *Chronic Café* espresso bar.

Le Sex Shoppe 12323 Ventura Blvd, Studio City ☎818/760-9352. LA's prime sex-paraphernalia dealer, with everything from magazines and videos to handcuffs and lingerie, catering to a mix of curious Westsiders and seedy regulars. One of six citywide branches.

Noisy Toys 8728 S Sepulveda Blvd, Westchester, just north of LAX ☎310/670-9957. A cacophonous shrine to percussion, loaded with drums and other instruments from around the world, including zithers, rain sticks, bongos, maracas, castanets, wooden whistles, tambourines, and didgeridoos. Best of all, you can sample each instrument at your leisure.

Off the Wall 7325 Melrose Ave, north of Mid-Wilshire ☎323/930-1185. Appealing mid-twentieth-century antiques cleaned up and sold as high-priced goods, from Bakelite jewelry to Fiestaware dishes, as well as faded consumer items like outdated board games and old telephones.

Plastica 8405 W Third St, Mid-Wilshire ☎323/655-1051. A one-of-a-kind shrine to all things plastic: shoes, boots, shirts, tank-tops, spectacles, and accessories, along with jewelry, furniture, handbags, pillows, and countless other cheap knickknacks.

Raven's Flight 5050 Vineland Ave, North Hollywood ☎818/985-2944. Tools of the trade for witches and pagans, including books on casting spells, magical herbs, ceremonial masks, druidic jewelry, and the ins and outs of joining Wiccan society. Located in the NoHo District.

Skeletons in the Closet 1104 N Mission Rd, Downtown ☎323/343-0760. Believe it or not, this is the LA County Coroner Gift Shop, selling everything from skeleton-adorned beach towels and T-shirts to toe-tag key chains – a great place to buy unique LA merchandise.

Vidiots 302 Pico Blvd, Santa Monica ☎310/392-8508. Easily one of LA's best video stores, providing an excellent selection of classics and current flicks, but also a good range of cult and bizarre films, strange government propaganda, and experimental art movies.

Wacko 4633 Hollywood Blvd, Hollywood ☎323/663-0122. The name says it all – freakish alternative comic books, odd-smelling candles, funky posters and toys, and various underground magazines. Part of a complex that includes the Soap Plant, where, along with soap, you can find body creams, fragrant oils, and bubble baths.

Zipper 8316 W Third St, north of Mid-Wilshire ☎323/951-9190. The height of chic and trendy gifts for Angelenos, and a good spot to pick up a gift from La-La Land for the folks back home: lacquered stone candles, stylish cocktail shakers, glazed terracotta bowls, quirky trinkets, and sleek lamps, glasses, and teacups.

Galleries

The Westside is the province of LA's top art **galleries** for painting, mixed-media, sculpture and, especially, photography. Indeed, snapping pictures is what a city based on the movie industry does best, and you're likely to find terrific retrospectives of artists like Weston and Stieglitz among the breakout shows of up-and-coming local shutterbugs. Keep in mind that the galleries listed below represent established art-houses in LA, and that by wandering through the right parts of Venice, Silver Lake, and Downtown's northeast fringe, you can often find art that's just as interesting and much cheaper. By taking a **tour** of such areas (on, say, the Venice Art Walk, p.343, or the Discovery Tour of the Arroyo Arts Collective, p.79) you can see what grassroots artists are currently up to – long before they reach the walls of the big-name galleries.

Armory Center for the Arts 145 N Raymond Ave, Pasadena ☎626/792-5101. Shows by young artists and retrospectives of local painters and photographers make this an enjoyable, fairly unpretentious spot. Located just north of Old Pasadena.

Beyond Baroque 681 Venice Blvd, Venice ☎310/822-3006. A gallery and art center that's as interesting and unpredictable as any place else in town, with a wide spectrum of performance art, fiction and poetry readings, assemblage and mixed-media, painting, drawing, photography and more. Also offers classes and tours of LA murals.

Center for Land Use Interpretation 9331 Venice Blvd, Culver City ☎310/839-5722, ⊛www .clui.org. Narrowly focused but fascinating

museum/gallery that looks at land use from various angles, notably time-lapse photography, satellite images, and even field trips to mudslide catch basins, aviation graveyards, and windswept eastern deserts.

DIRT Gallery 7906 Santa Monica Blvd, West Hollywood ☎323/822-9359. One of the better places on the Westside to discover the edgiest and most cutting-edge artworks in a variety of media. Some works are compelling, some aren't for the faint of heart.

Fahey-Klein 148 N La Brea Ave, Mid-Wilshire ☎323/934-2250. One of LA's institutional heavyweights, featuring much contemporary work, especially black-and-white photography. Don't be deterred by the forbidding, windowless exterior – the gallery is open and accessible most days of the week.

Gagosian Gallery 456 N Camden Drive, Beverly Hills ☎310/271-9400. A major name in LA art that occasionally shows big names like Lichtenstein, Miró, and Twombly, and is housed in a memorable modern shed designed by Richard Meier. But with prices in the stratosphere, you're better off window-shopping here.

Gallery 825 825 N La Cienega Blvd, West Hollywood ☎310/652-8272. Affiliated with the Los Angeles Art Association, a long-standing spot devoted to groundbreaking exhibits by emerging artists and thoughtful career retrospectives.

Gallery Figueroa 6122 N Figueroa St, Highland Park ☎323/258-5939, ⊛www.galleryfigueroa .com. One of the more prominent dealers in Northeast LA, where the wide-ranging shows include everything from photography and etchings to murals.

Gallery of Functional Art 2525 Michigan Ave, Santa Monica ☎310/829-6990. Noise-emitting clocks, ornamental wooden furniture, and funky, Space Age wall sconces are for sale at this Bergamot Station gallery, where form and function mix with intriguing results. One of the few galleries good for (well-behaved) kids to browse in.

Iturralde Gallery 116 S La Brea Ave, Mid-Wilshire ☎323/937-4267. Established and emerging Latino artists are usually on display here, with shows alternating between the work of talented locals and international figures.

Jan Kesner Gallery 164 N La Brea Ave, north of Mid-Wilshire ☎323/938-6834. This excellent and well-respected gallery features retrospectives of noted artists – many of them photographers – as well as openings by up-and-comers. By appointment only.

Judson Gallery 200 S Ave 66, Highland Park ☎323/255-0131, ⊛www.judsonstudios.com. A good place for checking out what's going on in Downtown's artsy northeastern fringe, heavy on contemporary stained glass as well as periodic exhibitions in a variety of media. Located in USC's former art and architecture school.

Koplin Del Rio 464 N Robertson Blvd, West Hollywood ☎310/657-9843. Elite art dealer specializing in etchings, paintings, and drawings, with an eye toward contemporary art from LA. One of many high-priced galleries scattered around this upscale section of town.

La Luz de Jesus 4633 Hollywood Blvd, Hollywood ☎323/666-7667. Connected to the Wacko strange-gift emporium (see opposite), and sharing its taste for the bizarre, perverse, experimental, and quirky in a variety of media, with many affordable prints and posters.

Los Angeles Contemporary Exhibitions 6522 Hollywood Blvd, Hollywood ☎323/957-1777. Also known as LACE, this institution hosts a wide-ranging selection of mixed-media, painting, drawing, and video work, while its community-outreach programs bring art to the masses.

Margo Leavin Gallery 812 N Robertson Blvd, West Hollywood ☎310/273-0603. This eclectic gallery is worth a look for what's new and trendy on the West Hollywood gallery scene, and features a Claes Oldenburg facade, *Knife Slicing Through Water* – ie, the stucco.

New Alchemy 6909 Melrose Ave, Hollywood ☎323/933-6912. A hip Melrose gallery offering dark, edgy work that is slightly less expensive than some galleries on the Westside.

Rosamund Felsen Gallery 2525 Michigan Ave, Santa Monica ☎310/828-8488. One of the bigger names in Bergamot Station, featuring established Southern California artists and more recent arrivals. The eclectic selection is often striking, but you can forget about buying anything: the prices here are always high.

Susanne Vielmetter/Los Angeles Projects 5795 W. Washington Blvd, Culver City ☎323/933-2117. Miracle Mile gallery showing contemporary artists, particularly those working in untraditional media, with a strong Southern California bent.

Track 16 2525 Michigan Ave, Santa Monica ☎310/264-4678. Politically oriented artworks tending toward mixed-media and assemblage, though you can also find traditional painted and sculpted works, with one message or another boldly attached.

Directory

Airports Bob Hope/Burbank ☎818/840-8847, ⊛www.bophopeairport.com; John Wayne/Orange County ☎949/252-5006, ⊛www.ocair.com; LAX ☎310/646-5252, ⊛www.los-angeles-lax.com; Long Beach ☎562/570-2600, ⊛www.longbeach.gov /airport; Ontario ☎909/937-2700, ⊛www .lawa.org.

Beach information Coastal weather conditions for Malibu ☎310/457-9701, Santa Monica ☎310/578-0478, South Bay ☎310/379-8471.

Coast Guard Search-and-rescue, Los Angeles/Long Beach ☎562/980-4444, Orange County/Newport Beach ☎949/834-3800.

Consulates UK, 11766 Wilshire Blvd #1200, West LA ☎310/481-0031, ⊛www .britainusa.com/la; Canada, 550 S Hope St, 9th Floor, Downtown ☎213/346-2700, ⊛www.dfait-maeci.gc.ca/los_angeles; Australia, 2049 Century Park East, Century City ☎310/229-4800, ⊛www.austemb .org/losangeles.html; New Zealand, 12400 Wilshire Blvd #1150, Westwood ☎310/207-1605, ⊛www.nzembassy.com.

Currency exchange Outside of banking hours, exchange offices are scattered inconveniently throughout town. Most reliable are those at LAX; hours vary by terminal (often daily until 11pm ☎310/649-2801).

Dental treatment The cheapest place is USC School of Dentistry, 925 W 34th St, South Central (☎1-888/USC-DENT, ⊛www.usc .edu/hsc/dental/patient_care) on the USC campus, costing $50–200. Turn up and be prepared to wait all day. You can also get emergency treatment at the LA Dental Society, 3660 Wilshire Blvd #1152 ☎213/380-7669, ⊛www.ladentalsociety.com.

Directory assistance Local ☎411 (a free call at pay phones); long distance ☎1 + area code + 555-1212.

Drugs Although hard drugs carry stiff penalties and jail time, possession of up to an ounce of marijuana is treated as a misdemeanor in California, and not often prosecuted. However, if you're a foreign national, even a minor drug bust could be a convenient excuse for the authorities to boot you from the country – or worse, place you on the government's "watch list" barring re-entry.

Electricity 110V AC. European appliances typically require two-pin plug adapters for lower US voltages.

Emergencies Dial ☎911. For less urgent needs: fire ☎323/890-4194; civil defense and disaster services ☎213/974-1120; police ☎213/625-3311; sheriff ☎213/526-5541; poison control center ☎1-800/777-6476; food poisoning reports ☎213/240-7821.

Food safety To inquire about a restaurant or grocery's food-safety rating, contact the LA County Department of Public Health at ☎626/430-5100, or visit ⊛lapublichealth .org/rating to view searchable, online reports from the last year.

Internet access Available from cyber-oriented coffee shops (see p.43), the *Newsroom Café* (p.288), many city libraries, and sit-down terminals near flight gates at LAX. Outside of libraries, expect to pay around 10–25¢ per minute to browse the Web.

Laundry Most hotels do laundry, but they charge quite a bit for the service. You're better off going to a laundromat or a dry cleaner (see *Yellow Pages* under "Laundromats").

Left luggage All Greyhound bus stations have left-luggage lockers for $1–2 a day, or $2.50 for larger lockers. See p.34 for station locations.

Libraries Downtown's Central Library is the city's finest (see p.75), with branches throughout LA. Other cities also have good main libraries, notably Beverly Hills (see p.126) and Santa Monica, 1343 Sixth St (☎310/458-8600, ⓦwww.smpl.org). Specialist libraries are quite common, too, such as the Margaret Herrick Library (p.94) for film-related materials, and the One Institute (see box, p.327) for gay and lesbian publications. For collegiate libraries, USC's Doheny (see p.165) and UCLA's Powell (see p.133) are among the best choices.

Measurements and sizes Measurements of length are in inches, feet, yards, and miles; weight in ounces, pounds, and tons. American pints and gallons are about four-fifths of imperial ones. Clothing sizes are two figures less than they would be in Britain (a British size 12 is an American size 10). To calculate your American shoe size, simply add one to your British size.

Medical care The following have 24-hour emergency departments: Cedars-Sinai Medical Center, 8700 Beverly Blvd, Beverly Hills ☎310/855-6517 or 423-8780, ⓦwww.csmc.edu; Good Samaritan Hospital, 1225 Wilshire Blvd, Downtown ☎213/977-2121, ⓦwww.goodsam.org; and UCLA Medical Center, Tiverton Drive at Le Conte Place, Westwood ☎310/825-2111, ⓦwww.healthcare.ucla.edu.

Mexican tourist office and consulate 2401 W Sixth St, 5th Floor, Downtown ☎1-800/44-MEXICO or 213/351-2069, ⓦwww.visitmexico.com. Call for general information or pick up a tourist card – necessary if you're crossing the border. Mon–Fri 9am–5pm.

Newspapers Newsstands are scattered throughout the region, and both USC's and UCLA's libraries have overseas publications. Day-old British and European papers are on sale in Hollywood at Universal News Agency, 1645 N Las Palmas Ave (daily 7am–midnight), and World Book and News, 1652 N Cahuenga Blvd (24 hours). See "The media," p.47, for a rundown of LA's various papers.

Pharmacies Late hours at Horton & Converse, 11600 Wilshire Blvd, West LA (until 2am; ☎310/478-0801) and at Kaiser's

West LA hospital, 6041 Cadillac Ave (24hr; ☎323/857-2151).

Post office The main Downtown post office, Alameda Station, is located at 760 N Main St (☎213/617-4405), next to Union Station. Open Mon–Fri 8am–7pm, Sat 8am–4pm; mail pick-up Mon–Fri 8am–3pm.

Public toilets Uncommon outside of hotels and restaurants, though found at malls and larger retailers. Street toilets are a rarity – and rarely clean.

Smog LA air quality can often be very poor and, especially in the valleys in late summer, sometimes quite dangerous. An air-quality index is published daily in the *Los Angeles Times* and if the air is really bad, warnings are issued on TV and radio. For more information contact the South Coast Air Quality Management District (☎1-800/CUT-SMOG, ⓦwww.aqmd.gov).

Smoking Frowned upon, perhaps more than in any other major US city. Considered antithetical to a healthy lifestyle by the majority of Angelenos, though a requisite badge of rebellion in counterculture clubs and cafés. Forbidden in restaurants and bars – though variably enforced.

Taxes LA sales tax is 8.25 percent; hotel tax variable, generally 14.5 percent.

Time Pacific Standard Time (PST), 3 hours behind US Eastern Standard Time and 8 or 9 hours behind GMT, depending on seasonal observance of Daylight Savings Time.

Tipping Generally 15 percent for restaurants, though upscale eateries may expect closer to 20 percent (still, it's up to you) and many restaurants will slap a flat 18 percent charge on parties of six or more. Generally $1 per carried bag at hotels and $1 per day for maid service (both with a minimum $2 tip).

Traffic Check AM radio news channels for frequent updates on which freeways are suffering from gridlock or congestion; if a highway section is particularly immobile, a "Sig-Alert" will be issued, meaning "avoid at all costs." Radio stations emphasizing traffic reports include KNX 1070 AM; also try ⓦwww.sigalert.com on the Internet.

DIRECTORY

(21)

Contexts

Contexts

History

T o casual observers, Los Angeles is a place with no sense of **history**, an ultramodern urban sprawl that lives up to its vapid stereotypes: the land of sunny skies, carefree surfers, and Hollywood movie stars. However, a potent countermyth has also emerged of dystopic LA, in which violent outbreaks and scandals are commonplace, and lying beneath the city's sunny surface is a dark and dangerous underbelly. Although both of these myths have some validity, what they most reveal is LA's sense of drama in viewing itself, and not just the Hollywood variety, either. Whether they see their city as a sunshine paradise or a necropolis, Angelenos tend to agree that their chosen city is a harbinger of things to come for the rest of America.

Prehistoric LA

Like other parts of the West Coast, the underlying **geology** that makes up the LA basin began as an **oceanic terrane**, basically a mobile chunk of land that pushed toward the North American landmass along the Pacific Plate. For 120 to 160 million years, the terrane came closer, drifting northward, and repeatedly rose above and sank below sea level, until it reached its current, above-ground position around five million years ago. By the time of the **Ice Age**, around 25,000 years ago, the LA region was literally an arcadia – a sylvan land of fertile, tree-covered plains, crystalline brooks and lakes, untamed rivers, and a temperate climate. Despite the idyllic conditions, a natural peril awaited the region's creatures in the form of the **La Brea Tar Pits**: dark, boggy pools that were visible evidence of the copious petroleum deposits in the region and which spelled doom for any animals that wandered into them. Sinking into the murky ooze, they remained preserved in the tar until they were unearthed in the modern era by **William Orcutt**, giving a vivid picture of the rich ecology of the time, when prehistoric LA was populated with the likes of saber-toothed tigers, giant ground sloths, mammoths, and even camels. The wide array of fauna and pristine environment would not last long, for as soon as humans began crossing into North America via the temporary land-bridge at the Bering Strait (about 18–25,000 years ago), such creatures were doomed to be prey for hunters or driven out of the area entirely, to become extinct in future eras.

Native peoples

For thousands of years prior to the arrival of Europeans, **native peoples** subsisted in different parts of the Los Angeles basin without too much difficulty. The dominant groups in the area were **Tataviam**, **Chumash**, and **Tongva** (whom the Spanish called Gabrieleño) peoples. Of these, the dominant tribes were the Chumash, who lived along the coast around modern-day Malibu and Ventura, and the Tongva, who occupied much of the central LA basin. These tribes, however, had little in common, and were an easy target for the **Spanish** conquerors and missionaries – although it's also true that they were wiped out by European-borne epidemics as much as by outright Spanish aggression.

Today, LA County is home to the greatest number of native peoples of any county in the US – up to two hundred thousand by some estimates, many migrating from other parts of the US. Indeed, most Native Americans in these parts are now Navajo, and little remains to mark the existence of the early tribes, aside from the faded remnants found at scattered archeological digs and the cultural treasures locked up behind glass in folk-art museums.

European discovery and colonization

The first explorer to use the name California was **Juan Cabrillo**, who sighted San Diego harbor in 1542, and continued north along the coast to Santa Catalina Island and the Channel Islands off Santa Barbara. He bestowed a number of other place names that survive, including, in the LA area, Santa Monica, and San Pedro Bay, named for the first Bishop of Rome. Other European explorers followed, charting the California coast and naming more of the islands, bays, and coastal towns, but it was the **Spanish**, moving up from their base in Mexico, who were to colonize Southern California and map out the future city of Los Angeles.

The Spanish occupation of California began in earnest in 1769 as a combination of military expediency (to prevent other powers from gaining a foothold) and Catholic missionary zeal (to convert Native Americans). Padre **Junípero Serra** began the missions, setting off from Mexico and going all the way up to Monterey; assisting him was **Gaspar de Portola**, a soldier who led the expedition into LA.

The first mission sited in Los Angeles was **Mission San Gabriel**, in 1771; from that beginning, Spanish military garrisons served to hold the natives, subject to the demands of Franciscan friars who ordered them to abandon their religious beliefs, cultural rituals, and languages. The penalties for disobedience were stiff: flogging with twenty to forty lashes was standard practice. While the Spanish were trying to "convert the savages," they were also decimating the native population, reducing their ranks by 95 percent over the course of 150 years. By World War I, fewer than 17,000 of them remained.

The Spanish era

Aside from abusing the natives, the Spanish who colonized Southern California effected the first crude designs for LA, which they established in 1781 at a site northwest of the current Plaza in Downtown. The city's original **pobladores**, or settlers, of which there were less than fifty, set a multicultural precedent for the region, as they were made up of a majority of black, mestizo, mixed-race, and native peoples, with the white Spanish being a distinct, though powerful, minority. The early **pueblo** (town), designed by California's governor **Felipe de Neve**, grew in short spurts, aided by the creation of the *zanja madre*, or "mother ditch," that brought water into town. Despite half-hearted efforts by the Spanish to make the settlement grow, it took a devastating 1815 flood for large-scale development to begin, starting with the construction of the current Plaza and its Plaza Church – La Placita – and the Avila Adobe.

△ Statue of Padre Junípero Serra, Mission San Gabriel

As the town grew from remote outpost to regional centerpiece, the power of the Spanish Crown began to fade. While the military and missions exercised official power, the functional operation of the little burg was increasingly the province of a small group of mestizo families whose names are still reflected in LA's street names – Sepulveda, Pico, and so on – along with a few white American expatriates who for various reasons found the region to their liking. By the early 1800s, the Spanish were playing only a *de jure* role in city administration; soon after, they would be forcibly removed from power.

Mexican rule

Mexico gained independence in 1821, calling itself the United States of Mexico, and over the next four years, the Mexican residents of Southern California evicted the Spanish and made the region into a territory of Mexico itself – Alta California.

The 24 subsequent years of Mexican rule were marked by some dramatic changes in governance and the social order – and the destruction and looting of many missions – but no end to the oppression of native peoples. The Tongva and others now found themselves at the bottom level of a new hierarchy, where rich land barons controlled huge parcels of land known as **ranchos** and reduced the natives to a state of near-serfdom. (Despite the ugliness that took place there, many of these ranchos survive in a reasonably preserved state, with copious gardens and elegant adobe architecture, making for an excellent starting point on any trip into LA history.)

Due to widespread social oppression and frequent clashes between the wealthy land bosses (often linked to internal politics in southern Mexico), the period was largely a chaotic one, well described by Richard Henry Dana, Jr in his book *Two Years before the Mast*. By the time Governor **Pio Pico** successfully established his Alta California capital in Los Angeles (long his preferred spot for governance), the period of Mexican rule was almost at an end, its demise assured by the factional struggles and laggardly ways of the ranch owners.

The Mexican–American War

From the 1830s onward, driven by the concept of **Manifest Destiny**, the popular, almost religious, belief that Americans had a divine or moral charge to occupy the country from coast to coast, the US government's stated policy regarding California was to buy all of Mexico's land north of the Rio Grande, the river that now divides the US and Mexico. When President James K. Polk went ahead and annexed Texas – still claimed by Mexico – war broke out. Most of the fighting in the **Mexican–American War** took place in Texas, though a few skirmishes occurred in Southern California.

By the summer of 1846, after the American capture of Monterey and San Diego, Pico and his colleagues had difficulty even finding significant numbers of loyal Mexicans to defend LA against the US. A truce was signed to avoid bloodshed and American troops walked into the city virtually unopposed. However, despite this relatively pacific start, the military chieftains left local government in the hands of the incompetent **Archibald Gillespie**, who promptly instituted martial law and just as quickly turned the populace against the American presence. The situation further degenerated, with outbreaks of local hostilities, and by the time Mexican general Andreas Pico and American "pathfinder" John C. Fremont signed the final **peace treaty** in January 1847 at Campo de Cahuenga, after several battles and much bloodshed, the chasm between the Mexican residents and their new American conquerors had grown considerably.

Early American rule

California was admitted to the US as the 31st state in 1850, a move quickly followed by the **1851 Land Act**, through which the new white settlers targeted the rancho owners, forcing them to legally prove their right to the land they had been granted. The ensuing legal battles left many of the owners destitute, and while the rancho boundaries and some of their elemental chunks continued to linger for up to a century or more, the central goal of the new settlers had been accomplished: the old-line Mexicans were driven out and replaced by a gringo elite. However, even as this process was taking place, and the latest real-estate magnates were consolidating their power, the city's social structure continued its slide into chaos.

For many good reasons, LA was called "**Hell Town**" in the middle of the nineteenth century. The lives of the native peoples got even worse, as they were subject to all manner of mob aggression and legal disenfranchisement. Because the city had no effective municipal authority, and because it was crowded with hordes of aggressive fortune-hunters who had failed in the northern gold rush, it became a magnet for violent criminals and other ne'er-do-wells, and was peppered with gambling halls, saloons, and brothels – a Wild West town decades before such a thing existed. The bellicose citizenry usually focused their rage against the groups at the bottom of the social hierarchy, tactics that eventually backfired when roving groups of Mexican bandidos, such as Tiburcio Vasquez, emerged to counter the threats.

The local situation got so bloody that "**vigilance committees**" were created to deal with the crime, which had reached the same levels as San Francisco even though LA only had a tenth as many people. The vigilantes summarily executed 32 people, and gave rise to even more extreme groups who would hunt down lawbreakers, real or imagined, and severely maim or kill them. The El Monte Rangers, an imported gang of Texas thugs, was perhaps the most notorious, though there were many others, and LA remained a city solidly under the thumb of mob rule until after the Civil War.

During the height of its social strife, the region managed to sketch the outlines of what would later become the metropolitan area. Post offices, banks, newspapers, and churches were a few of the emblems of encroaching civilization, and the activity of such pioneering entrepreneurs as **Phineas Banning** – the developer of the Wilmington harbor plan – also brought early growth to the city.

In 1860, LA's citizens chose the wrong side in the **Civil War**, casting only a meager 18 percent of their ballots for Abraham Lincoln, and soon became possessed by secessionist rage and racial hatred. Adding to the rancor, many in the city and region were clamoring to split from northern California and create their own autonomous enclave, where they wouldn't be subject to state or federal power. Thirteen thousand soldiers were stationed in Wilmington's Drum Barracks to ensure domestic order and also act against Southwest rebel activity and, later, quash native uprisings. Just as tellingly, a crowd of revelers gathered in LA after hearing news of Lincoln's assassination. Their celebration was broken up – but only with the aid of the federal soldiers.

Late nineteenth-century growth

The last three decades of the nineteenth century were an era of **rapid growth** and **technological change** in LA, principally because of three key factors: periodic real-estate booms that led to the subdivision of the old ranchos into smaller, more profitable chunks; the building of railroad lines externally, to places like San Francisco, and internally, from Downtown to the port at San Pedro; and most importantly, the mass arrival of Midwesterners.

From the 1870s, LA gained a reputation as a bastion of healthy living. While eastern American cities were notorious for sooty air and water pollution, LA was touted as a sunny, clean-air paradise where the infirm could recover from their illnesses and everyone could enjoy the fruits of the invigorating desert lifestyle. The **orange** was the perfect symbol of this new arcadia, and trees and citrus groves were planted by the thousands, ultimately leading to towns being named for oranges and walnuts, and streets for magnolias and white oaks. Huge numbers of Iowans and Kansans moved to the city in the Victorian era, spurred on as well by cheap one-way railroad tickets: thanks to a price war between the Santa Fe and Southern Pacific railroads, fares from Kansas City to LA dropped to a mere dollar; before long, the passenger cars were full of church-going Protestants seeking desert salvation.

The Midwesterners of the 1880s did much to displace lingering Hispanic influences, meanwhile exacerbating racial tensions, which flared up in such instances as the **anti-Chinese riot of 1871**. After a disagreement left a white man dead at the hands of a Chinese shopkeeper, a mob assembled and quickly set about attacking and murdering what Chinese residents it could get its hands on. While there were only about two hundred Chinese in LA at the time, the mob managed to strangle, shoot, stab, and hang 22 of them. In an ominous portent of LA-style justice, few of the perpetrators faced jail time, and those that did only served a year or so.

Beyond its racial animus and Midwestern migrations, LA was becoming an attraction of sorts for a few of the nation's more colorful characters. **Charles Fletcher Lummis** was the first of these, a fervent supporter of the rights of native peoples, yet also an isolationist who saw a looming threat from foreign immigration. Aside from that, Lummis was a bit of a crank who was so committed to his own notion of healthy living that he created a boulder house, "El Alisal," which still stands in Highland Park, and he took the unusual step of coming to LA from Cincinnati **on foot** – a distance of nearly three thousand miles. Lummis would be just one of many individualists to inhabit the LA region, including others like the Pasadena artisans who created "**Arroyo culture**" just after the turn of the century (an arts-and-crafts philosophy that owed much to Lummis; see box, p.202), and left-wing political activists like **Job Harriman**, whose commune in the northern desert town of Llano del Rio was intended to be the blueprint for a socialist utopia.

While the dreamers and artists experimented with alternative living, the politicians and businessmen were busy expanding the city by every means possible: the **harbor** was developed at San Pedro; **railway lines** were added throughout the region by Henry Huntington, through his electric Red Car transit system; and other entrepreneurs like Edward Doheny grew rich drilling for **oil** practically everywhere.

The early twentieth century: water and power

Around the turn of the century, LA's population reached 100,000; perhaps more important to the city's development, however, **William Mulholland** was put in charge of the city's water department. Mulholland was the catalyst for a water-stealing scheme that even now remains legendary: various bankers, publishing magnates, and railway bosses purchased large land holdings in the San Fernando Valley, and shortly thereafter, a small cadre of city bankers secretly began buying up land in California's distant Owens Valley, 250 miles away. By the time the northern farmers realized what had happened, the bankers had consolidated control over the valley watershed and were making plans to bring the bulk of the region's water to the seemingly drought-stricken citizens of LA. Seemingly is the key word, for modern evidence suggests that massive amounts of water were being deposited into the city sewers so area dams and reservoirs could drop precipitously, thus making it look like the region was on the verge of a severe drought.

Following the land grab, Mulholland built a **giant canal system** – one of the country's biggest public-works projects (see box, p.208) – that carried the stolen water to Southern California, but not LA proper. Instead, the aqueduct mysteriously ended in the San Fernando Valley and city politicians **annexed** the valley for housing, thus wiping out thousands of acres of fertile agricultural land and making the real-estate interests there – actually Downtown bankers and political powerbrokers who secretly bought up the land – wealthy beyond imagination. The entire enterprise surely ranks as one of the country's biggest municipal swindles, and one that the Owens Valley farmers did not soon forget. In the 1920s, when Mulholland and company set about acquiring more property for the canal system, the farmers responded by destroying sections of the system with carefully placed dynamite charges. This violence, coupled with the unrelated bursting of the St Francis dam north of LA – a catastrophe that killed more than four hundred people – destroyed Mulholland's reputation. However, by that time, his main work had already been accomplished: the aqueduct helped turn LA into a metropolis.

Accompanying the development of the modernizing city was the growth of **organized labor**. In 1910, a series of strikes at breweries and foundries crippled the city, and local labor was also responsible for nearly bringing socialist Job Harriman to power. However, when the main building of the *Los Angeles Times* – the right-wing organ of labor's archenemy **Harrison Gray Otis** – was bombed, a slow erosion of leftist support took place and ultimately led to defeat for Harriman, who then retreated to his northern desert commune.

World War I to the Great Depression

Metropolis or not, LA continued to display its regressive, provincial character in many ways, especially in its treatment of **minorities**. Chinese residents were still subject to all manner of exclusionary laws, as were the Japanese, and both were among the Asian immigrants targeted by the **1913 Alien Land Bill**, which kept them from purchasing further land tracts and limited their lease tenures. Finally, even though industrial production during World War I doubled the black population of the city, the total number of **African-Americans** was still fairly small (less than three percent of the population).

Despite its lack of progressive ideas, rapid growth continued, and after World War I, LA became quite a **tourist magnet** – long before the arrival of Disneyland. Sights like Abbot Kinney's pseudo-European Venice and the carnival midways in Santa Monica and Long Beach all drew good numbers of seasonal visitors, as did Santa Catalina Island and the Mount Lowe Railroad in the San Gabriel Mountains.

Soon, another great **wave of newcomers** began arriving, from all across America. By the 1920s, LA was gaining residents by one hundred thousand per year, most coming by car and flocking to **suburbs** such as Glendale, Long Beach, and Pasadena. **Petroleum** was adding to the boom, from places like Signal Hill to Venice, with oil wells popping up all over the region, usually without regard to aesthetics or pollution. Naturally, the wells helped fuel the explosive growth of the local **car culture**, which even in the 1920s had become a potent force, eventually displacing the Red Car mass-transit system. The quintessential symbol of the dynamic, forward-looking atmosphere of the time was **City Hall**, built in 1928 as a mix of classical and contemporary elements, and topped by none other than a small replica of one of the long-lost ancient wonders of the world – the Mausoleum at Halicarnassus. This was civic ego on a grand scale, a fitting reflection of the attitudes of the time, but also a symbolic portent of the 1930s.

Into this highly charged environment also came the first **movie pioneers**, whose typically Jewish backgrounds, and origins in the Eastern garment industry, were looked down on by the Downtown elite. Because of exclusionary housing laws, film titans like Adolph Zukor and Samuel Goldwyn developed the Westside as their base of operations, an action that had long-lasting effects. Even today, West Hollywood, Beverly Hills, and West LA remain the cultural focus of the city, with Downtown far behind, despite the constant financial efforts of the remaining Downtown elite to remedy the situation.

The boom years ended with the onset of the **Great Depression**. Banks collapsed, businesses went bankrupt, and Midwestern drought brought a new round of immigrants to Southern California, much poorer and significantly more desperate than their forebears. These hard times spawned a number of movements. Led by fiery evangelists like **Aimee Semple McPherson**, religious **cults** gained adherents by the thousands, Communist and Fascist organizations trawled for members among the city's more frustrated or simple-minded ranks, and the muckraker **Upton Sinclair** emerged as the greatest threat to LA's ruling hierarchy since Job Harriman.

With his **End Poverty in California (EPIC)** campaign, Sinclair frightened the upper crust across the region, and was countered not only by the usual Downtown stalwarts, but also by their Westside adversaries, the Hollywood movie bosses, who rightly perceived a danger in Sinclair's message to their control over the film industry and film-crew labor. Fraudulent newsreel propaganda (showing hordes of homeless men and various halfwits testifying their allegiance to Sinclair) helped speed Sinclair's demise in the gubernatorial contest, but no one could stop the tide of reform, which brought down LA's corrupt mayor **Frank Shaw** and his attendant cronies. The entire political and social mess was reflected in the most famous literary works of the time: Nathanael West's *Day of the Locust* and Raymond Chandler's detective fiction, all of which portrayed a morally decayed society on the verge of collapse.

World War II and after

By the time of **World War II**, LA was emerging as one of the top US sites for military hardware production and coastal defense. In San Pedro, Fort MacArthur, named after the father of one of the war's most famous generals, was the site of Battery Osgood, home to anti-aircraft guns on the watch for Japanese fighter planes. Similarly, at the man-made Terminal Island, the harbor area itself was a shipbuilding center, embodied by the presence of the hulking SS *Lane Victory*, one of the huge cargo ships that carried supplies for the Navy during the war.

The misery of the continuing Depression and the dark, paranoid atmosphere in the early part of the war exacerbated the underlying social tensions and unleashed new rounds of violence and oppression against the perceived enemies of white Protestants. Although Chinese citizens had suffered after Union Station was plunked on top of the destroyed, former site of Chinatown, it was the city's Japanese population who now received the full brunt of the region's, as well as the nation's, racial animus. One of Franklin Roosevelt's executive orders gave the green light to mass deportations of Japanese-American citizens, who were forcibly relocated to bleak desert **internment camps** for the duration of the war. Minorities who hadn't been shipped away made for fat targets as well, especially Mexican-Americans.

The **Sleepy Lagoon Murder case** – in which seventeen Hispanics were rounded up and sent to jail for a single murder, only to be later released by a disgusted appellate court – was but a prelude to the turmoil that would come to be known as the **Zoot Suit Riots**, named for the popular apparel Hispanic youth wore at the time, with wide stripes, broad, shoulders, and accessories like dangling watch-chains and low-slung hats. Over the course of several days in early June 1943, two hundred sailors on leave attacked and beat up a large number of Mexican-Americans – with the assistance of local police, who made sure that the black-and-blue victims were promptly arrested on trumped-up charges. The violence continued until it became a federal issue, causing a rift in international relations between the US and Mexico. After the chaos ended, the LA City Council responded aggressively to the ugly events – by banning the wearing of zoot suits.

Although anti-Asian and -Hispanic feelings still remained, the end of the war brought a shift in hostilities. A growing contingent of **black migrants**, drawn by the climate and defense-related jobs, became the focus of white wrath, and the reason was clear: from 1940 to 1965, the number of blacks in LA increased from 75,000 to 600,000. The white elite did what it could to marginalize the new residents – keeping blacks confined to eastern sections of town around Central Avenue and "redlining" them out of personal loans and business financing – but these tactics only served to heighten the hostility that would later erupt in mass violence.

In the meantime, LA was becoming one of the USA's largest cities, with the nonstop arrival of newcomers from across the country, the rebirth of the local economy, and the construction of a **vast freeway network** to replace the old Red Cars – due principally to a decline in public-transit users and active subversion by oil, gas, and automotive interests. Defense industries, notably in aerospace, began a decades-long dominion over the local economy, superseding, most notably, the movie industry, which experienced a sharp decline in the 1950s because of television's impact and governmental antitrust actions (see

"The rise of Hollywood," p.389). Not surprisingly, with the rise of the military-industrial complex, the LA region became a focus of Cold War defense as many hilltop sites, from San Pedro to the Santa Monica Mountains, were converted into command centers for launching missiles against nuclear bombers, and installations like the Jet Propulsion Laboratory and Edwards Air Force Base became the focus of a local economy still on a war footing.

Concurrently, suburbs like Orange County drew old-time residents from the heart of the city into expanding towns like Garden Grove, Huntington Beach, and Anaheim – where **Disneyland** also acted as a pop-culture beacon. The northern valleys traded orange groves for subdivisions and asphalt, and before long, the entire LA basin was swelling with people in every conceivable direction. In contrast, much of the wealth in the Hollywood and Mid-Wilshire sections of town, areas that had first been developed by middle-class automotive travel in the 1920s and 1930s, left with the "white flight" of bourgeois residents to the outlying suburbs, and the old commuter suburbs west of Downtown increasingly became part of the inner city and the new home of working-poor minorities.

The 1960s to the 1980s

As elsewhere in the country, the face of Los Angeles began changing dramatically in the 1960s. Not only was the freeway system stitching the entire basin into an interconnected network of automobile suburbs, but LA's own classic Art Deco and Historic Revival buildings were quickly disappearing to make way for the promise of shiny new superstructures. Places like **Bunker Hill** changed from shambling Victorian neighborhoods into auto-oriented corporate enclaves, poor Hispanic families were cleared out of Elysian Park to make way for Dodger Stadium, the old 20th-Century Fox movie lot was sold off to make way for the colorless high-rise towers of Century City, and the quaint homes of Playa del Rey were demolished to make way for expansion of LAX. However unpopular they were, many of these deals were, predictably, sealed behind closed doors, in the continuing atmosphere of secrecy and intrigue that pervaded city politics.

However, the type of right-wing leadership evident in LA's postwar politicians, such as the race-baiting mayor Sam Yorty, and the city's so-called **Committee of 25**, a business cabal that acted as a sort of shadow government from its California Club headquarters, got its comeuppance with 1965's **Watts Riots**. The riots – which started with the arrest of one Marquette Frye for speeding, lasted a week and ended with the arrival of 36,000 police and National Guard troops – caused $40 million worth of property damage and permanently dismantled white LA's beliefs about the perceived laziness of minorities and willingness to accept overt subjugation. While many blacks did not see, and still have not seen, a diminution in poverty levels, the old municipal overlords couldn't help but take notice at the potent brew of anger and frustration they had helped create.

Along with this, the late 1960s **protests** by student radicals, mostly against the involvement in Vietnam, and the emergence of flower power and hippie counterculture caused a dramatic break between generations – the staid Orange County parents versus their rebellious, pot-smoking kids. The colorful result led to an explosion of psychedelic music, left-wing political diatribe, untamed sexuality, and, occasionally, bursts of violence – evident with the Manson Family killings of 1969. These freewheeling attitudes were most evident in places like the Sunset Strip, then as now famed for its rock-music scene, and Topanga Canyon, which became a veritable hippie commune in places.

After much effort, the progressive forces in LA politics finally began to undermine the corrupt power structure that had ruled LA for nearly a century. Eight years after the riots, LA's first black mayor, **Tom Bradley**, was elected by a coalition of black, Hispanic, and Westside Jewish voters. The political success of these groups galvanized others into action on the LA political scene, notably women and gays. Accordingly, the *LA Times*, long a paragon of reactionary yellow journalism, underwent a historic change through the efforts of **Otis Chandler**, son of archconservative former publisher Harry Chandler, who turned the paper into a liberal icon with a range of world-class writers and critics.

Bradley's twenty-year tenure was also marked, less fortuitously, by the disappearance of LA's manufacturing base. South Central and Southeast LA ceased to be centers for oil, rubber, and automotive production, the San Fernando Valley saw its car plants close, and heavy industries like Kaiser's mammoth steel-making operation in Fontana shut down. Though this was somewhat tempered in the 1980s by the heavy investment of foreign money into Downtown real estate, the decade ended hard with the **demise of aerospace jobs**, which had provided the region with its military-industrial meal ticket since the early Cold War era.

Modern LA: the 1990s to the present

The early Nineties continued the hard times, which only got bleaker when black motorist **Rodney King** was videotaped being beaten by uniformed officers of the LA Police Department. The officers' subsequent acquittal by jurors in conservative Simi Valley sparked the April 1992 **riots**, which highlighted the economic disparities between rich and poor, along with the more obvious abuses of police power and privilege. Thirteen years on, the aftermath of the riots (which involved all races in mass chaos from South Central to Koreatown and were not simply black versus white) has not yet been fully realized or understood, and new initiatives promised by local and federal authorities to combat LA's endemic violence and poverty never materialized. Meanwhile, episodes like the **O.J. Simpson trial** have only served to further confuse matters. In 1995, Simpson, a black former football star, was acquitted of killing his wife and her friend, in what was termed the "Trial of the Century," an ugly and protracted affair in which public opinion was split along racial lines.

All these factors combined to make the first five years of the 1990s perhaps the bleakest since the Great Depression, and **natural calamities** – regional flooding, Malibu fires and mudslides, and two dramatic earthquakes – only added to the general malaise.

The rest of the decade was not nearly as dramatic. **Richard Riordan**, a multimillionaire technocrat, was mayor for eight years in the mid- to late-1990s and presided over a major **revival** in the city's economic fortunes and a **restructuring** of its economic base – aerospace and automotive industries giving way to tourism, real estate, and, as always, Hollywood. New property developments attempted to revitalize blighted sections of town, and even crime and violence tailed off marginally. However, the city's old demons continued to stir. More than anything else, the allegations behind the **Rampart police scandal** – where a group of corrupt police officers acted worse than the gangs they were trying to shut down – made people realize what truly awful elements still lurked under LA's glossy surfaces.

The 2001 mayoral election of bland, uninspiring bureaucrat James Hahn didn't help matters, but his appointment of former New York police reformer **William Bratton** to head the LAPD surprised many, giving hope that an outsider with no connection to the department's entrenched ways might be just the person to reform it, though this still remains more hope than reality. Four years later, Hahn was defeated in his re-election bid by **Antorio Villaraigosa** – amazingly, LA's first Latino mayor since 1872 – but the city's core problems remain the same as they ever have: a huge gap between the richest and poorest Angelenos (even more extreme than the national rate); much lingering hostility between the races; and the difficulty of expunging gang violence, drive-by shootings, and all those other nasty elements of urban life that have been more effectively dealt with in cities such as, say, New York. To add to all this, the **floods of winter 2005** – caused from historic levels of rainfall and resulting in countless mudslides and road closures – gave everyone a swift reminder that natural disasters weren't just limited to the 1990s.

Nonetheless, the metropolis is back on a much firmer economic footing than in the previous decade, and the ugly character of much LA design from the 1960s into the 1990s – a mix of concrete Brutalism and corporate glass towers – may slowly be changing with the arrival of a slew of high-profile **signature buildings**, including the Getty Center and Disney Hall. At the same time, the preservation of classic sections of town like Old Pasadena and Downtown's Spring Street and Broadway offers hope that the city may have finally learned from its mistakes in trying to demolish its past.

Considering all these factors, and with the movies again showcasing LA as a stereotypical land of ultra-brite smiles and perfect bodies, it may only be a matter of time before the migrants – white, black, and Hispanic – start arriving in droves once more. Despite the occasional rain and gloom, the Southern California dream is too vivid and blinding ever to be fully obscured.

The rise of Hollywood

To this day, the word **Hollywood** remains synonymous with the motion picture industry, even if the reality of that association has not always held true. What follows is a brief history of the movie business in Los Angeles and how the studio system took root, from its genesis to the beginning of its decline.

Westward migration

While we now think of Hollywood's emergence as a simple matter of abundant sun, low taxes, and cheap labor – all important factors, to be sure – the original reason the first filmmakers established themselves here was due to something much simpler: **fear**. But for the strong-arm tactics of Thomas Edison and company, the movie business might never have come to Southern California.

Edison and his competitors (companies like Biograph, Vitagraph, and Pathé, among many others) had by 1909 consolidated their various patents on film technology and processing to form what was known as "**the Trust**": the Motion Picture Patents Company (the MPPC). Although it didn't even last a decade (thanks to bad business practices and a federal antitrust suit), the MPPC did manage to scare off many directors and producers in the first years of its existence, including producer William Selig and director Francis Boggs, both of whom wanted to get as far away from the MPPC's seat of power, New York City, as they possibly could. Southern California was their choice, and more prominent film-industry figures soon followed, finding the taxes, labor costs, and abundant shooting locations much to their liking.

△ Hollywood's iconic badge, here since 1923

Early Hollywood

Thomas Ince, **Mack Sennett**, and **D.W. Griffith** were the early film legends who helped to establish Hollywood as the focus of the American movie business. Ince, with his studios in Culver City and Edendale, and his coastal "Inceville" north of Santa Monica, founded the elemental model of the studio system that was to hold sway for many decades: writers would prepare scripts in collaboration with directors and Ince himself, after which a tightly budgeted production would be filmed at prearranged locations, and a final cut of the movie would be edited. This sort of precise planning minimized the possibility of surprises during shooting, as well as ground-breaking or idiosyncratic storytelling, and contributed to the factory-like character of Ince's operation.

By comparison, Sennett's **Keystone Film Company** in Edendale, in East Hollywood, produced Keystone Kops comedies in less rigorous fashion. However, with production needs mounting, Sennett adopted his former colleague's model (both had worked for Triangle Films in Culver City) and went on to a two-decades-long career making his signature brand of wacky entertainment.

The largest creative presence in early Hollywood was, however, D.W. Griffith, who began as a theatrical actor and director of one-reel shorts and reached the peak of his fame with *Birth of a Nation*, a runaway hit in 1914 – despite its glamorization of the Ku Klux Klan, its epic length (2hr 40min), and its unprecedented $2 admission fee. Woodrow Wilson praised the film for "writing history with lightning," overlooking that its source was not actual history, but the bigoted ramblings of Southern preacher Thomas Dixon, on whose book, *The Clansman*, the movie had been based.

Generating a firestorm of controversy with the film, Griffith fired back at his critics with his next film, *Intolerance* – a bloated historical epic – but only succeeded at shooting himself in the foot. With its preachy moralizing and colossal sets loaded with Babylonian columns and squatting elephants, *Intolerance* became a buzzword for box-office failure and directorial narcissism. Long before this, Griffith would make a slow slide into obscurity in the 1920s, but not before he perfected the essential aesthetic components he developed with *Birth of a Nation*: close-ups, flashbacks, cross-cutting, and the like.

The birth of the big studios

In 1913, **Cecil B. DeMille**, an itinerant theatrical actor and director, came west to rent a horse barn for a movie. From this simple act, DeMille and his partners, glove-maker Sam Goldfish (soon to be renamed Goldwyn) and vaudeville producer Jesse Lasky, established the basis for the big studios that would follow. The film made in the barn (even as there were horses still in it) was *The Squaw Man*, which became a huge commercial triumph; DeMille became one of the early industry's most bankable directors of historical and biblical epics, and Lasky and Goldwyn later teamed with Adolph Zukor to create the colossus known as **Paramount Studios**.

Like other studios in the coming decades, Paramount used a number of tactics to push its product, including "block booking" (in which film packages, rather than individual films, were sold to exhibitors, thus maximizing studio revenue) and buying up theater chains across the country (to ensure exhibition spaces for its films). These influential practices served to consolidate the industry. By the end of World War I, three major studios had risen to dominance: Paramount, **Loew's**, and **First National** – though only Paramount would survive in name during the height of the studio system.

The 1919 creation of **United Artists (UA)** looked promising for actors and directors. This studio, formed by Douglas Fairbanks Sr, Mary Pickford, D.W. Griffith, and Charlie Chaplin, seemed to suggest a greater role might be in store for the creative individuals who actually made the films, instead of just the studio bosses and executive producers. Things didn't quite work out that way, and the next decade saw UA in the role of bit player, along with Columbia and Universal, principally because it didn't own its own theaters and had to rely on one of the major studios for booking its films. The one major development UA prefigured was the dominance of the **star system**, by which big-name actors (such as Fairbanks and Pickford), rather than writers, directors, or the story itself, would drive the production and marketing of studio product – a scheme that has barely changed in more than 85 years.

The golden age

The five largest studios from the 1920s to the 1940s were **Paramount**, the **Fox Film Corporation** (later 20th Century-Fox), **Warner Bros**, **Radio–Keith–Orpheum** (later RKO), and the biggest of them all, **Metro–Goldwyn–Mayer**, or MGM, which was controlled by the still-powerful Loew's corporation in New York. The majors used every method they could to rigidly control their operations, and they did much to industrialize the business, breaking down the stages of production and using specialists (editors, cinematographers, and so on) to create the product. The arrival of **sound** in the late 1920s further specialized the industry, and the possibility of a lone professional with a camera shooting a nationally released film vanished.

Ince's original system had been perfected into rigorous, clinical efficiency. Even the content of the movies was controlled, in this case because of **Will Hays**, formerly Postmaster General in the corrupt Harding administration, when a series of 1920s scandals (not least, Fatty Arbuckle's three trials for the murder-rape of actress Virginia Rappe) tarnished the industry and raised the specter of government censorship. Hays' major claim to fame was as the developer of the 1930 "**Hays Code**," a series of official proscriptions and taboos that the studios were supposed to follow, involving intimations of sex, miscegenation, blasphemy, and so on. Although Hays is often credited with enforcing movie-industry censorship, it was actually **Joseph Breen** who wielded the real censorial power starting in the mid-1930s, when the Code first began to be rigidly enforced. With Breen and the Catholic organization the **Legion of Decency** looking over its shoulder, Hollywood produced a brand of entertainment that was safe, fun, and mostly noncontroversial. That filmmakers like John Ford, Orson Welles, Howard Hawks, and Preston Sturges were able to make classic films in such a stifling environment says much about the degree of talent the studios were employing during this time – although the industry also produced many tepid, cloying melodramas and tiresome serials that followed the Code precisely and today remain almost unwatchable.

Although Hollywood was, as an industrial system, unmatched by any other production complex in the world, it was, even at its height, something of an illusory power. For while the most visible and glamorous of the movie industry's stars and bosses smiled for the paparazzi in Hollywood, the real **financial muscle** continued to come from New York City. Companies like Loew's, which were based there, had the power – infrequently used until the 1950s – to command studios like MGM to change their policies and even films, simply by applying pressure in the corporate boardroom. It was only the financial discipline of the Southern California tycoons, their ability to turn a handsome profit and their fear of the Wall Street honchos that kept Hollywood with a reasonable degree of autonomy. And when times turned bad, New York took over – firing even the all-powerful Louis B. Mayer in 1951.

The demise of the studios

The emergence of the **film noir** style at the end of World War II should have sounded a warning to the old studio system. With bleak storylines, chiaroscuro photography, morally questionable antiheroes and dark endings, film *noir* was an abrupt departure from many of Hollywood's previous aesthetic conventions. This stylistic change, and the postwar disillusion it reflected, preceded several major transformations that permanently altered the way the studios did business.

A case study: Hollywood's first and last major studio

Riding high on the heels of the success of their 1913 film, *The Squaw Man*, Cecil B. DeMille, Sam Goldwyn, and Jesse Lasky created **Paramount Studios** by merging their operation with **Adolph Zukor's Famous Players**, which owned property across Melrose Avenue at 650 N Bronson. By adopting the Paramount name and merging with twelve other movie companies three years later, the young company quickly became second in stature only to Culver City's MGM. It subsumed the facilities of **RKO Studios** when that company went under, and in its heyday, Paramount churned out more than a hundred films a year, and had biggies like the Marx Brothers, Cary Grant, D.W. Griffith, Marlon Brando, and countless others under contract. Moreover, it even possessed a "**house style**" of glossy cinematography, sleek sets, and smart dialogue, with impeccable directors like Ernst Lubitsch and Josef von Sternberg helping to define the very notion of the sophisticated, intelligent Paramount film.

Eventually, as with the other majors, Paramount's unique style would fade by the 1950s and the company found itself foundering. By 1967, the conglomerate **Gulf + Western** devoured the studio but later adopted its name to fully cash in on its snow-capped image and reputation. A surprising rebound was soon led by studio executive, and later independent producer, **Robert Evans**, who with his freewheeling style and mountainous ego would do much to recall the glory days of the company's golden age, this time in the late 1960s and early 70s. With Evans bringing the studio back to prominence with a slew of commercially and/or critically successful films like *Rosemary's Baby*, *Love Story*, *The Godfather*, and *Chinatown*, Paramount regained its stature as a major force in Hollywood. Today, as with its house style of old, Paramount's critical and commercial luster has dimmed considerably, until its movies now resemble those of any other studio owned by a media conglomerate – faceless, sterile diversions. However, even though it's now owned by another giant corporation, Viacom, Paramount continues to maintain one unique aspect that other studios have long since forsaken: its original Hollywood location.

The greatest threat to the system, the **federal government**, in its antitrust prosecution of Paramount, was beginning to dismantle the practices of block booking and theatrical ownership that had kept the majors in firm control over the exhibition of their films. The increasing power of independent producers, helped by this and other structural changes, also removed some of the majors' control over the industry, as did the increasing ability of actors to finally use the star system to their advantage by not allowing the studios to lock up their careers for interminable lengths of time (starting with Olivia de Havilland, who sued Warner Bros to get out of her contract and won in California's supreme court after a three-year legal battle). Along with these changes, **television** reduced film viewership by great numbers and the studio bosses had to resort to desperate devices like 3-D, widescreen, and Cinerama to try to lure back their audiences.

Furthermore, the institution that the Hays Code had censored, with the blessing of Congress, began to come under direct attack from McCarthyite politicians. The House Un-American Activities Committee (HUAC) dredged up information on the alleged presence of Communist and left-leaning groups in Hollywood, and many screenwriters, actors, and directors were either humiliated into testifying or found themselves on an internal **blacklist** that kept them from working.

After the HUAC proceedings, Hollywood was creatively damaged, but the government's activities didn't keep directors like Otto Preminger from challenging the Hays Code. Through a series of legendary battles, on films like *The Moon is Blue* and others, Preminger and other filmmakers succeeded in throwing off the yoke of the Code, which had been in place for more than thirty years. This change, combined with the diminishment of pressure groups like the Legion of Decency, further loosened the control of the studio bosses over movie content and later led to the establishment of the **ratings system** in place today.

The aftermath

By the end of the 1950s, the studio system, at least as it had been known, was finished, and it took many years for the majors to regain much of the ground they had lost. However, while the industry eventually **rebounded** – through greater international sales and the development of ancillary markets like cable TV and home video – and moviemaking has become profitable once more to the studios (if not necessarily for their investors), it's unlikely that the industry will see a return to Depression-era days, when each studio churned out hundreds of films per year and could afford to experiment occasionally with quirky low-budget projects or off-kilter genre pictures.

Currently, Hollywood only manages to pump out a few big-budget spectacles and a declining number of medium-budget flicks – often cumulatively less than twenty annual films per studio. Modern American filmmaking, driven by exorbitant **talent costs**, is quite different from the old mechanized industry between the wars. With much of today's production budgets going into the wallets of the top actors, many of the formerly essential costs – elaborate sets, casts of thousands, and so on – have had to be scaled back as expensive luxuries. To make up the difference, computer-enhanced **CGI** technology has led the way for cheaper, more cost-effective filmmaking – even though the results of such digitally generated image-making are often less than convincing. Moreover, television–film studio mergers, videotape sales, and multimedia production have only served to highlight the differences from the old way of doing business. In one way, though, the studios have reasserted their dominance: by buying innovative independent companies like Miramax, or establishing their own "art-house" divisions such as Fox Searchlight, they have ensured that risky, lower-budget productions come under their direct control, to their direct benefit – just like the old days.

LA on film

Since its birth in the 1910s, Hollywood has often searched its own backyard for compelling scenes and interesting stories. While not always successful in conveying the truth of LA to a film audience, Hollywood **films** have nevertheless helped define the city for domestic and foreign audiences alike. The list below focuses on films that best use their LA backdrop as well as key works in Hollywood film history, and films tagged with a ⊡ are particularly recommended.

Hollywood does Hollywood

Autofocus (Paul Schrader 2003). Memorably creepy portrait of mid-level actor Bob Crane, who played the sunny title character on TV's *Hogan's Heroes*, but was in reality a sex addict who ended up being murdered in a Scottsdale motel, in one of Tinseltown's still-unsolved mysteries.

The Bad and the Beautiful (Vincente Minnelli 1952). Kirk Douglas shines in one of his best roles, a megalomaniacal Hollywood producer whose machinations are described in retrospect by his associates and victims.

Barton Fink (Joel Coen 1991). Tinseltown in the 1940s is depicted by the Coen brothers as a dark world of greedy movie bosses, belligerent screenwriters, and murderers disguised as traveling salesmen. Allegedly based on the experience of playwright Clifford Odets.

The Big Knife (Robert Aldrich 1955). An incisive portrayal of Hollywood politics, in which a weak-willed actor can't get free from the tentacles of a hack director, despite the pleas of his wife. Based on a play by Clifford Odets and filmed like one as well.

Day of the Locust (John Schlesinger 1975). Somewhat awkward realization of the classic satire by Nathanael West. The author's vivid colors are rendered here as bland pastels.

See "Books," p.412, for a review of the source.

Ed Wood (Tim Burton 1994). The ragged low-budget fringes of Fifties Hollywood are beautifully re-created in this loving tribute to the much-derided auteur of *Plan 9 from Outer Space* and *Glen or Glenda*. Gorgeously shot in black and white, with a magnificent performance by Martin Landau as an ailing but vulgar Bela Lugosi.

Gods and Monsters (Bill Condon 1998). An interesting, fact-based tale of the final days of 1930s horror-film director James Whale, ignored by the moviemaking elite and slowly dying of malaise by his poolside in Hollywood. The title refers to a memorable Ernest Thesiger line from Whale's classic *Bride of Frankenstein*.

Good Morning, Babylon (Paolo and Vittorio Taviani 1987). Two restorers of European cathedrals find themselves in 1910s Hollywood, working to build the monstrous Babylonian set for D.W. Griffith's *Intolerance*, in this Italian story of the contribution of immigrants in early Tinseltown. Oddly enough, that same set has now been rebuilt in Hollywood – as part of a mall (see p.109).

Hollywood Canteen (Delmer Daves 1944). Based on an actual, eponymous Hollywood establishment where popular movie stars from the World War II era sang and danced to a bevy of toe-tapping tunes. Most of Warner Bros' stars were featured in the picture – those that wouldn't appear were labeled "unpatriotic."

Hollywood on Trial (David Helpern Jr 1976). This interesting documentary examines the early 1950s witch-hunts in Hollywood and the blacklisted screenwriters, actors, and directors.

Hurlyburly (Anthony Drazan 1998). David Rabe's acidic play about Hollywood players and hucksters is rendered in celluloid as a prattling pathos-fest, with much angst for Sean Penn and Chazz Palminteri and much ironic detachment for Kevin Spacey and Garry Shandling.

The Last Tycoon (Elia Kazan 1976). F. Scott Fitzgerald's unfinished, would-be masterpiece is here rendered as an interesting failure: a rich, opulent world of Hollywood gloss that translates into slow, clumsy storytelling.

★ **The Player** (Robert Altman 1992). Tim Robbins is a studio shark who thinks a disgruntled screenwriter is out to get him; he kills the writer (at South Pasadena's Rialto theater; see p.203), steals his girlfriend and waits for the cops to unravel it. A wickedly sharp satire about contemporary Hollywood, with some great celebrity cameos.

Postcards from the Edge (Mike Nichols 1990). Written by Carrie Fisher, an insider's look at behind-the-scenes Hollywood, with Meryl Streep as the drug-addicted daughter of pushy glamour-queen Shirley MacLaine – thinly veiled versions of Fisher and her mother, Debbie Reynolds.

Singin' in the Rain (Stanley Donen/Gene Kelly 1952). A merry trip through Hollywood set during the birth of the sound era. Gene Kelly, Donald O'Connor, and Debbie Reynolds sing and dance to many classic tunes, including *Good Morning*, *Moses*, and *Broadway Melody*.

A Star Is Born (William Wellman 1937; George Cukor 1954). Based on the film *What Price Hollywood?*, these adaptations tell the story of the rise of a starlet mirroring the demise of her Svengali. Janet Gaynor and Fredric March star in the 1930s version, Judy Garland and James Mason in the later. Both are worthwhile, while a 1977 remake with Barbra Streisand and Kris Kristofferson runs a very distant third.

The State of Things (Wim Wenders 1982). A European filmmaker sees his financing disappear while stranded in LA and is beset by boredom in his mobile home. Essential if you're a fan of Wenders or of music by the punk band X – then near their peak.

Sullivan's Travels (Preston Sturges 1941). A high-spirited comedy about a director who wants to stop making schlock pictures and instead create gritty portrayals of what he thinks real life to be. The first two-thirds are great, though the film ends in mawkish fashion.

★ **Sunset Boulevard** (Billy Wilder 1950). Award-winning film about a screenwriter falling into the clutches of a long-faded silent-movie star. William Holden was near the beginning of his career, Gloria Swanson well past the end of hers. Erich von Stroheim fills in nicely as Swanson's butler, and even Cecil B. DeMille makes a cameo appearance.

The Way We Were (Sydney Pollack 1973). Aside from the Barbra Streisand–Robert Redford pairing and cloyingly memorable songs, a worthwhile portrait of the dark days of the Red Scare and Hollywood blacklist of the 1950s.

What Price Hollywood? (George Cukor 1932). The template for the *A Star Is Born* movies that followed: Constance Bennett is the starlet, an ambitious waitress, and Lowell Sherman is the drunken director.

Whatever Happened to Baby Jane? (Robert Aldrich 1962). Bette Davis and Joan Crawford are former child stars who plot against one another in a rotting Malibu house. A fine slice of horror.

LA crime stories

Beverly Hills Cop (Martin Brest 1984). Still-amusing Eddie Murphy flick, in which the actor plays an unorthodox, fast-talking Detroit detective who takes LA by storm while trying to solve a murder case.

The Big Sleep (Howard Hawks 1946). One of the key *film noirs* of the 1940s, with Humphrey Bogart playing Philip Marlowe, and featuring a wildly confused plot – even screenwriter Raymond Chandler admitted he didn't know who killed a particular character – that ends up being subordinate to the crackling chemistry between Bogie and Lauren Bacall.

★ **Chinatown** (Roman Polanski 1974). One of the essential films about the city. Jack Nicholson hunts down corruption in this dark criticism of the forces that animate the town: venal politicians, black-hearted land barons, crooked cops, and a morally bankrupt populace. Great use of locations, from Echo Park to the San Fernando Valley.

Devil in a Blue Dress (Carl Franklin 1995). Terrific modern *noir*, in which South Central detective Easy Rawlins (Denzel Washington) navigates the ethical squalor of elite 1940s white LA and uncovers a few ugly truths about the city's leaders.

Double Indemnity (Billy Wilder 1944). The prototypical *noir*. Greedy insurance salesman Fred MacMurray collaborates with harpy wife Barbara Stanwyck to murder her husband and cash in on the settlement. Edward G. Robinson observes on the sidelines as MacMurray's boss.

Get Shorty (Barry Sonnenfeld 1995). Slick Miami gangster Chili Palmer, played by John Travolta, takes up residence in Tinseltown and decides he wants to become a movie producer, in this amusing adaptation of an Elmore Leonard novel.

The Glass Shield (Charles Burnett 1995). Institutionalized racism in the LAPD is brought under the harsh glare of director Burnett, one of the great chroniclers of LA's black urban underclass.

The Grifters (Stephen Frears 1990). A memorable film with Annette Bening, John Cusack, and Anjelica Huston playing the title characters – con artists hunting through the LA underworld for their next victims.

He Walked by Night (Alfred Werker 1948). This vérité-style crime story set in "the fastest growing city in the nation" starts with a random cop-killing in Santa Monica and ends with a manhunt through the 700-mile subterranean city storm-drain system, stunningly shot by torch-light by peerless *noir* cinematographer John Alton.

Heat (Michael Mann 1995). Stars big names like De Niro and Pacino, but this crime drama, which does include some stunning set-pieces (eg a Downtown LA shootout), is ultimately less than the sum of its parts, with a frustratingly predictable ending.

In a Lonely Place (Nicholas Ray 1950). One of the all-time great *noirs*, and an unconventional one at that. Humphrey Bogart is a disturbed, violent screenwriter who causes trouble for those around him, particularly girlfriend Gloria Grahame – at the time, the director's real-life ex-wife.

Jackie Brown (Quentin Tarantino 1997). A glorious return to form for Pam Grier, who, as a tough airline stewardess, plays the perfect foil for Samuel Jackson's smooth gangster. LA provides the dark, menacing backdrop.

LA Confidential (Curtis Hanson 1997). Easily the best of the contemporary *noir* films, a perfectly realized adaptation of James Ellroy's novel about brutal cops, victimized prostitutes, and scheming politicians in 1950s LA. Even the good guys, Russell Crowe and Guy Pearce, are morally questionable.

The Long Goodbye (Robert Altman 1973). Altman intentionally mangles *noir* conventions in this Chandler adaptation. Elliott Gould plays Marlowe as a droning schlep who wanders across a sun-drenched landscape of casual corruption, encountering bizarre characters like nerdy mobster Marty Augustine, played with relish by movie director Mark Rydell, and Sterling Hayden as a hulking alcoholic writer. Cameo by future governor Arnold Schwarzenegger – in his underwear.

Murder My Sweet (Edward Dmytryk 1944). One-time Busby Berkeley crooner Dick Powell changed his tune and became a grim tough-guy detective in the best work from this director, who was briefly blacklisted for his former communist ties, then ratted on his colleagues once he was released.

One False Move (Carl Franklin 1991). A disturbing early role for Billy Bob Thornton, as a murderous hick who kills some people in an LA bungalow with his girlfriend and a psychotic, nerdy colleague, then gets pursued by the LAPD and a small-town Arkansas sheriff.

Point Blank (John Boorman 1967). Engaging, somewhat pretentious art-house flick with Lee Marvin as a hit man out for revenge. Begins and ends in Alcatraz, but in between successfully imagines LA as an impenetrable fortress of concrete and glass.

The Postman Always Rings Twice (Tay Garnett 1946). Lana Turner and John Garfield star in this seamy – and excellent – adaptation of the James M. Cain novel, first brought to the screen as *Ossessione*, an Italian adaptation by Luchino Visconti. Awkwardly remade by Bob Rafelson in 1981 with Jessica Lange and Jack Nicholson.

To Live & Die in LA (William Friedkin 1985). A violent cult film with a plot having something to do with morally dubious characters and counterfeiting, but most remembered for its kinetic car chases and dark portrait of the sleek, cold LA of the 1980s.

Touch of Evil (Orson Welles 1958). Supposedly set at a Mexican border town, this *noir* classic was actually shot in a seedy, decrepit Venice. A bizarre, Baroque masterpiece with Charlton Heston playing a Mexican official, Janet Leigh as his beleaguered wife, and Welles himself as a bloated, corrupt cop addicted to candy bars.

True Romance (Tony Scott 1993). With a Quentin Tarantino plot to guide them, Patricia Arquette and Christian Slater battle creeps and gangsters amid wonderful LA locations, from seedy motels to the classic *Rae's Diner* in Santa Monica.

Apocalyptic LA

★ **Blade Runner** (Ridley Scott 1982). The first theatrical version may have flopped, but the re-cut director's version confirms the film's stature as a sci-fi classic, in which dangerous "replicants" roam the streets of a dystopic future LA and soulless corporations rule from pyramidal towers.

Earthquake (Mark Robson 1974). Watch the Lake Hollywood dam collapse, people run for their lives, and chaos hold sway in the City of Angels. Originally presented in "Sensurround!"

Falling Down (Joel Schumacher 1993). Fired defense-worker Michael Douglas tires of the traffic jams on the freeways and goes on a rampage through some of the city's less picturesque neighborhoods, railing at petty injustices and wreaking havoc at every turn.

Kiss Me Deadly (Robert Aldrich 1955). Perhaps the bleakest of all *noirs*, starring Ralph Meeker as brutal detective Mike Hammer, who tramples on friends and enemies alike in his search for the great "whatsit" – a mysterious and deadly suitcase.

Lost Highway (David Lynch 1997). A lurid, frightening take on the city by director Lynch, using nonlinear storytelling and actors playing dual roles, and which had critics screaming for the exits – but if you like Lynch, this is essential viewing.

Strange Days (Kathryn Bigelow 1995). In a chaotic, nightmarish vision of LA, Ralph Fiennes, Angela Bassett, and Juliette Lewis run around the city screaming-in the new millennium. More interesting as a reflection of mid-1990s LA angst than as compelling cinema.

★ **The Terminator** (James Cameron 1984). Modern sci-fi classic, with Arnold Schwarzenegger as a robot from the future sent to kill the mother of an unborn rebel leader. Bravura special effects and amazing set-pieces here were followed up with the director's 1989 sequel, *T2: Judgment Day*, in which Arnold becomes a good robot, and the less-inspired *T3*.

Volcano (Mick Jackson 1997). A memorably cheesy disaster flick in which a volcano pops up near the La Brea Tar Pits, and Tommy Lee Jones and Anne Heche fight the lava with gusto.

LA lifestyles

Bob & Carol & Ted & Alice (Paul Mazursky 1969). Once-daring, but still funny zeitgeist satire about wife-swapping and bed-hopping in hedonistic Southern California, starring Natalie Wood, Robert Culp, Elliott Gould, and Dyan Cannon as the titular foursome.

Boyz N the Hood (John Singleton 1991). An excellent period piece that cemented the LA stereotype as a land of gangs and guns, starring Cuba Gooding Jr in his first big role, and Laurence Fishburne as his dad.

Clueless (Amy Heckerling 1995). Jane Austen's *Emma* transplanted to a rich Southern California high school, with a fine performance by Alicia Silverstone as a frustrated matchmaker.

Dogtown & Z-Boys (Stacy Peralta 2002). Even if you have no interest in skateboarding, this is a fun, high-spirited look at the glory days of the sport, when a daring group of LA kids took to using the empty swimming pools of the elite as their own private skate-parks.

Endless Summer (Bruce Brown 1966). Still the template for all surf films, a riveting portrait of the sport at its 1960s zenith, when catching a killer break could mean the world, and the waves teemed with legends. Good photography and portrait of the surfing world from one of its movie pioneers.

Faces (John Cassavetes 1968). A vivid, unforgettable portrait of middle-aged angst in upper-middle-class LA, in which a married couple breaks apart amid a nocturnal land-scape of dive bars, dance clubs (the early *Whisky-a-Go-Go*), and hand-some estates – one of them the director's own home.

Ghost World (Terry Zwigoff 2001). Sardonic portrait of alienated high-schooler Thora Birch trying to find her place in a grim LA world of strip malls, pointless jobs, and adult lies. Based on an equally effective and groundbreaking comic strip.

Go (Doug Liman 1999). A kinetic joyride through LA's rave subculture told from three perspectives, includ-ing Sarah Polley's botching of an aspirin-for-Ecstasy drug sale, and Jay Mohr and Scott Wolf – as two secretly gay TV soap stars – stuck in a police sting operation.

Grand Canyon (Paul Mazursky 1992). An overly sentimental flick that many movie fans love anyway, made at the nadir of LA's self-loath-ing of the early 1990s, involving folks from various races and classes trying to get chummy and rediscover their humanity.

★ **The Limey** (Steven Soderbergh 1999). Gangster Terence Stamp wanders into a morally adrift LA looking for his daughter's killer, and finds the burned-out husk of former hippie Peter Fonda. Arguably this director's best work.

The Loved One (Tony Richardson 1965). An effective adaptation of Evelyn Waugh's pointed satire about the dubious practices of the funeral industry, inspired by a trip to Forest Lawn.

Magnolia (Paul Thomas Anderson 1999). A darkly affecting travelogue of human misery starring Jason Robards and Tom Cruise, among many others. The San Fernando Valley serves as an emotional inferno of abusive parents, victimized chil-dren, haunted memories, and a mysterious plague of frogs.

Mi Familia (Gregory Nava 1994). The saga of the Sanchez family, featuring fine performances by a range of Hollywood's best Hispanic actors, including Jimmy Smits, Edward James Olmos, and Esai Morales. Overly earnest and senti-mental in places, though.

Mi Vida Loca (Alison Anders 1993). Depressing ensemble piece about the hard lives of Latinas in Echo Park girl-gangs and the central reason the director won a prestigious MacArthur Fellowship.

★ **Pulp Fiction** (Quentin Taran-tino 1994). A successful collec-tion of underworld stories by cult director Tarantino. Set against a backdrop of downtrodden LA streets, bars, diners, and makeshift torture chambers.

The Rapture (Michael Tolkin 1991). Mimi Rogers plays an LA telephone operator who abandons her hedonistic lifestyle after hear-ing a fundamentalist group talking about the impending "Rapture," and becomes born again, ultimately head-ing into the desert to await Arma-geddon. Michael Tolkin's wonderfully literal film takes his premise just as far as it can go, and then some.

Riding Giants (Stacy Peralta 2004). One of the best of the current batch of surfing documentaries, showing the glories of the sport (with modern, high-tech equipment), the life stories of some of its bigger names, and that perennial California backdrop of sun and waves.

Safe (Todd Haynes 1995). In Haynes' brilliant tale of millennial unease and corporeal paranoia, Julianne Moore plays a San Fernando Valley homemaker with seemingly little inner-life and an opulent outer one, who is diagnosed with environmental sickness and finds refuge at a New Age desert retreat.

Short Cuts (Robert Altman 1993). Vaguely linked vignettes tracing the lives of LA suburbanites, from a trailer-park couple in Downey to an elite doctor in the Santa Monica Mountains. Strong ensemble cast bolsters the intentionally fractured narrative.

Slums of Beverly Hills (Tamara Jenkins 1998). Troubled teen Natasha Lyonne deals with growing pains in a less-than-glamorous section of

town, where a pill-popping cousin, manic uncle, weird neighbors, and her own expanding bustline are but a few of her worries.

Speed (Jan de Bont 1994). Ultimate LA action flick, in which a bus careens through the freeways and boulevards of the city – and will blow up if it slows below 50mph. Much better than its sequels.

Star Maps (Miguel Arteta 1997). Melodrama of immigrant life on the fringes of Hollywood. Carlos, who has grandiose dreams of movie stardom, is doing time in his father's prostitution ring, standing on street corners ostensibly selling maps to stars' homes – in reality selling his body for cash.

Swingers (Doug Liman 1996). Cocktail culture gets skewered in this flick about a couple of dudes who flit from club to club to eye "beautiful babies" and shoot the breeze like Rat Pack–era Sinatras. Many LA locales shown, including the *Dresden Room* and *The Derby*.

"Way-out" West

Barfly (Barbet Schroeder 1987). Mickey Rourke channeling writer Charles Bukowski in this liquor-soaked romp through LA's seedy world of low-lifes, fistfights, and general depravity.

Beach Blanket Bingo (William Asher 1965). A cult favorite – the epitome of sun-and-surf movies, with Frankie Avalon and Annette Funicello singing and cavorting amid hordes of wild-eyed teenagers.

The Big Lebowski (Joel Coen 1998). A bizarre Coen foray into LA, exploring the lower-class underbelly of the city – Jeff Bridges' "The Dude" and his pal John Goodman uncover mysteries, meet peculiar

characters, and do lots and lots of bowling.

Boogie Nights (Paul Thomas Anderson 1997). A suburban kid from Torrance hits the big time in LA – as a porn star. Mark Wahlberg, Julianne Moore, and Burt Reynolds tread through a sex-drenched San Fernando Valley landscape of the disco years.

Down and Out in Beverly Hills (Paul Mazursky 1986). A West Coast adaptation of Jean Renoir's classic *Boudu Saved from Drowning*, with homeless Nick Nolte salving the nerves of *nouveau riche* neurotics.

Escape from LA (John Carpenter 1996). In John Carpenter's alternative vision of the future, LA is cut off from the mainland by an earthquake and has been turned into a deportation zone for undesirables. Sent in to uproot insurrection, Kurt Russell battles psychotic plastic surgeons and surfs a *tsunami* to a showdown in a netherworld Disneyland.

Gidget (Paul Wendkos 1959). One of the most influential films about life in Southern California, for better or worse, establishing the emblematic LA images of teenagers playing in the sun, carefree romance, and high-flying surfing. The first of several in a series.

House on Haunted Hill (William Castle 1958). Not the clumsy remake, but the glorious Vincent Price original, with the King of Horror as master of ceremonies for a ghoulish party thrown at his Hollywood Hills estate – actually, Frank Lloyd Wright's Ennis-Brown house (see p.101).

Mayor of the Sunset Strip (George Hickenlooper 2003). Great, disturbing documentary about the title character, a former stand-in for one of the Monkees, legendary DJ, lounge denizen, and apparent man-child who can't seem to get his life together, despite being pals with people like David Bowie.

Minnie and Moskowitz (John Cassavetes 1971). Strange and amusing tale of two loners who find a very strained romance amid the city's hot-dog stands, low-rent theaters, and LA County Museum of Art. The director himself pops up in a dark cameo as a snide, cheating husband.

★ **Mulholland Drive** (David Lynch 2001). Told in the director's inimitable style, a nightmarish tale of love, death, glamour,

and doom in LA – in which elfin cowboys mutter cryptic threats, elegant chanteuses lip-sync to phantom melodies, and a blue key can unlock a shocking double identity.

Permanent Midnight (David Veloz 1998). A grim tour through the city's drug subculture, with Ben Stiller as your heroin-addicted guide. Based on the autobiographical novel by former sitcom-writer Jerry Stahl, who was responsible for *Alf*.

Repo Man (Alex Cox 1984). Emilio Estevez is a surly young punk who repossesses cars for Harry Dean Stanton. Very imaginative and fun, and darkly comic.

Seconds (John Frankenheimer 1966). One of Rock Hudson's better performances, as a bored suburbanite who gets a second chance at life transplanted into the body of a younger man. Bleak in its treatment of Southern California's swinging Sixties.

Shampoo (Hal Ashby 1975). Using LA as his private playground, priapic hairdresser Warren Beatty freely acts on his formidable, though nonchalant, libido. A period piece memorable for its 1970s look.

They Live (John Carpenter 1988). Ludicrous but entertaining horror flick, in which a drifter living on the outskirts of LA discovers that aliens are subliminally encouraging the city's rampant consumerism.

Valley Girl (Martha Coolidge 1983). Early Nicolas Cage flick, in which the actor winningly plays a new-wave freak trying to woo the title character (Debra Foreman) in a clash of LA cultures. Good soundtrack, too.

C

Drama and history

The Aviator (Martin Scorsese 2004). Engaging biopic in which the brilliant but troubled mind of Howard Hughes is vividly on display in mid-century LA, as the aircraft pioneer builds some of the world's fastest and biggest planes, dates Hollywood starlets, and battles rival executives and politicians, all while obsessively washing his hands and collecting jars of his own urine.

The Doors (Oliver Stone 1991). Val Kilmer plays the great Jim Morrison at the height of his 1960s debauchery, under the frenetic direction of Oliver Stone.

Fat City (John Huston 1972). Great, late Huston film starring Stacy Keach as a washed-up boxer and Jeff Bridges as his young, incompetent charge. Quietly and effectively depressing.

The Killing of a Chinese Bookie (John Cassavetes 1976). Perfectly evoking the sleazy charms of the Sunset Strip, Cassavetes' behavioral crime story is about a club-owner (Ben Gazzara) in hock to the mob – just one of his many great LA character studies.

La Bamba (Luis Valdez 1987). The fictionalized story of Ritchie Valens, the LA rocker who died in an untimely plane crash with Buddy Holly. Lou Diamond Phillips gives a compelling performance, despite looking nothing like Valens.

Less Than Zero (Marek Kanievska 1987). More valuable as a period piece than as inspired cinema, a depiction of the drug habits of fatuous LA youth. The book wasn't much better.

Nixon (Oliver Stone 1996). A long, dark look at the first president from Southern California (played by Anthony Hopkins), as well as the old-time LA suburbs where he grew up.

★ **Rebel Without a Cause** (Nicholas Ray 1955). Troubled-youth film, starring, of course, James Dean. A Hollywood classic with many memorable images, notably the use of the Griffith Park Observatory as a shooting location.

Stand and Deliver (Ramon Menendez 1988). Inspired by the story of East LA's miracle-working teacher Jaime Escalante, played effectively by Edward James Olmos. A somewhat moving film better suited for TV than the big screen.

They Shoot Horses, Don't They? (Sydney Pollack 1969). Gloomy story set during the Depression, in which contestants desperately try to win money in an exhausting dance marathon. Aptly reflects the fatalistic attitudes of the late 1960s.

To Sleep with Anger (Charles Burnett 1990). An interesting view of LA's overlooked black middle-class, directed with polish by a very underrated African-American filmmaker.

Tupac and Biggie (Nick Broomfield 2002). In-your-face documentary about the murders of rappers Tupac Shakur and Notorious B.I.G., implicating hip-hop producer Suge Knight and rogue elements of the LAPD.

Zabriskie Point (Michelangelo Antonioni 1970). Muddled, pretentious misfire from the director that nonetheless features some promising early work by Jack Nicholson and visually interesting shots of the LA basin.

Zoot Suit (Luis Valdez 1981). A simplified overview of the Sleepy Lagoon Murder case and resultant anti-Hispanic violence, told as a musical.

C

Books

n the **book** reviews below, publishers are listed in the format US/UK, unless the title is available only in one country, in which case the country has been specified. Highly recommended titles are signified by ⊕ . Out-of-print titles are indicated by o/p.

Travel and general

Mike Davis *Ecology of Fear* (Metropolitan Books/Picador). Despite containing certain factual errors, a compelling read about LA's apocalyptic style, focusing on gloom and doom in movies and literary fiction, the danger of earthquakes and fires, mountain-lion attacks, and even tornadoes.

Robert Koenig *Mouse Tales* (Bonaventure Press US). All the Disneyland dirt that's fit to print: a behind-the-scenes look at the ugly little secrets – from disenchanted workers to vermin infestations – that lurk behind the happy walls of the Magic Kingdom.

Anthony Lovett and Matt Maranian *LA Bizarro* (St Martin's Press US). Without a doubt the best alternative, off-kilter guide to the city: indispensable reading if you're touring LA's dingiest motels, grungiest bars, goofiest architecture, and most infamous death sites.

★ **Leonard Pitt and Dale Pitt** *Los Angeles A to Z* (University of California Press US). If you're truly enthralled by the city, this is the tome for you: six hundred pages of encyclopedic references covering everything from conquistadors to movie stars.

Kevin Roderick *The San Fernando Valley: America's Suburb* (Los Angeles Times Publishing US). A surprising and occasionally intriguing view of the history, geography, and culture of "The Valley," provided by one of its former denizens.

Alexander Vertikoff and Robert Winter *Hidden LA* (Gibbs-Smith). An architecture photographer and writer present their favorite unheralded sights in the metropolis, using glossy photos to highlight such spots as Monrovia's *Aztec Hotel* and the tomb of Henry Huntington.

John Waters *Crackpot* (Random House/Fourth Estate). The irreverent director of cult classics like *Pink Flamingos* and *Hairspray* takes you on a personalized tour of the city's seamy underside.

Paul Young *LA Exposed: Strange Myths and Curious Legends in the City of Angels* (Griffin US). Lurid Hollywood mysteries and sordid urban lore from the last century revealed in a fast-paced and readable style.

History and politics

Oscar Zeta Acosta *Revolt of the Cockroach People* (Vintage US/UK). The legendary model for Hunter S. Thompson's bloated "Dr. Gonzo," the author was in reality a trailblazing Hispanic lawyer who used all manner of colorful tactics to defend oppressed and indigent defendants. A striking, semi-autobiographical portrait of 1970s East LA, written just before the author's mysterious disappearance.

Lou Cannon *Official Negligence* (Times Press/Westview). One man's version of the 1992 riots, which lets the Rodney King–beating cops off easy while concentrating its attack against LA's political leadership and the upper brass of the LAPD.

Margaret Leslie Davis *Dark Side of Fortune: Triumph and Scandal in the Life of Oil Tycoon Edward L. Doheny* (University of California Press US). The best and most comprehensive volume available about a business giant of early twentieth-century LA, covering his rise to power via local petroleum fields, to his downfall in the Teapot Dome scandal.

Gordon DeMarco *A Short History of Los Angeles* (Lexicos US o/p). A 180-page summary of the major events and phenomena that have shaped the city, with particular regard to class and racial struggles. Excellent reading.

Robert Fogelson *The Fragmented Metropolis: Los Angeles 1850–1930* (University of California Press US). Deftly covers a hefty chunk of local history, with significant insight. A sweeping story from the early "Hell Town" to the go-go days of the 1920s.

Robert Gottlieb and Irene Wolt *Thinking Big: The Story of the Los Angeles Times* (Putnam US). An insightful look at the way the city's biggest and most important newspaper has reported and manipulated the news through the years.

Paul Greenstein et al *Bread and Hyacinths: The Rise and Fall of Utopian Los Angeles* (California Classics US). A chronicle of efforts to create communal living by some city activists, particularly the socialist and near-mayor Job Harriman.

Abraham Hoffman *Vision or Villainy: Origins of the Owens Valley–Los Angeles Water Controversy* (Texas A&M University Press US). An introduction to the messy business of water politics c.1900, a topic that still engenders debate and anger a century later.

Norman Klein *A History of Forgetting* (Verso US/UK). A good companion to Mike Davis's *City of Quartz*, uncovering some of the political ugliness and minority oppression that have characterized LA's past.

Lisa McGirr *Suburban Warriors: The Origins of the New American Right* (Princeton University Press US). The tale of how once-fringe right-wing activists in Southern California rose from the ashes of the 1960s to dominate state and, later, national politics, culminating with the presidency of Ronald Reagan and his various minions.

★ **Carey McWilliams** *Southern California: An Island on the Land* (Gibbs-Smith US). Still one of the most important books about the city ever written, detailing the social clashes and intrigues that rocked LA in the first half of the twentieth century. McWilliams brings special insight as the lead defense attorney in LA's shameful prosecution of the Sleepy Lagoon Murder case.

Harris Newmark *Sixty Years in Southern California: 1853–1913* (Houghton Mifflin US). One of the great nineteenth-century leaders of the Jewish community offers an insider's take on the region's politics as well as various secrets of the time.

Don Normark *Chavez Ravine, 1949* (Chronicle US/UK). Black-and-white photographs and a compelling narrative provide a vivid look at life in a rural Hispanic community on the fringes of Downtown LA, just before the area was paved over to make way for Dodger Stadium.

★ **Mark Reisner** *Cadillac Desert* (Penguin US/UK). An essential guide to water problems in the

CONTEXTS | Books

American West, with special emphasis on LA's schemes to bring upstate California water to the metropolis. One of the best renderings of this sordid tale.

Jack Smith *Jack Smith's LA* (McGraw-Hill US o/p). A collection of the author's wry, incisive columns for the *Los Angeles Times*, which details the daily life of the city and its many assorted urban characters.

Kevin Starr *Material Dreams: Southern California through the 1920s* (Oxford University Press US/UK).

The third of the author's multi-volume series on the history of LA, from the late rancho period to the years after World War II, and perhaps the most interesting, covering the city's boom years and its attendant scandals and colorful celebrities.

Jules Tygiel *The Great Los Angeles Swindle* (University of California Press US). A rather basic but adequate presentation of Southern California's 1920s petroleum scandals, focusing on Edward Doheny and his local connection to the national Teapot Dome debacle.

Urban theory

★ **Mike Davis** *City of Quartz: Excavating the Future in Los Angeles* (Vintage/Pimlico). A leftist counterpart to Kevin Starr's mainstream history (see above). Written in the early 1990s, Davis's descriptions of racial hatred, security-system architecture, shifty politicians, and industrial decay have dated somewhat, and his fact-finding methods have been questioned, but there's still plenty here worth reading.

Umberto Eco *Travels in Hyperreality* (Harvest/Picador). A pointed examination of "simulacra," and a nice literary time-capsule of Southern California life several decades ago, discussing such things as a now-closed museum in Orange County that re-created the great works of art as wax figurines.

William Fulton *The Reluctant Metropolis: The Politics of Urban Growth in Los Angeles* (Johns Hopkins University

Press US). A highly readable account of political and economic conflicts in contemporary LA, with notable sections on modern Chinatown and the aftermath of the 1992 riots.

Blake Gumprecht *The Los Angeles River: Its Life, Death and Possible Rebirth* (Johns Hopkins University Press US). The downhill history of the LA River, from its early days as a meandering stream to its final transformation into a bleak, lifeless flood-channel.

Merry Ovnick *Los Angeles: The End of the Rainbow* (Balcony Press US). A riveting account of the city's political and social struggles, as seen through its institutions and architecture.

W.W. Robinson *Ranchos Become Cities* (San Pasqual Press US). A chronicle of the changes that turned the old Mexican rancho system into subdivided plots of land fit for real-estate speculation, urban growth, and massive profit-taking.

Architecture

★ **Reyner Banham** *Los Angeles: The Architecture of Four Ecologies* (University of California Press US). The book that made architectural

historians take LA seriously, and still an enjoyable read. Valuable insights on the city's freeways, vernacular buildings and cultural attitudes circa 1971.

Margaret Leslie Davis *Bullocks Wilshire* (Balcony Press US). A long-overdue tribute to the hallmark example of LA's stunning Zigzag Moderne architecture, a Mid-Wilshire department store that's now been reincarnated as a law-school library.

David Gebhard and Harriette Von Breton *Los Angeles in the Thirties: 1931–1941* (Hennessey & Ingalls US). Great old black-and-white photos documenting LA's Streamline Moderne architecture.

★ **David Gebhard and Robert Winter** *Los Angeles: An Architectural Guide* (Gibbs-Smith US). Still the definitive guide to the city's architecture, covering a full range of structures from programmatic to Art Deco to modern. Gebhard's excellent *Romanza: The California Architecture of Frank Lloyd Wright* (Chronicle US) is another essential volume for LA architecture fans.

Philip Jodidio *Contemporary California Architects* (Taschen US/UK). An overview of the city's most vibrant and influential architects, including Frank Israel, Eric Owen Moss, and Frank Gehry. Somewhat lacking in analysis, but filled with splendid color images.

Sam Hall Kaplan *LA Lost and Found* (Hennessey & Ingalls US). Of interest for the excellent pictures that accompany this former newspaper critic's lament for the good old days of local architecture.

Esther McCoy *Five California Architects* (Hennessey & Ingalls US). This still-relevant 1960s book was the first to draw attention to LA's Irving Gill, an early twentieth-century forerunner of the modern style, as well as other important architects who practiced in Southern California.

Robert McGrew and Robert Julian *Landmarks of Los Angeles* (Abrams US). A large-format guide, with numerous large, glossy photos, listing LA's historic sights and structures.

Richard Meier *Building the Getty* (Knopf US/UK). Highly readable account of the conception and creation of the Getty Center, as told by its architect, the prince of modernism.

Charles Moore *The City Observed: Los Angeles* (Hennessey & Ingalls US). Twenty-year-old volume that's still worth a look for its maps, pictures, and anecdotes, plus recommendations to set you on your way to exploring the old-time nooks and crannies of LA.

Elizabeth A.T. Smith *Blueprints for Modern Living: History and Legacy of the Case Study Houses* (MIT Press US). An excellent compendium of essays and articles about the built and unbuilt homes of the Case Study Program (see box, p.119), with descriptions, diagrams, and photographs of each.

Music

Clora Bryant et al *Central Avenue Sounds: Jazz in Los Angeles* (University of California Press US). Vividly re-creating the bouncy, kinetic scene on Central Avenue in the mid-twentieth century, and telling a long-overdue story in LA's, and the nation's, musical history.

★ **Barney Hoskyns** *Waiting for the Sun: Strange Days, Weird Scenes and the Sound of Los Angeles* (Bloomsbury UK). Ironic, detached overview of pop and rock music history in the City of Angels, with well-written perspectives on such seminal figures as Brian Wilson and Arthur Lee, and a vivid account of how it all went wrong – thanks to drugs and violence – in the late 1960s and 70s.

Don Snowden *Make the Music Go Bang: The Early LA Punk Scene* (St Martin's Press US). One of the few volumes on a critical stage in local music history, this book is most valuable for its striking pictures from the 1970s, highlighting such bands as Black Flag, the Germs, and X.

Mark Spitz and Brendan Mullen *We Got the Neutron Bomb: The Untold Story of LA Punk* (Three Rivers Press US). Long-overdue recollection of the glory days of the local punk and thrash scene in the 1970s.

Danny Sugarman *Wonderland Avenue* (Little Brown/Abacus). The former Doors' publicist gives a mind-bending tour of the local rock scene from the late 1960s on, providing lurid accounts of famous and infamous figures.

Hollywood and the movies

Kenneth Anger *Hollywood Babylon* (Dell US/UK). Deliciously dark and lurid stories of sex scandals, bad behavior and murder in Tinseltown, written by the *enfant terrible* of 1960s experimental films. Not especially well written, but it holds your attention throughout.

Robert Berger *The Last Remaining Seats* (Hennessey & Ingalls US). An excellent photo guide to the extant movie palaces of Los Angeles, including many shots of theaters that are now closed to the public.

Peter Bogdanovich *Who the Devil Made It* (Random House/Arrow). Acclaimed book of conversations with great old Hollywood film-makers, including Alfred Hitchcock, Fritz Lang, and Howard Hawks.

David Bordwell, Janet Staiger and Kristin Thompson *The Classical Hollywood Cinema* (Columbia University Press/Routledge). Learn all about the techniques used by filmmakers and studios up to the 1960s: cross-cutting, eyeline-matches, the shooting axis, and other devices that you may not know by name, but have seen in countless movies.

Kevin Brownlow and John Kobal *Hollywood: The Pioneers* (Knopf US/UK). An intriguing look at the founders of American cinema in the

silent era, told from the points of view of an esteemed film historian and preservationist, and a prolific writer on movie topics.

Robert Evans *The Kid Stays in the Picture* (New Millennium US). Spellbinding insider's view of the machinations of Hollywood after the demise of the studio system, written with verve by one of LA's biggest egos and, it turns out, most compelling writers – the head of Paramount when that company was at its modern peak.

Carrie Fisher *Postcards from the Edge* (Pocket/Picador). The real-life Princess Leia had serious problems: a mother from hell, the pressures of teenage stardom, and the unstoppable force of the Hollywood Movie Machine. After caving in to chemical comfort, she cleaned up her act, rebuilt her relationship with Mom, and wrote this memorable book – a *Heart of Darkness* for 1980s Hollywood.

Otto Friedrich *City of Nets: A Portrait of Hollywood in the 1940s* (University of California Press/HarperCollins). Descriptions of the major actors, directors, and studio bosses of the last good years of the studio system, before TV, antitrust actions, and Joe McCarthy ruined it all.

Ian Hamilton *Writers in Hollywood: 1915–1951* (HarperCollins US/UK). A revealing look at screenwriters from the early days of the studio system up to its decline, with special focus on literary heavyweights like F. Scott Fitzgerald and William Faulkner.

Charles Higham *Hollywood Cameramen* (Viking/Secker & Warburg both o/p). A discussion of seven of the great masters of cinematography, whose work in lighting movie classics has been all too frequently overlooked by the general public. A classic read, with a few copies still floating around.

Gerald Horne *Class Struggle in Hollywood: 1930–1950* (University of Texas Press US). Excellent exploration of a commonly overlooked aspect of Tinseltown – the ongoing strife between labor unions and the studios, which culminates here with a dramatic strike and subsequent violence.

★ **Ephraim Katz** *The Film Encyclopedia* (Harper US/UK). The essential reference guide for anyone interested in the movies, providing valuable information on the old movie companies and countless studio-system bit players, along with more contemporary figures. The first, 1980, edition is the best.

Colin McArthur *Underworld USA* (Viking/Secker & Warburg both o/p). One of the best analyses of the Hollywood gangster film, as realized by directors from Fritz Lang to Don Siegel.

Corey Mitchell *Hollywood Death Scenes* (Olmstead Press US). A valuable guide to the seamy side of movieland, covering all the famous murders – from the Black Dahlia to Charles Manson – with pictures of the morbid sites, then and now.

Michael Munn *Hollywood Murder Casebook* (St Martin's US o/p). If the above book isn't enough for you, this book examines the gory details of Hollywood murders from a scientific viewpoint, with clinical efficiency.

Thomas Schatz *The Genius of the System* (Owl Books/Faber & Faber). A laudatory account of the big studios and bosses of the golden age of movies, covering the structure of the industry and detailing the major and minor players. A bit overbroad in its praise, but still a very worthwhile read.

★ **Alain Silver and Julia Ward** *Film Noir: An Encyclopedic Reference to the American Style* (Overlook US/UK). A large-format guide to the bleak films of the 1940s to the present, and an essential title that has gone through many editions. The best of author Silver's many excellent *noir*-related volumes.

Jerry Stahl *Permanent Midnight* (Warner/Process). When his employers on TV's *Alf* heard that star writer Stahl was spending more than his already-huge paycheck to support his heroin and other habits, they gave him a raise to cover the difference and keep him on the job. The result is another gritty descent into (and recovery from) Tinseltown drug hell.

Fiction

Eve Babitz *Eve's Hollywood* (Delacorte US o/p), *Slow Days, Fast Company* (Knopf US o/p), *LA Woman* (Simon & Schuster US o/p). Eye-opening, thinly veiled autobiographical portraits of Southern California in the 1960s and 70s, with all the drugs, sex, and rock'n' roll you can imagine, but described in a relaxed, almost wistful, manner. Though all are out of print, only the first is difficult to find online.

T.C. Boyle *Tortilla Curtain* (Penguin/Bloomsbury). Set in LA, this book boldly borrows its premise – a privileged white man running down a member of the city's ethnic underclass – from Tom Wolfe's *Bonfire of the Vanities*, but carries it off to great satiric effect.

Charles Bukowski *Post Office* (Ecco Press/Virgin). An alcohol- and sex-soaked romp through some of LA's festering back alleys, with a mailman surrogate for Bukowski as your guide. One of several books by the author exploring his encounters with the city's dark side.

★ **James M. Cain** *Double Indemnity, The Postman Always Rings Twice, Mildred Pierce* (Vintage/Picador). With Raymond Chandler, the ultimate writer of dark, tough-guy novels. His entire oeuvre is excellent reading, but these three are the best explorations of LA.

★ **Raymond Chandler** *Farewell, My Lovely, The Long Goodbye, The Lady in the Lake* (Vintage/ Penguin). All of these books, and several more, have been adapted into movies, but Chandler's prose is inimitable: terse, pointed, and vivid. More than just detective stories (centered on gumshoe detective Philip Marlowe), these are masterpieces of fiction.

Susan Compo *Life After Death and Other Stories* (Faber & Faber US/ UK). The club life of the black-clad members of the local goth-rock scene is the subject here, and the author's prose brings it to life in sordid detail.

Michael Connelly *Angels Flight* (Warner Books/Orion). A sixth volume of contemporary detective fiction featuring the LAPD investigator Harry Bosch, whose appropriate moniker casts him as a keen observer of LA's blood-curdling mix of corruption, public scandals, and violence.

Joan Didion *Play It as It Lays* (Farrar, Straus & Giroux/Flamingo). Hollywood rendered in booze-guzzling, pill-popping, sex-craving detail. Oddly, the author went on to write the uninspired script for a third adaptation of *A Star is Born*.

John Gregory Dunne *True Confessions* (Oldcastle/No Exit Press). The tale of an LA cop and his priestly brother, based in part on the city's notorious Black Dahlia Murder case. A first-rate book, made into a second-rate movie.

★ **James Ellroy** *The Black Dahlia, The Big Nowhere, LA Confidential, White Jazz* (Vintage/Arrow). The LA Quartet: an excellent saga of city cops from the postwar era to the 1960s, with each novel becoming progressively more complex and elliptical in style.

Steve Erickson *Amnesiascope* and *Arc d'X* (Henry Holt/Quartet Books). The two best of the author's wildly florid, postmodern novels about the city, featuring bizarre characters in surreal settings.

John Fante *Ask the Dust* (Black Sparrow/Rebel Inc.). The first and still the best of the author's stories of itinerant poet Arturo Bandini, whose wanderings during the Depression highlight the city's faded glory and struggling residents.

Robert Ferrigno *The Horse Latitudes* (Avon/Pocket Books both o/p). A drug-dealer-turned-academic begins a descent into a bizarre LA world when he encounters a corpse at his home, possibly left by his missing ex-wife.

David M. Fine *Imagining Los Angeles: A City in Fiction* (University of New Mexico Press US). Excellent overview of fiction set in LA, from early historic romances to detective novels to apocalyptic tales.

F. Scott Fitzgerald *The Last Tycoon* (Scribner/Penguin). The legendary author's unfinished final work, a major novel on the power and glory of Hollywood. Intriguing reading that gives a view of the studio system at its height. US edition features a reconstruction of what the finished version might have looked like.

Chester Himes *If He Hollers Let Him Go* (Thunder's Mouth Press/Serpent's Tail). A fine literary introduction to mid-twentieth-century race relations in LA, narrated by one Bob Jones, whose struggles mirror those of author Himes, who eventually ended up living in Spain.

Aldous Huxley *Ape and Essence* (Ivan R. Dee/Vintage). Imaginative depiction of post-nuclear LA, in which books are burned in Pershing Square for warmth and the *Biltmore* hotel is the site of an annual orgy.

Christopher Isherwood *Down There on a Visit* (University of Minnesota Press; Minerva). Incisive, involving read by a British expatriate, who penned much of his later fiction in and on Southern California.

Helen Hunt Jackson *Ramona* (New American Library/Avon). Ultra-romanticized depiction of mission life that rightfully criticizes the American government's treatment of Indians while showing the natives to be noble savages and glorifying the Spanish exploiters. Not particularly good reading, but a valuable period piece – and perhaps the most influential piece of fiction ever written about LA.

Gavin Lambert *The Slide Area* (Serpents Tail US). Seven short tales focusing on the dark side of Hollywood and LA's beachside towns, first published over forty years ago but still absorbing for its urban insights and lurid details.

Elmore Leonard *Get Shorty* (Harper/Penguin). Ice-cool mobster Chili Palmer is a Miami debt collec-

tor who follows a client to Hollywood, and finds that the increasing intricacies of his own situation are translating themselves into a movie script.

David Levien *Wormwood* (Hyperion o/p in US/Allison & Busby). Get a glimpse of the seamier side of the contemporary movie biz, following an up-and-coming story editor through the corporate ranks until he achieves utter exhaustion and, curiously, an addiction to absinthe.

Ross MacDonald *Black Money* (Vintage/Orion). Private detective Lew Archer pilots himself through the nasty underworld of LA society, both high and low. A captivating read.

Walter Mosley *Devil in a Blue Dress*, *A Red Death*, *White Butterfly*, *Black Betty*, *A Little Yellow Dog*, *Bad Boy Brawly Brown* (Washington Square Press/Serpents Tail). Six excellent modern *noir* novels featuring black private detective Easy Rawlins, who "does favors" from his South Central base. Mosley compellingly brings to life Watts and, later, Compton.

Kem Nunn *Tapping the Source* (Four Walls Eight Windows US o/p). One of the most unexpected novels to emerge from California beach culture, this eerie murder-mystery is set amid the surfing scene of Orange County's Huntington Beach.

Thomas Pynchon *The Crying of Lot 49* (HarperPerennial/Vintage). The hilarious adventures of techno-freaks and potheads in Sixties California, revealing among other things the sexy side of stamp collecting.

John Ridley *Love is a Racket* (Ballantine US/UK). A delightful slice of Hollywood hell, in which protagonist Jeffty Kittridge, slumming through the dregs of local society and being abused by countless predators, leads us on a darkly comic journey through LA's many bleak corners.

Geoff Ryman *Was* (Penguin US/UK). A pop-lit masterpiece that bizarrely updates and twists the *Wizard of Oz* for more contemporary times, creating a fascinating work of Southern Californian magical realism.

Danny Santiago *Famous All Over Town* (Plume/Putnam). A compelling portrayal of life in a struggling Hispanic community, set in the barrio of East LA, and featuring a cast of street gangs.

Budd Schulberg *What Makes Sammy Run?* (Vintage/Random House). Classic anti-Hollywood vitriol by one of its insiders, a novelist and screenwriter whose acidic portrait of the movie business is unmatched.

Mona Simpson *Anywhere but Here* (Vintage/Faber & Faber). Engaging story of a mother's desire to put her daughter on the fast track to Hollywood stardom. Made into a less inspired movie.

Upton Sinclair *The Brass Check* (University of Illinois Press US). The failed California gubernatorial candidate and activist author's vigorous critique of LA's yellow journalism and the underhanded practices of its main figures. Sinclair also wrote *Oil!*, about the city's 1920s oil rush, and *The Goose Step*, concerning collegiate life at USC.

Terry Southern *Blue Movie* (Atlantic Monthly Press/New American Library). Sordid, frequently hilarious take on the overlap between high-budget moviemaking and pornography, with the author's vulgar themes and characters cheerfully slashing through politically correct literary conventions.

Michael Tolkin *The Player* (Avalon US/UK). A convincing portrayal of the depravity and cutthroat dealings of the filmmaking community, with special scorn reserved for venal movie execs. Made into a classic flick by Robert Altman.

Gore Vidal *Hollywood* (Vintage/Abacus). The fifth volume in the author's "Empire" series about emerging US power on the world stage, this one focusing on the movie industry, its interaction with Washington bigwigs, and boundless capacity for propaganda.

Evelyn Waugh *The Loved One* (Back Bay/Penguin). The essential literary companion to take with you on a trip to Forest Lawn – here rendered as Whispering Glades, the pinnacle of funerary pretension and a telling symbol of LA's status-obsessed ways.

Nathanael West *The Day of the Locust* (New Directions/Penguin). The best novel about LA not involving detectives; an apocalyptic story of the characters on the fringes of the film industry, culminating in a glorious riot and utter chaos.

Glossaries

Architectural terms

Art Deco Catch-all term for Zigzag Moderne, Streamline Moderne, governmental WPA, and other styles, often identified by geometric motifs, sharp lines, and sleek ornamentation. See the Miracle Mile, pp.87-88.

Beaux Arts Turn-of-the-century movement imported from New York and Europe emphasizing Neoclassical symmetry, imposing dimensions, grand columns and stairways, and other features now associated with old-time banks. See the monumental Hall of Justice, p.65.

Brutalist Late-modern extreme architectural style first popularized in Britain and poorly executed in LA, emphasizing concrete, box-like construction, and utter lack of ornament and aesthetic interest. See any parking garage or 1960s government building.

Bungalow Prototypical style of home design in the early twentieth century, originating in the Far East but finding popularity in LA for its use of shingles, porches, and sloped roofs, and compact design. Although it was most often linked to the Arts and Crafts movement, many varieties can be spotted with Spanish Colonial, Mission, Continental, and even Moderne influences. See Bungalow Heaven in Pasadena, p.200.

Case Study Program Postwar design project initiated by *Arts and Architecture* magazine, which planned and sometimes constructed modern, affordable homes made principally of steel and glass. See box on p.119 for more details, or the Eames House in Pacific Palisades, p.218.

Corporate Modern Bland reduction of the original modern aesthetic, with glass curtain walls, boxy geometry, and an inhuman scale. Usually found with towering office blocks Downtown or in Century City, though sometimes inventive, as with the Library Tower, p.75.

Craftsman Early twentieth-century style, using exposed wood beams, overhanging rooflines, large shingles, cobblestones, and prominent fireplaces to create a rough-hewn look. See the Gamble House, p.201.

Deconstructivist Architecture that looks like it's falling apart or incomplete, characterized by irregular shapes, aggressive asymmetry, and lack of obvious coherence. See box on the work of Eric Owen Moss, p.141.

Folk Architecture Home-made structures created by untrained, self-taught builders, the Watts Towers being a glorious example, p.171.

Googie Free-spirited coffee-shop architecture, with bright colors, sharp curves and boomerang shapes, pitched roofs and neon trim. See *Pann's* in South Central, p.161, or *Bob's Big Boy* in Burbank, p.211.

High-Tech 1970s and 1980s variant on the machine aesthetic, characterized by exposed pipes and ducts and industrial decor. Few good examples survive locally, although the post-industrial Carlson-Reges Residence, p.79, comes close.

Historic-Revival The early twentieth-century use of various older architectural styles – notably Spanish Colonial in the 1920s. See box on the architectural firm of Morgan, Walls and Clements, p.88.

Mission Originally the unimposing, ranch-style buildings put up by the Spanish in the eighteenth and early nineteenth centuries, such as Mission San Fernando, p.214. Later a period-revival style that reached its height with 1920s housing; see Union Station, p.61, for its most monumental form.

Modern Clean, geometric design aesthetic, beginning in the 1920s and 1930s with houses built by R.M. Schindler, such as the architect's own home, p.122, and Richard Neutra, the Lovell House, p.91, and continuing on to today's exemplars like the Getty Center, p.135.

Moderne A popular architectural style that used Art Deco ornamentation and sleek lines to convey quiet elegance. See any glossy movie set from the 1930s, or Crossroads of the World, p.112.

Period-Revival See "Historic-Revival."

Postmodern Contemporary rehash of Neoclassical architecture, often in pastel colors. See Charles Moore's Civic Center in Beverly Hills, p.126.

Pre-Columbian Quirky 1920s architecture, employing blocky sunbursts, abstract floral motifs and stylized faces to create an ancient look for the modern city. See the *Aztec Hotel*, p.207, or almost any LA work by Frank Lloyd Wright.

Programmatic Buildings taking a particular, nonarchitectural shape, such as dogs, boots, rockets, and hats. See *Tail o' the Pup*, p.269, or *The Donut Hole*, p.271, for good examples.

Ranch Quintessential style of Southern California design, typically found in suburban homes with low-slung, single-story plans, open layouts with few interior walls, and abundant windows. Best seen in its grandest form at the ranch at Will Rogers State Historic Park, p.219.

Sculptural Architecture as art, often "molded" by the architect using computer-assisted design to create structures that would not be possible at a drafting table. Quite striking when successful, as in much of the work of Frank Gehry, especially Disney Hall, p.65.

Spanish Colonial Perhaps the quintessential style for housing architecture in LA, especially in the period-revival 1920s, emphasizing tiled roofs, wrought-ironwork, whitewashed walls, and romantic landscaping. See Villa Aurora, p.220.

Streamline Moderne Buildings resembling ocean liners and sometimes airplanes, borne of a 1930s worship of all things mechanical. See the Coca-Cola Bottling Plant, p.170.

Victorian General term for late-1800s housing styles – Eastlake, Queen Anne, Stick – few of which remain in the city. See Angelino Heights, p.77, or Heritage Square, p.79.

Zigzag Moderne A late-1920s version of Art Deco that had particular popularity in LA, with strong verticality, narrow windows, geometric ornamentation, and occasional use of pre-Columbian or Egyptian motifs. See Bullocks Wilshire, p.83.

LA movie-industry terms

Above the line Budgeted costs for actors, writers, directors, and producers.

Above the title Adjective or adverb referring to the placement of a major actor's film credit in studio advertising, often a contractual requirement.

Below the line Budgeted costs for camera, lighting, and all other technical and behind-the-scenes costs.

Below the title Except for major actors, where everyone else – supporting players, writer, director, and so on – gets named in studio

C

advertising for a film, typically near the bottom in fine print.

Block booking Old studio-system practice of forcing exhibitors to carry whole "blocks" of studio films, including many awful titles they would otherwise reject. Since declared an illegal monopoly practice by the US Supreme Court.

Blockbuster Now a well-known word for a big hit, its original meaning meant a film that appealed to all audiences and thus "busted" the "blocks" of disparate segments of viewers.

Box office The weekly money generated by a particular film. Also called the "take."

Completion bond Finishing funds for a film project, given by a financial entity who in return gets some degree of control over the film.

Development The branch of a film company responsible for bringing projects into existence in pre-production, often through working with writers to re-craft their scripts for the big screen and getting notable actors and directors, and sometimes producers, on board.

Development hell The much-feared limbo that a film project experiences during pre-production when the script suddenly requires multiple, contradictory revisions, prospective actors quit, or the studio loses interest. Every screenwriter's nightmare.

Green light A verb meaning to approve the actual production of a given film.

Gross profit The raw financial returns of a film before costs are subtracted, published on Mondays in the trade press and watched eagerly by Hollywood players.

High concept A movie plot that can be summarized on a cocktail napkin, or more specifically, by a single, basic sentence, eg "A chimpanzee detective solves crimes in Hollywood."

In the can A finished film project, symbolically sitting in its reel or canister. However, term does not mean the film is about to be released – projects can sit "in the can" for years, or never be released at all.

Independent Once applied to small companies operating outside the studio mainstream. Since such companies are now mostly controlled by the majors, the term currently refers to ultra-low-budget films and filmmakers. Also called "indie."

Lens Verb, mostly employed by the trade-industry press, meaning "to film." Possibly used this way only in Hollywood.

Lunch Verb meaning "to conduct business," and the place where business is conducted.

MPAA Acronym for the Motion Picture Association of America, the body that oversees the film-rating and classification board.

Oater Pejorative slang for Westerns – a nearly defunct genre.

Open Verb meaning "to begin playing" and, more importantly, "to draw an audience."

Player 1980s term for an important studio executive, film producer, or top director able to command financial respect throughout town and get a movie project "green lighted."

Points A percentage of profits taken from the gross earnings of a film, often as payment by actors and directors in lieu of salary.

Post Short for post-production: editing, adding sound effects, redubbing dialogue, and the like.

Preview Outside of LA, a short advertising clip, also known as a "trailer," preceding a film viewing. Within LA, an advance screening of a movie used to gauge an audience's response – positive or negative.

Scale Union-minimum wages that supporting players must accept to be involved with many productions, and that big-name actors will sometimes accept to be associated with a prestigious low-budget work or acclaimed director.

Sleeper A familiar term for an unheralded flick that manages to be a surprise hit.

Turnaround Occurs when a production company loses interest in a film project and either pawns it off on another company or shelves it for an indefinite period.

Vehicle Not an automobile, but a motion picture – often of limited creative value – that is used to forward the career of a major celebrity or rising actor. In the extreme, is known as a "vanity project."

Vertical integration The practice in the film world of owning the production, distribution, and exhibition parts of the industry – studios controlling every step of the process. Declared an illegal practice by the US Supreme Court in the 1950s but since loosened by Congress with the rise of cable TV, videotape, and digital filmmaking, and their financial overlap.

Travel
store

Rough Guides travel...

TRAVEL STORE

Rough Guides are available from good bookstores worldwide. New titles are
published every month. Check www.roughguides.com for the latest news.

...music & reference

Jordan
Kenya
Marrakesh
  DIRECTIONS
Morocco
South Africa, Lesotho
  & Swaziland
Syria
Tanzania
Tunisia
West Africa
Zanzibar

Travel Theme guides
First-Time Around the
  World
First-Time Asia
First-Time Europe
First-Time Latin
  America
Skiing & Snowboarding
  in North America
Travel Health
Travel Online
Travel Survival
Walks in London & SE
  England
Women Travel

Restaurant guides
French Hotels &
  Restaurants
London Restaurants

Maps
Algarve
Amsterdam
Andalucia & Costa
  del Sol
Argentina
Athens
Australia
Baja California
Barcelona
Berlin
Boston
Brittany
Brussels
Chile
Chicago

California
Corsica
Costa Rica & Panama
Crete
Croatia
Cuba
Cyprus
Czech Republic
Dominican Republic
Dubai & UAE
Dublin
Egypt
Florence & Siena
Florida
Frankfurt
Greece
Guatemala & Belize
Iceland
Ireland
Kenya
Lisbon
London
Los Angeles
Madrid
Mallorca
Marrakesh
Mexico
Miami & Key West
Morocco
New York City
New Zealand
Northern Spain
Paris
Peru
Portugal
Prague
Rome
San Francisco
Sicily
South Africa
South India
Sri Lanka
Tenerife
Thailand
Toronto
Trinidad & Tobago
Tunisia
Tuscany
Venice

Washington DC
Yucatán Peninsula

**Dictionary
Phrasebooks**
Czech
Dutch
Egyptian Arabic
European Languages
  (Czech, French,
  German, Greek,
  Italian, Portuguese,
  Spanish)
French
German
Greek
Hindi & Urdu
Hungarian
Indonesian
Italian
Japanese
Mandarin Chinese
Mexican Spanish
Polish
Portuguese
Russian
Spanish
Swahili
Thai
Turkish
Vietnamese

Music Guides
The Beatles
Bob Dylan
Cult Pop
Classical Music
Elvis
Heavy Metal
Hip-Hop
Irish Music
Jazz
Music USA
Opera
Reggae
Rock
Sinatra
World Music (2 vols)

Film Guides
Comedy Movies
Ganster Movies
Horror Movies
Sci-Fi Movies

Reference Guides
Books for Teenagers
Children's Books, 0–5
Children's Books, 5–11
Conspiracy Theories
Cult Fiction
Cult Football
Cult Movies
Cult TV
The Da Vinci Code
Ethical Shopping
iPods, iTunes & Music
  Online
The Internet
James Bond
Kids' Movies
Lord of the Rings
Macs & OSX
Muhammad Ali
PCs and Windows
Pregnancy & Birth
Shakespeare
Superheroes
Unexplained
  Phenomena
The Universe
Weather
Website Directory

Football 11s Guides
Arsenal 11s
Celtic 11s
Chelsea 11s
Liverpool 11s
Manchester United 11s
Newcastle 11s
Rangers 11s
Tottenham 11s

TRAVEL STORE

Also! More than 120 Rough Guide music CDs are available from all good book
and record stores. Listen in at www.worldmusic.net

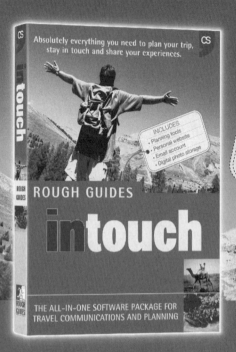

Absolutely everything you need to plan your trip, stay in touch and share your experiences.

INCLUDES
• Planning tools
• Personal website
• Email account
• Digital photo storage

A NEW CONCEPT IN TRAVEL

ROUGH GUIDES

intouch

THE ALL-IN-ONE SOFTWARE PACKAGE FOR
TRAVEL COMMUNICATIONS AND PLANNING

ROUGH GUIDES SOFTWARE
Share your adventures on the move

Rough Guides have launched **intouch**, a new all in one software package for planning your trip and staying in touch with people back home before, during and after your travels.

Create an itinerary and budget using on-screen information and maps, and take advantage of the diary to keep family and friends informed of your whereabouts.

The diary can be linked to your mobile phone so that you can send a text message, **intouch** will automatically send an email or cheap SMS to those listed on your account.

You can also post photos and diary entries online and then download them to make a journal on your return.

Rough Guides **intouch** is easy to install and you don't need to take anything with you – just hit the synchronize button and then use it from any internet café in the world.

Rough Guides **intouch** includes:
Planning tools
Free email address
Free personal website
Digital photo storage   And much more......

£5 OFF your purchase of Rough Guides **intouch** if you buy online at www.roughguidesintouch.com reference code: Rough Guide Books

Recommended retail price £24.99 available through leading retailers e.g. WH Smith, Waterstones and PC World

ROUGH GUIDES
not just travel

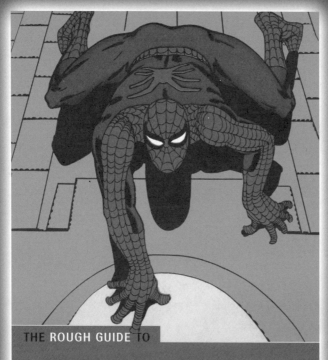

THE ROUGH GUIDE TO

Superheroes

THE COMICS ✳ THE COSTUMES ✳ THE CREATORS ✳ THE CATCHPHRASES

NOTES

NOTES

NOTES

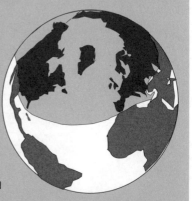

small print and

Index

A Rough Guide to Rough Guides

In the summer of 1981, Mark Ellingham, a recent graduate from Bristol University, was traveling round Greece and couldn't find a guidebook that really met his needs. On the one hand there were the student guides, insistent on saving every last cent, and on the other the heavyweight cultural tomes whose authors seemed to have spent more time in a research library than lounging away the afternoon at a taverna or on the beach.

In a bid to avoid getting a job, Mark and a small group of writers set about creating their own guidebook. It was a guide to Greece that aimed to combine a journalistic approach to description with a thoroughly practical approach to travelers' needs – a guide that would incorporate culture, history, and contemporary insights with a critical edge, together with up-to-date, value-for-money listings. Back in London, Mark and the team finished their Rough Guide, as they called it, and talked Routledge into publishing the book.

That first *Rough Guide to Greece*, published in 1982, was a student scheme that became a publishing phenomenon. The immediate success of the book – with numerous reprints and a Thomas Cook Prize shortlisting – spawned a series that rapidly covered dozens of destinations. Rough Guides had a ready market among low-budget backpackers, but soon also acquired a much broader and older readership that relished Rough Guides' wit and inquisitiveness as much as their enthusiastic, critical approach. Everyone wants value for money, but not at any price.

Rough Guides soon began supplementing the "rougher" information about hostels and low-budget listings with the kind of detail on restaurants and quality hotels that independent-minded visitors on any budget might expect, whether on business in New York or trekking in Thailand.

These days the guides – distributed worldwide by the Penguin Group – offer recommendations from shoestring to luxury and cover more than 200 destinations around the globe, including almost every country in the Americas and Europe, more than half of Africa, and most of Asia and Australasia. Our ever-growing team of authors and photographers is spread all over the world, particularly in Europe, the USA, and Australia.

In 1994, we published the *Rough Guide to World Music* and *Rough Guide to Classical Music*, and a year later the *Rough Guide to the Internet*. All three books have become benchmark titles in their fields – which encouraged us to expand into other areas of publishing, mainly around popular culture. Rough Guides now publish:

- Travel guides to more than 200 worldwide destinations
- Dictionary phrasebooks for 22 major languages
- History guides ranging from Ireland to Islam
- Maps printed on rip-proof and waterproof Polyart™ paper
- Music guides running the gamut from Opera to Elvis
- Restaurant guides to London, New York, and San Francisco
- Reference books on topics as diverse as the Weather and Shakespeare
- Sports guides from Formula 1 to Man Utd
- Pop culture books from *Lord of the Rings* to Cult TV
- World Music CDs in association with World Music Network

Visit **www.roughguides.com** to see our latest publications.

Rough Guide credits

Text editor: Stephen Timblin
Layout: Ankur Guha
Cartography: Manish Chandra
Picture editor: Jj Luck
Production: Julia Bovis
Proofreader: Diane Margolis
Editorial: London Kate Berens, Claire
Saunders, Geoff Howard, Ruth Blackmore,
Gavin Thomas, Polly Thomas, Richard Lim,
Clifton Wilkinson, Alison Murchie, Sally
Schafer, Karoline Densley, Andy Turner, Ella
O'Donnell, Keith Drew, Edward Aves, Nikki
Birrell, Helen Marsden, Joe Staines, Duncan
Clark, Peter Buckley, Matthew Milton, Daniel
Crewe; **New York** Andrew Rosenberg,
Richard Koss, Steven Horak, AnneLise
Sorensen, Amy Hegarty, Hunter Slaton
Design & Pictures: London Simon Bracken,
Dan May, Diana Jarvis, Mark Thomas,
Harriet Mills, Chloë Roberts; **Delhi** Madhulita
Mohapatra, Umesh Aggarwal, Ajay Verma,
Jessica Subramanian, Amit Verma
Production: ,Sophie Hewat, Katherine Owers

Cartography: London Maxine Repath, Ed
Wright, Katie Lloyd-Jones; **Delhi** Rajesh
Chhibber, Jai Prakash Mishra, Ashutosh
Bharti, Rajesh Mishra, Jasbir Sandhu, Karobi
Gogoi, Animesh Pathak
Online: New York Jennifer Gold, Suzanne
Welles, Kristin Mingrone; **Delhi** Manik Chauhan,
Narender Kumar, Shekhar Jha, Rakesh Kumar,
Lalit Sharma, Chhandita Chakravarty
Marketing & Publicity: London Richard
Trillo, Niki Hanmer, David Wearn, Demelza
Dallow, Louise Maher; **New York** Geoff
Colquitt, Megan Kennedy;
Delhi Reem Khokhar
Custom publishing and foreign rights:
Philippa Hopkins
Manager India: Punita Singh
Series editor: Mark Ellingham
Reference director: Andrew Lockett
PA to Managing and Publishing directors:
Megan McIntyre
Publishing director: Martin Dunford
Managing director: Kevin Fitzgerald

Publishing information

This fourth edition published January 2006 by
Rough Guides Ltd,
80 Strand, London WC2R 0RL
345 Hudson St, 4th Floor,
New York, NY 10014, USA
14 Local Shopping Centre, Panchsheel Park,
New Delhi 110017, India
Distributed by the Penguin Group
Penguin Books Ltd,
80 Strand, London WC2R 0RL
Penguin Putnam, Inc.,
375 Hudson St, NY 10014, USA
Penguin Group (Australia)
250 Camberwell Road, Camberwell,
Victoria 3124, Australia
Penguin Books Canada Ltd,
10 Alcorn Avenue, Toronto, ON
M4V 1E4 Canada
Penguin Group (New Zealand),
Cnr Rosedale and Airborne Roads,
Albany, Auckland, New Zealand

Typeset in Bembo and Helvetica to an original
design by Henry Iles.

Printed and bound in China.

© JD Dickey 2006

448pp includes index.
A catalogue record for this book is available from
the British Library.

ISBN-13: 978-1-84353-515-7
ISBN-10: 1-84353-515-7

SMALL PRINT

3   5   7   9   8   6   4   2

Help us update

We've gone to a lot of effort to ensure that
the fourth edition of **The Rough Guide
to Los Angeles** is accurate and up to
date. However, things change – places get
"discovered," opening hours are notoriously
fickle, restaurants and rooms raise prices or
lower standards. If you feel we've got it wrong
or left something out, we'd like to know, and if
you can remember the address, the price, the
time, the phone number, so much the better.

We'll credit all contributions, and send a
copy of the next edition (or any other Rough

Guide if you prefer) for the best letters.
Everyone who writes to us and isn't already a
subscriber will receive a copy of our full-color
thrice-yearly newsletter. Please mark letters:
"Rough Guide Los Angeles" and send to:
Rough Guides, 80 Strand, London WC2R
0RL, or Rough Guides, 4th Floor, 345 Hudson
St, New York, NY 10014. Or send an email to
mail@roughguides.com.

Have your questions answered and tell
others about your trip at
www.roughguides.atinfopop.com.

Acknowledgments

JD Dickey: Thanks go out to editor Stephen Timblin, who contributed much vigor, focus, and flair to this fourth edition of the book (as well as the second), and Andrew Rosenberg, who has always guided the LA project with steely eyes and a velvet touch. Thanks also are due to JD's wife and family; his travel contacts and coordinators in LA, including Marlene Armas-Zermeno, Tammy Lyn Phillips, Ann Flower, and Michelle Bolton; Music Center and Disney Hall representatives Kirsten Schmidt, Matt Velasco, and Lisa Hasenbalg; and to all the good people in the Rough Guide offices in London and Delhi, including Jj Luck for her excellent photo research, Manish Chandra and Maxine Repath for sterling work on the maps, Ankur Guha for spot-on typesetting, Diane Margolis for her excellent proofreading, and Daniel May and Umesh Aggarwal for their smooth production work.

Photo credits

SMALL PRINT

Index

Map entries are in color

INDEX

Map symbols

Maps are listed in the full index using colored text

-----	International border	Rocks	
--- -	State border	Marshland	
80	Interstate	Airport	
30	US Highway	Hotel	
1	Highway	Restaurant	
= = =	Road under construction	Campsite	
- - - - -	Pedestrianized road	Lighthouse	
	Steps	Bridge	
....	Tunnel	Museum	
	Railway	Information center	
—M—	Metrorail station	Building	
- - - - -	Walkway	Church	
— —	Ferry route	Stadium	
	River	Cemetery	
	Mountain range	Park/National or State Park	
▲	Peak	Beach	

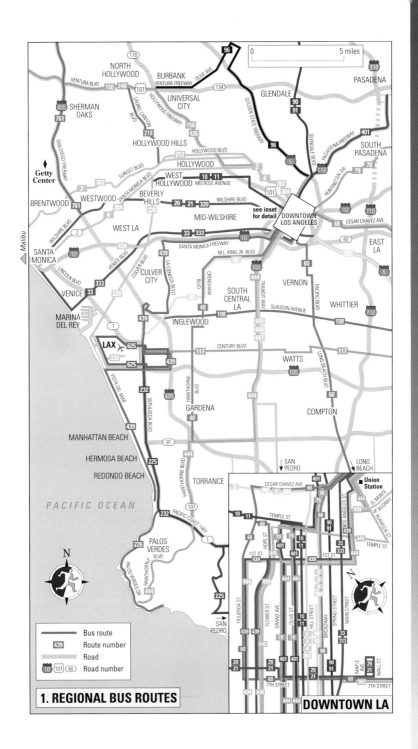

1. REGIONAL BUS ROUTES

DOWNTOWN LA

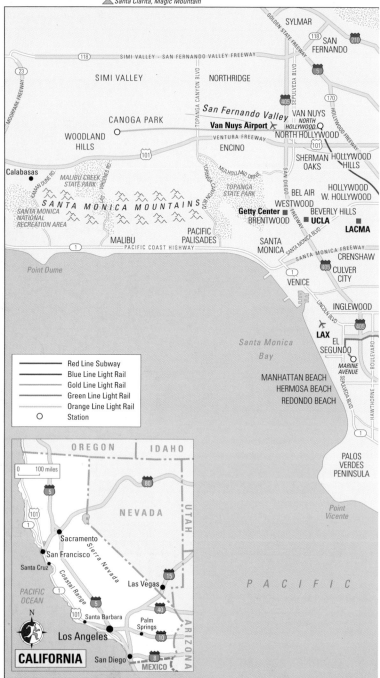

SYLMAR

SAN FERNANDO

SIMI VALLEY – SAN FERNANDO VALLEY FREEWAY

SIMI VALLEY

NORTHRIDGE

CANOGA PARK

San Fernando Valley

VAN NUYS
NORTH HOLLYWOOD

WOODLAND HILLS

Van Nuys Airport ✈

NORTH HOLLYWOOD

VENTURA FREEWAY

ENCINO

Calabasas

MALIBU CREEK STATE PARK

SHERMAN OAKS

HOLLYWOOD HILLS

MULHOLLAND DRIVE

TOPANGA STATE PARK

BEL AIR

HOLLYWOOD
W. HOLLYWOOD

SANTA MONICA MOUNTAINS

WESTWOOD

SANTA MONICA NATIONAL RECREATION AREA

Getty Center ■
BRENTWOOD

BEVERLY HILLS
■ UCLA

LACMA

MALIBU

PACIFIC PALISADES

SANTA MONICA

SANTA MONICA BLVD

SANTA MONICA FREEWAY

PACIFIC COAST HIGHWAY

CRENSHAW

Point Dume

CULVER CITY

VENICE

Santa Monica Bay

INGLEWOOD

LAX ✈

EL SEGUNDO

MARINE AVENUE

MANHATTAN BEACH
HERMOSA BEACH
REDONDO BEACH

Red Line Subway
Blue Line Light Rail
Gold Line Light Rail
Green Line Light Rail
Orange Line Light Rail
○   Station

PALOS VERDES PENINSULA

OREGON   IDAHO

0   100 miles

Point Vicente

NEVADA

PACIFIC

Sacramento

San Francisco

Santa Cruz

PACIFIC OCEAN

Sierra Nevada

Coastal Range

Las Vegas

UTAH

ARIZONA

N

101

Santa Barbara

Palm Springs

Los Angeles

CALIFORNIA

San Diego

MEXICO

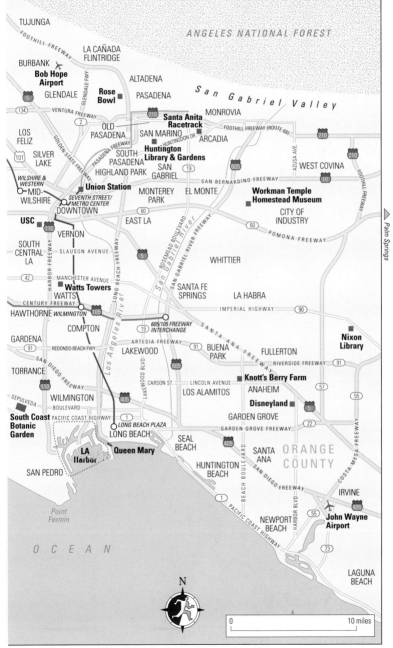

ANGELES NATIONAL FOREST

TUJUNGA

FOOTHILL FREEWAY

LA CAÑADA FLINTRIDGE

BURBANK

Bob Hope Airport

ALTADENA

San Gabriel Valley

GLENDALE

Rose Bowl

PASADENA

GLENDALE FWY

134

VENTURA FREEWAY

2

MONROVIA

210

Santa Anita Racetrack

FOOTHILL FREEWAY (ROUTE 66)

210

LOS FELIZ

OLD PASADENA

PASADENA FREEWAY

SAN MARINO

HUNTINGDON DR

ARCADIA

101

SILVER LAKE

GOLDEN STATE FREEWAY

SOUTH PASADENA

Huntington Library & Gardens

AZUSA AVE

WEST COVINA

WILSHIRE & WESTERN

HIGHLAND PARK

SAN GABRIEL

19

605

MID-WILSHIRE

Union Station

SEVENTH STREET/ METRO CENTER

MONTEREY PARK

EL MONTE

SAN BERNARDINO FREEWAY

10

FOOTHILL FREEWAY

USC

DOWNTOWN

60

Workman Temple Homestead Museum

VERNON

110

EAST LA

60

CITY OF INDUSTRY

SOUTH CENTRAL LA

SLAUSON AVENUE

5

POMONA FREEWAY

ROSEMEAD BOULEVARD

San Gabriel River

San Gabriel River Freeway

WHITTIER

42

MANCHESTER AVENUE

Watts Towers

SANTA FE SPRINGS

LA HABRA

HAWTHORNE

WATTS

WILMINGTON

CENTURY FREEWAY

105

IMPERIAL HIGHWAY

90

Los Angeles River

Long Beach Freeway

COMPTON

19

605/105 FREEWAY INTERCHANGE

SANTA ANA FREEWAY

Nixon Library

GARDENA

91

REDONDO BEACH FWY

ARTESIA FREEWAY

91

BUENA PARK

FULLERTON

RIVERSIDE FREEWAY

91

TORRANCE

110

SAN DIEGO FREEWAY

LAKEWOOD

605

LAKEWOOD BLVD

CARSON ST.

LINCOLN AVENUE

Knott's Berry Farm

57

55

SEPULVEDA

WILMINGTON

BOULEVARD

405

LOS ALAMITOS

ANAHEIM

Disneyland

5

South Coast Botanic Garden

PACIFIC COAST HIGHWAY

1

LONG BEACH PLAZA

GARDEN GROVE

22

GARDEN GROVE FREEWAY

LA Harbor

Queen Mary

LONG BEACH

SEAL BEACH

405

SANTA ANA

ORANGE COUNTY

SAN PEDRO

HUNTINGTON BEACH

BEACH BOULEVARD

SAN DIEGO FREEWAY

COSTA MESA FREEWAY

Point Fermin

1

PACIFIC COAST HIGHWAY

IRVINE

405

O C E A N

NEWPORT BEACH

HARBOR BLVD

55

John Wayne Airport

73

LAGUNA BEACH

N

0   10 miles

Palm Springs

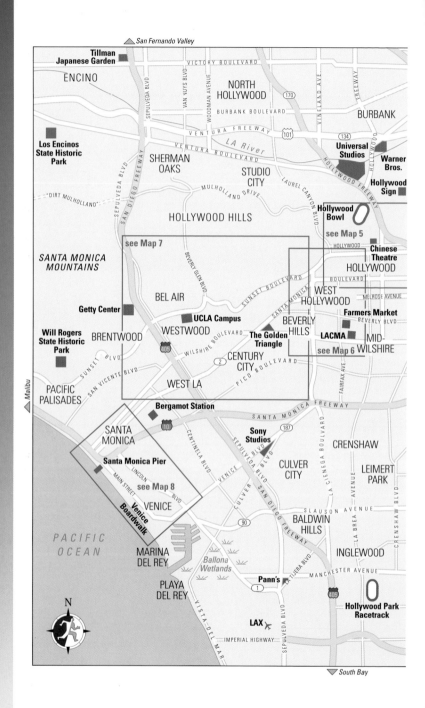

Angeles National Forest

0   5 miles

LA CAÑADA-FLINTRIDGE

GLENOAKS BLVD

OLIVE AVENUE

ALTADENA

Rose Bowl

Gamble House

PASADENA

210

VENTURA FREEWAY

GLENDALE

COLORADO ST

134

BRAND BLVD

COLORADO BLVD

Museum of the
American West

Griffith
Park

SAN FERNANDO ROAD

GOLDEN STATE FREEWAY

Eagle
Rock

OLD
PASADENA

Griffith
Observatory

HIGHLAND PARK

Huntington
Library and
Gardens

SAN
MARINO

LOS FELIZ BLVD

2

Southwest
Museum

SOUTH
PASADENA

BLVD

LOS FELIZ

SILVER
LAKE

SUNSET BLVD

PASADENA FREEWAY

Heritage
Square

HUNTINGTON DRIVE

ALHAMBRA

HYPERION AVE

5

110

GLENDALE FREEWAY

VALLEY

BOULEVARD

GARFIELD AVENUE

ATLANTIC BOULEVARD

ECHO
PARK

see Map 4

101

Dodger Stadium

SAN BERNARDINO FREEWAY

WILSHIRE BOULEVARD

WESTLAKE

CHINATOWN

KOREA
TOWN

Bullocks
Wilshire
Building

Union Station

10

EAST LA

710

PICO BLVD

LA City Hall
DOWNTOWN

BOYLE
HEIGHTS

Convention
Center

POMONA FREEWAY

60

WEST ADAMS

10

USC Campus

Exposition Park

M.L. KING JR. BLVD

SANTA ANA FREEWAY

WHITTIER BOULEVARD

The Citadel

VERNON

LA River

5

110

WESTERN AVENUE

VERNON

AVENUE

CENTRAL AVENUE

HARBOR FREEWAY

SLAUSON AVENUE

SOUTHEAST LA

GARFIELD AVENUE

ATLANTIC AVENUE

FLORENCE AVENUE

SOUTH
CENTRAL LA

WILMINGTON BLVD

ALAMEDA

42

PACIFIC BLVD

FLORENCE AVENUE

FIRESTONE BOULEVARD

710

DOWNEY

CENTURY BOULEVARD

STREET

LONG BEACH ROAD

WATTS

Watts Towers

IMPERIAL HIGHWAY

105

3. CENTRAL LA

San Gabriel Valley

Whittier

Orange County

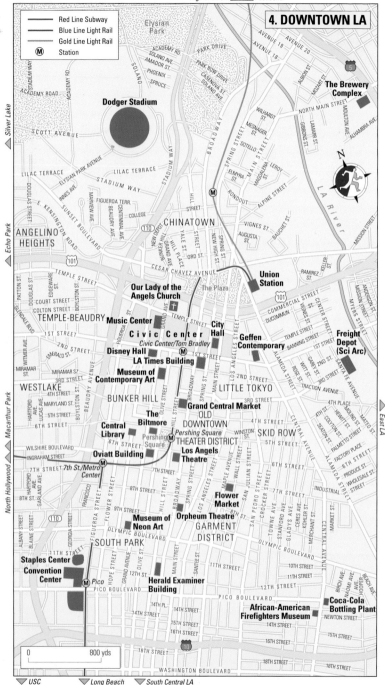

Red Line Subway
Blue Line Light Rail
Gold Line Light Rail
Ⓜ Station

Elysian
Park

AVENUE 19   AVENUE 20
AVENUE 18

ACADEMY RD.
SOLANO AVE.
AMADOR ST.
PHOENIX
SPRUCE

PARK DRIVE
PARK ROW DRIVE
CASENOVA ST.
SOLANO AVE.

ALBION ST.
MOZART ST.

**The Brewery
Complex**

STADIUM WAY
ACADEMY RD.
ACADEMY ROAD

WILHARDT
ST.
MESNAGER
ST.

NORTH MAIN STREET

MOULTON AVE.
ALHAMBRA AVE.
LAMAR ST.
GIBBONS ST.

Dodger Stadium

SCOTT AVENUE

BROADWAY
SPRING STREET
MAIN STREET

SOTELLO
ST.

LA River

LILAC TERRACE
STADIUM WAY
LILAC TERRACE

ELYSIAN PARK AVENUE
INNES AVE.
MARVIEW AVE.

DOUGLAS ST.
LUCAS AVE.
E. KENSINGTON ROAD

SUNSET BOULEVARD
FIGUEROA TERR.
BEAUDRY AVE.
CENTENNIAL AVE.
COLLEGE

ELMYRA
ST.

MAGDALENA
LEROY

ALPINE STREET

RONDOUT

ANGELINO
HEIGHTS

(101)

ANDERSON STREET
MISSION STREET

CHINATOWN
(110)
NEW HIGH ST.
YALE ST.
HILL ST.
HILL PLACE
GRAND AVE.
ORD ST.
NEW HIGH ST.
SPRING ST.

VIGNES ST.
BAUCHET ST.

AUGUSTA
ST.

RAMIREZ
ST.
KELLER
ST.

CESAR CHAVEZ AVENUE

**Union
Station**

(101)

COMMERCIAL STREET
VICKES ST.
DUCOMMUN

MYERS STREET
CENTER STREET

PATTON ST.
EDGEWARE ST.
DOUGLAS ST.
BOYLSTON ST.

TEMPLE STREET
COURT STREET
COLTON ST.
1ST STREET

**Our Lady of the
Angels Church**
The Plaza

TEMPLE-BEAUDRY **Music Center**
WITMER AVE.
LUCAS AVE.
EMERALD ST.
GLENDALE BLVD.

2ND STREET

TEMPLE STREET

FIGUEROA ST.
GRAND AVE.

Civic Center **City
Hall**

**Geffen
Contemporary**

TEMPLE STREET
BANNING STREET

**Freight
Depot
(Sci Arc)**

ANDERSON STREET
SANTA FE AVENUE

MIRAMAR
ST.
MIRAMAR ST.
3RD STREET

Civic Center/Tom Bradley Ⓜ
Disney Hall
LA Times Building
1ST STREET

LOS ANGELES STREET
MAIN STREET

1ST STREET
ROSE ST.
GAREY ST.
WITT ST.
2ND STREET
3RD STREET

WESTLAKE
HARTFORD
AVE.
MARYLAND AVE.
4TH STREET
5TH STREET
BOYLSTON ST.
BEAUDRY AVE.

**Museum of
Contemporary Art**

2ND STREET

LITTLE TOKYO

TRACTION AVENUE

BUNKER HILL

BROADWAY
OLIVE STREET
HILL STREET

Grand Central Market
3RD STREET

4TH PLACE
PALOMA ST.
4TH PLACE

6TH STREET

**The
Biltmore**

**OLD
DOWNTOWN**
4TH STREET

4TH STREET
HEWITT ST.
COLYTON ST.
SEATON ST.

CENTRAL AVENUE

MATEO ST.
PALMETTO STREET

WILSHIRE BOULEVARD
INGRAHAM STREET

**Central
Library**

Pershing Square Ⓜ
Pershing
Square
THEATER DISTRICT
WINSTON
ST.
5TH STREET

SKID ROW

6TH STREET
FACTORY PLACE
6TH STREET
PRODUCE ST.
WHOLESALE ST.

INDUSTRIAL STREET

Oviatt Building

**Los Angels
Theatre**

7TH STREET

7TH STREET
7th St./Metro
Center Ⓜ

MAPLE AVENUE
WALL STREET
SAN JULIAN STREET
SAN PEDRO STREET

HARTFORD AVE.
GARLAND AVE.

FRANCISCO ST.

8TH STREET

8TH STREET

7TH STREET
6TH STREET

INDUSTRIAL STREET
STREET

MARKET ST.

(110)

FIGUEROA STREET
FLOWER STREET

9TH STREET
BROADWAY
SPRING STREET
MAIN STREET

**Flower
Market**

CROCKER ST.
TOWNE AVE.
GLADYS AVE.
CERES AVE.
KOHLER ST.
MERCHANT ST.

CENTRAL AVENUE

**Museum of
Neon Art**

Orpheum Theatre
OLYMPIC BOULEVARD

**GARMENT
DISTRICT**

OLYMPIC BOULEVARD

ALBANY STREET
BLAINE STREET
GEORGIA STREET

SOUTH PARK

LOS ANGELES STREET

11TH STREET

10TH STREET

BIRCH AVE.
NAOMI AVE.
AVE.
BEACH AVE.
HOOPER

Staples Center
**Convention
Center**

Pico Ⓜ
PICO BOULEVARD
12TH STREET

HOPE STREET
GRAND AVENUE
OLIVE STREET

SANTEE ST.

11TH STREET

12TH STREET

**Herald Examiner
Building**

PICO BOULEVARD

**Coca-Cola
Bottling Plant**

14TH PL.   14TH STREET
15TH STREET
16TH STREET

**African-American
Firefighters Museum**
14TH STREET

NEWTON STREET

15TH STREET

0 ——————— 800 yds

18TH STREET
(10)
WASHINGTON BOULEVARD

18TH STREET

18TH STREET

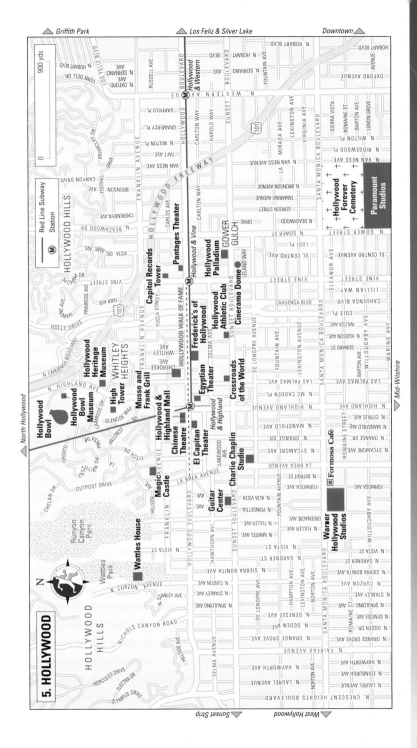

5. HOLLYWOOD

△ Griffith Park   △ Los Feliz & Silver Lake   Downtown △

900 yds
0

Ⓜ Red Line Subway
Ⓜ Station

HOLLYWOOD HILLS

Griffith Park

Runyon Canyon Park

Wattles Park

N

HOLLYWOOD HILLS

Hollywood Bowl
Hollywood Bowl Museum
Hollywood Heritage Museum
High Tower
Musso and Frank Grill
Hollywood & Highland Mall
Magic Castle
Chinese Theatre
El Capitan Theater
Guitar Center
Charlie Chaplin Studio
Wattles House

Capitol Records Tower
Pantages Theater
Frederick's of Hollywood
Hollywood Athletic Club
Egyptian Theater
Crossroads of the World
Cinerama Dome

Hollywood & Vine
Hollywood Palladium
GOWER GULCH

HOLLYWOOD WALK OF FAME

Formosa Café
Warner Hollywood Studios

Hollywood & Western
Hollywood Forever Cemetery
Paramount Studios

HOLLYWOOD FREEWAY

△ North Hollywood

▽ Sunset Strip   ▽ West Hollywood   ▽ Mid-Wilshire

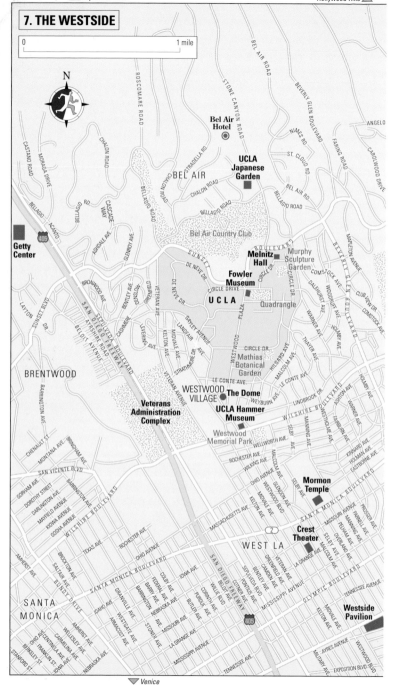

7. THE WESTSIDE

0   1 mile

N

Sepulveda Pass

ROSCOMARE ROAD

BEL AIR ROAD

STONE CANYON ROAD

BEVERLY GLEN BOULEVARD

ANGELO

CASTANO ROAD

MORAGA DRIVE

CHALON ROAD

Bel Air Hotel

BELTRADELLA RD.

NIMES RD.

ST. CLOUD RD.

FARING ROAD

CARGWOOD DRIVE

BEL AIR

UCLA Japanese Garden

CHALON ROAD

BEL AIR ROAD

BELLAGIO ROAD

BELLAGIO ROAD

BELLAGIO ROAD

CASCADE WAY

ASHDALE AVE.

GLENROY AVE.

Bel Air Country Club

405

Getty Center

SUNSET BOULEVARD

Murphy Sculpture Garden

Melnitz Hall

COMSTOCK AVE.

MARLETON AVENUE

BEVERLY GLEN BOULEVARD

DE NEVE DR.

CIRCLE DR.

Fowler Museum

DALEHURST AVE.

WOODRUFF AVE.

CLUB VIEW DR.

COMSTOCK AVE.

BRONWOOD AVE.

BENTLEY AVE.

WINSLOW

CASIMERE

LEVERING AVE.

VETERAN AVE.

BELOIT AVENUE

DE NEVE DR.

GAYLEY AVENUE

LANDFAIR AVE.

MIDVALE AVE.

KELTON AVE.

STRATHMORE AVE.

CIRCLE DRIVE

U C L A

Quadrangle

PLAZA

WESTWOOD

HILGARD AVE.

WARNER AVE.

THAYER AVE.

HOLMBY AVE.

CIRCLE DR.

LAYTON AVE.

SUNSET DR.

SAN DIEGO FREEWAY

SAN DIEGO BOULEVARD

AYRSHIRE ROAD

BRENTWOOD

Mathias Botanical Garden

LE CONTE AVE.

MALCOLM AVE.

LE CONTE AVE.

HOLMBY DR.

BARRINGTON AVENUE

VETERAN AVENUE

Veterans Administration Complex

WESTWOOD VILLAGE

The Dome

WEYBURN AVE.

LINDBROOK DR.

ASHTON AVE.

MANNING AVE.

WARNER AVE.

WESTHOLME AVE.

FAIRBURN AVE.

UCLA Hammer Museum

WILSHIRE BOULEVARD

SELBY AVE.

KINNARD AVE.

HOLMAN AVE.

EASTBORNE AVE.

CHENAULT ST.

BRINGHAM AVE.

MONTANA AVE.

Westwood Memorial Park

WELLWORTH AVE.

ROCHESTER AVE.

WILKINS AVE.

OHIO AVENUE

MALCOLM AVE.

GLENDON AVE.

WESTWOOD BLVD.

SELBY AVE.

GORHAM AVE.

DOROTHY STREET

DARLINGTON AVE.

BARRINGTON AVENUE

MAYFIELD AVENUE

KIOWA AVENUE

GOSHA AVENUE

WILSHIRE BOULEVARD

KELTON AVE.

MIDVALE AVE.

Mormon Temple

SANTA MONICA BOULEVARD

MISSOURI AVENUE

PROSSER AVE.

PARNELL AVE.

PELHAM AVE.

OVERLAND AVE.

SELBY AVE.

MALCOLM AVE.

ROCHESTER AVE.

OHIO AVENUE

MASSACHUSETTS AVE.

2

Crest Theater

VETERAN AVE.

LA GRANGE AVE.

WEST LA

AMHERST AVE.

SALTAIR AVE.

BROCKTON AVE.

BUNDY DRIVE

SANTA MONICA BOULEVARD

TEXAS AVE.

OHIO AVENUE

IDAHO AVE.

COLBY AVE.

IOWA AVE.

FEDERAL AVE.

BARRY AVE.

BARRINGTON

GRANVILLE AVE.

NEBRASKA AVE.

SAN DIEGO FREEWAY

SEPULVEDA BLVD.

BENTLEY AVE.

GREENFIELD AVE.

CAMDEN AVE.

PONTIUS AVE.

PURDUE AVE.

CORINTH AVE.

BUTLER AVE.

MISSISSIPPI AVENUE

OLYMPIC BOULEVARD

TENNESSEE AVENUE

SANTA MONICA

AMHERST AVE.

WELLESLEY AVE.

CARMELINA AVE.

STANFORD ST.

FRANKLIN ST.

BERKELEY ST.

OHIO AVE.

CENTINELA AVE.

IDAHO AVE.

NEBRASKA AVE.

WESTGATE AVE.

ARMACOST AVE.

STONER AVE.

LA GRANGE AVE.

MISSISSIPPI AVENUE

TENNESSEE AVENUE

BELLO AVE.

405

MIDVALE AVE.

KELTON AVE.

WESTWOOD BLVD.

AYRES AVENUE

MILITARY AVE.

EXPOSITION BLVD.

Westside Pavilion

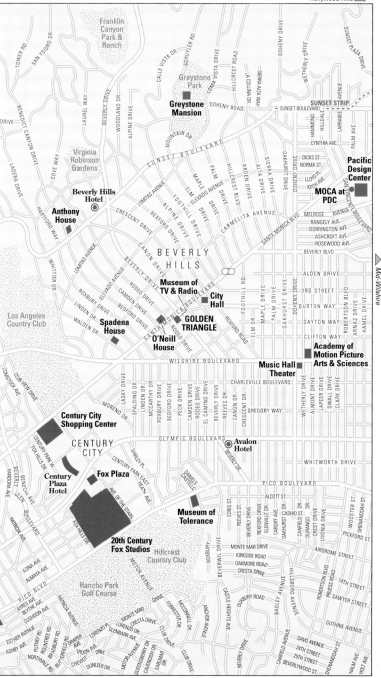

Franklin Canyon Park & Ranch

Greystone Park

Greystone Mansion

DOHEY ROAD

SUNSET BOULEVARD

CYNTHIA AVE

DICKS ST.
NORMA ST

Pacific Design Center

MOCA at PDC

Virginia Robinson Gardens

SUNSET BOULEVARD

MELROSE AVENUE
RANGELY AVE
DORRINGTON AVE
ASHCROFT AVE
ROSEWOOD AVE

Beverly Hills Hotel

Anthony House

CRESCENT DRIVE

CARMELITA AVENUE

BEVERLY BLVD

ALDEN DRIVE

**B E V E R L Y
H I L L S**

3RD STREET

BURTON WAY

Los Angeles Country Club

Museum of TV & Radio

City Hall

GOLDEN TRIANGLE

Spadena House

O'Neill House

DAYTON WAY

CLIFTON WAY

Academy of Motion Picture Arts & Sciences

WILSHIRE BOULEVARD

Music Hall Theater

CHARLEVILLE BOULEVARD

GREGORY WAY

Century City Shopping Center

OLYMPIC BOULEVARD

Avalon Hotel

WHITWORTH DRIVE

**C E N T U R Y
C I T Y**

Fox Plaza

Century Plaza Hotel

PICO BOULEVARD

ALCOTT ST.

Museum of Tolerance

PICKFORD ST.

20th Century Fox Studios

Hillcrest Country Club

AIRDROME STREET

KIRKSIDE ROAD
OAKMORE ROAD
CRESTA DRIVE

Rancho Park Golf Course

DUXBURY ROAD

GUTHRIE AVENUE

PICO BLVD

AYRES AVE
BLYTHE AVE
CUSHDON AVE

DAVID AVENUE
24TH STREET
25TH STREET
BEVERLYWOOD ST.

ESTHER AVENUE
ASHBY AVE

SAWYER STREET

18TH STREET

NORTHVALE RD

6. WEST HOLLYWOOD AND THE MIRACLE MILE

0   500 yds

Hollywood

Hollywood Hills

N

House of Blues

Schindler House/ MAK Center

Art + Design Museum

Whisky-a-Go-Go

Viper Room

The Roxy

Pacific Design Center

MOCA at PDC

Margo Leavin Gallery

SUNSET BOULEVARD
SANTA MONICA BOULEVARD
MELROSE AVENUE
SAN VICENTE BOULEVARD
LA CIENEGA BOULEVARD
FAIRFAX AVENUE
CRESCENT HEIGHTS BOULEVARD

FULLER AVENUE
MARTEL AVENUE
VISTA STREET
GARDNER STREET
N. CURZON AVENUE
HAMPTON AVENUE
LEXINGTON AVENUE
NORTON AVENUE
DE LONGPRE AVENUE
OGDEN DRIVE

N. FULLER AVENUE
N. MARTEL AVENUE
N. VISTA STREET
N. GARDNER STREET
N. SIERRA AVENUE
N. BONITA AVENUE
WILLOUGHBY AVENUE
N. CURZON AVENUE
N. STANLEY AVENUE
N. SPAULDING AVENUE
N. GENESEE AVENUE
N. OGDEN AVENUE
N. ORANGE GROVE AVENUE

CLINTON STREET
W. ROSEWOOD AVENUE

N. HAYWORTH AVENUE
N. EDINBURGH AVENUE
N. LAUREL AVENUE

N. HAYWORTH AVENUE
N. LAUREL AVENUE
N. CRESCENT HEIGHTS BLVD

HAVENHURST DRIVE
N. LA JOLLA AVE
N. HARPER AVE
N. SWEETZER AVENUE
ROMAINE STREET
N. FLORES AVENUE
N. KINGS ROAD
N. ORLANDO AVENUE
N. CROFT AVENUE
WARING AVENUE
N. ALFRED STREET

W. ROSEWOOD AVENUE
CLINTON STREET
N. CROFT AVENUE
N. ALFRED STREET

WOODSHILL TRL
MONTEEL RD.
WOODROW WILSON DR.
KINGS ROAD
CARLTON WAY
HAROLD WAY
QUEENS ROAD
MILLER DR.

OLIVE DR.
HACIENDA PL.
SIERRA TR.
N. KINGS ROAD
ALTA LOMA RD.
LONDONDERRY PL.
SUNSET PLAZA DR.
HORN AVE.
HOLLOWAY DRIVE
WEST KNOLL DRIVE
HANCOCK AVENUE
PALM AVENUE
LARRABEE STREET
CLARK ST.
N. WETHERLY DR.
OZETA
ST. IVES DR.
CORDELL DR.
CAROL DR.
DOHENY DRIVE

N. HAMMOND ST.
CYNTHIA ST.
HARRATT ST.
PHYLLIS AVE.
VISTA GRAND ST.
CINTHIA ST.
DICKS STREET
NORMA PLACE
ELEVADO AVE.
PACE AVE.
KEITH AVE.
LLOYD
MELROSE AVENUE
RANGLEY STREET
HUNTLEY DR.
N. WEST KNOLL ROAD
WESTMONT DRIVE
SHERWOOD DRIVE
WESTBOURNE DRIVE
PILGRIM DR.
HILLDALE AVE.
SAN VICENTE BLVD
EL TOVAR PL.
DORRINGTON AVENUE
LA PEER DR.
ROSSMORE AVE.
N. OAKHURST DRIVE

S FULLER AVENUE

S MARTEL AVENUE

S VISTA STREET

S GARDNER STREET

1ST STREET

OAKWOOD AVENUE

N STANLEY AVE

N SPAULDING AVE

N GENESEE AVE

N OGDEN AVE

N ORANGE GROVE AVE

BEVERLY BOULEVARD

HAUSER BLVD

BURNSIDE AVENUE

RIDGELEY DRIVE

HAUSER BLVD

MASSELIN AVENUE

SIERRA BONITA AVENUE

CURZON AVENUE

STANLEY AVENUE

ALANDELE AVE

SPAULDING AVENUE

WILSHIRE BOULEVARD

COLGATE AVE

S BURNSIDE AVE.

CURZON AVE. E.

S FULLER AVE.

S 6TH STREET

W 6TH STREET

BLACKBURN AVE

S ORANGE GROVE AVE.

CURZON AVE. W.

S ALANDELE AVE.

COLGATE

S OGDEN DR

S OGDEN DR.

Pan Pacific Park

CBS Television City

The Grove Mall

Farmers Market

La Brea Tar Pits/ Page Museum

Los Angeles County Museum of Art

Craft and Folk Art Museum

LACMA West

Museum of the Holocaust

Peterson Automotive Museum

FAIRFAX AVENUE

S FAIRFAX

CAPISTRAND WAY

N HAYWORTH AVENUE

S HAYWORTH AVENUE

N LAUREL AVENUE

S LAUREL AVENUE

DEL VALLE DR

MCCARTHY VISTA DR

WARNER DR.

AVENUE

1ST STREET

BLACKBURN AVENUE

4TH STREET

COLGATE AVENUE

DREXEL AVENUE

5TH STREET

MARYLAND DRIVE

LA JOLLA AVENUE

LINDENHURST DRIVE

6TH STREET

ORANGE STREET

FOSTER DR

CARRILLO DR

SLOAT DR

N SWEETZER AVENUE

KINGS ROAD

BEVERLY BOULEVARD

3RD STREET

S SWEETZER AVENUE

S ORLANDO AVENUE

COMMODORE

SANTA YNEZ WAY

SCHUMACHER DRIVE

OLYMPIC BOULEVARD

AVENUE

OAKWOOD

TOWER DRIVE

GALE DRIVE

HAMILTON DRIVE

Wilshire Theater

Center for Motion Picture Study

N LA CIENEGA BOULEVARD

GREGORY WAY

WESTBOURNE DR.

HUNTLEY DRIVE

SAN VICENTE

Beverly Center

LE DOUX ROAD

STANLEY DRIVE

CARSON ROAD

WILLAMAN DRIVE

HAMEL DRIVE

ARNAZ DRIVE

S VICENTE BOULEVARD

BONNER DR

BURTON WAY

BURTON WAY

Cedars-Sinai Hospital

Fine Arts Theater

WILSHIRE BOULEVARD

CHARLEVILLE BOULEVARD

BOULEVARD

GREGORY WAY

CHALMERS DRIVE

S ROBERTSON

CLARK DRIVE

SWALL DRIVE

LA PEER DRIVE

ALMONT DRIVE

WETHERLY DRIVE

OLYMPIC BOULEVARD

N ROBERTSON BLVD

ALDEN DRIVE

3RD STREET

BEVERLY BOULEVARD

ASHCROFT AVENUE

ROSEWOOD AVENUE

CLARK DRIVE

SWALL DRIVE

LA PEER DRIVE

ALMONT DRIVE

WETHERLY DRIVE

Academy of Motion Picture Arts & Sciences

Music Hall Theater

DRIVE

OAKHURST DRIVE

DOHENY

OAKHURST DRIVE

0   800 yds

8. SANTA MONICA & VENICE

California Avenue

Wilshire Boulevard

Arizona Avenue

Santa Monica Boulevard

Broadway

Camera Obscura

Third Street
Promenade

SANTA MONICA

18th Street
Arts Complex

Broadway

Colorado Avenue

Memorial
Park

Santa Monica
Place

Angels Attic

Olympic Boulevard
Santa Monica Freeway

Santa
Monica
Pier

Olympic Place

City Hall

Michigan Avenue

Delaware Avenue

Civic
Auditorium

Woodlawn
Cemetery

Pico Boulevard

Pico Boulevard

PACIFIC

Bay Park

Bay Street
Grant Street
Pacific Street
Pearl Street
Cedar Street

Bicknell Ave.
Pacific St.

Hotchkiss
Park

Joslyn Park

Strand St.

Pine Street
Maple Street

Santa
Monica
College

Hollister Avenue

Los Amigos
Park

Edgemar
Complex

Beach
Park

Ocean Park Blvd.

Ocean Park Boulevard

California
Heritage
Museum

Hill Street

Oak Street

Hill Street

Raymond Ave.

Ashland Ave.

Ashland Avenue

Ocean
Park

Pier Ave.

Sunset Ave.

Bryn Mawr

Pier Avenue
Marine Ave.

Marine Street

Navy St.
Ozone St.

Navy Street

Marine Street

Sunset Ave.

Dewey Street

Ballerina Clown

Machado St.

Rose Avenue

Rose Avenue

Chiat / Day / Mojo

Flower Avenue

Sunset Avenue

Sunset Avenue

Lake Way

Hopper
Studio

Vernon Avenue

Vernon Ave.
Indiana
Ave.

Morningside Way

Venice Boardwalk

Venice Beach

Indiana Avenue

Lake Way

Appleton Way

Brooks Avenue

Elkgrove Ave.

Preston Way

Brooks Ave.
Breeze Ave.

Broadway

Palms Blvd.

Westminster
Park

Westminster Avenue

Palms Blvd.

Vienna Way

San Juan Avenue

Santa Clara Avenue

California Avenue

Horizon Ave.

Millwood Ave.

Nowita Place

Windward
Colonnade

Market St.

Windward
Circle

Race Through The Clouds

Superba Ave.

Marco Pl.

Carlton Ave.

Muscle
Beach

Rialto Ave.

Grand Blvd.

Palms

Amoroso Pl.

Venezia

Lucille Ave.

VENICE

Superba Ave.

Victoria Ave.

Venice Boulevard

Grand Blvd.

Beyond Baroque
Arts Center

Amoroso Ct.

Venice Boulevard

Venice Way

Washington Way

Victoria Ave.

Zanja Street

Venice
Canals

Mildred Avenue

Boccaccio Ave.

Olive Avenue

Woodlawn Ave.
Crestmoore Pl.

Garfield Ave.

Harbor Street

Beach Ave.

Main St.

Coeur D'Alene Ave.

Van Buren Avenue

Ocean Ave.

Oxford Avenue

Grant Ave.

Bari Way

Harrison Ave.

28th St.

Sanborn Ave.

Washington Boulevard

Washington Boulevard

Venice
Pier

Howard St.

Beach Avenue

Admiralty Way

Dickson St.